Alan Simpson's DOS Secrets Unleashed

Alan Simpson's

DOS SECRETS UNLEASHED

SAMS
PUBLISHING

A Division of Prentice Hall Computer Publishing
11711 North College, Carmel, Indiana 46032 USA

To Susan, Ashley, and Alec.

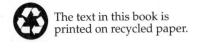

Overview

Contents

Alan Simpson's
DOS Secrets Unleashed

Contents

xxxi

Acknowledgments

Even though only a single author's name appears on the cover of the book, every book is a team project, and this book is no exception. I would like to give credit where it is due and thank the following people for their hard work and dedication.

On the publishing side, Stacy Hiquet, Dean Miller, Tad Ringo, Cheri Clark, and Gordon Arbuthnot were all instrumental in creating this book, as were the dedicated production team at Sams.

On the authorial side, talented writers David Haskin, David Rhodes, David Stryble, Tina and Andy Rathbone, and Elizabeth Olson contributed to the original manuscript. The talents and hard work of Neweleen Trebnik and Martha Mellor kept this manuscript moving along and on time.

Many thanks to my agent, Bill Gladstone of Waterside Productions, for keeping my writing career busy and productive. Thanks also to Matt Wagner of Waterside Productions.

And of course, many thanks to my wife Susan, daughter Ashley, and son Alec for being patient and supportive through yet another demanding "Daddy project."

About the Author

Alan Simpson is the author of more than 30 best-selling computer books in over a dozen languages worldwide. Currently there are about three million copies of his books in print.

Alan Simpson's years of microcomputer experience have allowed him to write in nearly every genre of computer literature: operating systems (DOS and Windows), database management systems (ACCESS, dBASE, and Paradox), spreadsheets (1-2-3 and Quattro), and word processing (WordPerfect). The success of his books is due to his unique ability to write clearly, concisely, and understandably about the uses and intricacies of even the most technical software programs.

Prior to becoming a full-time writer, Alan Simpson spent more than a decade as a freelance programmer and software consultant. He also taught introductory and advanced computer courses at the University of California-San Diego and San Diego State University.

Introduction

DOS 6, Microsoft's latest version of their highly popular disk operating system, offers fantastic additions to an already user-friendly version. DOS 6 features its familiar DOS Shell, which provides you with a greatly simplified graphical interface, as well as an enhanced online help system.

If you have problems with a sluggish hard drive due to fragmented files, DOS 6 introduces the new DEFRAG command—a real winner. You will find protecting your data as simple as choosing to install either the Windows or MS-DOS versions of the new Anti-Virus, Backup, and Undelete programs. To top it all off, DOS 6 features multiconfiguration capabilities—a real time-saver!

Is This Book for You?

The answer is "YES" if you are interested in learning about all the new features of DOS 6 or if you want to enhance your knowledge of Microsoft's disk operating system. This book is intended for the intermediate to advanced user. However, I've also included enough of the basics to bring the beginning user along for the ride.

This book is designed to take you from the most important "need to know" information to the more advanced (although to some extent, "nice to know") information. Therefore, you can read as far as you wish to learn what you want to learn and then keep the book around for future reference to find information on an "as needed" basis. Here's a summary of the contents of the book.

Part I: DOS Lives!

Part I gets you started on what's new to DOS 6 and answers the question, "Should I upgrade?" Basic DOS skills are presented here to teach you the essentials of locating and running programs—which is what using a computer is all about.

Part II: Setting Up DOS

This part focuses on getting it all started with DOS 6. You are presented with installation secrets and surprises, tips for achieving peak performance, and step-by-step instructions on setting up and effectively utilizing your new AUTOEXEC.BAT and CONFIG.SYS files.

Part III: Putting DOS to Work

Now that you've made a great start with DOS 6, keep it going with DOS essentials and tips, working from the command line and the DOS Shell, and creating simple batch programs. This part also teaches you how to create, edit, and work efficiently with files and directories.

Part IV: Optimizing and Tuning DOS

These chapters take you deeper into DOS and show you techniques for simplifying management of your hard disk, memory, and Windows environment. In this part you also learn how to implement three very important data protection programs: Anti-Virus, Backup, and Undelete.

Part V: Managing Your Standard Devices

Part V takes you inside your computer and DOS. You learn how to configure your equipment to your specific needs and maximize its use. Also in this part, you'll gain more control of your screen, disk, keyboard, printer, modem, and FAX.

Part VI: The Network Connection

In this part, Microsoft takes you beyond the lone PC and offers you the capability to optimize your computing resources by physically connecting your PC to your laptop (or another PC). I've also included a chapter on Workgroup Connection. Use this add-on program to further enhance your connection to such products as Windows for Workgroups.

Part VII: Programming for Non-Programmers

This part moves you into the realm of programming by describing the relatively easy creation of batch programs so you don't need a background or education in computer science to use this powerful technique. Using QBasic and other simple programming tools is greatly simplified with DOS 6.

Part VIII: Low-Cost and Free Software

These chapters teach you how to obtain and use shareware to enhance DOS. I have included a number of shareware products on three add-on disks that I hope will give you a well-rounded start with shareware. There are so many impressive shareware programs available these days that it is almost overwhelming.

Part IX: Customer Support

Appendix A presents instructions for installing DOS 6 on your computer. Appendix B lists solutions to common problems you may encounter from time to time. DOS error messages are detailed in Appendix C, along with possible resolutions. Finally, Appendix D provides information on how to get help beyond this book from Microsoft Support's online help system.

Features of the Book

I've included a number of special features in this book to help you get the most out of using it. These features include special icons to identify important sections of text, a tear-out reference card, and three disks packed with useful shareware programs.

Icons

The icons in this book identify sections that are dedicated to DOS 6 users, cautions, warnings, notes, and of course secrets! The following three icons are the most important ones:

> Want to know something not everybody knows? This book is jam-packed with secrets, so keep an eye out for them.

 This surprise icon is located at the end of each chapter. It denotes the troubleshooting section that details problems you might encounter and proposed solutions.

 This Version 6 icon marks the beginning of text that concerns Version 6 of DOS.

Endpapers

Inside the front cover you'll find a quick reference to the new features of DOS 6. You'll also find a tear-out card in the front of the book. This card has a DOS Command Survival Guide on one side and a DOS Shell Survival Guide on the other side.

Add-On Disks

Look at the great shareware programs I've included with this book! These disks are packed with programs that have been zipped. If you are not familiar with PKWare's PKZIP software, you'll soon find out what it is all about—it's included on the disks. See Part VIII, "Low-Cost and Free Software," for further details.

DOS Lives!

CHAPTER 1

DOS 6 Features Revealed

MS-DOS 6 is yet another giant step forward in the evolution of DOS, the most widely used personal-computer operating system in the world. In use for the past 12 years, MS-DOS has more than 100 million users worldwide. This latest version of DOS builds on and is compatible with all previous versions of DOS, but it adds unprecedented functionality in areas such as hard disk and memory management, networking capabilities, virus protection, and features specific to portable computers.

History of DOS

To fully appreciate the features of MS-DOS 6, you should understand how far DOS has evolved. From the introduction of version 1.0 in 1981, DOS has undergone more than 10 major revisions. Version 1.0 was designed for the IBM PC and supported single-sided floppy diskettes only. The first major revision of DOS, version 2.0, came in 1983 and added support for hierarchical directory structures and hard disks. Beginning a year later, versions 3.0 through 3.3 added support for 1.2M floppy drives, Microsoft networks, 3 ½-inch floppy drives, and multiple disk partitions.

Microsoft introduced version 4.0 in late 1988. This was the first release to add support for expanded memory and disk partitions greater than 32M. Most important, however, was that this was the first release of DOS to include a graphical *shell*. Using this interface, users could do almost all the things they used to do from the command line by pointing and clicking with a mouse.

The most powerful version of DOS came in 1991. With the release of MS-DOS 5.0, users of 386 and 486 computers got back tens, even hundreds, of kilobytes of conventional memory. The memory management capabilities of DOS 5 allowed DOS itself to load into *high* memory and allowed terminate-and-stay-resident (TSR) programs and device drivers to be loaded into *upper* memory. An upgraded shell allowed for task swapping, and a full-screen editor replaced the archaic EDLIN for creating and editing text files. QBasic was also added, a big improvement over BASIC.

What's New in MS-DOS 6

The latest version of DOS is very similar to DOS 5 at one level yet very different at another. The base functionality of DOS 6 builds on DOS 5—an easy and powerful shell, a full-screen editor, advanced memory management, and so forth. However, DOS 6 has become something that no version of any other operating system is or has ever been—a full-blown package of utilities and applications.

> The new and improved features of DOS 6 include memory management, hard disk management, network connectivity, configuration utilities, file management, laptop features, virus protection, and online help.

Memory Management

The memory management features of DOS 5 freed up lots of conventional memory for users of 386 and 486 computers. Now that DOS ran in the high memory area (HMA) and TSRs and device drivers could be loaded into upper memory (the region between 640K and 1024K), more memory became available for other applications. However, as more and more memory-resident programs needed to be loaded, the number of possible combinations quickly grew into the thousands. Deciding which combination of programs should be loaded high became a difficult, if not impossible, task.

MemMaker

DOS 6 adds a program called MemMaker that is designed to take the guesswork out of memory management. By simply running MemMaker, you can have your system analyzed and optimized for the best possible usage of high and upper memory.

You can run MemMaker in Express mode for the fastest and easiest results, or in Custom mode for control over specific issues, including optimizing memory for use with Windows.

Memory Management Utilities

MemMaker builds on commands that were available in DOS 5 but are significantly enhanced in DOS 6. The device driver that provides upper memory management, EMM386.EXE, and the internal commands LOADHIGH and DEVICEHIGH have been improved. For you, the user, to get a better picture of your system's memory and the applications that are running at any given moment, the MEM command has been enhanced as well.

MemMaker and the enhanced memory management utilities are covered in Chapter 15, "Getting the Most from Your Memory."

Hard Disk Management

As new versions of applications are released, they generally get larger. DOS 6 itself, for example, takes up much more disk space than did versions 3, 4, or even 5. Microsoft Windows and all the applications that run under it are extremely large as well. Although a large hard disk doesn't cost as much as it used to, it's still important to get as much out of your hard disk as you can.

DoubleSpace

DOS 6 includes a disk-compression utility called DoubleSpace. This utility can double your disk space by compressing files to about half their size. Suddenly your 40M hard drive looks like an 80M drive with no additional hardware!

The first time you run DoubleSpace, your hard disk is automatically compressed. DoubleSpace can even convert drives that were compressed with the popular Stacker utility. Running the DoubleSpace program at any time after initial setup gives you a full-screen utility to optimize and manage compressed drives.

Defragmenter

After the applications and data files on your hard drive have been used for a while, the process of changing, moving, or deleting files tends to spread them out over separate physical areas of the hard drive. Although they look and work the same to you, they might take longer to access because the hard disk must move around more to get the whole file.

Whereas DoubleSpace helps you manage the quantity of space available on your hard drive, the Defragmenter utility helps you manage the quality and speed of your hard drive usage. The Defragmenter application optimizes your hard drive so that all files are stored in contiguous areas on the disk, as opposed to being stored in fragments around the disk. This results in your files being accessed as fast as possible.

Disk Caching

DOS 6 includes an enhanced version of the SMARTDrive utility. SMARTDrive sets aside a portion of extended memory to act as a fast but temporary storage region for frequently accessed data.

Originally designed to speed up only disk reads, the SMARTDrive in DOS 6 includes caching of disk writes, which speeds up writing to files as well as reading from them.

The hard disk management utilities, including DoubleSpace, Defragmenter, and SMARTDrive, are covered in Chapter 14, "Hard Disk Management Made Simple."

Connectivity

From the smallest office to the largest corporation, personal computers are connecting to other personal computers. Local area networks are springing up everywhere, and DOS 6 can connect to them with the help of the Workgroup Connection.

Workgroup Connection

The Workgroup Connection provides you with the ability to share applications, data files, and printers with others in your workgroup. If your office uses any Microsoft network—Windows for Workgroups, LAN Manager, or Windows N/T—you can connect with the Workgroup Connection.

Using command-line utilities or a memory-resident pop-up utility, you can connect your local drive letters to directories on other people's desktops or on file servers in your workgroup. You can also reroute local printer ports to printers on other desktops or servers, gaining access to powerful and expensive shared printers around the workgroup.

Microsoft Mail

After you are connected to the network, you can also communicate with workgroup members using one of the 1990s most popular tools—electronic mail.

The Workgroup Connection includes Microsoft Mail for sending and receiving electronic mail within your workgroup. You can communicate with other users of the Workgroup Connection, Windows for Workgroups, or other networks that support Microsoft Mail.

If the network administrator has the proper hardware and software in place on the network, you can even exchange mail from your desktop with people in other workgroups, offices, companies, or even countries!

The Workgroup Connection is covered in Chapter 26, "Making the Workgroup Connection," and Microsoft Mail is covered in Chapter 27, "Keeping in Touch with Electronic Mail."

Configuration

There are two main components to a personal computer: hardware and software. There are also two major areas in which problems arise when adding new components or applications: hardware and software.

Troubleshooting Hardware

DOS 6 includes a powerful utility called Microsoft Diagnostics (MSD) that helps you identify what hardware is in your computer and how it is configured. Running this application often helps to determine which interrupts or base addresses are free or why an interface board is not working. Because most expansion cards also require device drivers or TSRs, Microsoft Diagnostics helps you troubleshoot software settings for DOS and Windows as well.

Managing Software

Adding new applications often means adding commands to the CONFIG.SYS and AUTOEXEC.BAT files. These files can quickly become messy and hard to troubleshoot, but more important, all commands in both files are executed each time you start your computer. You might find that you need different settings for different applications or for different users of the computer.

Multiple Configurations

Instead of hassling with keeping separate CONFIG.SYS and AUTOEXEC.BAT files for different purposes, you can use Microsoft's DOS 6 commands to manage multiple configurations in a single set of these start-up files. By separating the commands into *blocks* within the CONFIG.SYS and AUTOEXEC.BAT files, you can choose a particular configuration each time you boot your computer. For example, when you boot your computer, you can easily choose between Matt's and Martha's setup, or between a DOS-only and a Windows setup.

Start-Up Options

Troubleshooting these start-up files is infinitely easier with DOS 6. Instead of manually editing the CONFIG.SYS file each time you want to exclude a command, with DOS 6 you can step through the lines one at a time by pressing the F8 function key for an *interactive* start. Furthermore, instead of renaming or deleting the CONFIG.SYS and AUTOEXEC.BAT files to get a *clean* start, you can simply press the F5 function key to abort the start-up and drop you at a DOS prompt.

Batch Program Prompts

Within the AUTOEXEC.BAT (and any other batch programs you have), you might want to let users respond to questions before actions are taken; for example, "Which program do you want to start— Excel, Word, or Golf [E,W,G]?" DOS 6 provides a small program that enables you to do just that. When you use this program, called CHOICE, your batch programs become miniprograms.

All the configuration utilities are discussed in Chapter 13, "Customizing DOS."

File Management

Some of the biggest headaches of using DOS come from managing files, especially from the command line. The BACKUP and RESTORE commands are powerful but very hard to use. Files are hard to move around without both a COPY and a DEL command, and in fact, subdirectories can't be moved or deleted without lots of extra work. And have you ever deleted a file accidentally and not been able to recover it? DOS 6 attacks all of these problems head-on.

Microsoft Backup

Licensed from Symantec and based on the popular Norton utility, Microsoft Backup provides a DOS and Windows application to manage full, incremental, and differential backups. You can back up files to any DOS-supported device, including diskettes, removable drives, and even network drives. If you're using DoubleSpace, data is also backed up in compressed form, saving on the number of diskettes needed.

Managing Files and Directories

To help you better manage files and subdirectories from the command line, the new MOVE command enables you to move files and even entire subdirectories from one place to another. If you just want to delete a subdirectory, you can use the new DELTREE command.

> Using the DELTREE command, you can delete a whole tree structure without having to manually delete each branch.

Undelete

The Undelete utility has been significantly enhanced since DOS 5. It even includes an Undelete for Windows version. Licensed from Central Point Software, Undelete includes three levels of assurance: *Standard,* which enables you to undelete a deleted file immediately; *Tracker,* which uses a TSR and a control file; and *Sentry,* which requires a TSR and a hidden directory to keep track of all deleted files, even those on network drives.

All the file-management utilities, including Microsoft Backup, as well as the MOVE, DELTREE, and UNDELETE commands, are covered in Chapter 10, "Working with Files and Directories," and Chapter 14, "Hard Disk Management Made Simple."

Laptop Features

The number of laptop computers, and more recently notebook computers, has grown dramatically in the 1990s. The benefits of portability, however, are often offset by the inconvenience of having to swap floppy diskettes back and forth between the laptop and the desktop computer.

INTERLNK

DOS 6 includes a powerful new utility, called INTERLNK, to eliminate this hassle. With the proper parallel or serial cable, you can directly connect your portable computer to your desktop computer. The resources of the desktop, including drives and printers, become resources of the laptop. Simple DOS commands move files back and forth, and any application that is available on the desktop can be run on the laptop.

POWER

Although battery life has increased in most laptop and notebook computers, there is nothing more frustrating than being in the middle of a project and having your computer shut down. Conforming to the Advanced Power Management (APM) specification, Microsoft developed the POWER utility. This device driver, when used with a laptop or notebook that conforms to the APM specification, can save up to 25 percent on your battery.

Both of these utilities are covered in Chapter 28, "The POWER of INTERLNK."

Microsoft Anti-Virus

Over the past few years, thousands of users have learned the hard way that viruses are serious trouble. Ranging from simply annoying to totally destructive, viruses are a serious concern to all users of personal computers.

Included with DOS 6 is Microsoft Anti-Virus. Also licensed from Central Point Software, it includes a TSR to constantly monitor your computer for viruses and virus-like activity. It also provides both a full-screen DOS and a Windows utility to detect and clean up viruses from your PC. More than 1,000 viruses can be detected in memory, floppy drives, hard drives, and even network drives. Because the list of known viruses grows every week, Central Point Software makes update lists available to users of DOS 6.

Microsoft Anti-Virus is covered in Chapter 18, "Protecting Your System."

Getting Help

Finally, with all the new features of MS-DOS 6, you might be thinking that you won't be able to get anything done without carrying a big manual around with you. Although you will definitely need to look up new (and old) commands every now and then, the manual shouldn't be necessary. DOS 6 comes with a complete online reference, including syntax, notes, and examples for each command and device driver.

Troubleshooting

Although DOS 6 is relatively easy to install and use, problems often happen when you least expect them. To that end, I have tried to structure this book in a way that will help you quickly and easily find resolutions to any problems you may encounter.

If you have a problem:

■ Turn to the troubleshooting section located at the end of each chapter. There you will find a summary of problems and their resolutions for the specific information covered in the chapter.

■ Refer to Appendix B, "Solutions to Common Problems," to locate your problem and its probable resolution.

■ Refer to Appendix C, "DOS Error Messages and What to Do," when you encounter an error message and need help.

Summary

DOS 6 builds on DOS 5's easy and powerful shell, full-screen editor, advanced memory techniques, and so on. However, DOS 6 also is the first version of DOS to provide a full-blown package of utilities and applications. So what should you expect from DOS 6? You should expect the highest levels of reliability and compatibility. Microsoft again delivers features that are accessible to a wide range of users as well as flexible enough for advanced users to configure to their liking. Thank you, Microsoft!

Alan Simpson's
DOS
SECRETS
UNLEASHED

CHAPTER 2

Moving to DOS 6

As revealed in Chapter 1, DOS 6 contains many powerful new capabilities. You can base your decision about whether to upgrade to DOS 6 on whether you need those additional capabilities. This chapter will help you decide whether to upgrade from your current version of DOS and, if you do, what you need to make the upgrade successful.

Upgrading from DOS 5

The next two sections briefly discuss the benefits of these new features so that you can decide whether to upgrade.

New Utilities in DOS 6

DOS 6 includes several freestanding utility programs that you otherwise must pay extra for. Table 2.1 lists the new utilities and the needs they fill. If they fill a need for you, upgrading to DOS 6 might be worth your time and money.

Table 2.1. New DOS 6 utilities.

Your Need	DOS 6 Utility
Backing up files	Microsoft Backup for DOS and Windows
Optimizing memory usage	MemMaker
Increasing hard disk storage capacity	DoubleSpace
Speeding up your hard disk	DEFRAG
Computer virus protection	Microsoft Anti-Virus for DOS and Windows

Your Need	DOS 6 Utility
Protection against accidental file erasure	Microsoft UNDELETE for DOS and Windows
Conserving laptop battery power	POWER
Speeding up reading and writing files	SMARTDrive
Viewing hardware configuration	Microsoft Diagnostics (MSD)
Transferring files between computers	INTERLNK

Each utility listed in Table 2.1 could be a stand-alone software product.

You should seriously consider upgrading to DOS 6 if one of the following situations applies to you:

- You need a system for backing up your programs and data files. Hard disk failures are an inevitable calamity for computer users, and backing up your files is the best insurance you can have against losing important information. If you do not currently have a program for backing up your programs and data files, you could benefit from DOS 6's Microsoft Backup for both DOS and Windows. Chapter 18, "Protecting Your System," and Chapter 14, "Hard Disk Management Made Simple," provide detailed information about Microsoft Backup.

- You are running out of memory. Computer memory often is at a premium, particularly for those who use a lot of programs. This problem is especially acute with *lower* or conventional memory, or the first megabyte of RAM. If you run out of memory, programs might slow down or even cease to function. If this is a problem for you, MemMaker can provide you with the tools to fit more programs into memory. MemMaker is discussed in-depth in Chapter 15, "Getting the Most from Your Memory."

■ You have more programs and data files than you can store on your hard drive. Computer programs are getting more complex. As a result, they take more disk space to store. If you use a variety of programs, and if you create a lot of files with those programs, you can easily run out of disk space, no matter how large your hard drive is. DOS 6 includes DoubleSpace, which compresses program and data files so that more files can fit on your hard disk. In fact, with DoubleSpace you might be able to double your hard drive storage capacity. DoubleSpace is discussed in detail in Chapter 14, "Hard Disk Management Made Simple."

■ Your hard disk operates more slowly than it should. Over time, hard disk performance deteriorates as files become *fragmented*, or are split up and placed in multiple locations on your hard disk. DOS 6 includes DEFRAG, a tool for solving this problem. Chapter 14 also contains a detailed discussion of DEFRAG.

■ You regularly use a laptop computer powered by batteries. Battery-powered laptops make it easy to compute while you are on the go. However, laptop batteries always seem to run out of power too soon. The POWER program reduces the drain on laptop batteries, meaning you can use your laptop longer without recharging. Chapter 28, "The POWER of INTERLNK," has a detailed discussion of POWER.

■ You use both a desktop computer and a laptop. If you use a laptop computer part of the time and a full-sized desktop computer at other times, it is essential that the files on both computers be up-to-date. INTERLNK provides a fast, powerful way to move large numbers of files between two computers. INTERLNK is also discussed in detail in Chapter 28.

■ You want protection against computer viruses. Computer viruses can destroy all the work you store on your hard disk. They can even destroy your hard disk itself. DOS 6 comes with Microsoft Anti-Virus for DOS and Windows, which detects computer viruses and, in most cases, repairs any damage they have caused. Chapter 18, "Protecting Your System," contains a detailed discussion of Microsoft Anti-Virus.

■ You need protection against accidental erasure of files. Even computer professionals erase files by mistake from time to time. Microsoft UNDELETE for Windows and DOS gives you the ability to restore files that you accidentally have deleted. Additional details about Microsoft UNDELETE are also found in Chapter 18.

New Commands and Other Features

DOS 6 includes other new features besides the utilities described in the preceding section. When deciding whether to upgrade to DOS 6, think about whether any of the following new features will be useful to you:

■ A complete on-line help system for all DOS commands. The new MS-DOS HELP provides detailed information and examples about each DOS command. This information is useful for beginning and experienced DOS users alike. For more details about MS-DOS HELP, see Chapter 5, "Peak Performance in the DOS Environment."

■ The DELTREE and MOVE commands, which enable you to move or delete entire sections of your hard disk with a single command. Accomplishing these tasks with previous versions of DOS required sequences of commands. More detail about these commands is found in Chapter 10, "Working with Files and Directories."

■ The ability to start your computer in many different ways.
This enables you to customize your usage of DOS to meet
specific computing needs. You can find more detail about
the new support for multiple configurations in Chapter 13,
"Customizing DOS."

■ Added power in batch commands. The new CHOICE batch
program command adds versatility to batch commands by
enabling user input and other benefits. For more about
the CHOICE command, see Chapter 29, "Batch Programs
Unleashed."

Upgrading from DOS 2, 3, or 4

If you use a version of DOS that is even earlier than DOS 5, the array of additional features available in DOS 6 might be dizzying. The
preceding section outlined features that were added between DOS
5 and 6. If you upgrade to DOS 6 from an earlier version of DOS,
you will gain all those new features, plus many features that initially appeared in DOS 5. This section provides a brief summary of
these features.

Perhaps the most important innovation in DOS 5 was its capability to use the so-called high memory area of your computer's
random-access memory (RAM) to store program information. The
benefit of this capability is that it provides more memory for your
programs. If you are using an older version of DOS and regularly
run out of memory, upgrading to DOS 6 will help you. Details about
memory usage are found in Chapter 15, "Getting the Most from
Your Memory."

DOS 4 was the first version of DOS to include a Shell to provide
a graphical framework for managing your programs, files, and
drives. However, the DOS Shell was significantly upgraded for DOS
5, in both appearance and functionality. If you are using the DOS 4
Shell, or previous versions of DOS without a shell, the DOS Shell in
DOS 6 might be a good reason to upgrade. You can find details about

the DOS Shell in Chapter 8, "Using the Shell," Chapter 10, "Working with Files and Directories," and Chapter 14, "Hard Disk Management Made Simple."

The MS-DOS Editor was added to DOS 5 for editing many DOS-related files. This full-featured text editor makes creating and altering text files simple. Details about the MS-DOS Editor are included in Chapter 11, "Creating and Editing Files."

The DOSKEY utility added in DOS 5 remembers the commands you issue to DOS and makes them easily available to you again, meaning you don't have to retype commands you recently used. This is a tremendous time and effort saver for DOS command-prompt users. Details about DOSKEY are found in Chapter 13, "Customizing DOS."

DOS 5 included numerous improvements to the DIR command that enable you to sort the order in which it lists files. Details about DIR command capabilities are included in Chapter 9, "Using the Command Line."

DOS 5 added support for larger floppy and hard drives. Specifically, it provides support for more than two hard drives and for hard drive partitions larger than 32M. It also provided support for new high-capacity 2.88M floppy drives. You can find details about using larger storage devices in Chapter 21, "Maximizing Your Disk Drives."

For programmers, the MS-DOS QBasic program, added in DOS 5, provides a more robust BASIC programming environment than was previously available. Details about MS-DOS QBasic are found in Chapter 30, "A QBasic Primer."

Requirements for Upgrading

The following sections discuss what you need in order to upgrade to DOS 6.

Hardware Requirements

DOS 6 comes on high-density floppy disks. High-density 3 ½-inch floppy disks have a capacity of 1.44M, and high-density 5 ¼-inch floppy disks have a capacity of 1.2M.

If your computer's floppy drives read only low-density disks, you must order your DOS 6 disks from Microsoft. The DOS 6 package includes a coupon for ordering low-density disks.

As with previous versions of DOS, you can run DOS 6 on computers with only one floppy drive. Although computers with this configuration were relatively common in the early days of DOS and PCs, hard drives have been standard equipment on most PCs for years.

If you use an older PC with only one or two floppy drives and no hard drive, you can still use many of the features in DOS 6. However, many of the new features in DOS 6 are designed specifically for use with hard drives.

If you have a hard drive, you need at least 6M of free disk space for DOS 6 and all the accompanying programs. Note, however, that during the installation process, you can choose not to install all the DOS 6 programs.

If you do not use Windows, you can save hard disk space by not installing the Microsoft Backup, Anti-Virus, and Undelete programs for Windows.

DOS 6 runs properly with virtually any video configuration that is commonly available.

Memory Requirements

When PCs first became popular in the early 1980s, most computers came with 256K of RAM installed. However, over the years, computer programs have become more sophisticated and, as a result, require more memory than they used to. DOS is no exception. To install DOS 6, you need 420K of free memory.

Note, however, that most large applications you are likely to use will require even more memory. To run DOS and your applications most effectively, you should have at least 640K of memory installed in your computer.

 Troubleshooting

To avoid problems moving to DOS 6, you need to perform the following before installing DOS 6:

- Back up critical files. This is especially critical if you are using disk-compression software.

- Disable disk-caching and anti-virus programs. Edit your CONFIG.SYS and AUTOEXEC.BAT files and disable or remove startup commands for these programs if they are loaded when you start your computer.

- Disable automatic message services. These services, such as network pop-up or printing notification, display messages directly to your screen and are incompatible with DOS Setup.

- Run CHKDSK. CHKDSK enables you to check your computer's configuration to make sure you have enough memory, hard disk space, and so on.

- Review the READ.ME file. You can use a text editor or the command line to view this file which contains valuable, late breaking information that might not have been included in your DOS manuals. Once you install DOS 6, this text file is located in your MS-DOS directory.

Summary

This chapter helped you decide whether to upgrade to DOS 6. It described the benefits of all the new features in DOS 6. It also discussed minimum requirements for using DOS 6. Specifically, this chapter taught you the following information:

- You might want to upgrade if you need any of the new utility programs and commands included with DOS 6.

- DOS 6 includes freestanding utilities that protect and optimize your computer system.

- DOS 6 also includes new commands and capabilities to make your use of DOS more efficient.

- Many, but not all, of the new capabilities in DOS 6 are designed to optimize hard drives or memory usage.

Alan Simpson's
DOS
SECRETS
UNLEASHED

CHAPTER 3

Exploring the Basics of DOS

Computers are tools designed to perform one basic task: reading instructions. In this sense, a computer is similar to a cassette player. If you turn on a cassette player without music (stored on a cassette tape) in it, the cassette deck does nothing. When you put in a recorded cassette tape and press the Play button, the stereo plays whatever music the tape "tells" it to play, be it Beethoven or the Beatles.

Similarly, if you turn on a computer without a *program* (instructions) in it, the computer does nothing. However, when you "play" a program, the computer does whatever the program's instructions tell it to do, such as manage your business, create graphics, or help you write a book.

DOS is a very special program that makes many things possible on your personal computer. Every time you work with a personal computer, you are certain to use DOS.

This book discusses the newest version of DOS, DOS 6, in detail. This chapter, however, discusses computers in general and defines some common computer terms, such as *hardware, software, RAM,* and *DOS.* This will make the computer less mysterious and intimidating to newcomers and might refresh the memories of older, more experienced computer users.

Computer Hardware

Computer *hardware* is the stuff that you can see and touch and that would probably break if dropped on the floor. A microcomputer system usually consists of the computer itself and several *peripheral devices* (or simply *devices*), such as the video monitor, the printer, the keyboard, and perhaps others.

Virtually all microcomputer systems consist of a central unit (also called the system unit), a keyboard, and a video monitor. In the early days of PCs, you could buy a computer with only one *floppy disk drive* for storing programs and information. These days, however, nearly all PCs include a *hard drive* for storing information.

Other useful devices that you can attach to your computer include a printer, which provides *hard* (printed) copies of information from the computer; a *modem* (short for modulator/demodulator) for communicating with other computers via telephone lines; and a *mouse,* an optional device that enables you to interact with the computer without having to type on the keyboard.

A brief discussion of the functions of these peripherals follows.

The Keyboard

You use the keyboard to type information into the computer. The primary section of the keyboard is similar to a standard typewriter, except that the carriage-return key is replaced by a key labeled Enter or Return, or with the symbol ↵.

Besides the standard typewriter keys, most computer keyboards also include a numeric keypad (similar to that on an adding machine), cursor-control (arrow) keys, and function keys.

The Mouse

Mice sometimes are called *pointing devices* because they make it easy to point an on-screen cursor at specific parts of software programs and select commands and options. In many cases, mice also enable you to navigate through programs more easily and quickly than is possible with the keyboard.

A mouse should fit comfortably in your hand. A mouse has as many as three buttons that you press to initiate actions in your software or to confirm actions your software has asked you to take.

You can't use mice with all programs. And in most programs in which you can use mice, you also can use your keyboard to accomplish the same tasks.

Some programs are more "mouse-centric" than others. In other words, some programs make it harder to issue commands and navigate through screens with a keyboard than with a mouse.

These days, an increasing number of programs enable the use of mice. This is particularly true in graphical environments such as Microsoft Windows.

The Video Monitor

The video monitor (also called the *screen*, the *monitor*, the *display*, or the *VDT*) shows what you type at the keyboard and what the computer's response is. Some monitors can have only one color and display only alphanumeric characters. Such monitors are called *monochrome* monitors. Most monitors sold today, however, can show many colors, as well as display graphics images.

The Printer

Most computers have a printer attached to make *hard copies*, or print information on paper. If your computer has a printer attached, DOS (and this book) will help you use it to its fullest potential.

Various types of printers are available for modern microcomputers, such as the fast *dot-matrix* printer, the slower *daisy-wheel* printer, and the powerful and versatile *laser* printer.

Floppy Diskette Drives

The floppy diskette drive (or drives) on your computer plays a role similar to that of a turntable or cassette player on a stereo. Computer programs are stored magnetically on diskettes, in much the same way that music is stored magnetically on cassette tapes. As the drive spins the diskette within its casing, the computer reads information from and records information on the diskette.

Microcomputer diskettes come in two sizes—5$\frac{1}{4}$-inch floppy diskettes (or minidiskettes) and 3$\frac{1}{2}$-inch microfloppies (or microdiskettes). Your computer probably has at least one disk drive that is capable of handling one of these diskette sizes.

Some leeway is provided in using diskettes of different storage capacities within different disk drives. The basic rule is that a disk drive can use diskettes that are equal to or less than the drive's own total capacity. That is, a high-capacity drive can read both high-capacity and low-capacity diskettes. A low-capacity disk drive, however, can use only low-capacity diskettes.

General Care of Diskettes

Always handle diskettes with the label side up and your thumb on the label. This helps prevent you from touching the magnetic media (particularly on 5$\frac{1}{4}$-inch disks, on which the magnetic media is exposed in a large oblong cut-out section). This procedure also ensures that you insert the diskette into the drive correctly.

When you remove diskettes from your computer, keep them away from extreme temperatures, dust, dirt, coffee spills, pets or young children, and—most important—magnets. If you use 5$\frac{1}{4}$-inch diskettes, be sure to place the diskette back in its paper sleeve to keep dust and dirt off the exposed magnetic media.

Fixed Disks

Besides diskette drives, most computers also have a fixed disk (or *hard disk*, as it is often called). Unlike the drives that use diskettes, a fixed disk uses magnetic media that you cannot remove; it stays inside the fixed disk unit at all times.

A single hard disk can store as many programs as dozens, or even hundreds, of diskettes can. Whenever you buy a new software product (a program), you copy it onto your hard disk and then store the original floppy diskette in a safe place. In the future, when you want to use a program, such as an inventory manager or a form-letter generator, you don't need to bother with diskettes. Just select (or type) the name of your program, and it's immediately available for use.

Besides having great storage capacity, a hard disk drive operates at a much higher speed than diskette drives do, which in turn increases your productivity.

Directories

Because you can store so much information on a hard drive, DOS includes a method of dividing and subdividing the hard drive by creating *directories* and *subdirectories.* Directories and subdirectories provide structure for your hard disk so that you don't have to search long for your information when you need it.

One way of thinking about directories is to think of a file cabinet. You can place all your information on your hard drive just as you can place information in a file cabinet. However, you might want even more organization. With a file cabinet, you have drawers, and within each drawer are folders. Similarly, with a hard drive you have directories. Within each directory can be more directories, called subdirectories, which are like folders. Chapter 10, "Working with Files and Directories," and Chapter 14, "Hard Disk Management Made Simple," discuss organization of your hard drive in greater detail.

Files

All information that your computer uses is stored in *files.* Files, in turn, are stored on either floppy diskettes or hard drives. There are two basic kinds of files:

Program files store the instructions that make your programs work. Each program you use, including DOS, is composed of one or more files which control the activities of that program.

Data files contain the information you create using your programs. This information takes the form of documents created with your word processor or with any of the other kinds of programs described in later sections.

Disk Drive Names

Each disk drive is assigned a name, consisting of a single letter followed by a colon. The diskette drives are always named A: and B: (if your computer has only one drive, it is named A:). The first hard disk is always named C:. Note, however, that some computers have additional hard disks named D:, E:, F:, and so on.

Random-Access Memory

At the very heart of every computer is *random-access memory*, abbreviated RAM. (RAM often is called *main memory* or just *memory*.) RAM is composed of small electrical components called *chips*. These chips are mounted inside the main system unit and need never be removed.

When you first turn on your computer, most of RAM is empty. When you tell your computer to perform a particular job, it copies the program (instructions) required to perform that job from the disk into RAM. After the program is in RAM, the computer reads the program's instructions and behaves accordingly.

Why can't the computer just read the instructions directly from the disk without first copying them into RAM? There are a few reasons, but the most important reason is speed. Basically, RAM operates much more quickly than the disk drives. The computer copies a program into RAM before executing its instructions to ensure that everything goes at top speed. In this way, your work gets done as quickly and efficiently as possible.

If RAM is so much faster than the disk drives, why not just store everything in RAM and forget about the disk drives? Although disks store information *magnetically*, RAM stores information *electronically*. When you turn off the computer, or the electricity goes off, everything in RAM vanishes instantly! For this reason, RAM is said to be *volatile*. Also, RAM costs more than magnetic media.

DOS takes care of all the details of loading programs into RAM and executing instructions. When you want to use a program on your computer, all you have to do is type a *command* (usually one word) or press a button. DOS takes care of the rest.

Computer Software

I've already talked about how software provides instructions that tell the computer how to behave. When you buy software, it is stored on a diskette. To use the software, you enter a command that tells the computer to load that program into RAM and to execute its instructions.

Literally thousands of software products are available for modern microcomputers—everything from video games to accounting packages.

Word Processing

Word processing programs have virtually replaced the typewriter because they offer features that no typewriter can provide. With a word processor, you can easily move, copy, or delete words, sentences, paragraphs, or entire groups of paragraphs. You can even reformat an entire document (such as changing the margins or line spacing) with the press of a key.

Some word processors can check and correct your spelling and even suggest changes in your grammar. Most also provide capabilities for printing form letters, mailing labels, and envelopes.

Desktop Publishing

Desktop publishing programs turn your computer into a powerful typesetting machine. Using desktop publishing programs, you can produce printed pages with various print sizes and fonts, margin notes, embedded graphs, and other advanced printing features (such as those you see in this book).

Spreadsheets

If you've ever used a ledger sheet to work with financial data and have had to change an entry and recalculate the entire ledger sheet with your calculator, pencil, and eraser, you're sure to love spreadsheet programs. A spreadsheet program acts much like a ledger sheet, except that when you change any individual piece of information on the ledger sheet, the program instantly updates all the calculated values on the sheet for you.

Many spreadsheet programs also provide a graphics capability that enables you to instantly plot ledger information on a graph. Spreadsheets are great for projecting what-if scenarios, because you can experiment with any piece of information, such as interest rates or potential sales forecasts, and immediately see the results of your experiments.

Database Management Systems

Database management systems manage large volumes of information, such as mailing lists, customer lists, inventories, financial transactions, and scientific data. Using these programs, you can store, change, delete, sort, search, and print large volumes of information.

Most database management systems (abbreviated DBMS) also enable you to develop *applications* that you can tailor to your own business needs. For example, you could use a single database management system to manage your company's accounting, inventory management, personnel information, sales prospects, and customer lists.

Some database management systems also provide graphics capabilities that enable you to see information in the form of graphs, pie charts, and the like.

Accounting Packages

Accounting packages are programs specifically designed to aid in bookkeeping and accounting. Most accounting packages are modularized so that you can buy and use only what your company requires. Accounting packages usually consist of the following modules: General Ledger, Accounts Payable, Accounts Receivable, Time and Billing, Payroll, Job Costing, Inventory Control, and Manufacturing Planning.

Operating Systems

No matter which types of software you use, you must have an *operating system*. This program starts your computer and manages the flow of information to and from the various components, such as the diskettes, the hard disk, and the printer.

DOS, an acronym for Disk Operating System, is such an operating system. As you'll learn in coming chapters, DOS provides many services that are essential to your computer.

Computer Capacities

Suppose that a friend or a computer salesman shows you a computer, pats it gently atop the monitor, and says, "This baby has an 80386 microprocessor running at 20 megahertz, with 640K RAM, and an 80-meg hard disk." Unless you are already familiar with computer terminology, you might wonder whether this person is even speaking English! Yes, this person is speaking English and is describing how "big" and how fast the computer is. I will define these often-used computer buzzwords in the next sections.

Kilobytes and Megabytes

A single character of information occupies one *byte* of storage on a computer. Therefore, the word *cat* occupies three bytes. Most diskettes can store many thousands of bytes, so their capacities are often expressed in *kilobytes* (abbreviated *K* or *KB*). You can think of a kilobyte as 1,000 bytes (although, actually, it's 2^{10}, or 1,024 bytes). Hence, a 720K diskette can store 737,280 characters of information. Because the average typed, double-spaced page contains 2,000 characters, a 720K diskette can store approximately 360 typed pages (that is, 720,000/2,000 = 360).

Some diskettes, and certainly all hard disks, can store millions of bytes, and their capacities are measured in *megabytes* (abbreviated *M* or *MB* when written, or expressed as the word *meg* when spoken). A megabyte is equal to a thousand kilobytes, or approximately one million bytes. Therefore, an 80M (that is, 80 meg) hard disk can hold about 80,000,000 characters, or about 80,000 typewritten pages.

In case you insist on absolute accuracy, I should mention that a megabyte is actually 1,024 kilobytes, or 1,048,576 bytes.

RAM also stores information, but rarely as much as is on a hard disk or even on diskettes. Remember, RAM stores a copy only of the program that you are currently using. Therefore, you need only as much RAM as your computer's largest program requires.

Megahertz

Besides the storage capacity of a computer, *clock speed* is an important factor. All computers operate with an internal *clock*. Each time the clock "ticks," the computer does a tiny bit of work. The speed at which the clock ticks is measured in *megahertz* (abbreviated *MHz*). One megahertz equals one million ticks per second.

The maximum clock speed of a computer is closely related to the model number of the microprocessor that the computer uses. The five microprocessors used in IBM-compatible microcomputers are the 8086, the 8088, the 80286, the 80386, and the 80486 models. The 8086 and 8088 are somewhat obsolete, however, and release of the next-generation chip, called the Pentium chip, was imminent as this book went to press.

The first-generation microprocessor (for IBM-compatible micro-computers) was the 8088, which runs at a clock speed of 4.77 MHz. The next-generation microprocessor was the 8086, which operates at a top speed of about 8 MHz. The next-generation microprocessor was the 80286, which operates at speeds up to about 20 MHz. The newer 80386 and 80486 models can operate at speeds in excess of 60 MHz.

> Even though programs do not require a specific clock speed, some programs run only on computers that use an 80286, 80386, or 80486 microprocessor.

So Where Does DOS Fit In?

I've already mentioned that DOS is an operating system—a specialized set of programs that you use to start and operate your computer. It is DOS that actually coordinates all the components of your computer, even to the point of getting other programs into RAM and starting them running.

Much of what DOS does occurs automatically, behind the scenes where you do not have to be concerned with it. But DOS definitely enables you to perform important and useful tasks, including those in the following list:

■ Run applications programs, such as business programs, graphics programs, word processors, spreadsheets, and any other program you want to use.

■ Organize large amounts of information for quick and easy retrieval.

■ Format diskettes and copy information to them to share with coworkers or for use on other computers.

■ Make backup copies of information on your hard disk so that if you ever accidentally erase information, you can get it back.

■ Add new components—such as a mouse, a modem, or a laser printer—as your system grows.

■ Internationalize your computer for printing in foreign-language alphabets.

Starting Your Computer and DOS

You can't start, or *boot up,* a computer without DOS or some other operating system. That's because when you turn on the computer, it immediately searches its disk drives for an operating system. If the computer cannot find an operating system, it has no operating instructions, so it does nothing.

Because there are so many different types of computers and different versions of DOS, the start-up procedures for your particular computer cannot be specified here. However, this chapter explains general start-up procedures and shows you how to determine the version of DOS that is installed on your computer.

Installing DOS

 If you experience a problem during the start-up procedure, see the "Troubleshooting" section near the end of this chapter for advice.

Before you can use DOS, you need to install it on your computer. Chapter 4, "Installation Secrets and Surprises," contains a more detailed and technical discussion of installing DOS, and general installation instructions are found in Appendix A.

Starting DOS with a Hard Disk

If your computer has a hard disk and DOS has been installed to start from the hard disk, the steps for starting DOS are simple:

1. Be sure that any floppy diskette drives are empty. If the disk drive has a latch (or door), put it in the open position.

2. Turn on the computer (as well as the monitor and the printer) by turning on all the appropriate knobs and switches.

3. Wait until the computer finishes its power-on tests (most computers sound a beep at this point).

4. Skip to the section titled "Entering the Date and Time."

Starting DOS Without a Hard Disk

If your computer has no hard disk (or if DOS is installed so that it must be started from a floppy diskette), the following steps start DOS:

1. Insert the DOS Start-up disk in drive A: or drive B:.

2. Turn on the computer (as well as the monitor and printer) by turning on all the appropriate switches.

3. Wait until the computer finishes its power-on tests and sounds a beep.

4. Proceed with the next section.

Entering the Date and Time

Depending on the setup of your computer and the version of DOS you are using, your screen might ask you to enter the current date and time before proceeding. If your computer does not have a battery-driven clock to keep track of the date and time when the computer is off, DOS will probably ask for the current date by displaying a message similar to this:

```
Current date is Tue 1-01-1980
Enter new date (mm-dd-yy):
```

As always, the blinking cursor to the right of the colon (:) indicates that DOS is waiting for you to enter the current date. Type the current date using the format mm-dd-yy (for example, 6-1-93 for June 1, 1993). Press the Enter key (labeled as ↵, Enter, or Return) on your keyboard.

Next, DOS probably displays a message similar to this:

```
Current time is 1:04:43.47p
Enter new time:
```

Again, the blinking cursor indicates that DOS is waiting for you to enter the time. Even though DOS displays the time down to a hundredth of a second, you can type just the hour and minute, using a *p* to indicate PM. For example, type 9:30 for 9:30 a.m., or 4:30p for 4:30 in the afternoon. Press Enter after typing the time.

Note that versions of DOS before DOS 5 expect you to enter the time in 24-hour (military) format, in which morning hours up to noon are expressed as usual, but after noon, each hour has 12 added to it. For example, the hour for 1:00 p.m. is 13, for 2:00 p.m. the hour is 14, and so on until 11:00 p.m., which is hour 23. Midnight is expressed as hour zero (0).

What happens next depends on the version of DOS that is currently installed on your computer, as well as how DOS is installed. If you are using a version of DOS prior to version 4, you will see the DOS *command prompt*, which usually appears as a single letter followed by a greater-than sign, such as A> or C>. (See Figure 3.1.) Your screen might show additional information, such as the version of DOS in use and copyright notices.

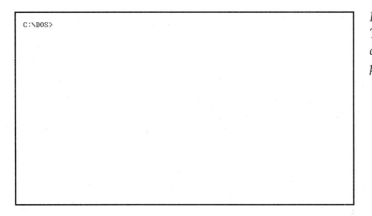

```
C:\DOS>
```

Figure 3.1.
The DOS
command
prompt:

If you are using DOS Version 4 or later, your screen might show the *DOS Shell,* which displays much more information. The Shell program in DOS 4 is quite different from that in DOS 5 and 6. Figure 3.2 shows the DOS 6 Shell when it is first activated.

For the time being, assume that your computer is displaying the DOS prompt. The next section shows you how to determine which version of DOS is currently installed on your computer (in case it is not already displayed on your screen).

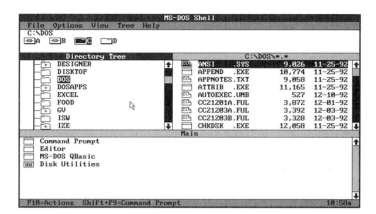

Figure 3.2.
The DOS 6
Shell.

Determining Your Version of DOS

Although this book focuses on the newest version of DOS (version 6), it also can be used with DOS 3 and later versions. If your screen is now displaying the DOS prompt (for example, A> or C>) with a blinking cursor to the right, you can easily determine what version of DOS is in control by following these steps:

1. Type VER.

2. Press Enter.

> When typing DOS *commands,* such as VER, you can use uppercase, lowercase, or a combination of upper- and lowercase letters.

The screen now displays a brief message similar to this one:

```
MS-DOS Version 6.0
```

Don't be concerned if the message you see is worded differently; the important fact is that the correct version number appears.

The DOS Shell

Look again at Figure 3.2 to see how the DOS 6 Shell looks on your screen when it is first activated (although your particular screen might look slightly different).

The DOS Shell, which is available only in DOS Version 4 and higher, provides a more convenient method for interacting with DOS. It is called a Shell because, in a sense, it surrounds the complicated inner workings of DOS and enables you to interact with DOS in a simplified, graphical manner.

As mentioned earlier, the Shell used in DOS 5 and 6 is significantly different from the DOS 4 Shell.

Determining Your DOS Version from the Shell

Here is a quick way to determine which version of DOS you are using, even if the Shell is currently displayed on your screen:

1. Press Shift+F9 (hold down the Shift key and press the F9 key, then release both keys) to leave the Shell.

2. Type VER and press Enter. Note the DOS version number on your screen.

3. Type EXIT and press Enter to return to the Shell.

Starting the DOS Shell from a Hard Disk

If your computer has a hard disk and you are certain you are using DOS Version 4 or greater, start the DOS Shell by typing DOSSHELL at the command prompt and pressing Enter. The DOS Shell that appears on your screen resembles the Shell shown in Figure 3.2.

Troubleshooting

If your computer does not start or operate properly, determine which of the following descriptions most accurately represents your problem, and then try the suggested solution.

- If the screen displays the message `Non-System disk or disk error Replace and press any key when ready`, you have inserted a disk in drive A: or B: that is not capable of starting DOS. If, on your computer, DOS starts from the hard disk, remove all floppy diskettes and reboot your computer. If you want to start your computer with a floppy diskette, place the correct Start-up disk in drive A: or drive B:. If you've installed DOS Version 4 or greater, insert the copy labeled Start-up. If you use DOS Version 3.3, insert the disk labeled Start-up or Start-up/Operating. If you are using an earlier version of DOS, use the disk labeled DOS— not the one labeled DOS Supplemental Programs. After you insert the disk and close the drive latch (if the drive has a latch), press any key to try starting DOS again.

- If the computer seems to start but nothing appears on-screen, be sure you have turned on your monitor, and then turn the brightness knob clockwise to illuminate the screen. If this action does not help, turn off the computer and monitor and be sure all the wires are properly plugged into the back of the computer and into the wall socket. Then turn on the computer and the monitor again.

- If nothing happens when you turn the power switch on the computer (for example, you cannot even hear the fan running), return the switch to the off position, and be sure everything is plugged in according to the directions in your computer's operation manual. Then try again. If you plug all your computer plugs into a plug-in strip, or a single device that accepts multiple plugs, make sure the strip is turned on.

■ If all else fails, refer to your computer's operation manual
and the DOS manual for additional start-up procedures.

Summary

This chapter examined the basic components of computer hardware
and software and discussed the purpose of each element. This chapter also described how DOS works with your computer system and
defined several computer buzzwords that you might have heard (or
eventually will encounter) in your work with computers. Specifically, this chapter taught you:

■ Computer hardware consists of the physical components of
your computer, such as the central processing unit, the
keyboard, the monitor, and other optional devices.

■ Programs, which tell the computer how to behave, are
stored magnetically on hard disks and diskettes.

■ Floppy diskette drives allow the computer to read information from and record information on diskettes.

■ A fixed disk (or hard disk) is an optional device that can
store copies of programs and information from many
dozens, or even hundreds, of diskettes.

■ RAM (random-access memory) is the part of the computer
that stores whatever program you are using at the moment.

■ Software is the name given to programs (that is, instructions) used in RAM and stored magnetically on disks.

■ The amount of software that a diskette, hard disk, or RAM
can store is measured in bytes (each of which holds a single
character), kilobytes (about 1,000 bytes), and megabytes
(about 1,000,000 bytes).

■ The speed at which a computer operates is measured in
megahertz, abbreviated MHz.

■ DOS (an acronym for Disk Operating System) is a special set of programs that your computer needs to get started and to use all other types of programs.

■ The DOS Shell is available only in version 4 and greater of DOS.

■ A blinking cursor next to the command prompt indicates that DOS is waiting for you to type a command and then press the Enter key.

Setting Up DOS

Alan Simpson's
DOS
SECRETS
UNLEASHED

CHAPTER 4

Installation Secrets and Surprises

Installing DOS, in most cases, is a simple operation. You insert the Setup disk in your floppy drive, type SETUP, and then watch the screen and respond to prompts until the installation is complete. See Appendix A, "Installing DOS," for detailed instructions.

This chapter describes the considerations you should be aware of before you install DOS 6. Also in this chapter, you are given guidelines for configuring your system to take advantage of DOS 6 features for data protection.

Preparing Your Installation

You need to do several things before you install any program, and DOS 6 is no exception. For example, you need to make sure you have enough disk space to store the program. You might need to disable certain memory-resident programs that can interfere with your installation. And you should decide which, if any, files you need to back up before you begin.

> Before you can use DOS 6, you must run the Setup program. You cannot boot your computer from the DOS 6 Setup floppy disks, because files on these disks are compressed. Setup decompresses the files as it copies them to your hard disk. See "Using the Uninstall Disks" or "Creating a Bootable Floppy" sections in this chapter.

Checking the README.TXT File

The README.TXT file that comes with your Setup disks contains information about installing DOS 6 on systems with specific hardware configurations. You should, for example, consult this file before running Setup on a drive that uses disk-compression soft-ware such as Stacker or SuperStor. It's a good idea to consult this file regardless of your hardware configuration—just to be safe.

To view the README.TXT file, type the command

```
TYPE A:README.TXT ¦ MORE
```

This command displays the contents of README.TXT and pauses scrolling as screens are filled. As an alternative, type

```
EDIT A:README.TXT
```

to load the file with the DOS 6 text editor. You can then take advan-tage of capabilities of searching and replacing, and of configuring the display.

Determining Available Disk Space

One of the first things you should know about installing DOS 6 might be surprising. DOS 6 requires a minimum of 4.2M of disk space. If you install DOS 6 with all the included utilities, such as Undelete, Anti-Virus, and Backup, you will need a little more than 8M for installation. This is a significant increase over DOS 5, which required just under 3M. So one of the first things you should do is make sure you have enough disk space.

Use the CHKDSK utility to check your available disk space. At the DOS prompt, type

```
CHKDSK drive
```

This command scans the drive you specify and displays a summary report.

If you do not have sufficient disk space, you can proceed in two ways. First, you can free up more space by deleting files you don't need. Or, use a custom installation and install a minimum configu-ration that works with your available space.

> You also can use the DoubleSpace program to automatically increase the amount of free space on your disk.

Disabling Memory-Resident Programs

Certain memory-resident programs can interfere with the DOS 6 setup programs and produce unpredictable results. The following types of programs should be disabled before you run Setup:

■ Disk-Caching programs, such as Windows SMARTDRIVE, PC Tools, PC-CACHE, and Norton Utilities NCACHE.

■ Delete protection programs, such as PC Tools UNDELETE and Norton Utilities UNERASE.

■ Anti-virus programs, such as PC Tools ANTI-VIRUS.

■ Automatic message services, such as network pop-ups or printing notifications that are output directly on your screen.

To disable these programs, use a text editor to edit your CONFIG.SYS and AUTOEXEC.BAT files. Find the commands that load these programs. Insert * or REM in front of these commands. When you boot, these commands are not executed. After you have installed DOS, delete the * or REM notations to return to your previous configuration.

Backing Up—to B: or Not to B:

The DOS 6 documentation tells you to back up your entire hard drive before running Setup. The Setup program even displays a message prompt telling you the same thing. Regular backups should be a part of your overall computing strategy. Sooner or later, something in your system is going to fail. So if you haven't backed up for a while, or if you just want the maximum level of security and confidence, follow these instructions. Back up your hard drive.

At times backing up is required, such as when you repartition your hard drive before installing. Consider also doing a full backup if you are installing DoubleSpace data compression software. Incidentally, repartitioning a drive destroys all the data on it.

Weigh these caveats against this tip: *you might not need to back up your entire drive before running Setup.* If you have copies of your program disks and recent work files, you can save a lot of time and trouble. The Setup program presents little risk of losing data.

Using the Uninstall Disks

When you install DOS 6, you are prompted to use two blank disks labeled Uninstall #1 and Uninstall #2. These disks are used to restore the previous version of DOS in case you encounter problems installing DOS 6.

> If you use 3½-inch floppies, you need only one Uninstall disk.

The primary purpose of the Uninstall disks is to safeguard your files while you are installing DOS 6. The first time you run Setup, a directory named OLD_DOS1 is automatically created. DOS files from the previous version are copied to this directory, from which they are available until they are deleted. Setup also copies your CONFIG.SYS and AUTOEXEC.BAT files to the Uninstall disks and renames them CONFIG.DAT and AUTOEXEC.DAT. There is also a program, UNINSTAL.EXE, which restores your previous version of DOS.

To restore your previous version of DOS, follow this procedure:

1. Insert the Uninstall Disk #1 in drive A:.

> If you uninstall after you install DoubleSpace, you will lose your data on the DoubleSpace drive. Be sure to back up your data.

2. Press Ctrl+Alt+Del to restart your computer and boot from the Uninstall disk.

3. Follow screen instructions to restore the previous version of DOS.

Another major benefit of the Uninstall disks is that you can use them to boot your computer if you have problems with your hard drive. To start your computer using the Uninstall disks and not restore the previous DOS version, follow this procedure:

1. Insert the Uninstall Disk #1 in drive A:.

2. Press Ctrl+Alt+Del to restart your computer and boot from the Uninstall disk.

3. When the Uninstall screen appears, press F3 twice to quit the Uninstall program and go to the DOS prompt.

Creating a Bootable Floppy

Your Uninstall disks can be used for emergencies. A better way to go, though, is to create a bootable floppy disk with DOS 6. Then if something goes wrong, instead of reverting to the previous DOS version you can boot up with DOS 6. In addition, if you reformat or repartition your hard disk after creating the Uninstall disks, you won't be able to use them to restore your system. It's excellent practice, then, to create a bootable floppy disk.

In the past, you could boot your computer from the DOS disks that came with the program. This is no longer true. The disks shipped with DOS 6 (and DOS 5) contain compressed files and won't work on their own. The files must be expanded before they can be read and executed. The easiest way, then, to create a bootable floppy is to use the SYS command after DOS 6 is installed on your hard disk. For example, the command

```
SYS A:
```

copies the system files and COMMAND.COM to a formatted floppy disk in drive A:. You can format the floppy and add the system files by typing

```
FORMAT /S
```

on an unformatted floppy.

> Label your bootable floppy SYSTEM or EMERGENCY, and keep it handy. You can make this disk even more valuable by copying other DOS files onto it. For example, keep a current copy of your CONFIG.SYS and AUTOEXEC.BAT files on it to configure your system when you use the floppy to boot.

You might want to copy your mouse driver and any other important device drivers onto the floppy as well. If you do, edit the CONFIG.SYS and AUTOEXEC.BAT files on the bootable floppy to modify the path designations for these drivers. Change

```
C:\DOS\MOUSE.SYS
```

to

```
A:\MOUSE.SYS
```

so that the system knows where to find your mouse driver when it boots from the floppy.

Put the CHKDSK.EXE program on your emergency disk. Then you can run it to diagnose the hard drive that's causing the problem. Put FORMAT.COM on it in case, regrettably, you're ever compelled to reformat your hard drive. You can also copy BACKUP.EXE and RESTORE.EXE onto it to save files, if possible, from the problem drive.

Installing DOS 6 on Floppies

An alternative to creating an emergency disk is to create an entire set of DOS 6 disks. This way you have access from floppy disks to all DOS utilities.

To be doubly safe, you might do both—create an emergency disk and a set of DOS 6 floppies. This should keep you ready for any contingency.

Creating a set of DOS 6 disks on floppies requires three diskettes labeled STARTUP/SUPPORT, HELP/BASIC/UTILITY, and SUPPLEMENTAL. Type the command

```
SETUP /F
```

and then follow the screen instructions, inserting and swapping diskettes as directed. Or see Appendix A, "Installing DOS," for complete details.

Don't use a floppy with a previous version of DOS to boot your computer. You can damage the information on your hard drive if you do. It's good practice before you install DOS 6 to find all your old emergency start-up disks and label them clearly. If you need to, use the VER command to check which version of DOS is on the disks. Then put them away somewhere remote, or reformat them. Don't keep them where they can be reached if your hard disk fails—don't make it too easy to panic and reach for the closest disk. Make sure you use the emergency start-up disk with the current version of DOS.

Installing DOS 6 Manually

You might need to install DOS 6 manually for computers with certain types of partitions or disk-partitioning software. The easiest way to do this is to first create a set of DOS floppy disks. Next, follow these steps:

1. Quit Setup.

2. Insert the STARTUP/SUPPORT disk in your floppy drive.

3. Restart your computer by pressing Ctrl+Alt+Del.

4. Type SYS C: (for drive C:).

5. Create a directory for files from the previous DOS version by typing MD C:\OLD_DOS.

6. Type COPY C:\DOS*.* C:\OLD_DOS to copy the old files to the new directory.

7. Type DEL C:\DOS*.* to delete the files in your \DOS directory.

8. Copy the DOS 6 files from your floppies to your hard disk by typing COPY A;*.* C:\DOS.

9. Repeat step 8 for all three DOS 6 floppies.

Manually Expanding DOS 6 Files

As stated previously, the files on the DOS 6 Setup disks are compressed and must be expanded, or decompressed, before they can be read and executed. From time to time, you might find you need to copy one or more files from the Setup disks onto your hard disk. If you've created a set of DOS 6 floppy disks, you can copy the files you need from these disks.

However, if you haven't created a set of DOS 6 floppy disks, you can still expand Setup files manually using the DECOMP.EXE program. The program called DECOMP (for decompress) is usually found in your DOS directory. To decompress and copy the BACKUP.EXE file on drive A:, for example, use the following command structure:

```
DECOMP A:BACKUP.EX_ C:\DOS\BACKUP.EXE
```

Notice the EX_ extension on the source file. The compressed files on the Setup disks are given an underscore (_) at the end of their extensions. When you decompress the files, you must specify the substitute character.

Data Recovery Guidelines

The way you configure your DOS environment has a profound effect on the way your computer works for you. DOS 6 contains several features you can use to protect your data against inadvertent or malicious destruction.

Use the following guidelines for configuring your system for maximum recoverability. Then see Chapter 18, "Protecting Your System," for comprehensive instructions.

Creating an Emergency Disk

As stated previously, you can use the Uninstall disks created during Setup to start your computer in the event your hard drive fails. You can also create a bootable floppy that contains important DOS utilities that can be used for troubleshooting. Then if your system crashes, you can use the emergency disk to restart your computer and, hopefully, to restore your hard drive. Be sure to update your emergency disk any time the configuration of your system changes.

Running the MIRROR.COM Program from Your AUTOEXEC.BAT File

The MIRROR.COM program saves a copy of your file allocation table (FAT) and can be used to recover lost files if your FAT is corrupted. By running MIRROR from your AUTOEXEC.BAT file, you create backups of your FAT each time you start your computer. In addition, put the MIRROR.COM program on your emergency disk.

Making Regular Backups

No data recovery technique is foolproof. Having regular backups is your best protection against data loss.

Using Undelete to Protect Your Files

Having followed the previous guideline, the Undelete program provides excellent protection against accidental deletion of files. Undelete provides three levels of protection, depending on your requirements and available disk space. See Chapter 18, "Protecting Your System," for a complete discussion.

Optimizing Your Hard Disk Regularly

The DEFRAG.EXE program maximizes the efficiency of your disk accesses by rearranging your files into contiguous units. When your computer writes files to disk, it uses any available disk sectors. As you work, your files become fragmented. To access them, your computer must locate and read many noncontiguous sections. Run DEFRAG regularly to eliminate file fragmentation. Not only does this make locating files easier for your computer, but it also significantly increases your chances of recovering them in the event they are accidentally deleted.

Protecting Your Computer Against Viruses

Computer viruses can cause irrecoverable loss of data. DOS 6 includes two versions of Anti-Virus—one for DOS, and one for Windows. Use these programs to protect your system against infestation by viruses. Again, see Chapter 18 for complete instructions.

After DOS 6 Is Installed

After you've installed DOS 6, it's excellent practice to give your system a brief trial run to make sure everything is working correctly. Here's a brief list of things to do to check your installation:

1. Restart your computer to make sure that you get a DOS prompt.

2. Make sure your system is recognizing all your drives. Use the DIR command for each drive, and check that the number of bytes shown is correct for each.

3. Start an MS-DOS application. Make sure it works without problems. Open a file, save it, print it. If you use a mouse, make sure it responds to your manipulations.

4. If you use Windows, start it. Make sure it appears correctly on your screen. Run a Windows application and repeat step 3.

If you encounter problems, see Appendix A, "Installing DOS," for complete instructions on installing and troubleshooting DOS 6.

 # Troubleshooting

The following are the most common error messages you might encounter while installing DOS 6:

■ `Your computer uses a disk compression program`

You will not be able to uninstall DOS 6 during or after Setup if your computer uses a disk-compression program on its startup drive. After you setup DOS 6, replace your disk-compression program with the Microsoft DoubleSpace compression program. Be sure to back up your data files before you run Setup.

■ `Your computer uses a disk compression program and does not have enough free disk space to set up MS-DOS`

Your uncompressed drive, indicated by Setup, must have at least 512K of free disk space. Delete unnecessary files or move files to another drive until you have 512K free. Use the CHKDSK command to view the number of available bytes free on your uncompressed disk.

■ `Your computer uses password protection`

If your computer uses a password protection program, you must exit Setup, disable the program, restart your computer, and run Setup again.

■ `Cannot find a hard disk on your computer`

This message displays if your hard disk is incompatible with Setup or is supported by a device driver, or if your hard disk isn't functioning properly. You need to contact Microsoft Product Support Services for information.

■ Too many Primary Partitions or Incompatible Primary DOS
  Partition

If one of these messages displays, repartition your hard
drive and restart the installation program.

Summary

Although DOS 6 normally installs without problems, you need to
consider several strategic issues. First, make sure you have enough
disk space. Check the README.TXT file for any hardware-specific
issues you might encounter. You might not need to perform a complete backup. But you should create, at minimum, an Uninstall disk
or, preferably, a full-featured emergency disk you can use to restart
your computer in the event of hard disk failure. Use the data recovery features of DOS 6 to protect your data. After you install DOS 6,
make sure you can run your applications, open files, save files, print
files, and use your mouse correctly.

Alan Simpson's
DOS
SECRETS
UNLEASHED

C H A P T E R 5

Peak Performance in the DOS Environment

Peak system performance results from setting up the DOS environment so that programs run quickly and data is located efficiently. Optimizing your system with DOS 6 involves managing memory and disk space, and using the command prompt skillfully.

This chapter presents the basic concepts of configuring your system and setting up the DOS environment. It also presents some fundamental guidelines and simple techniques you can use to increase your computing power.

Understanding System Resources

System resources that directly affect performance are discussed in the following sections. These resources are covered:

- Processor type and speed
- Memory
- Available disk space

Your Processor's Effect on Performance

Your processor is a microchip that acts as the main, functional component of your computer. It handles program instructions, performs calculations, and generally runs the show. For IBM-PCs and compatibles, there are many types of processors, which can be grouped into the broad categories of 286, 386, and 486 machines. The higher the number, the faster the processor.

Processor speed, also called *clock speed*, refers to the rate at which instructions are routed through your computer's processing chip. This speed is expressed in megahertz (MHz). You have little control over your computer's processing speed. Some machines, for example, are designed to operate in turbo mode, which can be switched on and off. Also, certain 486 motherboards contain empty sockets designed to accept clock-doubling chips. So a 25 MHz 486 machine can be upgraded to 50 MHz. In the absence of an upgrade socket, however, your only option for increasing processor speed is to replace your motherboard. In this case, it might be just as cost-efficient to replace the entire system and take advantage of upgraded monitors, disk drives, and other components.

Memory and Performance

Random-access memory (RAM) provides temporary storage for applications and data. In general, the more memory you have, the faster your applications can run. After data and instructions are loaded into RAM, they can move around your system without hesitation.

In general, you can't have too much memory. However, there is a price/performance ratio at which it does not make sense to add memory. For example, adding 2M to a 1M machine gives a greater percentage of improvement than adding 2M to a 16M machine. Each system has a unique price/performance ratio. The only drawback to RAM is that it is volatile—its contents are lost when you exit programs or turn off the computer.

Understanding Memory

Before information is processed or displayed on-screen, it is first brought into memory. Application and data files are stored on your hard disk. Before your application displays any type of menu, all or part of its instructions are loaded into memory (see Figure 5.1). The application might then open a data file, bringing all or part of it into memory for processing. Reading application instructions and data from disk is a relatively slow, mechanical operation. So the more memory you have, the fewer disk accesses are required.

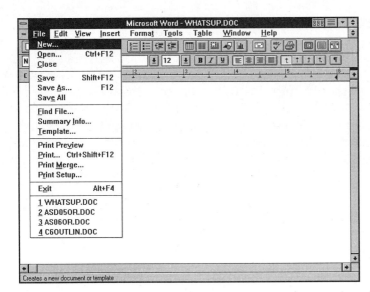

Figure 5.1.
A typical menu
display.

As software evolves, memory demands grow. Windows, as an example, requires a minimum of 2M of RAM just to load and run. For peak performance, 4M or more are recommended.

Types of Memory

The more program instructions and data you can stuff into memory, the faster your system operates. Several types of memory are installed on personal computers:

- Conventional memory

- Extended memory

- Expanded memory

- Upper memory

All of these memory areas function the same, storing data and program instructions temporarily. Programs use these areas for specific purposes. You can assign programs to load into specific areas. To do this, you must first load memory managers such as HIMEM.SYS and EMM386EXE. These programs are designed to facilitate the moving of programs and data into and out of extended and expanded memory. See Chapter 15, "Getting the Most from Your Memory," for more information.

In general, the first guideline to use when configuring your memory is this—conserve conventional memory.

The more conventional memory available, the faster your applications run. Most DOS programs today can run only in conventional memory, even though they might use extended and expanded memory for temporary storage. For peak performance, load DOS, device drivers, and other terminate-and-stay-resident (TSR) programs into extended or expanded memory areas. Use the DEVICEHIGH and LOADHIGH commands to install programs and drivers into upper memory areas (refer to Chapter 15 for more information on these commands).

Use the MEM utility to determine the memory configuration of your system.

Use the MemMaker utility to optimize your memory configuration.

The second guideline is to use only what's necessary. Remove any unnecessary drivers or TSRs from your AUTOEXEC.BAT and CONFIG.SYS files.

Disk Management and Performance

The way you organize your disk storage also affects system performance. When your computer accesses data from a disk, a mechanical read/write head travels over the disk, reading directories until the file is located. By optimizing your disk storage, you can decrease the frequency of disk accesses and increase the speed of the accesses required.

> See Chapter 14, "Hard Disk Management Made Simple," for a comprehensive discussion of hard disk management and its effects on performance.

Install a Disk Cache

A disk cache is a section of memory DOS sets aside for use as a holding area between the disk and RAM. Instead of repeated reads and writes, the cache holds information until it can be moved efficiently or until the cache is full. Although caching programs do consume valuable memory resources, they usually can be loaded into extended or expanded memory to minimize this disadvantage.

> Use the SMARTDRV.EXE device driver to install a disk cache with DOS 6.

Consider a RAM Disk

A RAM disk, also called a virtual disk, is a section of RAM that your computer uses as if it were another disk drive. A RAM disk can improve performance significantly, especially for disk-intensive applications. Create a RAM disk, for example, and use it to store the dictionary for your spell checker. Then spell-check a large document. The improvement in performance is dramatic.

Unlike physical drives, such as your C: drive, RAM disks are erased completely when your computer is turned off. Each time you turn on your computer, you must copy files to the RAM drive. Then, any files you create or edit on your RAM drive must be copied to a physical drive if you want to save them permanently.

Use the RAMDRIVE.SYS device driver to install a RAM drive with DOS 6.

If you include your RAM disk in your PATH statement, make sure it's the first directory in the path. Otherwise, your system will search physical drives before locating files in RAM.

Make Sure Your DOS Directory Is in Your *PATH* Statement

The PATH statement in your AUTOEXEC.BAT file specifies a search path DOS follows when searching for program and data files. DOS won't be able to execute external commands unless it knows where to find them. By default, Setup creates a \DOS directory for these commands and includes this directory in the PATH statement.

Use Batch Programs and a Simple *PATH* Statement

Keep your PATH statement short; limit it to the directories you access most frequently. Put the directories you use most often at the beginning of your PATH statement. Use batch programs for programs or files in other directories. For example, suppose you produce a monthly newsletter using a page-layout program called AUTHOR. The batch program

```
c:
cd AUTHOR
AUTHOR
```

eliminates repeated and unnecessary searches of the \AUTHOR directory. Make sure your PATH statement does include the directory in which you store your batch programs.

To view your PATH statement, at the command prompt, type

```
PATH
```

Optimize Your Directory Structure

A hard drive is a large storage area that stores comparatively small files. Therefore, the better the hard drive is organized, the quicker your system can locate what it needs. Chapter 14 details complete guidelines for organizing your directory structure. Here's a quick review:

- Keep your root directory clean. AUTOEXEC.BAT and CONFIG.SYS are the only two files that absolutely must be in the root directory. Use subdirectories to organize other files into categories.

- Do not use more than three levels of subdirectories. A broad, shallow directory structure is much more efficient than one that is narrow and deep.

- Limit the number of files in subdirectories. Create more subdirectories if the number of files in any directory becomes excessive.

Think of your hard drive as a warehouse in which you need to store thousands of small items. By grouping similar items and drawing a clear, logical map of their locations, you can find items without walking up and down the aisles unnecessarily. By doing the same with your disk storage, your computer can find what it needs efficiently.

The DOS Environment and Performance

Regardless of how truly optimized your memory and disk strategies, and even if you're a confirmed Windows user, you can always improve your computing power by executing tasks from the DOS command line (the ubiquitous C:> prompt). If you're addicted to your mouse, consider a typing tutor to improve your keyboarding skills.

By learning the concepts and implementing the strategies presented in this section, you can set up your DOS environment for maximum results.

Your Configuration Files—CONFIG.SYS and AUTOEXEC.BAT

Two files contain instructions that directly control your system configuration—CONFIG.SYS and AUTOEXEC.BAT. Every time you boot your computer, it reads these files and follows their instructions. DOS 6 creates both of these files during Setup and sets them according to the parameters of your system. With few exceptions, you can use the Setup-created files with little concern.

As you add or change components and programs, these files should be updated to maintain performance. Most applications today make changes to CONFIG.SYS and AUTOEXEC.BAT files automatically. Pay close attention to these changes.

For example, consider again the AUTHOR program. You use it once a month to produce a newsletter. You notice, however, that AUTHOR's installation program has added the \AUTHOR directory to the beginning of your PATH statement. So you move the \AUTHOR entry to the end of your PATH statement. Or you remove the \AUTHOR designation completely and load the program using the batch program described in the previous section.

You might also want to modify your configuration files temporarily to perform specific tasks. When you defragment your hard drive, for example, you need to disable any installed disk-caching utilities by deleting or disabling the appropriate commands in your CONFIG.SYS or AUTOEXEC.BAT files.

If you find yourself modifying your CONFIG.SYS files frequently, you can take advantage of DOS 6's capability to create multiple configurations that you can select from when you boot. See Chapter 13, "Customizing DOS," for more information.

Learning to Edit Your Configuration Files

Changing your configuration, then, involves editing your CONFIG.SYS or AUTOEXEC.BAT files, or both. Doing this requires an editing program that can read and write in the ASCII format. Any word processor such as WordPerfect or Word for Windows can do the job. But changing your configuration usually involves minor changes to one or two lines of text. Also, at times you'll need to change your configuration temporarily to perform a task, then revert to your previous configuration.

You might want to disable your disk cache to optimize your hard disk. This requires the following steps:

1. Edit your AUTOEXEC.BAT file to disable the command that loads your disk cache program.

2. Reboot your computer.

3. Run your disk-optimization program.

4. Edit your AUTOEXEC.BAT file again to reenable your disk cache.

5. Reboot your computer.

Keep in mind that CONFIG.SYS and AUTOEXEC.BAT are read only when you boot your system. You must reboot every time you make changes to these files.

Editing Your Configuration with EDIT

DOS 6 includes a straightforward, easy-to-use text editor called EDIT (EDIT.COM). This editor loads quickly and includes a full complement of text-editing features. Using EDIT, you can change CONFIG.SYS and AUTOEXEC.BAT with a minimum of fuss. Figure 5.2 shows the DOS text editor that lets you edit text files with "point and click" convenience.

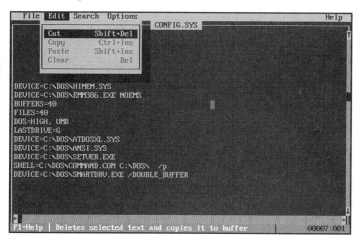

Figure 5.2.
The DOS text editor.

Using EDIT is a lot like using other DOS commands. At the prompt, enter the name of the command along with the file name (optional) of the file you want to edit. To edit your CONFIG.SYS file, type the line

```
edit CONFIG.SYS
```

The editor opens and automatically loads the CONFIG.SYS file. Make changes using pull-down menus and function keys. Save, exit, and reboot.

You can disable commands in your configuration files without deleting them. Simply insert the * character or the REM command at the beginning of the command line you want to disable. To reenable the command, simply delete the * or REM.

When you use * to disable commands in your configuration files, your system might display one of two error messages when you reboot:

```
Bad Command or File Name (for AUTOEXEC.BAT)
```

or

```
Unrecognized Command in CONFIG.SYS
```

Ignore these error messages. Remove the * or REM notation when you want to reenable the command line.

Editing Your Configuration with Your Word Processor

You can also edit your configuration files with word processing programs such as WordPerfect, Microsoft Word, Word for Windows, and many more. Edit the file as you would any other. When you save your changes, however, you must specify the ASCII, or Text Only, format (see Figure 5.3). Word processing formats include special characters and formatting commands that cause problems in configuration files.

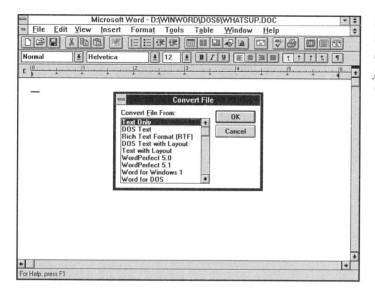

*Figure 5.3.
Save your
configuration
file in Text
Only format.*

Using Windows SYSEDIT to Edit Your Configuration

If you're running Windows, you can use SYSEDIT as your system configuration editor (see Figure 5.4.). To load this editor, click the appropriate icon, or enter SYSEDIT in the Windows Run dialog box. CONFIG.SYS, AUTOEXEC.BAT, and the Windows configuration files, SYSTEM.INI and WIN.INI, are automatically loaded into different windows. SYSEDIT is quick and easy, takes advantage of Windows' mouse capabilities, and makes automatic backups with the .SYD extension.

To create an icon for SYSEDIT, follow these steps:

1. Open the Program Manager window.

2. Click the Main icon to open the Main window.

3. Pull down the File menu and select New.

4. Choose Program Item; then click OK.

5. Type System Editor in the Description field.

6. Type `C:\WINDOWS\SYSTEM\SYSEDIT.EXE` in the Command Line field.

7. Click OK.

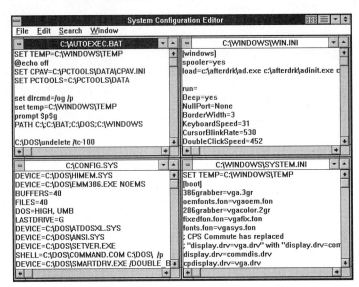

Figure 5.4.
The SYSEDIT
program for
Windows.

Optimizing Your CONFIG.SYS File

When you boot your computer, DOS first carries out instructions contained in your CONFIG.SYS file. In general, these commands determine your hardware configuration and reserve memory space for specific programs and tasks. You can edit your CONFIG.SYS file to change your configuration as needed.

At an absolute minimum, your CONFIG.SYS file should contain two commands—FILES and BUFFERS. These commands are used to allocate memory space for disk input and output (BUFFERS), and to determine the number of files that can be opened simultaneously (FILES).

Chapter 6, "Getting It All Started with AUTOEXEC.BAT and CONFIG.SYS," presents basic considerations for your CONFIG.SYS files. See Chapter 13 for more advanced customization procedures.

The rule of thumb for FILES and BUFFERS, though, is the more the better, as long as you have enough memory.

Remove Unnecessary Device Drivers to Streamline Performance

Device drivers in CONFIG.SYS are used to load programs into memory that control devices. DOS treats hardware components, such as printers and keyboards, as well as software modules such as disk-caching programs, as devices. The DEVICE command is used to load device drivers. In viewing your CONFIG.SYS file, you might see commands like

```
DEVICE=C:\DOS\ANSI.SYS
```

Each driver takes up a small amount of memory. For peak performance, then, eliminate any installed drivers you don't need. DOS Setup might load drivers such as INTERLNK.EXE, the INTERLNK network server, and DBLSPACE.SYS, a disk-compression utility. If you aren't connected to a network, or if you have enough disk space without compressing data, delete these and any other unnecessary drivers from your CONFIG.SYS file. (Note that if the disk you're working with was compressed, you must keep DBLSPACE.SYS in.)

Optimizing Your AUTOEXEC.BAT File

When you boot your computer, and after CONFIG.SYS instructions have been executed, DOS reads and executes the commands contained in your AUTOEXEC.BAT file. The primary function of these commands is controlling the way COMMAND.COM interacts with the user. An AUTOEXEC.BAT file is optional. If your system doesn't have one, when you boot, DOS prompts you for the time and date, then displays the C:> prompt. Again, see Chapters 6 and 13 for more information on AUTOEXEC.BAT.

Customizing Your *PROMPT*

The PROMPT command in your AUTOEXEC.BAT file controls the appearance of your command prompt. Without a PROMPT command, the prompt for your C: drive looks like

```
C:>
```

even when you change the current directory. You must always re-member your current directory or enter the DIR command to dis-play its name. Typing the command

```
PROMPT $P$G
```

changes the prompt to include the current directory path. This com-mand is added to your AUTOEXEC.BAT file automatically during setup. You can also use / options to display time and date, use multiple-line prompts, and enter your own text.

Streamline Your *PATH* Statement

The PATH statement in your AUTOEXEC.BAT specifies the directo-ries and order in which DOS searches for executable files. Your PATH statement should be short and should include only those directo-ries you use frequently.

Loading Start-up Programs

AUTOEXEC.BAT is a batch program; it reads and executes com-mands one command at a time. Therefore, use it to load programs automatically when you start your computer. If you're an accoun-tant, for example, you might add the start-up command for your spreadsheet program. Then, each time you boot your computer, your spreadsheet is loaded automatically. For Windows users, the simple command

```
win
```

at the end of your AUTOEXEC.BAT file loads Windows with each boot.

You can also load TSR programs through AUTOEXEC.BAT. These programs are discussed in the following section.

Boosting Performance with TSRs

Terminate-and-stay-resident (TSR) programs, also called memory-resident programs, are loaded into memory, where they wait until they are called to perform their tasks. Some TSRs are called with a designated keystroke combination, or hotkey. Others are called in response to specific conditions or actions. Consider screen savers as an example. These programs remain in memory until a specific condition arises—a designated period of inactivity. In addition, most screen savers can be activated with a hotkey, such as Ctrl+Shift+S.

TSRs are powerful tools for boosting your system's performance. Because they reside in memory, they are accessed instantly when called. In addition, you can load a custom set of TSRs to configure your system to your needs. And finally, TSRs are convenient; you can have several available at your fingertips at all times.

TSR Conflicts

Occasionally, conflicts arise when two or more TSRs try to occupy the same memory address or are assigned the same hotkey. Other conflicts might occur between TSRs and an application running in the foreground. Usually, when this happens your system freezes, or fails to respond to keyboard or mouse input. If you install a new TSR and your system suddenly crashes, you can bet that the new program has caused the problem.

Resolving these conflicts involves removing or reconfiguring the offensive TSR. You can isolate problems by loading TSRs one at a time and testing after each is loaded. DOS 6 provides capabilities for individually confirming TSRs loaded through CONFIG.SYS. These capabilities are explained in Chapter 13.

TSRs in DOS 6 That Can Make a Difference

DOS 6 includes several TSRs that can improve the overall performance of your system. All are discussed in other chapters of this book. Here's a quick review of some frequently used DOS TSRs:

- DOSKEY facilitates the entry and execution of repetitive DOS commands.

- DOSSHELL is a graphical interface that makes it easy to perform housekeeping tasks such as copying and moving files, formatting disks, and running programs.

- FASTOPEN speeds access to frequently used files.

- UNDELETE protects files against accidental deletion.

- SMARTDRV is a disk-caching program.

- VSAFE protects your computer against infection by viruses.

Performance Guidelines for the DOS Environment

Now that you've learned the basics of system performance, use the following tips and guidelines to optimize your DOS environment and maximize the speed and efficiency of your computing.

Master the DOS Shell

Earlier in this chapter, you learned that all users can benefit from knowing how to get things done from the command prompt. Although this statement is true, many users might feel that it's just not worth the effort. On the other hand, there are times when Windows and other graphical-user-interface programs are too slow or too complicated. For those users, the DOS Shell was created (see Figure 5.5).

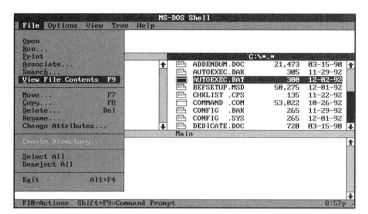

Figure 5.5.
The DOS 6
Shell.

The DOS Shell is a program that fits around the main portion of DOS (hence the name, shell). The Shell lets you run programs and manage files and disks with "point and click" convenience. Instead of mastering the unforgiving structures of keyboard commands, you can make selections from menus and dialog boxes to accomplish your tasks.

For example, suppose you're working in your C: directory and you want to view a list of all files with the .DOC extension in the D:\WINWORD\WIP directory. Using the keyboard, you would type the following commands:

```
d:
cd WINWORD\WIP
dir *.DOC
```

Looks fairly simple, and it is. But if you type WNWORD rather than WINWORD, the command isn't recognized, and you must type all 15 keystrokes again. Now, consider the same operation performed through the Shell:

1. Click on the D: drive icon.

2. Click on the WINWORD\WIP directory in the tree list panel.

3. Pull down the Options menu, and choose File Display Options.

4. In the Name text box, type `*.DOC`.

5. Click OK.

Notice that in this procedure the only text typed is `*.DOC`. All other steps are performed using the mouse or the Tab and arrow keys to select commands. And if, in the preceding example, you want to view `*.DOC` files in another directory, you simply click on that directory on the tree list. From the command prompt, you would have to repeat all three commands, and again risk the frustration of imperfect commands.

The DOS Shell reduces virtually all DOS tasks to a simple matter of pointing and selecting. It eliminates the frustration of living up to the unforgiving demands of the command prompt.

Using the DOS Shell, you can

- Take advantage of mouse capabilities when working with files and file groups.

- Run programs.

- Launch programs and associated data files automatically.

- Set up different configurations of the same program for different tasks.

- Run several programs simultaneously.

- View file contents without opening files.

- Search for files according to specified parameters.

See Chapter 8, "Using the Shell," for comprehensive explanations of the Shell's features and capabilities.

Alphabetize Your Directory Listings

Large groups of file names are much easier to grasp if they are sorted alphabetically. At the command-line prompt, type

```
dir /on /p
```

or place this entry in your AUTOEXEC.BAT file:

```
set dircmd=/on /p
```

> The /on switch in the preceding example might be mislead-
> ing. It refers to "options-name" rather than indicating
> something has been turned on from the command line.

To sort directories by subdirectories first, then by file names, at
the command-line prompt type either the characters

```
dir /og /p
```

or the characters

```
set dircmd = /og /p
```

Adding the /p parameter to any of the previous command entries causes your directory displays to pause when the screen is full
and prompt you for a keystroke before another screen is displayed.
This prevents large directory listings from scrolling off the screen
faster than you can read them.

Use Wildcards to Specify Files

Wildcards are nifty shortcuts for specifying groups of files. They are
used most often—but not exclusively—at the command line. They
also can be used in many dialog boxes in the Shell and the Windows
Run dialog box. A good way to illustrate the use of wildcards is with
the DIR command, as explained next. It's also a safe way of experimenting with wildcards, because it's possible to lose files if
wildcards are misused with commands like COPY.

Using Wildcards with *DIR*

You are probably familiar with the DIR command used to display
all files in a directory:

```
dir *.*
```

The wildcard (*) represents up to eight characters in a file name,
and three characters in a file extension. Thus, to see all files with a

.DOC extension, type

```
dir *.doc
```

The files that are displayed include TEMP.DOC, ABC.DOC, GOODWORK.DOC, and so on.

You can also use the ? wildcard to represent a single character. For example, type

```
dir chap?
```

to display CHAP1, CHAP1.DOC, CHAP1.BAK, CHAP2, CHAP2.DOC, CHAP2.BAK, and so on, but not CHAP11, CHAP12.DOC, or CHAP12.BAK. Notice that because no extension is specified, files with and without extensions are displayed. Additionally, keep in mind that ? might not represent any character. For example,

```
dir ????
```

displays YOUR.DOC as well as MY.DOC.

You also can use both wildcards together to specify groups of files. For example, suppose you have a directory with files like DEPT12.WK1, DEPT12.DOC, DEPT13.DOC, and DEPT13.WK1. Type the command

```
dir ????12.*
```

to display files relating to DEPT12. Also displayed are files such as NEW12.TXT and V12.JAG. But if you use a *12.* wildcard in this example, you'll see the same files as if you used the *.* wildcard. Remember, the * represents up to eight characters in a file name.

You can exclude groups of files by using the minus sign (-) wildcard. For example, suppose you want to display all files in a directory except those with a .TMP extension. You would use the command

```
DIR *.* -*.TMP
```

Commands That Recognize Wildcards

You can use wildcards with the following commands:

```
ATTRIB
BACKUP
COPY
CHKDSK
COMP
DEL
DIR
ERASE
PRINT
REN
REPLACE
RESTORE
XCOPY
```

You can also use wildcards with the RECOVER command, but exercise extreme caution.

Use DOSKEY to Perform Repetitive Tasks

DOSKEY is a powerful TSR utility that simplifies entering and executing commands from the command prompt. A previous section illustrates the frustration of entering commands with long path designations only to have to start over because one character is mistyped or misplaced. Indeed, it is this frustration that led to the popularity of mouse-oriented programs such as Shell and Windows.

For dedicated command-line users, it's DOSKEY to the rescue!

DOSKEY can be added to your AUTOEXEC.BAT file or loaded from the command prompt with the simple entry

```
doskey
```

When loaded, DOSKEY remains in memory and works magic at the command prompt. DOSKEY remembers what commands you have used and makes them available for you to use again. It lets you call up previously used commands and edit them for current tasks. It also lets you issue several commands on a single line.

Using DOSKEY to Recall Previous Commands

When DOSKEY is loaded and is memory-resident, you can take the following actions:

- Press the ↑ key to recall the previous command. Press Enter to execute that command.

- Press ↑ repeatedly to scroll through all previous commands.

- Press ↓ to reverse the direction of your scrolling.

- Press F7 to view a numbered list of all previously issued commands. To execute a command from this list, press F9, type the number of the command, and then press Enter twice.

- To issue several commands at once, type the commands on a single line, and separate them by pressing Ctrl+T after each command. The paragraph symbol (¶) appears on your screen after each command. Press Enter to execute the string of commands.

- Use the ← and → keys to move back and forth along a command line for editing. Without DOSKEY, you can only use Backspace and retyping.

- To select previously issued commands quickly, press ESC, then F8, and then type the first few letters of the command you want to locate. Press F8 repeatedly to scroll through all commands beginning with the letters you typed.

- Press → or F1 to insert the previous command one character at a time. To modify that command, type the characters to change as needed.

■ To modify a previously issued command, press F2 and type a character. The portion of the previous command, up to the character you typed, is inserted. Type your changes, then press F3 to insert the remaining portion of the previous command.

The last bulleted item bears illustration. Suppose, for example, you typed

```
copy *.doc d:\backup
```

You could then press F2 and press . to display

```
copy *.
```

Then you could type txt and display

```
copy *.txt
```

Finally, by pressing F3 you would display the rest of the original command:

```
copy *.txt d:\backup.
```

Mastering DOSKEY can eliminate "command-line frustration." Keep in mind that it must be memory-resident to work.

Use Command-Line Help Screens

If all else fails, you can access an excellent built-in productivity tool called the HELP utility. You can access it from the Shell by pulling down the Help menu and selecting a category. From the command prompt, type

```
help command
```

in which command is the name of the command for which you want additional information. DOS 6 Help screens explain command formats and list all the available options for executing the command in exactly the way you want.

Troubleshooting

You need to keep in mind that your computer and DOS are designed to be general-purpose tools. That is, using DOS effectively is not merely a matter of pushing the right button at the right time. Instead, using DOS effectively is a matter of knowing what tools are available and how and when to use those tools to solve a particular problem.

This chapter presents many DOS 6 tools you can use to solve your particular problems. Here is a brief list of those tools and the chapters you should review for more specific troubleshooting information:

- DOS Shell—Chapter 8, "Using the Shell"

- File Management—Chapter 10, "Working With Files and Directories"

- System Configuration—Chapter 13, "Customizing DOS"

- Memory Utilization—Chapter 15, "Getting the Most From Your Memory"

- Windows—Chapter 16, "Setting Up DOS for Windows"

- Batch Programs—Chapter 29, "Batch Programs Unleashed"

Summary

System performance is controlled by your system's resources and by the way these resources are configured. Two major factors in determining performance are memory and disk storage. Conserving conventional memory and taking full advantage of upper memory areas can improve performance significantly. After your system is configured, you can use simple techniques to optimize your DOS environment, both in the DOS Shell and at the command prompt.

Alan Simpson's
DOS
SECRETS
UNLEASHED

C H A P T E R   6

Getting It All Started with CONFIG.SYS and AUTOEXEC.BAT

Your computer uses six files to boot. IO.SYS, MSDOS.SYS, and DBLSPACE.BIN are hidden, and COMMAND.COM is a program file. These four are left alone under normal circumstances. The other two, CONFIG.SYS and AUTOEXEC.BAT, contain instructions that configure your computer. You can use these files to customize your system.

CONFIG.SYS, as its name implies, is DOS' configuration file. It's a text file that contains commands which control how DOS operates, allocates memory for disk and file storage, and configures hardware devices such as keyboards, monitors, printers, memory, and the like.

AUTOEXEC.BAT is also a text file, but its .BAT extension tells DOS that it's a batch program—an executable file. DOS runs AUTOEXEC.BAT after executing the commands in CONFIG.SYS. The primary function of AUTOEXEC.BAT is to control the way COMMAND.COM interacts with you.

Both CONFIG.SYS and AUTOEXEC.BAT are optional files. Your computer will start without them, prompt you for the time and date, and then display the command prompt.

In the preceding chapter, you learned that DOS 6 Setup automatically creates CONFIG.SYS and AUTOEXEC.BAT files. These files configure DOS according to your system's hardware components, memory (type and amount), available disk space, and other factors. In this chapter, the essential CONFIG.SYS and AUTOEXEC.BAT commands are explained. Then sample files are provided. You can use these files as models for building your own CONFIG.SYS and AUTOEXEC.BAT files.

This chapter focuses on basic concepts and techniques. Experienced users can skip to Chapter 7, "DOS Essentials and Tips." Advanced techniques for CONFIG.SYS and AUTOEXEC.BAT are presented in Chapter 13, "Customizing DOS."

Viewing Your CONFIG.SYS and AUTOEXEC.BAT Files

Figures 6.1 and 6.2 show CONFIG.SYS and AUTOEXEC.BAT files created by Setup.

```
C:\>type config.sys
DEVICE=C:\DOS\HIMEM.SYS
DEVICE=C:\DOS\EMM386.EXE NOEMS
BUFFERS=40
FILES=40
DOS=HIGH, UMB
LASTDRIVE=G
DEVICE=C:\DOS\ATDOSXL.SYS
DEVICE=C:\DOS\ANSI.SYS
DEVICE=C:\DOS\SETVER.EXE
SHELL=C:\DOS\COMMAND.COM C:\DOS\ /p
DEVICE=C:\DOS\SMARTDRV.EXE /DOUBLE_BUFFER

C:\>
```

Figure 6.1.
A typical
CONFIG.SYS
file created by
Setup.

```
C:\>type autoexec.bat
SET TEMP=C:\WINDOWS\TEMP
@echo off
SET CPAV=C:\PCTOOLS\DATA\CPAV.INI
SET PCTOOLS=C:\PCTOOLS\DATA

set dircmd=/og /p
set temp=C:\WINDOWS\TEMP
prompt $p$g
PATH C:\;C:\BAT;C:\DOS;C:\WINDOWS

C:\DOS\undelete /tc-100
C:\DOS\doskey /bufsize=512 /overstrike
C:\DOS\smartdrv 2048 512 /q
gmouse

C:\>
```

Figure 6.2.
A typical
AUTOEXEC.BAT
file created by
Setup.

Notice the TYPE command at the command prompt in these figures. There are two ways to view your configuration files. You can either load them into a text editor or use the TYPE command at the command prompt, as shown in the following lines:

```
TYPE CONFIG.SYS
TYPE AUTOEXEC.BAT
```

> You use the /P option if your files are too long to be displayed on a single screen.

You can use the CONFIG.SYS and AUTOEXEC.BAT files created by Setup with minimum risk. At times, however, it pays to be able to view these files and make simple changes quickly. In general, your configuration files might need to be changed at these times:

- When you add a new hardware component or reconfigure an existing one.

- When you install application programs.

- When you want to change the way DOS operates to suit your needs or preferences.

Consult the appropriate hardware manuals for information on installing and configuring drivers for hardware components. Also, be aware that most application programs automatically change CONFIG.SYS and AUTOEXEC.BAT files when they are installed. Pay close attention to these changes. Know how they affect your system's overall performance, and be ready to edit your configuration files if needed.

CONFIG.SYS—The Essential Commands

CONFIG.SYS commands either configure your system or load device drivers. Many commands can be used in CONFIG.SYS, but the list of truly essential commands can be narrowed to four:

```
FILES
BUFFERS
DEVICE
DEVICEHIGH
```

The structure and execution of these commands are discussed in the following sections.

Using *BUFFERS* and *FILES* to Allocate Memory

The number of BUFFERS and FILES set by the respective commands in your CONFIG.SYS file control how your system's memory is allocated. A rule of thumb for both commands is that more is better. This is because many applications rely heavily on disk accesses. The more FILES and BUFFERS you have set, the more quickly your applications will run.

If you're unhappy with your system's performance, try setting your FILES and BUFFERS higher. Reboot to see whether the changes make a difference.

The *FILES* Command Structure

The FILES command is used to specify the number of files DOS can have open simultaneously. The format is

```
FILES=n
```

in which *n* is the maximum number of files you want DOS to be able to keep open at the same time. So if you want to set 20 as the maximum number of files that can be opened at once, type

`FILES=20`

> If you don't use the `FILES` command, the default value is 8. However, 8 might be too low. Try 30 to start with.

The *BUFFERS* Command Structure

The `BUFFERS` command sets the number of file buffers DOS uses. File buffers are memory areas set aside for storing information, as data is read from or written to the disk. The format for the `BUFFERS` command is

`BUFFERS=n,m`

in which *n* is the number of files DOS uses, and *m* is the number of buffers in the secondary buffer cache. Typically, the number of buffers is set to the same number as the number of files, and the buffer cache is from 0 to 8, with the default set to 0. So if you want to set 20 as the number of buffers DOS uses, type

`BUFFERS=20,0`

Working together, `FILES` and `BUFFERS` are the most important part of your CONFIG.SYS file in determining performance—at least as concerns applications that access your hard disk repeatedly. Assigning `FILES` and `BUFFERS` does take up memory, but the loss of memory usually is compensated by increased performance.

Understanding Devices and Drivers

To DOS, everything is a device. Drives are devices, your keyboard is a device, and so are your monitor and printer. DOS devices can be input-output, input-only, or output-only devices. Disk drives are input-output devices, and printers are output-only devices.

Because DOS treats everything as a device, you can copy information between devices just as you would between disk drives. For example, the command

```
COPY AUTOEXEC.BAT PRN
```

sends the AUTOEXEC.BAT file to your standard printer (PRN)—a DOS device. Using the same principle, you can create files from your monitor screen.

Or suppose you want to create an AUTOEXEC.BAT quickly. Try this:

```
COPY CON AUTOEXEC.BAT
```

This command tells your computer to copy information from one device, your monitor (CON for console), to a file named AUTOEXEC.BAT, which is stored on another device, your hard drive. (The current directory is used unless a path is specified.) All information entered on-screen is copied to a file named AUTOEXEC.BAT. Signal the end of the file with DOS' end-of-file character, generated by pressing Ctrl+Z or F6. Press Enter to return to the command prompt.

Using *DEVICE* and *DEVICEHIGH* to Load Drivers

The DEVICE command is used to load installable device drivers into conventional memory areas; DEVICEHIGH, to load into high memory areas. Device drivers are programs which control devices that DOS doesn't know about. When installed, devices can communicate and transfer data back and forth.

Using *DEVICE* to Load Drivers

The DEVICE command is used to install device drivers into conventional memory. The format for this command is

```
DEVICE=[path][driver name]
```

in which *path* is the directory location of the driver file, and *driver name* is the name of the driver file. DOS comes with several device drivers. For example, to set up a RAM drive, type

```
DEVICE=C:\DOS\RAMDRIVE.SYS
```

Unless you specify a path, DOS assumes that the device driver is in the root directory. Because it's best to keep your root directory uncluttered, always keep your drivers in a directory specified in your PATH statement, or include a path at the command prompt.

Using *DEVICEHIGH* to Load Drivers into Upper Memory

You can load device drivers into upper memory areas, provided upper memory is available. Loading drivers into upper memory frees conventional memory for use by other programs. For peak performance, load as many drivers as possible into upper memory. If you're a Windows user, be careful not to use too much upper memory, because Windows uses it extensively.

Keep in mind that upper memory is also a device. Therefore, before you can load other drivers into upper memory, you must first load your upper memory drivers into conventional memory. HIMEM.SYS and EMM386.EXE are two upper memory drivers, also called memory managers, included with DOS 6.

> If you use DEVICEHIGH and no upper memory is available, the command functions the same as DEVICE.

The format for the DEVICEHIGH command is

```
DEVICEHIGH=[parameters][path][driver name]
```

in which *parameters* specifies the region and size of the upper memory blocks used to load the driver, *path* specifies the directory location of the driver, and *driver name* is the name of the driver file. The parameters you can use to load devices into upper memory are shown next.

> These parameters require hexadecimal notations and knowledge of your memory allocation. Use them only if you're familiar with these concepts. For complete information, see Chapter 15, "Getting the Most from Your Memory."

■ /L:[*region1*],[*minsize1*];[*region2*],[*minsize2*]; [...]

The /L switch specifies one or more areas of memory (regions) into which the driver is loaded. By default, the driver is loaded into the largest free upper memory block (UMB). When loaded with this switch, the driver can use only the specified region. Because some drivers require more than one area, you must specify a value for *region2*. Separate values for multiple regions with a semicolon (;). MemMaker sets these for you automatically.

Some drivers require more memory when running than when loaded. DOS loads drivers into a UMB in the specified region only if that region contains a UMB larger than the driver's load size. Use the [*minsize*] parameter to ensure that the driver is not loaded into a UMB that is too small to run it.

■ /S

The /S switch shrinks the UMB to its minimum size while the driver is loading. This switch can be used only in conjunction with the /L parameter, and it affects only UMBs for which a minimum size is specified.

DOS 6 Device Drivers

DOS 6 includes the following device drivers:

ANSI.SYS—enables extra control features for the screen and keyboard according to specifications created by the American National Standards Institute (ANSI).

DISPLAY.SYS—is used with laptop computers to control screen displays.

DBLSPACE.SYS—is used, when loaded with DEVICEHIGH, to move the DoubleSpace driver to upper memory.

DRIVER.SYS—creates a logical drive you can use to refer to a physical disk (especially one not supported by your ROM BIOS) and configures it according to parameters you specify.

EGA.SYS—is used for EGA monitors.

EMM386.EXE—simulates expanded memory on a 386 or higher machine with extended memory.

MemMaker automatically installs EMM386.EXE on machines that can use it.

HIMEM.SYS—is an extended memory manager for 286 or higher systems with extended memory. DOS 6 Setup automatically loads this device on systems that can use it.

RAMDRIVE.SYS—creates a RAM disk. You can load RAMDRIVE into upper memory using DEVICEHIGH. You can also configure its size and other parameters using optional switches.

SETVER.EXE—is used to simulate previous DOS versions by applications that are incompatible with the current DOS version.

SMARTDRIVE.EXE—is a disk-caching program used for hard-disk controllers that can't work with EMM386.EXE, and for Windows running in 386-Enhanced mode.

AUTOEXEC.BAT—The Essential Commands

AUTOEXEC.BAT is a batch program that is run after DOS executes the instructions in CONFIG.SYS. You can add any command to your AUTOEXEC.BAT file that you would normally use at the command prompt. You can use standard batch commands to execute conditional tasks, to display prompts, and to provide input during execution. In addition, you can include commands to run any program automatically when you start your computer.

The following two commands are considered essential for AUTOEXEC.BAT files:

```
PROMPT
PATH
```

See Chapter 12, "Simple Batch Programs," for instructions on creating and running batch programs.

Customizing Your *PROMPT*

Use the PROMPT command to control the appearance of the command prompt. The format for the PROMPT command is

PROMPT [*text*] $[*option*] $[*option*] [...]

in which *text* is an optional text string and $*option* notations are used to configure the prompt according to the parameters described in Table 6.1.

Table 6.1. The PROMPT command options.

Option	Action
$B	Displays the pipe symbol (¦)
$D	Displays the current date
$E	Displays the escape character
$G	Displays the greater-than symbol (>)
$H	Backspaces one character
$L	Displays the less-than symbol (<)
$N	Displays the current drive
$P	Displays the current drive and path
$Q	Displays the equal symbol (=)
$T	Displays the current time

Option	Action
$V	Displays the DOS version number
$$	Displays the dollar sign ($)
$_	Starts a new line

For example, suppose you wanted a prompt that looked like this:

```
Today's date: Mon 01-22-95
C:\DOS>
```

You would type the following PROMPT command:

```
PROMPT Today's date: $D$_$P$G
```

Setting Your *PATH* Command

Your PATH command specifies a search path that DOS follows when looking for executable files. DOS looks for executable, or program, files any time you enter a command to load a program. If the directory of the program file is in your PATH command, you can load that program from any directory on that drive.

The format for the PATH command is

```
PATH [drive:directory;]
```

in which *drive:directory;* tells DOS which directory to search.

By default, DOS searches only the current directory. So although it is wise to keep as short a PATH as possible, you should at least have your root, \DOS, and \BAT directories in your PATH command, as in

```
PATH C:\;\DOS;\BAT
```

To display your current search path, type

PATH

at the command prompt. To clear your path settings and use the default (current directory only) setting, type

PATH ;

A Sample CONFIG.SYS File

To better understand the concepts discussed in this chapter, consider the following sample CONFIG.SYS file:

```
DEVICE=C:\DOS\HIMEM.SYS
DEVICE=C:\DOS\EMM386.EXE NOEMS
BUFFERS=40
FILES=40
DOS=HIGH
DEVICE=C:\DOS\ATDOSXL.SYS
DEVICE=C:\DOS\SMARTDRV.EXE /DOUBLE_BUFFER
```

In this example, line 1 loads the HIMEM.SYS driver—the extended memory manager.

Line 2 loads the EMM386.EXE driver. The NOEMS parameter provides access to upper memory areas without simulating expanded memory.

Line 3 sets the number of file buffers to 40.

Line 4 sets the maximum number of files that can be opened at the same time to 40.

Line 5 loads the DOS command module into upper memory.

Line 6 loads the ATDOSXL.SYS driver, which controls an installed hard-disk device.

Line 7 loads the SMARTDrive driver. SMARTDrive is a disk-cache program that should be loaded when you are using Windows in 386-Enhanced mode. The /DOUBLE_BUFFER parameter enables double buffering, which is required to run Windows in 386-Enhanced mode under certain conditions (see Chapter 5, "Peak Performance in the DOS Environment").

A Sample AUTOEXEC.BAT File

The following sample provides a further illustration:

```
SET TEMP=C:\WINDOWS\TEMP
@ECHO OFF
PROMPT $P$G
PATH C:\;C:\DOS;C:\BAT;C:\WINDOWS
C:\DOS\UNDELETE /TC-100 /LOAD
C:\DOS\DOSKEY /BUFSIZE=512 /INSERT
GMOUSE
DOSSHELL
```

In this example, line 1 sets an environment variable for the temporary files used by the Windows program.

Line 2 turns off the screen display. The remaining commands are not seen at the command prompt as they are read. The results of their execution, however, are displayed.

Line 3 configures the prompt to display the current path and the greater-than (>) symbol.

Line 4 sets the search path to include the root directory, as well as the \DOS, \BAT, and \WINDOWS directories.

Line 5 loads the Undelete program, which protects files from accidental deletion. The /TC-100 parameter specifies that the C: drive is protected using the delete tracking method, and that 100 file entries are tracked before they are purged. The /LOAD parameter loads Undelete memory-resident.

Line 6 loads DOSKEY, a keyboard enhancement program. The /BUFSIZE=512 switch sets at 512 bytes the size of the buffer used to store commands and macros. The /INSERT switch acts like the Ins key on your keyboard. When it is activated, text typed at the DOS command line is inserted into existing text. The default setting is Overstrike.

Line 7 loads the GMOUSE.COM device driver, which controls mouse functions.

Line 8 loads the DOS Shell interface. With this line, the Shell is loaded automatically every time you boot your computer.

Starting DOS

Even though starting your computer is a simple matter of flipping a switch, there are some considerations worth mentioning. When your computer gets power, it searches for DOS, first in your floppy drives and then in your hard disk. If the computer can't find DOS or another operating system, it does nothing. After DOS is loaded, the computer carries out the instructions contained in CONFIG.SYS, and then AUTOEXEC.BAT, provided those files are in the root directory.

You can use Setup to create a set of DOS floppies. If your hard disk malfunctions, you can boot using the Start/ Support disk and then perform troubleshooting.

Starting DOS from a Hard Disk

If your computer has a hard disk and DOS has been installed, the boot procedure is simple:

1. Make sure all floppy drives are empty.

2. Turn on the computer and all components (monitor, printer, external peripherals, and so on).

Your computer performs its power-on tests, loads DOS, and then looks for the CONFIG.SYS and AUTOEXEC.BAT files.

Starting DOS from a Floppy Disk

You can boot your computer from any floppy that has been formatted with the /S option and has the COMMAND.COM file on it. Formatting with the /S option installs the hidden files, IO.SYS and MSDOS.SYS.

To start DOS from a floppy, take the following steps:

1. Insert the DOS floppy into the drive. You might also have to close the drive door.

2. Turn on the computer and all components (monitor, printer, external peripherals).

Your computer performs its power-on tests, loads DOS, and then looks for the CONFIG.SYS and AUTOEXEC.BAT files, just as it does when booting from a hard disk.

Most computers today are equipped with hard disks. So the only time you need to boot from a floppy is when you're troubleshooting your system. Sometimes a clean boot is required, meaning DOS is started without executing any configuration instructions from CONFIG.SYS and AUTOEXEC.BAT.

Copy your CONFIG.SYS and AUTOEXEC.BAT files onto the DOS Start/Support disk as CONFIG.SAV and AUTOEXEC.SAV (or use any extension you prefer). You can do a clean boot using this disk without changes. To restore your configuration, rename the files CONFIG.SYS and AUTOEXEC.BAT.

In addition, there are alternative methods for starting DOS 6 that can be extremely helpful when troubleshooting your system. These are explained in Appendix A, Installing DOS 6.

The Warm Boot—A Three-Finger Salute

When you make changes to the CONFIG.SYS and AUTOEXEC.BAT files, you need to reboot your computer before the changes will take effect. Turning power off and on is abrasive to your system. If you must do so, wait 30 seconds after you turn the power off to give your hard disk time to stop spinning. A better way is to use a warm boot—press Ctrl+Alt+Del. Your computer skips its power-on tests and loads DOS, CONFIG.SYS, and AUTOEXEC.BAT in the regular way.

 Troubleshooting

Having problems with your AUTOEXEC.BAT or CONFIG.SYS files can spell disaster. If either of these two files is configured incorrectly, your computer will either run slowly, refuse to run your programs, or worse yet, not work at all. Here are a few tips to help you correctly configure both of these files:

- Don't put any extraneous information in the AUTOEXEC.BAT or CONFIG.SYS files, because DOS tries to interpret everything in these files as a command. If you add comment lines, use the REM command so DOS doesn't try to interpret your comments as commands.

- Be extremely careful if you use a RAM disk for temporary files. Microsoft Windows often creates files larger than one megabyte in the TEMP directory when printing files with a variety of fonts. This doesn't matter if you have enough memory for a huge RAM disk.

- If you encounter a Bad command or filename, File not found, or Syntax error, and the message is not preceded by a reference to a line in your CONFIG.SYS file, you need to make changes to your AUTOEXEC.BAT file.

- If your PROMPT command is too long to fit on the screen, let it wrap to the next line. Do not insert returns where you think the line should break, because DOS doesn't know how to interpret the second line and part of your prompt will be lost.

- Just because you can use 127 characters for your PATH command doesn't mean you should. For infrequently used executable files, it may be faster to create a batch file or include the path at the command prompt to run those executables.

- The DOS Setup program makes more extensive changes to your configuration files than previous versions. In particular, if you use a 80386 or 80486 computer with more than 640K of memory, Setup installs several commands in CONFIG.SYS to manage memory.

- If you have an 8086 or 8088 microprocessor, you won't be able to use SMARTDrive because you don't have the required type of memory.

Summary

Use CONFIG.SYS and AUTOEXEC.BAT to configure your computer to your own tastes. When you boot, your computer loads DOS and then looks for and executes the instructions within these files. You can boot your computer from your hard disk or a floppy disk that has been properly prepared. You might need to boot from a floppy when troubleshooting your system.

Putting DOS
to Work

Alan Simpson's
DOS
SECRETS
UNLEASHED

C H A P T E R 7

DOS Essentials and Tips

Now that you have DOS 6 properly installed on your computer, this chapter covers the basics of starting to use DOS. DOS offers two ways in which to work: You can launch programs, manage files, and do other tasks from the command prompt, also known as the DOS prompt. Or you can use the shell program included with DOS. This chapter covers the basics of these two options, and it provides information about files, programs, and how DOS stores information in your computer. Chapter 8, "Using the Shell," provides more detail about using the DOS Shell, and Chapter 9, "Using the Command Prompt," provides more detail about using the command prompt. Part IV offers advanced topics about managing files as well as using the command prompt and DOS Shell.

Files

Any program or collection of data stored on a computer disk is saved in a file. The name is appropriate: just as a filing cabinet contains many different files (typically stored in manila folders), a computer disk also stores many different files.

Computer disks can store two types of files:

- *Program files* (or *programs*) contain instructions that tell the computer what to do and how to do it.

- *Data files* (or *text files*) contain data (information), such as names, addresses, letters, and inventory or bookkeeping data.

Every file on a disk, whether program or data, has a name that can consist of two parts: a *base name* (mandatory) followed by an *extension* (optional). The base name can be one to eight characters long. The optional extension always starts with a period (.) and can contain as many as three additional characters. File names cannot contain blank spaces. Following are some examples of legal file names:

APPEND.EXE	IBMDOS.COM
LETTER_1.TXT	9.WKS
SALES.DAT	GRAPH

In the first example file name, APPEND is the base name, and
.EXE is the extension. As a rule of thumb, the file's base name describes the contents of the file, and the extension usually describes
the type of information in the file.

> Certain types of files typically use specific extensions. For
> example, files with extensions .COM and .EXE are always
> program files. Files with the .BAT extension are always a
> special kind of file called a batch program (see Chapter 12,
> "Simple Batch Programs"). Similarly, files with .DOC and
> .TXT as extensions typically are text files.

The Directory Tree

> Chapter 14, "Hard Disk Management Made Simple,"
> discusses the best techniques for organizing the information
> on your computer's hard disk into directories.

A hard disk can store hundreds, or even thousands, of files. To make
it easier to manage a large number of files, you can use DOS to divide the hard disk into *directories*, each of which contains its own
set of related files.

To help you further refine how you manage files, each directory
can have *subdirectories*. The structure of directories and subdirectories on a disk is often referred to as the *directory tree*. Every
hard disk and diskette contains an initial directory called the root
directory. DOS automatically assigns the simple name \ to this root
directory. Any additional directories (and subdirectories) you create are thought of as being "below" the root directory.

The files in subdirectories are usually related to the files in the directories above them, and they also are usually loosely related to each other. For example, your word processing program files might be located in a directory called WP. A subdirectory below the WP directory might be called DOCS and could contain all your letters, memos, and other data you created with your word processor.

The same rules that apply for naming files apply to naming directories and subdirectories. Each directory or subdirectory name can be up to eight characters long. You also can have a period and a three-character extension in directory and subdirectory names, although this is not a common practice.

> As with file names, give directories and subdirectories names that are descriptive of their contents. That is why it makes sense, for example, to name the subdirectory in which you keep your word processing documents DOCS. If you want, you can subdivide even further. For example, you can create subdirectories under the DOCS called LETTERS, MEMOS, and REPORTS.

Exploring the DOS Shell

The DOS Shell provides a convenient and comprehensive method for interacting with DOS. The name "shell" is appropriate because, in a sense, it surrounds the complicated inner workings of DOS and lets you interact with DOS in a simplified, graphical manner.

Starting the Shell

Start the DOS Shell at the command prompt by typing DOSSHELL and then pressing Enter. The DOS Shell that appears on your screen will resemble Figure 7.1, although it will look somewhat different depending on your monitor and the files and directory structure.

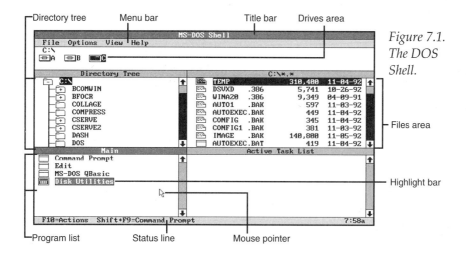

Figure 7.1. The DOS Shell.

The DOS Shell is a convenient environment in which to manage your files and disks as well as to launch programs. As Figure 7.1 shows, the DOS Shell provides graphical details about the contents of your disks. It also enables you to launch commands and programs without having to memorize how to do so at the command prompt. Chapter 8," Using the Shell," goes into greater detail about using the DOS Shell.

Elements of the DOS Shell

The main elements of the DOS Shell are labeled in Figure 7.1. More detail about the DOS Shell is available in Chapter 8, "Using the Shell." The following list summarizes the main elements of the Shell:

Title bar—shows the name of the current screen or window.

Menu bar—shows the names of available pull-down menus (File, Options, View, Tree, and Help).

Drives area—displays the names of disk drives available on your computer. Double-clicking on a drive provides on-screen information about that drive, its directories, and files.

Directory tree—lists the directory structure of the current disk drive.

Files area—lists the files in the currently selected directory.

Program list—displays the contents of the Main program group, which includes programs such as QBASIC and the Editor (discussed later), and program groups such as Disk Utilities (also discussed later).

Highlight bar—indicates the currently selected option. You move this about the screen to make selections.

Status line—shows helpful keys available at the moment.

Mouse pointer—appears if you have a mouse installed and moves in whatever direction you move the mouse.

You can easily move from one area of the Shell to another using either your mouse or your keyboard.

Using the DOS Shell Help System

The DOS Shell has a built-in *help system* to provide immediate answers to questions and solutions to problems. There are three ways to access the help system:

- Press the F1 key at any time when you're in the Shell.

- Select the Help command button from the current dialog box (if any).

- Select Help from the Menu bar to access the Help pull-down menu.

Figure 7.2 shows a typical screen from the DOS Shell help system.

The first two methods generally provide *context-sensitive* help. Context-sensitive help displays information relevant to the part of the DOS Shell in which you are working. The third option, using the Help menu, provides access to the same help screens, but through more general means.

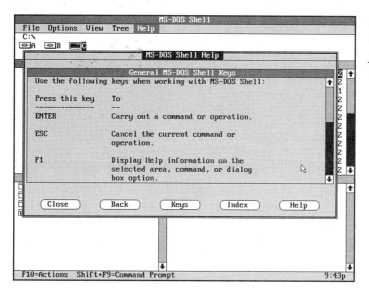

Figure 7.2.
A help screen
from the DOS
Shell.

Exploring the Command Prompt

As an alternative to using the DOS Shell, you can use the command prompt to interact with DOS. In earlier versions of DOS (prior to DOS 4), the command prompt was the only way to interact with DOS.

> See Chapter 8, "Using the Shell," for a discussion about the advantages of using both the command prompt and the DOS Shell.

Basic Command Prompt Usage

The DOS command prompt typically shows the current drive and directory, followed by a greater-than sign (>) and a blinking cursor.

For example, on hard disk drive C:, the command prompt for the root directory might look like

```
C:\>
```

or

```
C:\DOS>_
```

if \DOS is the current directory.

Typing a command at the command prompt involes two steps:

1. Type the complete command (you can use the Backspace key to back up and make corrections).

2. Press Enter to send the completed command to the computer.

About Commands

You type commands at the command prompt to tell DOS what to do and how to do it. Each DOS command has its own syntax, which consists of a *verb* (also known as the *command name*). Following the command name, there might be *parameters*, which are what the command operates on. After the parameters, there might be switches, which further refine the way the command operates.

When entering a command, you type the command verb first, followed by a blank space and the parameters, if any, followed by another blank space, and any switches. I'll use the DIR command as a simple example because it works with or without parameters and switches.

In its simplest form, DIR can be entered by itself at the command prompt:

```
DIR
```

That command tells DOS to show the names of all the files on the current drive and directory. Figure 7.3 shows the results of typing the DIR command while in the \DOS directory.

```
(continuing C:\DOS)
CHKDSK    EXE     16216 10-26-92    6:00a
CHKSTATE  SYS     38752 10-26-92    6:00a
CHOICE    COM      1754 10-26-92    6:00a
COMMAND   COM     53022 10-26-92    6:00a
COMP      EXE     14282 04-09-91    5:00a
CONFIG    UMB       331 11-04-92    9:42a
COUNTRY   SYS     17069 10-26-92    6:00a
DBLSPACE  BIN     63868 10-26-92    6:00a
DBLSPACE  EXE    286338 10-26-92    6:00a
DBLSPACE  HLP     35342 10-26-92    6:00a
DBLSPACE  INF      1113 10-26-92    6:00a
DBLSPACE  SYS       217 10-26-92    6:00a
DEBUG     EXE     20634 10-26-92    6:00a
DEFRAG    EXE     74505 10-26-92    6:00a
DEFRAG    HLP     16809 10-26-92    6:00a
DELOLDOS  EXE     17710 10-26-92    6:00a
DISKCOMP  COM     10636 10-26-92    6:00a
DISKCOPY  COM     11879 10-26-92    6:00a
DISPLAY   SYS     15792 10-26-92    6:00a
DOSHELP   HLP      5743 10-26-92    6:00a
DOSHELP   EXE     11401 10-26-92    6:00a
DOSKEY    COM      5883 10-26-92    6:00a
Press any key to continue . . .
```

*Figure 7.3.
Results of
using the DIR
command.*

You can add a parameter to the DIR command if you want. For example, if there is a floppy drive in drive B: and you want to see the names of the files on the disk, you enter the command

`DIR B:`

In this case, DIR is the verb, or command, and B: is the parameter that determines the drive upon which the DIR command acts. Note the blank space between the verb and the parameter.

DIR also accepts several switches. For example, the /P switch tells DIR to display its information one "page" (screenful) at a time. To add the /P switch to the previous example, you would type

`DIR B: /P`

Notice the blank space between the parameter and the switch, just as there was a blank space between the verb and the parameter.

Make sure all commands are in the *command-parameter-switch* order, with a space between each element. If you use any other order, the command will not work.

Although DOS commands are not sensitive about whether you use capital letters, they are very sensitive about spaces between and within the elements of the command. The only spaces in a command should be between commands, parameters, and switches. If you do not follow this rule, DOS will not process your command and will give you an error message that says `Bad command or file name`.

Chapter 9, "Using the Command Prompt," discusses using the command prompt in greater detail.

Internal and External Commands

There are two basic types of DOS commands: *internal* and *external*. Internal commands are part of the DOS command processor, COMMAND.COM. Because COMMAND.COM is loaded into memory when you start your computer, internal commands are stored in memory and are always accessible from the command prompt. `DIR` is an example of an internal command.

External commands are actually small programs located on your hard disk, probably in the directory in which you store DOS. An example of an external command is the `CHKDSK` command. Like any program, DOS must be able to find the programs that constitute external commands. Using the `PATH` command (see Chapter 5, "Peak Performance in the DOS Environment") is the simplest way to ensure that DOS can always find its own external commands so that you can use them.

Using Online Documentation

DOS 6 provides help about commands in two ways. You can get quick help from the command prompt. In addition, a new feature in DOS 6, the MS-DOS Help system, is a DOS program that provides detailed help about commands.

Help from the Command Prompt

Help from the command prompt is most useful if you are familiar with the command you want to use but cannot remember its exact syntax or optional parameters and switches. To get quick help with the syntax for the DIR command, at the command prompt, type

    DIR /?

The screen displays a description of the command and its syntax along with a brief description of parameters and switches. Figure 7.4 shows the help screen for the DIR command after you type DIR/? at the command prompt.

```
Displays a list of files and subdirectories in a directory.

DIR [drive:][path][filename] [/P] [/W] [/A[[:]attribs]] [/O[[:]sortord]]
    [/S] [/B] [/L] [/C]

  [drive:][path][filename]   Specifies drive, directory, and/or files to list.
  /P          Pauses after each screenful of information.
  /W          Uses wide list format.
  /A          Displays files with specified attributes.
  attribs    D  Directories    R  Read-only files        H  Hidden files
             S  System files   A  Files ready to archive  -  Prefix meaning "not"
  /O          List by files in sorted order.
  sortord    N  By name (alphabetic)       S  By size (smallest first)
             E  By extension (alphabetic)  D  By date & time (earliest first)
             G  Group directories first    -  Prefix to reverse order
             C  By compression ratio (smallest first)
  /S          Displays files in specified directory and all subdirectories.
  /B          Uses bare format (no heading information or summary).
  /L          Uses lowercase.
  /C          Displays file compression ratio if on a compressed drive.

Switches may be preset in the DIRCMD environment variable.  Override
preset switches by prefixing any switch with - (hyphen)—for example, /-W.

C:\COLLAGE>
```

Figure 7.4. Command prompt help for the DIR command.

In the help screen, items in square brackets ([]) are optional. Hence, for the DIR command, the [path], [drive:], and [filename] parameters as well as all the switches are optional. Note, however, that if you want to use an optional parameter or switch, you don't type the brackets.

DOS commands can be finicky. You must type the command and optional parameters and switches correctly, or the commands will not execute. Command prompt help is a fast way to get help about a command if you understand

> the command but are not sure about the syntax. The MS-DOS Help system, described in the next section, is more useful if you don't understand either the command or its syntax.

The MS-DOS Help System

The quick help system is useful for both beginners and experienced users, but it is still incomplete. MS-DOS Help, a free-standing program you can access from the command prompt, provides more comprehensive information about commands. Whereas command prompt help information is terse and focuses on syntax, MS-DOS Help offers more detail. Besides details about syntax, it provides examples of how to use a particular command and notes about how to make your use of the command more productive. The MS-DOS Help program provides tools to search for specific information and the capability to jump from one bit of information to other, related bits of information.

To use MS-DOS Help for more information about the DIR command, at the command prompt type

```
HELP DIR
```

Figure 7.5 shows the first screen you see after asking for help about the DIR command. Note that information about syntax is more complete in MS-DOS Help than in the command prompt help system.

Figure 7.5 shows the main elements of MS-DOS Help screens. The following list also summarizes those elements:

File menu—provides options for printing help screens and for leaving MS-DOS Help.

Search menu—enables you to search for help about specific commands and enables you to repeat the preceding search.

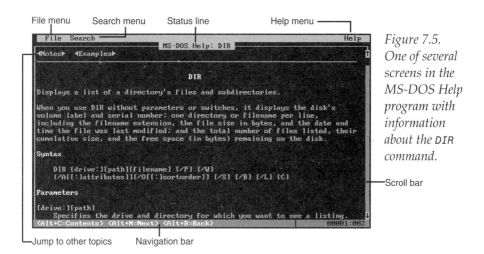

*Figure 7.5.
One of several
screens in the
MS-DOS Help
program with
information
about the DIR
command.*

Status line—lists the item currently being described.

Help menu—provides help about using MS-DOS Help.

Jump to other topics—enables you to jump to more help
about a specific command.

Scroll bar—enables you to use a mouse to view more information when the information takes more than a single
screen.

Navigation bar—enables you to move around within the MS-
DOS Help system.

To access menus in the MS-DOS Help program, either click the
menu item with your mouse or press Alt plus the first letter of the
menu. For example, press Alt+F to pull down the File menu.

MS-DOS Help enables you to jump from the current screen to
more information either about the same command or about related
commands, parameters, or switches. Although not present for all
topics, the Jump to Related Topics bar enables you to move to more
information about a specific command. You also can jump from
words within the main text of a help screen. Topics from which you
can launch a jump are in parentheses. On color monitors, the parentheses appear in green.

Use the Tab key to move the cursor forward between words from which jumps can be launched. Use Shift+Tab to move the cursor backward between jump launching points. To jump to the related information, press the Enter key. Or double-click on any jump launching point to move to the related information.

For example, with the cursor on the word <Examples> at the top of the screen shown in Figure 7.5, you can press Enter to jump to a screen of examples of the actual use of the DIR command (see Figure 7.6). You also can double-click on the word <Examples>.

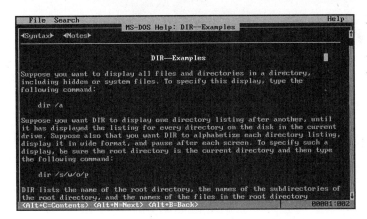

Figure 7.6.
The examples
screen for the
DIR command.

The Navigation bar enables you to move among help topics or find information about any topic. You can press

Alt+C, or double-click Alt+C in the Navigation bar, to view a list of all help topics available in MS-DOS Help. You can jump from that list to the specific topics using the techniques described previously.

Alt+N, or double-click Alt+N in the Navigation bar, to go to the next help screen.

Alt+B, or double-click Alt+B in the Navigation bar, to go to the help screen you previously viewed.

Because MS-DOS Help is a separate program, you must exit it just as you would exit any other program. To exit, select Exit from the File menu.

DOS Programs

External commands also are called DOS programs. DOS programs
help you perform common tasks related to DOS. DOS programs are
accessed by commands typed at the command prompt, the same as
internal commands. An example of a DOS program is the CHKDSK
program, which tells how much memory you have used and how
much you have remaining, both in your computer's random-access
memory (RAM) and on your disks.

> Do not run the DOS FORMAT.COM program until you've
> thoroughly read Chapter 21, "Maximizing Your Disk
> Drives." This program prepares your disks to receive more
> data. The first step in this process is eliminating all existing
> data on your disks.

Application Programs

You undoubtedly have programs other than DOS available on your
computer. A computer is like a tape player, and programs are like
cassette tapes. A tape player has little intrinsic value without tapes
to play. Similarly, after you buy a computer, you must buy programs
to run on it.

To start an application program, you must type a command at
the command prompt just as you do with DOS commands. With
application programs, as with DOS programs, you must type the
name of the primary program file for that program. That file usually has the .EXE or .COM file extension, although occasionally you
can launch a program by using a file with the .BAT extension. You
must read the application program's documentation to learn what
to type at the command prompt.

You do not have to type the extension to launch programs. You need to type only the base name. When you type the base name and press Enter, DOS automatically searches for programs with the .EXE, .COM, or .BAT extension and launches them. For DOS to do this, however, either you must type the name from the directory in which the program is located, or that directory must be included in the DOS path. For more information about the PATH command, see Chapter 5, "Peak Performance in the DOS Environment."

Like DOS commands, application programs can often accept parameters and switches. For example, if you load your word processor by typing WP, you might be able to load a specific file at the same time by adding a parameter such as

```
WP myfile.doc
```

Likewise, you might be able to add a switch, such as one to tell your word processor to run in monochrome rather than color, by typing

```
WP myfile.doc /m
```

These examples are fictitious. For specific information about loading your applications, consult the documentation for those applications.

Although application programs often require you to learn different techniques for effective use, most programs provide instant help when you press the F1 key.

Troubleshooting

This section discusses common problems you might encounter while beginning to use DOS from either the command prompt or the DOS Shell.

■ If you type a DOS command and DOS responds with the message `Bad command or file name`, you might have incorrectly spelled either the command or any of the command's parameters and switches. Another common problem is placing a space where it does not belong in the command or failing to place a space where one does belong. Press Esc and retype the command, being precise about the syntax.

If you are sure you have typed the command correctly but still receive a `Bad command or file name` message, chances are that you have encountered one of two problems:

1. DOS cannot find the external command on your disk. Read about the `PATH` command in Chapter 5, "Peak Performance in the DOS Environment."

2. The external command is missing from your hard disk. Go to the directory in which DOS is stored, and use the `DIR` command to get a list of all the files in the directory. Look for the external command you typed.

■ DOS displays the message `Abort, Retry, Ignore` or `Abort, Retry, Fail`. This error occurs when you type a command that the computer cannot carry out, such as when you attempt to access an empty floppy disk drive.

1. If you can correct the cause of the problem based on the brief message that appears above the `Abort, Retry, Ignore` or `Abort, Retry, Fail` message, do so and then press `R` to retry the command.

2. If you cannot correct the situation, press I to select
   Ignore, or press F to select Fail (whichever is displayed
   on your screen as an option). The message Current
   drive is no longer valid displays at the command
   prompt. You must then switch to a valid drive. For
   example, if you have a hard disk named C:, type C:
   and press Enter. If your disk drive A: contains a
   diskette, type A: and press Enter. The command
   prompt redisplays the current drive name.

■ DOS displays the message General failure reading drive
  followed by a drive name (such as A). If you get this
  message while trying to use a diskette drive, the diskette in
  the drive either is not formatted, and therefore cannot be
  accessed yet, or is faulty. Try a different diskette or see
  Chapter 21, "Maximizing Your Disk Drives," for formatting
  techniques.

Summary

This chapter has provided basic information about the DOS command prompt and the DOS Shell, as well as about files and how DOS
stores them. To summarize the most important issues covered in this
chapter:

■ Files either contain information that tell your computer
  what to do and how to do it, or they contain data, such as
  letters, spreadsheets, or database information.

■ To store information, DOS places files on your disk in a
  structure called a directory tree. A directory tree consists of
  a root directory and additional directories and subdirectories below the root that contain data and program files.

■ To manage files and launch commands, you can use either
  the command prompt or the DOS Shell.

■ To get help about commands from the command prompt, either use command prompt help by typing the command at the command prompt followed by /?, or use the MS-DOS Help program by typing HELP followed by the command name at the command prompt.

■ To get help about using the DOS Shell, press the F1 key at any time when you're in the Shell. You also can select Help from the Menu bar to access the Help pull-down menu or select the Help command button from the current dialog box (if any).

Alan Simpson's
DOS
SECRETS
UNLEASHED

CHAPTER 8

Using the Shell

Chapter 7 explained about using DOS from either the command prompt or the DOS Shell. This chapter provides more details on getting the most out of the DOS Shell. You will learn how to move around efficiently in the DOS Shell and how to use its graphical environment to manage your files, launch programs, and accomplish many tasks with DOS. Finally, you will learn how to use the DOS Shell to launch more than one program at a time and switch among open programs. Chapter 13, "Customizing DOS," discusses how to customize the Shell to best suit your needs. Chapter 10, "Working with Files and Directories," and Chapter 14, "Hard Disk Management Made Simple," provide specifics about using the DOS Shell to manage files and your hard drive.

To Shell or Not to Shell

The method you use for navigating through DOS is a matter of personal preference. There is no right answer about whether the command prompt or the DOS Shell is better. Still, each environment has its advantages. This section provides an overview of those advantages.

Deciding whether to use the command prompt or the DOS Shell need not be an either/or decision. Nor need it be a hasty decision. You might want to take a week or two and switch between the two environments, using the command prompt for a few days and then using the DOS Shell for a few days. After a while, your natural preferences will become clear. Don't be surprised if you find you are more comfortable doing some tasks at the command prompt and others with the DOS Shell.

Advantages of the DOS Shell

The DOS Shell shields you from having to memorize commonly
used DOS commands. It enables you to use such basic commands
as Copy and Delete without having to remember the syntax. Most
commonly used DOS commands are easily available from the DOS
Shell's menus.

Some users find it easier to manage their files with the DOS Shell
because it provides a graphical representation of their computing
environment. The overall structure of the hard disk, and the files
stored on the hard disk, are readily visible, which many people find
comforting.

Several functions are available with the DOS Shell that are not
available from the command prompt. The most visible of these special functions is the Task Swapper, which enables you to keep two
or more programs open simultaneously and switch among them
with a simple keystroke. For people who use many different programs, the Task Swapper can be a significant time and effort saver.

Another advantage is that the DOS Shell enables you to launch
programs without having to remember how to launch each program
from the command prompt. Techniques for launching programs
from the DOS Shell are described later in this chapter.

Advantages of the Command Prompt

In general, the command prompt is more straightforward than the
DOS Shell and provides users with greater power when managing
their DOS environment. For example, although many commonly
used commands are easily accessible from the DOS Shell, the command prompt remains the only way to execute many less-commonly
used commands.

Many of the new features and programs added to DOS 6, such as the Defrag and Memmaker programs, cannot be launched from the DOS Shell. Nor is it as easy to modify commands with parameters and switches using the DOS Shell.

Some users maintain that the command prompt is a simpler environment, even if there is more to memorize. They say that it is easier and faster to launch a program, exit the program, and start another from the command prompt than it is to set up the DOS Shell to work precisely the way they want. In addition, because many DOS functions can't be started from the DOS Shell, switching between the two environments often becomes necessary, which many people find tiring.

Navigating the DOS Shell

This section describes how to move around in the DOS Shell using both a mouse and the keyboard.

About Mice

If you have a properly installed mouse, the mouse pointer appears on your DOS Shell screen. If you are using the DOS Shell in graphics mode, the pointer appears as an arrow. If you are using text mode, the pointer appears as a block.

Although your mouse probably has two or three buttons on it, only one button is active in the DOS Shell. Usually, this is the leftmost button. Some mice, however, come with software that enables you to switch buttons, which often provides greater comfort for left-handed users.

For the sake of clarity, the following terms will be used to discuss how to operate your mouse:

Click—Roll the mouse pointer to the option you want, and then press and release the active mouse button once.

Double-click—Roll the mouse pointer to the option you want, and then press and release the active mouse button twice in rapid succession.

Drag—Roll the mouse pointer to the option you want, and then hold down the active mouse button while rolling the mouse.

You can use the mouse to change active windows simply by clicking on the new window. For example, if you are in the Directory Tree area and want to work in the File List area, click anywhere in the File List area and that becomes the active window.

About the Keyboard

Many operations in the Shell require combination keystrokes. Whenever you see two keystrokes separated by a plus (+) sign, it means to hold down the first key while you press the second key. For example, the keystroke combination Shift+Tab means "Hold down the Shift key and press the Tab key."

Usually in the DOS Shell, you use the Tab key to move ahead to the next element or window, and you use Shift+Tab to move backward. For example, if you currently are working in the directory tree area of the DOS Shell and you want to work in the File List area, press the Tab key once. To move backward to the directory tree window, press Shift+Tab.

About Scroll Bars

A scroll bar appears to the right of any window that contains more information than can fit into that window. The purpose of a scroll bar is to let you scroll through multiple screens of information.

The mouse is necessary to use the scroll bar. To scroll down one line at a time, click once on the down arrow at the bottom of the scroll bar. To scroll up one line at a time, click once on the up arrow at the top of the scroll bar.

The box between the up and down arrows indicates your position in the document. To move up one screen at a time, click in the scroll bar above the position box. To move down one screen at a time, click in the scroll bar below the position box. You also can click on the position box and drag the box up or down in the scroll bar to move to another part of the document.

If you don't have a mouse, use the PgUp key to move up one screenful at a time and the PgDn key to move down one screenful at a time. To move up one line at a time, use the ↑ key, and use the ↓ key to move down one line at a time.

Using the Menu Bar

The Menu bar provides access to commands. You can use either the keyboard or the mouse to access the Menu bar.

Using the mouse, click on the menu item you want. The menu with all its options drops down. Then click on the option you want. If an option is not available, it is grayed out. In Figure 8.1, the Program/File Lists view is grayed out. It is not available because that is the current view.

*Figure 8.1.
The View
menu with
one item
grayed out.*

To access menus and options using the keyboard, first press the Alt key or F10. When you do this, the first letter in each menu name on the Menu bar becomes underlined. Press the underlined letter of the menu you want, and the full menu drops down. One letter in each available menu option is underlined. (If you are in text mode, as opposed to graphical mode, the letter might be highlighted or brightened.) Pressing a highlighted or underlined letter in the menu activates that command. If you inadvertently select an option you don't understand, press Escape to back out of that selection.

Changing the View

You can set the DOS Shell to view or hide different elements. Most of the figures in this book show the Shell screen with the default view. You can change the view easily to whatever best suits your needs at the moment. Here's how:

1. Select View from the Menu bar (either by clicking that option or by pressing Alt+V).

2. Select any of the five views:

   Single File List—Removes the program area from the screen. Use this option when you want to see a longer Directory tree and Files List.

   Dual File Lists—Presents two independent drive, directory, and files areas. This option is useful for moving and copying files across drives and directories. Figure 8.2 shows this view.

   All Files—Displays all files on the drive as though they were all one directory. The name, size, directory location, and other information about the currently highlighted file is displayed to the left. This option is useful for operations that involve files from multiple directories.

   Program/File Lists—The default setting shows the Drives, Directory Tree, Files, and Program areas.

   Program List—Displays the Program List area.

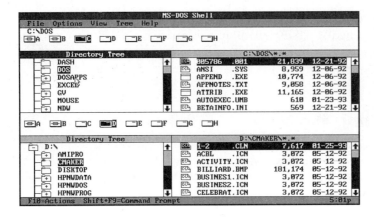

*Figure 8.2.
The Dual Files
List view in the
DOS Shell.*

When you change views, the DOS Shell automatically uses the new view until you change the view again. You do not have to specifically save the new view for the DOS Shell to use it in the future.

Another window that might appear on your screen is the Active Task List. Turn this window on and off by selecting Enable Task Swapper from the Options pull-down menu. The Task Swapper is discussed in greater detail later in this chapter.

The best way to determine which view is best for you is to try them all for a time. For many people, a preference for one view or another emerges based on their natural work style. Other people do not develop such a preference, but rather switch among views depending on their tasks.

About Dialog Boxes

Another tool for communicating with DOS is the dialog box, so named because the box (or window) requests information, which you provide. For example, if you select File Display Options from the Options pull-down menu, you'll see the dialog box shown in Figure 8.3. The figure also points out some items that often appear in dialog boxes.

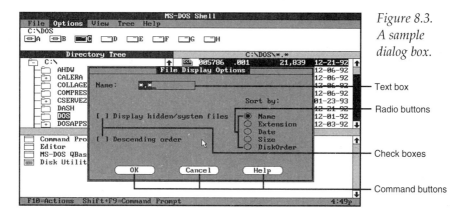

Figure 8.3. A sample dialog box.

Navigating a Dialog Box

Using a mouse, move between elements in a dialog box by clicking on the new element. With the keyboard, use the Tab and Shift+Tab keys to move forward and backward between elements. Within the elements of the dialog box

- Press ↑, ↓, →, or ← to move from option to option.
- Press Enter to select the currently highlighted option.

Using Text Boxes

A text box requires that you type some text. In some cases, the text box already contains suggested text, such as *.* in the sample dialog box shown in Figure 8.3.

To use a text box with a mouse, take these steps:

1. Click wherever you want to start typing within the text box.

2. Type text.

If you are using the keyboard rather than a mouse, take these steps:

1. Press Tab or Shift+Tab until the cursor gets to the text box. If text is already in the text box, it will be highlighted.

2. If you want to replace all the text in the box, type the new text.

3. If you want to insert text into the box, position the cursor where you want to insert text (using the → and ← keys), and type the new text.

If you open a text box that already has text in it, it is either the last text entered into that box or the text the DOS Shell places in the box by default. If you enter information into a text box, it stays there until you change it or exit the DOS Shell. After you exit and return to the DOS Shell, the information in the box reverts to the default. The default might be either text, such as the *.* in Figure 8.3, or an empty text box.

Table 8.1 lists keys you can use to make changes to text in a text box.

Table 8.1. Keys used with text boxes.

Key(s)	Effect
→ ←	Moves to the left or right through existing text.
Del	Deletes the character over the cursor.

Key(s)	Effect
Backspace	Deletes the character to the left of the cursor.
Tab (or Shift+Tab)	Moves to the next or previous item in the box, if any.

Using Radio Buttons

Some dialog boxes contain a set of mutually exclusive options, such as the Sort by: options in the sample dialog box in Figure 8.3. The buttons you use to select such options are called radio buttons because, as with a push-button car radio, pressing one button automatically unpresses another.

To use radio buttons with a mouse, click the button you want. If you are using a keyboard, take the following steps:

1. Press Tab or Shift+Tab until you get to the radio button area.

2. Press ↑ or ↓ to move to the option you want.

3. Press Tab or Shift+Tab to move to the next area, or press Enter to record the change.

Using Check Boxes

Some dialog boxes also offer check boxes in which you can turn the option either on, by placing an X in its check box, or off, by removing the X from its check box. The check box itself is simply a pair of brackets, like this: [ ]. The settings in Figure 8.3 for Display hidden/ system files and Descending order are check boxes.

To use check boxes with a mouse, click anywhere on the option or the box to place or remove the X.

With a keyboard, take these steps:

1. Press Tab or Shift+Tab until the cursor gets to the check box.

2. Press the Spacebar to place or remove the X.

Using Command Buttons

A list of command buttons appears at the bottom of most dialog boxes. The command buttons carry out one of three actions: accept changes you've made in the dialog box and exit the dialog box, cancel any changes and exit the dialog box, or get help. As shown in Figure 8.3, those command buttons usually are called

> OK
> Cancel
> Help

To select a command button with a mouse, click it once. With the keyboard, press Tab or Shift+Tab until the button you want is selected (a small underline appears in the button). Then press Enter to select that button.

Running Programs from the Shell

One of the best uses of the DOS Shell is as a launching pad for your programs. The DOS Shell provides various ways to run DOS and application programs.

Running a Program

From the DOS Shell, the procedure for running DOS programs and the procedure for running application programs are essentially the same. As an example, run the CHKDSK program as described next.

CHKDSK is a DOS program that reports how much memory you have used and how much remains on your disks and in random-access memory. It is stored with the file name CHKDSK.EXE.

Assuming that you are starting from the initial DOS Shell screen (which displays both the File List and the Program List), use the following steps to run the CHKDSK program:

1. If you have multiple hard drives, select the drive on which DOS programs are stored (typically drive C) from the Drives area.

2. Select the directory in which you store your DOS programs from the Directory Tree area of the Shell. Typically, this is the \DOS directory.

3. If you are using a mouse, double-click on CHKDSK.EXE in the Files area, and the program executes. If you are using the keyboard, press Tab to move to the Files area of the screen, and then use the ↓ or ↑ key to move the highlight bar to the CHKDSK.EXE file name.

4. When CHKDSK.EXE is highlighted (as shown in Figure 8.4), press Enter. (If you have a mouse, you can use the scroll bar to locate the CHKDSK.EXE file and double-click the file name.)

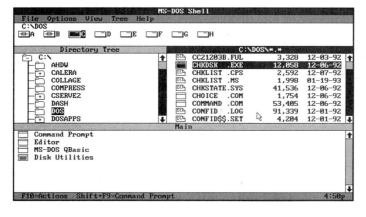

Figure 8.4. The CHKDSK.EXE file name is highlighted.

The program executes, and the screen displays information about your computer's memory (RAM) and the current hard disk or diskette.

Running Programs from the File List

Rather than going through file directories to find the program files you want to launch, you can launch files from the Program List.

The Program List displays programs, and groups of programs, that are available from the Shell. See Figure 8.4 for a view of the DOS Shell and the File List. The Program List is visible only in the Program/File Lists and Program List views of the Shell.

> Be careful not to clutter your Program List. To avoid clutter, either include only those programs you run most frequently, or categorize your programs into several groups. If you list all your programs in your Program List, it will take longer to find the ones you want.

Initially, the Program List displays the Main program group (the title "Main" appears at the top of the window). It's also likely that your program list contains at least three programs (Command Prompt, Editor, and MS-DOS QBasic) and one group of programs (Disk Utilities).

To run a program listed in the Program List, follow these instructions:

- Double-click on the program you want to run. If you are using the keyboard rather than a mouse, press Tab until the highlight bar is in the Program List window.

- If the program you want to run is in a group other than the one that's currently displayed, select the appropriate group name, either by double-clicking its name or by moving the highlight bar to the name and pressing Enter.

■ Select the name of the program you want to run, either by double-clicking its name or by moving the highlight bar to the name and pressing Enter.

You can use the same basic techniques to run a program in a particular group. To run a program, for example in the Disk Utilities group, carry out the following steps:

1. Move the highlight bar to the Disk Utilities group name and press Enter (or double-click Disk Utilities if you are using a mouse). The names of programs in the Disk Utilities group are displayed.

2. Launch the program either by double-clicking or by using the ↓ or ↑ keys until the program you want is highlighted and then pressing Enter.

3. Exit the program you have launched.

4. To get back to the Main group, highlight Main and press Enter, or double-click the Main option.

Adding Programs to the File List

The procedures for adding programs to the Program List and adding a group to the Program List are similar.

To add a program to the Program List, follow these steps:

1. Make sure the Main window is the currently active window.

2. Select New from the File menu.

3. Select the Program Item button to add a program, or select the Program Group button for adding a group. Then select OK. Figure 8.5 shows the dialog box for adding a new program.

4. In the Add Program dialog box, carry out the following actions:

Type the program title. This is the title as it will appear in the Program List.

Type the command needed to launch the program, with any parameters and switches. For example, to launch your word processor, the appropriate command might be WP.EXE. Check the documentation accompanying the program to learn the name of the program file.

Type the directory in which the program is located.

Type a shortcut key to be used for switching among programs with the Task Swapper, described later in this chapter.

Indicate whether there should be a pause after exiting the program and returning to the DOS Shell.

When you first add a program to a group, always be sure the Pause after exit box is checked. That way, if you make a mistake in the dialog box, you can see the error message, which in turn might help you solve the problem.

If desired, type a password to be required for accessing the program.

If desired, select Advanced options to fine-tune how the program runs. The Advanced options include memory and video options. It usually is not necessary to set these options.

5. Select OK.

Figure 8.5 shows the dialog box for adding an item to the Program List. Figure 8.6 shows the dialog box for adding a program.

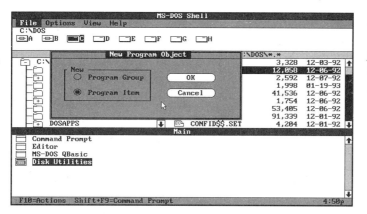

Figure 8.5.
The dialog box
for adding an
item to the
Program List.

To have the DOS Shell prompt you for a specific file name or other command-line parameters after you launch a program from the Program List, type the parameter %1 after the command name in the Commands text box in the Add Program dialog box, shown in Figure 8.6. Be sure to place a space between the command and the parameter. After you click OK, fill out another dialog box with information about how you want the DOS Shell to prompt you for a file name. This procedure saves you from having to search for a specific file after you have loaded your program.

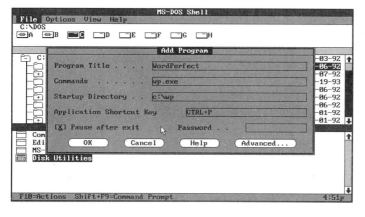

Figure 8.6.
The dialog box
for adding a
program to the
Program List.

If you choose a password for launching a program (or group) from the Program List, hide a copy of the password in a safe place. You will be unable to launch the program or group if you forget the password.

If you have a file you must open frequently, you can have a listing in Program List that will load that file automatically. To do this, add a parameter after the file name in the Add Program dialog box. The parameter should state the path and file name of the file you want to open. Check with your application's documentation to make sure your program supports loading files in this way.

Adding Groups to the File List

To add a group to the Program List, follow these steps:

1. Make sure the Main window is the currently active window.

2. Select New from the File menu.

3. Select the Program Group Item radio button in the New Program Object dialog box, shown in Figure 8.5.

4. Fill in the text boxes in the Add Group dialog box (Figure 8.7). The only mandatory item in the dialog box is the title of the group. You can use any title you want. The title in Figure 8.7, Applications, would be appropriate for a group containing your most-used application.

5. Click OK.

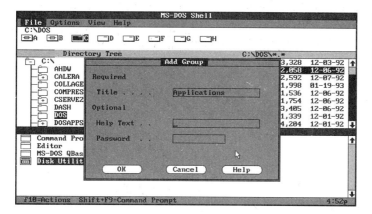

Figure 8.7.
The Add
Group dialog
box.

To add programs to a group, follow these steps:

1. Select the program group in the Program List either by double-clicking on the group name in the Program List or by highlighting the group name and pressing Enter.

2. Add programs as described previously.

Deleting Items from the File List

To delete a program or group from the File List, take the following steps:

1. Highlight the item you want to delete.

2. Select Delete from the File menu.

3. Select Delete this Item.

4. Select OK.

To delete a group, you first must delete all the programs in the group.

Running Programs by Dragging

Yet another technique for running some programs is to use the mouse to drag a data file to its program. By a data file, I mean a file that contains data which a program created, such as a document created with your word processing program or a spreadsheet created with your spreadsheet program.

To use this technique, you must be able to recognize which data files belong to which programs. Furthermore, this procedure does not work with all programs. You might have to experiment and do a little research in your application's documentation to determine whether you can use this technique. The general procedure is as listed here:

1. In the Files List, highlight the data file you want to work with.

2. Hold down the left mouse button and drag the file to the program you want to use. (If the program is not currently visible, keep holding down the left mouse button, and move to the arrows at the top or bottom of the scroll bar for the Files List to scroll.)

3. When you see the program file, move the highlight bar to it, and release the mouse button.

4. You might see a dialog box asking for confirmation. If so, click Yes to continue with the operation.

If the data file and program are on separate drives or directories, use the Dual File Lists view to drag a data file to its program.

When mastered, this technique can save a lot of time. If, for example, you are a WordPerfect user, you could drag a WordPerfect document file to the WordPerfect program (WP.EXE); then when WordPerfect started, it would automatically load your document file.

Running Programs by Association

Another method of running programs is by associating certain data files with the programs that create them. This is one of the most convenient techniques that the DOS Shell offers.

In simple terms, this technique involves associating a certain file name extension with a specific program. After you create the association, whenever you select the data file from the Files List, the DOS Shell will know to launch both the application and the file on which you double-clicked.

For example, you might want to associate the .WK1 file name extension with Lotus 1-2-3. After you make the association, any time you double-click on a file with the .WK1 extension, the DOS Shell launches Lotus 1-2-3 and the file you selected.

To associate a file with a particular extension, follow these steps:

1. In the Files List area, highlight a file with the extension you want to associate.

2. Select Associate from the Files menu.

3. In the dialog box, type the full path and file name of the application to which you want the files associated. Figure 8.8 shows the Associate File dialog box.

4. Select OK.

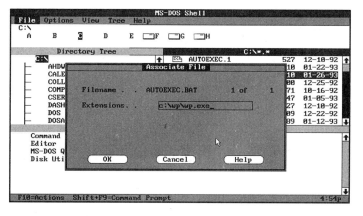

*Figure 8.8.
The Associate
File dialog box.*

The techniques of associating files and launching programs from the File List are not mutually exclusive. When you want to start your application with a specific data file, the file-association technique is faster. When you want to start a new document, launching from the File List works better.

Starting More Than One Program at a Time in the Shell

The DOS Shell enables you to perform several operations you can't perform from the command prompt. One of the most useful Shell-only operations is called task swapping.

The practical uses for this time-saving feature are many. Without this capability, if you are using one program and want to see data in another program, you must exit the first program, start the second, view the data, exit the second program, and then start the first again. The DOS Shell, however, enables you to start two or more programs and then swap between the programs or the Shell with a single key combination.

Enabling the Swapper

Before you can take advantage of task swapping, you must first enable the Task Swapper. To do this, follow these instructions:

1. Press Alt+O or select Options in the Menu bar to pull down the Options menu.

2. Select Enable Task Swapper.

The Enable Task Swapper option is a toggle. It has only two states: enabled or disabled, on or off. To toggle the option off (disable the Task Swapper), follow the previous steps exactly. Select the option once to turn it on; select it again to turn it off.

If you pull down the Options menu again, you'll notice that a diamond-like bullet appears to the left of the Enable Task Swapper option when it is enabled. That bullet symbol is used throughout the DOS Shell to signify that an option is on, or active.

> The default is to have the Task Swapper disabled. However, when you understand how it operates, there are no disadvantages to enabling the Task Swapper and allowing it to stay enabled. This has the advantage of ensuring that the Task Swapper always is available for use.

The Active Task List Display

After you enable the Swapper, the Program List section of the Shell divides into two areas: one titled Main (or the active program group name) and the other called the Active Task List. The Active Task List lets you know which programs you have already started and, therefore, which programs are currently open.

If your Shell is currently displaying the Program List view, the Active Task List occupies the entire right side of the screen (see Figure 8.9); if you are using the Program/File Lists view, the Active Task List section is a small box in the lower-right corner of the screen (see Figure 8.10).

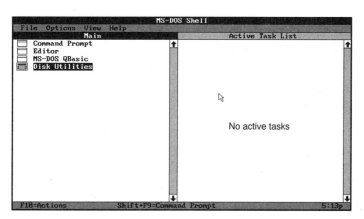

Figure 8.9. The Active Task List box in the Program List view.

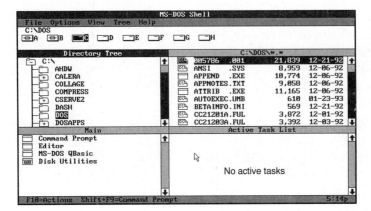

Figure 8.10.
The Active
Task List
box in the
Program/File
Lists view.

How the Task Swapper Operates

After you've enabled the Task Swapper, you can start a program and then press a key combination to return to the Shell, from which you can start another program. You can repeat this process as many times as necessary.

Although all the programs you have started are technically open, they are not all active. Only the currently selected program is actually running. What about the other unselected programs?

Assume that you've started a program from the Shell and then issued the command that swaps you back to the Shell. DOS immediately takes a snapshot of that program and the condition it was in and saves that information to a disk file. Then it starts the Shell program. When you return to the previously started program, DOS exits the Shell and reloads the saved disk file into memory. This restores your computer's memory to its previous state (which includes the program and data that was stored there before you switched to the Shell), and that program resumes running.

You cannot start a spreadsheet recalculation or large printing task, for example, and assume that the operation will continue after you switch to another program. When you leave the current program, DOS suspends its activity and restores that activity only when you switch back to the program. Only one program can be running at a time.

Swapping Between Programs

To run multiple programs available from the Active Task List, first be sure the Enable Task Swapper option in the Options menu is on, and then use the following general steps:

1. If your monitor is not displaying the Active Task List, select Program/File Lists from the View menu.

2. Start a program in the usual manner, using either the Files List or the Program List, as described previously in this chapter.

3. After your program completes all of its start-up operations and is active, press Alt+Tab, Alt+Esc, or Ctrl+Esc. This causes DOS to return to the Shell.

The Active Task List on the screen now includes the name of the program you just left. You can use steps two and three to start another program. Each new program name is listed in the Active Task List.

To switch to an already running (open) program, select its name from the Active Task List. With the mouse, double-click the program name; with the keyboard, Tab to the Task List, use the arrow keys to highlight the program name, and press Enter.

A faster way to switch between programs is with shortcut keys. You can assign shortcut keys in the Add Program dialog box (Figure 8.6) that you must fill out to add a program to the Program List. Then, after the program is open, you have to press only the shortcut key combination to switch back to that program. Notice that the shortcut key for the Editor in Figure 8.11 is Ctrl+P.

Closing Open Programs

If you finish using a program and no longer need to swap to it, exit (close) that program as you normally would. After the program ends, DOS returns you to the Shell, from which you can switch to another program. Note that the Active Task List no longer displays the name of the program you just closed.

You cannot exit the Shell until you have closed all open programs. You must select the programs one by one from the Active Task List, exiting them in the usual fashion. When the Task List no longer displays any program names, you can exit the Shell.

You can, however, temporarily get to the command prompt by pressing Shift+F9 or by selecting Command Prompt from the Main program group, even while programs are listed in the Active Task List. Remember, however, that when you temporarily exit the Shell in this manner, you type the EXIT command (not DOSSHELL) at the command prompt to get back to the Shell.

Never turn off the computer while programs are still open (while their names are displayed in the Active Task List box). If you do, you probably will lose the data you entered into those programs. Always close those programs and exit the Shell before turning off your computer.

If a program ever locks up, or freezes so that you can't exit it as you normally would, use the following steps to recover:

1. Press Alt+Esc to return to the Shell.

2. Highlight the program's name in the Active Task List. With the mouse, click the name once; with the keyboard, Tab to the Task List, and use the arrow keys to position the highlight over the name.

3. Press the Del key.

This is a last-resort procedure! Figure 8.11 shows the warning message that DOS displays before you delete a program from the Task List. Although this procedure closes the program, it might cause you to lose some of the data you've entered. It also destabilizes DOS and can disrupt future operations. After you have deleted the program name, immediately close any other programs that are open, exit the Shell, and then reboot your computer.

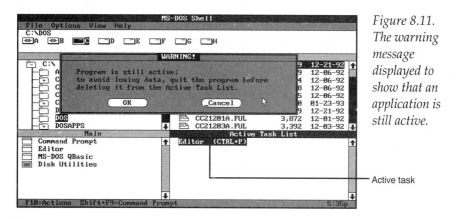

Figure 8.11. The warning message displayed to show that an application is still active.

Active task

Back to the Defaults

After you activate the Task Swapper, it remains enabled even in future DOS Shell sessions until you turn it off. If you want to disable the Task Swapper now, you must first empty the Active Task List by ending any running programs. Then select Enable Task Swapper from the Options pull-down menu.

Getting Help in the DOS Shell

Extensive help for using the DOS Shell is available from the Help menu. As with all other menus, you can access the Help menu by clicking on the word Help in the Menu bar or pressing Alt plus the first letter of the menu name, in this case, Alt+H. Figure 8.12 shows a typical screen from the DOS Shell help system, in this case, the screen describing keys used for navigating the DOS Shell.

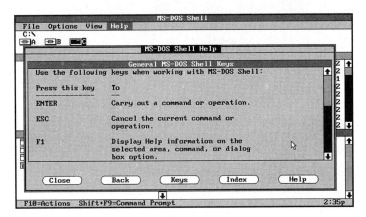

Figure 8.12.
A typical help screen from the DOS Shell.

The Help menu offers the following options:

Index—an index of all general topics covered by the DOS Shell help system.

Keyboard—help with using the keyboard to navigate through the DOS Shell.

Shell Basics—the basics about the Shell and how to access commonly used features.

Commands—explanations of menu options in the DOS Shell.

Procedures—basic procedures, such as how to choose menu commands.

Using Help—help using the DOS Shell help system.

About Shell—basic information about the DOS Shell program.

Exiting the DOS Shell

If you want to switch to the command prompt, you need to exit the Shell. There are two ways to exit the Shell and get to the command prompt:

Full exit—The Shell is removed from memory, and any current temporary settings are lost. You have access to all memory when the command prompt appears.

Partial exit—The Shell and all its current (temporary) settings remain in memory. The command prompt appears and all commands are acceptable; available memory is limited, however.

Making a Full Exit

Unless the Shell is doing something, such as running several programs, you'll probably want to make a full exit to DOS when you need to get to the command prompt. That way, you'll have full access to all your computer's memory.

> You cannot make a full exit from the Shell if tasks are running. You must close all running programs before you can make a full exit.

To make a full exit, use one of the following methods:

- Pull down the File menu from the Menu bar, and select Exit.

- As a shortcut, press the F3 key.

To return to the Shell after making a complete exit, you must load the DOS Shell again.

Making a Temporary Exit

If you need to make a temporary exit from the Shell to access the command prompt (for example, when several tasks are running), use one of the following methods:

- Select Command Prompt from the Program List.

- Press Shift+F9.

The command prompt appears, and you can enter any valid DOS command. However, the Shell and any other programs you had running remain at least partially in memory. This is sometimes known as shelling to DOS.

To return to the Shell after making a partial exit, follow these steps:

1. Type EXIT.

2. Press Enter.

If a copy of the Shell is in memory and you try to access the Shell with the DOSSHELL command, you load yet another copy of the Shell into memory instead of coming back to the original Shell. This action causes you to run out of memory sooner, and because you're loading a new instance of the Shell, you might not return to the same Shell environment you left.

If you ever find yourself at the command prompt and can't remember which method you used to exit the Shell, I suggest you first type EXIT (and press Enter) to return to the Shell. If a copy of the Shell is not already in memory, nothing happens. Now you can just type DOSSHELL and press Enter to load a new copy of the Shell without wondering whether this is the first or second copy of the Shell in memory.

Troubleshooting

If you experience problems during this chapter, try to locate the problem in the following section, and then follow the suggested solution.

■ If you cannot get the DOS Shell running, one of two things is probably wrong:

1. You are using an old version of DOS that does not include the DOS Shell.

2. The subdirectory in which you store your DOS programs, including the DOS Shell, is not in your DOS Path. (Read about the PATH command in Chapter 5, "Peak Performance in the DOS Environment.") If this is the problem, you can still start the DOS Shell by switching to the directory in which DOS files are stored (usually C:\DOS). Then type DOSSHELL and press Enter.

■ If your DOS Shell screens look dramatically different from the ones shown in this chapter, one of two things is probably wrong:

1. Your view is different from the view in the screen shots in this book. Changing your view in the Options menu, as described in this chapter, should rectify that situation.

2. You are running the DOS Shell from DOS 4. Although the DOS Shell included with DOS 5 looks very similar to the DOS Shell in DOS 6, the DOS 4 Shell looks different.

■ If none of the arrow keys, nor the PgUp or PgDn keys, works on your keyboard, press the Num Lock key once to unlock the numbers on the numeric keypad. Then try the arrow keys again.

■ If you cannot get your mouse to work in the DOS Shell, be sure it is properly connected, following the instructions that

came with the mouse. Also, make sure the driver that
allows your mouse to operate is loaded. First check your
mouse documentation for the name of the mouse driver file.
Then look for that file on your hard drive. It likely will be
either in your root directory or in the directory in which you
store your DOS programs. If you do not find the driver,
reinstall it following the directions in your mouse documentation. If you do find the mouse driver, make sure it is
loaded in either your AUTOEXEC.BAT or your
CONFIG.SYS file.

■ If you cannot switch from one program to another, one of
two things might be wrong:

1. The shortcut key you selected for the program you
   want to switch to is being used for some function in
   your current application. If this is the case, you must
   change shortcut keys.

2. You might be using an application that was developed
   before the DOS Shell and that does not work with the
   Task Swapper. If that happens, call your software
   reseller or software vendor for an update.

Summary

This chapter provided details about using the DOS Shell. To summarize the most important issues covered in this chapter:

■ Whether to use the DOS Shell or the command prompt is a
matter of personal preference. There is no right answer.

■ You can move from area to area in the DOS Shell either by
clicking on the new area with the mouse or by using the Tab
and Shift+Tab keys to move forward and backward between areas.

■ Scroll bars enable you to move quickly in screens that
contain more than a single screenful of information.

■ You can change the way you view the DOS Shell by selecting different views from the Options menu.

■ You often communicate with the DOS Shell and with DOS itself with dialog boxes. Elements of dialog boxes include text boxes, radio buttons, check boxes, and command buttons.

■ You can run programs from the DOS Shell by clicking on the appropriate program file name either in the Files List area or in the Program List area.

■ Specific files can be loaded with programs by dragging the file to its program or by associating certain types of files with specific programs.

■ You can use the Task Swapper to load more than one program at a time and then switch among all loaded programs.

■ You can temporarily exit from the DOS Shell by either selecting Command Prompt from the Program List or pressing Shift+F9.

■ You can permanently exit from the DOS Shell by either selecting Exit from the File menu or pressing F3.

Alan Simpson's
DOS
SECRETS
UNLEASHED

Using the Command Prompt

The command prompt is where you tell DOS what to do and how to do it. It is the most direct way to interact with DOS. In fact, until the DOS Shell was introduced in DOS 4, it was the only way to interact with DOS. This chapter provides details about using commands at the command prompt and discusses some commonly used commands. It also discusses ways to get more power out of the command line by using pipes and filters. For more information about fine-tuning your use of the command line, see Chapter 13, "Customizing DOS."

Command-Line Basics

Using commands is a two-step process. First you type the command. Then you press Enter to send it to the computer for processing.

Upper- and Lowercase Letters in Commands

DOS doesn't care whether you type commands in upper- or lowercase letters, so you can use them interchangeably. That is, as far as DOS is concerned, DIR, dir, and Dir are the same thing.

Don't forget, though, that you cannot use the letter *l* for the number *1*, nor the letter *O* for the number *0*.

Command Shortcuts

Shortcut keys can help you enter the same or similar commands repeatedly or make a correction to a faulty command that produced an error message. Those keys are listed in Table 9.1.

Table 9.1. The editing keys used with commands.

Key(s)	Effect
F1 or →	Retypes one character from the previously entered command.
F2	Retypes all the characters up to the character you type next.
F3	Retypes the entire preceding command, from the right of the current cursor position.
F4	Moves up to the next character you type without copying any characters.
Backspace or ←	Deletes the character to the left of the cursor.
Insert (Ins)	Inserts the next characters typed into the preceding command. You can then press F3 to bring back the rest of the preceding command.
Esc	Cancels all characters up to the point at which you press Esc, places a backslash at that point, and advances the cursor one line. You can start over and then type your corrected command. When you press Enter, the \ and all characters to the left of it are ignored.

Repeating Groups of Commands

As you work at the command prompt, you often will need to repeat commands. F3 retypes your most recent command, but what if you want to reuse a command you used previously? DOS includes a special utility called DOSKEY that lets DOS remember a long series of commands. DOSKEY is discussed in greater detail in Chapter 13, "Customizing DOS."

Pausing and Canceling Commands

Some commands produce several pages (screens) of information. For example, if you use the DIR command in a subdirectory with many files, the listing of files will scroll off the screen.

You can halt the scrolling of the screen by pressing Ctrl+S or Pause. Pressing any key (or Ctrl+S) then resumes the scrolling. Or, as discussed in the next section, you can use the MORE command filter, which provides information one screenful at a time.

If you want to terminate a command altogether while it is displaying text on the screen, press Ctrl+Break or Ctrl+C. These keys, however, only stop a command in its tracks; they cannot undo a command that has already completed its job.

How to Modify Commands

You have already learned how to use parameters and switches to modify commands. Three other tools also are available to modify commands: *filters, pipes,* and *wildcards.*

Filters and Pipes

Programs or commands that rearrange the output of DOS commands are called *filters.* Filters often are used with other commands.

To separate commands from filters when they are used together, you must use a character called a *pipe.* The ¦ character, called pipe, is Shift+\ on most keyboards (hold down the Shift key and press \). When a pipe is used, a filter, which may be a command in its own right, can change, or redirect, the output created by the first command.

For example, the output from the DIR command described in this chapter often results in more than one screenful of information. You can use the filter MORE to make sure DOS provides only one screenful of information at a time. Because you are using two commands at the same time, you must separate them with a pipe. One example is

```
C:\DOS> DIR ¦ MORE
```

By typing the command in this way, you get only one screenful of information at a time—the next screen does not appear until you press a key (see Figure 9.1).

```
Press any key to continue . . .

(continuing C:\DOS)
ATTRIB     EXE    15796 10-26-92   6:00a
AUTOEXEC   UMB      391 11-04-92   9:44a
BCCMBIAP             0 11-09-92   6:44p
BCCMBIBF          1900 11-09-92   6:44p
CHKDSK     EXE    16216 10-26-92   6:00a
CHKSTATE   SYS    38752 10-26-92   6:00a
CHOICE     COM     1754 10-26-92   6:00a
COMMAND    COM    53022 10-26-92   6:00a
COMP       EXE    14282 04-09-91   5:00a
CONFIG     UMB      331 11-04-92   9:42a
COUNTRY    SYS    17069 10-26-92   6:00a
DBLSPACE   BIN    63868 10-26-92   6:00a
DBLSPACE   EXE   286338 10-26-92   6:00a
DBLSPACE   HLP    35342 10-26-92   6:00a
DBLSPACE   INF     1113 10-26-92   6:00a
DBLSPACE   SYS      217 10-26-92   6:00a
DEBUG      EXE    20634 10-26-92   6:00a
DEFRAG     EXE    74505 10-26-92   6:00a
DEFRAG     HLP    16809 10-26-92   6:00a
DELOLDOS   EXE    17710 10-26-92   6:00a
— More —
```

*Figure 9.1.
The DIR
command used
with the MORE
filter.*

Wildcards

You can place the wildcard characters (? and *) in file names when you are using commands from the command prompt. Using wildcards means you don't have to use the same command many times when your commands are acting on files with similar names.

The DOS wildcard symbols are

?   Matches any single character in a base name or an extension.

*   Matches any group of characters in a base name or an extension.

When you combine the wildcard characters with regular characters, you create what is called an ambiguous file name. For example, the ambiguous file name M*.* isolates all file names that begin with M. The M* matches file names that begin with M followed by any characters, and .* matches any extension.

Wildcards work well when you are using a command that works on multiple files with similar names. For example, if you wanted to copy the files SAMPLE1.TXT and SAMPLE2.TXT from the C:\WP directory to the C:\FILES directory, you could type

```
COPY C:\WP\SAMPLE?.TXT C:\FILES
```

The two files have similar names, varying only in one character. The ? character replaces any character in its position in either the base name or the extension.

Figure 9.2 shows the result of typing the DIR command with the * wildcard as follows:

```
C:> DIR *.EXE
```

The * character stands for any characters in the base name.

```
(continuing C:\DOS)
INTERSVR EXE    37266 10-26-92   6:00a
JOIN     EXE    17870 04-09-91   5:00a
LABEL    EXE     9390 10-26-92   6:00a
MEM      EXE    30470 10-26-92   6:00a
MEMMAKER EXE   117611 10-26-92   6:00a
MSD      EXE   158428 10-26-92   6:00a
MWUNDEL  EXE   130032 10-26-92   6:00a
NLSFUNC  EXE     7052 10-26-92   6:00a
OPSETUPT EXE    77312 10-26-92   3:44p
POWER    EXE     8052 10-26-92   6:00a
PRINT    EXE    15656 10-26-92   6:00a
QBASIC   EXE   256217 10-26-92   6:00a
RECOVER  EXE     9146 04-09-91   5:00a
REPLACE  EXE    20226 10-26-92   6:00a
RESTORE  EXE    38294 10-26-92   6:00a
SETVER   EXE    12015 11-03-92  10:30a
SHARE    EXE    10912 10-26-92   6:00a
SIZER    EXE     5489 10-26-92   6:00a
SMARTDRV EXE    44121 10-26-92   6:00a
SMARTMON EXE    28672 10-26-92   6:00a
SORT     EXE     6938 10-26-92   6:00a
SUBST    EXE    18478 10-26-92   6:00a
Press any key to continue . . .
```

Figure 9.2.
*The screen created by using the DIR command with the * wildcard.*

You can use wildcard characters only to substitute for characters in file names—never for drive, directory, or subdirectory names.

As you gain experience using DOS wildcards, you'll notice what an advantage it is to name related files with file names that have a similar pattern. You can name files that store quarterly data in a haphazard manner, such as 1992QTR1.DAT, QTR2-92.INF, and 92-3-QTR.TXT. But if you name them haphazardly, you cannot use ambiguous file names to perform operations on these files as a group. However, if you rename the files using a consistent format, such as QTR1-92.DAT, QTR2-92.DAT, and QTR3-92.DAT, you can more easily display or manage these related files using the ambiguous file names QTR?-92.DAT or QTR*.DAT.

Commonly used DOS commands are discussed in the next section. You can use wildcards with any command in which you must designate specific files.

DOS File Management Commands

This section describes some of the more commonly used DOS file-management commands and their most common uses. A comprehensive reference of DOS commands is available in your *DOS User's Manual*.

COPY

The COPY command takes files in a directory or floppy drive, called the *source,* and copies them to another disk or directory, called the *destination.* The COPY command can also be used to combine ASCII text files. After you have completed use of the COPY command, the files will be located both in the old location and in the new location.

The DOS Shell contains a MOVE command that copies files to the new location and automatically eliminates them from the old location. Until DOS 6, there was no similar command that you could execute from the command prompt. DOS 6 introduces the MOVE command, as detailed in Chapter 10, "Working with Files and Directories."

COPY is an internal command. The syntax is

```
COPY [source path][source filename] [destination path]
    [destination filename]
```

You do not have to include a source or destination path if your current directory is either the source or the destination. Nor do you have to include a destination file name if the file name does not change.

Following are some samples. These commands all copy MYFILE.DOC from the C:\WP directory to the C:\OLDFILES directory.

The following command is executed from the source directory, so the source path is not included in the command:

```
C:\WP> COPY MYFILE.DOC C:\OLDFILES
```

The next command is executed from a third directory (in this case, the root directory), so both the source and the destination paths are included:

```
C:\> COPY C:\WP\MYFILE.DOC C:\OLDFILES
```

The next command is executed from the destination directory, so the source path is included:

```
C:\OLDFILES> COPY C:\WP\MYFILE.DOC
```

The following command is similar to the previous one, except the file in the destination directory is given a different name from the file in the source directory:

```
C:\OLDFILES> COPY C:\WP\MYFILE.DOC NEWFILE.DOC
```

Sometimes it is useful to have a second copy of the same file. You can use the COPY command to do this by copying the file to another name. For example, the command COPY MYFILE.DOC MYFILE.BAK creates an identical file in the same subdirectory. You can then work with the original file knowing that if something goes wrong, you have another copy of the file easily available.

The following command combines two files, MYFILE.DOC and THATFILE.DOC, into a third file called NEWFILE.DOC. You should carry out this procedure only with ASCII files. Using non-ASCII files, such as word processing documents, can lead to unpredictable results.

```
C:\WP> COPY MYFILE.DOC + THATFILE.DOC NEWFILE.DOC
```

Remember that the COPY command overwrites any file with the same name without warning. To avoid overwriting an existing file when you use the COPY command, first use the DIR command to see whether a file with the same name exists in the destination directory.

When you are done copying files, DOS displays a message telling you how many files were copied.

If you want to make sure that your copy command was carried out precisely, use the /V (for verify) switch. Copies of files can be improperly made because of disk failures, fluctuations in power supplies, or similar problems. The /V switch verifies that the COPY command was carried out without problems. Note, though, that using this switch means that the COPY command will take slightly longer to execute.

Two related commands are DISKCOPY and XCOPY. DISKCOPY makes an exact copy of a diskette onto another diskette. XCOPY is like the COPY command but offers many more options, such as the capability to copy only files that you changed since a particular date. XCOPY also can copy files from subdirectories beneath the current directory, creating subdirectories as needed on the destination disk.

ERASE (DELETE)

The ERASE command eliminates designated files from your disk. If you prefer, you can use the DELETE command, which has the same effect. The ERASE command syntax is similar to that of the COPY command, except there is no destination directory.

ERASE is an internal command. Its syntax is

ERASE [*path*][*filename*]

Here are two examples:

C:\WP> DELETE MYWORK.BAK

No path is included because the command was started from the directory in which the file is located.

```
C:\> DELETE c:\wp\mywork.bak
```

The path is included in this example because the command was started from a directory other than the one in which the file is located.

> After you erase a file, it often is possible to get it back using the UNDELETE command (discussed in Chapter 18, "Protecting Your System"). But to avoid the uncertainty, you might want to get into the habit of using the /P switch with the ERASE command. This switch asks you to confirm that you want to delete the file or files you have designated, giving you time to avoid making a thoughtless error.

DIR

The DIR command displays a list of file names in a designated directory. By default, along with each file name, DIR displays the size of the file in bytes, as well as the date and time of the most recent change to the file. It also lists the names of subdirectories directly below the designated directory.

DIR is an internal command. It takes various parameters and switches, but the syntax is

```
DIR [path][filename]
```

Here are a couple of examples:

```
C:\WP> DIR
```

provides a list of all files in the C:\WP directory.

```
C:\> DIR C:\WP
```

provides the same result as the first example, but the path was added because the command was launched from another directory.

If there are many files in the directory, they scroll off the screen before you can read them all. Also, the files are unlikely to be listed in an order that you find useful. The MORE filter, discussed previously in this chapter, is one way to solve this problem. Another way is to use a variety of switches with the DIR command.

The /P switch pauses with each screenful of file names and waits for you to press a key before giving you another screenful. The /W switch lists file names and subdirectories, but in a wide-screen format of as many as five columns across the screen. You can use these switches together or separately.

For the most part, the other switches control the information displayed and the order in which it is displayed.

The following two switches were first included in DOS 5. If you are using a previous version of DOS, these switches are not available to you. After each switch, you can add values that further refine the action of the switch.

- /A displays files only with the specified attributes. You can specify which attributes you want to display by placing a colon after the switch and then typing any of the following values:

  - reverses the actions of the attribute values listed in the following lines.

  A displays names of files that will be archived during the next backup.

  D displays directory names.

  H displays hidden file names.

  R displays read-only file names.

  S displays system file names.

If you don't add a value to the /A switch, DIR lists all files, even system and hidden files.

> If you use more than one value, do not separate the values with spaces.

- /O specifies the order in which DIR displays file and directory names.

    - reverses the actions of the order values listed in the following lines.

    N sorts alphabetically by name.

    E sorts alphabetically by extension.

    D sorts by date and time, earliest first.

    S sorts by size, smallest first.

    G sorts with directories grouped before files.

    Here, then, is a sample DIR command using these switches:

```
DIR C:\ /A:A /O:N
```

This command results in a directory listing for the root directory showing files that will be archived in the next backup, sorted alphabetically by name.

> Although these switches provide a lot of flexibility to create hundreds of useful customized directory listings, they are not easy to memorize. Instead, you can use the DIRCMD environmental variable in your AUTOEXEC.BAT file so that any time you use the DIR command, DOS executes the options you prefer. For more details about the DIRCMD environmental variable, see Chapter 13, "Customizing DOS."

RENAME (REN)

The RENAME command, which can be shortened in commands to REN, changes the name of a file. It has no effect on the contents of the file. Nor can you use the RENAME command to change the location of a file; this command assumes that the file will continue to be stored on the same disk and directory.

> You cannot rename a file to a name that already exists on the specified drive or directory. If you try, you receive the error message Duplicate file name or File not found.

The syntax of RENAME is

```
RENAME [drive][path][old filename] [new filename]
```

For example,

```
RENAME MYFILE.DOC MYFILE.TXT
```

changes the name of MYFILE.DOC to MYFILE.TXT.

TIME and DATE

These two commands set your system's time and date. Having an accurate time and date is important because many programs use them as a means of recording when data was created or altered.

Both commands are internal. The syntax is

```
DATE [current date]
```

To change the current date to February 19, 1993, type

```
DATE 02-19-1993
```

To check the date, type DATE at the command prompt. The command displays the current system date and gives you a chance to change it. If you do not want to change the date, press Enter.

> Dates are entered with a dash between the month, day, and year. The TIME command, described next, uses colons between hour, minute, and second.

Because time is based on a 24-hour clock, the hour can be entered as a number between 0 (for midnight) and 24. Or you can add A or P to designate a time as a.m. or p.m.

```
TIME [hour:minute:second][A¦P]
```

For example,

```
TIME 08:10:17
```

sets your system time to 10 minutes and 17 seconds past 8 a.m. The line

```
TIME 08:10:17 p
```

sets the system time to 10 minutes and 17 seconds past 8 p.m. Alternatively, you can type TIME 20:10:17.

As with DATE, you can type TIME at the prompt to get the current time and an opportunity to change it. If you choose not to change the current time, press Enter.

TYPE

The TYPE command displays the contents of a file. If the file you display contains only ASCII text characters, the output is quite readable. However, if you use TYPE with a program, spreadsheet, database, or some word processing files, the contents will consist of strange graphics characters (such as happy faces), and the computer might even beep.

If you execute the TYPE command and want to stop it before it is finished, press Ctrl+Break (or Ctrl+C). This is useful if you use the TYPE command on a large program file and you get gibberish and beeps on your screen for quite a while. Or you might use the TYPE command on a long ASCII file but decide you don't want to view the entire file.

TYPE is an internal command. The syntax is

```
TYPE [drive][path][filename]
```

Some examples of the TYPE command follow:

```
TYPE READ.ME
```

enables you to view the file READ.ME if it is located in the current directory.

```
TYPE C:\WP\DOCS\READ.ME
```

adds a drive and path, enabling you to read the file if it is in another directory, in this case C:\WP\DOCS.

For viewing longer files, you might want to add the ¦MORE filter, described earlier in this chapter. This shows only one screenful of information at a time. To get another screenful of information, press any key.

The following example uses the ¦MORE filter to limit output to one screen at a time:

```
TYPE READ.ME ¦MORE
```

You also can print the information you view with the TYPE command by adding >PRN to the command. The following example sends the output to the printer:

```
TYPE READ.ME > PRN
```

Memory-Management Commands

This section describes some of the more commonly used DOS memory-management commands and their most common uses. A comprehensive reference of DOS commands is available in your *DOS User's Manual*.

CHKDSK

CHKDSK (pronounced "check disk") tells you how much disk space and random-access memory you are using, and how much you have left. It also checks for flaws in the disk and can even correct some of the flaws.

CHKDSK is an external command. The syntax is

```
CHKDSK [drive][path][filename]
```

If you do not add parameters, CHKDSK acts on the currently active drive.

CHKDSK produces a status report that contains the following information:

Disk volume

Date the disk was formatted

Disk volume serial number

Total disk space in bytes

Number of hidden files and the amount of disk space they occupy

Number of directories and the amount of disk space they occupy

Number of user files and the amount of disk space they occupy

P A R T   I I I

Putting DOS to Work

Total disk space available

Number of bytes in each allocation unit

Number of allocation units on disk

Total amount of system memory

Amount of available system memory

Figure 9.3 shows the results of using the CHKDSK command.

```
D:\>chkdsk d:

Volume ZELIG 3       created 08-31-1992 4:04p
Volume Serial Number is 1963-53DB

124389376 bytes total disk space
112979968 bytes in 19 hidden files
   30720 bytes in 15 directories
 3096576 bytes in 45 user files
 8282112 bytes available on disk

    2048 bytes in each allocation unit
   60737 total allocation units on disk
    4044 available allocation units on disk

  655360 total bytes memory
  467056 bytes free

D:\>
```

*Figure 9.3.
Results of
using the
CHKDSK
command
without adding
switches.*

If you add the /F switch, CHKDSK finds any clusters in the file allocation table (FAT) that are not allocated to a file and displays the prompt

Convert Lost chains to file (Y/N)?

If you type N in response, CHKDSK ignores the lost clusters (chains). If you type Y, CHKDSK recovers the clusters and places them in a file named FILE*nnnn*.CHK in the root directory of the disk. The *nnnn* designation is a series of numbers beginning with 0000 and incremented sequentially with each .CHK file. After you check the files and retrieve any useful information, you can erase them.

You can use the /V switch to display the drive, path, and file name for all files on the disk.

You can redirect the output from CHKDSK to the printer by adding >PRN, or to a file by adding >`filename.ext`. However, do not redirect output to a file when you use the /F switch.

Some examples of the CHKDSK command follow.

```
CHKDSK
```

This example executes the CHKDSK command for the current drive.

```
CHKDSK C:
```

This example provides CHKDSK information for the C: drive if you currently are on another drive.

```
CHKDSK /F
```

This example finds and fixes lost clusters on the current drive.

```
CHKDSK /V >PRN
```

This example shows the path and file names for all files in the current drive and sends the results to the printer.

MEM

MEM displays the amount of memory that is currently in use and the amount that remains available. It also can provide an itemized list of memory usage in conventional memory, upper memory blocks (UMBs), and extended memory. Some programs are loaded into memory and are always available. Some of these programs can be loaded into the upper memory area with the LOADHIGH and DEVICEHIGH commands. This makes more lower, or conventional, memory available for your programs.

Depending on the switches you use, MEM can list the programs that are using each type of memory and how much of each type of memory each program is using. If your computer has extended memory, or memory in excess of 1M, MEM also tells you how much total extended memory you have and how much is available.

MEM is an external command. The syntax for the MEM command is simple:

MEM

As you can tell from Figure 9.4, the MEM command provides general information about the usage and remaining availability of different types of memory.

```
C:\>mem

Memory Type        Total =  Used  +  Free

Conventional        640K    184K      456K
Upper                99K     57K       42K
Adapter RAM/ROM     285K    285K        0K
Extended (XMS)     7168K   2352K     4816K

Total memory       8192K   2877K     5315K

Total under 1 MB    739K    240K      499K

EMS is active.
Largest executable program size        456K   (467232 bytes)
Largest free upper memory block         39K    (40112 bytes)
MS-DOS is resident in the high memory area.

C:\>
```

Figure 9.4.
Results of the
MEM command
without any
additional
parameters or
switches.

To get more detailed information about memory usage, use the /CLASSIFY switch. This tells you which programs are using memory and how much conventional and UMB memory they are using. Because this command will likely produce more than one screen of information, a good way to use the /CLASSIFY switch is

MEM /C ¦MORE

The /CLASSIFY switch can be activated simply by typing /C. The ¦MORE filter gives you only one screenful of memory information at a time. The result of the MEM /CLASSIFY command is shown in Figure 9.5.

You can get even more detail by using the /DEBUG switch (which can be abbreviated as /D). This provides information about not just programs, but also internal device drivers and other drivers installed in memory. A new DOS 6 switch is /F, which lists free areas of conventional and upper memory. Also new to DOS 6 is /M, which shows how specific program modules are using memory.

```
Modules using memory below 1 MB:

Name         Total      =    Conventional  +    Upper Memory

MSDOS        17245   (17K)      17245   (17K)         0    (0K)
HIMEM         1104    (1K)       1104    (1K)         0    (0K)
EMM386        3072    (3K)       3072    (3K)         0    (0K)
SMARTDRV     30832   (30K)       2400    (2K)     28352   (28K)
STACKER      45120   (44K)      45120   (44K)         0    (0K)
COMMAND       2912    (3K)       2912    (3K)         0    (0K)
SMARTCAN     10144   (10K)      10144   (10K)         0    (0K)
SNAP        105920  (103K)     105920  (103K)         0    (0K)
SETVER         656    (1K)          0    (0K)       656    (1K)
SHARE         8352    (8K)          0    (0K)      8352    (8K)
IMOUSE       10848   (11K)          0    (0K)     10848   (11K)
FASTOPEN      5616    (5K)          0    (0K)      5616    (5K)
DOSKEY        4144    (4K)          0    (0K)      4144    (4K)
Free        510864  (499K)     467408  (456K)     43456   (42K)

Memory Summary:

Type of Memory       Size      =     Used      +      Free
— More —
```

*Figure 9.5.
Results of the
MEM /CLASSIFY
command.*

Disk Navigation and Management Commands

This section describes some of the more commonly used DOS navigation and management commands and their most common uses. A comprehensive reference of DOS commands is available in your *DOS User's Manual*.

CHDIR (CD)

The CHDIR (or Change Directory) command changes you to a different directory or displays the name of the current directory.

CHDIR, which can be abbreviated in commands as CD, is an internal command. Its syntax is

CHDIR [*drive*][*path*]

For example,

C:\> CHDIR C:\WP\DOCS

switches you from the root directory on drive C: to the \WP\DOCS subdirectory. Typing the command

C:\WP\DOCS> CHDIR \

switches you from the \WP\DOCS subdirectory to the root directory.

Switching to a specific directory on another drive requires two separate commands. One command switches you to the other drive. For example, to switch from C: to D:, type D:. The other command switches you to the specific directory. To make this switch, use the CHDIR command. You can use this command from your original drive (C:). For example, you can type CHDIR D:\LOTUS from the C: prompt. Then when you switch to the D: drive, you will be at the \LOTUS directory.

If your prompt does not tell you which directory you are in, typing the CHDIR command will tell you.

The double dot symbol (..) is an abbreviation for the parent directory when used with the CHDIR command. For example, if you are in the C:\WP\DOCS subdirectory and you want to go to the C:\WP directory, type CD .. (the space is not mandatory). If you want to switch to the C:\WP\ARCHIVE subdirectory, you can type CD ..\ARCHIVE.

MKDIR (MD)

The MKDIR (or Make Directory) command creates a new directory. Used without parameters, except for the directory name, the command makes a new directory under your current directory.

The MKDIR command, which can be abbreviated as MD, is an internal command. Its syntax is

```
MKDIR [drive][path][directory name]
```

To make a new directory called TEMP directly below the root directory, type

```
C:\> MKDIR TEMP
```

To make a new directory directly below the root directory on drive D: called TEMP, type

```
C:\> MKDIR D:\TEMP
```

To create a subdirectory beneath the C:\WP directory called ARCHIVE, type

```
C:\WP> MKDIR ARCHIVE
```

RMDIR (RD)

The RMDIR command is the opposite of the MKDIR command—it removes directories from your hard drive.

The syntax of RMDIR, which is an internal command, is

```
RMDIR [drive]path
```

You cannot remove the current directory—to remove the current directory, you must first move to another directory. If you are in the parent directory to the one you want to remove, type

```
RMDIR [directory name]
```

Otherwise, you must specify the full drive and path.

The directory you are trying to remove must be empty before you can remove it with RMDIR. If it is not empty, you get the error message Invalid path, not directory or Directory not empty. A new DOS 6 command, DELTREE, removes a directory, subdirectories, and all files within them. This command is detailed in Chapter 10, "Working with Files and Directories."

Troubleshooting

This section lists common problems you might encounter as you issue commands from the command prompt. If you encounter any of these problems, try to resolve them with the suggested solutions.

■ When you try to copy or delete files on a floppy disk, you receive the error message Write protect error writing to drive A: Abort, Retry, Fail?

This message means you probably tried to act on a file located on a disk that was write-protected. To correct the problem, remove the disk from the floppy drive. If it is a 5¼-inch floppy disk, remove the write-protect tab from the notch on the side of the disk. If it is a 3½-inch floppy disk, look for the tab located in one of the top corners of the disk. With the back of the disk toward you, eliminate write protection by moving the tab from the up position to the down position.

■ You copy a file and no error message appears, but you can't find the file in the destination directory.

You probably used the wrong destination path in the command. Try the COPY command again, being careful to be precise. To find the missing file, first look in the root directory, a common destination for such errors. If that fails, use the FIND command in the File menu of the DOS Shell to find the missing file (see Chapter 8, "Using the Shell").

■ The ERASE command does not work, even though you type the command properly at the command prompt, or perform the operation correctly from the DOS Shell.

The file you are trying to erase probably has its attributes set to read-only. From the command prompt of the directory in which the file is located, type ATTRIB -R [filename] to change the file's attributes to read/write. Then try the ERASE command again.

■ If you try to create a new directory using the MKDIR command and you get the error message Unable to create directory, one of the following errors has occurred:

A directory with the same name already exists.

A file with the same name as the directory already exists.

You specified a parent directory that does not exist.

The disk is full.

The root directory contains the maximum number of files.

■ If you try to eliminate a directory and you get the error message Invalid path, not directory or Directory not empty, one of the following errors probably has occurred:

You have mistyped the name of the directory.

There are still files in the directory.

If you correct these problems and still cannot remove the directory, there probably are hidden files in the subdirectory. To unhide a file, switch to the subdirectory where it is located. Change the attribute with the command ATTRIB [filename] -H, and then erase the file. If you are not sure of the name of the hidden file, type ATTRIB *.* -H. This unhides all files.

Summary

This chapter provided details about using the command prompt and discussed commonly used commands. To summarize the most important issues covered in this chapter:

■ Commands are not case sensitive. You can type commands in upper- or lowercase.

■ The function keys provide ways to automate entering commands.

■ If your command causes more than one screenful of information, you can pause the scrolling by pressing Ctrl+S or the Pause key.

■ You can modify commands by using pipes and filters. A filter is a command entered at the same time as a primary command and separated by the pipe figure ¦.

■ Common commands include

COPY, which takes files in a directory or floppy drive and copies them to another directory or disk.

DELETE, which deletes designated files from your disk.

DIR, which displays a list of file names in the designated directory.

RENAME, which changes the names of files.

TIME and DATE, which set your system's time and date.

TYPE, which displays the contents of a file.

CHKDSK, which tells how much disk space and random-access memory you are using, and how much you have left.

MEM, which displays the amount of memory currently in use and the amount that remains available.

CHDIR, which changes you to a different directory.

MKDIR, which creates a new directory.

RMDIR, which removes directories from your hard drive.

Working with Files and Directories

This chapter discusses how to work with your files and directories by making, viewing, copying, erasing, moving, renaming, and protecting them. These general file and directory management techniques will be useful in all your future work with your computer and DOS. In fact, you'll probably use some of these techniques every time you sit down at the keyboard.

Working with Your Files

If DOS 6 is installed on your computer, you can use the DOS Shell to perform file management operations. The basic procedure is as follows:

1. Be sure that you are using one of the File List only screens or that the cursor is in the File List section of the Program/ File Lists screen.

2. Select a file (or files) for the operation.

3. Select the appropriate operation from the File pull-down menu.

Figure 10.1 illustrates the general procedure (discussed in more detail with each operation).

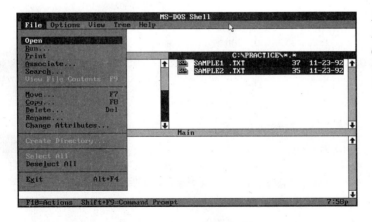

Figure 10.1.
Performing file
operations with
the DOS 6
Shell.

All DOS users who prefer the command prompt can use several built-in DOS commands for these operations, including XCOPY, COPY, RENAME, DEL or ERASE, and TYPE. Remember, built-in commands are available in DOS at any time, so you can perform these operations on any disk drive and in any directory.

If you have problems doing these exercises, refer to the Troubleshooting section near the end of the chapter. DOS Shell users can also press the F1 key or select the Help menu to display help on-screen.

Rules for Naming Files

When you start creating, copying, and renaming files, remember that DOS imposes certain restrictions on file names and that all file names must abide by these rules. This holds true even if you create files with an application program, such as a spreadsheet, a database-management system, or a word processor.

Following are the basic rules for creating file names:

- The base name for the file can be no more than eight characters long and cannot contain blank spaces.

- You can include an optional three-letter extension—preceded by a period—with any file name.

- You should restrict file names to only letters, numbers, hyphens (-), and underscores (_). (Use the period only to separate the base name from the extension.) The following characters can never be used in a file name: " . / \ [ ] : * < > ¦ + : , ?.

- Do not use any of these reserved device names as one of your custom file names: CLOCK$, CON, AUX, COM1, COM2, COM3, CON, LPT1, LPT2, LPT3, NUL, PRN.

Try to use meaningful file names that describe the contents of the file. For example, instead of assigning the file name X.DAT to your first-quarter 1993 data file, use the more meaningful file name QTR1-93.DAT.

As much as possible, try to use a similar pattern of file names for related files. (For example, you might use QTR1-93.DAT, QTR2-93.DAT, QTR3-93.DAT, and so on, for files that store quarterly data.) This makes it easier to manage the files as groups when you are copying, moving, or erasing them.

■ Avoid using the file name extensions `.BAT`, `.COM`, and `.EXE`, because these extensions are reserved for programs. (You'll learn how to create your own .BAT program files in Chapter 12, "Simple Batch Programs.")

Examples of valid and invalid file names are shown in Table 10.1.

Table 10.1. Examples of valid and invalid file names.

File Name	Status
ACCT_REC.DAT	Valid
X.ABC	Valid (but not very descriptive)
LEDGER.WKS	Valid
ABC-CO.LET	Valid
1990SUMM.TXT	Valid

File Name	Status
READ.ME	Valid
PRNT.TXT	Valid
GENERAL-LEDGER.DAT	Invalid (base name is too long)
MY LETTER.DOC	Invalid (contains a blank space)
MY.LET.DOC	Invalid (contains two periods)
PRN.TXT	Invalid (PRN is a DOS device name)

File Name Extensions

You can assign any extension to a file name when you create a file. However, many application programs automatically assign their own extensions to file names. Some examples of commonly used file name extensions and the types of information that those files hold are listed in Table 10.2.

Table 10.2. Examples of commonly used file name extensions.

Extension	Contents
.BAT	A DOS batch program (discussed in Chapter 12)
.COM	A program that DOS can run
.EXE	A program that DOS can run
.TXT	Written text
.DOC	A document (written text)

continues

195

Table 10.2. continued

Extension	Contents
.BAK	A backup (copy) of another file
.BAS	A BASIC program
.BMP	A Windows 3 bit-mapped (graphics) file
.WKS	A Lotus 1-2-3 (version 1) spreadsheet
.WK1	A Lotus 1-2-3 (version 2) spreadsheet
.XLS	A Microsoft Excel spreadsheet
.MSP	A Microsoft Paint picture
.DBF	A dBASE database
.DB	A Paradox database
.OVL	An overlay file

Hands On: Creating Some Sample Files

To perform some of the file management techniques in this chapter, you first need to create a few simple practice files, named SAMPLE1.TXT and SAMPLE2.TXT. There are many ways to create files on your computer. I'll demonstrate a somewhat primitive technique in this chapter, only because the sample files are small and the technique is simple. As you gain experience with your computer, you'll probably want to use a word processor or EDIT, the DOS 6 full-screen editor (discussed in Chapter 11, "Creating and Editing Files"), to create larger text files and programs.

If your computer has a hard disk, place these practice files in the PRACTICE directory. If your computer does not have a hard disk, place the sample files on a blank formatted diskette. To create these files, follow the appropriate steps for your particular computer:

1. If you are using DOS 6, press the F3 key (or Alt+F4) to exit the Shell and display the command prompt.

> If you plan to return to the Shell after performing the subsequent steps, press the Shift+F9 keys in lieu of step 1. This temporarily exits you from the Shell and gives you the DOS command prompt. When you finish the following steps, type Exit and press Enter to return to the Shell.

2. If your computer has a hard disk, type C: and press Enter to access the hard disk. (If you haven't created the PRACTICE directory, type CD \ and press Enter to go to the root directory. Type the command MD PRACTICE and press Enter to make a directory named PRACTICE.) Then type CD \PRACTICE and press Enter to change to the PRACTICE directory.

3. If your computer does not have a hard disk, place a blank formatted diskette in drive B:. Then type B: and press Enter to access drive B:.

4. Type the command COPY CON SAMPLE1.TXT, and press Enter.

5. Type the sentence This is the first sample text file. (Use the Backspace key to make corrections if necessary.)

6. Press Enter.

7. Press Ctrl+Z or press F6. This displays a ^Z on your screen.

8. Press Enter again.

After DOS displays the message 1 file(s) copied, the command prompt reappears. DOS has copied the sentence you typed on-screen into a file named SAMPLE1.TXT. To create the second sample file, follow these steps:

1. Type COPY CON SAMPLE2.TXT and press Enter.

2. Type the sentence I am the second sample text file. (Again, use the Backspace key to make corrections if necessary.)

3. Press Enter.

4. Press Ctrl+Z (or F6), and then press Enter.

You have now created the two practice files you will use in later examples in this chapter. You did so by COPYing text from the CONsole (screen) to a file.

If you had previously exited the Shell by pressing F3 or Alt+F4, type DOSSHELL and press Enter to return to the Shell. If you had pressed Shift+F9, type Exit to return to the Shell. If you do not have a hard disk, be sure your Shell diskette is in drive A:. Then type A: and press Enter to access that drive. When the A> command prompt appears, type the command DOSSHELL and press Enter.

Selecting Files for Operations in DOS 6

You must display the File List section of the DOS Shell to perform the following file operations. To do so, choose any of the display options except Program List from the View menu.

If you are using DOS 6, you often need to select files from the Files area before you perform an operation. Therefore, I'll review the general techniques for selecting file names. As with all DOS 6 operations, you can use either the keyboard or a mouse to select file names, as summarized in the following lists.

Take the time to learn both ways (keyboard and mouse) just in case your mouse "dies" and you don't have immediate access to another one. It is very frustrating and can be very unproductive if you don't know the keyboard method.

To select a single file using the keyboard, take the following steps:

1. Using the keyboard, press the Tab key until the highlight moves to the Files List of the screen.

2. Then use the ↓, ↑, PgUp, or PgDn keys to move the highlight bar to the file you want to select.

To select a single file with a mouse, take the following steps:

1. Move the mouse pointer to the name of the file you want to select in the Files List area.

2. Click once.

To select all the file names in the Files List, choose Select All from the Files pull-down menu.

To select two or more consecutive files using the keyboard, follow these steps:

1. Press the Tab key until the highlight bar gets to the File List area.

2. Use the ↓, ↑, PgUp, and PgDn keys to scroll the highlight to the first file you want to select.

3. Hold down the Shift key, then press ↓ or ↑ to highlight adjacent file names.

4. When the file names you want to select are highlighted, release the Shift key.

To select two or more consecutive files using the mouse, follow these steps:

1. Move the mouse pointer to the name of the first file you want to select, and click once.

2. Hold down the Shift key, and click the last file in the group. (If you need to use the scroll bar to display more file names in a long list, continue holding down the Shift key as you scroll through the list.)

To use the keyboard to select two or more nonconsecutive files on nonconsecutive groups of files, follow these steps:

1. Press the Tab key until the highlight moves to the Files List.

2. Then use the ↓, ↑, PgUp, and PgDn keys to move the highlight bar to the first file you want to select.

3. Press Shift+F8 to initiate the Shell's Add mode, in which you can add file names to the current list of selections. (Note that the word ADD appears on the Reference bar at the bottom of the screen.)

4. Use either keyboard technique described previously for selecting individual or groups of file names from the Files List.

When the Shell is in Add mode (Shift+F8), you can press the Spacebar to select a file and to deselect a selected file.

To use the mouse to select two or more nonconsecutive files or non-consecutive groups of files, follow these instructions:

1. Select the first file name by single-clicking it.

2. Select additional file names by holding down the Ctrl key and single-clicking additional file names.

3. Select additional groups of adjacent file names by keeping the Ctrl key held down, holding down the Shift key, clicking the last file name in the group of adjacent file names, and then releasing the Shift (but not the Ctrl) key.

On a graphics screen, a *selected* file is displayed with its icon in reverse video (that is, white on black rather than black on white). For example, in Figure 10.1, the files SAMPLE1.TXT and SAMPLE2.TXT are currently selected. On a text screen, selected files are represented by a right-pointing triangle to the left of the file name.

If you temporarily leave the Shell (Shift+F9) and perform any file or directory manipulations, such as deletions, undeletes, renames, and so on, you need to update the Shell's directory- and file-tracking files when you return to the Shell by selecting the Refresh option of the pull-down View menu. This also updates the Shell's display.

Deselecting Files

If you want to deselect one or more selected files, follow these instructions:

1. If you are in the Add mode and using the keyboard, move the highlight bar to the name of the file you want to deselect, and press the Spacebar.

2. If you're using a mouse, hold down the Ctrl key and click the name of the file you want to deselect.

3. To deselect all the currently selected file names, select Deselect All from the File pull-down menu.

Spacebar Versus Enter

Notice that when selecting files for an operation, as in this chapter, you always press the Spacebar. In other chapters, you see how highlighting a program file name in the Files List and pressing Enter is used to run a program.

If you accidentally press Enter rather than the Spacebar while trying to select a file name, or if you double-click rather than single-click your mouse when selecting a file name, DOS assumes that you are attempting to run the file as though it were a program.

This minor (and common) mistake results in one of two actions. If the file you specify is not a program (or a file associated with a program), DOS beeps to inform you that it cannot open the file. However, if the file that you specify is an executable program (or a file associated with a program), DOS runs it.

To recover from this situation, exit the program (if necessary), and press a key when DOS displays the `Press any key to return to MS-DOS Shell` prompt at the lower-right corner of your screen. When DOS redisplays the File List, use the ↑ and ↓ keys or click once with your mouse to properly select the appropriate file name.

Viewing the Contents of a File

DOS contains a built-in command you can use to look at the contents of any file. However, the contents of many files (particularly programs) might appear on-screen as strange characters or cause the computer to beep, because they contain instructions that only the computer can read.

Here are the general steps for viewing the contents of a file:

1. Select the drive and directory on which the file you want to view is stored in the Directory Tree areas of the Shell.

The View File Contents option is available on the File pull-down menu only when a single file name is selected in the Files area.

2. Highlight or single-click the name of the file you want to view in the Files List area of the Shell.

3. Select View from the pull-down menu.

4. When you finish viewing the contents of the file, press Escape or select Restore View from the View pull-down menu.

Press F9 as a shortcut method of displaying the contents of a single file.

If you'd like to try this feature on your own, follow the steps to view the contents of the SAMPLE2.TXT file you created earlier. It appears on your screen as shown in Figure 10.2.

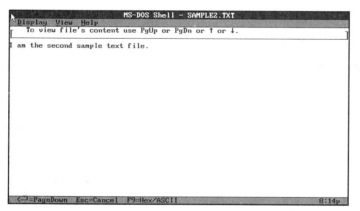

Figure 10.2. The contents of the SAMPLE2.TXT file displayed in ASCII format.

Because the SAMPLE2.TXT file is so small, you can see its entire contents. However, when viewing larger files, you might need to use the PgUp and PgDn keys or the ↑ and ↓ keys to scroll through the file, as the message at the top of the screen indicates.

Notice in the Title bar at the top of the screen that DOS indicates that you are currently viewing the SAMPLE2.TXT file. Also notice that the Menu bar now offers three choices: Display, View, and Help.

To switch between the ASCII (text) and Hex displays, you can press the F9 key, as noted in the bottom line of the screen.

With the Display menu, you can choose to view a file either in ASCII format (as straight characters and symbols, as shown in Figure 10.2) or in Hexadecimal format, which enables you to examine program files in great detail. If you now select the Hex option from the Display menu, you see the screen shown in Figure 10.3. The left column of numbers represents the locations of the data in the file, the middle column shows the data in the file as two-digit hexadecimal (base 16) numbers, and the right column shows the numbers as ASCII characters. (The dots represent all hex values that are not standard ASCII characters.)

```
                        MS-DOS Shell - SAMPLE2.TXT
 Display  View  Help
     To view file's content use PgUp or PgDn or ↑ or ↓.

   000000    4920616D   20746865   20736563   6F6E6420      I am the second
   000010    73616D70   6C652074   65787420   66696C65      sample text file
   000020    2E0D0A                                         ...




 ←┘=PageDown  Esc=Cancel  F9=Hex/ASCII                              8:44p
```

Figure 10.3.
The contents of
SAMPLE2.TXT
displayed in
hexadecimal
format.

The View pull-down menu in the View File Contents screen provides the option Repaint Screen (for example, to remove network messages) and the option Restore View (to return to the Shell).

The Help menu is the same as it is in the File and Program Lists. After viewing the contents of the file, press Esc or select the Restore View option from the View menu to return to the File List screen.

If you are using an earlier version of DOS or the optional DOS 6 command prompt, you can use the TYPE command to view the contents of a file. Use this method to look at the contents of the SAMPLE2.TXT file.

> Because DOS always requires that you press Enter after typing a command, from now on I'll use the term *enter* to mean *type the command and then press Enter.*
>
> For example, when I say, "Enter the command TYPE SAMPLE1.TXT," that means you should type the command TYPE SAMPLE1.TXT and press the Enter key when you are at the command prompt. (If you are at the Shell, don't forget to first exit to the command prompt by pressing F3.)

1. If your computer doesn't have a hard disk, be sure to access drive B: by entering the command B:.

2. If your computer has a hard disk, be sure to change to the PRACTICE directory by entering C: to get to drive C: and then entering CD \PRACTICE to get to the PRACTICE directory.

3. Enter the command DIR to verify that the SAMPLE2.TXT file is on the current drive and directory.

4. Enter the command TYPE SAMPLE2.TXT.

After DOS shows the contents of the file, it redisplays the command prompt, as shown in Figure 10.4. (Your screen might also show preceding commands.)

```
C:\>CD\PRACTICE

C:\PRACTICE>DIR

 Volume in drive C is CC DISK
 Volume Serial Number is 1976-6AC6
 Directory of C:\PRACTICE

             <DIR>     11-23-92   5:25p
             <DIR>     11-23-92   5:25p
SAMPLE1  TXT        37 11-23-92   7:47p
SAMPLE2  TXT        35 11-23-92   7:48p
        4 file(s)         72 bytes
                    83908608 bytes free

C:\PRACTICE>TYPE SAMPLE2.TXT
I am the second sample text file.

C:\PRACTICE>
```

*Figure 10.4.
The contents
of the
SAMPLE2.TXT
file are dis-
played.*

Remember that if you attempt to view the contents of a program with the TYPE command, your screen displays strange symbols and might beep repeatedly. However, this does not harm the file; the information is stored as codes that only the computer can read.

There are many times when the file that you want to read contains more display lines than your monitor can display on one screen. When you enter the TYPE command at the command prompt, your monitor begins scrolling so fast that you cannot read the file data. An excellent way to see the contents of a large file is to enter the command as TYPE SAMPLE2.TXT ¦ MORE. This command line "pipes," or directs, the output of the TYPE command (in this case, SAMPLE2.TXT) to the program MORE, which displays one screen of output at a time.

Copying Files

Much of your work with DOS involves the copying of files. In fact, copying files is one of those truly basic procedures that every computer user seems to perform nearly daily. You make these copies for any or all the following reasons:

- To back up important files.

- To transfer files between the hard disk and diskettes or between different sizes of disks (if your computer has both 5¼-inch and 3½-inch disk drives).

- To use the same set of files on more than one computer.

XCOPY and COPY are both file copying commands that you can enter at the command prompt. They approach the copying process differently, and each method has its advantages and disadvantages. In most cases, if you are at the command prompt and need to copy multiple files, I would recommend that you use XCOPY, because it is faster and more flexible during most copy operations. If you are going to copy one file, it usually doesn't matter which copy program you choose.

I also recommend that you use the DOS Shell as the preferred method of command entry if it is available. The Shell provides an important feature that COPY and XCOPY do not— the Shell warns you before you overwrite another file.

Using the Shell to Copy Files

The Shell offers two procedures for copying files: a general procedure through standard menu selections, and another using the mouse to drag a copy of the file to a new location—a very Macintosh-like action.

After the copy process begins within the Shell, you cannot break out of it or cancel the command with the Esc or Ctrl+C keys. If you change your mind in the middle of copying a large directory to another, you might as well sit back and wait, unless, as a desperation move, you press the Ctrl+Alt+Del keys or your computer's reset button.

Here is the general procedure for copying files via the Shell:

1. In the Files List area of the Shell, select the file or files you want to copy (as described under the previous heading "Selecting Files for Operations in DOS 6").

2. Select Copy from the File pull-down menu.

3. When the Copy File dialog box appears, type the destination of the copies (for example, type A:\ if you want to copy the selected files to the root directory of drive A:).

4. Press Enter or select OK.

When making copies, you need to know two simple things: the *source* of the file that you want to copy (that is, the file's location) and the *destination* of the copy (that is, where you want to place the copy of the file). When you specify the source and location, DOS makes the following assumptions:

If you don't specify a drive, DOS assumes the current drive.

If you don't specify a directory, DOS assumes the current directory.

If you don't specify a file name in the destination, DOS assumes that it can give the copied file the same name as the original file.

You can place the wildcard characters ? and * in file names when you use the command prompt to copy groups of files, such as *.BAK to copy all files with the .BAK extension or *.* to specify all the files on a particular directory.

Because no two files in the same drive and directory can have the same name, attempting to copy a file to the same drive, directory, and file name results in DOS displaying a message to the effect that a file cannot be copied to itself.

A handy copy-related program available at the command prompt is the REPLACE command. You can use the REPLACE command when you just want to copy updated files in one directory or disk back over the original files in another directory or disk. It can also be used to copy files that exist in the source directory, but do not exist in the destination directory.

This information might make copying sound more complicated than it is, but copying files is pretty simple and straightforward as long as you keep the source and destination clearly fixed in your mind. The sections that follow describe specific techniques for copying files. I describe the general menu operation first.

Making Backup Copies

This section describes procedures used to create backup file copies using copy facilities. Procedures relating to backing up files, directories, and disks with backup utility programs are covered in Chapter 18, "Protecting Your System."

Often it's a good idea to keep two copies of the same file on a directory. That way, if you accidentally delete a copy or make modifications to it that you later change your mind about, you have the other copy of the file to work with.

Use the following technique to copy SAMPLE1.TXT to a file named SAMPLE1.BAK on the PRACTICE directory. In this case, you are placing the copy on the same drive and directory as the original file, so you must give the copy a unique name (SAMPLE1.BAK in this example). Here are the exact steps to follow:

1. At a DOS Shell File List screen, be sure that the SAMPLE1.TXT and SAMPLE2.TXT file names are displayed in the Files area. (If they are not, use the usual techniques to access the appropriate drive and directory.)

2. Move the highlight to the SAMPLE1.TXT file name in the Files area (or just click that file name with your mouse).

Press F8 as a shortcut method of displaying the Copy dialog box.

3. Select Copy from the File pull-down menu.

4. When the dialog box appears, press the End or ← key to move the cursor to the end of the suggested destination.

5. Type \SAMPLE1.BAK so that the dialog box looks like Figure 10.5. (You must use the backslash to separate the file name from the directory name.)

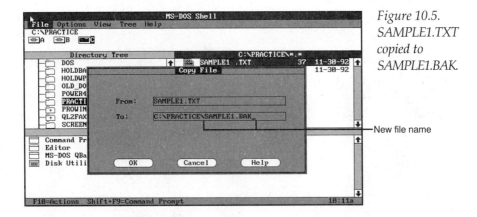

Figure 10.5. SAMPLE1.TXT copied to SAMPLE1.BAK.

6. Press Enter or click OK to perform the copy.

When DOS is finished copying, it lists the SAMPLE1.BAK file name in the Files area. Now, on your own, try repeating the general procedure outlined in steps 1 through 6, but this time copy SAMPLE2.TXT to a file named SAMPLE2.BAK. When you finish making the second copy, your screen looks like Figure 10.6. (You can use the View File Contents option on the File pull-down menu to verify that the copied files match the originals.)

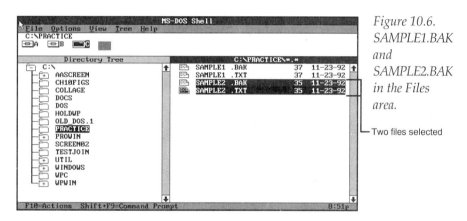

Figure 10.6.
SAMPLE1.BAK and SAMPLE2.BAK in the Files area.

─ Two files selected

Copying Files from the Command Prompt

To make copies from the command prompt, use the COPY command followed by the source file name (the original) and the destination file name (the copy). To store copies of SAMPLE1.TXT and SAMPLE2.TXT in file names SAMPLE1.BAK and SAMPLE2.BAK, you could use the following two COPY commands (remember to press Enter after typing each command):

```
COPY SAMPLE1.TXT SAMPLE1.BAK
COPY SAMPLE2.TXT SAMPLE2.BAK
```

As a shortcut to using several commands to copy multiple files, you can use wildcards, provided that the names of the files being copied have a similar format. The file names SAMPLE1.TXT and SAMPLE2.TXT have a similar format, with only one character differentiating the two names. Therefore, you can make copies of both files in a single operation by specifying SAMPLE?.TXT as the source name and SAMPLE?.BAK as the destination name. Here are the exact steps to follow:

1. If your computer has a hard disk, type the command CD \PRACTICE to access the PRACTICE directory.

2. If your computer does not have a hard disk, insert the diskette that contains the sample files into drive B:. Then type the command B: to access the diskette in drive B:.

3. Be sure that the sample files are indeed on the current drive and directory by entering the command DIR to view all file names.

4. Type the command COPY SAMPLE?.TXT SAMPLE?.BAK.

DOS displays the name of each original file as it makes the copies; then, it ends the process with the message 2 file(s) copied. To verify that you now have two new files named SAMPLE1.BAK and SAMPLE2.BAK, enter the DIR command. (Also, verify that the copies contain exactly the same text as the originals by using the TYPE command to view the contents of each file.)

Copying to a Different Directory (Same Drive)

In some situations, you might want to store copies of files in multiple directories. To do so, you specify a file name as the source of the copy and a directory name as the destination. (The copied file will have the same name as the original file.)

You can copy several files to a new directory in a single operation. To demonstrate this procedure, store copies of SAMPLE1.TXT and SAMPLE2.TXT on the PRACTICE\TEST directory (which is currently empty). Use the following steps as appropriate for your version of DOS. (If your computer does not have a hard disk, you can create these files and directories on a diskette, or you can skip to the section "Copying to Different Disk Drives.")

To use the DOS Shell to copy the SAMPLE1.TXT and SAMPLE2.TXT files to the PRACTICE\TEST directory, follow these steps:

1. Select the PRACTICE directory from the Directory Tree area of the Shell.

2. Select both the SAMPLE1.TXT and SAMPLE2.TXT file names by highlighting one, pressing Shift+F8, and using the arrow keys and Spacebar combination to highlight the other. (Or you can click one with your mouse and then hold down the Ctrl key while clicking the other.)

3. Select Copy from the File pull-down menu.

4. Press End and type \TEST to change the suggested destination to C:\PRACTICE\TEST, as shown in Figure 10.7. (You must use the backslash to separate the directory names.)

5. Press Enter or select OK.

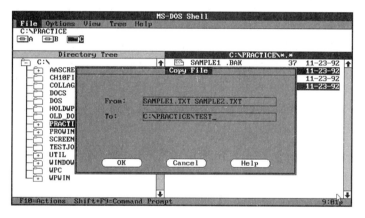

Figure 10.7. Dialog box to copy files to the PRACTICE\TEST directory.

When the operation is complete, the dialog box disappears. To verify that the PRACTICE\TEST directory now contains copies of SAMPLE1.TXT and SAMPLE2.TXT, move the highlight to the Directory Tree area and select the TEST directory name. Note the names of the two copied files in the Files area of the screen.

Copying to a Different Directory by Dragging

You can also use the Shell to copy files by dragging them to a new location.

The procedure for copying files to a different directory is simple:

1. Hold down the Ctrl key.

2. Select all the files you want to copy by clicking them.

3. When you click the last file to be moved, do not release the left button.

4. With the left button still depressed, drag the file icon to the Directory Tree area.

5. When the file icon is on the name of the directory to which you are copying the files, release the left button and then release the Ctrl key.

6. Select the Yes button in the Confirm Mouse Operation dialog box.

How does this procedure work? To find out, repeat the example in the preceding section. To use the mouse to copy the SAMPLE1.TXT and SAMPLE2.TXT files into the TEST subdirectory, follow these steps:

1. Hold down the Ctrl key.

2. Click SAMPLE1.TXT.

3. Click SAMPLE2.TXT, but do not release the left mouse button.

4. Drag the mouse cursor into the Directory Tree area. Notice that a three-line file icon appears in place of the mouse cursor.

5. Position the file icon on the TEST subdirectory name. Release the left mouse button and then the Ctrl key. The Shell now displays the Confirm Mouse Operation dialog box, shown in Figure 10.8.

6. Press Enter (or select Yes) to tell the Shell to copy the files to
   C:\PRACTICE\TEST.

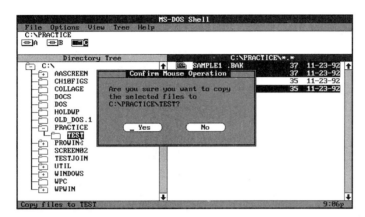

*Figure 10.8.
Confirm
Mouse
Operation
dialog box
to copy
SAMPLE1.TXT
and
SAMPLE2.TXT
to the TEST
directory.*

You can copy one file or an entire directory of files with the same
easy procedure.

> You can quickly display a list of all the files that appear in
> each directory on your disk by typing the TREE command as
> follows:
>
> TREE \ /F ¦ MORE
>
> Or to print a listing of all the files, type
>
> TREE \ /F > PRN

To copy files to a new directory using the command prompt,
specify the name of the file (or use wildcard characters to indicate a
group of files) as the source, and specify the drive and directory
name as the destination. For example, to copy SAMPLE1.TXT and
SAMPLE2.TXT to the TEST directory (beneath the PRACTICE directory), follow these steps:

1. Type the command CD \PRACTICE to access the PRACTICE directory.

2. Type the command COPY SAMPLE?.TXT C:\PRACTICE\TEST.

DOS displays the names of the files as they are copied and then ends the operation with the message 2 file(s) copied. To verify that the TEST directory indeed contains these new files, change to the directory by entering the command CD TEST, and then enter the DIR command to view the names of files stored there.

Note that both the PRACTICE and the PRACTICE\TEST directories contain copies of the SAMPLE1.TXT and SAMPLE2.TXT files. Even though the files share the same name and content, they are completely independent of each other. Hence, changing or deleting these files on one directory has no effect on the copies on the other directory.

Copying to Different Disk Drives

> Some application programs are *copy-protected* with a structure that enables them to be used on only one computer. Although DOS can copy such programs, the copies will not work on different computers.

Copying files from one disk (or diskette) to another is one of the most common types of copying. If your computer has a hard disk, you use this basic procedure to copy application programs from their original diskettes onto your hard disk. You also use this technique to copy files from your hard disk to diskettes, an operation that enables you to store extra backups or use files on other computers.

If your computer doesn't have a hard disk, use this procedure to copy files from one diskette to another so that you can store the copies in a safe place as backups. Or you can copy files from one diskette to another so that you can use the same files on multiple computers.

Using Shell Menus to Copy Files to a Disk

To copy a file from one disk drive to another, specify the file or files that you want to copy as the source, and specify the disk drive that you want to copy to as the destination. You can also specify a directory on the destination disk drive, but it must be the name of an existing directory. (DOS will not automatically create a new directory while copying files.) If you do not specify a directory on the destination drive, DOS places the copies in the current directory of that drive (usually the root directory).

To practice this procedure, copy the files SAMPLE1.BAK and SAMPLE2.BAK to a new diskette. To do so, you need a blank formatted diskette (in addition to the one you might have used in earlier exercises). To prepare for the procedure, set up the diskettes in this way:

■ If your computer does not have a hard disk, insert the source diskette (the one with SAMPLE1.BAK and SAMPLE2.BAK on it) in drive B: and insert the blank formatted diskette in drive A:.

■ If your computer has a hard disk, insert the blank formatted diskette in drive A:.

Now, follow the appropriate steps for your computer:

1. At the File List screen, be sure to access the PRACTICE directory on your hard disk (or drive B: if you have no hard disk).

When the Shell is in Add mode (Shift+F8), you can press Spacebar to select a file or press it again to deselect a highlighted file.

2. Select the SAMPLE1.BAK and SAMPLE2.BAK file names by highlighting one, pressing Shift+F8, and using the arrow keys and Spacebar combination to highlight the other (or by clicking one with your mouse and then holding down the Ctrl key while clicking the other).

3. Press F10 or Alt, and then press Enter to access the File pull-down menu.

4. Select Copy....

> You must specify a directory for the operation, even if it is only the root directory.

5. Hold down the Del (or Delete) key until the suggested destination is completely erased; then type the new destination A:\, as shown in Figure 10.9.

6. Press Enter.

When copying is complete, the dialog box disappears from the screen.

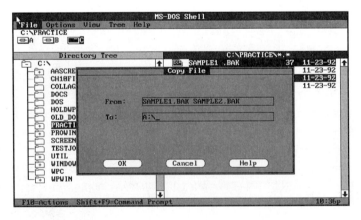

Figure 10.9. Dialog box to copy SAMPLE1.BAK and SAMPLE2.BAK to drive A:.

Precautions for Copying Files

Before you start copying files on your own, keep in mind this important point: If you copy a file to a disk drive or directory that already contains a file of the same name, the copied file replaces the original file.

For example, suppose that a directory named ACCT_REC contains a file named CUSTLIST.DAT that lists 1,000 customer names and addresses. Now, suppose that you create another file named CUSTLIST.DAT in a directory named INVENTRY, but this file lists only two customer names and addresses.

Finally, suppose that you decide to copy the CUSTLIST.DAT file from the INVENTRY directory to the ACCT_REC directory. If you do so, the 1,000 names and addresses in CUSTLIST.DAT will be lost forever because DOS will *overwrite* (replace) the original CUSTLIST.DAT file on the ACCT_REC directory with the copy from the INVENTRY directory.

DOS 5 and 6 helps protect users from potential problems of this type. Whenever you copy a file using the DOS Shell File List, DOS first checks the destination drive or directory to see whether it already contains a file with the same name as the one it's about to copy. If DOS finds a file on the destination with the same name and the Confirm on Replace confirmation option is on, DOS presents the warning shown in Figure 10.10.

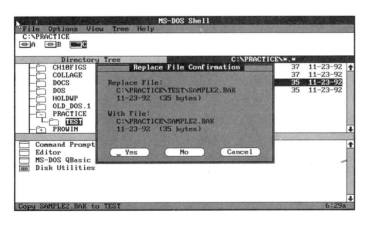

Figure 10.10. The DOS 6 Replace File Confirmation dialog box warns you about overwriting an existing file.

As you can see, the Replace File Confirmation dialog box warns you when it is about to overwrite an existing file. The `Replace File:` message at the top of the box tells you the path, name, creation date, and size of the file that the copy operation will overwrite. The `With File:` message displays the same information about the file that you are currently copying.

In the example in Figure 10.10, the dialog box warns you that the SAMPLE2.BAK file in the \PRACTICE\TEST directory will be overwritten by the SAMPLE2.BAK file from the \PRACTICE directory. If you select Yes, DOS replaces the file on the destination with the new copy and then proceeds to copy other files (if any). If you select No, the file is not copied, and DOS proceeds to copy other files (if any). If you select Cancel, DOS cancels the entire current copy operation.

This Replace File Confirmation dialog box can save you from inadvertently overwriting a new file with an old one. Whenever you see this box, check the dates and the sizes of the two files. The date specifies when the file was created or last modified; the size tells you how many characters the file contains. In general, you rarely want to copy an older file over a newer one or a smaller file over a larger one.

When you work at the command prompt, DOS (any version) gives no warning when a copy procedure is about to replace an existing file—DOS simply replaces the file! Therefore, you should always check the destination directory (or drive) to see whether it contains a file that has the same name as the one you are about to copy. (Use the `DIR` command to do so.)

For example, say that you are planning to copy CUSTLIST.DAT from the INVENTRY directory to the ACCT_REC directory. (Because your computer probably does not have these directories, you cannot try this right now; this is just a hypothetical example.) Before you rush into the copy procedure, you decide to check the destination directory to see whether it already contains a file with this name. You type the command

```
DIR C:\ACCT_REC\CUSTLIST.DAT.
```

Now, suppose that DOS informs you there is already a file named CUSTLIST.DAT on the ACCT_REC directory, and DOS displays the file name and the following information:

```
Directory C:\ACCT_REC
CUSTLIST    DAT        35000    03-15-93    3:22p
```

You must now ask yourself, "Should I proceed with this copy, thus overwriting (replacing) the CUSTLIST.DAT file's contents with the INVENTRY directory's CUSTLIST.DAT file?"

To answer this question, you would first look at the basic file information for CUSTLIST.DAT on the INVENTRY directory. To do so, you would type the command DIR CUSTLIST.DAT (you don't need to specify the drive and directory if you are already accessing the INVENTRY directory), and DOS might show you the following information about that file:

```
Directory C:\INVENTRY
CUSTLIST    DAT        50    06-20-93    8:00a
```

The DOS 6 Replace File Confirmation dialog box automatically displays file dates and sizes when you are about to overwrite an existing file.

In this example, you would be wise not to copy CUSTLIST.DAT from the INVENTRY directory to the ACCT_REC directory for one very important reason: As you can see in the two directory displays, the CUSTLIST.DAT file in the ACCT_REC directory contains 35,000 bytes (characters), whereas the CUSTLIST.DAT file in the INVENTRY directory contains only 50 bytes. If you were to proceed with the copy, you would lose at least 34,950 characters in the CUSTLIST.DAT file in the ACCT_REC directory. This could, indeed, be a rather unpleasant loss (particularly if you had no backups of the file being replaced).

Remember, even if you are planning to copy a group of files with a single XCOPY command, you can check the destination directory to see whether it already contains files with the same names as the files being copied. For example, suppose that you plan to copy *.TXT (all files with the extension .TXT) from the PRACTICE directory to the PRACTICE\TEST directory. To preview the current (PRACTICE) directory to see what files will be copied, type the command DIR *.TXT. To check the destination directory for files with similar names, type the command

```
DIR C:\PRACTICE\TEST\*.TXT
```

Renaming Files

As you gain experience using your computer and DOS wildcards, you'll notice what an advantage it is to name related files with file names that have a similar pattern. For example, suppose that you store quarterly data for your business in separate files. If you were to name these files in a haphazard manner, such as 1993QTR1.DAT, QTR2-93.INF, and 93-3-QTR.TXT, you could not use ambiguous file names to perform operations on these files as a group. However, if you renamed the files using a consistent format, such as QTR1-93.DAT, QTR2-93.DAT, and QTR3-93.DAT, you could more easily display or manage these related files using the ambiguous file names QTR?-93.DAT or QTR*.DAT.

It's easy to use DOS to rename a file, and you don't need to worry about accidentally replacing an existing file with a new one, because DOS will never allow you to do so. When you change the name of a file, the new name must be unique in the current directory (or diskette). If the new name is not unique, DOS displays a warning message and refuses to continue the operation.

Renaming Files from the Shell

You can use the usual DOS wildcard characters, ? and *, to simultaneously rename several files. To demonstrate, try renaming the SAMPLE1.BAK and SAMPLE2.BAK files on the PRACTICE directory to SAMPLE1.OLD and SAMPLE2.OLD. Use the following steps for your version of DOS:

1. If your computer has a hard disk, select the PRACTICE directory from the Directory Tree area of the File List screen.

2. If your computer does not have a hard disk, be sure that disk drive B: contains the diskette that has the SAMPLE1.BAK and SAMPLE2.BAK files on it. Then select B from the Drives area.

3. Select the SAMPLE1.BAK and SAMPLE2.BAK file names by highlighting one, pressing Shift+F8, and using the arrow keys and Spacebar combination to highlight the other. (Or click one with your mouse and then hold down the Ctrl key while clicking the other.)

4. Press F10 or Alt, and press Enter to pull down the File menu.

5. Select Rename….

   The Rename File dialog box appears on your screen, as shown in Figure 10.11. Notice that the box displays the current name for the file, a blank box for entering a new name for the file, and a counter that keeps you informed of the number of operations you are performing. (In Figure 10.11, for example, SAMPLE1.BAK is 1 of 2, the first of two files that you are going to rename.)

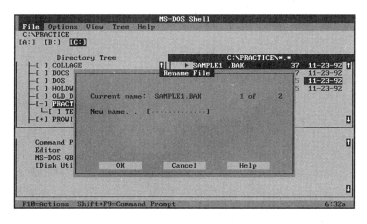

*Figure 10.11.
The Rename
File dialog box.*

You must remember to enter a complete file name for each file. After you type the new file name and press Enter, DOS prompts you to rename the next file, until you've provided a new name for each selected file. (If you decide not to rename a particular file, press Enter without typing a new name.) As usual, you can also press F1 (or select the Help button) for help or press Esc to cancel the entire request.

To proceed with the renaming exercise, follow these steps:

6. Type SAMPLE1.OLD and press Enter.

7. Type SAMPLE2.OLD and press Enter.

The Files area of your screen now displays the two files with the new names you provided.

> You can abbreviate the RENAME command as REN.

Renaming Files from the Command Prompt

To rename files from the command prompt, use the RENAME command followed by the current name, a blank space, and the new name, as shown in this syntax line:

RENAME currentname newname

You can use wildcard characters to rename a group of files, but you need to exercise a little caution when doing so, as demonstrated later. For now, rename SAMPLE1.BAK and SAMPLE2.BAK to SAMPLE1.OLD and SAMPLE2.OLD by following these steps:

1. If your computer has a hard disk, enter the command CD \PRACTICE to change to the PRACTICE directory.

2. If your computer does not have a hard disk, be sure the diskette in drive B: has the SAMPLE1.BAK and SAMPLE2.BAK files on it, and access drive B: by typing the B: command.

3. Type RENAME SAMPLE?.BAK SAMPLE?.OLD.

4. Press Enter.

To verify the results of the procedure, type the DIR command to display the new files' names. As the directory display shows, DOS renamed the SAMPLE1.BAK and SAMPLE2.BAK files to SAMPLE1.OLD and SAMPLE2.OLD. Because you used the wildcard character ?, both files were included in the renaming operation.

In the future, when you use wildcard characters to rename groups of files, keep in mind one important rule: Don't shorten the names of two or more files using a single RENAME command. The reason for this rule is straightforward. Suppose that you attempt to rename SAMPLE1.OLD and SAMPLE2.OLD to SAMP1.OLD and SAMP2.OLD using the single command RENAME SAMPLE?.OLD SAMP?.OLD.

The problem here is that DOS does not know the last character in the file name (that is, 1 or 2), which is the character that makes each file name unique. It therefore renames the first file to SAMPL.OLD. Then, it also attempts to name the second file SAMPL.OLD. When DOS sees that the file name SAMPL.OLD is already in use, it displays the error message Duplicate file name or file not found and cancels the renaming of the second file. (If you then entered the DIR command to see the names of files, you would see that only one of the files was renamed.)

If you want to shorten the names of several files, you must rename each file individually. Hence, in this example, rather than using the command RENAME SAMPLE?.OLD SAMP?.OLD, you would need to type the following two commands:

```
RENAME SAMPLE1.OLD SAMP1.OLD
RENAME SAMPLE2.OLD SAMP2.OLD
```

Also keep in mind that you cannot provide a new drive or directory location for a file while renaming it. For example, the seemingly logical command RENAME C:\PRACTICE\SAMPLE1.TXT A:SAMPLE1.BAK displays the error message Invalid parameter, because the command attempts to rename a file in the PRACTICE directory while trying to move the file to the diskette in drive A:. Such operations are simply not allowed with the RENAME command. (However, the command COPY C:\PRACTICE\SAMPLE1.TXT A:SAMPLE1.BAK would work; it would leave SAMPLE1.TXT intact on the PRACTICE directory, while also putting a copy of that file—with the name SAMPLE1.BAK—on the diskette in drive A:.)

Deleting Files

From time to time, you probably will want to delete (or erase) files to make room for new ones or to unclutter your disks. However, if you are using any version of DOS before version 5.0, you should be careful when deleting files because after you do, there is no turning back. That is, as soon as you erase a file, it is permanently gone! DOS erases a file very quickly, so even if it took you days, weeks, or even two months to create a file, DOS can zap it into oblivion before you can say, "Whoops!"

If you are using DOS 6, you can use the UNDELETE command to recover accidentally deleted files. However, you must recover the deleted files immediately. If you perform other DOS operations, such as creating, copying, or combining files, you might overwrite the data in the deleted files, thus losing the information forever. (See the next section for an overview of how to undelete files in DOS 6.)

As with the other basic file operations discussed in this chapter, you can erase several files during a single operation. However, when doing so, you must exercise extreme caution to ensure that you do not inadvertently erase more files than you intended. Techniques that illustrate caution are built into the following exercises, which show you how to safely erase the SAMPLE1.OLD and SAMPLE2.OLD files.

Deleting Files from the Shell

The basic technique for using the DOS Shell to erase files is the same as it was for other operations, except that you must be absolutely sure you've selected only the files that you want to erase. You do this by first deselecting all files, as discussed in the following steps:

1. Be sure that you are still accessing the PRACTICE directory if you are using a hard disk, or if your computer has no hard disk, that your current drive is drive B:.

2. With the File List screen displayed, press F10 or Alt, and then press Enter to pull down the File menu.

3. If the Deselect All option is available, select it. (If the option is shaded and unavailable, there are no selected files, so you can press the Esc key to close the menu.)

4. Now that you know that there are no selected files (which you might have otherwise overlooked), press Tab (or use your mouse) to move to the Files area of the screen.

5. Select the SAMPLE1.OLD and SAMPLE2.OLD files using the usual technique.

Press the Del key as a shortcut method of displaying the Delete dialog box.

6. Press F10 or Alt, and then press Enter to pull down the File menu.

7. Select Delete....

8. DOS displays the Delete File dialog box, which contains the names of the files to delete. Press Enter to proceed.

The Delete File Confirmation dialog box provides options that enable you to delete the current file (select Yes), skip (don't delete) the current file (select No), or cancel the entire operation (select Cancel), as shown in Figure 10.12. DOS displays a confirmation dialog box for each file that you previously selected for deletion. (This is an added precaution in case you forget to deselect all files before selecting new files for this operation.)

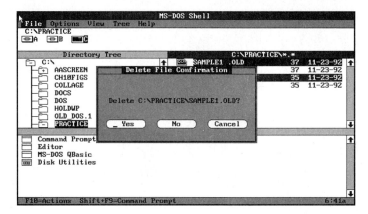

Figure 10.12. Options to delete a file or to cancel deleting a file.

To delete the file whose name is shown next to the `Delete` prompt, select Yes by clicking the button with your mouse or by moving the underline cursor to that option and pressing Enter. To complete this exercise, proceed with the following steps:

9. Select Yes to delete SAMPLE1.OLD.

10. When the options appear for SAMPLE2.OLD, again select Yes to delete the file.

After DOS erases both files, it redisplays the File List screen. Note that SAMPLE1.OLD and SAMPLE2.OLD are no longer listed in the Files area, as Figure 10.13 shows.

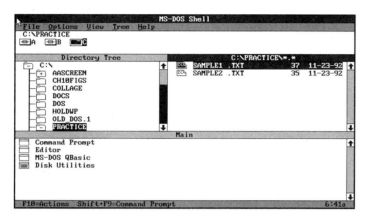

*Figure 10.13.
SAMPLE1.OLD
and
SAMPLE2.OLD
have been
deleted.*

Deleting Files from the Command Prompt

To delete files from the command prompt, use the DEL (or ERASE) command followed by the name of the file you want to delete.

You can also use ambiguous file names to delete multiple files. For example, to delete SAMPLE1.OLD and SAMPLE2.OLD, you could use the command DEL SAMPLE?.OLD or the identical command ERASE SAMPLE?.OLD, but before you do so, look at some precautionary steps you can take so that you don't accidentally erase other files:

1. If your computer has a hard disk, be sure to change to the PRACTICE directory by typing CD \PRACTICE. If your computer does not have a hard disk, be sure that the diskette containing SAMPLE1.OLD and SAMPLE2.OLD is in drive B:, and access the drive by entering the B: command if necessary.

2. Before erasing SAMPLE?.OLD, first type the command DIR SAMPLE?.OLD to see which files fit this ambiguous file name pattern.

3. In this case, you should see only two file names, SAMPLE1.OLD and SAMPLE2.OLD (in addition to the usual information that the DIR command provides).

231

4. Because SAMPLE1.OLD and SAMPLE2.OLD are indeed the two files you want to erase, type the command DEL SAMPLE?.OLD and press Enter.

5. Type DIR to see the names of remaining files, which will not include the deleted SAMPLE1.OLD and SAMPLE2.OLD files.

As mentioned at the beginning of this section, if you are using a version of DOS other than DOS 5 or 6, you need to exercise caution when erasing files, because after you do erase files, they are gone forever (which, of course, is a very good reason for always making backup copies of important files!). However, at a deeper, more technical level, the file is not really deleted. Instead, DOS changes the first character in the file name to make the file "invisible" and ready to be replaced by a new file. When you save a new file in the future, DOS then overwrites the invisible file with the new file's contents.

> You can also protect files from being accidentally erased as discussed in the section "Protecting Files," later in this chapter.

DOS 5 was the first version of DOS to provide a built-in feature to locate and recover these invisible files. Therefore, you can undelete an accidentally deleted file, as you will see in the next section. However, if you are using an earlier version of DOS, all hope is not lost; several third-party vendors offer undelete utilities that work with files in DOS 3 and 4. If you don't own DOS 5 or 6, you should seriously consider purchasing one of these products for your computer. Do so now, before an accident actually occurs.

Remember, even if you use DOS 6 or own an unerase program, up-to-date backup copies of files are still the best way to protect yourself from accidentally losing files.

Undeleting Files with the DOS 6 *UNDELETE* Command

The new DOS 6 UNDELETE command has a Windows version and an MS-DOS version. See Chapter 18, "Protecting Your System," for a detailed explanation on using the UNDELETE command from Windows or the command prompt. You can now undelete files on a network and undelete a directory and its files.

When DOS deletes a file, it doesn't really erase the data from the disk; it just changes the first character of the file name (to a Σ—a lowercase sigma) so that other DOS commands don't "see" the file. Although the information is still on the disk immediately after you erase the file, DOS commands no longer recognize that it is there, and they quickly overwrite the data with the new or modified files that you later save to disk.

> When you're sure that you are not going to want to UNDELETE your files, you can speed up DOS's file searches by XCOPYing all of your files (XCOPY ignores inactive files) in a given directory to a temporary directory. Erase your files in the original directory, remove the directory, re-create your original directory name (now, minus the inactive-deleted file information), and copy all of your files from the temporary directory back into your newly created "original" directory.

The UNDELETE command searches for file names that start with a Σ so that you can restore the first character of the file name to a letter that DOS commands can recognize. Immediately thereafter, DOS can again perform operations on that file.

The basic use of the command is quite simple, and if it is used immediately after a deletion, it is always effective. However, if you save, copy, or alter even one file after a deletion, your chances of recovering the deleted file decrease dramatically, because the new or revised file might overwrite part of the deleted file.

If you use the UNDELETE command immediately after accidentally erasing a file or files, the following brief procedure always recovers all the deleted files in the current directory:

1. Be sure that the current directory is the directory that contains the deleted files.

2. Type UNDELETE. (If DOS responds with a Bad command or file name error message, type the full path name C:\DOS\UNDELETE.)

3. When UNDELETE asks whether you want to recover the specified file, press Y (for Yes).

4. When UNDELETE prompts you to enter the first character of the file, press the original first letter. (If you can't remember the original first letter, press any valid character that will create a unique name in the current directory.)

Repeat the previous steps until you have undeleted all the files that you want to recover.

In the previous section, you deleted two files—SAMPLE1.OLD and SAMPLE2.OLD. Now assume that you haven't performed any other file operations and that PRACTICE is still the current directory. If you follow the steps in the preceding numbered list (entering S at both of the Enter the first character of the filename prompts), your screen will resemble Figure 10.14.

```
C:\PRACTICE>UNDELETE

UNDELETE - A delete protection facility
Copyright (C) 1987-1993 Central Point Software, Inc.
All rights reserved.

Directory: C:\PRACTICE
File Specifications: *.*

    Delete Sentry control file not found.

    Deletion-tracking file not found.

    MS-DOS directory contains    2 deleted files.
    Of those,    2 files may be recovered.

Using the MS-DOS directory method.

    ?AMPLE1  OLD       37 11-23-92  7:47p  ...A  Undelete (Y/N)?Y
    Please type the first character for ?AMPLE1 .OLD:
```

Figure 10.14.
Using
UNDELETE to
recover two
deleted files.

Type the DIR command to see that the two files have indeed been undeleted.

If you want to undelete a specific file (even if it is in another directory or on another drive), type the path and/or file name after the UNDELETE command. For example, if you are currently in the \DOS directory and want to undelete the SAMPLE1.OLD file in the PRACTICE directory, type

UNDELETE \PRACTICE\SAMPLE1.OLD

and answer the prompts accordingly.

Combining Files

You can copy and combine (merge) several individual text files into a single new file. This can be handy when, for example, you've created several files containing names and addresses and you want to create a larger file combining all the names and addresses. The DOS 6 Shell does not provide any means of combining files, but all versions of the DOS command prompt do. The basic technique for combining files is to use the COPY command.

> XCOPY will not concatenate (combine) files.

You must list as the source of the copy the names of files to be combined, separated by a plus (+) sign. You must provide as the destination a new, unique file name. Look at an example that combines the SAMPLE1.TXT and SAMPLE2.TXT files:

1. If you are using the DOS 6 Shell, press the F3 key to exit the Shell and display the command prompt.

2. Be sure to access the correct drive or directory; type the command CD \PRACTICE if you have a hard disk, or type B: if you don't have a hard disk.

3. Type the command COPY SAMPLE1.TXT+SAMPLE2.TXT COMBO.TXT. (Note the plus sign that joins the source files and also note the blank space in front of the new file name COMBO.TXT.)

4. To verify that the command worked, type DIR to view the file names.

5. To view the contents of the new COMBO.TXT file, type the command TYPE COMBO.TXT.

The TYPE command displays the contents of the COMBO.TXT files:

```
This is the first sample text file.
I am the second sample text file.
```

> You should combine only *text* files. Never try to combine program files (that is, those with the file name extension .EXE or .BAT.). If you combine program files, the resulting "program combination" file probably will not work at all, or if it does, it might do very strange things to your computer!

If you are a DOS 6 user, return to the DOS Shell now by typing the command DOSSHELL and pressing Enter. (If you do not have a hard disk, be sure to insert the Shell diskette in drive A:, access drive A: by typing A: and pressing Enter, and then type DOSSHELL and press Enter).

Moving Files

As you gain experience in using your computer, you might occasionally decide to change the directory tree structure of the hard disk to better organize your files. When you do so, you probably will want to move, rather than copy, files from one directory to another.

The DOS 6 File List has a built-in menu option for moving files. However, earlier versions of DOS do not have a move command, so with those versions you must move files using the following two-step operation:

1. Copy the file to the new directory.

2. Erase the file from the original directory.

The New DOS 6 *MOVE* Command

The new DOS 6 MOVE command is a powerful file management command. This command is useful for moving files from one directory to another when you no longer want the file to reside in the original directory. It also can rename directories and files during the move.

In previous versions of DOS, moving files from one directory to another required copying the files to the new directory and then deleting them from the original directory. The MOVE command combines those commands into a single command.

MOVE is an external command. Its basic syntax is

```
MOVE [directory][path][filename] [new directory]
[new path][new filename]
```

For example, if you want to move TESTIT.DOC from the C:\WP\DOCS directory to the C:\TEST directory, type

```
MOVE C:\WP\DOCS\TESTIT.DOC C:\TEST
```

You can use wildcards to move more than one file at a time. For example,

```
MOVE C:\WP\DOCS\TEST*.DOC C:\TEST
```

moves all files with the .DOC extension to the C:\TEST directory. Of course, if you are in the C:\WP\DOCS directory, don't type the paths.

The MOVE command can change the names of directories. To re-name the C:\TEST subdirectory to C:\NEWTEST, type

```
MOVE C:\TEST C:\NEWTEST
```

The MOVE command also can change the name of a single file during the move operation. Using the same example, to change the name of TESTIT.DOC to TESTGOOD.DOC while moving it, type

```
MOVE C:\WP\DOCS\TESTIT.DOC C:\TEST\TESTGOOD.DOC
```

The MOVE command works with files in which the hidden attribute is on. This means that when you use wildcards with the MOVE command, you also might inadvertently move hidden files that are required to be in the source directory.

Moving Files from the Shell

Try a simple example. Move the new COMBO.TXT file from the PRACTICE directory to the PRACTICE\TEST directory. (These steps are described for a hard disk computer, but if you created these directories on a diskette, you can follow the instructions by substituting the correct drive name.) Follow the appropriate steps for your version of DOS:

1. Select PRACTICE from the Directory Tree to change to the PRACTICE directory.

2. Select COMBO.TXT from the Files area of the screen.

> Press F7 as a shortcut method to a different directory. You cannot specify a drive or another directory in the source.

3. Press F10 or Alt, and then press Enter to pull down the File menu.

4. Select Move….

5. Press the End key and type \TEST to change the destination to C:\PRACTICE\TEST, as shown in Figure 10.15.

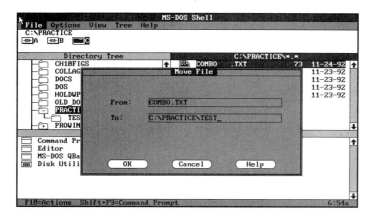

Figure 10.15. Dialog box to move COMBO.TXT to the TEST directory.

6. Press Enter to start the operation.

When DOS finishes the operation, COMBO.TXT is no longer displayed in the Files area. If you move the highlight to the Directory Tree area of the screen and select TEST to change to that directory, you'll see that COMBO.TXT is now stored on that directory.

With the mouse-only procedure, use the Alt key to move files; use the Ctrl key to copy files.

DOS 6 users also have the ability to move files graphically—that is, to literally move a file's icon (and the file itself!) to a new location. This is similar to the mouse-only copying procedure discussed earlier in this chapter. However, instead of holding down the Ctrl key during the operation, you hold down the Alt key.

To see how this procedure works, repeat the previous example (move COMBO.TXT back to the PRACTICE directory). Use the mouse to move the COMBO.TXT file into the TEST subdirectory, as described in the following steps:

1. Hold down the Alt key.

2. Click COMBO.TXT, but do not release the left mouse button.

3. Drag the mouse cursor into the Directory Tree area. Notice that a three-line file icon appears in place of the mouse cursor. (You can release the Alt key now.)

4. Position the file icon on the TEST subdirectory name, and release the left mouse button. The Shell now displays the Confirm Mouse Operation dialog box, shown in Figure 10.16.

5. Press Enter (or select Yes) to tell the Shell to move the file to C:\PRACTICE\TEST.

If you switch to the PRACTICE\TEST directory and look in the Files area, you will see that COMBO.TXT has been moved into the TEST directory. Click the PRACTICE directory to verify that the file is no longer there.

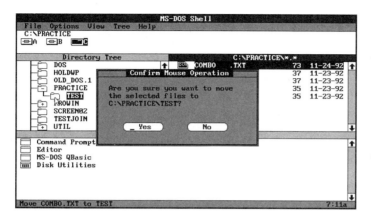

Figure 10.16.
Confirm
Mouse
Operation
dialog box
to move
COMBO.TXT
to the TEST
directory.

Notes on Move/Copy by Dragging

When using your mouse to move/copy files by dragging, keep a few points in mind:

- If you hold down the Ctrl key while dragging files, the result is always a copy (easy to remember because both *Ctrl* and *Copy* begin with the letter C).

- If you hold down the Alt key while dragging files, the result is always a move.

- If you don't hold down either Ctrl or Alt while dragging a file, the result depends on where you drag the file to:

  If you drag the files to a different directory on the same drive, the result is a move.

  If you drag the files to a different drive, the result is a copy.

This might seem confusing, but it's just DOS's way of trying to be intuitive. The most common reason for dragging a file from one directory to another on the same drive is to move it; hence that's the default if you don't hold down Ctrl or Alt when dragging. The most common reason to drag a file to a different drive is to make a copy, so that's the default if you don't hold down Ctrl or Alt in that situation.

241

Protecting Files

Each file on your diskette or hard disk is assigned several attributes. Whenever you store a new file or a copy of an existing file onto your disk, DOS automatically assigns that file the attribute read-write, which means that you can change or delete the file at any time. However, you can reset the attribute of any file to read-only, which means that you can view and use the contents of the file, but not change or delete the file.

Changing a file's attribute to read-only is a good way to ensure that the file is never accidentally erased. However, because setting the read-only attribute also prevents you from changing the file, it is inconvenient for data files that you need to update regularly (such as mailing lists, bookkeeping data, and so on). On the other hand, files that you never change (such as application programs and DOS programs) are good candidates for read-only protection.

Take the time to protect your word processing forms (letter formats, invoice formats, and so on) with the read-only attribute. Due to the many manipulations of these files, they are subject to accidental modification.

To practice using this technique, change the attribute of the SAMPLE1.TXT and SAMPLE2.TXT files in the PRACTICE directory to read-only, and then you can see what happens when you try to erase those files.

Protecting Your Files from the Shell

To protect your files from the Shell, take the following steps:

1. Be sure that the File List is displayed on your screen and that you are accessing the PRACTICE directory (if you have a hard disk) or that you are accessing the drive containing

the diskette with SAMPLE1.TXT on it (if you don't have a hard disk).

2. Move to the Files area, and select the SAMPLE1.TXT and SAMPLE2.TXT files in the usual manner.

3. Press F10 or Alt, and then press Enter to pull down the File menu.

4. Select Change Attributes....

5. At the Change Attributes dialog box, select the first option to change the selected files one at a time (see Figure 10.17).

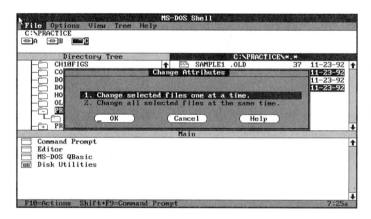

Figure 10.17. This Change Attributes dialog box appears when you select more than one file.

DOS displays the next Change Attributes dialog box on your screen, as shown in Figure 10.18. Note that each file has four attributes that you can change; however, for the time being, I'll confine the discussion to the read-only attribute. As you are instructed on-screen, to change an attribute, you must move the highlight to it using the ↑ or ↓, and then press the Spacebar.

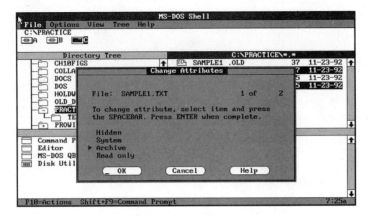

Figure 10.18. This Change Attributes dialog box shows four attributes for each file.

6. Press ↓ to move the highlight to the Read only option.

7. Press the Spacebar (or click the option once with your mouse) to select the attribute. Note that a right-pointing triangle to the left of the option indicates that the read-only attribute is now turned on. (The Archive attribute might also be turned on; to turn it off, highlight Archive and press the Spacebar. Note that pressing the Spacebar toggles an option on and off.)

8. Press Enter to set the attribute of that file to read-only.

9. Repeat the procedure with the next file. When you press Enter, you will return to the File List.

Just to experiment, try to erase SAMPLE.TXT now. Follow these steps:

1. Select the PRACTICE directory from the Directory Tree area of the Shell.

2. Select the SAMPLE.TXT file name.

3. Select Delete... from the File pull-down menu. Notice the dialog box that appears, as shown in Figure 10.19.

4. Select No (or press Esc) to avoid deleting the file.

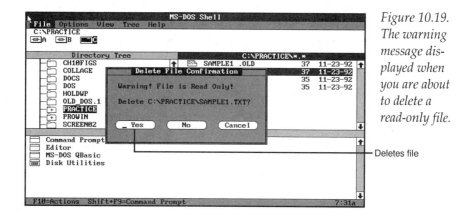

Figure 10.19.
The warning
message dis-
played when
you are about
to delete a
read-only file.

As you can see, changing a file to read-only gives you an extra level of protection against accidentally deleting an important file.

Protecting Your Files from the Command Prompt

DOS 6 users who prefer the command prompt can use the ATTRIB (short for ATTRIBUTE) program to change a file's attribute. To the right of the ATTRIB command, you place the following symbols to assign or remove the read-only attribute:

+R (to turn on the read-only attribute)

-R (to turn off the read-only attribute)

To the right of the +R or -R symbol, specify the file (or an unambiguous file name) to which you want to assign the attribute. Here are the exact steps for changing the attribute of SAMPLE1.TXT to read-only (+R):

1. If your computer has a hard disk, type the command CD \PRACTICE to access the PRACTICE directory (or type B: to access the diskette that contains SAMPLE1.TXT).

2. Type the command ATTRIB +R SAMPLE1.TXT.

245

Although nothing appears to happen because DOS just redisplays the command prompt, see what happens when you try to erase the file. Type the command ERASE SAMPLE1.TXT. DOS displays a message because you cannot erase a file (via the command prompt) that has the read-only attribute assigned to it. (Type the DIR command to prove to yourself that the file has not been erased.)

> ATTRIB is not a built-in command; DOS needs to have access, via a PATH statement, to the ATTRIB.EXE file to run the program.

Resetting the Read-Write Attribute from the Shell

At times you might need to change a file's attribute back to read-write so that you can modify or erase the file. Use the same basic procedure you used to turn on the read-only attribute. Because you really do not need to protect the SAMPLE1.TXT and SAMPLE2.TXT files, using the following steps changes them back to read-write files:

1. Select SAMPLE1.TXT and SAMPLE2.TXT from the Files area of the File List screen.

2. Press F10 or Alt, and then press Enter to pull down the File menu.

3. Select Change Attributes....

4. Select the option Change selected files one at a time.

5. Highlight Read only and press the Spacebar (so that the triangle marker disappears).

6. Press Enter.

Repeat the procedure with the next file.

Resetting the Read-Write Attribute from the Command Prompt

To reinstate the Read-Write attribute by way of the command prompt, use the -R option with the ATTRIB command:

At the command prompt, enter the command ATTRIB -R SAMPLE1.TXT.

SAMPLE1.TXT no longer has the read-only attribute turned on, so you can change it or erase it at the command line.

The ATTRIB command can be used to find any file on your disk by typing ATTRIB [*path*] [*filename*] /S. The /S parameter includes files in all subdirectories below the current directory.

Working with Your Directories

A hard disk can store many hundreds, or even thousands, of files. To make it easier to manage a large number of files, you can use DOS to divide the hard disk into *directories*, each of which contains its own set of related files.

Like file names, directory names can have only as many as eight characters and cannot contain blank spaces. A directory name can have a three-character extension, but to prevent directory names from being confused with file names, people rarely use extensions with directory names.

Individual directories can be further divided into subdirectories. You might think of subdirectories as areas within a file drawer in a filing cabinet (or directory) that are marked off with dividers. Subdirectory names follow the same conventions as directory names. That is, they can be as many as eight characters long, cannot contain spaces, and generally do not include an extension.

Chapter 14, "Hard Disk Management Made Simple," discusses the best techniques for organizing the information on your computer's hard disk into directories.

The Directory Tree

The *structure* of directories and subdirectories on a disk is often referred to as the *directory tree*. Every hard disk and diskette contains an initial directory called the *root* directory. DOS automatically assigns the simple name \ to this root directory. Any additional directories (and subdirectories) that you create are considered to be "below" the root directory.

Now before I move on to other topics, take a minute to review the following important information:

- A disk drive contains a disk and usually has a letter name (such as A: or C:).

- To organize information on a disk, you can subdivide the disk into directories and subdirectories.

- Every directory contains its own unique set of files.

As you'll see, it's pretty easy to explore the disk drives (usually called simply *drives*), directories, and files on any computer system.

Expanding and Collapsing Branches

Each directory beneath the root directory is sometimes referred to as a *branch* in the tree. To avoid cluttering the Directory Tree area with too much information, *subdirectories* (directories that branch off directories other than root) are not initially displayed in the Directory Tree area. Instead, if a branch leads to still other branches, its icon contains a plus sign (+).

If a branch is already expanded, its icon contains a minus sign (–) as a reminder that you can collapse that branch if you want. It there are no subdirectories beneath the particular directory, its icon is empty.

There are several ways to expand and collapse directory tree branches to view more or fewer directory levels, as explained in the following sections.

Expanding One Level

■ To expand a branch one level, click the + icon next to the directory name, or highlight the directory name and then press +, or select Expand One Level from the Tree menu.

■ To collapse an expanded branch, click the – icon next to the branch name, or highlight the branch name and then press -, or select Collapse Branch from the Tree menu.

When a branch is expanded, you can select any subdirectory name that appears to view the names of files on that subdirectory simply by selecting the subdirectory name. Either move the highlighter with the ↓ or ↑ key, or click the name of the subdirectory.

Fully Expanding a Branch

Rather than just viewing one additional level of subdirectories, you can fully expand a branch to see all levels. To do so, follow these steps:

1. Highlight the name of the directory you want to expand.

2. Press * or select Expand Branch from the Tree menu.

Fully Expanding All Branches

If you want to fully expand all the branches in the directory tree, take the following action:

Select Expand All from the Tree menu.

Even though there is no Collapse All option to return to the one-level view of the tree, you can quickly return to that level by collapsing and then expanding the root directory.

If you have several directories on a disk drive, you might want to select that drive and practice some of the techniques just described, just to get a feel for it.

Creating Directories

It's easy to create a directory on a disk, but there is one important point that you need to keep in mind when creating your own directories: When you create a new directory, DOS automatically creates it below the current directory.

As you know, the root directory is the highest-level directory in any directory tree. All directories that you create are below the root directory in the tree. In the exercise that follows, you will create a new directory, named EXAMPLE, on hard disk drive C:. This directory will be one level beneath the root directory.

Creating Directories from the Shell

If you are using DOS 6 and the DOS Shell is displayed on your screen, follow these steps to create the EXAMPLE directory:

If you are using a mouse, use the usual point-and-click method to perform steps 1–5.

1. In the Drives area of the Shell, select the drive on which you want to create the directory (that is, C: or A:).

2. In the Directory Tree area of the Shell, select the root directory by moving the highlight to the top of the tree.

3. Select Create Directory… from the File pull-down menu.

4. When you see the Create Directory dialog box, type EXAMPLE, the new directory name.

5. Press Enter or click OK to create the directory. Note that your new directory name, EXAMPLE, is in the directory tree.

Because the EXAMPLE directory that you just created is new, it does not yet contain any files. To verify this, change to the directory and see for yourself. From the Shell, select the directory name EXAMPLE from the Directory Tree area of the File System. The Files area displays the message No files in selected directory.

Creating Directories from the Command Prompt

To create a new directory, use the MKDIR (often abbreviated MD) command (both are short for Make Directory). To ensure that the new directory is created one level below the root directory, follow these steps exactly:

1. Go to the drive where you want to create the directory (that is type C: to switch to drive C: or type A: to switch to drive A:), and press Enter.

2. To go to the root directory, type the command CD \ and press Enter.

3. Next, type the command MD EXAMPLE and press Enter.

4. To view the new directory tree, type TREE and press Enter.

Remember, you can type the command TREE > PRN to print the directory tree.

To verify that the newly created EXAMPLE directory does not yet contain any files, follow these simple steps:

1. Type CD EXAMPLE and press Enter.

2. Type DIR and press Enter.

DOS displays a screen similar to this:

```
Directory of C:\EXAMPLE

.            <DIR>     01-21-93    9:38a
..           <DIR>     01-21-93    9:38a
        2 File(s)              0 bytes
                    xxxxxxxx bytes free
```

The bottom line of the DIR command says that there are 2 File(s) on this newly created directory, and it appears as though these are named . and .. However, . and .. are not truly files. Instead, they are shortcut names for the current and parent (higher-level) directories.

Creating Subdirectories

As mentioned earlier, DOS automatically places any new directory that you create beneath the current directory in the tree. Therefore, to create a subdirectory, you merely change to the parent directory (the one that you want to be above the new subdirectory) and follow the same steps that you did to create the EXAMPLE directory, but using the new subdirectory names. As an example, create a subdirectory named TEST beneath the EXAMPLE directory.

Renaming Directories

You can use DOS 6 to change the name of a directory easily. Rather than work through a sample exercise to demonstrate this technique (which you probably will not use often, except to correct a misspelled directory name), I'll outline the general techniques for future reference. (You don't need to try the following steps if you don't want to change a directory name.)

> You cannot use the RENAME command to rename directories at the command prompt. To change the name of a directory at the command prompt, you must carry out four separate actions: make a new directory using the MD command, copy all the files from the old directory to the new directory, erase all the files in the old directory, and remove the old directory name using the RD command. It is much easier to use the Shell!

To rename a directory using the DOS 6 Shell, you first need to ensure that no file names in the Files area are selected (otherwise, DOS renames the selected files rather than the directory). Here are the general steps you need to follow:

1. Access the File List screen.

2. Select the directory you want to rename from the Directory Tree (by highlighting it or by clicking the directory name with your mouse).

3. Press F10 or Alt, and then press Enter to pull down the File menu.

4. If the Deselect All option is available for selection, select it to ensure that no files are selected. (You would then need to redisplay the File pull-down menu.)

5. Select Rename....

6. When the Rename Directory dialog box appears (as shown in Figure 10.20), type the new name for the directory.

7. Press Enter.

You can also use the MOVE command to rename a directory as discussed earlier.

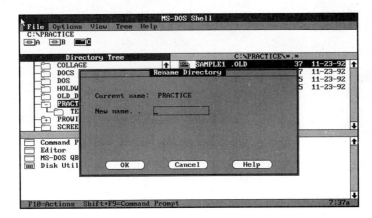

Figure 10.20.
Dialog box to
rename a
directory.

After DOS completes the operation, the Directory Tree immediately displays the new directory name that you specified.

Deleting Directories with the DOS 6 *DELTREE* Command

You can use the new command DELTREE to delete a directory and all subdirectories below it, including the files in those directories. In previous versions of DOS, you first had to go to the lowest-level subdirectory, delete all the files, and then move up one level and delete the subdirectory. This process had to be repeated until all the files and directories were deleted.

DELTREE does all of that with one command, including deleting files for which the hidden, read-only, and system attributes are set. DELTREE is an external command. Its syntax is

DELTREE [/Y] [*drive/path*]

The /Y switch tells DELTREE to withhold warnings when you are about to delete a directory. To use DELTREE, you must be in the directory above the directory you want to eliminate.

> Don't use the /Y switch with DELTREE unless you are confident you will never make a mistake. Deleting a directory and all its subdirectories is a powerful action. Being prompted about whether you want to delete the directory might take an extra second or two, but it provides one more safeguard against mistakenly taking the wrong actions.

 # Troubleshooting

If you make an error while working with your files and directories, DOS probably will display one of the following error messages. Try using the suggested solutions to correct the error.

- `Access denied:`

  DOS displays this error message when one of the following problems arises:

  You tried to change or delete a read-only file. (Turn off the read-only attribute, using techniques described in the section "Resetting the Read-Write Attribute at the Command Prompt" in this chapter.)

  You tried to create a file or directory using an invalid name. (Use a different name, avoiding the reserved device names and illegal characters.)

  You tried to create or rename a directory or file using a name that is already in use. (Use the TREE or DIR command to see whether the directory or file name already exists.)

■ Bad command or file name

Usually, you've tried to run a program that is not in the current directory or diskette and is not in the PATH statement, or you've misspelled a command. Use the DIR command to search for the directory that contains the file, and then try again, being sure to include the complete location and name of the file you want.

■ Duplicate file name or file not found

During a renaming operation, DOS was unable to find the file that you want to rename or was unable to rename the file because the file name already existed in the current directory. Use the DIR command to check current file names to determine which error is creating the problem; then, retry the command using an acceptable file name.

■ File cannot be copied onto itself

The source and destination in a copy operation are identical, thus asking DOS to store two files with the same name in the same directory. Try again, being sure to specify a valid source and destination for the copy operation.

■ File creation error

Either there is not enough room left on a diskette to store the new file or you exceeded the maximum number of directory entries for the disk.

■ File not found

The file name specified in a command does not exist in the current directory or diskette. You are accessing the wrong directory or diskette, or you misspelled the file name, or the file specified is a system or hidden file. Check the Files area in the DOS 6 File List, or use the DIR command to see whether the file exists in the current directory or diskette.

■ `Invalid drive specification`

You specified a disk drive (such as D: or B:), but there is no such drive on your computer. Try again, using a valid disk drive name.

■ `Invalid filename or file not found`

You tried to create or rename a file using an illegal file name. DOS also displays this error when you try to use the wildcard characters ? or * in a TYPE command, which can only accept a single, unambiguous file name.

■ `Invalid Keyword`

DOS does not recognize your path separator. It should be a backslash (\).

■ `Invalid switch`

A switch specified in your command is not available with the current command. Also caused by using a forward slash (/) rather than a backslash (\) in directory names.

■ `No subdirectories exist`

You ran the TREE command from a directory that has no subdirectories. Type the command CD \ to access the root directory, and then retry the TREE command.

■ `Path not found`

Your command specified the name of a directory that does not exist. Check your spelling, or use the TREE command to check the directory tree for the correct path name.

■ `Syntax error`

You used the wrong format when you typed a command. Try again, being sure to use blank spaces, backslashes, and punctuation marks carefully. Also, be sure to put file names for the command in their proper order.

■ Unable to create directory

You tried to create a file or directory using an invalid name. (Use a different name, avoiding the reserved device names and illegal characters.)

■ Write-protect error writing drive n --Abort, Retry, Fail

You tried to store a new file on a diskette that is write-protected. Press A to abort the command, and then remove the write-protect tab from the diskette.

Summary

This chapter discussed the basic techniques needed for making, viewing, copying, renaming, deleting, moving, and protecting files and directories. I'll review the basic techniques presented in this chapter:

■ Regardless of which application programs you use on your computer, your file and directory names need to conform to the rules imposed by DOS: an eight-character maximum length with no blank spaces or illegal characters, followed by an optional period and extension.

■ To protect files from accidental change or erasure at the command prompt, use the syntax ATTRIB +R *filename* to turn on the read-only attribute. From the Shell, turn on the read-only attribute by selecting Change Attributes... from the File pull-down menu.

■ From the command prompt, use the syntax TYPE *filename* to view the contents of a file. To view the contents of a file from the Shell, select a single file name from the Files area, and then select the View File Contents option from the File pull-down menu. (Press F6 as a shortcut method of viewing a file.)

■ At the command prompt, use the syntax COPY [source] [destination] to copy files. From the Shell, use the Copy... option in the File pull-down menu to copy a selected file (or files) to a new name on the current directory or to the same name in a different directory or disk drive. (Press F8 as a shortcut method of copying a file.)

■ To erase (delete) files at the command prompt, use the syntax DEL filename or ERASE filename. From the Shell, to delete files using the File List, select the files to delete, and then select the Delete... option from the File pull-down menu. (Press Del as a shortcut method of deleting a file.)

■ Use the new DELTREE command to delete a directory along with its subdirectories and the files within these directories.

■ To combine files into a single new file, use the syntax COPY file1+file2+file3 newfilename in which files to be combined are joined by plus signs, and newfilename is the name of the resulting combined file. You cannot combine files from the Shell.

■ Use the new MOVE command for moving files from one directory to another when you no longer want the file to reside in the original directory. You can also rename directories and files during the move.

To move files to a new directory or disk by dragging a file icon to a new location, hold down the Alt key, select the file or files, drag the file icon to the new directory or drive, and then release the left mouse button.

C H A P T E R   1 1

Creating and Editing Files

DOS and other applications require the use of special files to configure your usage of hardware and software. Although these files are critical for running your computer and your programs, they typically are simple ASCII text files. The two best-known of these files are CONFIG.SYS and AUTOEXEC.BAT. However, several other text files also are critical to running your computer. Many applications now require configuration files with .INI extensions that store a variety of program settings. And batch programs (see Chapter 12, "Simple Batch Programs") also are ASCII text files.

You must use an editor to change these special files. Hundreds of editors are available for DOS microcomputers. They range from complex word processing programs, such as WordPerfect, to small desktop text editors that come with programs such as PC Tools Deluxe. In addition, DOS comes with a somewhat simplified text editor, EDIT, which was first introduced in DOS 5.

Another editor, EDLIN, is a decade-old line editor that was both clumsy and difficult to use. DOS 6 no longer includes the EDLIN editor, although most previous versions of DOS included it.

EDIT is a good way to edit DOS text files. Optionally, you can use your favorite word processor, as long as you remember a few basic rules.

This chapter provides some tips about using a word processor to edit DOS files and shows you how to use the DOS EDIT program.

Using a Word Processor to Edit DOS Text Files

The most important rule to remember when using a word processor to edit DOS text files is to save your files in ASCII format. Most word processors insert invisible, and usually proprietary, application-specific, formatting characters into their normal files.

The formatting characters are necessary to make documents attractive. However, formatting characters can cause confusion to DOS. DOS files, such as your AUTOEXEC.BAT file, that are saved in the proprietary format of a word processor could cause error messages such as Bad command or file name to appear when they execute. This has been known to drive many computer users half crazy, because they cannot see the formatting characters that DOS sees, and therefore they cannot figure out what is wrong.

There are ways to tell whether formatting characters are in what should be plain ASCII text files. Perhaps the easiest is to use the TYPE command to view the contents of a file. Figure 11.1 illustrates that typing the command TYPE C:\AUTOEXEC.BAT shows peculiar characters which indicate that the file is not an ASCII text file.

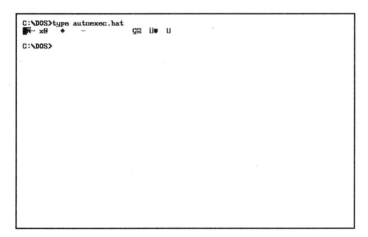

Figure 11.1. The TYPE command's view of a non-ASCII file.

DOS Shell users can see whether a text file contains formatting characters by using the View File Contents option in the File menu. The View File Contents option just shows text when it views an ASCII file. As Figure 11.2 shows, when non-ASCII files are viewed, they are shown in so-called hexadecimal format.

```
┌──────────────── MS-DOS Shell - AUTOEXEC.BAT ───────────────┐
│ Display  View  Help                                         │
│ ┌─ To view file's content use PgUp or PgDn or ↑ or ↓. ──────┐
│ │ 000000   DBA52D00  78400904  00000000  2D000000  ▋N-.x@.....-...  │
│ │ 000010   00000000  00000000  80010000  9A030000  .......ç...ü...  │
│ │ 000020   550A0000  00000000  00000000  00000000  U.............  │
│ │ 000030   00000000  1A020000  00000000  00000000  .............  │
│ │ 000040   00000000  00000000  00000000  00000000  .............  │
│ │ 000050   00000000  00000000  00000000  59010008  .........Y...  │
│ │ 000060   00005901  59090000  00005909  00000000  ..Y.Y....Y...  │
│ │ 000070   59090000  00005909  00000000  59090000  Y.....Y....Y..  │
│ │ 000080   8E006709  00001200  79090000  00007909  ..g....y.....y.  │
│ │ 000090   00000000  79090000  00007909  00000000  .....y....y...  │
│ │ 0000A0   79090000  8A008309  00000A00  79090000  y.....â.....y..  │
│ │ 0000B0   00008D09  00004900  D6090000  0000D609  ..ì...I.π.....π. │
│ │ 0000C0   00000000  D6090000  0000D609  00000000  ...π....π.....  │
│ │ 0000D0   D6090000  0000D609  00000000  D6090000  π....π....π..  │
│ │ 0000E0   0000D609  00000000  D6090000  0200D009  ..π....π...+.  │
│ │ 0000F0   00000000  D8090000  0000D809  00000000  ...+....+....  │
│ │ 000100   D8090000  0000D809  00000000  D8090000  +....+....+...  │
│ │ 000110   1E00F609  00003400  2A0A0000  2B00F609  ..÷...4.*...+.÷. │
│ │ 000120   00000000  59090000  00000000  00000000  ....Y.......  │
│ │ 000130   F6090000  0000F609  00000000  00000200  ÷.....÷.......  │
│ └─ ←┘=PageDown  Esc=Cancel   F9=Hex/ASCII                7:11p ─┘
```

Figure 11.2.
A non-ASCII
text file viewed
with the View
File Contents
option in the
DOS Shell.

Virtually all word processors have the option to save files as pure ASCII text files. Make sure if you use a word processor to edit a DOS file that you use this option.

Never use a word processing program to edit a program file with the .COM or .EXE extension. These files are not DOS text files.

Using EDIT to Edit DOS Text Files

EDIT was introduced in DOS 5; if you have an earlier version of DOS, you must use another text editor.

You can use the DOS Editor (referred to as EDIT) to edit DOS text files. This full-screen text editor is easy to learn, comes with extensive online help, and performs several sophisticated operations, such as global search-and-replace and block operations.

EDIT always stores its files in ASCII text format, so you never have to worry about formatting characters being embedded in your files.

Running EDIT

The EDIT program is stored in a file named EDIT.COM. This program should have been placed in your DOS directory when you installed DOS. To start EDIT from the DOS Shell, follow these steps:

1. Select Editor in the Program List near the bottom of the screen by double-clicking or by highlighting and pressing Enter.

2. When the File to Edit dialog box appears, type the complete location and name of the file you want to edit (for example, C:\AUTOEXEC.BAT) and press Enter (or select OK).

If you use the command prompt, type EDIT and press Enter. If you want to load a specific file automatically, type the command, a space, and the path and name of the file you want to edit. For example, type:

```
EDIT C:\AUTOEXEC.BAT
```

The file you specified (if it exists) appears on-screen, ready for editing, as shown in Figure 11.3.

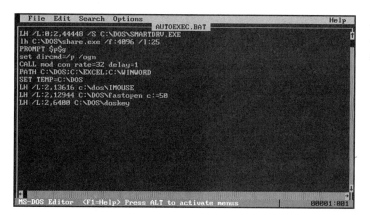

Figure 11.3. EDIT's editing screen.

Using EDIT's Help Screens

Like the Shell, EDIT offers context-sensitive help. You can get to the help screen by pressing F1 at any time or by selecting Help from the upper-right corner of the screen (by clicking or pressing Alt+H).

EDIT also offers a Survival Guide, which you can view by pressing F1 when no menu or option is selected. You can also access the Survival Guide by running EDIT without providing the name of the file to edit (either by entering the command EDIT alone at the command prompt or by leaving the Open File dialog box empty when starting EDIT from the Shell).

Navigating in the Survival Guide, and the entire EDIT help system, is similar to navigating in the MS-DOS help system, described in Chapter 7, "DOS Essentials and Tips."

Basic Menu Operations

Using EDIT's menus is similar to using the menus in the DOS Shell. From the keyboard, take the following steps:

1. Press the Alt key or F10 to activate the Menu bar.

2. Press the first letter of the menu you want to view.

3. Use the arrow keys to position the highlight bar on the option you want, and then press Enter.

As with the DOS Shell, if you are using a mouse, simply point to and then click in the Menu bar on the name of the menu you want to view. Then point to and click on the menu option you want.

Typing in EDIT

For practice, start a new file in EDIT called PRACTICE.TXT. Before you begin typing text in your practice file, you should realize that EDIT is not a word processor—you will not want to use it to create lengthy or complex documents. EDIT's most noticeable limitations are:

No word wrap—When you type more than 80 characters on one line, the words don't automatically wrap to the next line. Instead, your characters are entered on the same line, and your screen display shifts to the right.

No undo feature—If you accidentally delete a block of text, you cannot recover it; you have to retype the entire block.

No automatic backup—When you change an existing file and then quit the editor, EDIT does not create a backup of the original file.

The word-wrap limitation requires an additional comment. If you load ASCII files created by word processors that do not insert carriage returns at the end of their screen lines (that is, that use automatic word wrap), EDIT extends those lines off the right side of the screen until it reads a carriage return. Thus, your document might have a width of several thousand characters—not an ideal size for viewing on an 80-column display! When you use your word processor, remember to press ↵ at the end of each line (instead of relying on automatic word wrap) so that your document won't have such wide lines.

To create a practice file, type the following text. (Remember, you must press Enter at the end of each line of text to move to the next line. Press Enter twice if you want an extra blank line.)

```
Knowledge is of two kinds.
We know a subject ourselves,
or we know where we can find
information about it.

Boswell, Life of Johnson,
1775
```

When you finish, your screen should look like Figure 11.4.

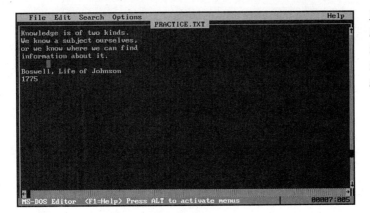

Figure 11.4. Some sample text typed on the EDIT screen.

I will refer to this sample file at times in the rest of this chapter.

Cursor Movement in EDIT

In EDIT, you use two sets of keyboard commands for most actions—a Microsoft set and a WordStar-compatible set. If you already know the WordStar editing commands, you can use most of the functions of EDIT immediately. Table 11.1 includes the complete list of keyboard commands for moving the editing cursor through your text.

Table 11.1. EDIT's cursor-movement keys.

Action	Microsoft Keystrokes	WordStar-Compatible Keystrokes
Left one character	←	Ctrl+S
Right one character	→	Ctrl+D
Left one word	Ctrl+←	Ctrl+A
Right one word	Ctrl+→	Ctrl+F
Up one line	↑	Ctrl+E
Down one line	↓	Ctrl+X
First indention of current line	Home	
Beginning of current line	Ctrl+Q,S	
Beginning of next line	Ctrl+Enter	Ctrl+J
End of line	End	Ctrl+Q,D
Top of screen	Ctrl+Q,E	
Bottom of screen	Ctrl+Q,X	
Sets bookmarks (maximum of 4)	Ctrl+K,0–3	
Accesses set bookmarks	Ctrl+Q,0–3	

EDIT has a built-in feature—bookmarks—that you can use to move the cursor quickly around the screen. Bookmarks are preset locations in your document that you can access by a simple combination of keys.

For example, to set a bookmark, move the cursor to a location in the first line on your screen, and press

Ctrl+K

Then press a number from 0 through 3. If, for example, you place the 0 bookmark in line 1 and the 1 bookmark in line 6, you can instantly move the editing cursor to bookmark 0 by pressing

Ctrl+Q, 0

and then quickly move to bookmark 1 by pressing

Ctrl+Q, 1

You can insert as many as four bookmarks on a screen at any time. Although you probably don't need this feature on a standard 25-line display or if you use a mouse, it can be helpful for keyboard users with high-resolution VGA monitors. Note that the bookmarks do not stay with the file after you quit the editor.

Text Scrolling in Edit

EDIT also has both Microsoft keystrokes and WordStar-compatible keystrokes for scrolling text when you have more text than can fit on a single screen (see Table 11.2).

Table 11.2. The text-scrolling keys.

Action	Microsoft Keystrokes	WordStar-Compatible Keystrokes
Up one line	Ctrl+↑	Ctrl+W
Down one line	Ctrl+↓	Ctrl+Z
Up one page	PgUp	Ctrl+R
Down one page	PgDn	Ctrl+C
Left one window	Ctrl+PgUp	
Right one window	Ctrl+PgDn	

If you are using a mouse, you also can use the vertical scroll bar (or drag the white part of the scroll bar, called the Slider box) to move toward the beginning or end of your file. You click the horizontal scroll bar (or drag the Slider box) to move the display right or left on a long line.

Because EDIT doesn't have word wrap but can load documents with lines longer than 80 columns, you might need to use the Ctrl+PgDn key combination (or click the horizontal scroll bar with the mouse) to view the text at the end of a long line.

Editing a Document

EDIT includes a full array of editing commands. However, for editing simple files, such as AUTOEXEC.BAT and CONFIG.SYS, or for jotting down quick notes, you can get by with a few basic editing keys. Type your text and erase any mistakes with the commands listed in Table 11.3.

Table 11.3. The basic editing keys in EDIT.

Key	Purpose
Backspace or Ctrl+H	Delete character to the left of the cursor
Del or Ctrl+G	Delete character at the cursor
Ctrl+T	Delete from the cursor to the end of the word
Ctrl+Y	Delete entire line
Ctrl+QY	Delete from the cursor to the end of the line
Ins or Ctrl+V	Switch between Insert and Overwrite modes

Selecting (Highlighting) Text

You can more efficiently perform most editing operations that involve more than a few characters if you select, or highlight, the text first. To select text, follow these instructions:

1. Position the cursor on the first (or last) character you want to select.

2. Hold down the Shift key.

3. Move the cursor in the appropriate direction using the arrow keys.

Or, using a mouse, move the mouse cursor to the beginning of the text you want to highlight, and drag to the end of the text you want to highlight.

Table 11.4 lists all of EDIT's text-selection keys.

Table 11.4. The text-selection keys.

Action	Microsoft Keystrokes	WordStar-Compatible Keystrokes
Left one character	Shift+←	
Right one character	Shift+→	
Left one word	Shift+Ctrl+←	
Right one word	Shift+Ctrl+→	
Current line	Shift+↓	
Line above	Shift+↑	
Screen up	Shift+PgUp	
Screen down	Shift+PgDn	
To beginning of file	Shift+Ctrl+Home	
To end of file	Shift+Ctrl+End	

To cancel a selection (to "unselect" selected text), press any cursor movement key. Or if you are using a mouse, click anywhere in the EDIT window.

Block Operations on Selected Text

To move text, highlight the text you want to move, and then select Cut from the Edit menu. Move the cursor to the point at which you want to insert the text, and select Paste from the Edit menu.

To copy text, highlight the text and select Copy from the Edit menu. Move the cursor to the point to which you want to copy the text, and select Paste from the Edit menu.

To delete text, highlight the text and select Cut or Clear from the Edit menu, or merely press the Del key. Using the Cut option saves the material to the Clipboard, whereas using Clear or the Del key does not save the material to the Clipboard.

When you use the Cut or Copy options, material is placed on the Clipboard. Material on the Clipboard can be pasted back into the document. However, EDIT, like most programs, keeps only one body of information on the Clipboard at a time. If you place one item on the Clipboard, it disappears for good when you place another item on the Clipboard.

Table 11.5 lists all the pertinent commands for these basic EDIT editing procedures and other related operations.

Table 11.5. The insert and copy keys.

Action	Microsoft Keystrokes	WordStar-Compatible Keystrokes
Toggles Insert and Overstrike modes	Ins	Ctrl+V
Copies selected text to the Clipboard	Ctrl+Ins	
Moves selected text to the Clipboard	Shift+Del	
Moves current line to the Clipboard	Ctrl+Y	
Moves text from cursor to the end of line to the Clipboard	Ctrl+Q,Y	
Pastes contents of the Clipboard to current cursor position	Shift+Ins	
Inserts a blank line below the cursor position	End+Enter	
Inserts a blank line above the cursor position	Home,Ctrl+N	

Finding Text

EDIT also contains easy-to-use Find (search) and Change (global search-and-replace) commands. For example, if you want to see whether your text uses the word *we,* first pull down the Search menu, and then select the Find option. Notice that the word at the current cursor location (in your text) automatically is inserted into the Find What field. (See Figure 11.5.)

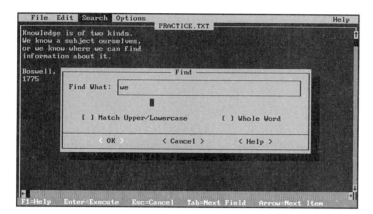

Figure 11.5.
The Find box
in EDIT.

In this case, type we in the Find What field. You can specify a string of as many as 127 characters. For strings longer than the box, characters scroll to the left.

Next, tab to the Match Upper/Lowercase check box. You use this check box to specify whether the search should be case-sensitive. If you select this check box (by clicking it with the mouse or by tabbing to it and pressing the Spacebar), EDIT will find only two matches for we (in the third line). If you don't check this box, EDIT will find three matches—because it also finds the We in the second line.

Finally, tab to the next check box, Whole Word. If you check this box, the search finds strings only if entire words match other entire words; that is, a search for we finds only that word. However, if you do not check the box, a search for we not only finds We and we, but also the we in Boswell (in the second to last line).

After you enter your settings, select OK. A highlight in the work area immediately selects the first occurrence of your text (if any exists). To see whether the document contains other occurrences of your text, select the Repeat Last Find option from the Search menu, or press the F3 function key.

275

Notice that the cursor highlights each instance of your string and cycles through the document again if you continue to press F3.

Replacing Text

If you need to change all occurrences of a string, you can use the global search-and-replace feature called Change (see Figure 11.6).

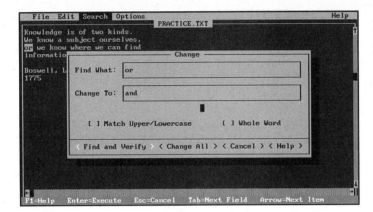

Figure 11.6. The Change box in EDIT.

For example, if you decide to change the word *or* to the word *and* throughout the document, highlight an instance of or in the text, and then select Change from the Search menu. Notice that EDIT has already inserted the word into the Find What field. (You also can type the word into the field.)

Next, tab to the Change To field and type and. The string in this field replaces all occurrences in the document of the string in the Find What field (or). Again, be careful with the settings you choose for the Match Upper/Lowercase and Whole Word check boxes. If you don't select Whole Word, some global replaces can produce unpredictable results. For example, this exercise would result in the following "word":

Infandmation

That's probably not what you had in mind.

After you've filled in all the fields and set the check boxes, begin the search-and-replace operation by selecting either the Find and Verify or the Change All button at the bottom of the dialog box. If you are sure you want to replace every instance of a string, select Change All. EDIT changes all occurrences of the string in your document and then displays a dialog box telling you that the operation is complete. Select OK to return to the work area.

If you are not sure whether to change every occurrence of a string, select the Find and Verify button. Table 11.6 summarizes EDIT's Find and Change commands.

Table 11.6. The find and change keys.

Action	Microsoft Keystrokes	WordStar-Compatible Keystrokes
Find (searches for text)		Ctrl+L
Repeat Last Find	F3	Ctrl+Q,A
Change (changes text)		Ctrl+Q,F

Printing a Document

When you finish typing and editing your text, you might want to print a copy of your efforts. To do so, select the Print option from the File menu. This opens the Print dialog box (shown in Figure 11.7), which displays the following two option buttons:

```
( ) Selected Text Only
(·) Complete Document
```

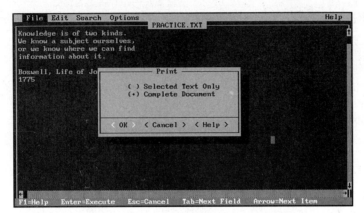

Figure 11.7.
The Print
dialog box in
EDIT.

If you have not selected (highlighted) any text in the document, EDIT makes the Complete Document button the default option. (The bullet within the parentheses indicates which button is currently active.) However, if you previously highlighted text within the document, EDIT displays the Selected Text Only option as the default.

Saving a File

To save a document, select Save from the File pull-down menu.

Because you specified the name of the file (PRACTICE.TXT) before you began this example session, EDIT automatically saves your text (including any changes) to that file. After EDIT saves your work to disk, it redisplays the main work area.

If you start EDIT without specifying a file name, and then type some text, and then try to save the file using the Save option, EDIT displays a Save dialog box.

The Save dialog box contains several fields. If you want to save your file in the current directory (which is listed below the words File Name), type a valid DOS name into the File Name field, and then press Enter or select OK. If you want to specify another directory or drive, move the cursor to the Dir/Drives field, and use the up- and down-arrow keys to select the appropriate path name for the file. If you are currently in a subdirectory, select the .. symbol to move to the parent, or next higher, directory. (Of course, you can always type the complete path name into the File Name box without accessing the Dir/Drives field.) After you enter the correct name and location, select OK.

Creating a New Text File

To start a new file, select the File menu and then choose the New command. If you have made changes to your previous file but have not saved them, EDIT prompts you to do so.

EDIT immediately saves the changes, closes the file, and opens a new file. Because you have not yet named this new document, the title area near the top of the screen reads Untitled.

To exit EDIT after you've created and saved your file, select the File menu (Alt-F), and then press X or select the Exit option. This returns you to the command line if you started EDIT from the DOS prompt, or to the DOS Shell if that is where you started.

If you have not yet saved your changes to disk, EDIT opens the Save dialog box to enable you to do so. If you have saved your work and not altered it, you exit immediately.

Customizing the Editor

The Options selection in the Menu bar pulls down a menu that enables you to change some EDIT display settings. If you have a color monitor, you can select the Display option to change the current

EDIT screen colors. You can also use this option to change two other display settings.

Both the EDIT.COM and QBASIC.EXE programs use the same initialization file: QBASIC.INI. Therefore, any display changes you make to EDIT (such as changing colors) automatically affect the default QBASIC screen, and vice versa.

Changing Colors

When you select Display from the Options menu, the dialog box that appears is divided into two main sections—the Colors field and the Display Options field. The highlighted colors in the Foreground and Background boxes of the Colors field are your current color selections.

To change colors, move the flashing underline cursor to the Background box, and use the arrow keys (or the scroll bars) to move the highlight, thus changing the EDIT background color. Notice that the left side of the Colors field actually shows the new color (and the current foreground color) as it will look on your screen.

Remember that whatever changes you make in this dialog box are saved in the QBASIC.INI initialization file and also affect the QBASIC environment.

Other Display Options

If you use a mouse, be sure that the scroll-bars check box has an X in it. If you use the keyboard, you can turn off the scroll bars by toggling off the X. This gives you an extra column and row in which you can type text.

Inside the horizontal and vertical scroll bars is a small box that moves as you move the cursor through your document. This Slider box is a helpful indicator of your current location in a lengthy document. Because the scroll bars offer this convenient feature, you might want to keep scroll bars displayed even if you are not using a mouse.

The Tab Stops field determines how many spaces a Tab keystroke advances the cursor. The default setting is eight spaces, an indention used by many programmers. If you use EDIT strictly for writing DOS files, notes, and letters, you might want to reset this field to five spaces, a standard paragraph indention.

When you finish changing the settings in the Display dialog box, select OK to initiate your changes. Select Cancel to return to the original settings.

Specifying a Help Path

The Help Path option enables you to set the path to the EDIT.HLP file in case you are using the EDIT program in a directory other than the directory that contains the help file. You probably won't need to set this field, because the default installation places both EDIT.COM and EDIT.HLP in the \DOS directory. It also specifies this directory in the system PATH command set in your AUTOEXEC.BAT file. However, if you decide to relocate the help file to another directory, you can specify that directory name in this dialog box.

Command-Line Switches

You can control some of EDIT's display features when you start the program from the command line. The following switches to the EDIT command modify the setup of the editor's display:

/B enables you to use a monochrome monitor with a color graphics card or see EDIT in monochrome on a color monitor.

/G executes a fast update of a CGA monitor. If your monitor displays flickering dots, your hardware doesn't support this option. You will have to restart EDIT without the /G option.

/H displays the maximum number of lines your hardware permits.

/NOHI enables you to use a monitor that does not support high intensity. Do not use this switch with Compaq laptop computers.

If you have an EGA or a VGA monitor, you probably will use the /H switch often. This switch lets EDIT display 43 (EGA) to 60 lines (VGA) of text at a time, which is most helpful when you are creating or editing long documents and want to see as much text on-screen as possible. To use this switch (or any of the others), type a command line similar to the following line:

```
EDIT filename /H
```

 ## Troubleshooting

The following problems might occur as you edit DOS files. Look for the solution here, and follow instructions to solve the problem.

- If you get a Bad command or file name error message, you might have tried to run a program (perhaps EDIT) that is not available on the current drive or directory. Try a different diskette, disk drive, or directory.

- If DOS ignores changes in your AUTOEXEC.BAT or CONFIG.SYS file, one of following problems might have occurred:

  You might have accidentally saved the file in a directory other than the root directory where AUTOEXEC.BAT and

CONFIG.SYS belong. A likely mistake would be to save these files in the directory in which EDIT is located, typically the \DOS directory. Find the files and copy them to the appropriate directory.

If you were using a word processor, you might have saved the files in a proprietary format which DOS was unable to read. Reopen the files with your word processor, and save them in ASCII format.

You expected the changes to these files to go into effect immediately. However, they will not go into effect until you reboot your computer.

Summary

As you read future chapters, you might want to create or edit DOS text files, particularly the CONFIG.SYS and AUTOEXEC.BAT files. To do so, use any text editor, any word processor, or the DOS EDIT editor. In summary:

- If you use a word processor, you must save your file as an ASCII text file.

- The easiest way to see whether a file contains word processing formatting characters is to use the DOS Shell's View File Contents option or the command prompt TYPE command.

- If a text file contains formatting characters, you must remove them or DOS will not be able to read the file.

- The DOS 6 full-screen EDIT editor never stores formatting characters in a file.

- After editing either the CONFIG.SYS or the AUTOEXEC.BAT file, be sure to store these files in the root directory of the appropriate hard disk drive or diskette; otherwise, DOS ignores any changes you've made.

Alan Simpson's
DOS SECRETS UNLEASHED

CHAPTER 12

Simple Batch Programs

Batch programs are DOS text files that contain a group, or batch, of commands that DOS executes in sequence. This chapter provides the basics about batch programs and shows you how to create and run them. Chapter 29, "Batch Programs Unleashed," provides more detail about batch programs.

Why Are Batch Programs Important?

Batch programs are important because they can save time and effort. Batch programs can execute a series of commands flawlessly, freeing you from having to type each command without error and in the correct sequence. They also can automatically respond to certain conditions so that, in effect, they think for you.

The best-known batch program is the AUTOEXEC.BAT file. This file automatically runs when you start your computer and sets your computer to run the way you want. If you want your prompt to look a certain way, you can include that information in the AUTOEXEC.BAT file. If you want to be asked whether to run a specific program when you start your computer, that too can be included in the AUTOEXEC.BAT file.

AUTOEXEC.BAT is the only batch program that runs automatically. When you start your computer, DOS looks for a file called AUTOEXEC.BAT and automatically runs it. All other batch programs have to be either started from the command prompt or called from within other batch programs.

Batch programs can be as simple as one-line files that load a particular program. Or they can be complex programs that, for example, install and configure application programs.

Writing batch programs is similar to writing simple programs. DOS includes several programming commands you can include in batch programs that control the timing, presentation, and execution of commands in your batch program. These are discussed in detail in Chapter 29, "Batch programs Unleashed." But many batch programs are relatively simple affairs that don't use many of those tools.

Creating and Storing Batch Programs

Batch programs must be stored as ASCII text files. Therefore, you can use any of the techniques described in Chapter 11, "Creating and Editing Files," to create and edit your own batch programs. The name you assign to a batch program must follow the basic rules of all DOS file names—no more than eight characters in length, no blank spaces, and no punctuation other than the underscore and hyphen. The file-name extension must be .BAT.

When naming a batch program, do not give it the same base name as a .COM or an .EXE file. For example, if you have the dBASE program on your computer, do not create a batch program named DBASE.BAT. Otherwise, when you enter the command DBASE, DOS runs only DBASE.BAT or DBASE.EXE, but not both. Whether it runs DBASE.BAT or DBASE.EXE depends on the current directory and PATH statement. On any single directory, DOS gives priority first to a file with the .COM extension, then to a file with the .EXE extension, followed by a file with the .BAT extension. For example, if the current directory contains both a file named DBASE.EXE and a file named DBASE.BAT, the DBASE.EXE file will be executed when you type DBASE and press Enter.

On the other hand, if you have files named DBASE.COM and DBASE.BAT in two different directories, DOS runs whichever one it encounters on the current directory. If neither of those files is in the current directory, DOS runs whichever one it encounters first in the current PATH statement, regardless of whether it has the .COM, .EXE, or .BAT extension.

Although you shouldn't give batch programs the same base name as a program file, you still should give your batch programs names that are easy to remember. For example, if your batch program starts dBASE, you can name your batch program DBF.BAT. DBF is the extension used for dBASE data files. A batch program that loads WordPerfect can be called DOC.BAT for similar reasons. These names are easy to remember and refer to a specific application, but don't duplicate the application's base file name.

Because batch programs provide useful tools to make your work easier, they should be stored where they are easily accessible. Keep in mind, however, that if a batch program includes any DOS external commands, such as CHKDSK, TREE, SORT, FIND, or MORE, the associated DOS program files (CHKDSK.COM, TREE.COM, SORT.EXE, FIND.EXE, and MORE.COM) must also be accessible from the current drive, directory, or path.

Remember that DOS executes commands in a batch program exactly as though they were typed at the command prompt. Therefore, if your batch program contains a misspelled command or an external command that is not available from the current drive, directory, or defined path, DOS displays the usual Bad command or file name error message when it attempts to execute that command.

To ensure easy access, you might want to create a directory under the root directory called \UTILS and store all your batch programs there. To make sure that these batch programs are always accessible, place the \UTILS directory in your PATH statement. Assuming you do not give your batch programs the same base name as your program files, you then can launch your batch programs from any directory.

Creating Your Own Batch Programs

You'll create several useful batch programs in this chapter. Table
12.1 shows the external DOS commands used by the sample batch
programs. Before you continue, make sure that these program files
are stored on your hard drive. They should have been installed in
the same directory as all your other DOS programs, typically the
C:\DOS directory.

Table 12.1. External DOS commands used by the sample batch programs.

Command Used	File Required
CHKDSK	CHKDSK.EXE
EDIT	EDIT.COM*
FIND	FIND.EXE
MORE	MORE.COM

* Required only if you use EDIT to create and edit batch programs.

A Simple Practice Batch Program

A good practice batch program is one that is simple to create and
use. I'll start with a batch program that contains only two simple
commands—DIR /W and VER. You can name this simple batch program D.BAT. Admittedly, D.BAT won't dazzle you with its power;
still, it demonstrates many of the fundamental principles of batch
programs.

To use the DOS EDIT editor to create this batch program, see the
following steps. (If, instead, you use another editor or word processor, remember to save the file in ASCII text format.)

1. Type EDIT \UTILS\D.BAT and press Enter.

2. Type DIR /W in the first line and press Enter.

3. Type VER.

4. To pull down the File menu, press Alt+F.

5. To exit EDIT, press X.

6. Press Y to save your changes and end the EDIT program.

7. To verify that the file was saved, type TYPE \UTILS\D.BAT and press Enter.

The batch program that appears on-screen consists of the following two lines:

```
DIR /W
VER
```

Running Your Batch Program

To run a batch program, use the same basic technique that you use to run any program—type the file name without the extension, and press Enter. In this example, press D and then press Enter.

You can also use the DOS Shell to run the D.BAT batch program. First, use the File List to access the drive or directory that contains the file. Then highlight D.BAT in the Files List and press Enter (or double-click the mouse).

This batch program displays a wide listing of the file names on the current diskette or directory (the DIR /W command) and then the current version of DOS (the VER command), as shown in Figure 12.1. (Your screen, of course, shows different file names.) Note that the figure shows the exact series of events that took place.

Although this is not a terribly exciting batch program, it does provide one convenience: whenever you want to see a wide directory listing, you enter the letter D at the command prompt, rather than DIR /W. You save a few keystrokes, which is very handy if you don't like to (or can't) type.

If you made a mistake and your batch program does not work properly, use EDIT (or another text editor) to make corrections.

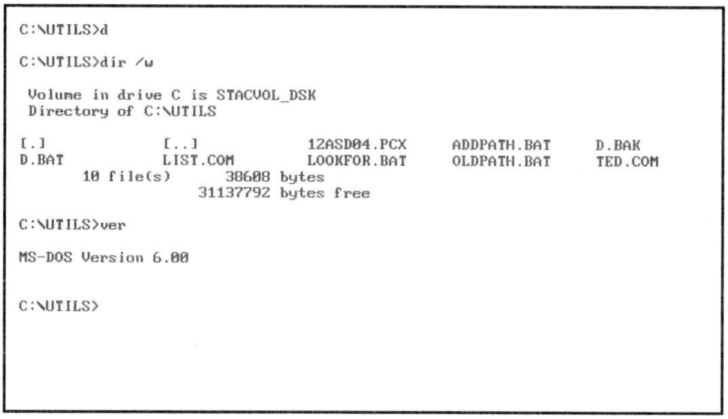

```
C:\UTILS>d

C:\UTILS>dir /w

 Volume in drive C is STACVOL_DSK
 Directory of C:\UTILS

[.]            [..]            12ASD04.PCX     ADDPATH.BAT     D.BAK
D.BAT          LIST.COM        LOOKFOR.BAT     OLDPATH.BAT     TED.COM
        10 file(s)       38608 bytes
                      31137792 bytes free

C:\UTILS>ver

MS-DOS Version 6.00


C:\UTILS>
```

*Figure 12.1.
Results of
running the
D.BAT batch
program.*

Basic Batch Program Techniques

The following sections describe basic batch program techniques you can use when creating batch programs.

Using Echo to Display Text

You can include the ECHO command to send a message from a batch program to the screen. For practice, modify the simple D.BAT batch program so that it sends the rather frivolous message That's all folks! to the screen after it executes the DIR /W and VER commands. Here are the steps to follow if you are using the EDIT editor:

1. At the DOS command prompt, type EDIT \UTILS\D.BAT and press Enter.

2. To move the editing cursor to the end of the file, press Ctrl+End or click on the third line with the mouse.

3. Type ECHO That's all folks!.

4. Select Exit from the File menu. Press Y to save your changes.

5. To verify that the file was saved, type TYPE \UTILS\D.BAT and press Enter.

To run your modified D.BAT batch program, type D at the command prompt and press Enter. Your new batch program still displays a wide directory of file names and shows the current DOS version number. In addition, these lines appear beneath the file names:

```
C\UTIL>ECHO That's all folks!
That's all folks!
```

The ECHO command displayed the That's all folks! message, but it did so twice, as Figure 12.2 shows. That happened because DOS automatically displays commands stored in batch programs before it executes them. That is, DOS displayed the entire command ECHO That's all folks!, executed that command, and displayed the results of the command—the sentence That's all folks!.

```
C:\UTILS>d

C:\UTILS>dir /w

 Volume in drive C is STACVOL_DSK
 Directory of C:\UTILS

[.]            [..]           12ASD04.PCX    ADDPATH.BAT    D.BAK
D.BAT          LIST.COM       LOOKFOR.BAT    OLDPATH.BAT    TED.COM
       10 file(s)       38634 bytes
                     31129600 bytes free

C:\UTILS>ver

MS-DOS Version 6.00

C:\UTILS>echo That's all folks!
That's all folks!

C:\UTILS>
```

*Figure 12.2.
Results of
running the
D.BAT batch
program with
the ECHO
command
added.*

Preventing Double Echoes

If you are using DOS 3.3 or later, you can prevent DOS from displaying a command before executing it by preceding the command with an @ symbol. (If you are using an earlier version of DOS, you can do so by putting the command ECHO OFF at the top of the batch program, as discussed in the section "Hiding All Commands" later in this chapter.)

If you are using DOS 3.3 or later, use the following steps to change the ECHO command in the D.BAT batch program to @ECHO:

1. Type EDIT \UTILS\D.BAT and then press Enter.

2. Move the editing cursor to the third line of the file, and at the beginning of the line, type the @ symbol.

3. Select Exit from the File menu. Press Y to save your changes.

4. To verify that the file was saved, type TYPE \UTILS\D.BAT and press Enter.

To run the new batch program, press D and Enter. This time, notice that the That's all folks! message appears only once, at the bottom of the list of file names, as shown in Figure 12.3.

```
C:\UTILS>d

C:\UTILS>dir /w

 Volume in drive C is STACVOL_DSK
 Directory of C:\UTILS

[.]              [..]             12ASD04.PCX    ADDPATH.BAT    D.BAT
D.BAK            LIST.COM         LOOKFOR.BAT    OLDPATH.BAT    TED.COM
       10 file(s)        38596 bytes
                      31129600 bytes free

C:\UTILS>ver

MS-DOS Version 6.00

That's all folks!

C:\UTILS>
```

Figure 12.3.
The @ECHO
message
appears only
once in
D.BAT.

Using Remarks to Comment Batch Programs

Although the D.BAT file is relatively simple, batch programs can be quite large and complicated (as you will see in later examples). To make it easier for you—and for others who use your batch program—to understand the purpose of commands in the batch program, add *comments* (also called *remarks*) to the file. A comment is like a note to yourself. DOS realizes that the comment is only for humans to read and therefore completely ignores it.

To add a comment to a batch program, start the line with the command REM (short for remark).

> The REM command is also a useful debugging tool for temporarily deactivating commands in batch programs and your CONFIG.SYS file. For example, if you are having trouble running DOS as you would like and you suspect that a driver or program is causing a compatibility problem, use your editor and type REM at the beginning of the line in which that program or driver is listed. When you restart your computer, that driver or program does not load. If DOS then operates as you want, you have found the problem.

If you are using DOS 3.3, you can use the command @REM to put a comment in a batch program, which prevents DOS from displaying the remark when it executes the batch program. You can test this now by adding a comment to the D.BAT batch program using the following steps:

1. Type EDIT D.BAT and press Enter.

2. Move the editing cursor to the third line of the file, or click on the first character of the third line with the mouse.

3. To insert a comment above the third line (if you are using DOS Version 3.3 or later), type the command @REM Show closing message.... (If you are using an earlier version, leave out the leading @ sign.) Press Enter.

4. Select Exit from the File menu, and press Y to save your changes.

5. To verify that the file was saved, type TYPE \UTILS\D.BAT
   and press Enter.

You can test the D.BAT batch program by entering the command
D at the command prompt. If you are using DOS 3.3 or later and
added the @REM command, you will see that the D.BAT file does its
job without displaying the comment to the right of the REM command.

Later examples use REM comments to label each batch program
with a name and a general purpose. These comments at the top of
the file make it easier for you to determine which batch program
you are viewing in the figures in this book.

Hiding All Commands

Regardless of which version of DOS you are using, you can prevent
batch program commands from being displayed before execution
by adding the ECHO OFF command to the top of your batch program.
ECHO OFF tells DOS not to echo the commands to the command
prompt, but instead to display the results of the commands.

If you are using DOS 3.3 or later, you can make the first command in your batch program @ECHO OFF, which prevents even the
ECHO OFF command itself from being echoed. To test the ECHO OFF
command, add the command to D.BAT. Your batch program should
now contain the following commands (but without the @ signs if you
are using DOS 3.2 or earlier):

```
@ECHO OFF
DIR %1 /W
VER
@REM Show closing message...
@ECHO That's all folks!
```

When you enter D to run the batch program, notice that the commands from the batch program are not displayed; only the results
of each command appear on-screen, as Figure 12.4 shows.

```
C:\UTILS>d

 Volume in drive C is STACVOL_DSK
 Directory of C:\UTILS

 [.]            [..]            ADDPATH.BAT     D.BAT        D.BAK
LIST.COM     LOOKFOR.BAT     OLDPATH.BAT     TED.COM
      9 file(s)        25778 bytes
                       31145984 bytes free

MS-DOS Version 6.00

That's all folks!
C:\UTILS>
```

Figure 12.4. Only the results of commands from D.BAT are displayed.

Don't include the ECHO OFF or @ECHO OFF command when you first build a batch program. You are better off seeing the commands as they are executed so that if the batch program fails to run properly, you can see which command caused the error. Only after you have created, tested, and perfected your batch program should you insert the ECHO OFF or @ECHO OFF command at the top of the file.

For the remaining batch program examples in this book, I assume that you are using one of the later versions of DOS 3.3 or later. That is, I include @ signs in front of certain commands to prevent them from being echoed on-screen.

Interrupting a Batch Program

You can stop any executing batch program by pressing Ctrl+Break or Ctrl+C. DOS then displays the message Terminate batch job? (Y/N)?. Press Y to stop the batch program execution and return to the command prompt, or press N to resume the batch program execution.

Passing Parameters to a Batch Program

So far, the D.BAT file is little more than a shortcut for typing the longer command DIR /W and displaying the current DOS version number. However, it lacks one feature that the DIR command offers: the capability of specifying types of files. For example, with DIR, you can enter a command such as DIR *.EXE /W to limit the listing of files to those that have the .EXE extension. However, if you enter the command D *.EXE, DOS still lists the names of all the files in the current diskette or directory because it ignores the *.EXE.

Change the D.BAT file so that it accepts and uses a parameter (additional text entered at the command prompt), such as the *.EXE specifier in the previous example. The basic technique is to use percent variables as placeholders for additional command-line entries. The first extra entry is always named %1, the second is named %2, and so on. When you type a batch program name and additional parameters on the command line, each parameter passed to the % variables must be separated by a blank space.

To permit a single parameter to be passed to the DIR command in the D.BAT file, edit the first line of the file to read

```
DIR %1 /W
```

Type TYPE \UTILS\D.BAT and press Enter to check the contents of the batch program. If you are using DOS 3.3 or later, your batch program should contain the following commands (with all the blank spaces in the right places):

```
DIR %1 /W
VER
@REM Show closing message...
@ECHO That's all folks!
```

If you are using version 3.2 or earlier of DOS, your D.BAT batch program should look the same, but without the @ symbol in front of the REM and ECHO commands.

Now, try using a file specifier with the D command. For example, when you enter the command D *.COM, DOS now displays only the names of files (if any) on the current directory that have the extension .COM. If D.BAT is the only file on your current directory, try viewing the contents of a different directory. For example, type the command

D C:*.COM

to view the .COM files on the root directory of your hard disk. Or type the command

D C:\DOS*.COM

to view the names of the .COM files on your hard disk's DOS directory.

D.BAT now has the flexibility of the DIR command. That's because the parameter you type next to the D command gets passed to the DIR command in your batch program. For example, look closely at Figure 12.5; notice at the top of the screen that I entered the command D C:\DOS*.COM to view .COM files in the DOS directory. Also notice that the batch program substituted the C:\DOS*.COM parameter into its own DIR command (in place of the %1 variable).

```
C:\UTILS>d c:\dos\*.com

C:\UTILS>dir c:\dos\*.com /w

 Volume in drive C is STACVOL_DSK
 Directory of C:\DOS

CHOICE.COM      COMMAND.COM     DISKCOMP.COM    DISKCOPY.COM    DOSKEY.COM
DOSSHELL.COM    EDIT.COM        FORMAT.COM      GRAPHICS.COM    HELP.COM
KEYB.COM        LOADFIX.COM     MODE.COM        MORE.COM        MOUSE.COM
SYS.COM         TREE.COM        UNFORMAT.COM    VSAFE.COM
        19 file(s)      320644 bytes
                      31121408 bytes free

C:\UTILS>ver

MS-DOS Version 6.00

That's all folks!

C:\UTILS>
```

*Figure 12.5.
Results of
entering* D
C:\DOS*.COM.

What happens if you enter the old D command without specifying a drive, directory, or file name? The batch program acts exactly as it did before. DOS substitutes nothing for %1, so the command that DOS executes is again DIR /W.

Try passing two parameters to the D batch program. Notice that when you type the command

D *.* /S

the /S has no effect, because it is a second optional parameter on the command line (that is, a blank space separates it from the first parameter, *.*). D.DAT ignores this second parameter because the batch program contains no %2 variable to handle it.

> For some batch programs, you might want to add more variables than you immediately need. This enables you to make more sophisticated use of the batch program later.

Creating Some Sample Batch Programs

Now that you have some basic tools to help you create and develop batch programs, you can move ahead and start creating more practical and more powerful batch programs.

A Batch Program to Search for Files

By using the CHKDSK and FIND commands, you can search every directory on a hard disk. For example, entering the command CHKDSK /V ¦ FIND /I "budget" displays all the files that contain the name budget. However, wouldn't it be easier if you could perform this operation by typing a simple command such as LOOKFOR BUDGET?

> Actually, I wanted to name this batch program FIND.BAT so that I could type the command FIND BUDGET, but because DOS already includes a program named FIND.EXE, this would have created a conflict.

The LOOKFOR.BAT batch program uses three external commands: CHKDSK, FIND, and MORE. Remember, these are external commands and require access to the CHKDSK.COM, FIND.EXE, and MORE.COM files. As discussed earlier in this chapter, these files must be either in the same directory from which you run the batch program or in a directory specified in the PATH command.

1. Type EDIT LOOKFOR.BAT and press Enter.

2. Type @REM **************** LOOKFOR.BAT (type any number of asterisks). Press Enter.

3. Type @REM Searches all directories for a file. Press Enter.

4. Type @ECHO Did you remember to use UPPERCASE? Press Enter.

5. Type @ECHO (press Ctrl+C to cancel) and press Enter.

6. Type @ECHO Searching... and press Enter.

7. Type CHKDSK /V ¦ FIND /I "%1" ¦ MORE and press Enter.

8. Select Exit from the File menu, and press Y to save your changes.

9. Type TYPE LOOKFOR.BAT and press Enter to view the file.

Figure 12.6 shows the completed LOOKFOR.BAT batch program. The asterisks in the first line of the batch program are decorative: They make the name of the batch program stand out. The second line is an explanation of what the batch program does. The three @ECHO commands display messages on-screen as the batch program is executing (as you will soon see).

DOS also offers the /S switch with the DIR command, which you can use instead of CHKDSK /V. Type DIR *.* /S rather than CHKDSK /V.

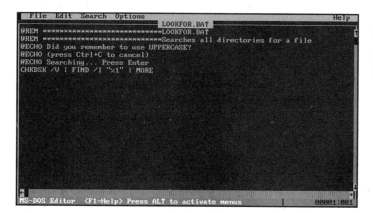

Figure 12.6.
The
LOOKFOR.BAT
batch program.

Notice that in the last command, the %1 variable is not surrounded by blank spaces within the quotation marks of the FIND
command. This is because when you enter a command such as
LOOKFOR BUDGET, you want the word BUDGET to be inserted into the
FIND command without any blank spaces, as follows:

CHKDSK /V ¦ FIND /I "BUDGET"

If you had inserted blank spaces in this example during execution, as shown next,

CHKDSK /V ¦ FIND /I " %1 "

the substitution would result in

CHKDSK /V ¦ FIND /I " BUDGET "

The FIND command would then look for the word BUDGET surrounded
by blank spaces. Of course, because file names cannot contain blank
spaces, the command would never find a matching name.

Notice that the CHKDSK command line includes the MORE
command. This ensures that DOS pauses if LOOKFOR displays
more file names than can fit on one screen. A single keystroke then displays the next screenful of names. (MORE does
not affect the display if all the file names fit on one screen.)

Test this batch program by using LOOKFOR to display the names of all files that have the .BAT extension. Enter the command

```
LOOKFOR .BAT
```

(Be sure to use uppercase letters for .BAT.) After you press Enter (and perhaps wait a while), your screen displays all file names that have the .BAT extension. Figure 12.7 shows the results. Note that the results will be different on your computer.

```
C:\UTILS>LOOKFOR .BAT
(press Ctrl+C to cancel)
Searching... Press Enter

C:\DOS\211FDOSC.BAT
C:\DOS\2592DOSC.BAT
C:\DOS\2E83DOSC.BAT
C:\DOS\5CCBDOSC.BAT
C:\DOS\AUTOEXEC.BAT
C:\GU\GUROCLR.BAT
C:\GU\GUROSET.BAT
C:\STACKER\STACDOS5.BAT
C:\UTILS\ADDPATH.BAT
C:\UTILS\D.BAT
C:\UTILS\OLDPATH.BAT
C:\UTILS\LOOKFOR.BAT
C:\WINDOWS\WAVE\X.BAT
C:\AUTOEXEC.BAT

C:\UTILS>
```

Figure 12.7.
Results of the
LOOKFOR .BAT
command.

Notice at the top of the figure that you can see where I entered the command LOOKFOR .BAT. The next three lines display messages from the ECHO commands in the batch program. The command CHKDSK /V ¦ FIND ".BAT" ¦ MORE is the final command that the batch program executes. Note that the .BAT parameter was substituted into the command in %1 position. The remainder of the screen shows the locations and names of all the files on my hard disk with the .BAT extension.

If your LOOKFOR.BAT batch program is working properly, you might want to insert the @ECHO OFF commands as the first line. This prevents the CHKDSK command line from being displayed on-screen when you use LOOKFOR.BAT in the future.

Because the FIND command does not support the wildcard characters ? and *, you cannot use these with your new LOOKFOR command. However, you can enter any partial file name to achieve the same basic result. For example, LOOKFOR MYTEXT displays all file names that contain the characters MYTEXT. The command LOOKFOR .C displays all file names that contain .C (such as .COM, .CHK, .COS, and so on).

Changing the Path

Suppose that you use many different programs on your computer, and you often need to change your PATH setting. For example, suppose your AUTOEXEC.BAT file assigns the path

```
PATH C:\DOS;C:\WP;C:\UTILS
```

and this path is adequate for your usual needs. Occasionally, however, you use programs that require an expanded path. Rather than force DOS to always search these seldom-used directories, you just type the new PATH command as you require it.

If you regularly need to retype this command, you will find it very tiring. Wouldn't it be better if you could just enter a command like ADDPATH C:\DBASE to add C:\DBASE to your current PATH setting? You can easily create a batch program to provide this feature.

Accessing the DOS Environment

DOS stores the current settings for various commands in an area of memory called the DOS environment (or environment for short). You can examine the contents of the environment at any time. Enter the command SET at the command prompt. DOS then displays your system's environment, as in the following example (yours will be different):

```
COMSPEC=C:\DOS\COMMAND.COM
APPEND=C:\DOS
PROMPT=$P$G

PATH=C:\DOS;C:\WP;C:\UTILS
```

A batch program can copy any information from the environment if you specify the environment variable name within percent signs. For example, if you insert %PATH% in a batch program and then later execute the file, the current path would be substituted for %PATH%. (You'll soon see an example of this.)

A batch program can also use the SET command to store information in the environment. In fact, you can even store information in the environment from the command prompt. To see an example of this, follow these steps:

1. At the command prompt, type SET VAR1=TEST and then press Enter.

2. Type SET and press Enter.

The first step creates an environmental variable called VAR1, which contains the word TEST. The second command displays the current contents of the environment, which now includes

VAR1=TEST

To remove the new variable from the environment, type the command

SET VAR1=

and press Enter. (Enter the SET command again to verify that the variable has been removed.)

What are the practical implications of this? As you'll see, both the %PROMPT% variable and the SET command play an integral part in the new ADDPATH.BAT batch program. Use the following steps to create ADDPATH.BAT:

1. Type EDIT ADDPATH.BAT and press Enter.

2. Type @REM *************** ADDPATH.BAT (use any number of asterisks). Press Enter.

3. Type @REM Extends the current path. Press Enter.

4. Type @REM and remembers the previous path. Press Enter.

5. Type SET EXPATH=%PATH% and press Enter.

6. Type PATH %PATH%;C:\%1 and press Enter (if you do not have a hard disk named C:, substitute a different drive name).

7. Type @ECHO Path is now %PATH% and press Enter.

8. Select Exit from the File menu, and press Y to save your changes.

The complete ADDPATH.BAT file should match Figure 12.8. To understand how it works, assume that the current path is

H:\TEMPS;C:\DOS;C:\WP51;C:\UTILS

and that you run the batch program by typing the command ADDPATH DBASE. The first command following the comments substitutes the current path for %PATH% so that the command actually becomes

SET EXPATH=H:\TEMPS;C:\DOS;C:\WP51;C:\UTILS

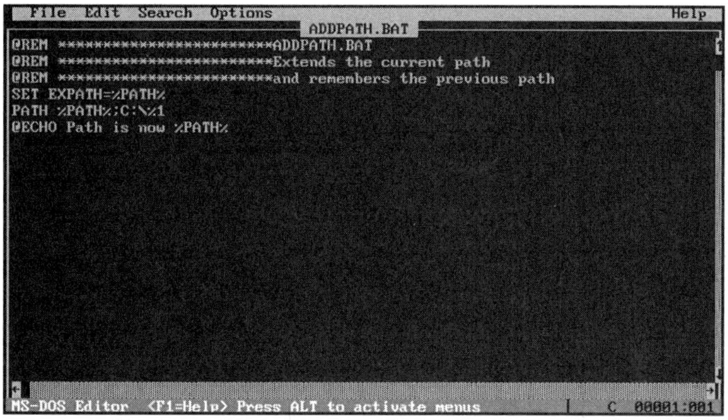

Figure 12.8.
The
ADDPATH.BAT
batch program.

Then when the command executes, it stores the current path setting in the environment using the variable name EXPATH. (This variable is important in the next batch program you will create, which enables you to undo a change made by ADDPATH.)

Then the current path is again substituted for %PATH% in the next command, so that line becomes

PATH H:\TEMPS;C:\DOS;C:\WP51;C:\UTILS;C:\%1

PART III
Putting DOS to Work

Next, the parameter from the command line, DBASE in this example, is substituted into the position held by %1 so that the command is finally expanded to

PATH H:\TEMPS;C:\DOS;C:\WP51;C:\UTILS;C:\DBASE

After both substitutions are made, DOS executes the complete command, which defines the new path as

H:\TEMPS;C:\DOS;C:\WP51;C:\UTILS;C:\DBASE

The last command, @ECHO Path is now %PATH%, displays the new PATH setting on-screen.

Try using this batch program. First, type the command PATH and press Enter to view your current PATH setting on-screen. Then enter the ADDPATH command with the name of any other directory on your hard disk. For example, you might type the command

ADDPATH WINDOWS

Your screen shows quite a bit of activity, as Figure 12.9 shows. To see whether ADDPATH did its job, type the command SET when the command prompt reappears. Notice that the environment now contains both the new path (next to PATH=) and the previous path (next to EXPATH=), as shown at the bottom of the figure.

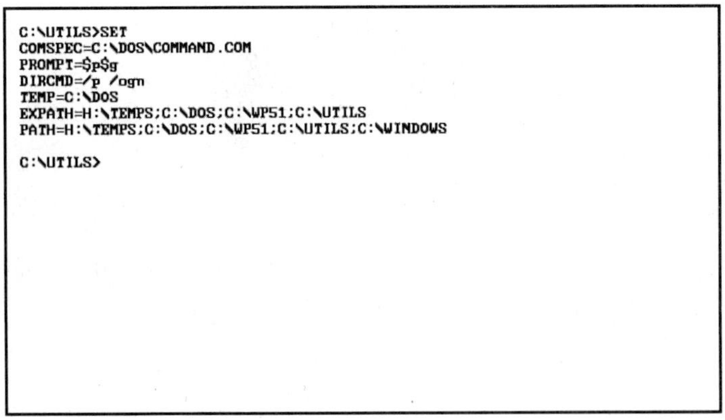

```
C:\UTILS>SET
COMSPEC=C:\DOS\COMMAND.COM
PROMPT=$p$g
DIRCMD=/p /ogn
TEMP=C:\DOS
EXPATH=H:\TEMPS;C:\DOS;C:\WP51;C:\UTILS
PATH=H:\TEMPS;C:\DOS;C:\WP51;C:\UTILS;C:\WINDOWS

C:\UTILS>
```

Figure 12.9.
Results of the command
ADDPATH
WINDOWS.

306

If your ADDPATH command is working properly, you can clean up its display by adding the @ECHO OFF command to the top of the batch program.

Restoring the Original Path

The OLDPATH.BAT batch program is the opposite of ADDPATH: it removes the last-added directory name from the path list. It's particularly handy for correcting a mistake. For example, suppose that while using ADDPATH, you add the drive name to the directory name out of habit. Because ADDPATH automatically adds the drive name, entering a command such as ADDPATH C:\WINDOWS produces this faulty new path:

```
C:\DOS;C:\WP;C:\UTILS;C:\C:\WINDOWS
```

Notice that there is an extra C:\ before the WINDOWS directory name. DOS can't handle this, so you need to correct the path definition. The OLDPATH.BAT batch program enables you to make this correction just by typing the command OLDPATH (rather than by retyping the entire PATH command). To provide feedback, OLDPATH also shows you that it has reinstated the current path to

```
C:\DOS;C:\WP;C:\UTILS
```

After running OLDPATH.BAT, you need only enter the correct command, ADDPATH WINDOWS, for DOS to set up the new, correct PATH command.

To create the OLDPATH.BAT batch program, follow these steps:

1. Type EDIT OLDPATH.BAT. Press Enter.

2. Type @REM **************** OLDPATH.BAT and press Enter.

3. Type @REM Removes the latest addition to the PATH. Press Enter.

4. Type PATH %EXPATH% and press Enter.

5. Type @ECHO Path is back to %PATH% and press Enter.

6. Select Exit from the File menu, and press Y to save your changes.

Your OLDPATH.BAT batch program should match the file in Figure 12.10. The first two lines are comments. In the next command, the previously defined path (which, you recall, was stored in the EXPATH environmental variable) is substituted for %EXPATH%. Therefore, the command expands to PATH C:\DOS;C:\WP;C:\UTILS (using the preceding example path) when DOS executes it. This resets the PATH definition to the preceding definition. The last command displays the new current path definition.

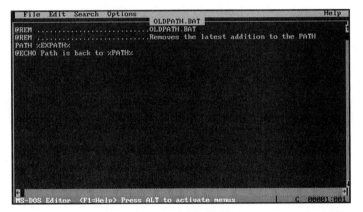

Figure 12.10. The OLDPATH.BAT batch program.

You can run the OLDPATH batch program only after you've used the ADDPATH batch program to add a new path because ADDPATH creates the EXPATH variable. To test this batch program, type the command OLDPATH at the command prompt. (This batch program accepts no parameters.) Notice that the path you added with the previous ADDPATH command is now removed from the PATH definition. To further verify this, type either the command PATH or the command SET.

Any changes you make with ADDPATH.BAT and OLDPATH.BAT will be in effect until you either use ADDPATH.BAT again or restart your computer. Neither of these batch programs make changes to the PATH definition in your AUTOEXEC.BAT file, so the AUTOEXEC.BAT PATH statement executes each time you start your computer.

ADDPATH for Multiple Disk Drives

As it is currently designed, ADDPATH.BAT can be run only on a computer that has a hard disk drive named C:. If you want your ADDPATH.BAT batch program to enable you to include other hard disk drives, change the line

```
PATH %PATH%;C:\%1
```

to

```
PATH %PATH%;%1
```

When using this new ADDPATH batch program, you must include the drive name with the ADDPATH command. For example, to add the PARADOX4 directory from drive F: to the current PATH setting, you must type the command

```
ADDPATH F:\PARADOX4
```

 Troubleshooting

If you experience problems during this chapter, try to locate the exact problem in the following sections, and then follow the suggested solutions.

■ You try to run a batch program, but it does not execute. Try the following actions to correct this problem:

Retry the command. You might have merely typed it wrong at the command prompt.

Make sure that the batch program is accessible from your current location. If you store all your batch programs in a specific directory, such as \UTILS, make sure that directory is in your PATH statement.

Try to find the batch program itself. If you can't find it anywhere, you failed to save it properly when you created the batch program. Or perhaps you inadvertently mistyped its name.

Examine your batch program for misspellings. This includes improper spaces in elements such as parameters.

■ You get a Bad command or file name message when you run a batch program. Either of the following errors might be occurring:

The program your batch program is calling is not accessible. Make sure that the directory in which the file is located is in your PATH statement or, if it is not, that your batch program changes to the appropriate directory before starting the file.

The program your batch program is calling is no longer on your hard drive. Remember to update your batch programs when you delete programs from your computer.

Summary

This chapter discussed the basics of creating your own commands via batch programs. The basic techniques you've learned here will enable you to create nearly any batch program you might require. Remember, any command you can type at the command prompt can be placed in a batch program. This includes commands that run other programs, such as DBASE, WP, or EXCEL.

In Chapter 29, "Batch Programs Unleashed," you'll expand your knowledge of batch programs by learning about commands that are allowed only in batch programs. But first, review the important points discussed in this chapter.

- Any commands you normally enter at the command prompt can be stored as a group in a batch program.

- Batch programs must have the extension .BAT and should not have the same name as any file with a .COM or an .EXE extension.

- You execute all the commands in a batch program by running the file exactly as you would run any other program on your computer.

- To prevent a command from appearing on-screen before it is executed, precede the command with an @ character (versions 3.3 and later).

- You can pass parameters from the DOS command line to your batch program by using the names %1, %2, %3, and so on as placeholders.

- To stop the execution of a batch program, press Ctrl+C or Ctrl+Break.

- You can have a batch program read information from the environment by surrounding variable names with % signs.

Optimizing and Tuning DOS

C H A P T E R   1 3

Customizing DOS

In the previous chapters, you learned the basics of how to use DOS and the DOS Shell. This chapter provides details about how to customize DOS and the DOS Shell to get the most power out of them. Specifically, you will learn about new features in DOS 6 that provide many options for configuring DOS when you start your computer. You will learn how to speed up your usage of the DOS Shell. You also will learn three ways to customize your keyboard to add power and speed to your DOS operations.

Alternative Ways of Starting DOS

Usually, when you start your computer, DOS executes the contents of your CONFIG.SYS and AUTOEXEC.BAT files. So unless you change those start-up files, your computer will start the same way every time.

However, at times you might want your computer to start with a different configuration—different sets of loaded drivers, launched programs, or environment variables. Here are some examples of situations in which you might want different configurations when you start your computer:

■ You are having problems that are causing your computer to behave erratically, and you want to track down and fix the cause of those problems. To do this, you often will want to start your computer "clean." That is, you want to start your computer with absolutely no drivers loaded or programs launched. Doing so enables you to see how your computer behaves without these elements. You then can load drivers and programs one at a time until your computer misbehaves, enabling you to isolate the problem.

■ You sometimes run an application that requires a lot of memory, and you want the option to load only the commands and drivers that are absolutely necessary so that your application has sufficient memory to run efficiently.

■ You want one configuration for running a graphical environment, such as Windows, and another configuration if you are only running in the DOS environment. Often, different drivers and programs are appropriate for those different environments. Previously, you had to load all the drivers and programs for both environments, which increased the danger of memory shortages and compatibility conflicts.

■ You share a computer with somebody, and the two of you have different configuration needs. For example, the person with whom you share the computer prefers Windows and you do not. Or you prefer to use some terminate-and-stay-resident (TSR) utilities that remain in memory until they are needed, but the person with whom you share does not want to use them.

DOS 6 includes three new ways to bypass or customize the use of your CONFIG.SYS and AUTOEXEC.BAT start-up files. When you start your computer with DOS 6, you can carry out these actions:

Completely bypass your start-up files. This provides you with a clean start-up.

Specify which commands in your CONFIG.SYS file you want DOS to carry out. You also can tell DOS whether it's to execute the AUTOEXEC.BAT file.

Develop start-up options that define different environments, and then, from a menu, choose the set of options you want to execute.

Completely Bypassing Your Start-Up Files

If you want to start your computer without loading any of the elements in your CONFIG.SYS or AUTOEXEC.BAT files, take the following steps:

1. Restart your computer.

2. When you see the message Starting MS-DOS..., press and release F5. You also can hold down the Shift key.

Your computer then starts without any commands or drivers being loaded.

Keep in mind that the Starting MS-DOS... message appears only briefly as your computer starts. If you do not press the appropriate key in time, you must reboot and try again.

Starting your computer this way means you will not be able to do many of the things you typically do. For example,

- Any programs or devices that require device drivers loaded in your CONFIG.SYS file will not work properly if you bypass your start-up files. For example, your mouse might not work.

- Programs that use expanded or extended memory either will not run or will use lower memory (the initial 640K of memory). That is because the drivers that enable use of expanded and extended memory will not be loaded.

- Environment variables will not be set. For example, you will not have an active PATH statement. Also, your command prompt will be C>, no matter what directory you are in.

- DOSKEY macros that you place in batch programs to be started by your AUTOEXEC.BAT file will not be available to you.

- DOS will not automatically load programs into high memory, which means you will most likely have less conventional memory than with running CONFIG.SYS.

Confirming CONFIG.SYS Commands

With this option, DOS asks whether each command in your CONFIG.SYS file should be carried out. It then asks whether the entire AUTOEXEC.BAT file should execute as a whole. For this option, follow these instructions:

1. Restart your computer.

2. When you see the message Starting MS-DOS..., press and release the F8 key.

3. DOS asks you a series of questions about whether you want to carry out specific commands. For example, you might be asked,

   ```
   Files=40 [Y,N]?
   ```

   Press Y if you want DOS to carry out that command, or N if you do not want DOS to carry out that command.

4. After you have answered all the questions about commands in your CONFIG.SYS file, DOS asks,

   ```
   Process AUTOEXEC.BAT [Y,N]?
   ```

   Press Y if you want your AUTOEXEC.BAT file to execute or N if you do not want it to execute. Figure 13.1 shows an example of this option.

You are not asked whether you want each of the commands in your AUTOEXEC.BAT file to execute. If you select Y to have your AUTOEXEC.BAT file execute, the entire AUTOEXEC.BAT file runs as it normally does.

```
     Total upper memory available  . . . . . .      99 KB
     Largest Upper Memory Block available  . .      95 KB
     Upper memory starting address . . . . . .    B000 H

     EMM386 Active.

     BUFFERS=30,0 [Y,N]?Y
     FILES=60 [Y,N]?Y
     LASTDRIVE=G [Y,N]?Y
     FCBS=4,0 [Y,N]?Y
     DEVICE=C:\DOS\SETVER.EXE [Y,N]?Y
     SHELL=C:\DOS\COMMAND.COM C:\DOS\  /P [Y,N]?Y
     STACKS=9,256 [Y,N]?Y
     DEVICEHIGH=C:\DOS\DBLSPACE.SYS [Y,N]?Y
     INSTALL=C:\COLLAGE\SNAP.EXE [Y,N]?Y




     Process AUTOEXEC.BAT [Y,N]?
```

Figure 13.1.
The option for
processing
your
AUTOEXEC.BAT
file.

Multiple Configurations

DOS 6 enables you to select from among multiple configurations that you set up in advance. With this new option, DOS displays a menu when you start your computer. From the menu you can choose the configuration you want for the current computing session.

The menu consists of the following elements:

A numbered list of configuration options. Use the ↑ and ↓ keys to scroll among the options, and press Enter to make your selection.

A box in which to type the number of the menu option you want.

A line reminding you that you still can press F5 to bypass all start-up files, or F8 to be asked whether you want individual components of your CONFIG.SYS file to be executed.

You define the form and content of the menu at the top of the CONFIG.SYS file. The section in the CONFIG.SYS file in which this occurs is called the menu block. All the different configurations from which you can choose are created in sections of the CONFIG.SYS file called configuration blocks. To help you create the menu and configurations, DOS 6 adds six new commands:

```
INCLUDE
MENUCOLOR
MENUDEFAULT
MENUITEM
NUMLOCK
SUBMENU
```

Each configuration block is a CONFIG.SYS file in its own right. It can contain any commands and parameters that ordinarily go in a CONFIG.SYS file.

Figure 13.2 shows an example of the CONFIG.SYS file that created the multiple configuration menu discussed in the next section.

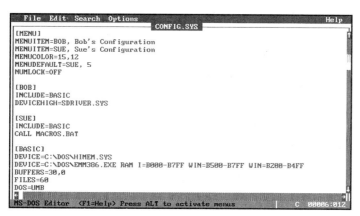

Figure 13.2.
A
CONFIG.SYS
file for multiple
configurations.

The next section starts at the top of the CONFIG.SYS file and creates a start-up menu. The section after that walks you through the process of creating the various configurations.

The Menu Block

The menu block, located at the top of the CONFIG.SYS file, defines the contents and form of the menu. The first line of the menu block, called the menu header, is simple:

```
[MENU]
```

The next several lines begin with one of two new DOS 6 commands—MENUITEM or SUBMENU. Lines that begin with these commands list the name of the associated configuration block, followed by the description of the configuration as you want it to appear in the start-up menu. For our example, assume you are setting up different configurations for different people. The first MENUITEM command might be

```
MENUITEM=BOB, Bob's Configuration
```

In this example, BOB is the name of the configuration block located later in the CONFIG.SYS file, and Bob's Configuration is how that option will appear in the start-up menu.

The configuration block name can contain as many as 70 characters but cannot contain spaces. Nor can it include slashes (\ or /), commas, semicolons, equal signs, or square brackets. The menu text can be as long as 70 characters and can contain any characters.

You will need a line, beginning with the MENUITEM or SUBMENU command, for each configuration or submenu you want to list in the start-up menu. You do not, however, have to place all configurations in the start-up menu, as discussed later.

Creating submenus also is discussed later in this chapter.

If Sue also gets a configuration, you add the line

```
MENUITEM=SUE, Sue's Configuration
```

After you have listed all the menu items, you can add three optional lines.

The first optional line in the menu block defines the color of the start-up menu using the MENUCOLOR command. An example of the menu color command is

```
MENUCOLOR=15,12
```

The first parameter lists the color of the menu text. The second parameter lists the color of the menu background. Table 13.1 lists the values for the colors used with the MENUCOLOR command. As you can tell from the table, the previously listed command creates a menu with white text on a red background.

Table 13.1. Colors used with the MENUCOLOR command.

Number	Color
0	Black
1	Blue
2	Green
3	Cyan
4	Red
5	Magenta
6	Brown
7	White
8	Gray
9	Bright blue
10	Bright green
11	Bright cyan
12	Bright red

continues

Table 13.1. continued

Number	Color
13	Bright magenta
14	Yellow
15	Bright white

> If you do not include a color line, DOS automatically selects a rather mundane combination of gray letters on a black background.

The second optional line in a menu block specifies a default configuration and the time that can elapse before that configuration is automatically launched, if you do not choose an option first. A sample of that line is

```
MENUDEFAULT=BOB, 30
```

This line means that BOB is the default configuration, and it will be launched 30 seconds after start-up if you do not select a configuration during that time. Notice that the start-up menu screen has a timer in the lower-right corner. If you use the MENUDEFAULT command, that timer counts down until you select an option or until it launches the default configuration.

The final optional line involves the Num Lock key. You can set the Num Lock key to be ON or OFF. A sample of that line is

```
NUMLOCK=OFF
```

This ensures that, during start-up, the Num Lock key is OFF. If you do not include this line, your system defaults determine whether the Num Lock key is ON or OFF.

Now you can see an entire menu block put together in one place:

```
[MENU]
MENUITEM=BOB, Bob's Configuration
MENUITEM=SUE, Sue's Configuration
MENUCOLOR=15,12
MENUDEFAULT=BOB, 30
NUMLOCK=OFF
```

If you are in the process of developing new configuration blocks but have not yet finished them, you still can name them and include them in the CONFIG.SYS file without including them in the menu block. There is no harm in doing this; such configurations will not be executed, but they will be available for future editing. You must remember, however, to include the configuration block header in unused configuration blocks, or the information in the unfinished configuration will be executed as part of the configuration block directly above it.

Creating Submenus

Each menu can contain a maximum of nine menu items. If you have more than nine items, or if you simply want to categorize the configurations in your menu further, you can create submenus.

For example, you might want a menu item called CONFIGURATIONS FOR USERS. By selecting that option from the start-up menu, you can get an additional menu, or submenu, that lists the configurations for your various users.

To create submenus, use the SUBMENU command in the menu block. For example,

```
SUBMENU=USERS, Configurations for Users
```

Figure 13.3 shows the CONFIG.SYS file with the SUBMENU command.

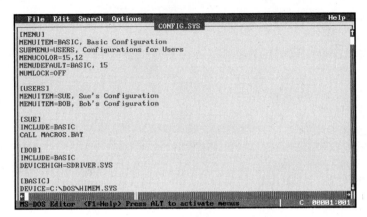

```
 File  Edit  Search  Options                                    Help
                         CONFIG.SYS
[MENU]
MENUITEM=BASIC, Basic Configuration
SUBMENU=USERS, Configurations for Users
MENUCOLOR=15,12
MENUDEFAULT=BASIC, 15
NUMLOCK=OFF

[USERS]
MENUITEM=SUE, Sue's Configuration
MENUITEM=BOB, Bob's Configuration

[SUE]
INCLUDE=BASIC
CALL MACROS.BAT

[BOB]
INCLUDE=BASIC
DEVICEHIGH=SDRIVER.SYS

[BASIC]
DEVICE=C:\DOS\HIMEM.SYS

 MS-DOS Editor  <F1=Help> Press ALT to activate menus       C  00001:001
```

Figure 13.3. A CONFIG.SYS file that creates a start-up menu with submenus.

When you use the SUBMENU command in the menu block, you then must create a configuration block with the name of the submenu. In this case, the submenu block is named USERS, as shown in Figure 13.3.

If you select the BASIC configuration option on your start-up menu, it executes when you select it. However, if you select the CONFIGURATIONS FOR USERS option, you get another menu, or submenu, asking you to choose between configurations for Bob and Sue.

Creating Configuration Blocks

In the example just discussed, you must create four configuration blocks—one for BASIC, one for the USERS submenu, and one each for the BOB and SUE configurations.

The first line in each configuration block is the name of the block in squared brackets ([ ]). This is called the configuration block header. Here's an example:

[BOB]

Everything after the block name until either the next block name or the end of the file is part of that configuration. Each configuration block is a CONFIG.SYS file unto itself. As a result, anything you put into a CONFIG.SYS file can be placed in a configuration block. You use the same commands, parameters, and switches, with one exception.

That exception is the INCLUDE command, another new command in DOS 6. The INCLUDE command allows the commands in one configuration to be carried out in another configuration. For example, in the BOB configuration, the command

```
INCLUDE=BASIC
```

carries out all the commands in the BASIC configuration in addition to any other commands listed in the BOB configuration.

Use the INCLUDE command to save time and ensure accuracy. If you have commands that must be carried out in all configurations, place them in a universal configuration with a name like BASIC. For example, if your FILES, BUFFERS, and PATH commands will remain the same for all configurations, place those three commands in the BASIC configuration. You can then use the INCLUDE=BASIC command in all your other configurations. This way, you won't have to type all the commands for each configuration, and you can be assured that the commands are entered accurately in each configuration.

Which commands fit best in universal configurations, such as BASIC, and which commands vary among configurations? Candidates for a universal configuration include FILES and BUFFERS, which take relatively little memory and which, after they're set, rarely affect performance of an application. On the other hand, device drivers required to connect to a network can require a lot of memory but aren't necessary in every situation. The low-impact commands often work well in universal configurations because they can be used in all configurations. Commands that affect the performance of your computer but which aren't always needed are placed only in those configurations in which they are needed.

There is still another use for a universal configuration block with a name like BASIC. Many application programs place commands specific to those programs at the end of the CONFIG.SYS file during installation. If you place the BASIC configuration last, all additions to your CONFIG.SYS file will become part of that configuration. Those commands, in turn, are carried out in each configuration, assuming you have used the INCLUDE=BASIC command in each configuration. If you don't include a catchall configuration as the last configuration in your CONFIG.SYS file, commands added to the end of the file will be carried out by only the last configuration block.

> As you create different configurations for different purposes, make sure to test each configuration to ensure that it achieves the results you desire. For example, if you create a configuration to maximize your available memory, use the MEM /C /P command to examine the effect of your configuration.

Modifying Your AUTOEXEC.BAT for Multiple Configurations

Just as you might want different CONFIG.SYS files for different purposes, you also might want different AUTOEXEC.BAT commands for each configuration. To do this, you use *branching* batch commands within the AUTOEXEC.BAT file. This section provides an overview of this process; it is discussed in detail in Chapter 29, "Batch Programs Unleashed."

Branching commands are used in batch programs and in full-fledged development languages. They tell the computer that if one condition occurs, a specific action is performed, and if another condition occurs, a different action is performed.

The primary command you use to customize the start-up of your AUTOEXEC.BAT file is the GOTO command. You use this command in combination with a command-line variable.

We all perform branching commands in our everyday lives; for example:

If the refrigerator is empty, go to the grocery store.

If the refrigerator is full, start (go to) making dinner.

The GOTO command can react to specific commands, or it can react to variables. With GOTO commands in your AUTOEXEC.BAT file, if a certain condition is met, AUTOEXEC.BAT goes to a specific section of commands. This section of commands is called a *subroutine*.

Variables are discussed in Chapter 12, "Simple Batch Programs."

When a specific configuration is selected from a start-up menu, DOS creates an environment variable named CONFIG. The name of the configuration block you selected is attached to the CONFIG environment variable. If you select the BOB configuration, for example, and you use the SET command, you see the line

CONFIG=BOB

In this way, %BOB% becomes the variable. Using the GOTO command, the AUTOEXEC.BAT file can then respond to this variable by automatically skipping to a section of the file, or subroutine, called BOB.

An AUTOEXEC.BAT file designed to handle variables has several parts:

At the beginning of the AUTOEXEC.BAT file, list the commands you want executed no matter which subroutines are selected.

Then add the GOTO "%CONFIG%" command. This directs the AUTOEXEC.BAT file to go to a special section, or subroutine, that responds to the variable. Each section must end with a GOTO END command. For example, if the BOB configuration was selected in the start-up menu, this line goes to (or branches to) the section (or subroutine) of the AUTOEXEC.BAT file called BOB.

Then list the subroutines associated with each variable. Each subroutine is a mini-AUTOEXEC.BAT that can use all the commands you ordinarily use.

End the AUTOEXEC.BAT file with the END subroutine.

Each set of commands, or subroutine, begins with a line that starts with a colon (:), followed by the name of the subroutine. For example,

```
:BOB
```

defines the start of the BOB subroutine. The lines that follow, until either the end of the file is reached or another GOTO command starts, are executed as part of the BOB subroutine.

You can end the AUTOEXEC.BAT file with a one-line subroutine called

```
:END
```

The :END subroutine ends execution of the AUTOEXEC.BAT file. Simple subroutines typically end with the command

```
GOTO END
```

Figure 13.4 shows a sample AUTOEXEC.BAT file that responds to multiple configurations.

> Only one option can be executed. If the BOB configuration is selected, the BOB subroutine is executed. If the SUE configuration is selected, the SUE subroutine is executed.

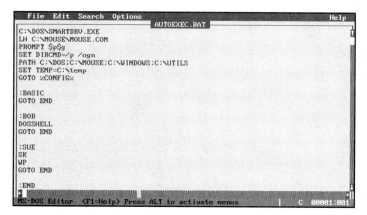

```
 File  Edit  Search  Options                              Help
                    ┌───────── AUTOEXEC.BAT ─────────┐
C:\DOS\SMARTDRV.EXE                                   ↕
LH C:\MOUSE\MOUSE.COM
PROMPT $p$g
SET DIRCMD=/p /ogn
PATH C:\DOS;C:\MOUSE;C:\WINDOWS;C:\UTILS
SET TEMP=C:\temp
GOTO %CONFIG%

:BASIC
GOTO END

:BOB
DOSSHELL
GOTO END

:SUE
SK
WP
GOTO END

:END
                                                     ↕
MS-DOS Editor  <F1=Help> Press ALT to activate menus    C  00001:001
```

Figure 13.4. An AUTOEXEC.BAT file using the GOTO command to respond to different configurations.

Customizing the Shell

This section discusses methods for customizing the DOS Shell to make it work precisely the way you want.

Adding Your Own Commands and Groups to the Program List

You learned in Chapter 8, "Using the Shell," how to add programs to the Program List of the DOS Shell. But you also can add commands and groups of commands as well as applications. Although the DOS Shell's menus enable many commands and functions, they do not enable all the commands you are likely to use. Adding commands to the Program List decreases the number of times you must temporarily exit the DOS Shell to execute commands at the command prompt.

Some DOS 6 programs cannot be started from the DOS Shell under any circumstances. For example, never start the DEFRAG program from the DOS Shell. That program, and any other program that makes fundamental changes to memory or your hard drive, must be started from the command prompt only after you have fully exited the DOS Shell.

Note

In some cases, you can run a command from the DOS Shell Program List, but not one or more of the parameters for that command. For example, you can add the CHKDSK command to the Program List, but you cannot use the /F parameter, which finds and then optionally fixes lost clusters.

You can add commands to the Program List just as you add an application program. Or if you add multiple commands, you might prefer to add a group to the Program List to contain the new commands.

Notice in Figure 13.5 that the Program List Main group includes a new group named Commands.

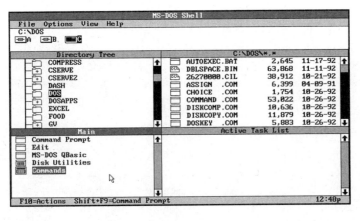

Figure 13.5.
A new group added to the Program List screen.

Selecting the new Commands option displays a new group of options, as Figure 13.6 shows. Selecting an option from this group runs a specific command.

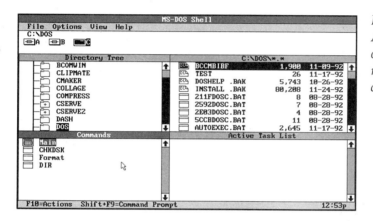

Figure 13.6.
A new group
of options for
running
commands.

The process for adding a group to the DOS Shell is described in Chapter 8, "Using the Shell." Here's a review of those steps:

1. Display the higher level group screen. For example, if you want the new Commands group to be accessible from the Main group screen, be sure that the Main group screen is displayed and that the highlight is in the Program List area.

2. From the pull-down menu, select the New... option.

3. In the New Program Object dialog box, select the Program Group button. This displays the Add Group dialog box, which you fill out.

4. Select a group title that briefly describes the contents of the new group. It can be as many as 23 characters long and can contain blank spaces and punctuation marks.

5. You optionally can add your own help message to a group. After you add the message, your help text appears in the Help window whenever you highlight the group title and press the F1 key. You can type as many as 255 characters,

including spaces and punctuation, to the Help box. Later, when the DOS Shell displays your help text, it automatically formats the text to fit inside the Help window.

6. If you want to limit access to the new group, you can assign a password to it. The password can be as many as 20 characters long and can contain blank spaces. Keep in mind that after you assign a password, only people who know the password will be able to gain access to the group.

> If you forget the password for a group, you can edit the group's password= line in the DOSSHELL.INI file to change or delete the password. An obvious caution: Because you can edit a password in the DOSSHELL.INI file, your password is not very secure.

Adding Commands and Programs to Groups

When you first create a new group, it doesn't contain any programs or commands. Here's a review of the process of adding a new program or command to the group:

1. Select New from the File menu. Then select Program Item. This option is the default selection.

2. Fill out the Add Program dialog box. This dialog box contains two required items: Program Title and Commands. The other items are optional.

3. In the Commands box, enter the command that you type at the command prompt. See the next section about adding parameters to your commands.

4. Type as many applications or commands as you desire in your new group.

You now can access commands and applications from within the DOS Shell that you previously accessed only from the command prompt. Note that, in most cases, running a command or an application from the DOS Shell automatically causes you to temporarily exit from the DOS Shell.

Adding Parameters to Commands

In the DOS Shell, you can add parameters to commands. When you select a command, the DOS Shell displays a dialog box in which you fill in the parameter. This is useful for common commands that take parameters, and when it is time-consuming to load specific files from within the application. To set the DOS Shell to prompt you for parameters, carry out these steps:

1. Select New from the File menu.

2. Select Program Item from the dialog box.

3. In the Commands text box, type the command, then a space and a replaceable parameter. The first parameter is %1. You can use as many as nine parameters.

4. After you select OK, you are asked to fill out information for each parameter. The dialog box asks you to supply the text that will be included in the dialog box which prompts you for the parameter. Figure 13.7 shows that dialog box, with sample information filled in.

If you always use the same parameter when you launch the command, specify that parameter in the Default Parameters text box. Then that parameter will automatically be placed in the text box in the parameter dialog box.

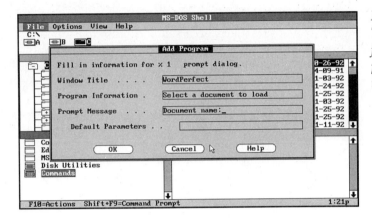

*Figure 13.7.
The dialog box
for establishing
parameters in
the DOS Shell.*

After you specify that a command be run with parameters, whenever you launch that command from the Program List, the dialog box that you helped create asks you for the parameters. Fill the parameter information into the dialog boxes. Note that the dialog box in Figure 13.8 includes the text entered in Figure 13.7.

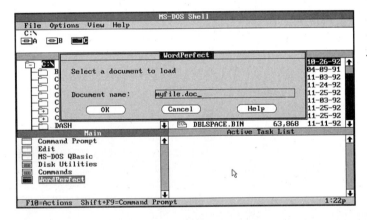

*Figure 13.8.
A dialog box
for variables.*

After you fill in the dialog boxes with parameters, your command is executed with the parameters you selected.

Most programs enable you to load a specific file at the same time you load the program by specifying the file name as a parameter. However, some programs do not have this capability; therefore, you cannot use parameters with those programs from the DOS Shell. Check the documentation for your application to find out whether it can be used with parameters.

Making Applications Faster

Two ways to make your applications run faster are by using short-cut keys and by pausing when leaving applications.

Using Shortcut Keys

The Task Swapper is an excellent way to increase efficiency when you use several different applications. Basic use of the Task Swapper is described in Chapter 8, "Using the Shell." You can increase your efficiency even more by using shortcut keys to jump between open applications. Using shortcut keys, you merely have to press a key to go directly to a different program.

Assigning shortcut keys to programs listed in the Program List is easy. You can select a shortcut key when you first add a program to the Program List. Shortcut keys should start with Ctrl, Alt, Ctrl+Alt, Ctrl+Shift, or Alt+Shift. To assign a shortcut key after the program has been added, first highlight the program. Then select Properties from the File menu. In the Application Shortcut Key box, select the shortcut key combination you want.

337

To do this, you must actually press the key combination instead of trying to type the name of the key combination. In other words, if you want to assign the shortcut key Ctrl+E to an application, press the Ctrl key and then the E key.

Note that several key combinations are reserved by DOS and can't be used as shortcut keys. Those key combinations are listed here:

Ctrl+M	Shift+Ctrl+M
Ctrl+I	Shift+Ctrl+I
Ctrl+H	Shift+Ctrl+H
Ctrl+C	Shift+Ctrl+C
Ctrl+[	Shift+Ctrl+[
Ctrl+Num5	Shift+Ctrl+Num5
Alt+Esc	Shift+Alt+Esc
Alt+Tab	Shift+Alt+Tab
Ctrl+Esc	
Ctrl+Home	
Ctrl+End	
Alt+F4	

The shortcut keys are listed in the Active Task List to help you remember them. However, because you can't see the Active Task List when you are in your application, at first you might want to list all the shortcut keys and their related applications on a piece of paper you keep near your keyboard.

Pausing When Leaving Applications

When you leave an application, you are prompted to press a key before you return to the DOS Shell. This is the DOS Shell default, but you can switch this default off so that you can exit programs faster.

To switch this default off, highlight the program you want to change. Then select Properties from the File menu. Then clear the Pause After Exit option by eliminating the X from the check box. Finally, select OK.

Getting More Information on the Screen

You can operate DOS faster and more efficiently if there is more information on-screen. The DOS Shell makes it easy to change your display to get more information on-screen.

The DOS Shell can be set to operate in either text mode or graphics mode. Functionally, there is no difference between the two modes, although they appear somewhat different.

The default for both modes is to show 25 lines of information on the screen at a time. However, you can change this by selecting Display from the Options menu. The dialog box enables you to select displays with 25, 43, or 50 lines in text mode. It also enables you to select displays of 25, 30, 34, 43, and 60 lines in graphics mode.

Graphics adapters can display both graphics and text modes. However, monochrome adapters can display the DOS Shell only in text mode. Also, you might be unable to use all the display options if you have a monochrome adapter. This depends on the capabilities of your graphics adapter.

Increasing the number of lines of information your monitor displays can increase productivity, but it also can increase eyestrain. Be aware of this fact, and switch to fewer lines of display if you begin to suffer from eyestrain.

Figure 13.9 shows a default graphics screen, which displays 25 lines of information. Figure 13.10 shows a graphics screen that has 43 lines of information.

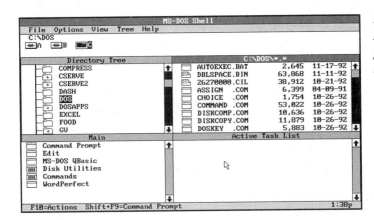

*Figure 13.9.
A default
graphics
screen.*

*Figure 13.10.
A graphics
screen with
additional lines
of information.*

Power Tips for the File List

The DOS Shell offers many advanced features to simplify managing directories and files on your computer. Using the DOS Shell to manage files and directories is discussed in detail in Chapter 14, "Hard Disk Management Made Simple." This section, however, details how to manage the File List, which, in turn, enables you to manage files and directories efficiently.

Arranging File Names

By default, DOS displays the names of all files alphabetically. To rearrange the order of the display, select File Display Options from the Options menu.

Notice that there are four fields, or areas, that you can change.

Name—text box that enables you to specify which files to display. The default specification (*.*) displays all files.

Display hidden/system files—enables the Shell to list files that have their hidden or system attributes set.

Descending order—reverses the normal order of a listing. For example, if you check this box, the File List first displays files that begin with *Z* and ends the list with files that begin with *A*.

Sort By—consists of five option buttons. Select an option and press Enter. The options and their effects are described in Table 13.2.

Table 13.2. The Sort By options for displaying file names.

Option	Effect
Name	File names are displayed in alphabetical order (the default selection).
Extension	File names are displayed in alphabetical order by extension.
Date	File names are displayed in descending date order (that is, the most recently created or modified files are displayed first).
Size	File names are displayed in descending (largest to smallest) order by size.
DiskOrder	File names are displayed in the order in which they were stored in the directory.

Quickly Selecting Groups of File Names

Rearranging file names is only one way to speed your management of large groups of files. By changing the Name: section in the Display Options dialog box from *.* to a more descriptive ambiguous file name, you can quickly isolate groups of file names for an operation.

For example, suppose you want to copy files with the extensions .TXT and .BMP from the current directory to a diskette. Instead of painstakingly selecting each file individually, you use the Display Options dialog box to show only files with those extensions.

Selecting Files from Different Directories

In some operations, you might need to select files that are stored on separate directories (or disk drives). To do so, you must execute two basic steps:

1. Pull down the Options menu and enable the Select Across Directories option.

2. View the file names of two drives or directories by selecting Dual File Lists from the View pull-down menu.

You then can select files in more than one directory at a time and launch commands, such as Copy or Delete, that deal with those files.

Using the Dual File Lists screen and a mouse, you can drag an icon to copy or move a file from one directory to another directory on another drive.

You can also use the multiple file list to display the source and destination directories for Copy and Move operations.

Selecting Files from Three or More Directories

Even though you cannot split the File List screen into more than two windows, you can still select files from more than two directories, as long as the Select Across Directories option is enabled. Because using two windows isn't valuable when you are working with more than two directories, switch back to the single File List screen by selecting Single File List from the View menu.

Next, select Display File Options... from the Options pull-down menu. Type a file specifier in the Name: box that identifies the types of files you want to select. Now you can use the usual techniques to access various directories and to select files from each directory. Because the Select Across Directories option is enabled, DOS remembers all the files you select from each directory. This enables you to move freely from directory to directory so that you can select whatever files you need.

To select more than one file in a directory, first highlight a file. Then, while pressing the Ctrl key, click on each subsequent file you want to highlight.

Eliminating Confirmation Messages

When you select a large group of files and then copy or erase them, the DOS Shell stops and asks for permission to erase or overwrite existing files. The DOS Shell also asks for permission to copy or move a file when you use a mouse to drag that file to a new location. If you always take precautions before these operations and you are certain you want to copy, delete, or move the selected files, the constant checking for permission can become tiresome.

To prevent DOS from asking for permission before deleting or erasing a group of files, select Confirmation... from the Options menu to display a dialog box.

Turning off any of these options means you can carry out operations without having to confirm them.

Customizing the Keyboard with DOSKEY

DOSKEY, introduced in DOS 5, is a powerful tool for DOS command-line users. DOSKEY enhances command-line capabilities in four ways:

- Remembers previously used commands and makes it easy for you to reuse them without having to retype them.

- Uses enhanced command-line editing to modify earlier commands without retyping.

- Uses the command separator to place several commands on a single line.

- Uses the macro generator to create, run, and save macros, which are like your own custom DOS internal commands.

The following sections cover all these DOSKEY features.

Activating DOSKEY

To activate DOSKEY from the command prompt, type

```
DOSKEY
```

and press Enter. Optionally, add the command DOSKEY to your AUTOEXEC.BAT file if you want DOSKEY's features to be available every time you start your computer.

When you run DOSKEY, the program installs itself in memory and creates a buffer (a portion of memory) to hold commands and macros. The program and buffer occupy 4K of memory. If you are using a computer with an 80286 or greater processor, you might be able to load DOSKEY into reserved memory so that it doesn't use any conventional memory.

Chapter 15, "Getting the Most from Your Memory," explains how to use LOADHIGH to load DOSKEY into reserved memory, thus saving space in conventional memory for other programs.

Selecting a Buffer Size

By default, DOSKEY creates a 512-byte (½K) memory buffer in which it stores your previous commands and any macros you create. If the length of your average DOS command is between 10 and 16 characters, the default DOSKEY buffer can store approximately 32 to 50 commands. If you type more commands than the buffer can hold, DOSKEY stores the most recent and deletes the oldest.

Remember too that the buffer must also store macros. If you use many macros (each of which can be as long as 127 characters), DOSKEY might not have much memory left to store the DOS commands that you type on the command line.

If you want to set aside more memory for the buffer, you can include the /BUFSIZE= switch when you start DOSKEY. For example, the following command sets aside 1K of buffer space for DOSKEY:

```
DOSKEY /BUFSIZE=1024
```

If your computer has limited memory and you use few macros, you might want to reduce the DOSKEY buffer to conserve memory for your programs.

Reusing Recorded Commands

One of the easiest, and most useful, features of DOSKEY is its command-line history, so called because it records a history of commands entered at the command prompt. You can repeat any previous command in this history without retyping, which can be a real time-saver in situations in which you need to use the same command or commands repeatedly.

For example, say that during your current session, you checked your directory listing, changed directories, formatted a disk, ran a program, and then copied some files to a floppy diskette and cleared your screen. With DOSKEY, you can display, edit, or reuse all of these recorded commands.

There are two ways to use the command-line history. You can cycle through them using the ↑ and ↓, or you can press the F7 function key to display your command-line history. Figure 13.11 shows a typical command-line history that results from pressing the F7 key.

Table 13.3 lists all the keys you can use to redisplay recorded commands.

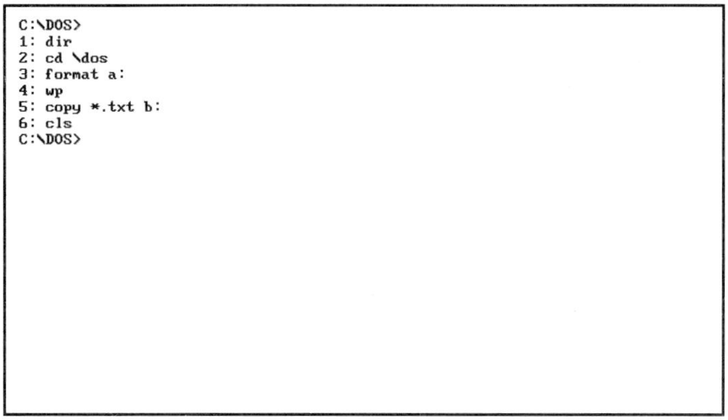

```
C:\DOS>
1: dir
2: cd \dos
3: format a:
4: wp
5: copy *.txt b:
6: cls
C:\DOS>
```

*Figure 13.11.
A sample
command-line
history.*

Table 13.3. Recalling command lines.

Key	Function
↑	Scrolls backward through recorded commands
↓	Scrolls forward through recorded commands

continues

347

Table 13.3. continued

Key	Function
PgUp	Displays the first command in the buffer
PgDn	Displays the last command in the buffer
F7	Displays all commands in the buffer
F8	Searches for commands that start with the text you specify
F9	Recalls a command by its number
Alt+F7	Deletes all commands from the buffer

For a quick reminder of DOSKEY options and keys, you can type DOSKEY /? at the command prompt. For even more detail, you can type HELP DOSKEY.

If you want to redisplay a command that you previously used, you can press the ↑ or ↓ keys to cycle through the commands, or the PgUp or PgDn keys to see the first or last commands stored in the buffer.

However, DOSKEY offers two faster methods. You can press F7 to redisplay a numbered list of all your commands, press F9, and then type the number of the line you want to recall. Or you can type the first few characters of the command and press F8.

For example, suppose that the seventh command of your current session was COPY C:*.TXT A:, and you want to redisplay the commands. Here's one way to do this:

1. Press F7, which displays a numbered list of stored commands.

2. Press F9, which displays the Line number: prompt.

3. Press 7, which selects the command COPY C:*.TXT A: (numbered as 7:).

4. Press Enter, which displays the seventh command on the current command line.

Or use these steps:

1. Press c.

2. Press F8 to display the first command in the buffer that starts with a C.

3. Continue pressing F8 until you display the command COPY C:*.TXT A:.

For step 1, you can type more characters—such as CO or COP—to limit the search to a more specific command name.

At this point, you can press Enter to execute that command, or you can edit the command line with DOSKEY's expanded command-line editing features, discussed in the next section.

The last command in Table 13.3, Alt+F7, erases all the commands stored in the DOSKEY memory buffer. You don't really need to use this command; DOSKEY automatically deletes the oldest stored commands when the buffer fills so that your most recent commands are always available.

Editing Recorded Commands

DOSKEY expands your command-line editing options and facilitates your editing of any command line currently stored in the DOSKEY memory buffer. Table 13.4 lists all the keys DOSKEY uses to edit commands.

Table 13.4. Keys used to edit commands.

Key	Function
→←	Positions the cursor to any character in the command
Home	Moves to the start of the command
End	Moves to the end of the command
Ctrl+←	Moves back one word
Ctrl+→	Moves forward one word
Backspace	Deletes the character to the left of the cursor
Del	Deletes the character at the cursor
Ctrl+End	Deletes all characters from the cursor to the end of the line
Ctrl+Home	Deletes all characters from the cursor to the beginning of the line
Ins	Inserts newly typed characters at the cursor position
Esc	Erases the currently displayed command

By default, DOSKEY is in overstrike editing mode; that is, any text you type replaces existing text. However, DOSKEY also has an insert mode in which the characters you type are inserted into text without overwriting the original text. Pressing the Ins key switches between insert and overstrike modes.

To put DOSKEY into insert mode for the current command, press the Ins key. The overstrike-mode cursor is an underline; the insert-mode cursor is a block.

> To start DOSKEY in insert mode, use the command DOSKEY
> /INSERT. Then, whenever you edit a command line, your
> characters are inserted into the current line. If you press Ins,
> you temporarily start overstrike mode; however, when you
> edit a new command, DOSKEY defaults to insert mode.

Entering Several Commands on One Command Line

With DOSKEY installed, you can also type multiple commands on a single line, up to a maximum of 127 characters. To do so, you must press Ctrl+T between each command. A paragraph symbol (¶) appears where you press Ctrl+T.

For example, to change the system date and time, you can type the command

```
DATE ¶ TIME
```

in which ¶ is generated by pressing Ctrl+T. You don't need to insert spaces before and after the character. When you press Enter, each command runs in left-to-right order. Figure 13.12 shows the results of multiple commands placed on the same line.

```
C:\DOS>DATE ¶ TIME
C:\DOS>DATE
Current date is Wed 11-25-1992
Enter new date (mm-dd-yy):

C:\DOS> TIME
Current time is  2:06:14.99p
Enter new time:

C:\DOS>
```

Figure 13.12. Two commands on the same line.

This feature can be handy, especially when you combine it with the procedures you learned for recalling and editing stored commands. For example, assume that you created several memos in the current directory of your hard disk and then saved them on a blank disk with the command

```
FORMAT B: /F:720 ¶ XCOPY *.TXT B: /V /M
```

which formats a 720K 3½-inch floppy diskette in drive B: and then copies all new or changed files (with the /M switch) to that diskette.

> Why have multiple commands on the same line? One advantage, using the example cited previously, is that the lengthy process of formatting and then copying becomes one operation; you don't have to wait for formatting to be completed before copying. Another advantage, of course, is that you redisplay and modify this lengthy command to format another disk and copy other files, as described earlier in the "Reusing Recorded Commands" section.

Although all the DOSKEY features I've discussed so far are easy and convenient, the most powerful feature of all is macros.

DOSKEY Macros

A macro is a set of commands executed as a single command. In this sense, macros are similar to batch programs. However, there are differences between macros and batch programs:

- DOSKEY macros are stored in memory rather than on disk, which means that they run a little faster, but also disappear when you turn off the computer.

- Whereas a batch program consists of many commands on separate lines, DOSKEY macros have all their commands on one line, with each command separated by Ctrl+T.

- There's no limit to the length of a batch program, but a macro cannot exceed 127 characters in length.

- You can terminate a batch program by pressing Ctrl+C or Ctrl+Break once, but these keys terminate only the current command in a macro.

- The replaceable parameters in batch programs are expressed as %0 through %9. In macros, you use $* through $9. Macros also use unique characters for piping and redirection (see Table 13.5).

- You cannot use the common GOTO and ECHO OFF batch program commands in macros.

- Neither a batch program nor another macro can start a macro. A macro can, however, start a batch program, and a batch program can create macros.

Creating and Executing Macros

To create a macro, use the format

```
DOSKEY name=command $T command $T ...
```

in which *name* is the name of the macro, *command* is the command that the macro is to execute, and $T separates multiple commands, if any. A blank space must separate the DOSKEY command and the macro name that follows it; all other blank spaces are optional.

Execute the macro as you do any command. Type the name of the macro at the command prompt, along with any parameters and switches.

Macro Piping and Redirection

You cannot use the >, <, ¦ characters in macros for redirection and piping. Instead, you must use special symbols that stand for these characters, as shown in Table 13.5.

Table 13.5. Redirection and piping characters used in macros.

Character	Macro Equivalent	Purpose
<	$L or $l	Redirects input
>	$G or $g	Redirects output
>>	GG or gg	Appends output to a file
¦	$B or $b	Redirects output from one command to another

Other Special Characters

Character	Macro Equivalent	Purpose
¶	$T or $t	Separates commands
$	$$	Represents the $ (dollar sign) symbol
%1 through %9	$1 through $9	Represent replaceable variables
	$*	Special replaceable variable that accepts all text on the command line after the macro name

The macro codes are easy to remember because they are all mnemonics. For example, $L is the Less-than symbol, $G is the Greater-than symbol, $B is the vertical Bar symbol (pipe), $T separates Two commands, and $* uses the DOS "all" character (*) to mean "all text on the command line." Upper- and lowercase differences don't matter.

Use these codes in macros exactly as you use the literal characters in a batch program or the command line. That is, if the command you want to execute needs the >> redirection character, use the code GG in your macro. The GG is automatically converted to >> when you execute the macro.

Some Sample Macros

Following are a few sample macros to give you an overview of the kinds of things you can do with macros, as well as some specific examples to work with.

Macros to Shorten Commands

The simplest macros are those that execute a longer command using a shorter one. For example, if you are tired of typing DOSSHELL every time you want to switch from the command prompt to the DOS Shell, you create a macro named DS (or just D, for that matter) that starts the DOSSHELL. To create the DS macro (assuming DOSKEY has been loaded by now), type

```
DOSKEY DS = DOSSHELL
```

and press Enter.

To test the macro, type DS and press Enter. (Press F3 to return to the command prompt after you get to the Shell.) Don't forget that the DS macro you just created is available for the current session only; it will be erased when you reboot or turn off the computer. I'll describe how to make macros more permanent in a moment.

Macros to Customize Commands

Another handy feature of macros is the capability of customizing an existing command to your liking. For example, when you type the MEM command, you see a brief report of the status of memory. To get a more complete report without it whizzing by too quickly to read, type MEM /C ¦ MORE.

You can easily create a DOSKEY macro that executes the command the way you want, simply by typing MEM.

```
DOSKEY MEM = MEM /C $B MORE
```

Remember that the $B in the macro is converted automatically to the split vertical bar (pipe) at execution time.

A Note on Macro Names

Even though MEM is a normal DOS command, the MEM macro is executed automatically when you type MEM as a command. That's because whenever you type a command at the command prompt, DOS first checks to see whether a macro has the same name as the command you entered. If so, DOS executes the macro.

If you really want to run the original MEM command to get a brief report on the status of memory, simply press the Spacebar before typing the command so that there is a blank space between the command prompt and the command.

Macros That Accept Variables

Like batch programs, a macro can contain replaceable parameters that take on a value from the command line, like many normal DOS commands. For example, the normal DOS COPY command can take any source or destination, which provides unlimited capabilities for copying files.

To mimic this capability of accepting data from the command line in macros, use $1, $2, and so on, through $9, as placeholders (technically called replaceable parameters) for text that comes from the command line.

To demonstrate, create a macro that, like the TYPE command, can type the contents of any file. Instead of displaying the contents at breakneck speed on-screen, this TYPE macro pauses after each screenful of text. Name this macro STYPE (for Slow Type).

To create the macro, at the command prompt type the command

```
DOSKEY STYPE = TYPE $1 $B MORE
```

and press Enter.

> Replaceable variables in batch programs are preceded by the % symbol; replaceable variables in macros are preceded by the $ symbol.

This creates a macro called STYPE that executes the command TYPE *filename* ¦ MORE. You can enter the *filename* parameter when you enter the command at the command prompt (as with the normal TYPE command). You insert the file name where the $1 placeholder appears. The $B MORE becomes ¦ MORE when the macro is executed so that the display pauses after each screenful of text.

Displaying Available Macros

If you forget which macros are available at the moment or forget the name of a particular macro, type this command at the command prompt:

```
DOSKEY /MACROS
```

This command can be abbreviated to DOSKEY /M. A list of all current macros is displayed, as in Figure 13.13.

Editing Macros

The command you type to create a macro is recorded just like any other command you type at the command prompt. Therefore, you can change any existing macro by using the keys listed in Table 13.3 to locate the macro command and then using any of the keys listed in Table 13.4 to make your changes. Optionally, you can retype the macro definition from scratch, using the same name. The new macro replaces the old one instantly.

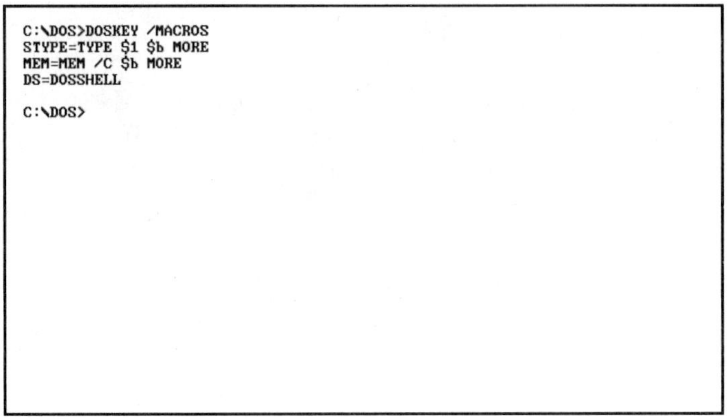

```
C:\DOS>DOSKEY /MACROS
STYPE=TYPE $1 $b MORE
MEM=MEM /C $b MORE
DS=DOSSHELL

C:\DOS>
```

Figure 13.13.
A sample list of
DOSKEY
macros.

Deleting Macros

To delete a macro, use the format

DOSKEY *macroname* =

in which *macroname* is the name of the macro you want to delete. Entering this command sets the macro equal to "nothing," which essentially erases the macro.

DOSKEY provides an easy shorthand method to delete all your current macros—press Alt+F10.

Batch Program Commands in Macros

Macros are very similar to batch programs. You can use most of the batch program commands described in Chapter 12, "Simple Batch Programs," and Chapter 29, "Batch Programs Unleashed," in your macros as well. The only two batch commands that don't work in macros are GOTO and ECHO OFF.

GOTO, as described in Chapter 29, tells a batch program to go to another line in the file and begin executing instructions there. More specifically, it tells the batch program to go to a *label,* or named section of the batch program. Obviously, then, GOTO won't work in a macro, because there are no labels. Macros, after all, are one-line entities. However, a macro can call a batch program using the CALL command.

Because the ECHO OFF command doesn't work within a macro, you will always see your macro commands typed before they are executed. (In case you are wondering, preceding the macro commands with the @ symbol won't suppress the displays either.)

Making Macros Permanent

As I've mentioned, all macros are erased from memory the moment you turn off or reboot your computer. Obviously, this is a major inconvenience if you create a handy supply of macros, because it necessitates creating all of your macros every time you restart your computer.

The solution to the inconvenience of losing macros when you turn off your computer is to create a batch program, named MACROS.BAT perhaps, that can create all your favorite macros at once, even automatically each time you start your computer. Here's the general procedure:

1. Use the DOSKEY /MACROS command to display all current macros but reroute the output to a batch program, C:\DOS\MACROS.BAT, for example. To do that, type

   ```
   DOSKEY /MACROS > C:\DOS\MACROS.BAT
   ```

2. Edit MACROS.BAT to ensure that all syntax is correct. Remember to add the DOSKEY command, plus a space, at the beginning of each line.

3. In the future, type the command MACROS to re-create all your macros, or include the command CALL MACROS in your AUTOEXEC.BAT file to re-create all macros automatically at the beginning of each new session.

359

Using the > symbol to redirect information to a file or the printer (or >> to append information to a file) works at the command prompt. If you want to redirect information within a macro, you must use $G or GG instead of > or >>.

Figure 13.13 showed a series of commands displayed by using the DOSKEY /MACROS command. Figure 13.14 shows the file in EDIT created by redirecting those commands. Note that the DOSKEY command has been added to the beginning of each line.

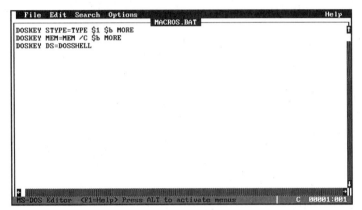

Figure 13.14.
The
MACROS.BAT
file in the
EDIT program.

Adding New Macros to MACROS.BAT

After creating a new macro at the command prompt, you might want to add that macro to your MACROS.BAT file to make it a permanent macro. To do so, use the same basic techniques you used to create the original MACROS.BAT file. For example, suppose that you type the following command to create a macro that ejects the current page from the printer when you type FF (for form feed) at the command prompt:

```
DOSKEY FF = ECHO ^L $G PRN
```

To add that macro to your MACROS.BAT file, reroute the output from `DOSKEY /MACROS` or `DOSKEY /HISTORY` to your C:\DOS\MACROS.BAT file, making sure to use the append (>>) redirection character. This appends the single command to the end of the specified file. For example,

```
DOSKEY /H ¦ FIND "DOSKEY FF" /I >> C:\DOS\MACROS.BAT
```

finds the macro you want and appends it to the end of C:\DOS\MACROS.BAT. You then update MACROS.BAT. Figure 13.15 shows the new batch program.

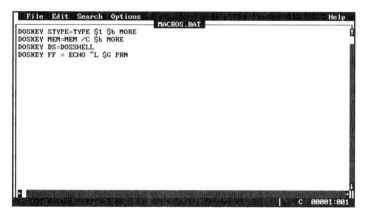

Figure 13.15. The MACROS.BAT file with the new FF macro definition added.

Converting Batch Programs to Macros

Many batch programs also will run as macros. This brings up an interesting question: Which of your batch programs should you convert to macros, and which should you leave as batch programs? Use the following guidelines to determine whether to create a macro or a batch program.

Use a Macro if

You want immediate access to the custom command from any drive or directory.

You want to customize an existing DOS command (as in the MEM macro described earlier).

361

You have adequate free memory to store it.

The command is fewer than 127 characters.

Use a Batch Program if

You use the command rarely.

Your command must make a decision and branch to an alternate location (that is, if it uses GOTO).

Your computer is short on memory and you don't want to increase the size of the DOSKEY buffer to handle the new command.

The command requires more than 127 characters.

The batch program is better, safer, or more "bulletproof" than the shorter macro version.

Running Multiple DOSKEY Sessions

With DOS 6, you can keep multiple versions of DOSKEY in memory at the same time; each memory-resident DOSKEY program maintains its own buffer of commands and macros. Although the practical implications of multiple DOSKEYs might be few, it's worth knowing how this works if you are a power user who runs multiple instances of the command prompt.

To start a new DOSKEY buffer with its own commands and macros, without replacing the original DOSKEY, you first need to get to a secondary DOS command prompt. There are a few ways to do so:

1. Start the Shell and then temporarily exit the Shell by pressing Shift+F9 or by selecting Command Prompt from the Program List.

2. Run a program and then temporarily exit that program to the DOS command prompt.

3. At the command prompt, type COMMAND and press Enter.

No matter which technique you use to get to the secondary command prompt, you can use the following command to install a new DOSKEY buffer:

```
DOSKEY /REINSTALL
```

Or if you're using reserved memory (discussed in Chapter 15, "Getting the Most from Your Memory"), you can type this command:

```
LOADHIGH DOSKEY /REINSTALL
```

With the following message, DOS reports that it has created a new copy of DOSKEY:

```
DOSKEY installed.
```

The new DOSKEY buffer in the secondary shell contains none of the previous commands typed at the command line; it is a totally new copy of DOSKEY, and its buffer is initially empty. You can now load a new set of macros, which are completely independent of the macros in your original version of DOSKEY. If you run the MEM command as follows

```
MEM /C ¦ MORE
```

and scroll through the list of programs in memory, you will notice two copies of DOSKEY.

To get back to your original DOSKEY buffer and macros, you first need to type the command EXIT at the secondary command prompt to leave that prompt. Then exit the current program or Shell as you normally do so that you're back to the original DOSKEY and command prompt. To verify your return, press F7 to list commands, or type DOSKEY /MACROS to list current macros.

Customizing the Keyboard Using ANSI.SYS

Many years ago when computers were all room-size giants, the American National Standards Institute (ANSI) developed a standardized coding system for managing the interface among keyboards, computers, and monitors. They did so to make software more portable; that is, so that programs can be used without modification on many types of computers and monitors.

DOS comes with a device driver, stored in a file named ANSI.SYS, that uses the ANSI coding system to send characters and images to your screen.

To see whether your computer is currently set up to accept ANSI codes, you have to use the TYPE command to view the contents of your CONFIG.SYS file.

If your computer can accept ANSI codes, the CONFIG.SYS file contains the command DEVICE= followed by the location and name of the ANSI.SYS file. For example,

```
DEVICE=C:\ANSI.SYS
```

> Some programs require that your CONFIG.SYS file load the ANSI.SYS file. These programs' documentation will inform you of this requirement.

If your CONFIG.SYS file does not set up the ANSI.SYS device driver, you can easily edit the file to load it by adding the line

```
DEVICE = C:\DOS\ANSI.SYS
```

After you change the CONFIG.SYS file, remember that modifications do not take effect until you reboot your computer. However, from then on, DOS automatically issues these commands every time you start your computer.

If your CONFIG.SYS file includes the DEVICE=ANSI.SYS command, you can customize your keyboard to perform special tasks. It's extremely unlikely that you want to redefine one of the standard keys, such as making the A key generate the letter Z (although you could do so if you had the desire). A more practical application is to use the procedure to assign functions to special key combinations that are not already defined by DOS, such as Ctrl+F3 or Alt+F7.

To change function keys, use the PROMPT command followed by an escape sequence, because you cannot generate Esc from the keyboard. However, you must also include a code that indicates the key you want to redefine, the character or characters you want the key to display (enclosed in quotation marks), the number 13 (which is the code for the Enter key), and finally, a lowercase *p*, which signals the end of the sequence. This syntax is as follows:

```
PROMPT $e[0;key number;"characters to type";13p
```

The numbers used to specify keys that you might want to redefine are listed in Table 13.6. Those marked with an asterisk already serve useful functions in DOS (and particularly the DOS Shell), so avoid redefining those keys.

Table 13.6. Numbers assigned to function keys.

Key	Number	Key	Number	Key	Number	Key	Number
F1*	59	Shift+F1	84	Ctrl+F1	94	Alt+F1*	104
F2*	60	Shift+F2	85	Ctrl+F2	95	Alt+F2	105
F3*	61	Shift+F3	86	Ctrl+F3	96	Alt+F3	106
F4*	62	Shift+F4	87	Ctrl+F4	97	Alt+F4	107
F5*	63	Shift+F5	88	Ctrl+F5	98	Alt+F5	108
F6*	64	Shift+F6	89	Ctrl+F6	99	Alt+F6	109
F7	65	Shift+F7	90	Ctrl+F7	100	Alt+F7	110
F8	66	Shift+F8	91	Ctrl+F8	101	Alt+F8	111
F9*	67	Shift+F9*	92	Ctrl+F9	102	Alt+F9	112
F10*	68	Shift+F10	93	Ctrl+F10	103	Alt+F10	113

* Already assigned a function by DOS.

Suppose that you want to redefine the Shift+F10 key (number 93) so that it displays the names of files when you press it. First, type the following command at the command prompt:

```
PROMPT $e[0;93;"DIR";13p
```

After you press Enter, the command prompt is no longer visible, so type the command PROMPT PG to redisplay it.

To test your new function key assignment, press Shift+F10 (hold down the Shift key and press the F10 key). Your screen displays the names of files on the current drive or directory.

Awkward commands that are difficult to remember are especially good candidates for redefinition as function keys. For example, to use the GRAPHICS command to prepare a wide-carriage IBM Personal Graphics Printer to print graphics screens, you might need to type the command GRAPHICS GRAPHICSWIDE /R /PRINTBOX:LCD. The following command assigns the appropriate command to the Shift+F8 key:

```
PROMPT $e[0;92;"GRAPHICS GRAPHICSWIDE /R /PRINTBOX:LCD";13p
```

After you initially type the command, your prompt disappears. You can type another PROMPT command, such as PROMPT PG, to bring back your original command prompt.

To set up your printer to print graphics displays, you need only press Shift+F8. Note, however, that the function key works only during the current session (before you turn off the computer) and only if the GRAPHICS.COM program is available from the current drive and directory.

As with DOSKEY macros, however, you can create a batch program of any key changes you create in this way. You can either start that batch program from the command prompt or call it from your AUTOEXEC.BAT files.

Assigning Multiple Commands to a Function Key

You can assign two or more commands to a function key, as long as you use the 13 (Enter) code to separate them. For example, the following command sets up the Shift+F7 key so that it first clears the screen (CLS) and then displays a wide directory listing (DIR /W):

```
PROMPT $e[0;90;"CLS";13;"DIR /W";13p
```

Resetting the Function Keys

To reset a function key to its original definition, follow the 0;*key number* portion of the command with a semicolon and a repeat of the 0;*key number*. For example, to reset the Shift+F10 key (number 93) to its original definition, type the command

```
PROMPT $e[0;93;0;93p
```

Customizing with Commercial Keyboard Programs

In addition to the methods discussed previously in this chapter, you can also use commercial and shareware keyboard macro programs to customize your keyboard. Most of these programs enable you to redefine a key by recording a series of keystrokes. By recording your moves, you don't have to deal with long strings of strange symbols.

In addition to helping with DOS, many keyboard macro programs can be used within your application programs. This means that complex or lengthy keystroke combinations required to carry out many functions can be assigned to either a single key or a key combination.

Talk to your software vendor for the names and manufacturers of keyboard macro programs.

Setting Keyboard Speed with the *MODE* Command

Many users upgrade to faster computers or faster video subsystems to increase the speed and responsiveness of their computers. You also can increase the speed and responsiveness of your keyboard with a simple command. To do this, use the MODE command, which is used to configure various devices.

In this case, the MODE command can be used to change what is called the typematic rate of your keyboard, or the rate at which keystrokes are repeated if you hold down a key. This might not seem important at first, but a sluggish keyboard can make using many applications seem sluggish and can try your patience.

MODE can be used to perform many different tasks, and the syntax for each task is somewhat different. The syntax for adjusting your typematic rate is

```
MODE CON: RATE=r DELAY=d
```

CON: refers to the keyboard. The rate is the speed with which a character repeats itself on-screen when you hold down the key. You can type a number between 1 and 32 for the rate. The default is 20 for most keyboards, although it is 21 for IBM PS/2-compatible keyboards.

If you set a rate, you also must set a delay. The delay is the amount of time that elapses between the time you hold down a key and the time it starts to repeat. You can type a number between 1 and 4, with the default being 2. Entering 1 means the delay will be .25 of a second. This goes up in increments of .25 second, with the maximum delay being one full second for the setting 4.

So a typical entry is

```
MODE CON: RATE=25 DELAY=1
```

This produces a faster response rate than the defaults.

The typematic rate is a matter of taste. For many, the fastest setting (RATE=32 DELAY=1) is too fast and results in typing errors when more characters appear than were intended. For others, the fastest typematic rate is quite comfortable. Some people find slower typematic rates frustratingly slow, whereas others find that slower rates more closely approximate the feel of a typewriter. This is an easy command to experiment with from the command prompt. Set different levels and simply type commands at the prompt for a while until you find a comfortable typematic rate.

 Troubleshooting

If you run into problems trying the techniques in this chapter, one of the following solutions might help you.

■ If you use multiple configurations and your start-up menu does not include the options you meant to include, try these adjustments:

Examine your CONFIG.SYS file to make sure the spelling and syntax of the menu block is correct.

Make sure that the configuration block you expected is included in the CONFIG.SYS file and that it is properly designated as a configuration block.

Make sure that the spelling of the configuration block is the same in the menu block as it is at the top of the configuration block.

■ If a configuration selected from the start-up menu executes more commands than you expect, make these checks:

Check your CONFIG.SYS file to see whether an application program has added commands to the end of the file. If this is the case, you can place those commands in a specific configuration block, if appropriate. You also can place the added commands in a universal configuration, with a name like BASIC, that is used as part of other configurations when you use the INCLUDE=BASIC command.

Make sure that the misbehaving configuration block begins with a block header, which is the name of the configuration in square brackets.

■ If you add commands or applications to the Program List of the DOS Shell and those commands or applications don't execute as expected, one of the following problems has likely occurred:

You entered the command syntax incorrectly. Reexamine the Commands text box in the Properties dialog box.

You are trying to run a DOS command that cannot execute from the DOS Shell. Examples of such commands are DEFRAG and CHKDSK /F.

■ If you try to use a shortcut key to switch from one application to another in the DOS Shell, but the shortcut key does not work, you might be faced with one of the following problems:

You have not enabled the Task Swapper and therefore cannot use shortcut keys. If this is the case, exit your application, enable the Task Swapper in the DOS Shell Options menu, and restart the application.

The shortcut key to jump to another application is reserved by your current application. If this is the case, change the shortcut key designation in the Properties dialog box.

Your application does not support the use of shortcut keys. This can happen with older DOS applications. If this is the case, you might want to call the software vendor and upgrade to a newer version.

■ If your screen acts erratically after you have switched to a DOS Shell video mode that shows more than 25 lines at a time, your video adapter or monitor might not be able to handle the new setting. Switch back to a setting that places fewer lines of information on the screen.

■ If you expect a DOSKEY macro to be available and it isn't (and you are sure you typed the macro name properly at the command prompt), one of the following problems might have occurred:

You restarted your computer and forgot that DOSKEY macros are kept in memory and are lost when you turn off your computer. If this happened, you must re-create the macros.

You placed your DOSKEY macros in a batch program, but you forgot to execute the batch program. Type the batch program name at the command prompt, and your macros will be available.

You have assigned that macro name to another macro.

■ If you routinely type one letter but get two or more letters entered, your typematic rate is set too fast. Use the MODE command to slow down your typematic rate.

Summary

This chapter has taught you about several ways to customize your use of DOS and the DOS Shell. Specifically, it taught you:

■ DOS 6 provides alternative ways to start your computer with DOS, including the capability to

Completely bypass your start-up files, providing you with a clean start-up.

Specify which commands in your CONFIG.SYS file you want DOS to carry out.

Develop several start-up options that define different environments, and then, from a menu, choose the set of options you want to execute.

■ To customize the DOS Shell to help you work faster and more efficiently. A number of tips were provided to

Customize the Program List.

Use applications faster.

Get more information on your screen.

Improve your efficiency when you use the File List.

■ To use the power of DOSKEY to provide

A command-line history to display, edit, and run previous commands.

Enhanced editing of commands.

A command separator so that you can place several commands on a single line.

A macro generator to create, run, and save macros.

■ To customize the use of your keyboard by using ANSI.SYS to assign multiple commands to a function key.

■ To speed up your keyboard's typematic rate, or slow it down, by using the MODE CON command.

Alan Simpson's

DOS SECRETS UNLEASHED

C H A P T E R 1 4

Hard Disk Management Made Simple

A hard drive that is well managed, organized, and optimized can make your computing life more efficient and enjoyable. This chapter provides techniques for managing programs and data files more quickly and efficiently. It also tells you how to increase the storage capacity of your hard disk and how to safeguard against hard disk disasters by backing up your files with the new Microsoft Backup program. This chapter also provides techniques for speeding up your hard drive.

Tips for Managing Programs and Files from the DOS Shell

The following sections provide tips for managing your programs and files from the DOS Shell.

Arranging File Names

By default, DOS displays the names of all files in alphabetical order in the File List of the DOS Shell. You can rearrange the order of the display by pulling down the Options menu from the Menu bar and selecting File Display Options…. Doing so displays the File Display Options dialog box, shown in Figure 14.1.

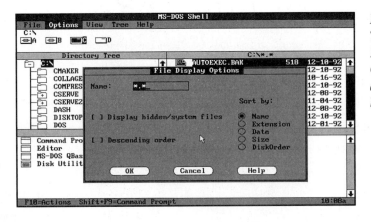

Figure 14.1.
The File
Display
Options
dialog
box.

Notice that there are four fields that you can change. Initially, the cursor is in the Name: box, which enables you to specify which files to display. The default specification (*.*) displays all files.

The next field, Display hidden/system files, enables the Shell to list files that have their hidden or system attributes set. To check this box, move the cursor to the box, and click the left mouse button. Many utility programs create hidden files that contain important information about your directories and internal DOS files. For example, DOS uses two system files (which are also hidden) and requires that they be stored in your root directory. Ordinarily, checking this box is of questionable value. After all, you know the hidden files were hidden from you for a reason—they are so important that they should not be tampered with.

Still, sometimes hidden files become unnecessary—for example, when you eliminate the program that placed them there in the first place. To make them visible in the Files List, select Display hidden/ system files.

The next field, Descending order, reverses the normal order of a listing. For example, if you check this box (using the same procedure as with the previous box), the File List first displays files that begin with Z and ends with files that begin with A.

The Sort by: field has five option buttons. The effects of the various options are described in Table 14.1.

Table 14.1. Options for displaying file names.

Sort by Option	Effect
Name	File names are displayed in alphabetical order (the default selection).
Extension	File names are displayed in alphabetical order by extension.

continues

Table 14.1. continued

Sort by Option	Effect
Date	File names are displayed in descending date order (that is, the most recently created or modified files are displayed first).
Size	File names are displayed in descending (largest to smallest) order by size.
DiskOrder	File names are displayed in the order in which they were stored in the directory.

These options are useful for managing files several ways. For example, if you want to see groups of files with the same extension, select the Extension option.

Suppose that you want to see which files have been created or changed today (or recently). Select the Date option in the Sort by: section, and DOS displays all the files most recently created or modified first.

Quickly Selecting Groups of File Names

Rearranging file names is only one way to manage large groups of files. By changing the Name: section in the File Display Options dialog box from *.* to a more descriptive ambiguous file name, you can quickly isolate groups of files for an operation.

For example, suppose that you want to copy some of the files with the extensions .TXT and .BMP from the current directory to a diskette. Instead of painstakingly selecting each file individually, use the File Display Options dialog box to make the procedure a quick and easy one.

Searching All Directories for a File

As you add directories and files to your hard disk, it becomes increasingly difficult to remember where every individual file is stored. You can use the DOS Shell File List to locate specific files quickly and easily, even if you do not know the exact file name you are looking for.

For example, suppose that you wrote a letter to a person named Smith, and named the file SMITH, but you do not remember the extension or the directory in which you stored the letter. First, you must display the All Files screen, which displays all file names in all directories. To do so, follow these steps:

1. Select the All Files option from the View menu.

2. Select Display File Options from the Options menu, and change the file specifier to SMITH.*. Press Enter.

The File List shows the names of all files that match the SMITH.* ambiguous file name. However, notice that the area which used to show the Directory Tree now displays specific file and directory information instead.

Other Features of the All Files Screen

You can use the File List's All Files screen to manage your files much as you use the normal single-directory file display. This is a great tool when you want to perform an operation on all directories, such as copying or deleting a group of files.

If your computer has multiple disk drives, select New drives from the Drives area at the top of the screen, and then select files from the multiple drives. DOS keeps track of all the files selected on all drives and directories. To do this, you must toggle on the Select Across Directories option in the Options menu. After you finish selecting files, DOS enables you to perform file operations that might involve several disk drives and dozens of directories.

The All Files screen also displays important information about your disk, as summarized in Table 14.2. You can also view the information presented in Table 14.2 without displaying the File List's All Files screen. To do so, move the highlight to any file name in the Files List, and then pull down the Options menu and select Show information. A window appears showing the requested information.

If you want to switch between the All Files screen and the standard screens so that you can select files from both, make sure the Select Across Directories option is enabled. Otherwise, DOS automatically deselects all files when you switch from the All Files display to other displays.

Table 14.2. Information displayed by the All Files view.

Heading	What Is Displayed
File Name	Name of the currently highlighted file
Attr	Attributes assigned to the file:
	a—Placeholder for any unassigned attribute
	r—Read-only attribute
	h—Hidden attribute is on
	a—Archive attribute is on
Selected	Drives that have been accessed
Number	Number of selected files on each drive
Size	Combined sizes of selected files

Heading	What Is Displayed
Directory Name	Directory that the highlighted file is stored on
Size	Amount of disk space used by the files in the directory
Files	Number of files stored on the directory
Disk Name	Electronic label assigned to disk (if any)
Size	Total storage capacity of disk
Avail	Total available disk space remaining on disk
Files	Total number of files stored on disk
Dirs	Total number of directories on disk

Tips for Managing Programs and Files from the Command Prompt

The following sections detail tips for managing programs and files from the command prompt.

The *DELTREE* Command

DOS 6 includes a powerful new command, DELTREE, that deletes a directory and all subdirectories below it, as well as the files in those directories. Previously, to eliminate a directory and its subdirectories, you first had to go to the lowest-level subdirectory, delete all the files, and then move up one level and delete the subdirectory. This process had to be repeated until all the files and directories were deleted.

DELTREE does all of that with one command, including deleting files for which the hidden, read-only, and system attributes are set. DELTREE is an external command. Its syntax is

```
DELTREE [/Y] [drive/path]
```

The /Y switch tells DELTREE to withhold warnings when you are about to delete a directory. To use DELTREE, you must be in the directory above the directory you want to eliminate.

Don't use the /Y switch in DELTREE unless you are confident you will never make a mistake. Deleting a directory and all its subdirectories is a powerful action. Being prompted about whether you want to delete the directory might take an extra second or two, but it provides one more safeguard against mistakenly taking the wrong actions.

The *MOVE* Command

Another powerful new file-management command in DOS 6 is the MOVE command. This command is useful for moving files from one directory to another when you no longer want the file to reside in the original directory. It also can rename directories and files. See Chapter 10, "Working with Files and Directories," for a detailed discussion of this command.

Refining the *COPY* Command

DOS Version 3.2 and all later versions include a program named XCOPY.EXE (for eXtended COPY) that can help you more specifically select files for copying. Two of this command's eight optional switches are particularly handy:

/D:date—Copies files that were created or changed on (or after) a specified date.

/S—Copies all files from the current directory and all subdirectories beneath it. This is similar to the MOVE command, but it leaves files in the source directory after the copy is completed.

Suppose that at the end of the day, you want to copy new and modified files from your hard disk onto a floppy diskette in drive A:. Furthermore, you've been working with files only in the \FINANCES and \FINANCES\SALES directories. Assuming that today's date is March 30, 1993, and that you are currently accessing the \FINANCES directory, type the following command to copy only the files that were created or modified on (or after) the current date:

```
XCOPY *.* A: /D:03-30-93 /S
```

The /D: switch followed by a date specifies the date to copy. The /S switch tells XCOPY to copy all files in the current directory and any subdirectories. If you start the XCOPY command from the root directory and use the /S switch, DOS copies all files from all directories on the disk.

Note that the current date is specified in the mm-dd-yy format. However, if you are using an international version of DOS, use the appropriate format for your dates, as displayed by the DATE and DIR commands.

Sorting the *DIR* Command

By default, the DIR command displays file names in the order they were created, the oldest files first and the newest files later. If you prefer a more organized sort order, choose from two options: use the SORT command in combination with the DIR command, or use one of the switches added to the DIR command (see Figure 14.2). If you find a sort order you prefer, you also can use the DIRCMD environment variable command in your AUTOEXEC.BAT file to make it the default.

```
ATTRIB    EXE     11165 11-25-92    6:00a
AUTOEXEC  UMB       527 12-10-92    9:57a
CC21201A  FUL      3072 12-01-92    9:10p
CC21203A  FUL      3392 12-03-92    3:29p
CC21203B  FUL      3328 12-03-92    4:45p
CHKDSK    EXE     12058 11-25-92    6:00a
CHKLIST   CPS      2592 12-07-92    1:37p
CHKSTATE  SYS     41536 11-25-92    6:00a
CHOICE    COM      1754 11-25-92    6:00a
COMMAND   COM     53405 12-01-92    6:00a
CONFID    LOG     91339 12-01-92    9:10p
CONFID$$  SET      4204 12-01-92    9:10p
CONFID$$  SLT      3440 12-01-92    9:10p
CONFIG    UMB       470 12-10-92    9:55a
COUNTRY   SYS     17066 11-25-92    6:00a
DBLSPACE  BIN     65402 12-01-92    6:00a
DBLSPACE  EXE    294588 12-01-92    6:00a
DBLSPACE  HLP     35851 11-25-92    6:00a
DBLSPACE  INF      1546 11-25-92    6:00a
DBLSPACE  SYS       217 11-25-92    6:00a
DEBUG     EXE     15715 11-25-92    6:00a
DEFAULT   BAK      4223 12-03-92    9:30a
DEFAULT   SAV      2016 12-03-92    9:30a
-- More --
```

*Figure 14.2.
The results of
using the SORT
command with
the DIR
command and
the MORE filter.*

The SORT command is a filter because it rearranges output. The ¦ character, called pipe, must be used with a filter. The ¦ character is Shift+\ on most keyboards. For example, to list file names in alphabetical order in the DIR display, type the command

DIR ¦ SORT

You can redirect the output to a printer by typing the command

DIR ¦ SORT > PRN

With the DIR command, you can use an internal switch to duplicate the previous operations. (See Chapter 9, "Using the Command Line," for more details about the DIR command.)

For example, to list a directory's file names in alphabetical order, type the DIR command with the /O: option:

DIR /O:N

The /O: (or "option") switch enables you to display files by name (N), extension (E), date and time (D), size (S), and with directories listed before files (G). If you place a minus sign (-) before any of these letters, you reverse the order of the display. For example, the command

DIR /O:-N

displays files in reverse alphabetical order (for example, names starting with Z display first, and names starting with A display last).

Displaying Files from a Certain Date

The DIR command can display all the files on a directory that were created or last modified on a certain date. This is handy when you are looking for a file that you created earlier today or yesterday but cannot remember the full name of the file.

The first step is to use the CD command to change to the directory on which the file is stored. Note that the format of the date used in the command must match the format displayed by the DIR command. Most versions of DOS use the mm-dd-yy format. However, some international versions of DOS might require the dd-mm-yy format (that is, 30-04-91) or the yy-mm-dd format (91-04-30). To determine the appropriate date format for your version of DOS, type the DIR command and look at the date assigned to each file.

Next, use the DIR command followed by the pipe (¦), the FIND command, and the date you're interested in enclosed in quotation marks. For example, to display the names of files created on March 30, 1993, type the command

```
DIR ¦ FIND "03-30-93"
```

Searching All Directories for a File

It is possible to search all the directories on your hard disk for a file from the command prompt. However, if you have an older, slower computer, the search can be quite time-consuming. Nonetheless, the technique is a valuable one, and it can come in handy in certain situations.

It is a common error to mistakenly save a file to another directory. For example, if you are using an application program and the last directory you saved to was the C:\TEMP directory, typically, that is the directory your application will save to the next time, unless you tell your program differently. The result might be that you save the file but do not know which directory it is located in.

The CHKDSK command provides an optional /V switch that displays the names of every file on the hard disk. You can also use the

CHKDSK /V command with the FIND command to restrict the search to a particular file name or a string of characters.

To search all the directories on your hard disk for a file named BUDGET, use the command

```
CHKDSK /V ¦ FIND "BUDGET"
```

Notice that you must separate the two commands with the pipe character (¦), you must enclose the file name you are searching for in double quotation marks, and you must type the file name in uppercase letters. This is the basic syntax of all searches.

After a pause (which might be either a few seconds or a few minutes), your screen displays the locations and names of all files that contain the name BUDGET. If your missing file appears on the list, you know exactly where to find it.

Of course, another common error that might prevent you from finding a file is misspelling the file name while saving it, but not realizing you've made such an error. For example, you might have typed BUDHET, rather than BUDGET, when you saved the spreadsheet.

You cannot use the * and ? wildcard characters with the FIND command, but you can narrow or broaden the search by searching for more or fewer characters. For example, the command

```
CHKDSK /V ¦ FIND "BUD"
```

displays all file (and directory) names that contain the letters *BUD*.

The CHKDSK and FIND commands are also handy for finding program files that have a particular extension, such as .COM or .EXE. For example,

```
CHKDSK /V ¦ FIND ".COM"
```

displays the names of all files on all directories that have the .COM extension. The command

```
CHKDSK /V ¦ FIND ".EXE"
```

displays the names of all files on all directories that have the .EXE extension. Figure 14.3 shows the results of such a search.

```
C:\CMAKER\CMAKER.EXE
C:\CMAKER\IMOVER.EXE
C:\COLLAGE\ALTOFF.EXE
C:\COLLAGE\ALTON.EXE
C:\COLLAGE\COLLAGE.EXE
C:\COLLAGE\S.EXE
C:\COLLAGE\SAVE.EXE
C:\COLLAGE\SHOW.EXE
C:\COLLAGE\SNAP.EXE
C:\COLLAGE\VIEW.EXE
C:\COMPRESS\LHA.EXE
C:\COMPRESS\PKARC.EXE
C:\COMPRESS\PKUNZIP.EXE
C:\COMPRESS\PKXARC.EXE
C:\COMPRESS\PKZIP.EXE
C:\COMPRESS\PPK.EXE
C:\CSERVE\CIM.EXE
C:\CSERVE\CIMUTIL.EXE
C:\CSERVE\MAKEINI.EXE
C:\CSERVE2\CIM.EXE
C:\CSERVE2\MAKEINI.EXE
C:\DASH\DASH.EXE
C:\DASH\DASHGRP.EXE
-- More --
```

Figure 14.3. The results of searching for all files with the .EXE extension.

If your search presents more files than can fit on-screen, you can redirect the output to the printer instead. Merely use the > PRN symbol, as in the following example:

CHKDSK /V ¦ FIND ".EXE" > PRN

Or to pause after each screenful of information, use this command:

CHKDSK /V ¦ FIND ".EXE" ¦ MORE

DIRCMD

If you usually prefer the output of your DIR commands to be displayed in a certain way, use the DIRCMD environment variable to preset your preference whenever you start your computer. As with the PATH environment variable, place the DIRCMD in your AUTOEXEC.BAT file so that it is always available.

To establish this preference, you use the DIRCMD command with the SET command, along with any valid DIR switches and parameters. For example, placing the command

```
DIRCMD=/P /O:GN
```

in your AUTOEXEC.BAT file means that unless you tell DOS otherwise, whenever you use the DIR command, output from the DIR command will be listed one screen at a time (the /P switch), with directories before files (the /O:G switch), and with both directories and files in alphabetical order (the N parameter).

As with other environment variables, you can always override the preset selection simply by using a different command from the command prompt. For example, if you want a wide display of your files, use the DIR /W command. Remember, though, that you must explicitly override switches designated with the DIRCMD command. For example, typing DIR /W still results in alphabetized listings of directories and files, presented one page at a time. The only difference is that the listing is presented in wide format. If you want files listed in another order, for example by date of creation, you must use the appropriate parameters. The next section discusses displaying files on the basis of creation date.

Directory Navigation Tips

The following sections provide tips on navigating around your disk directories.

Using the Root Directory Name

Chapter 9, "Using the Command Line," and Chapter 10, "Working with Files and Directories," cover the basics of using the MKDIR (or MD) command to create new directories, and the CHDIR (or CD) command to change directories.

You get a little more control over these commands by specifying the root directory name (\) as the starting point for the operation. For example, suppose that you are accessing a directory with the path name PRACTICE\TEST. If you type the command MD FI-NANCES, DOS automatically creates the new directory beneath the current directory so that the full directory path actually becomes PRACTICE\TEST\FINANCES.

However, if you type the command MD \FINANCES, DOS uses the root directory as the starting point, thus placing the FINANCES directory one level below the root. In other words, entering the command MD \FINANCES is a shortcut for typing the following two commands:

```
CD \
MD FINANCES
```

You can also use the root directory as the starting point for a CHDIR, or CD, command. The following examples show how different uses of the root directory (named \) affect the CD command:

> CD FINANCES—Changes to the FINANCES directory only if that directory is exactly one level below the current directory.

> CD \FINANCES—Changes to the FINANCES directory from any level, provided that the FINANCES directory is exactly one level below the root directory.

> CD \SALES\FINANCES—Changes to the FINANCES directory (beneath the SALES directory) from any directory on the disk (that is, regardless of the current directory).

Keep in mind that there is no quick-and-easy way to simultaneously access both a different drive and directory in a single command. For example, if you are currently accessing floppy disk drive A:, you cannot type the command C: \SALES\FINANCES to change to the SALES\FINANCES directory on drive C:. Instead, you must first change drives and then change directories, by typing the following two commands:

```
C:
CD \FINANCES\SALES
```

The . and .. Shortcuts

The DIR command displays two "file" names (. and ..) at the top of a directory listing. The . and .. are symbols— . is an abbreviation for the current directory, and .. is an abbreviation for the parent directory. You can use these symbols as shortcuts in your commands.

For example, suppose that your current directory path is \SALES\FINANCES. To move up to the \SALES directory from FINANCES, you need type only the CD.. command, which takes you up another level.

You can use the .. symbol in any command. For example, suppose that you want to copy all the files from the \FINANCES\SALES\1992 path to the lowest directory on the \FINANCES\SALES\1993 path. If \FINANCES\SALES\1992 is the current directory, type either the command

```
COPY *.* \FINANCES\SALES\1993
```

or the much shorter command

```
COPY *.* ..\1993
```

(because .. fills in the parent directory named \FINANCES\SALES).

The . command can be used to specify the current directory's name. For example, suppose that your current directory path is \FINANCES\SALES and you want to copy all of the SALES files to the next lower directory (on the \FINANCES\SALES\1993 path). Instead of typing the lengthy command

```
COPY *.* C:\FINANCES\SALES\1993
```

use . to stand for the current directory by typing the command

```
COPY *.* .\1993
```

The . symbol can also be used to specify all the files on a directory, as a shorthand way of saying *.*. For example, if you really want to take a shortcut, you can type the command

```
COPY . .\1993
```

rather than

```
COPY *.* .\1993
```

Furthermore, if the destination for the copy is the name of a directory that is exactly one level below the current directory, you really need not specify the parent directory or even the .. symbol. Hence, if the current path is \FINANCES\SALES and you want to copy all its files to the \FINANCES\SALES\1993 subdirectory, the ultimate shortcut command would be

```
COPY . 1993
```

Tips for Creating an Efficient Directory Tree

The purpose of dividing a hard disk into directories is to organize your files for easier access. If you create directories haphazardly, your files eventually become difficult to keep track of. To avoid making a maze of your hard disk, keep in mind the following tips as you create your directory structure.

Tip #1: Don't Clutter the Root Directory

The initial DOS installation procedure automatically creates the root directory and stores a few files on it. You might find it tempting to use the root directory as a sort of dumping ground for all your files, or perhaps for those stray files that do not seem to belong in any other directory.

> The only files that really need to be in the root directory are AUTOEXEC.BAT, CONFIG.SYS, and a few others that DOS placed there when it was installed.

Cluttering the root directory with extra files is like throwing manila file folders into a big unmarked cardboard box. Instead of using the large cardboard box approach, store all your information in clearly marked file drawers (that is, directories). DOS itself even stores most of its files in its own directory, usually the C:\DOS directory.

Tip #2: Keep All DOS Programs in a Single Directory

This tip is similar to tip #1: After a program installs itself in a directory, leave those files alone and do not store other files in those directories. When you start creating and storing your own files, create and use your own directories. Usually, data files are best placed below the directories that store program files. For example, if your word processor is stored in C:\WP, you might want to place your documents in a subdirectory, C:\WP\DOCS.

Tip #3: Install Application Programs in the Recommended Directories

Most programs come with installation programs. Most installation programs suggest a drive and directory for that program. Usually, that is the default installation directory.

When you install an application program on a hard disk, use the directory name that the program's documentation recommends. Otherwise, you might find it difficult using that program's manuals, which often assume that you followed their recommendations.

Tip #4: Make the Directory Tree Broad and Shallow

DOS enables you to be creative when constructing a directory tree. You can create subdirectories beneath directories, sub-subdirectories beneath subdirectories, and so on. However, the deeper you go in this scheme, the longer the path names become, and the harder they become to remember and type. (There is also a 66-character limit to any path.)

Another reason for keeping the directory tree broad and shallow is to provide easy access to all related files. For example, suppose that you use dBASE IV and Lotus 1-2-3. You store these programs in the directories that the manuals advise—dBASE and 123.

Now, assume that you need to create two new directories, one for storing accounts receivable data and one for inventory data. You decide to name these directories ACCT_REC and INVENTRY. Further assume that you use dBASE to handle some information in both accounts receivable and inventory data, and Lotus 1-2-3 to handle the rest of the data.

Given all this information, you have two options for creating the directory tree. A deep structure has directories containing accounts receivable and inventory files beneath each of the program directories. The problem with that directory tree is that it artificially divides the accounts receivable and inventory data into four separate directories: DBASE\ACCT_REC, DBASE\INVENTRY, 123\ACCT_REC, and 123\INVENTRY.

A better directory tree for organizing the various programs and your business data would have each directory on the same level (that is, the tree is shallower than the one previously discussed). All inventory data, whether created by Lotus 1-2-3 or dBASE IV, goes into the INVENTRY subdirectory. The same is true for your accounts receivable information.

The shallower directory tree has the distinct advantage of organizing both the accounts receivable files and the inventory files into their own clearly named directories. The files are not artificially divided into subdirectories that are dependent on individual application programs. If you change inventory data, you need only do so on one directory.

Given this new tip, you might be wondering when you would ever want to create a subdirectory. Actually, using a subdirectory makes sense when all the files on it are relevant only to the parent directory. If other types of data, such as quarterly data projections, are created only by Lotus 1-2-3, it makes sense to create a subdirectory, perhaps called QTR_BUDG, under your 123 directory.

Tips for Creating an Effective Search Path

As I have mentioned previously, if you attempt to run a program that is not in the current directory (or drive), DOS displays the error message Bad command or file name. This is inconvenient, if not maddening.

The solution to this problem is the all-important PATH command. This command tells DOS to look in other directories if it cannot find the requested program in the current directory. The syntax of the PATH command is

PATH d:pathname;d:pathname;d:pathname...

in which

   d: is the name of a drive

   pathname is the name of a directory on the drive

   ; separates each drive and directory name

To the right of the PATH command, list as many drive and directory names or pathnames as you want. Just remember to separate
each sequence with a semicolon and restrict the total number of
characters on the line to 127.

Include the root directory in the search path by including its
name (\) in the PATH command. For example, the following PATH
command tells DOS to search both the root and the DOS directories of drive C:

```
PATH C:\;C:\DOS
```

The order of directory names in the PATH command affects the
time that DOS requires to find a particular program. A little planning can ensure that DOS locates and runs your programs as quickly
as possible. That planning is the topic of the next section.

Planning the Perfect Path

First, remember that the PATH command searches only for *executable*
files, which always have the file-name extension .BAT, .COM, or
.EXE. Therefore, it serves no purpose to include in the PATH command directories that contain only data files.

Second, keep in mind that DOS searches all the directories—from
left to right—in the PATH command, until it finds the program you
requested. For example, suppose that you set up your PATH command as follows:

```
PATH C:\DOS;C:\WP;C:\WINDOWS;C:\DBASE
```

When you run the dBASE program from another directory, for
example, DOS first searches the current directory for the dBASE
program. Then it looks in the DOS directory, the WP directory, the
WINDOWS directory, and finally, the dBASE directory.

Therefore, consider two factors when determining the order of
the directories in your PATH command:

- How many files are in each directory
- Which programs you use most often

If a particular directory contains many files, list it as the last directory in the PATH command so that it is searched as a last resort, when DOS determines that no other directory contains the requested program.

If you use one program far more frequently than other programs, list its directory (or pathname) first in the PATH command. That way, its directory is the first one searched. For example, as a writer and programmer, I use my word processing program more than any other, and therefore, I always list its directory first in my PATH command.

Don't include every directory that contains a program in the PATH command. Include only those directories that contain program files you are likely to use from the command prompt. If directories contain programs that are loaded by the AUTOEXEC.BAT, CONFIG.SYS, or batch programs, don't include them in the PATH command. DOS takes longer to process PATH statements.

Do not put any blank spaces—other than the one immediately to the right of the PATH command in your list of directories. DOS stops reading directory names from the PATH command when it encounters a blank space.

How to Enter a *PATH* Command

Type the PATH command at the command prompt at any time. Note, though, that if you use the DOS Shell, you have to make a full exit before you type the PATH command. Type

PATH

to have DOS display the current path. DOS displays either the message No Path, if no path has been defined, or the currently defined path. After you define a new path by typing the PATH command, the new path is in effect until you reboot or define a different path.

Rather than type the PATH command each time you start the computer, include the PATH command in your AUTOEXEC.BAT file. That way, DOS automatically defines the path for you when it boots the computer.

Positioning the *PATH* Command in AUTOEXEC.BAT

You can place the PATH command anywhere in the AUTOEXEC.BAT file, as long as the entire command is no longer than 127 characters and no other commands are on the same line. Always remember, however, that if you are using the DOS Shell, the DOSSHELL command must be the last command in the AUTOEXEC.BAT file.

Figure 14.4 shows a sample AUTOEXEC.BAT file that includes the command

```
PATH C:\WP;C:\DOS;C:\UTILS;C:\DBASE;C:\WINDOWS
```

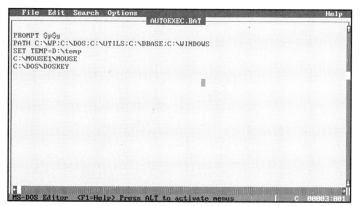

Figure 14.4. A sample AUTOEXEC.BAT file with a PATH command.

Notice also that the sample AUTOEXEC.BAT file includes the command C:\MOUSE1\MOUSE. This line runs the mouse driver program (named MOUSE.COM in this example), which installs the mouse when the computer first boots up. Because the MOUSE1 directory is not included in the preceding PATH command, DOS must be told the exact location of the MOUSE.COM program (C:\MOUSE1 in this example) so that it can find and execute the MOUSE.COM program.

Understanding the Effects of a *PATH* Command

Remember, DOS refers to the PATH command only when you attempt to run a program that is not in the current directory. PATH has no effect on file displays in the DOS Shell, or on the output of the DIR command.

Furthermore, DOS uses the PATH command only when searching for a program to run; it does not search for a file specified in conjunction with a command. For example, if you type the command TYPE MYFILE.TXT at the command prompt to view the contents of a file named MYFILE.TXT, DOS searches PATH for the TYPE command, but it searches only the current directory for the MYFILE.TXT file, regardless of the PATH search path.

Backing Up Your Files

Regularly backing up your files protects you against accidental erasures, disk failures, and a host of other problems that can endanger your data. Horror stories abound of computer users who labored for hours, days, even weeks to create files, only to have their work destroyed by a hard disk failure or other calamity. Many computer professionals claim that it is just a matter of time until such a calamity occurs.

DOS 6 includes special backup programs for both command-prompt users and those who use Windows. Although this section primarily discusses procedures for using the Microsoft Backup for MS-DOS program, the principles and virtually all procedures are the same for both programs.

Microsoft Backup for MS-DOS Basics

Microsoft Backup for MS-DOS is more than just an external command. It is a full-featured application program in its own right. It enables you to back up files to floppy drives or other storage devices. You then can restore the backed up files to their original locations. Its options enable you to configure the way you back up and restore files.

First I'll discuss some general issues related to backing up your files. Then, I'll discuss many of the options for customizing your usage of Microsoft Backup. Finally, I'll discuss the actual procedures you will use for backing up and restoring files.

To avoid confusion, you need to know that even though the name of the program is Microsoft Backup, there is no separate program for restoring backed up files. The restore function is included as part of the Microsoft Backup program.

One additional note about backing up. Microsoft Backup backs up and restores files to floppy disks, as well as to other removable drives and network drives. For the sake of simplicity, I will discuss backing up only to floppy drives. The principles are the same for backing up to floppy drives as they are for backing up to network drives or removable drives, such as those from such vendors as Bernoulli.

If you are using new floppy disks for your backups, don't bother to format them first. Microsoft Backup automatically formats them and can even use its own method of formatting, which allows it to store information faster and in less space.

Different Types of Backups

Microsoft Backup provides three distinct ways to back up your files. Each serves a different purpose, and each has advantages and disadvantages. This section gives an overview of those different types of backups. The next section will help you decide on the best strategy for your situation using the different types of backups.

Full Backups

When you choose to do a *full backup,* Microsoft Backup backs up every file you select. For example, if you want to back up your entire drive C:, this is the option you use. You also could use a full backup for all files of a particular type. For example, you might want to use a full backup for all your word processing documents.

The main disadvantage of full backups is that they take a lot of time. Also, full backups can be inefficient. A full backup backs up every file you select. As a result, it backs up files that have not changed since the last time you backed up. The next two options were designed to deal with this situation.

Incremental Backups

Incremental backups back up only files that you have changed since the last time you used Microsoft Backup. Using this option, you can save time by performing a full backup periodically, but doing an incremental backup regularly, perhaps every day. In this way, you back up all your files, but on a daily basis you back up only the files that have changed.

Incremental backups are an excellent way to make sure you save all revisions of files. If you have an important file that is changed regularly, and you want access to all the revisions, make sure you save each version of the file by using incremental backups.

One potential disadvantage of incremental backups is that each incremental backup requires its own set of disks. For example, suppose you perform a full backup, then the next day you do an incremental backup of files that have changed. The following day, you do another incremental backup. You now have three sets of backup disks: The original full backup and two sets of incremental backup disks. If you do daily incremental backups for a month, you will have 30 sets of backup disks. If something happens and you must restore all the files to your hard drive, you must restore 30 sets of backup files. The next option, differential backups, provides a slightly different solution.

Differential Backups

Differential backups back up all files that have changed since the last full backup. In other words, after a differential backup, you will have a set of backup disks for your full backup, and only one additional set of backup disks created by your differential backup. This lessens the number of backup disks you must maintain, and it makes restoring files simpler. On the other hand, you will not have backup copies of each version of the files that are being revised.

Backup Strategies

The three types of backups discussed in the preceding section provide much flexibility when you look for the best system for backing up your files. This section discusses three strategies for backing up your files. The strategy you select should reflect the way you work with programs and files, and the time you have available for backing up.

Note that although a full backup of an entire hard disk can take some time, incremental and differential backups typically should not take more than a few minutes a day. When the inevitable happens and you lose data, those few minutes can save work that took days and weeks to create.

One thing remains constant in the discussion of various backup strategies: whichever strategy you select, back up frequently. A good habit to learn is backing up your files at the same time every day. At first, you might need to set an alarm to remind yourself. Eventually, however, backing up at a specific time becomes second nature, and you can be assured that the work you lose in case of a hard disk disaster will be minimal.

Strategy 1: Full and Differential Backups

If you work with the same files day in and day out, you might want to adopt the strategy of first doing a full backup, then doing differential backups every day. For example, this is an effective strategy if you are a budget analyst and you typically work with a small handful of Lotus 1-2-3 files. It is time-effective because each backup copies only a relatively small number of files.

This also is a good strategy for those who do not need to track revisions of individual files. Incremental backups are best for tracking revisions of files, but they also require multiple sets of backup disks.

Strategy 2: Full and Incremental Backups

A very thorough but sometimes faster way to back up your files is to first perform a full backup of your entire hard drive, and then do incremental backups every day. This is a thorough method because it not only backs up every file you select, but also backs up multiple versions of the same files.

This is a good backup strategy if you create a lot of different files every day. For example, if your work at the computer consists mostly of writing letters and memos, you might want to use this strategy. That is because you will back up only those files you have created or changed since the last incremental backup. By contrast, a differential backup backs up all files you have changed or created since the last full backup. If you create a lot of files and use differential backups, the amount of time you spend backing up will increase every day.

The disadvantages of this method are that it requires more disks than other methods, and it can take more time than a differential backup when you have to restore your entire hard drive.

Strategy 3: Backing Up Only Data Files

People who rebel against the idea of spending the time to perform a full backup of a hard drive sometimes back up only data files. Although this provides the least amount of protection in case of disaster, it is the fastest method on a day-to-day basis.

With this strategy, for example, if you primarily use dBASE IV and WordPerfect, you would back up only files with the .DBF and .DOC extensions. Unless you have a lot of these files, you probably will want to do a full backup of the selected files every day. This means you will have only one set of disks to manage.

If you have a lot of individual files, however, you might want to first perform a full backup on all your .DOC and .DBF files, then choose either an incremental or a differential backup for everyday usage.

This strategy also is appropriate if you are a power user and you regularly change the programs on your hard disk and the configuration of your computer. In such a case, full backups, which are done only periodically, are quickly out-of-date.

Remember, though, that if you use this strategy and your hard disk crashes, you must first reload all your application programs manually before you restore your data files. This method will save you time every day but will cost you time in an emergency.

Configuring Microsoft Backup for MS-DOS

Before you put your backup strategy to work, you must select various settings and options. These are stored as *setup files*. Setup files include information about which drives, directories, and files you want to back up. Setup files also include information about the drives to which you want to back up your files. You also will select which type of backup you want to do, as well as other options.

Two other types of files created during the backup process are *backup sets* and *backup catalogs.* Backups sets are the files stored on the backup disks. A backup set includes a copy of the backup catalog, which contains all relevant information about the individual files you have backed up. The backup catalog also is stored on your hard drive. When it is time to restore files, you first load the appropriate backup catalog. The catalog then tells the Restore portion of Microsoft Backup where specific files are, and into which directories they should be restored.

How Backup Catalogs Are Named

Backup catalog files appear to have strange names. For example, a typical name for a backup catalog might be CD31112A.INC. To the uninitiated, this might not be a descriptive file name. But this file name tells you a lot about this catalog, as explained here:

C—The first drive backed up by the set described by the catalog.

D—The last drive backed up by the set described by the catalog.

3—The last digit of the year, as determined by your system date. In this case, the year would be 1993.

11—The current month.

12—The current day of the month.

A—Reflects the number of backups made during the day. *A* means that this is the first backup made on the C: and D: drives on that particular day.

INC—Reflects the type of backup made. In this example, the backup was an incremental backup. The extension .FUL stands for a full backup; .DIF stands for a differential backup.

The Configure Window

The opening screen of Microsoft Backup enables you to go to the backup or restore sections of the program, to compare files you already have backed up to the source files on your hard disk, or to configure the way you want Microsoft Backup to look and act. Figure 14.5 shows the screen you see when you first start Microsoft Backup.

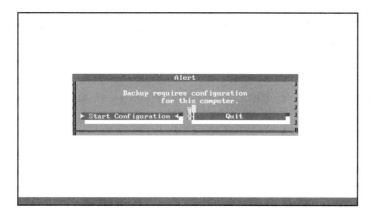

Figure 14.5. The Microsoft Backup opening screen.

If you select Configure, you will see the screen shown in Figure 14.6.

As Figure 14.6 shows, the Configure option from the opening screen enables you to adjust video and mouse settings, tell Microsoft Backup about the drives you are using for your backup and restore procedures, and run a compatibility test to make sure that your system can optimally use Microsoft Backup. It is best to set these options before you begin to use Microsoft Backup.

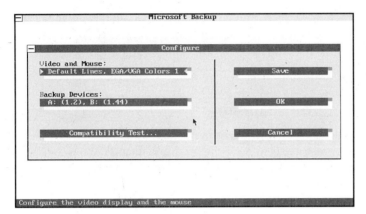

Figure 14.6.
The Configure
screen of
Microsoft
Backup.

Options to Ensure Reliable Backups

Microsoft Backup provides three ways to make sure your backups are safe and reliable. Two of those methods, *data verification* and *error correction codes,* are available from the Disk Backup Options dialog box, which you access from the Backup window.

The third option to ensure the reliability of backups, the Compare command, is available from the opening dialog box. This option compares the backed up files to the original files to make sure that none of the files was corrupted during the backup process.

To get to the Disk Backup Options dialog box, select Backup from the opening screen. This takes you to the Backup window, shown in Figure 14.7.

In the Backup window, select Options. The Disk Backup Options dialog box is shown in Figure 14.8. Other options in this dialog box are discussed in the next section.

When you select data verification from this dialog box, Microsoft Backup compares the backed up files to the original files on your hard drive during the backup process. This slows down the process but provides an added level of reliability. By comparison, the Compare command examines both backed up and original files after you have performed the backup.

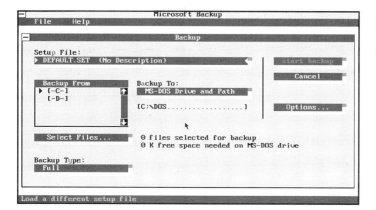

Figure 14.7.
The Backup
window.

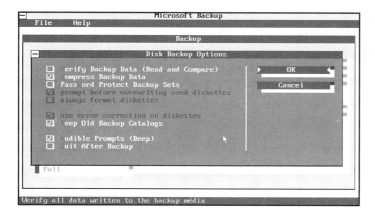

Figure 14.8.
The Options
dialog box.

Data verification also is available when you are restoring data. It works in the same way as for backups, but in reverse. You can switch this option on from the Disk Restore Options menu in the Restore window.

Error correction codes add special codes to backup floppy disks. The purpose of these codes is to make restoring your data easier if the backup set is damaged.

Other Backup Options

The other options in the Backup Options dialog box are as listed next:

Compress Backup Data—Compresses files on the backup disks. This allows more data to be stored on disks. Although compression decreases the number of backup disks you will need, it also can decrease backup speed.

Password Protect Backup Sets—Prevents unauthorized personnel from restoring or comparing backed up information. You must remember your password, or you will be unable to restore (or compare) your data.

Prompt Before Overwriting Used Diskettes—Warns you that information already exists on your backup disks and gives you the chance to switch disks or overwrite the information.

Always Format Diskettes—Formats all backup disks, every time they are used. This makes sure that the backup floppy disks always are formatted properly, but it takes more time. Even if you do not select this option, Microsoft Backup formats disks that are unformatted or incorrectly formatted.

Keep Old Backup Catalogs—Normally, when you perform a full backup, Microsoft Backup erases all previous catalogs. If you want to keep track of your previous backup operations, select this option.

Audible Prompts (Beep)—Tells Microsoft Backup to beep whenever it needs you to do something, such as insert the next diskette during a backup operation.

Quit After Backup—Automatically exits Microsoft Backup when the backup is completed.

Creating Setup Files

In the previous sections, you learned the basics about Microsoft Backup and how to configure it. Now it is time to create setup files. Setup files include specific instructions about how you want Microsoft Backup to back up your files.

A setup file is the combination of files that you select to back up, and other configuration options you select. Each setup file has its own name. For example, you could call the set in which you conduct a full backup FULL_BAK.

Typically, you will want more than one setup file. For example, besides the FULL_BAK set, you also might want a setup file for incrementally backing up data files. The procedures discussed in this section can be used to create as many different setup files as you want.

Microsoft Backup already comes with a setup file called DEFAULT.SET. Some of the configuration options in DEFAULT.SET are based on information the program gathered during the compatibility test during your initial configuration. DEFAULT.SET assumes that you want to make a full backup and save your files to floppy disks on drive A:. However, it has selected no files to back up.

Because Microsoft Backup loads the Default setup file unless you tell it otherwise, it makes sense to make the Default setup file one you use most frequently. If you perform a full backup every several weeks but do a differential backup every day, make the Default setup file the one that performs your differential backup.

After you have selected options from the Disk Backup Options dialog box, in the Backup window select which drive you want to back up to. Although most people back up to floppy drives, you should select the specific drive letter to which you want to back up.

Next, select the type of backup you want. When you are done with this process, it is time to select the files you want to back up

whenever you select this particular configuration. The procedure
for selecting files is discussed in the next section.

Selecting Files to Back Up

For each setup file, you must tell Microsoft Backup which files you
want to back up. This takes several steps. For this example, assume
that you are changing the DEFAULT.SET to make incremental backups of all files that have changed since the last backup session. Further, you want to exclude from the backup all files with the .BAK
extension.

To select files, first select the drive on which the files are located.
Notice that in Figure 14.9, the Backup From window indicates that
there are two drives, [-C-] and [-D-].

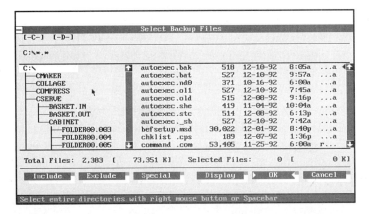

*Figure 14.9.
The Select
Backup Files
window.*

If you want to back up files from multiple drives, go
through the following procedure for each drive on which
files are located.

If you want to back up all files on that drive, either double-click the
drive letter or, with the drive letter highlighted, press the Spacebar.
After you do this, the words *All files* appear next to the drive letter.

If you want to select specific files to back up, select the Select Files option. You will see a screen like the one shown in Figure 14.9.

The left side of the Select Backup Files window shows the directories on the drive you selected. The right side of the window displays all the files in the directories. Move between the windows (and the options at the bottom of the window) by pressing Tab to move forward and Shift+Tab to move back. Or click your mouse on the area or button you want.

You can select files one at a time, or automatically. To select files manually, first select the directory you want in the directory list. If you want to select all files in the directory, press the Spacebar or double-click the directory name. If you want to select individual files within a directory, move to the files area and either double-click your mouse or press the Spacebar on the files you want. Notice that a check mark appears to the left of files you have selected.

The manual method is the best way to select specific files. However, this method is not useful if you will create files later that you also want to back up. For example, if you choose to back up MYFILE.DOC and you later create a file called NEWFILE.DOC, only MYFILE.DOC is backed up.

Because of this, in most cases, you will use automatic file selection. To use this method, select Include at the bottom of the Select Backup Files window. You will see the Include Files dialog box, shown in Figure 14.10.

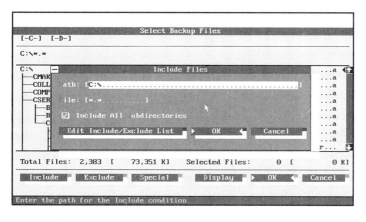

Figure 14.10. The Include Files dialog box.

In this example, type C:\ in the Path: text box and *.* in the File: text box. Make sure that the Include All Subdirectories option is checked. Then select OK. You have just told Microsoft Backup to include all files on your C: drive when it performs a backup.

Remember, though, that you also want to exclude all files with the .BAK extension. To do this, select the Exclude option at the bottom of the Select Backup Files window. The Exclude Files dialog box, shown in Figure 14.11, is similar to the Include Files dialog box.

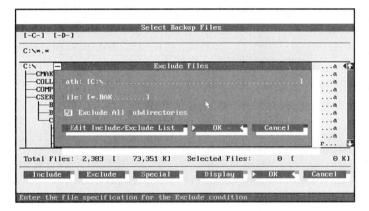

Figure 14.11.
The Exclude
Files dialog box
in Microsoft
Backup.

Again, type C:\ in the Path: text box, and make sure that you have checked the Exclude All Subdirectories option. This time, however, type *.BAK in the File: text box. Then select OK.

These two operations have told Microsoft Backup to back up all files on the C: drive except those with the extension .BAK. Notice in Figure 14.12 that all files except those with the .BAK extension have checks next to them.

You can add more files to include or exclude by repeating this process. Remember that you must go through this process for each drive from which you want to back up files. You can edit existing include or exclude settings by selecting the Edit Include/Exclude List from the bottom of the Include Files or Exclude Files dialog boxes.

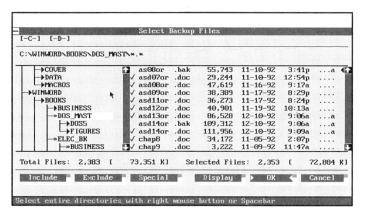

Figure 14.12.
Files included
and excluded
for backup.

Although using the include or exclude files options is fast, it is not the best method in every instance. You might want a setup file in which you back up only certain files. This might be true if you work with the same files all the time. If you are a budget analyst who typically works with only four or five Lotus 1-2-3 files, for example, you would not necessarily want to back up all files in your Lotus directory with the .WK1 extension. Manual selection is the best way to select files in such a situation.

When you return to the Backup window, the Backup From box tells you that some files have been selected from drive C:. Remember that you must repeat this process for drive D: and any other drives that contain files you want to back up.

When you are done selecting drives and files, and you have selected all other options, save your setup file by selecting Save from the File menu. Because the DEFAULT setup file automatically was loaded when you started Microsoft Backup, selecting Save from the File menu saves this new setup under the name DEFAULT.SET. Select Save As from the File menu to save your configuration with another name.

Although you will want a configuration for a full backup and a configuration for either an incremental or a differential backup, you also can develop different configurations for other purposes. For example, as discussed previously, you might work with a small number of critically important files each day. If you want to back up those files twice a day, create a setup file that performs a full backup of only those few files. Backing up a few files will take only a minute, but you can be assured that in case of a disk failure or other catastrophe, you have not lost too much work.

Creating a setup file with no files selected for backup can save you time when you need to back up specific files on a one-time basis. This is handy, for example, when a colleague who also uses Microsoft Backup asks you for a specific file, and that file is too large to fit on a single diskette. Load the setup file in which you have specified no files, manually select just that one file, and perform the backup. When you exit Microsoft Backup and you are asked whether you want to save the setup file, select No. That way, you won't accidentally back up that same file the next time you use that setup file.

Backing Up Files

You have now configured Microsoft Backup and have selected the files to include and exclude in DEFAULT.SET. Perhaps you have added additional setup files. Now it is time to back up your files.

First, start Microsoft Backup from the command prompt. Unless you specify otherwise, Microsoft Backup automatically loads

DEFAULT.SET. If you want to use a different setup file, select Open setup from the File menu, and select the setup file you want.

Microsoft Backup accepts command-line parameters for setup files. You can load a particular setup file from the command prompt by typing MSBACKUP followed by a space and the setup file name.

After you select your setup file, start the backup procedure by selecting the Start Backup button. Microsoft Backup prompts you to insert new disks until the backup is complete.

Keep your backup diskettes in a safe place and in proper order. Because they are your last line of defense against hard drive disasters, proper disk care is essential. Do not keep your diskettes in rooms that are too hot or too cold or that are smoky. Also keep them away from magnetic devices.

You periodically might want to perform a complete backup and keep those backup disks at an off-site location. If disaster, such as a fire, strikes your home or office, backup disks located near your computer will likely be destroyed along with everything else. Storing a set of full backup disks in another location is added insurance against that type of disaster.

Restore Options

When it is time to restore files to your hard drive, select the Restore option from the opening screen. With a few exceptions, the Restore window, shown in Figure 14.13, is similar to the Backup window.

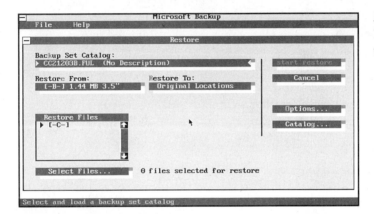

Figure 14.13. The Restore window.

Microsoft Backup is an ideal way to transfer files between computers. For example, if your home computer and work computer both have Microsoft Backup, back up your relevant data files, then restore them on your home computer. The same concept is true if you use both a desktop computer and a notebook computer.

If you select Options, the Disk Restore Options dialog box gives you the following choices:

Verify Restore Data (Read and Compare)—Verifies that the data being restored to a hard drive is identical to that stored on the backup disk.

Prompt Before Creating Directories—Warns you if the backup disks create a directory. This could occur if you backed up your hard drive, deleted a directory, and then restored files.

Prompt Before Creating Files—Prompts you if the restore process places new files on your hard drive.

Prompt Before Overwriting Existing File—Warns you if you are about to overwrite an existing file on your hard drive with a file with the same name from the backup set.

Restore Empty Directories—Determines whether directories that are empty should be restored to your hard drive.

Audible Prompts (Beep)—Determines whether Microsoft Backup beeps when it needs you to perform an action, such as changing diskettes.

Quit After Restore—Determines whether you automatically exit Microsoft Backup after you are done restoring files.

There are additional options in the Restore window. First, you must select the backup catalog. To select a catalog, select the Catalog option and select the catalog you want; then select Load.

Next select the type of disk you will use from the Restore From dialog box. Then select the destination for the restored files. Here are your options:

Original Locations—Restores files to the directories from which they were backed up.

Other Drives—Restores files to drives other than the one from which they were backed up. You are asked to provide the new drive.

Other Directories—Restores files to directories other than the ones from which they were backed up. You are asked to provide the new directories.

The catalog file for each backup session is stored on your hard drive, typically in the same directory as your Microsoft Backup program files. It also is stored on the last floppy in each set of backup disks. Even if the catalog file is not available on your hard drive, you can retrieve it by selecting the Retrieve option from the Select Catalog dialog box. Then follow the instructions in the dialog boxes that follow. You must use this technique when you back up files on one computer and restore them to another. And, of course, you must use this technique if your catalog files are inadvertently lost from your hard drive.

Restoring Your Files

After you have chosen all the options related to restoring files, you must select the files to restore.

The drives shown in the Restore Files selection box reflect only those drives from which files were backed up by any given setup file. If you have two drives named C: and D: but you backed up files only from the C: drive, that is the only drive that appears in the Restore Files selection box.

To restore all files that were backed up from that drive, either double-click the drive letter, or highlight the drive letter and press the Spacebar. Notice the message that appears stating how many files will be restored.

If you want to restore only specific files, select the Select Files option. You will see a window with all the directories on the left side and all the individual files in each directory on the right side. Select the files you want to restore in the same way that you selected files to back up in the Backup window. When you are done, select OK. Then, in the main Restore window, select Start Restore, and follow the on-screen directions.

Using Microsoft Backup for Windows

Although the focus of this chapter has been on Microsoft Backup for MS-DOS, procedures for using Microsoft Backup for Windows are nearly identical. You might notice a few differences in the contents of dialog boxes, but the basic procedures for all operations are the same.

When you installed DOS 6, you had the opportunity to install Microsoft Backup for MS-DOS, Microsoft Backup for Windows, or both. The installation program also gave you the same options for the Microsoft Anti-Virus and the Undelete programs (discussed in Chapter 18, "Protecting Your System"). If you installed Microsoft Backup for Windows, or either of the other two Windows-based programs, the DOS installation program automatically created a special program group for Microsoft applications in your Windows Program Manager.

To access Microsoft Backup for Windows, first double-click the Microsoft Applications group icon, and then double-click the Microsoft Backup icon.

One cosmetic difference between the two programs is that whereas the DOS version starts from an opening screen from which you choose Backup, Restore, Compare, or Configure, the Windows version takes you directly to the Restore window. In this window, however, there are large icons for selecting among the Restore, Compare, and Configure options. Figure 14.14 shows the backup window for Microsoft Backup for Windows.

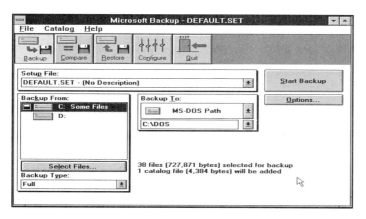

Figure 14.14. Microsoft Backup for Windows.

One advantage of using Microsoft Backup for Windows is that it can perform backups while you are doing other tasks in Windows. In Windows parlance, the backup program operates in the background. You can start your backup procedure, then switch to another application, such as your word processor or spreadsheet. When Microsoft Backup for Windows needs you to perform an action, such as change disks, it beeps and gives you a screen message with instructions. This is a handy feature for long backup procedures because it means you can get on with your other business while backing up your files.

You also can run Microsoft Backup for MS-DOS while you are using Windows. If you do this only occasionally, select Run from the File menu of the Program Manager, and type in the full path and file name. For example, in most cases, type

```
C:\DOS\MSBACKUP
```

with an optional setup file as a parameter. If you want to run Microsoft Backup for MS-DOS from Windows regularly, create a special file, called a Windows PIF file, that customizes the way DOS applications run. You also will probably want to create an icon within the Windows Program Manager to launch Microsoft Backup for MS-DOS. To perform these functions, consult your Windows User's Guide.

> The same setup files can be used by both the Windows and the MS-DOS versions of Microsoft Backup. This is useful to know if you use Windows but also spend a lot of time working from the command prompt.

Speeding Up Your Hard Drive

You will get more work done if your hard disk operates more quickly. DOS includes ways to increase the speed of your hard drive. This section discusses those techniques.

DEFRAG Basics

When you copy a file to your hard drive, DOS often divides it and places different portions of the file in different locations of the drive. However, your hard drive works more efficiently and faster if all elements of your files are next to each other, or *contiguous*. That is because the hard disk does not have to spend so much time finding and then loading all the different parts of a file.

As you add and subtract files from your hard disk, it becomes harder for DOS to make all the elements of your files contiguous. As a result, your files, and your hard disk, become *fragmented*. That is to say, an increasing number of your files are spread out to various locations on your hard disk. As this problem worsens, the performance of your hard disk noticeably decreases. A symptom of this problem is that the hard disk drive in-use light remains on for increasingly longer periods as it reads files.

DOS 6 includes a new program called DEFRAG to deal with this problem. DEFRAG examines your hard drive for the location of all elements of your files and then repacks—or defragments—your hard drive so that all the elements of your files are contiguous.

It is a good idea to run DEFRAG periodically. If you create and delete a lot of data files, run DEFRAG every few days. Most computer users, however, should run DEFRAG every week or two. If you disk was badly fragmented, you will notice a significant increase in performance after you run DEFRAG.

Never run DEFRAG from either the DOS Shell or Windows. Nor should you start DEFRAG from the DOS prompt if you have only temporarily exited, or shelled, from a program. Run DEFRAG only from the command prompt after you have permanently exited all other programs. Failing to do so could result in damage to your files. DEFRAG usually warns you if you try to load it improperly. But to make sure you avoid any problems, run DEFRAG only after permanently exiting all programs.

Running DEFRAG

DEFRAG is easy to run. First, as stated previously, fully exit all programs. At the command prompt, type

```
DEFRAG [drive] [switch]
```

Both the drive parameter and the switches are optional. If you do not specify a drive, DEFRAG asks when it starts which drive you want to defragment. The switches tell DEFRAG how to conduct the defragmentation process. Switches are discussed later in the section "The Optimize Menu." The screen asking which drive you want to defragment is shown in Figure 14.15.

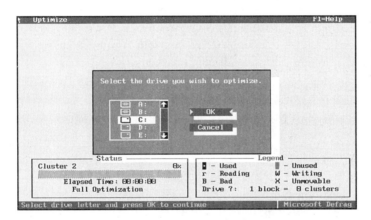

Figure 14.15. DEFRAG asks which drive you want to defragment.

DEFRAG examines all the files on the hard drive you select. It also gives you a brief report about the level of disk fragmentation and a suggested course of action. You can begin the defragmentation process immediately or use the menus for additional options. Figure 14.16 shows the main DEFRAG screen of a moderately defragmented hard drive. Most of the main screen is devoted to the *disk map*, which provides a graphical representation of your hard drive and shows the level of fragmentation. Each square represents a sector of the hard drive.

If DEFRAG finds that your hard disk contains lost allocation clusters, it stops and tells you to fix the problem by

using the CHKDSK /F command from the command prompt.
Lost clusters are portions of programs or files that DOS
thinks are not attached to their related programs or files.
The CHKDSK /F command is discussed in Chapter 9, "Using
the Command Line."

If you choose to proceed, the defragmentation process can take
just a minute or two, or it can take a lot longer, depending on the
level of defragmentation. When you are done, the disk map shows
a more ordered hard drive, as shown in Figure 14.17.

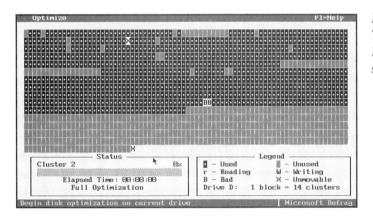

*Figure 14.16.
The main
DEFRAG
screen.*

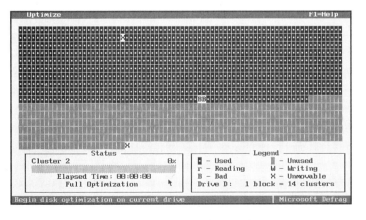

*Figure 14.17.
The disk
map after
defragmentation.*

The Optimize Menu

The DEFRAG program contains only one menu, the Optimize menu. It includes options that determine how the program conducts the defragmentation process. The Optimize menu is shown in Figure 14.18.

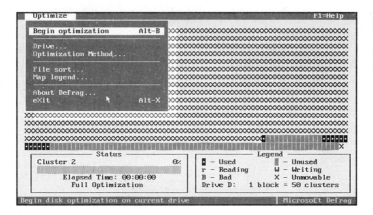

*Figure 14.18.
The Optimize
menu of
DEFRAG.*

The menu options are as listed here:

Begin Optimization—Begins optimization. You also can use the shortcut key, Alt+B.

Drive—Selects the drive to defragment.

Optimization Method—Leads to the Select Optimization Method dialog box. There are two options in this dialog box:

Full Optimization. Optimizes the entire hard drive and then packs all the files together. It results in a disk map in the main DEFRAG screen in which all files are packed together with no spaces. This option takes longer than unfragmenting files only. You can start this option from the command line with the /F switch.

Unfragment Files Only. Defragments only the files that need it. Because it doesn't repack the entire hard drive, you might see gaps in the disk map when you are done, such as the disk map in Figure 14.17. You can start this option from the command line with the /U switch.

File Sort—Leads to the File Sort dialog box, which sets parameters for sorting files within directories during the defragmentation process. Because this does not affect the physical placement of files on your hard drive, there usually is no need to change the default setting of Unsorted.

Map Legend—Describes the various elements of the disk map in the main DEFRAG screen.

Exit—Exits the program. The shortcut key is Alt+X.

SMARTDrive Basics

SMARTDrive is a *disk cache* program that can dramatically speed up your system. Disk caches work by temporarily storing data from your applications in a special section of RAM called a cache. When your application needs that information again, it is recalled from the cache rather than from your hard drive. Because RAM operates much faster than your hard drive, your application works much faster when you are using a disk cache.

SMARTDrive can speed up disk operations by temporarily storing information that your application reads from the hard disk. It also can temporarily store information that must be written to your disk, such as information you change when you are using an application program. It later writes the information to the disk when your computer requires fewer system resources, such as when you are not typing.

Larger disk caches can temporarily store more information in memory for later use. Thus, larger disk caches mean your computer operates faster.

SMARTDrive caches are placed in *extended memory*. Extended memory is memory in excess of 1M. (Extended memory is discussed in greater detail in Chapter 15, "Getting the Most from Your Memory.")

Using SMARTDrive

Include the command for SMARTDrive in your AUTOEXEC.BAT file so that it is activated every time you start your computer. However, it also can be loaded from the command prompt.

The syntax for SMARTDrive is

```
SMARTDRV [cache drives] [element size] [initial cache
 size] [windows cache size] [buffer size] /[switches]
```

This might seem like a complicated syntax. But SMARTDrive lives up to its name: it examines your system when it loads and, in many cases, adjusts its settings accordingly. As a result, most users don't need to set parameters and switches. The following paragraphs discuss each element of the syntax.

If you don't specify drives to cache, SMARTDrive automatically applies read and write caches to all hard drives and only write caches to floppy drives. CD-ROM and network drives are ignored. These options make sense in most situations. If you want to change the default, list the drive letter followed by + or -. The + enables read and write caching for the drive you designate, and the - disables all caching for a particular drive. For example, the command

```
SMARTDRV B+ D-
```

enables write caching for floppy drive B: and disables all caching for hard drive D:.

The element size is the number of bytes of information that SMARTDrive moves to and from the cache at a time. The options are 1024, 2048, 4096, and 8192 bytes. The default is 8192 bytes. Again, there should be no reason to change the default, although it might be useful in some cases in which conventional memory (memory below 1M) is very tight. That is because a small element of SMARTDrive is placed in conventional memory, and the amount of memory you designate for this parameter comes from that lower memory. Because the amount of memory involved is relatively small, do not change the default unless your lower memory is in extremely short supply.

The initial cache size refers to the size of the cache when Windows is not running. The Windows cache size refers to the amount of that cache that is dedicated to Windows when you start Windows. As mentioned previously, the larger the cache size, the better. However, Windows requires extended memory for uses other than SMARTDrive. As a result, if you have 2M of extended memory and you devote all of it to SMARTDrive, you soon will run out of memory for other functions when you are in Windows.

Because finding the balance between initial cache size and Windows cache size can be confusing, SMARTDrive does the work for you. When you start SMARTDrive, it examines how much memory you have. If you have not set specific initial or Windows cache sizes, it automatically sets them as shown in Table 14.3.

Table 14.3. SMARTDrive's default settings for initial cache size and Windows cache size.

Extended Memory	Initial Cache	Windows Cache
Up to 1M	All extended memory	0 (no caching)
1M to 2M	1M	256K
2M to 4M	1M	512K
4M to 6M	2M	1M
6M+	2M	2M

In most cases, there is no reason to change SMARTDrive's cache size settings. If you need to do so, however, simply put the value, in kilobytes, in the command line.

There also are several switches for use with SMARTDrive. The /B and /Q switches are used when SMARTDrive loads. Use the other switches from the command line after SMARTDrive has been started to alter the way it operates or to get information about SMARTDrive.

Table 14.4 is a brief description of available switches for the SMARTDRV command.

Table 14.4. SMARTDrive switches.

Switch	Function
/B:*buffersize*	Specifies size of the read-ahead buffer, which allows SMARTDrive to read additional disk information. The default is 16K.
/C	Writes all information from the cache to the disk. Used from the command prompt if SMARTDrive already is loaded.
/L	Prevents SMARTDrive from loading into reserved memory.
/Q	Prevents SMARTDrive from displaying error and status messages when it loads.
/R	Writes the contents of the cache to disk and restarts SMARTDrive.
/S	Provides information about the status of SMARTDrive and statistics about how well it is functioning.

The /S switch is particularly useful for showing how effectively SMARTDrive is working. It provides information about how often information was used from the cache (called a *cache hit*) and how often information had to be used directly from the hard drive (called a *cache miss*). Even with small caches, there should be at least twice as many hits as misses. If your cache regularly falls below that mark, adjust the cache size and other parameters.

Using SMARTDrive with Double Buffering

In some cases, you might have to use a feature of SMARTDrive called double buffering. You might need double buffering if you run either the EMM386.EXE memory manager or Windows in enhanced mode and you also use

- A hard disk or other device that uses a SCSI (small computer system interface).

- ESDI (enhanced system device interface) hard drive.

- An MCA (microchannel architecture) device.

Double buffering provides compatibility between these devices and SMARTDrive.

It is easy to find out whether you need double buffering by loading it and then checking to see whether SMARTDrive is using it. First, in your CONFIG.SYS file, add the line

```
DEVICE=C:\DOS\SMARTDRV.EXE /double_buffer
```

and restart your computer. At the command prompt, type

```
SMARTDRV
```

You will see information about the operation of SMARTDrive. The heading in one of the columns of information is Buffering. If any of the entries in that column says Yes, you need double buffering. If one or more of the entries in that column use the - character, SMARTDrive could not tell whether double buffering was needed. In either case, leave the new command in your CONFIG.SYS file. If all the entries in the column say No, remove the entry from your CONFIG.SYS file. Removing the entry saves you a little conventional memory.

Notes About SMARTDrive and Memory

SMARTDrive automatically loads itself into the reserved upper memory area if memory is available there. Because of that, you do not have to use the LOADHIGH command with SMARTDRV.EXE.

Because SMARTDrive caches are stored in extended memory, you must load an extended memory manager in your CONFIG.SYS file. In most cases, install the device driver HIMEM.SYS, which is

427

included with DOS 6. If you use another extended memory manager, it must conform to what is called the Lotus/Intel/Microsoft/AST Extended Memory Specification (XMS). Chapter 15, "Getting the Most from Your Memory," contains details about HIMEM.SYS.

Using RAMDrive

A RAM drive is a dedicated portion of RAM that masquerades as a disk drive. Special device drivers loaded in the CONFIG.SYS file are used to set up RAM drives. When the drivers are loaded, your computer thinks it has an additional drive. You can copy files to the RAM drive, create directories and subdirectories, or do virtually any task that you can do with an ordinary disk drive of that size.

There are two main differences between RAM drives and regular drives. First, because RAM drives are temporary drives, any information you place in a RAM drive disappears when you turn off your computer. Second, because a RAM drive really is a sleight-of-hand trick that uses RAM, which is faster than a physical medium such as a hard drive, RAM drives are faster than regular drives.

Because RAM drives are faster, they can play a role in speeding up your system. For example, if you have an application that is particularly slow, you might be able to speed it up by loading it in a RAM drive. Consult your application's documentation to find out whether the program supports this and, if so, which files must be placed in the RAM drive.

Another way to improve system speed—although it can be risky—is to place large data files in a RAM drive. With some applications, large files can be cumbersome and require a lot of disk accesses, which can slow down your system quite a bit. Placing the file in a RAM drive can speed things up. But a huge caution is worth repeating: Any information you save to a RAM drive disappears when you turn off your computer. Make sure you frequently save data files located on a RAM drive to a physical hard disk.

DOS 6 includes the RAMDRIVE.SYS device driver for creating a RAM drive. To use it, load it in your CONFIG.SYS file. The syntax is

```
DEVICE=RAMDRIVE.SYS [disk size] [sector size] [number of
 entries] /switches
```

Disk size refers to the size of your RAM drive in kilobytes. If you do not specify a size, RAMDrive creates a 64K RAM disk. A RAM drive can be as large as the memory you devote to it.

Sector size refers to the size of each sector on the drive. You can use any size up to 512 bytes, which is the default.

Number of entries refers to the number of files you can place in the RAM drive's root directory. You can use any number between 2 and 1024, although the default of 64 entries is used if you do not specify a number.

The /E switch places the RAM drive in extended memory. The /A switch places the RAM drive in expanded memory. Details about extended and expanded memory are in Chapter 15, "Getting the Most from Your Memory." If you don't use extended or expanded memory, RAMDrive uses conventional memory, which typically is in short supply.

You can have as many RAM drives as you want. Your only limitation is available memory.

Remember, it is risky, but sometimes useful, to place data files in a RAM drive. If you do this, see whether the application that created the data files supports macros to automate multiple keystroke operations. If so, develop a macro that saves the data file both to your physical hard drive and to your RAM drive in the same operation. Use the macro whenever you save your file to minimize your risk of losing data stored in your RAM drive.

Increasing Your Disk Storage

You don't have to purchase a new hard drive to get more storage capacity for your files. You can increase the amount of space available on your hard disk by compressing files. Special compression programs can squeeze programs so that you can fit more information on the same amount of disk space. This section discusses techniques for reclaiming hard disk space by using compression programs, as well as other techniques to increase your storage capacity.

Increasing Your Disk Capacity with DoubleSpace

One of the most powerful new features in DOS 6 is the DoubleSpace utility. DoubleSpace compresses and uncompresses your files as you use them, which dramatically increases the amount of storage capacity of your hard drive. As the name implies, in many cases DoubleSpace doubles the capacity of your hard drive.

When in place, DoubleSpace works in the background. When you issue a command from the command prompt or from within a program that requires a file, DoubleSpace automatically uncompresses that file, returning the file to its regular size. When you are done using that file, DoubleSpace recompresses the file. Even though this sounds like a lot of activity, in most cases DoubleSpace will not slow down your computer—for the most part, you will not even notice that DoubleSpace is operating.

DoubleSpace can compress your existing drives and all the files on them. For example, if you choose to compress your existing C: drive, it compresses each file on that drive. That process can take quite a while, depending on how many files are located on the drive. When this procedure is completed, commands such as DIR or CHKDSK will show that you have about twice as much disk space available as you had before.

DoubleSpace also can take free space on an existing drive and create a new, empty disk drive. Usually, the new compressed disk drive is designated with the next available drive letter. In other words, if you already have C: and D: drives, a new compressed drive will be the E: drive.

DoubleSpace Behind the Scenes

In most cases, other than knowing about the additional storage capacity, you won't even know that DoubleSpace is working. Behind the scenes, though, DoubleSpace is working hard to compress and uncompress your files and present the illusion that nothing about your system has changed.

DoubleSpace does not actually create new drives. Instead, a portion of your existing uncompressed drive, called the *host drive*, is used to store a large hidden file created by DoubleSpace that looks and acts like a drive. The host drive is usually your uncompressed C: drive, although when DoubleSpace is done, it will not appear as such.

If you compress your C: drive, DoubleSpace makes the large hidden file look and act like your regular C: drive. If you create a new compressed drive from an existing free space, it too is a hidden file stored on the host drive that acts just like a regular disk drive.

This all begs a question. Say you have only one drive, C:. If you compress that drive, what then appears to be your C: drive really is a large hidden file on your "real" uncompressed C: drive. So, in effect, your compressed C: drive is a phony! What happens to the "real" uncompressed C: drive? After all, DOS won't permit two drives with the same letter.

Here's where DoubleSpace uses some sleight of hand. First, DOS assigns the compressed drive a new drive letter. If you have only a C: drive and you compress it, technically the compressed drive is the D: drive, and the real uncompressed drive, or the host drive, remains the C: drive. However, because all your files are on the compressed drive, this would greatly confuse batch programs, PATH commands, and a wide variety of other commands and settings.

To avoid this confusion, DoubleSpace swaps drive letters so that the compressed drive becomes drive C: and your uncompressed drive becomes drive D:. The result is that everything appears normal to the user except that you now have a new, uncompressed drive called D:. DoubleSpace creates the illusion that your C: drive is the same as it always was and that the D: drive is new.

It is a trick that would make even the greatest magician proud. In virtually every case, using DoubleSpace makes no changes in the way you work or the way in which commands and applications function. The only visible difference is that you have significantly more available disk space.

> There is no need to apply a disk-cache program, such as SMARTDrive, to a compressed drive if you already have applied the cache to the normal uncompressed drive. That is because the compressed drive really is part of the compressed drive, as discussed previously.

Using DoubleSpace

> DoubleSpace makes fundamental changes to your hard drive. These changes will not endanger your data. They also can be reversed, but it is time-consuming and risky to do so. Do not use DoubleSpace, particularly to compress existing drives, unless you are ready to consider these changes as permanent.

To start DoubleSpace, at the command prompt type

```
DBLSPACE
```

The first time you start DoubleSpace, you are asked whether you want to proceed, get more information, or exit. If you proceed, you will see the opening screen shown in Figure 14.19.

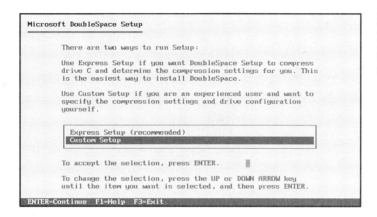

*Figure 14.19.
The
DoubleSpace
opening screen.*

You can choose between Express Setup and Custom Setup. Express Setup compresses your entire hard drive using DoubleSpace default settings. If you want to compress your entire hard drive, select Express Setup, and DoubleSpace will do all the work for you.

Custom Setup provides more options, including the option to create a compressed drive out of free space on your existing drive. Another option is to compress a specific hard drive, but not others. Custom setup also enables you to specify how much uncompressed disk space you want remaining when compression is completed.

Creating a new drive out of existing free space is a good way to start using DoubleSpace. Because this procedure does not compress existing data, it is faster to create new drives and easier to delete the new drive later.

As you start the custom installation process, the screen shown in Figure 14.20 asks you to select some options.

DoubleSpace asks how much of the host drive should remain uncompressed. You always must leave some uncompressed space because some files require it. DoubleSpace suggests that you leave 2M uncompressed on your host drive. DoubleSpace also asks you what letter you want to call the new drive. As a rule, use the next available drive letter, which DoubleSpace will suggest. After you are finished with this screen, DoubleSpace creates the new drive.

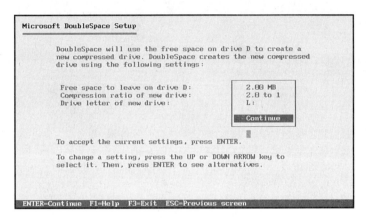

Figure 14.20. Options for creating a new compressed drive

One notable file that requires uncompressed space is the permanent swap file for Windows. Windows, like most programs, temporarily stores information on the hard drive. Because this information is stored only temporarily, it is placed in what is known as a swap file. Windows can use any available uncompressed space as temporary swap files. However, you get better performance with a permanent swap file, which is a portion of uncompressed hard drive dedicated to that purpose. If you already have a permanent swap file when you begin to compress your hard disk, DoubleSpace finds it and automatically places it on uncompressed disk space. However, if you use Windows and have not selected a permanent swap file, consider reserving uncompressed disk space for that use later. Reserve at least 8M and as much as 14M of uncompressed disk space for this purpose.

DoubleSpace Menu Options

After you have created compressed drives, you can use DoubleSpace menu options to alter and monitor what you have done.

The File menu includes the following commands:

Info—Provides information about all your drives, both compressed and uncompressed. It provides an overview of the capacity and available space of each drive.

Change size—Enables you to make compressed drives larger or smaller. If you select this option, a dialog box shows the largest and smallest possible sizes for the drive you select. Keep in mind that even empty space on compressed drives is compressed. If you have a compressed drive with 10M of free space and you eliminate that free space by making the compressed drive 10M smaller, it shows up as only 5M of free space on the uncompressed drive.

Change ratio—Enables you to change the expected compression ratio. This makes changes only for the purpose of reporting free and used space on compressed drives. This does not actually change the compression ratio. Some files are more compressible than others. For example, bit-mapped graphics files compress much more than program files. If you have many highly compressible files, you will want to ensure more accurate reporting of disk space by increasing the compression ratio.

Mount and Dismount—Enables you to make existing compressed drives either available or unavailable for use.

Format—Enables you to format a compressed drive. Note that formatting destroys all information currently on that drive. Do not format a compressed drive unless it is absolutely necessary, and back up all information on that drive before you do so.

Delete—Deletes a compressed drive. All information on that compressed drive will be lost permanently. If you choose this option, make sure the compressed drive is fully backed up.

The Compress menu repeats options you have seen before. You can compress an existing drive, or you can create a new drive out of free space on an uncompressed drive.

The Tools menu provides utilities to make DoubleSpace operate more efficiently. Here are the menu options:

Defragment—Enables you to defragment a compressed drive. Use this option, and not other disk defragmenters, such as DOS DEFRAG, to defragment compressed drives. Using other programs could damage your compressed drive.

Chkdsk—Examines the integrity of a compressed drive and provides information similar to that provided by using the CHKDSK command from the command prompt. Note, however, that you also can use the CHKDSK command from the command prompt for information about a compressed drive.

Stacker—Converts drives already compressed by the popular Stacker disk-compression program into DoubleSpace drives.

Options—Enables you to set parameters such as the last drive letter that can be used for compressed drives and the number of removable drives, such as floppy drives, on which you want to use DoubleSpace.

Compressing Individual Files

If you don't want to use DoubleSpace but still want more disk storage capacity, use a file-compression utility to compress individual files.

Unlike DoubleSpace, file-compression utilities do not automatically compress and uncompress files as you use them. Rather, you must issue a command to compress and uncompress files each time you want to use them. For that reason, this procedure is best used on files that you rarely use.

The most popular programs for compressing and uncompressing files are shareware programs. For more information about shareware and how to obtain it, see Chapter 32, "Using Shareware to Enhance DOS," and Chapter 33, "How to Obtain Shareware." The most popular shareware compression programs are PKZIP, PKARC, and LHARC. A number of shareware programs are included with this book.

You can store files compressed by compression utilities on compressed drives created by DoubleSpace. However, the compressed files will not become more compressed just because they are stored on a DoubleSpace drive. In all likelihood, the utility will compress the files about as much as possible.

Deleting Unnecessary Program Files

As with your home, a periodic housecleaning is a good thing for your hard drives. Many users add and delete programs and files from their hard drives regularly. It is a good idea every now and then to review the contents of your hard drives and delete any unnecessary programs and data files. The DOS Shell is a good tool for this task because its Directory List and File List make it easy to view large numbers of files and directories at a glance.

You should remember a couple of common-sense guidelines when you do your housecleaning:

- Before you begin, do a full backup of your hard drive. It is common to get into a "cleaning frenzy" and accidentally delete files that are needed later. I have done it myself (more often than I want to admit!).

- Make absolutely certain that you never again need the data files you are deleting. You always can reload an application file if you need to. But when data files are gone, they are gone forever.

A good target for deletion are temporary files that applications sometimes leave behind on your hard drive. If you see files with the .TMP extension, you can eliminate them. The SET command used with the TEMP or TMP environment variable designates a specific directory for temporary files. If you have not used that command, temporary files are likely to be located either in the root directory or in the directory containing the program files.

Never eliminate files with .TMP extensions if you have only temporarily exited, or shelled, from an application, the DOS Shell, or Windows. Many programs place temporary files on your hard drive when you temporarily exit them. If you temporarily exit a program and then delete the related temporary files, you run the risk of damaging programs and data files that were open when you made your temporary exit.

Deleting DOS Files

You might find that you don't need all the files that DOS places in the \DOS directory. For example, if you do not use an 80386 or greater computer, you cannot use the following programs:

EMM386.EXE
MEMMAKER
RAMDRIVE.SYS
SMARTDRV.SYS

DOS also includes files that support languages other than English. If you do not need international language support, you can eliminate these files:

NLSFUNC.EXE
GRAFTABL.COM
KEYB.COM
*.CPI

COUNTRY.SYS
DISPLAY.SYS
KEYBOARD.SYS
PRINTER.SYS

You also can delete files with the .BAS extension. These are sample files that accompany QBasic. Finally, you can delete the programming tool EXE2BIN.EXE if you do not plan to do any programming.

 # Troubleshooting

Look in this section for a description of problems that might arise while you are using any of the techniques described in this chapter. Then, try the suggested solutions.

- You try to load a program but get a `Bad command or file name` error message even though you are certain you have placed the program's directory in your PATH statement. This problem usually is related to syntax. Examine your PATH statement and make sure you have precisely followed the syntax discussed in this chapter. Common problems include those listed here:

    Placing a space between directories in the PATH command. The only space in the command should be after the command PATH.

    Misspelling a directory name in the PATH command.

    Forgetting to place a semicolon between directories in the command.

- To make more space on your hard drive, you delete all the files from a directory, then try to remove the directory. However, you get the error message `Invalid path, not directory` or `Directory not empty`. The likely problem is that there are files in the directory in which the Hidden attribute is turned on. This prevents you from seeing the directory when you use the DIR command. To see whether this is the problem, use the DOS Shell and select File Display Options from the Options menu. Make sure the Display hidden/system files check box has an X in it, and select OK. You will now see all files, even hidden files. If you see that there is a hidden file in the subdirectory, you can change the attribute by selecting Change Attributes from the File menu.

■ An application won't run after you have used the MOVE command with wildcards to move files from the source directory to another directory. You might have accidentally included files in the MOVE command with the Hidden attribute set to on. Your application will not run if those files are required to be present in the source directory. If you know which hidden files are required, go to the destination and move the hidden file back. If you do not know which hidden files are required to run your application, either consult your application's documentation for that information or reinstall the program.

■ You restore files you have backed up with Microsoft Backup. However, a specific file you need is not restored. One of the following problems is likely the cause:

1. When creating your setup file, you selected specific files, thinking that all files in the same subdirectory with the same extension also would be saved. However, you must use the Include command with wildcards to make sure that all files of a specific type are backed up. You can only correct this problem in the future.

2. You mistakenly used a different setup file than you thought you were using when you backed up. Again, you can only correct this problem for future use of Microsoft Backup.

3. You properly used the Include and Exclude commands to back up certain files from one drive, but

failed to use those commands to back up similar files on another drive. You must separately set files to be backed up for each drive. For example, just because you included all files with the .DOC extension for backup from the C: drive, files with the same extension on the D: drive will not be backed up until you specifically include them.

■ You try to load files into a RAM drive, but you get an error message stating Invalid drive specification. This indicates that your RAM drive was not created. This could occur because of one of the following reasons:

1. You mistyped the DEVICE command for the RAMDrive in the CONFIG.SYS file. To test for this, type the DEVICE command from the command prompt and see whether it creates the RAM drive. If so, you have corrected the problem.

2. You do not have adequate memory to load either the device driver or the RAM drive itself. Use the MEM /C command to see whether the RAMDrive was loaded into memory. The MEM /C command also reports whether you have enough memory available for the RAM drive itself, either in extended memory or in low memory, whichever you selected when you loaded the RAMDrive driver. If you do not have sufficient memory, try again by reloading your computer with fewer devices and programs that require the use of memory.

Summary

In this chapter, you have learned the following information:

■ How to use the PATH command effectively so that you can launch programs without having to go directly to the directory in which they are located.

■ How to create an efficient directory tree structure that makes it faster and simpler to manage your programs and files.

■ Tips and techniques for managing directories and files from both the DOS Shell and the command prompt.

■ How to use the new Microsoft Backup program to back up your files as insurance against disk disaster.

■ Various techniques to speed up your hard disk performance, including these techniques:

1. Using the SMARTDrive disk-caching program included with DOS 6.

2. Using the DEFRAG program to make your hard drive more mechanically efficient by placing all elements of files in close proximity to each other.

3. Using a RAM disk to create a temporary disk drive in RAM to speed up your operations.

■ How to increase your disk storage capacity by taking the following actions:

1. Using DoubleSpace to compress and uncompress files on your hard drive as you use them, which can double your disk capacity.

2. Compressing individual files that you do not use often.

3. Eliminating unnecessary files from your hard drive.

CHAPTER 15

Getting the Most from Your Memory

Disk storage and memory allocation are the two major factors determining system performance. And, while today's computers and programs tout themselves as being "hands off" or self-configuring, the very numbers and types of hardware and programs available can be staggering, both to you and to your computer's capabilities for keeping everything running smoothly.

Therefore, the more you know about disk storage and memory, and the more you are able to control them, the better your system will work. The previous chapter covers the basics of hard disk management. This chapter describes the basics of memory and memory configuration.

In this chapter, the focus is on using the capabilities of DOS 6 to configure memory for peak performance. Indeed, possibly the best reason for upgrading to DOS 6 (or DOS 5) is to take advantage of its memory-handling capabilities. That is, by using the speed of memory (as opposed to disk storage), and by eliminating unnecessary reliance on disk storage, you optimize overall computing.

Your Computer's Memory

Your computer's main memory (RAM) consists of RAM chips. These chips are located on the system board, or motherboard, and carry thousands, or millions, of switches, or transistors. Each switch has two states, *on* and *off*, corresponding to the 1 and 0 values of a data bit. Thus, each switch represents one data bit. As you know, eight bits make up a byte, and each byte represents one data character.

The switches in RAM chips operate, literally, at the speed of electricity. As you might guess, this is extremely fast, especially compared to the mechanical workings of disk storage.

Your computer also contains ROM (read-only memory) chips. These chips are programmed to perform a specific task. When you turn on your computer, for example, it performs certain self-tests. Routines for these tests and other power-up tasks are contained in ROM memory (see Figure 15.1).

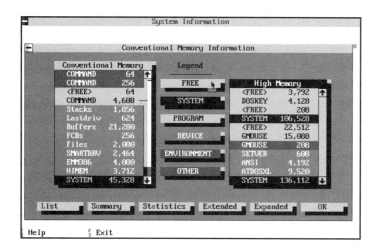

Figure 15.1.
A memory
allocation map.

Types of Memory

There are several types of memory. This section presents a quick review.

DOS was written for the original IBM PC (with the Intel 8088 microprocessor) introduced in 1981. This machine could only access 1 megabyte (1024K) of RAM. Because all PCs since have maintained compatibility with the original system, all DOS computers adhere to this standard. Even 286-based machines that can use up to 16M of RAM, and 386-based machines that can use up to 4 gigabytes, are still limited to the 1M standard established by the original PC.

The first megabyte of RAM is comprised of *conventional memory* and *upper memory*, or high memory.

Conventional Memory

Within the first, basic megabyte of RAM, conventional memory is the first 640K. Conventional memory is devoted to DOS for running programs and storing data.

Upper Memory

The remaining 384K of the first megabyte, the area between 640K and 1M, is called upper memory. Much of this area is assigned to the video display, the hard disk controller, and your PC's BIOS.

There is memory left over that can be used to optimize your system. This is explained in the "How Memory is Used" section later in this chapter.

High Memory

High memory is the first 64K of extended memory. It is used by some applications and by Windows. You can also run DOS in the high memory area, thereby freeing conventional memory for other programs.

Extended Memory

Extended memory, or memory above 1M, is available on 286 and higher computers, like IBM ATs and their clones. Extended memory is controlled by the extended-memory manager, a program whose main function is to keep two or more programs from using the same memory addresses at the same time. DOS 6 (like DOS 5) includes two extended-memory managers—HIMEM.SYS and EMM386.EXE.

Expanded Memory

Expanded memory is obtained by using an expanded-memory board (or card) that conforms to the Lotus, Intel, and Microsoft (LIM) standard, also known as the Expanded Memory Specification, or EMS. This specification was developed in response to user demand to handle large spreadsheets. With expanded memory, a special device driver, the expanded-memory manager, swaps 16K pages of memory to available upper memory. All PCs can use expanded memory, provided the expansion card and appropriate device driver are installed.

How Memory Is Used

Different memory areas are used for different purposes. Your computer keeps track of memory by assigning an address to each memory position. For example, the first 128K above the 640K address position, or the address positions from 640K to 768K, is usually used to manage the video display. Other memory addresses are used to store program instructions until they are executed and data is needed to execute them.

As you know, DOS is a program. When you boot your computer, DOS (or a portion of it) is loaded into RAM automatically. This portion, incidentally, contains the internal DOS commands like COPY, DIR, and so on. External commands, like FORMAT, must first be read from disk. The memory area used, or allocated, for DOS cannot be used for other programs. Memory that is not allocated can be used for other purposes.

To determine the amount of available (non-allocated) memory, subtract allocated memory from total memory.

Use the CHKDSK or MEM command to see how your computer's memory is allocated. See the section "Determining Your Memory Configuration" later in this chapter.

When you run a program, a copy of that program is loaded into memory, from which it can be accessed and executed speedily. For example, when you use your word processing program, a copy of it is stored in memory. When you exit your word processor and load your spreadsheet program, the copy of the word processor is erased and a copy of your spreadsheet is loaded.

Available memory determines the size of the program(s) you can load. Therefore, in the above example your spreadsheet is loaded only if there is enough memory available. If not, an Insufficient Memory error message is displayed. This is also the reason why, until Windows, you could only run one program at a time. It's also the reason certain types of programs have been developed that use memory in special ways. These memory-resident and shell programs are discussed briefly in the following sections. Then, determining your memory configuration is explained.

Memory-Resident Programs

Some programs remain in memory after you start them, even if you are not actively using them. Instead of releasing their memory when they quit, memory-resident programs stay in memory and continue to occupy a portion of it. The command prompt returns and you can run additional programs—the memory-resident programs are still available.

Memory-resident programs provide you with functions lacking in DOS or other applications. They can add new commands to DOS, modify the way the computer works, display the time (or other messages) on the screen, or operate a special pop-up utility when you press a specified hotkey or keystroke combination. Sidekick, for example, is a memory-resident program that provides an appointment calendar, telephone directory, and other functions in response to certain hotkeys. You can call up these functions by pressing the appropriate hotkey, even if you're in another program and not at the DOS command prompt.

Memory-resident programs are often called *TSRs*, for *terminate-and-stay-resident*. Typically, TSRs are loaded into RAM from the top down, with each succeeding TSR loaded beneath the previous one. DOS keeps track of TSR locations and accesses them as needed. TSRs, obviously, take memory space and reduce the amount of available memory.

> DOS 6 provides capabilities for loading TSRs into upper memory areas, freeing up conventional memory for use by other DOS programs. This is discussed in the "Conserving Conventional Memory" section later in this chapter.

Shell Programs

Some programs have the ability to quit and leave themselves intact and in memory. You can leave these programs and go to the DOS prompt or another application, then return to the original program using a simple command. The DOS PROMPT applet in Windows is a shelling program, for example. Click the DOS PROMPT icon and the command prompt is displayed. You can then run DOS commands as you would normally. However, instead of loading Windows again, just type EXIT and you are returned to Windows, which you loaded previously.

> The drawback to this arrangement is that Windows remains in memory, so you don't have much RAM left to run programs.

For a quick demonstration of shelling, use this procedure:

1. At the command prompt, enter the name of the DOS command processor. That is, type C:\COMMAND.COM (see Figure 15.2). You are now in a second, shelled version of the DOS command processor.

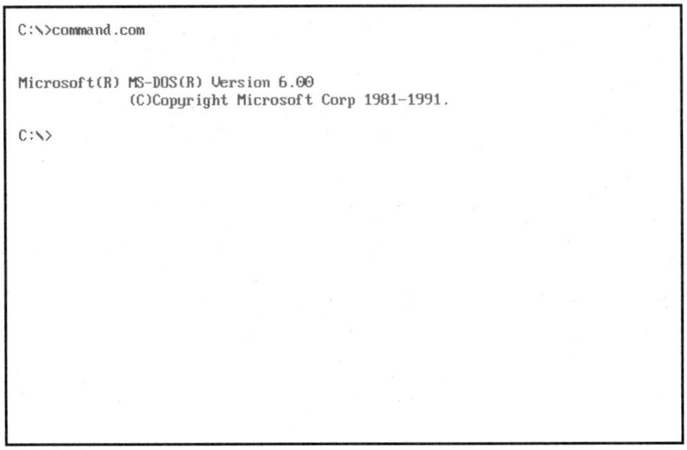

```
C:\>command.com


Microsoft(R) MS-DOS(R) Version 6.00
          (C)Copyright Microsoft Corp 1981-1991.

C:\>
```

Figure 15.2.
Results
displayed after
typing the
name of the
DOS command
processor at the
command
prompt.

2. To further illustrate, type PROMPT Test Prompt - Shell Mode $g at the command prompt. The prompt is changed only in the shelled version of DOS (see Figure 15.3).

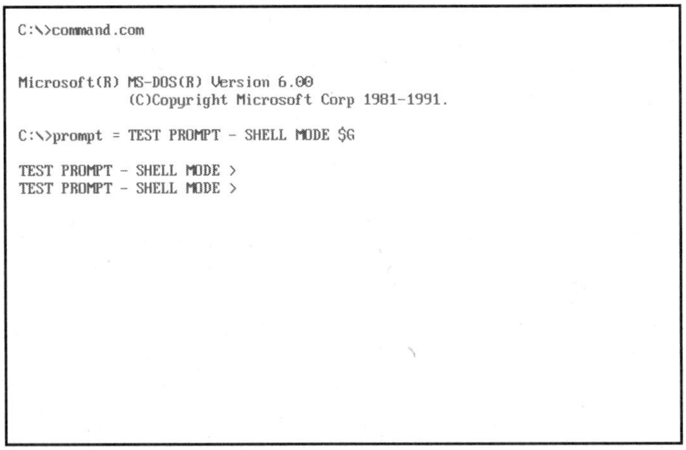

```
C:\>command.com


Microsoft(R) MS-DOS(R) Version 6.00
          (C)Copyright Microsoft Corp 1981-1991.

C:\>prompt = TEST PROMPT - SHELL MODE $G

TEST PROMPT - SHELL MODE >
TEST PROMPT - SHELL MODE >
```

Figure 15.3.
The changed
command
prompt in the
shelled version
of DOS.

3. To prove this, type EXIT. The shelled version is unloaded and your original prompt returns.

Understanding the concepts of memory-resident and shell programs can increase your computing power, as can customizing your memory configuration. Before you're ready to do this, however, you may need a quick way of determining your memory configuration.

Determining Your Memory Configuration

DOS 6 (and DOS 5 before it) provides a handy utility you can use to determine your memory configuration—the MEM command. Type MEM at the DOS prompt to display your memory configuration. Figure 15.4 shows a typical MEM display. Notice that each type of memory is broken down according to Total, Used, and Free memory space.

```
C:\>MEM

Memory Type        Total =  Used  +  Free
----------------   ------   -----    -----
Conventional        640K     174K     466K
Upper                59K      33K      26K
Adapter RAM/ROM     325K     325K       0K
Extended (XMS)     4096K    4096K       0K
                   ------   -----    -----
Total memory       5120K    4628K     492K

Total under 1 MB    699K     207K     492K

EMS is active.
Largest executable program size     465K  (476512 bytes)
Largest free upper memory block      22K   (22528 bytes)
The high memory area is available.

C:\>
```

*Figure 15.4.
A typical
memory
configuration
display.*

You can also use the MEM command to generate a detailed report of how every program you run is placed in conventional and high memory by adding the /C option to the MEM command line. For example, type MEM /C to generate a report similar to the one shown in Figure 15.5.

```
Modules using memory below 1 MB:

 Name        Total    =    Conventional  +   Upper Memory

 MSDOS       72845  (71K)    72845  (71K)         0   (0K)
 HIMEM        3728   (4K)     3728   (4K)         0   (0K)
 EMM386       4096   (4K)     4096   (4K)         0   (0K)
 SMARTDRV     2480   (2K)     2480   (2K)         0   (0K)
 COMMAND      4976   (5K)     4976   (5K)         0   (0K)
 UNDELETE     9632   (9K)     9632   (9K)         0   (0K)
 SAVE        80800  (79K)    80800  (79K)         0   (0K)
 ATDOSXL      9568   (9K)        0   (0K)      9568   (9K)
 ANSI         4240   (4K)        0   (0K)      4240   (4K)
 SETVER        656   (1K)        0   (0K)       656   (1K)
 GMOUSE      15328  (15K)        0   (0K)     15328  (15K)
 DOSKEY       4144   (4K)        0   (0K)      4144   (4K)
 Free       503392 (492K)   476832 (466K)     26560  (26K)

Memory Summary:

 Type of Memory      Size     =     Used      +      Free

 Conventional      655360  (640K)   178528  (174K)   476832  (466K)
Press any key to continue . . .
```

*Figure 15.5.
Detailed
memory
configuration
report.*

Don't run MEM /C from the DOS Shell. Your results will not be accurate.

You can also use the following options to obtain even more de-tailed listings of your memory allocation:

/CLASSIFY or /C lists programs currently loaded into memory, the program areas they occupy (conventional, upper, and so on), summarizes overall memory use, and lists the largest free memory blocks.

/DEBUG or /D lists the programs and internal drivers currently loaded into memory, as well as the size, segment address, and type for each module.

/FREE or /F lists the free areas of conventional and upper memory, the segment address and size of each free area, and the largest free upper memory block in each region of memory. These also summarize overall memory use.

> The /FREE or /F option can by used with the /PAGE option, but not with other MEM options.

Thus far in this chapter, you have learned the types of memory and how to determine the memory configuration of your computer. The next section presents guidelines for customizing your memory configuration for maximum speed and performance.

Memory Configuration in a Nutshell

If the terms (conventional, upper, extended, expanded, high) presented above seem confusing and overlapping, there's a simple reason: they are confusing and overlapping. Before you attempt to optimize your memory configuration, then, it might help to know exactly what you can do to manage memory in your computer.

Here's what you can do to manage memory, depending on the type of computer you have. Once you know what's possible, you can use the following section to focus on guidelines for optimizing your memory configuration.

■ If you have a 386 or higher computer, you can control your extended memory with two extended-memory managers: HIMEM.SYS and EMM386.EXE. Both managers let you load DOS into high memory (using the DOS command) and put TSR programs and device drivers into high memory using the LOADHIGH and DEVICEHIGH commands. You can also create a RAM disk with RAMDRIVE.SYS, and a disk cache with SMARTDRV.EXE.

> You need to use a combination of the HIMEM.SYS, DOS=UMB, and EMM386.SYS programs and drivers to prepare the upper memory blocks. When you've done so, you can use the DEVICEHIGH and LOADHIGH commands to load device drivers and TSR programs into upper memory, thereby conserving a substantial amount of conventional memory (RAM) for other programs, such as spreadsheets and word processors.

- If you have a 286 or higher machine, like an IBM AT or clone, you can put DOS in high memory with HIMEM.SYS. You can create a RAM disk with RAMDRIVE.SYS and a disk cache with SMARTDRV.EXE. You cannot use EMM386.EXE, nor can you load device drivers and TSRs into upper memory.

- If you have an 8088-type machine, like an IBM XT or clone, you can create a RAM disk (if you have expanded memory) and a disk cache, but you can't load DOS or TSR programs into high memory.

Guidelines for Optimizing Memory

This section presents general guidelines for optimizing your computer's memory configuration. Once you familiarize yourself with these concepts, read the remainder of this chapter. It focuses on the procedures you can use to customize your memory configuration.

Use these guidelines when configuring your memory. Each guideline is explained in detail in separate sections that follow.

- Activate expanded or extended memory, if you have it.

- Conserve conventional memory.

■ Load DOS into high memory, if possible.

■ Use DEVICEHIGH and LOADHIGH to install drivers and memory-resident programs into extended memory.

■ Use a disk cache to speed overall disk storage and retrieval.

■ Use a RAM disk, when feasible, to speed disk-intensive operations.

■ Run the MemMaker program to optimize overall performance.

Activating Extended and/or Expanded Memory

Adding extended or expanded memory to your computer isn't enough. You must instruct your computer to use them. Do this by installing the appropriate extended-memory manager or expanded-memory manager.

Activating Extended Memory

To use extended memory, you must first physically install it in your computer. That is, if you have no extended memory, or if you want to install additional memory, you must buy and install the appropriate memory chips. Then you must install the appropriate software drivers for the extended-memory managers. Remember, extended-memory managers handle the interactions between DOS and extended memory.

There are two extended-memory managers: HIMEM.SYS and EMM386.EXE.

HIMEM.SYS provides access to extended memory. For 286, 386, and 486 machines, the DOS Setup program automaticlly installs HIMEM.SYS. There are many parameters and switches you can use to customize HIMEM.SYS. Enter the command DEVICE = [*drive*][*path*]HIMEM.SYS in your CONFIG.SYS file. Normally, when your computer loads HIMEM, you'll see a message like this:

```
HIMEM:DOS XMS Driver, Version 3.09 - 07/24/92
Extended Memory Specification (XMS) Version 3.0
Copyright 1988-1992 Microsoft Corp

Installed A20 Handler number 1.
64K High Memory Area is available.
```

If you don't see a message like this, and DOS doesn't report that you already have an extended-memory manager installed, check the DEVICE command in your CONFIG.SYS file to make sure there are no errors.

> While there are many parameters and switches you can add to this command to customize HIMEM, it's default values work sufficiently with most machines. Use these options only if HIMEM fails to operate properly without them. Consult your DOS manual for instructions.

EMM386.EXE performs two functions for 386 and 486 machines. First it provides access to the upper memory (between 640K and 1M) area. Use it to increase available conventional memory by loading device drivers and memory-resident programs in upper memory. EMM386.EXE can also use extended memory to simulate expanded memory. Some programs are designed to run most efficiently in expanded memory. The EMM386 driver lets you run these programs on machines with extended, rather than expanded, memory.

Use EMM386.EXE on 386 and 486 machines to take advantage of available upper memory areas. If you don't use programs requiring expanded memory, enable the /NOEMS switch from the command line.

> A hassle-free method for installing the EMM386 driver is to run the MemMaker program. New to DOS 6, MemMaker analyzes your system's memory and installs the

> appropriate drivers. All parameters and switches are set
> automatically. Instructions for running MemMaker are
> given in the section "Optimizing Your System by Running
> MemMaker" later in this chapter.

When EMM386.EXE loads, you should see a message like the
one in Figure 15.6.

```
C:\>emm386.exe

MICROSOFT Expanded Memory Manager 386   Version 4.45
Copyright Microsoft Corporation 1986, 1992

   Available expanded memory . . . . . . . .   4288 KB

   LIM/EMS version . . . . . . . . . . . . .   4.0
   Total expanded memory pages . . . . . . .   292
   Available expanded memory pages . . . . .   268
   Total handles . . . . . . . . . . . . . .   64
   Active handles  . . . . . . . . . . . . .   1
   Page frame segment  . . . . . . . . . . .   D000 H

   Total upper memory available  . . . . . .    0 KB
   Largest Upper Memory Block available  . .    0 KB
   Upper memory starting address . . . . . .   C000 H

EMM386 Active.

C:\>
```

*Figure 15.6.
EMM386
confirmation
screen.*

If you don't see a message like this, and DOS doesn't report that
you already have an extended-memory manager installed, check the
DEVICE command in your CONFIG.SYS file to make sure there are
no errors.

Activating Expanded Memory

Activating expanded memory is similar to activating extended
memory in that both operations involve installing a software driver,
or device driver, usually through your CONFIG.SYS file.

Most memory expansion boards are shipped with a proprietary
device driver. Use the DEVICE command to install this driver. See

your hardware documentation for complete instructions. For 386 and 486 machines, use the EMM386.EXE driver to simulate expanded memory. See the previous section, "Activating Extended Memory."

> The /NOEMS switch disables expanded memory simulation. Be sure this switch is disabled if you need to simulate expanded memory. To disable this command, delete the /NOEMS character string from the DEVICE=EMM386.EXE command line.

Conserving Conventional Memory

All programs require conventional memory; thus, the more you make available, the less programs require disk accesses and the faster they can run. You can increase available conventional memory by minimizing the amount used by DOS, device drivers, and memory-resident programs.

First, edit your CONFIG.SYS and AUTOEXEC.BAT files, removing any unnecessary memory-resident programs and drivers.

> The DOS installation procedure, as well as many application installation programs, often adds unrelated or redundant drivers and modules. Make sure you're loading only what you need.

Then you can load part of DOS into high memory using the DOS=HIGH command (see the following section). You can also use DEVICEHIGH and LOADHIGH to load device drivers and memory-resident programs into upper memory.

Loading DOS into High Memory

The DOS=HIGH command takes about 60K of the DOS program and tucks it into the high memory area. You can set this command to manage upper memory blocks (UMBs) into which you can load drivers and memory-resident programs using DEVICEHIGH and LOADHIGH.

> Optimizing memory in the Windows environment differs slightly in that Windows uses extended memory, extensively. If you use Windows, consider leaving DOS in conventional memory. There is little or no difference in overall performance.

The *DOS=HIGH* Command

To load DOS into high memory, enter the DOS=HIGH command in your CONFIG.SYS file, using the following format. You can place this command anywhere in the CONFIG.SYS, as long as it comes after the HIMEM.SYS and EMM386.EXE driver commands.

```
DOS=[HIGH | LOW[,UMB | NOUMB]]
```

As you can see, there are two switches:

HIGH or LOW specifies the location for DOS. Use HIGH to load about 60K of DOS into the high memory area, and free up that much space in conventional memory. Use LOW (default) to keep all of DOS in conventional memory.

UMB or NOUMB specifies whether DOS manages the upper memory blocks created by an extended-memory manager (such as EMM386.EXE). UMB activates DOS as the UMB manager. NOUMB (default) disables the managing of UMB by DOS.

Loading Drivers and Memory-Resident Programs into Upper Memory

You can save precious memory by loading device drivers and program managers into upper memory. To do this, you must first do the following:

- Activate extended memory by loading the HIMEM.SYS driver. Do this with a DEVICE command in your CONFIG.SYS file.

- Create upper memory blocks by loading the EMM386.EXE driver. Do this also with a DEVICE command in your CONFIG.SYS file.

- Designate DOS or another UBM provider to manage the upper memory area. Designate DOS using the DOS=UMB command in your CONFIG.SYS file.

You don't need to load DOS high to use it to manage UMBs, even though the command DOS=HIGH UMB is commonly used to do both.

Device drivers are loaded into upper memory using the DEVICEHIGH command in your CONFIG.SYS file. To load memory-resident programs into upper memory, use the LOADHIGH command in either your CONFIG.SYS or AUTOEXEC.BAT files.

Here are some *do's* and *don'ts* to consider when loading drivers and programs into upper memory:

- *Don't* load HIMEM.SYS and EMM386.EXE into high memory. It simply won't work. Remember, these are the programs that control access to high memory areas.

- *Do* use the MEM command to determine an optimum configuration. Optimizing memory is a trial-and-error process. The MEM command provides concise summaries of memory allocations. Use MEM reports to evaluate the effectiveness of changes and adjustments.

■ *Do* load memory-resident programs manually if you encounter problems. Some programs don't run properly in upper memory. Disable the LOADHIGH command in your AUTOEXEC.BAT file and run the program (in conventional memory) from the command prompt.

■ If you're using Windows, *don't* load too much into upper memory. Windows runs best with large areas of upper memory available. If you fill up upper memory with drivers and programs, you won't get optimum performance when running Windows.

■ *Don't* load memory-resident programs before Windows. If you do, they won't be available through Windows. Instead, put these programs in a Windows program group and start them from the Program Manager.

Device Drivers You Can Run in Upper Memory

The following device drivers can be loaded into upper memory: ANSI.SYS, EGA.SYS, DISPLAY.SYS, DRIVER.SYS, MOUSE.SYS, PRINTER.SYS, RAMDRIVE.SYS, and SMARTDRV.SYS

Memory-Resident Programs You Can Run in Upper Memory

DOS 6 includes the following memory-resident programs that can be loaded into upper memory: DOSKEY.COM, DOSSHELL.COM, GRAPHICS.COM, KEYB.COM, MODE.COM, NLSFUNC.EXE, PRINT.EXE, and SHARE.EXE. You can also load other third-party programs like SideKick and other pop-up programs.

Be aware that some third-party programs are not designed to work in upper memory.

Loading Device Drivers Using *DEVICEHIGH*

The `DEVICEHIGH` command loads device drivers into the upper memory area, freeing conventional memory for use by other programs. Using `DEVICEHIGH` is virtually the same as using the `DEVICE` command. Both commands perform the same function; the difference is the destination of the driver being loaded.

> If upper memory is not available, the `DEVICEHIGH` command functions identically to `DEVICE`. Drivers are loaded into conventional memory.

For example, suppose you use a device driver named DRIVEME.SYS and want to load it into upper memory, and that DRIVEME.SYS is in the C:\DOS directory. You would add the command

```
DEVICEHIGH=C:\DOS\DRIVEME.SYS
```

to your CONFIG.SYS file after the HIMEM.SYS and EMM386.EXE driver commands. By default, DOS loads the driver into the largest available upper memory block and makes all other UMBs available for the driver's use.

> For maximum performance, use `MEM /C` to display the memory area occupied by installed drivers. Make a list of them and their sizes, then load them through your CONFIG.SYS in order from the largest to the smallest.

Loading Memory-Resident Programs Using *LOADHIGH*

Use the `LOADHIGH` command to load memory-resident programs into upper memory. This is another way of making more conventional memory available for other programs. You can use the LOADHIGH command in both CONFIG.SYS and AUTOEXEC.BAT files. LOADHIGH installs programs into the upper memory area, provided there is sufficient space. If space is insufficient, the program loads into conventional memory.

For example, suppose you want to load DOSKEY into upper memory. Use the command:

```
LOADHIGH DOSKEY
```

Of course, this command assumes that DOSKEY is either in the root directory or a directory specified in the PATH command (otherwise the path must be specified).

DEVICEHIGH and *LOADHIGH* Options

DEVICEHIGH and LOADHIGH obviously perform similar functions. For both commands, there are two switches that can be set, and parameters for configuring each switch. These switches are described in this section.

The /L switch can be used to specify the region or regions of upper memory into which you want to load the device or program. By giving the region number after the /L switch, the driver or program is loaded into the largest UMB in that area. You can specify more than one region, as may be required for some drivers and programs. Also, because some programs require more memory running than when loaded, you can specify a minimum UMB size into which the driver can be loaded. Normally, DOS loads a driver or program into a UMB in the specified region only if the UBM is larger than its size at loading.

Type MEM /F at the command prompt to list the available areas of upper memory. Type MEM /M [*driver name*] to find out how the driver uses memory.

For example, suppose you know that DRIVEME.SYS needs more than one memory area, and that although its load size is 15K, it requires 32K to run properly. You type the MEM /F command and determine that regions 1 and 3 are available. You would add the following command to your CONFIG.SYS file:

```
DEVICEHIGH=C:\DOS\DRIVEME.SYS /L1,32;3,32 /S
```

The /S switch shrinks the UMB to its minimum size while the driver is loading for more efficient use of memory. This switch must be used with the /L switch. It's a tough call deciding whether using this switch improves performance. Even the DOS documentation gives little or no criteria on which to base your decision. Therefore, it might be best to set these switches using the MemMaker program, as detailed in the section "Optimizing Your System by Running MemMaker" later in this chapter.

Installing a Disk Cache

Disk caches, like RAM drives, can be installed on virtually any IBM PC or clone with extended or expanded memory. A disk cache is a part of memory that DOS sets aside to hold recently accessed data and program modules. Because most programs use the same data and program routines repetitively, a disk cache speeds up the overall performance of your system by decreasing the number and increasing the efficiency of disk accesses.

The disk cache driver included with DOS 6 is SMARTDRV.EXE. It can be used in extended or expanded memory, but will not work in conventional memory. When you install DOS 6, the Setup program adds the SMARTDRV command to your AUTOEXEC.BAT file so that it loads automatically each time you boot your computer.

If a SMARTDRV command isn't included in your AUTOEXEC.BAT file and you have a hard drive and extended or expanded memory on your system, add one manually. Use this format:

```
[drive][path]SMARTDRV.EXE [drive[+][-]] [E:ElementSize]
[InitCacheSize] [WinCacheSize] [B:BufferSize] /C /R /L /Q /S
```

As with most DOS commands, you must specify the drive and path for the SMARTDRV.EXE file if it's not in the PATH command. Also, the default configuration of parameters and options may work sufficiently on your machine. The options that are available include:

drive—Specifies the letter of the disk drive for which caching is enabled. If no drive is specified, hard drives cached for read and write operations, floppies for read operations only, and CD-ROM, network drives, compressed drives, and Microsoft Flash memory-card drives are ignored.

path—Specifies the directory location of the SMARTDRV.EXE file.

drive[+][-]—Enables (+) or disables (-) caching for specified drives. For example, A- disables caching on the A drive.

/E:*ElementSize*—Specifies, in bytes, the size of the cache that SMARTDrive moves at one time to or from the disk. The larger the value, the more conventional memory is used by SMARTDrive. Valid values include 1024, 2048, 4096, and 8192.

InitCacheSize—Specifies, in kilobytes, the size of the cache when SMARTDrive starts (before Windows is loaded). The default value is 256K. In general, the larger the cache, the less frequently SMARTDrive needs to read information from the disk. Your system's overall performance improves. If you do not specify a value, SMARTDrive sets a value according to your system's configuration.

WinCacheSize—Specifies, in kilobytes, the amount the cache is reduced when Windows is loaded. SMARTDrive automatically reduces the size of the cache to free up memory when Windows is loaded. The default values for *InitCacheSize* and *WinCacheSize* are as follows:

Memory Configuration	InitCacheSize	WinCacheSize
Up to 1M	1M	None (no caching)
1M to 2M	1M	256K
2M to 4M	2M	512K
4M to 6M	2M	1M
6M or more	2M	2M

If you set the *InitCacheSize* smaller than the *WinCacheSize*, the *WinCacheSize* value is used for *InitCacheSize* as well.

/B:*BufferSize*—Specifies the size of the read-ahead buffer. SMARTDrive reads enough information to fill this buffer, and then holds it there until it's ready to be moved into the cache. When it is ready, it is available from memory instead of disk, providing even greater improvements in speed and performance. The larger the value of this buffer, the more conventional memory is used by SMARTDrive.

/C—Writes the contents of the cache back to the hard disk. SMARTDrive normally waits for periods of reduced activity to write information from memory to disk. You can use this option from the command prompt, for example, if you need to turn off your computer and want to make sure all cached information is saved to disk. When you run this option, be sure to wait until all disk activity has stopped before turning off your machine.

SMARTDrive writes all cached information to the hard disk if you perform a warm boot (by pressing Ctrl+Alt+Del). You will lose cached information if you turn the power off or press your Reset button, unless you run SMARTDrive from the command prompt with the /C switch enabled.

/R—Clears the contents of the cache and restarts SMARTDrive.

/L—Prevents SMARTDrive from loading into upper memory, even if upper memory blocks (UMBs) are available. Use this option to reserve UMBs for other programs.

/Q—Quiet mode, represses status and error display when SMARTDrive is loaded.

/S—Displays status information about the SMARTDrive. Consider the following sample SMARTDrive command:

```
C:\DOS\SMARTDRV.EXE A- B- 2048 1024
```

In this example, SMARTDrive is set up to create a cache for read/write operations on the C drive, and to exclude drives A and B. In addition, the size of the cache on loading (*InitCacheSize*) is set for 2048K; and the cache is reduced to no less than 1024K when Windows is loaded.

Using a RAM Disk to Speed Disk-Intensive Operations

A *RAM disk*, also called a *virtual disk*, is a section of RAM that your computer uses as if it were another disk drive. A RAM disk can improve performance significantly, especially for disk-intensive applications.

To illustrate the power of a RAM disk, create one and use it to store the dictionary for your spell checker, and then spell check a large document. The improvement in performance is dramatic. Follow these general procedures:

1. Create a RAM disk by adding the RAMDRIVE.SYS driver to your CONFIG.SYS file.

2. Copy your spellcheck dictionary to the RAM disk. RAMDRIVE automatically assigns the next highest drive designation. For example, if your last hard drive is labeled C:, the RAM disk is assigned D:.

> You may need to set the configuration of your word processor so that it accesses the spellcheck dictionary on your RAM disk.

3. Copy the file to be checked to the RAM disk.

4. Check spelling in the file according to normal procedures.

5. If you have made changes to the file or the spellcheck dictionary, they must be copied back to your hard drive. RAM disks are volatile. Their contents are lost when you reboot or turn off your computer.

Loading the RAMDRIVE.SYS Driver

To create a RAM disk, add the RAMDRIVE.SYS driver to your CONFIG.SYS file as follows:

```
DEVICE=[drive][path]RAMDRIVE.SYS [disksize] [sectorsize]
[NumEntries] /E /A
```

Use the following parameters and switches to customize your RAM disk to your individual requirements:

/A—Creates the RAM disk in expanded memory.

/E—Creates the RAM disk in extended memory.

disk size—Specifies, in kilobytes, the size of the disk.

sector size—Specifies, in bytes, the size of the disk sectors. If you specify sector size you must also specify disk size. Default is 512.

NumEntries—Specifies the number of file and directory entries (combined) you can add to your RAM disk. To use this specification, you must also specify a disk size and sector size. The limit specified is rounded up to the boundary determined by sector size. The default is 64.

If there is not enough memory to create a RAM disk as specified, RAMDRIVE attempts to create one with 16 entries. If you end up with a limit that differs from your specification, chances are you are running out of memory.

For example, suppose you want to create a 1024K RAM disk in extended memory, and that the RAMDRIVE.SYS driver is in your C:\DOS directory. Use this command:

```
DEVICE=C:\DOS\RAMDRIVE.SYS 1024 /E
```

If you include your RAM disk in your PATH statement, make sure it's the first directory in the path. Otherwise, your system will search physical drives (a mechanical operation) before locating files on the RAM disk (an electronic operation).

Optimizing Your System by Running MemMaker

The MemMaker program included with DOS 6 simplifies configuring your system. The MemMaker program performs several valuable, and potentially confusing, functions, including:

- Evaluating your system configuration

- Determining the optimum placement of DOS, device drivers, and memory-resident programs

- Editing your CONFIG.SYS and AUTOEXEC.BAT files so that, when you reboot, your system is configured according to what it sees as your best arrangement

MemMaker's primary objective is to conserve conventional memory by moving as much as it can into upper memory areas. Windows users can then choose to ignore this section. MemMaker may reduce the amount of available extended memory, a valuable commodity for Windows.

MemMaker provides an UNDO function that enables you to go back to the way things were before you ran it. However, it's still wise to make backup copies of your CONFIG.SYS and AUTOEXEC.BAT files before you begin. Then do the following:

- Verify that all your equipment and software is working properly.

- Eliminate any unnecessary program commands from your CONFIG.SYS and AUTOEXEC.BAT files.

- Exit Windows, DOSSHELL, or any other program. This is different than, for example, loading the DOS Prompt routine in Windows by clicking its icon.

MemMaker runs in two modes: *Express* and *Custom.* Express mode runs automatically with little user input. Custom mode provides menus of settings from which you can make choices and exercise greater control over the operation.

MemMaker also provides an excellent way to learn about configuring your system. Make a copy of your CONFIG.SYS and AUTOEXEC.BAT files, use them to evaluate the changes MemMaker makes to these files. If you don't run Windows (or a windowing program), print your files so they can be viewed side by side.

When you load MemMaker you're immediately asked whether you want to run in Express or Custom mode. Use the Express mode until you're comfortable. Use Custom mode if:

- You have an EGA or VGA monitor

- You do not use Windows or DOS applications in Windows

- You know that none of your programs require expanded memory

In this section, procedures are given for running MemMaker in Express mode. Then, changes typically made by MemMaker are explained, followed by procedures for running Custom mode.

Running MemMaker in Express Mode

To run MemMaker in Express mode, follow these steps:

1. At the command prompt, type:

   MEMMAKER

   The Welcome to MemMaker screen is displayed, as shown in Figure 15.7.

```
Microsoft(R) MemMaker
_____

Welcome to MemMaker.

MemMaker makes more conventional memory available by moving memory-
resident programs and device drivers into the upper memory area.

While running MemMaker, you will be able to make some choices.
MemMaker displays options in highlighted text. (For example, you can
change the "Continue" option below.) To accept the highlighted
option, press ENTER.  To choose a different option, press the
SPACEBAR until the option you want appears, and then press ENTER.

For help while you are running MemMaker, press F1, or see Chapter
X, "Making More Memory Available," in the MS-DOS User's Guide.

            Continue or Exit? Continue



ENTER=Accept Selection  SPACEBAR=Change Selection  F1=Help  F3=Exit
```

*Figure 15.7.
The
MemMaker
welcome
screen.*

2. Press Enter to continue.

3. Press Enter to choose Express mode. (Pressing the Spacebar changes the selection to Custom mode.)

4. MemMaker prepares your system for evaluation, which it does during a boot operation. Press Enter to restart your computer and continue.

   MemMaker analyzes your drivers and programs as they are loaded, and determines the best way to load each one.

If your system locks up during this restart, there is some type of conflict between MemMaker and one of your programs. Turn your computer off and on, MemMaker recovers and continues.

When your boot procedure is completed, MemMaker makes changes to your CONFIG.SYS and AUTOEXEC.BAT files to implement what it has determined is your optimum configuration. A displayed message prompts you to restart again with the new configuration.

If you have a menu program (like XTREE or Point and Shoot) that loads automatically, exit it and continue. To disable your menu program, delete its command from your AUTOEXEC.BAT file.

5. Press Enter to restart your computer. The message asks you to watch carefully for any error messages or unusual displays. Depending on the speed of your system, this may be easier said than done. If something isn't working properly, though, you'll probably know it by the way your system acts.

6. Your computer restarts again. A prompt asks you if your system is working properly. If yes, press Enter and go to step 8. If no, press the Spacebar to change the selection to No. Then press Enter.

7. If you chose No in the previous step, you are given two choices for exiting MemMaker:

   ■ Select Exit to quit MemMaker without undoing the changes it has made. This option lets you troubleshoot your system. Do this by viewing your CONFIG.SYS and AUTOEXEC.BAT files. Look for discrepancies and inconsistencies and edit them as needed. You can also load a program to see how it works. For example, if you believe your mouse program is causing the problem, load a mouse-based program and see how it responds.

Even if you exit without undoing changes, you are given the opportunity to do so the next time you run MemMaker.

Your CONFIG.SYS file at this point contains a CHKSTATE command added by MemMaker. Normally, MemMaker removes this command before it completes running. You can delete it now without consequence.

■ Select Undo to quit MemMaker and restore previous versions.

8. When MemMaker has completed, press Enter to quit and return to the command prompt.

Now that MemMaker has optimized your system, use a text editor or viewing program to browse through your CONFIG.SYS and AUTOEXEC.BAT files. The changes typically made by MemMaker are described in the next section.

Changes Made by MemMaker

MemMaker adds new commands and edits existing commands in your CONFIG.SYS and AUTOEXEC.BAT files.

Changes in Your CONFIG.SYS File

MemMaker typically makes the following changes to your CONFIG.SYS file:

■ The DEVICE commands for the HIMEM.SYS and EMM386.EXE memory managers are added, if they are not there already.

■ A DOS=UMB command is added, if it is not already there.

■ MemMaker adds switches to an existing EMM386.EXE command line to configure it for optimum performance. If the existing command line contains the RAM or NOEMS switch and you are running in Express mode, the line is unchanged. If you are running in Custom mode and you enable the Set Aside Upper Memory For EMS Page Frame option, MemMaker adds the RAM switch to the command line. If you choose not to enable this option, or if there is insufficient upper memory to hold the page frame, MemMaker adds the NOEMS switch.

■ DEVICE commands are changed to DEVICEHIGH commands for device drivers that can be run in upper memory. The /L switch is included, or added to existing device commands, and a memory region is specified for each driver. The /S switch may be added at MemMaker's discretion.

■ MemMaker adds a CHKSTATE.SYS driver to your CONFIG.SYS file, and then removes it before it completes running. You may see a DEVICE=CHKSTATE.SYS command if you exit the program without undoing changes made. Delete it and continue.

■ MemMaker uses a SIZER program to evaluate memory requirements for drivers as they load. The SIZER command appears at the beginning of each command line. You might, but probably won't, see this command. If you do, it can be deleted without consequence.

Changes in Your AUTOEXEC.BAT File

MemMaker typically makes the following changes to your AUTOEXEC.BAT file:

■ For programs that can run in upper memory, MemMaker adds the LOADHIGH command to the beginning of each command line. The /L switch is included, or added to existing LOADHIGH commands, and a memory region is specified for each program. The /S switch may be added at MemMaker's discretion.

■ MemMaker uses a SIZER program to evaluate memory requirements for programs as they load. The SIZER command appears at the beginning of each command line. You might, but probably won't, see this command. If you do, it can be deleted without consequence.

■ MemMaker adds a command line to start itself the next time you boot. You may see this command if you exit the program without undoing changes made. Delete it or leave it in, depending on how you wish to proceed.

When to Run MemMaker in Custom Mode

While Express mode works fine for most systems, you may be able to free even more conventional memory by running MemMaker in Custom mode. The list that follows describes situations in which you should use Custom mode, and recommends actions to be take to achieve maximum performance.

■ If you have an EGA or VGA monitor, enable (answer *Yes* to) the option Use monochrome region (B000-BFFF) for running programs?.

■ If you run Windows, but don't run non-Windows applications in Windows, disable (answer *No* to) the option Optimize upper memory for use with Windows?.

■ If your system locks up when MemMaker initiates a restart, enable the option Specify which drivers and TSRs to include in the optimization process. This option lets you verify the loading of each driver and program. Use it to isolate and identify the problem.

■ If you know you don't run any programs that require expanded memory, enable the option Set aside upper memory for EMS page frame?.

Running MemMaker in Custom Mode

To run MemMaker in Custom mode, follow these steps:

1. Exit Windows or any other shell program, if necessary. At the command prompt type:

    MEMMAKER

2. The Welcome screen is displayed. Press Enter to continue.

3. Press the Spacebar to change the selection to Custom mode. Press Enter to continue.

4. The Advanced Options screen is displayed. Use the up-arrow and down-arrow Keys to move among the options. Use the Spacebar to change selections. Press Enter to accept your changes and move to another option.

> Be sure to check each option and know what it means. The default selections may change your current configuration. For example, the default for the Set aside upper memory for EMS page frame option is Yes. If your current EMM386.EXE command line contains the NOEMS switch, it is changed by MemMaker.

5. When you have made your selections, press Enter to continue.

MemMaker Advanced Options

The following advanced options are available in Custom mode:

■ Specify which drivers and TSRs to include in optimization process?

Answer *No* (default) if your system restarts without problems.

Answer *Yes* if your system locks up during restart. When you restart again, you are prompted to verify the loading of each device driver and memory-resident program in your configuration files. Enter Y to load or N to exclude each driver and program. If you answer Y (Yes), MemMaker loads and optimizes the driver or program according to its memory requirements.

■ Set aside upper memory for EMS page frame?

When you run MemMaker it sets up the EMM386.EXE driver to simulate expanded memory. It does this by reserving 64K of upper memory for use as the EMS page frame. Answer *No* if you don't run programs that require expanded memory.

Answer *Yes* (default) if you know you have programs that need expanded memory.

■ Scan the upper memory aggressively?

Some computers are "sensitive" when they have upper memory blocks (UMBs) in memory addresses C800 through DFF. Answer *No* if your computer locks up during a restart initiated by MemMaker. MemMaker limits its search for available UMBs to "non-sensitive addresses."

Answer *Yes* (default) if you do not experience problems during restart. MemMaker searches the entire upper memory area for available blocks.

■ Optimize upper memory for use with Windows?

Answer *Yes* (default) if you run Windows but don't normally run non-Windows (DOS) applications in Windows. MemMaker automatically optimizes upper memory for Windows, but may reduce the amount of conventional memory available.

Answer *No* if you regularly run non-Windows applications with Windows. No conventional memory is taken up, leaving it available for non-Windows applications.

■ Use monochrome region (B000-BFFF) for running programs?

Answer *Yes* (default) if you have an EGA or VGA monitor that doesn't need the memory addresses (B000-BFFF) to function properly. MemMaker determines whether these areas can be used to run programs, and then configures your memory managers to use them.

Answer *No* if you have a monochrome or Super-VGA monitor that uses these memory addresses.

■ Keep current EMM386 memory exclusions and inclusions?

Answer *Yes* (default) to prevent any changes from being made to the exclusion and inclusion parameters previously specified for the EMM386.EXE driver. Answering *Yes* preserves current parameters.

Answer *No* to have MemMaker edit the existing parameters to what it determines is an optimum arrangement. This may free up additional conventional memory.

> Enable this option if your computer locks up during restart after you run MemMaker with this option disabled.

■ Move Extended BIOS Data Area from conventional to upper memory?

The Extended BIOS Data Area (EBDA) normally occupies the end of conventional memory. Answer *Yes* (default) to move the EBDA to upper memory, freeing conventional memory for other programs.

Answer *No* to leave the EBDA in conventional memory, especially if you suspect moving it to upper memory is causing your system to lock up.

Undoing Changes Made by MemMaker

To reiterate, MemMaker makes changes to your CONFIG.SYS, AUTOEXEC.BAT, and (sometimes) SYSTEM.INI files. If these changes cause problems, usually your system locks up during restart. If this happens, it's a simple procedure to undo MemMaker changes. You can then run MemMaker again in Custom mode and attempt to identify and rectify the problem(s).

To undo MemMaker changes, follow these steps:

1. Quit Windows and other programs. At the command prompt (and not a shell version of it) type this command:

   ```
   MEMMAKER /UNDO
   ```

   MemMaker loads and prompts `Restore original files or exit?`

2. Press Enter to choose the restore option. Press Enter again to continue. Your computer restarts and restores the previous versions of CONFIG.SYS AUTOEXEC.BAT.

   To exit without undoing changes, press the Spacebar to change the selection, press Enter to quit.

Troubleshooting

Using upper memory can affect dramatic improvements in the performance of most machines, but it can be tricky. Your computer's environment is sensitive to conflicts. Your programs are given exact memory addresses into which they can load. If these addresses are unavailable, or if two programs attempt to occupy the same addresses, problems arise. The main indication that something is wrong is that your system locks up while booting or running an application.

If you encounter problems, it may be that a driver or program is not designed to run in high memory. However, it may very likely be an installation or configuration error. Use the following checklist to identify and resolve problems.

If you experience problems in you CONFIG.SYS and AUTOEXEC.BAT files—such as programs or drivers won't load into upper memory—check the following items:

■ Be sure your CONFIG.SYS contains commands that load the appropriate memory manager(s). Verify that your CONFIG.SYS file contains lines similar to the following, in the following order):

```
DEVICE=C:\DOS\HIMEM.SYS
DEVICE=C:\DOS\EMM386.EXE
DOS=HIGH,UMB
```

The EMM386.EXE command line also may contain the NOEMS or RAM switches, and other switches and parameters.

■ Be sure your drivers are loaded using the DEVICEHIGH (instead of DEVICE) command. Otherwise, your drivers are loaded into conventional memory.

■ Be sure that programs are loaded using the LOADHIGH command in your AUTOEXEC.BAT file. Otherwise, your programs are loaded into conventional memory.

If you have problems starting or restarting your computer after you make changes to CONFIG.SYS or AUTOEXEC.BAT files, watch your screen for error messages. If you see one, try to determine which program is trying to load when it appears. If you see an error message and the system completes its boot procedure, edit your CONFIG.SYS or AUTOEXEC.BAT file to load the driver or program in conventional memory.

If your computer locks up during booting, see if there are error messages that identify the source of the problem. If you can determine the source, boot your system from a floppy disk, edit the offending command, and then restart from your hard drive.

If you cannot locate the source of the problem, follow these procedures to locate it:

1. Reboot your system from a floppy disk.

2. Use the MEM /C command to determine your available upper memory. Make a note of this figure (it gives you a rough idea of how many programs can be loaded into upper memory) and of the amount of memory occupied by each driver.

3. Edit your CONFIG.SYS file. Use the DEVICEHIGH command to load the largest driver into upper memory.

4. Reboot your system.

5. If your system reboots without problem, load the next largest driver into upper memory. If your system locks up, reboot from a floppy. Then edit your CONFIG.SYS file, changing `DEVICEHIGH` to `DEVICE` on the command line for the troublesome device. If the reboot is successful, load the next largest driver into upper memory.

6. Repeat steps 3 through 5 until all the drivers from your CONFIG.SYS file are loaded.

7. Edit your AUTOEXEC.BAT file to load the largest memory-resident (TSR) program into upper memory.

8. Reboot your system.

9. Follow the guidelines in step 5, loading one TSR at a time until you either locate the problem or load all programs into upper memory. Load programs in order from largest to smallest.

As you execute this procedure, use the `MEM /C` command frequently to monitor the changes in your memory allocation.

Some common error messages you might come across while trying to optimize your memory configuration are detailed here. Solutions are suggested as well.

■ Can't Access High Memory: The A20 Handler

If you get an error message saying DOS can't access the high memory area, verify that your `DEVICE` command is correct. If you still have problems, it may be a conflict with your A20 Handler. Without becoming overly technical, the A20 handler provides access to high memory; and different computers use different types of A20 handlers. DOS 6 is designed to work with the A20 handlers on most machines, but you might have one that it doesn't recognize.

To remedy this situation add a `/MACHINE:[code]` switch. The *code* designation identifies the A20 handler used by your machine. You can find the code for your machine in your hardware manual.

■ High Memory Area (HMA) Already In Use

If you see this message, one of your programs is attempting to use more high memory than is available. If you see it, free up high memory by loading DOS, device drivers, and/or memory-resident programs into conventional memory until sufficient high memory is available.

If your CONFIG.SYS file contains a DOS=HIGH,UMB command, change it to DOS=UMB. The UMB switch is required because it tells DOS to manage the upper memory blocks (UMB), which it can do from conventional or high memory areas.

Summary

Loading device drivers and memory-resident programs can improve your system's performance by increasing available conventional memory for use by other programs. Use the MEM command to evaluate and monitor your memory allocation. Make sure the HIMEM.SYS and EMM386.EXE memory managers are loaded. Then, use the DOS, DEVICEHIGH, and LOADHIGH commands to load DOS, device drivers, and memory-resident programs into upper memory. You can also boost performance using a disk cache (SMARTDRV.EXE) or a RAM disk (RAMDRIVE.SYS). DOS 6 includes an intuitive program, called MemMaker, which evaluates your system and configures it to load as many drivers and programs as possible into upper memory.

Alan Simpson's
DOS
SECRETS
UNLEASHED

CHAPTER 16

Setting Up DOS for Windows

Microsoft spent plenty of time and effort making sure not only that Windows runs well under DOS 6, but that it runs better under DOS 6 than under any other DOS version. For the most part, they've succeeded.

First, Windows is a DOS program—a multifaceted DOS program, but still a program that runs under DOS. That means that most of the enhancements Microsoft applied to your DOS programs apply to Windows as well. Many of the memory management techniques discussed elsewhere in this book make Windows run faster and more powerfully. This chapter discusses the special advantages Microsoft added to DOS 6 specifically to enhance Windows.

What DOS 6 Offers Windows

DOS 6 added Windows versions of the standard DOS utilities, giving Windows users one less reason to access the DOS Shell for housekeeping or disk maintenance chores. DOS 6 contains Windows versions of SMARTDrive, Backup, Anti-Virus, and Undelete. DOS 6 puts icons for these programs in a new Microsoft Tools Program Group, available in the Program Manager.

A new Tools pull-down menu in the File Manager also allows access to those utilities, as does the button bar in the Windows for Workgroups File Manager.

Also, Microsoft saves you disk space not only through compression, but by planning ahead. The DOS 6 Setup program asks whether you want the Windows versions, the DOS versions, or both versions of Backup, Undelete, and Anti-Virus. By choosing just the Windows versions, thus leaving out the redundant DOS versions, you can save some disk space.

If you're running Windows, consider buying a tape backup system. The DOS 6 Backup application for Windows requires that you place floppy disks in your computer to

> back up your data. Because most hard drives that contain
> Windows are fairly large, this process can require dozens of
> disks and several hours. Tape backup units record your
> hard drive's data onto cassette tapes; some even work in the
> background. Remember, the easier it is to backup your hard
> drive, the more often you'll get around to doing it.

Installing DOS 6 if Windows Is Already Installed

DOS 6 is very much aware of Windows. During the installation process, DOS 6 searches your hard drive for an existing copy of Windows. If it finds one, it places icons for the DOS 6 Windows utilities Backup, Undelete, and Anti-Virus directly into the Program Manager. You'll see the new Microsoft Tools Program Group waiting for you the next time you load Windows.

DOS 6 also adds a Tools menu item to the File Manager. DOS 6 updates your AUTOEXEC.BAT and CONFIG.SYS files so they refer to the more current versions of HIMEM.SYS and SMARTDrive. In fact, to avoid any conflicts, you should delete the versions from your Windows 3.1 directory.

Installing Windows 3.1 if DOS 6 Is Already Installed

DOS 6 contains the most recent copies of two important utilities, SMARTDrive and HIMEM.SYS, but Windows 3.1 doesn't know that. So, if you're installing Windows 3.1 over DOS 6, Windows tries to change your AUTOEXEC.BAT and CONFIG.SYS files so that they refer to the Windows 3.1 versions of SMARTDrive and HIMEM.SYS. (Those older versions are in the Windows 3.1 directory.)

Check your AUTOEXEC.BAT and CONFIG.SYS files after installing Windows; make sure they refer to the SMARTDrive and HIMEM.SYS files in your DOS 6 directory, not your Windows directory.

Swap Files

While Windows works, it copies information from your computer's memory to the hard drive. Windows then uses this *virtual memory* as RAM to run more programs at once.

To create this virtual memory, Windows creates one of two kinds of swap files—*permanent* or *temporary*. A permanent swap file is a portion of your hard drive set aside for Windows' exclusive use. It consists of a hidden file on your hard drive. Windows works faster with a permanent swap file, but there's a catch: the permanent swap file stays around, consuming part of your hard disk space, even when Windows isn't running.

The alternative is a temporary swap file—a file Windows creates when Windows starts, and deletes when you exit Windows. The trade-off is that Windows runs more slowly with a temporary swap file. If you have enough hard disk space, consider letting Windows create a permanent swap file on your hard drive. Unfortunately, neither Stacker nor DOS 6 DoubleSpace can compress this portion of your hard drive.

You can only create a permanent swap file out of your uncompressed hard disk space. If you try to create a permanent swap file on a compressed hard drive, Windows sends you an error message.

Try not to use DoubleSpace until *after* you install Windows. That way, Windows can create its permanent swap file on an uncompressed portion of your hard drive. When DoubleSpace goes to work, it will leave your Windows permanent swap file uncompressed, and compress the rest of your hard drive instead.

Managing Memory with MemMaker

The key to making DOS programs run smoothly under Windows is to manage your memory appropriately. In the past, Windows owners were forced to make meticulous changes to their system files, trying to find the right combination of memory settings for the best performance. DOS 6 automates much of this task with MemMaker.

The DOS 6 program, MemMaker, automatically tries out various memory configurations and then chooses the one that works best for your particular setup. Sometimes MemMaker simply changes the order of the commands in your AUTOEXEC.BAT and CONFIG.SYS files. Other times, it changes their settings by changing their parameters—adding special codes before or after the commands to subtly change their performance.

> Don't bother trying to run MemMaker under Windows; DOS 6 won't let you. Windows' presence in the background would only confuse the MemMaker program while it tried to sort out the best possible memory configuration.

MemMaker can work its magic with Windows in mind. Even if you choose MemMaker's Express Setup option, MemMaker automatically optimizes your computer's upper memory to work best with Windows. In fact, if you *don't* plan to run Windows, choose MemMaker's Advanced Options; from there, answer No to the Optimize upper memory for use with Windows? question. That conserves your computer's upper memory for use by other programs.

If necessary, MemMaker changes Windows' SYSTEM.INI file to reflect any needed changes in memory settings.

If you use Windows and Windows programs exclusively, you might not need MemMaker. MemMaker maximizes conventional memory for DOS programs by shovelling programs out of conventional memory and into extended memory, which is the type of memory Windows uses. If you plan to access the DOS Shell while in Windows (or run DOS programs by themselves), feel free to use MemMaker. If you don't use any DOS programs at all, don't bother with MemMaker. Running it will just hinder Windows' performance.

Optimizing **CONFIG.SYS** for Windows

As described earlier in this book, the CONFIG.SYS file strongly affects your computer's performance. Here's a look at the CONFIG.SYS file as it pertains to Windows.

Device Drivers

Every piece of your computer's hardware—the mouse, fax cards, sound cards, and others—is considered a *device* by your computer. To customize how that device works, DOS looks for a *device driver* in your CONFIG.SYS file. Drivers are small programs that let your computer communicate with that device. Here's how some of your drivers affect Windows.

HIMEM.SYS

DOS 6 installs this driver on any computer with an 80286 or higher processor and extended memory. The HIMEM.SYS driver manages your computer's extended memory, dishing it out to programs that need it.

HIMEM.SYS has some special command-line settings, but the default settings work well with Windows on most computers.

The line containing HIMEM.SYS must appear first in your CONFIG.SYS file, before any other device drivers. Most people make HIMEM.SYS their first or second line.

IF you install Windows 3.1 over DOS 6, Windows tries to change that line so it refers to the HIMEM.SYS in the Windows directory. Don't let it do that. Make sure you're using the HIMEM.SYS file with the most current date, which is probably the one in your DOS 6 directory.

RAMDRIV.SYS

This device driver takes some of your RAM and converts it into a *virtual* hard drive. It works just like a regular hard drive, but much faster. It's also much more volatile: it will disappear if your computer loses power.

If you have more than 8 megabytes of RAM, consider turning some of it into a RAM drive, as described in Chapter 5, "Peak Performance in the DOS Environment." By using this RAM drive as your TEMP file storage area (described later in this chapter under the AUTOEXEC.BAT file settings), you can speed up Windows' Print Spooler, as well as other operations. Be sure to set up your RAM drive to contain at least 2 megabytes, however, or else you might run out of room, especially when working with large files in Word for Windows.

Unless you do a lot of printing, you might be better off leaving out the RAMDRIV.SYS setting and simply handing your extended memory over to Windows for running programs. The less extended memory Windows has at its disposal, the less efficiently it runs your programs.

MemMaker will replace many of your DEVICE= statements with the word DEVICEHIGH=. This addition will load your device driver into upper memory, freeing additional conventional memory for running DOS applications under Windows.

Finally, it bears repeating that a RAM drive may look and act like a hard drive, but it exists only in your computer's memory. When your computer is turned off (either by the on/off switch or through an accidental power failure), all information in the RAM drive is erased.

Don't confuse a RAM drive with a Windows swap file; they're the opposite of each other. A RAM drive creates a virtual hard drive out of memory, making for a very speedy hard drive. A swap file creates virtual memory from your hard drive. This virtual memory works much slower than real memory, but sometimes Windows needs memory space more than it needs hard disk space.

EMM386.EXE

This program, when loaded as a device in your CONFIG.SYS file, can convert some of your computer's extended memory into expanded memory for programs that need that type of memory. It also lets you load programs and device drivers into *upper memory blocks* (UMBs).

MemMaker automatically puts the EMM386.EXE driver into your CONFIG.SYS file. Also, as part of its optimization technique,

MemMaker grabs extra portions of memory for exclusive use by Windows. For instance, look at the following line from a CONFIG.SYS file:

```
DEVICE=C:\DOS\EMM386.EXE RAM WIN=DD00-DFFF WIN=DA00-DCFF
```

Here, the memory ranges listed after the WIN= sections are extra memory that MemMaker has activated for use by Windows.

> Most of the extended memory settings specified by EMM386 in the CONFIG.SYS file take precedence over the memory settings in Windows SYSTEM.INI file. If the two files have conflicting instructions, Windows uses the ones in the CONFIG.SYS. That means that if you change those settings in the SYSTEM.INI file, they have no effect when EMM386.EXE is loaded.

Other CONFIG.SYS Settings

These next few CONFIG.SYS settings aren't device drivers, but they can affect Windows performance just as much.

- FILES—This line sets the number of files DOS allows a program to open at one time. Because Windows usually deals with a lot of programs and files at the same time, make sure the line FILES=30 appears in your CONFIG.SYS file. The default is 8; if you have problems under Windows, try increasing the number to 40, 50, or more. Don't get carried away, however. Larger numbers in the FILES setting translate to less memory available to other applications. Choose the setting you need—and no higher.

- BUFFERS—You probably won't need to worry about the BUFFERS command when running Windows. It's an older form of disk cache that essentially has been replaced on 386-class machines by SMARTDrive. Some communications programs bring an exception to this rule, however.

■ STACKS—Each time a piece of your computer's hardware—a mouse for instance—needs some processing time from your computer's CPU, it generates something called an *interrupt*. If Windows is busy when the interrupt signal comes in, the interrupts "stack up." Sometimes this can cause problems—your mouse might hang the system, for instance.

Therefore, when Windows installs itself, it adds the line STACKS=9,256 to your CONFIG.SYS file. This allows for nine stacks of 256 bytes of conventional memory. This default setting should work adequately for running Windows.

If you see an Internal Stack Overflow message when running Windows in 386-Enhanced mode, try slowly increasing the number 256; if that doesn't work, try slowly increasing the number 9.

Optimizing AUTOEXEC.BAT for Windows

Your AUTOEXEC.BAT file contains commands you would like your computer to perform every time you turn it on. You can load frequently accessed utilities, for instance, or you can add the single line WIN to the bottom of the AUTOEXEC.BAT file to load Windows automatically.

Here's a look at how certain settings in your AUTOEXEC.BAT file can affect Windows performance under DOS 6.

SMARTDRV.EXE

SMARTDrive works as a disk-caching program. Computers can read information from RAM more quickly than from a hard disk. Therefore, when Windows reads information from the hard drive, the information also heads for a special area in your computer's memory known as a *cache*. Then, if Windows needs the information again, it reads it from the cache, which is faster than re-accessing it from the slower hard drive.

DOS 6 automatically installs SMARTDrive in your AUTOEXEC.BAT file. Chapter 14, "Hard Disk Management Made Simple," discusses SMARTDrive in detail. If you're running Windows in 386-Enhanced mode (or if you're running EMM386.EXE), DOS 6 installs SMARTDrive's "double-buffering" feature by putting SMARTDrive in your CONFIG.SYS file, as well. The double-buffer provides compatibility for hard-disk controllers that have trouble working with Windows in 386-Enhanced mode.

You may not need the double-buffering feature, however. Here's how to check. Use MemMaker, and then run Windows for a few days with the double-buffering feature in place. (DOS 6 normally adds double-buffering if you're running Windows.) At the command prompt, type SMARTDRV and press Enter. Look at the column labeled *Buffering*. If you see the word *yes* anywhere in that column, you need double-buffering—leave that line in your CONFIG.SYS file. If every line says *no*, you can safely remove the SMARTDrive line from your CONFIG.SYS file.

SET

The SET command places something called a *variable* into your DOS environment. A variable is a special portion of memory set aside to hold temporary information. For example, programs can look at these variables to find special settings. Windows introduces a variable called TEMP by placing this line in your AUTOEXEC.BAT file:

```
SET TEMP=C:\DOS
```

This assumes that your DOS files are stored on your C: drive, as they are on most computers. Now, when Windows creates temporary files—to store files while printing, for instance—it checks the TEMP variable to see in what directory they should be stored. In this case, Windows would store them in your DOS directory.

To see what environment settings are currently active, type SET at any DOS prompt.

For tips on changing your DOS prompt under Windows with the SET command, see Chapter 17, "Secrets of the Windows Program Information Files (PIFs)."

The default setting of TEMP=C:\DOS lets Windows pour all its temporary, "garbage" files directly into your DOS directory. These TEMP files will then mingle unobtrusively with your DOS programs. To keep your TEMP files separate from your DOS files, create a TEMP subdirectory from your DOS directory; then change the TEMP variable to TEMP=C:\DOS\TEMP. When you're not using Windows, you can look in your DOS\TEMP directory to see if Windows forgot to delete some of its temporary files. If there are any left, feel free to delete them. Make sure you are out of Windows first, however, and not just shelled to DOS.

PATH

The PATH setting is the other AUTOEXEC.BAT file setting altered during a Windows installation. Directories listed after the PATH command in your AUTOEXEC.BAT file can be searched from any command prompt. Windows, therefore, places its WINDOWS directory in your PATH setting. That way, you can type WIN to start Windows, even if you aren't currently in the Windows directory—DOS finds the WIN.COM program in the Windows subdirectory and loads it.

SHARE

Windows doesn't automatically place the DOS program SHARE in your AUTOEXEC.BAT file, but you should. Normally used on networks, SHARE prevents you from opening a file that's currently being used by another program. Because Windows runs many programs at once, it's easy to accidentally open the same file in a different window. Then, when you save both versions, one will overwrite the work you've done with the other.

To prevent this, add the following line to your AUTOEXEC.BAT file:

```
INSTALL=C:\DOS\SHARE.EXE
```

Then, should you mistakenly start to open a file for a second time, Windows will flash an error message telling you that the file is already open.

Mouse Command Line

Most mouse installation programs place a mouse driver in either your AUTOEXEC.BAT or CONFIG.SYS file. However, because Windows contains its own mouse driver, the extra mouse driver merely consumes valuable memory space. If you plan to use Windows *exclusively*, feel free to remove any other mouse driver you might find in your AUTOEXEC.BAT or CONFIG.SYS files. Beware, however—if you shell to DOS, you won't find mouse support for those DOS programs under Windows. Only remove the mouse driver if you *never* use DOS programs.

Watch Out for These DOS Commands and Programs

Several DOS commands aren't intended to be run at the same time Windows is running. If you try to run them from within Windows, you'll probably receive a DOS error message before any harm is done. Still, avoid taking any chances by avoiding the following DOS commands and programs.

APPEND, ASSIGN, JOIN, and SUBST

These commands play tricks on the way DOS recognizes drives and directories. These commands can work well for DOS applications, but not when running under Windows. Avoid them. If you want to create or delete virtual drives with SUBST, you can exit Windows, safely use the command, and then load Windows again.

CHKDSK /F

CHKDSK can discover and fix errors in the way files are stored on your hard drive. However, if it tries to fix an error while running under Windows, you may lose some data. The /F option on the command line tells CHKDSK to fix the errors, so avoid that option under Windows. Exit Windows (don't just shell to DOS) before using the CHKDSK command.

DBLSPACE

DOS 6 won't let you run the DoubleSpace program under Windows. It needs to be run from a DOS session instead.

Also, when running the DoubleSpace program, be sure to leave enough uncompressed space available to accommodate Windows' permanent storage file. Depending on the size of your hard disk, your amount of RAM, and the size of your Windows programs, leave anywhere from 1M to 8M free for Windows to use as a permanent swap file. You create Windows' permanent storage file under the 386-Enhanced setting in the Control Panel. The storage file lets Windows run faster. Windows treats the file as virtual memory, using it to swap information back and forth as you open and close programs.

DEFRAG

The DEFRAG program reorganizes your hard disk by moving pieces of files closer to each other to speed up access time. This reorganization will confuse Windows, however. Don't try to run DEFRAG from either Windows or the Shell.

Don't know if you're in Windows or in a DOS Shell? Just type EXIT at the C:\> prompt before entering any other command. If you return to Windows, you were in the Shell. If the command prompt just looks confused, your safely sitting at the DOS prompt.

VSAVE

The DOS virus checker, VSAFE, needs to be disabled before you begin installing Windows; otherwise, it will mistake some of Windows' installation commands for damaging viruses. VSAFE is a memory-resident program that's loaded from your AUTOEXEC.BAT file. To disable it, either remove it completely from the AUTOEXEC.BAT file or add the letters REM to the beginning of the line, like this:

```
REM VSAFE.EXE
```

Save your AUTOEXEC.BAT file and then reboot your computer. With the REM, VSAFE won't be loaded, and you can safely install Windows. After installing Windows, exit the program, remove the REM portion, and reboot your computer to restore VSAFE.

DOS Shell

The DOS Shell adds a point-and-click interface to your DOS programs and commands. You can start programs from the Shell and return to the Shell when the program's finished, but don't start Windows from the Shell. Windows needs to start all by itself at the command line so it can properly organize your computer's memory.

Feel free to start the Shell from within Windows. You can either make the Shell an icon in one of your Program Groups, or you can run the Shell from the command line.

> The DOS RENAME command enables you to change a file's name. It won't, however, enable you to rename a directory or subdirectory. A quick way to do that is to use Windows File Manager. Highlight the name of the directory you want to change, and choose Rename from the File pull-down menu. Type in the new name and click OK to complete the process.

WINA20.386

Windows 3.0 required the WINA20.386 file to run in Enhanced mode under DOS 5.0. If you've upgraded to Windows 3.1, you can safely remove this file from your hard drive.

Starting Windows from the Command Prompt

To start Windows, you type WIN at the command prompt. However, you can start Windows different ways by adding different switches after the word WIN. Here's a look at the switches and what they do:

WIN /S or WIN /2 starts Windows 3.1 in standard mode.

WIN /3 starts Windows 3.1 in 386-Enhanced mode, but only if there's enough extended memory available.

WIN : bypasses Windows' opening screen, saving a second or two of idle time.

Troubleshooting

DOS 6 is designed to provide the technology necessary to make Windows perform at its best. If you encounter problems, perhaps the following tips can help.

- When you are running Windows, do not use the following commands:

  APPEND
  DBLSPACE
  DEFRAG
  EMM386
  FASTOPEN
  MEMMAKER
  MSCDEX
  NLSFUNC
  SMARTDRV
  SUBST
  VSAFE
  CHKDSK with the /F option

- If you use Windows exclusively, do not install DOS versions of Anti-Virus, Backup, or Undelete. The Windows versions of these programs require less disk space.

- Your program will run more effectively if you do not use RAMDRIVE.SYS. This will free up more extended memory for Windows. You do not need RAMDRIVE.SYS if you plan to do a lot of printing.

- Don't forget that the EMM386 settings in the CONFIG.SYS file take precedence over the memory settings in your Windows SYSTEM.INI file.

- Be sure to remove HIMEM.SYS and SMARTDRV from your Windows directory. DOS 6 Setup updates AUTOEXEC.BAT and CONFIG.SYS with the current versions of these two files which must reside in your DOS directory.

Summary

Strangely enough, DOS 6 gives Windows users one less reason to use DOS. It provides Windows versions of utilities such as Backup and Undelete, so Windows users no longer have to shell to the DOS command line for housekeeping chores. It's one more step toward making Windows 3.1 a complete, command-line–free environment.

- Don't install DoubleSpace until after you make allowances for Windows' permanent swap file. That file can't exist on compressed hard drive space.

- If you don't ever shell to DOS, and you don't run any DOS programs under Windows, don't bother with DOS MemMaker program. That program primarily optimizes your conventional memory for use with DOS programs, not Windows.

- One of the first lines to appear in your CONFIG.SYS file must be HIMEM.SYS. This must appear before any other device drivers are listed.

- DOS 6 contains the latest versions of HIMEM.SYS, SMARTDrive, and EMM386.EXE. If you install Windows 3.1 over DOS 6, Windows tries to insert its older versions of these files. Check the dates of these files after you install Windows to make sure you're using the most recent, DOS 6 versions.

- Before installing Windows over DOS 6, place the word REM in front of the line VSAFE.EXE. VSAFE can confuse Windows during the installation process, so you must temporarily disable VSAFE. Remove the REM after installing Windows to reactivate VSAFE.

- Perhaps the easiest way to rename a DOS directory is through Windows File Manager. Highlight the directory you would like to change, and press Alt+F+N. Then type in the new name and press Enter.

Alan Simpson's
DOS
SECRETS
UNLEASHED

Secrets of the Windows Program Information Files (PIFs)

Windows works well with Windows programs, but it sometimes has difficulty running DOS programs. Those programs simply weren't designed to work with Windows. To accommodate the special needs of a DOS program, Windows lets you keep that program's special settings in something called a *Program Information File* (*PIF*).

Whenever you tell Windows to run a program ending in .EXE, .COM, or .BAT, it looks for a .PIF matching the name of the program. For example, the settings required to run Lotus Magellan would be stored in a PIF called MG.PIF, so Windows would search for that file.

This chapter examines the best way to run DOS programs, under Windows, through Windows' PIF editor—the program that creates PIFs to track a DOS program's settings.

What's a PIF?

PIFs contain information on a program's location on the hard drive, the type and amount of memory it needs, what ports it needs, and other vital information. Some DOS programs come with their own PIF, written by the program's manufacturer to ensure its success under Windows. To start the program under Windows, double-click that program's PIF—it contains all the information Windows needs to make it run successfully.

Do You Need a PIF?

A large number of DOS programs don't need a PIF. You can start them from the File Manager with a double-click, just like any other program. The programs that require a PIF usually have special needs. Telecommunications programs, for example, sometimes need control over a computer's COM port. Other DOS programs have special memory requirements, because they weren't designed to work with Windows' special ways of parceling out extended memory.

If your DOS program didn't come with a PIF, try to double-click on its name in the File Manager to see if it works anyway. If you receive an error message, it's time to turn to the PIF editor and tell Windows your DOS program's special needs.

Even if a program comes with a PIF, you might want to change some of its settings by using the PIF editor. You can make the DOS program launch in a Window, for example, instead of always taking up the full screen.

Making Windows Create PIFs Automatically

When Windows sets itself up on your computer, it searches through your hard drive for any DOS programs it recognizes. Windows 3.1 comes with pre-configured PIFs (as well as icons) for many popular DOS programs. After installing a DOS program

1. Double-click the Windows Setup icon.

2. Choose the **S**et up Applications... option from the **O**ptions pull-down menu.

3. Press Enter at the next screen.

Windows will repeat its search of your hard drive, looking for any recognizable DOS programs.

Look in the list for your newly installed DOS program. If it's in the list, Windows can create a PIF allowing it to run correctly. If it's not there, you'll probably have to create your own using the PIF editor.

The PIF Editor

The PIF editor is a Windows accessory program that creates or changes PIFs. You'll find its icon in the Main Program Group in the Windows Program Manager. Double-click the icon, and the PIF editor will load. However, because Windows can run in two modes—Standard or 386-Enhanced—the PIF editor looks different depending on the current operating mode (see Figure 17.1 and Figure 17.2).

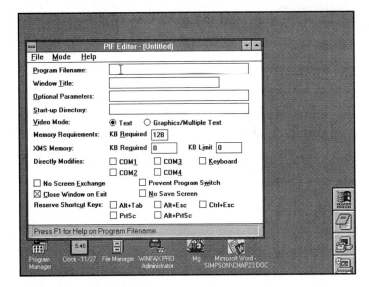

Figure 17.1.
The PIF editor
in Standard
operating
mode.

Standard Mode

When Windows runs in Standard mode, DOS programs must use the full screen. Under Standard mode, Windows doesn't run DOS programs in a window, and you can't copy information from the programs to the Clipboard.

Also, DOS programs can't multitask under Standard mode. When on the screen, the program takes up almost all of Windows' resources. When sitting as an icon at the bottom of your screen, the program hardly uses any processor time at all. When in Standard mode, Windows merely switches its attention from DOS program to DOS program, called *task-switching*—the programs can't keep running in the background.

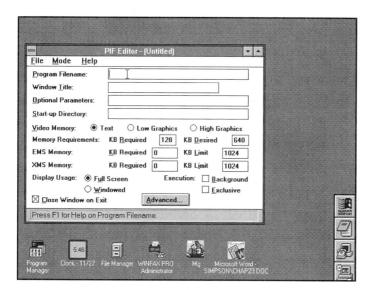

Figure 17.2. The PIF editor in 386-Enhanced mode.

386-Enhanced Mode

In 386-Enhanced mode, Windows uses the 386 chip's special powers to create several virtual DOS computers and runs them simultaneously. That means several DOS programs can run at the same time—a DOS communications program can download a file in the background while you type words into a word processing program in the foreground.

Because the DOS programs work so differently under the two different modes, the PIFs for those DOS programs also differ. Under 386-Enhanced mode, the PIF editor does everything it does under Standard mode, but adds one main feature: you can adjust a DOS program's multitasking times.

Each PIF actually has two settings: one for standard mode
and one for 386-Enhanced. To see them both, switch between the two using the **M**ode pull-down menu. From
there, you can click either **S**tandard or 386-Enhanced.

PIF Settings

Although the PIF editor's dozens of settings can seem overwhelming at first, it has a decent, context-sensitive help system. If you're
stumped as to what the "XMS Memory Locked" setting means, for
example, click that setting and press F1. Windows' help system will
explain a little more about that particular command.

Also, there's no set "right answer" for what PIF settings will
work for you. They'll change not only according to your particular
computer's hardware (memory, CPU power, and so on), but the type
of programs you're running at a particular time. Don't be surprised
if much of a PIF's performance depends on trial and error.

Standard Mode Options

Here's a look at the options available under the Standard mode.

■ **P**rogram Filename:—Type the name of the program that
  needs the PIF. To be on the safe side, include the program's
  complete name and path in this box.

■ Window **T**itle:—Windows uses the program's file name for
  the title, both when the program is running in a window or
  as an icon. If you prefer a different title, type that name in
  this box.

> Keep your titles short; that keeps the words from overlapping when icons appear next to each other.

■ **O**ptional Parameters:—Here you can type anything you want to place automatically after the program's name at the DOS command line. For example, you could type the name of a file you would like to load automatically when the program comes to the screen.

> Type a single question mark in this box, and Windows will prompt you for new parameters each time you load the DOS program.

■ **S**tart-up Directory:—Some DOS programs need to know where their supporting files are located. Type the name of that directory here.

> There's no reason why you can't make more than one PIF for the same program. For example, to make your DOS word processor open in a different directory, make a new PIF and type the new directory name in the **S**tart-up Directory box. Make a different PIF for each directory you want to use. Then you can just double-click that directory's PIF instead of having to change directories after your DOS program loads.

■ **V**ideo Mode:—Here you can choose between Text and Graphics/Multiple Text. Choose Text for DOS programs that use text displays only. Choose Graphics/Multiple Text if your program uses Graphics. (The section "386-Enhanced Mode Options" later in this chapter describes additional options.)

To save memory, first try setting the PIF with Text mode only. Then try switching back and forth from Windows to your DOS program. If the screen is garbled, switch to the Graphics/Text option.

■ Memory Requirements:—In the KB **R**equired box, type the amount of conventional memory that the program requires. You'll often find this information printed along the side of the program's box. (The 386-Enhanced mode offers an additional option here.)

Start with the minimum amount here, which is 128K. Windows automatically allocates more if needed, and setting the number too high robs memory from your other applications.

■ XMS Memory:—In the KB Re**q**uired box, type the amount of extended memory your program must have. In the KB Limit box, type the maximum amount of extended memory you can spare. Be sure your program actually uses extended memory before you allocate some. If your program doesn't need extended memory, type 0 in the KB Re**q**uired box.

■ Directly Modifies:—Windows usually controls your computer's serial ports and keyboard. Here you can give a DOS program complete control of a serial, or COM, port. Click the box next to the COM port that the program needs to control, or if you want your DOS program to control the keyboard buffer, click the **K**eyboard box. Beware, however, that giving the DOS program complete control means no other programs can use those facilities until you completely exit your DOS program. Also, clicking any of these options disables any Windows shortcut keys.

> As with many other PIF settings, try running your program
> without these settings checked. If you encounter problems,
> go back and set them.

- No Screen **E**xchange—Normally, you can use the Print
  Screen key to send snapshots of the screen to the Clipboard.
  Click this option, however, if you wish to save a little
  memory by disabling that feature.

- Prevent Program S**w**itch—Windows normally lets you
  switch from one program to another, even if your currently
  running DOS program is utilizing the full screen. If you
  don't need to switch between programs, click this box to
  save memory for your DOS application.

- **C**lose Window on Exit—If you want Windows to leave you
  at the DOS prompt when the DOS program closes, make
  sure a check doesn't appear in this box.

- **N**o Save Screen—If you're desperate for extra memory, try
  this option. Windows normally saves the screen's information in memory so that it can update the screen when
  necessary. If your DOS program has a "redraw screen"
  function, or can automatically update the screen, click this
  box. If it causes problems, click there again to remove the X
  mark and disable the feature.

- Reserve Shortcut Keys:—Several key combinations tell
  Windows to perform a specific task. For instance, holding
  the Ctrl key while pressing Esc brings up the Task List box,
  listing all the open programs. However, some DOS programs use these special key combinations for their own
  functions. If you want to reserve these keys for your DOS
  program, click their boxes. If you want these keys to call up
  Windows functions instead, leave them clear.

386-Enhanced Mode Options

These options appear in the 386-Enhanced mode of the PIF editor. Many of the options are the same as in the Standard mode, but a few differ subtly. Also, because the 386-Enhanced mode offers so many options, a click of the Advanced button brings up another screen.

■ Program Filename:—Type the name of the program in this box. Include the program's complete name and path.

■ Window Title:—Windows normally uses the program's file name for the title, both when running in a window or as an icon. If you prefer a different title, type that name in this box.

Keep your titles short; that keeps the words from overlapping when icons appear next to each other.

■ Optional Parameters:—Here you can type anything you want automatically placed after the program's name on the DOS command line. For instance, you could type the name of a file you would like to automatically load when the program comes to the screen.

Type a single question mark in this box, and Windows will prompt you for the parameters each time you load the DOS program.

■ Start-up Directory:—Some DOS programs need to know where their supporting files are located. Type the name of that directory here.

- **Video Memory:**—The 386-Enhanced mode offers more settings here than in Standard mode. Choose Text for DOS programs that use text displays only. Low Graphics works for CGA displays, and High Graphics, the most-used setting, works best for most EGA and VGA displays.

> To save memory, first try setting the PIF with Text mode only. Then try switching back and forth, from Windows to your DOS program. If the screen is garbled, switch to the Low or High Graphics option.

- **Memory Requirements:**—In the KB **R**equired box, type the amount of conventional memory the program requires. You'll often find this information printed along the side of the program's box. In the KB **D**esired box, type the amount of conventional memory you want available for your DOS program.

> Start with the minimum amount of conventional memory in the KB **R**equired box, which is 128K. Windows automatically allocates more memory if needed, and setting the number too high robs memory from your other applications.

- **EMS Memory:**—Under 386-Enhanced mode, Windows can simulate expanded memory for DOS programs that require it. Check your program's manual to see how much expanded memory it requires, and enter that amount in the **K**B Required box. If you're not sure, leave it blank and run the program. If it doesn't run properly, slowly increase the number until it works correctly. Under the KB **L**imit, enter the maximum amount of expanded memory you want that program to have. If you don't enter a limit, some programs will try to grab all the available expanded memory for themselves. (And why shouldn't they? They think they have the whole computer to themselves.)

If you want the program to have all the expanded memory it needs, type -1 in the KB Limit box. To keep it from grabbing any expanded memory at all, type 0 in the box.

- XMS Memory:—Here type the amount of extended memory your program must have in the KB Required box; type the maximum amount of extended memory you can spare in the KB Limit box. Be sure your program actually uses extended memory before you allocate some. If your program doesn't need extended memory, type 0 in the KB Required box. If you want to give it all the extended memory it needs, type -1 in the box. This can slow down your system considerably, however, so don't use this setting often.

- Display Usage:—Not found when under Standard mode, this setting enables you to choose between two options— running your DOS program in a window, or letting it have the entire screen. Some DOS programs don't behave well in a window. For example, the colors don't look right, the mouse doesn't work, or other problems surface. Others run just fine. Experiment between the two settings until you find the one that works best. The Execution: setting enables you to choose between Background or Exclusive. Neither setting robs you of the ability to switch to other programs; Background just means your DOS program will continue to function while you work with other programs, and Exclusive means that the program has Windows' full attention while it's the currently open window.

You can change all of these settings on the fly by pressing Alt+Spacebar, as described in the section "Making DOS Programs Run Faster" later this chapter.

■ **Close Window on Exit**—This setting works just as it does in Standard mode. If you want Windows to leave you at the DOS prompt upon exiting the DOS program, make sure there's no check mark in this box. Otherwise, you return to Windows when the program finishes.

386-Enhanced Mode Advanced... Settings

Not found under Standard mode, the Advanced... settings open the door to a plethora of puzzling PIF options (see Figure 17.3).

Figure 17.3. The PIF editor's Advanced options in 386-Enhanced mode.

■ **Multitasking Options**—One of the most confusing advanced options, the **B**ackground Priority: and **F**oreground Priority: boxes enable you to determine how much CPU time to

devote to your DOS program, both when it's running in the
background and when it's the currently active window.
Setting the number to 10000 gives the program exclusive
access to CPU resources. Setting it to 0 doesn't give it any
access. The default settings usually work well. The only
way to see if a different setting will work better is to
experiment.

> Click the **Detect Idle Time** box to have Windows shut off
> CPU access to DOS programs that don't seem to need
> access. If this causes problems, however, turn off the option.

- Memory Options—These four settings prepare Windows
  for dealing with your DOS program's advanced memory
  requirements. For the most part, don't check the boxes for
  EMS Memory Locked, XMS Memory Locked, or Lock
  Application Memory. When these boxes are checked,
  Windows won't swap that program's expanded or extended
  memory to the hard disk. That means your memory-
  resident programs will have their customary "instant"
  access to it, but this will slow down the rest of your system.
  Click the Uses High Memory Area box if your DOS program uses it.

- Display Options—Like many PIF options, you can leave all
  these boxes blank unless the DOS program's screen becomes garbled when switching back and forth to Windows.
  EGA modes seem to prefer the High Graphics mode.

Other Options

Here are some other options under the 386-Enhanced mode.

- Allow Fast **Paste**—Keep the Allow Fast **Paste** box checked
  unless your DOS program can't handle incoming streams of
  text from the Clipboard.

■ Allow **C**lose When Active—Don't check the Allow **C**lose
When Active box unless your DOS program never writes to
a disk; otherwise, Windows closes the program automatically when you exit Windows, regardless of whether your
work is saved or not.

■ Reserve **S**hortcut Keys:—Don't check any of the boxes
under Reserve **S**hortcut Keys unless your DOS application
needs those shortcut keys for its own use. You can type
your own shortcut key in the **A**pplication Shortcut Key: box.
For example, by pressing Ctrl+D while in the box, you can
return to that open DOS program in a sea of windows by
pressing Ctrl+D.

Don't expect too much from the Application Shortcut key.
First, your DOS program must already be open before you
can switch to it by pressing that key combination. Second,
Windows uses a lot of key combinations for itself, and you
might accidentally choose a conflicting set. You might do
better to merely press Ctrl+Esc to call up the Task List; then
choose your DOS application from the pop-up list.

Making DOS Programs Run Faster

Although the PIF settings enhance DOS performance each time you
load the programs, you can speed up a program under special circumstances. For example, if you want to run a DOS program and
don't really care about keeping your Windows options open in the
background, hold down the Alt key and press the Spacebar. The
menu shown in Figure 17.4 will pop up.

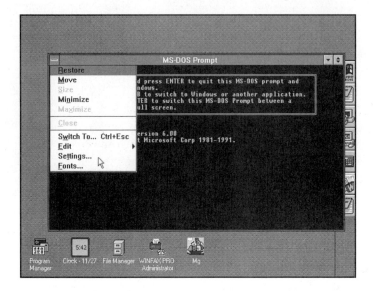

*Figure 17.4.
Hold down Alt
and press the
Spacebar to
bring up a
quick DOS
menu.*

When the DOS menu appears, press T (or click on Settings... with your mouse) to view the DOS Settings... menu shown in Figure 17.5.

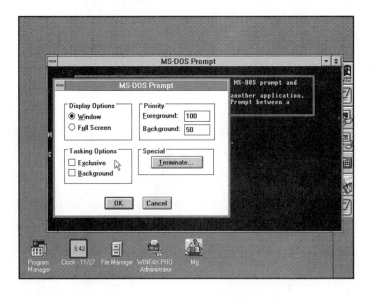

*Figure 17.5.
The DOS
Settings...
menu.*

From here you can click the Exclusive box to give your program all your CPU's attention. None of your other programs will continue to process information in the background, but most of the time they're not really working in the background anyway.

Note that you can also change the program's Priority, or the amount of access time the CPU devotes to it, just as with the PIF. You can also choose the Terminate option to purge a "frozen" DOS program from your system. Use this only as a last resort, however, as it can lead to unstable memory settings.

Shelling to DOS from Windows

When switching to a DOS prompt from within Windows, you can specify a startup file other than the usual C:\AUTOEXEC.BAT file. Open your DOSPRMPT.PIF file—the one with COMMAND.COM in the Program Filename: box—and place the following line in the Optional Parameters: box:

```
/K \drive\path\filename
```

Substitute the program you want to run for *filename* (complete with its \drive and \path), and Windows will run that program immediately before returning you to a DOS prompt. This is especially handy for running batch programs.

Sometimes it's hard to remember whether you've shelled to DOS through Windows or if you're actually in DOS (and Windows isn't waiting in the background). To make it easier to remember, use the WINPMT variable. For instance, put this line in your AUTOEXEC.BAT file:

```
set winpmt=Type "Exit" to return to Windows.$_$p$g
```

Now, when you shell to DOS, your prompt says the following:

```
Type "Exit" to return to Windows.
C:\>
```

Then you'll never forget you're still in Windows when you're staring at a DOS prompt.

 # Troubleshooting

Running your DOS programs in Windows is possible with PIFs. However, much of the program's performance depends on simple trial and error when defining the program's PIF settings.

If you receive an error message when you try to start a DOS program in Windows, you have two alternatives:

- Use Windows Setup to determine if a preconfigured PIF is available for your DOS program.

- If there is no pre-configured PIF, use the PIF Editor to create a PIF file containing your program's special settings.

Summary

Windows sometimes has difficulty running DOS programs, which were never designed to run in Windows' multitasking environment. To accommodate a DOS program's special needs, Windows lets you keep that program's special settings in something called a *PIF*, or Program Information File. With the proper PIF, most DOS programs can run under Windows.

- Windows can automatically create a PIF for the most popular DOS programs. From the Windows Setup icon, choose the **S**et up Applications... option from the **O**ptions pull-down menu. Windows then searches your hard drive, creating PIFs for any recognizable DOS programs.

- Even if a DOS program runs fine without a PIF, a PIF can customize how it runs. A PIF can tell a DOS program to boot in a window, for instance, instead of filling the entire screen.

■ You can create several different PIFs for the same DOS program. Each different PIF can tell that program to use a different default opening directory, for instance.

■ Each PIF has two modes, Standard and 386-Enhanced, although these two modes aren't initially obvious. The same PIF can set different options for both of these modes.

■ Unfortunately, much of a PIF's performance depends on trial and error. Different DOS programs run differently depending not only on the type of computer, but on the other programs currently running. Feel free to experiment with a PIF's settings until they work best with your particular setup.

■ A PIF controls how a DOS program behaves, but you can change several PIF settings on the fly. Hold down the Alt key and press the Spacebar to see a menu of changeable settings—font size, full screen/window toggle, and other handy options.

■ It's difficult to tell when you're running straight DOS or merely shelled to DOS through Windows. DOS 6 fixes this with the WINPMT variable. Place this variable in your AUTOEXEC.BAT file to change your DOS prompt when shelled to Windows. It's one of the handiest Windows features offered by DOS 6.

Alan Simpson's
DOS
SECRETS
UNLEASHED

Protecting Your System

Over the years, experienced computer users have relied on a roster of data protection programs and utilities to safeguard their work. These utilities, sold as separate software packages or bundled into "integrated" utilities, diminish the frustration of losing an important file to a careless deletion or a malicious virus.

Microsoft has streamlined data protection under DOS 6 by bundling three optional utilities with the operating system—Microsoft Backup, Anti-Virus, and Undelete.

DOS 6 actually contains six data protection utilities—a DOS version and a Windows version of each program.

Because they're optional, you can install and run these programs under DOS, Windows, both—or not at all. This chapter discusses DOS 6's provisions for backing up data, preventing viruses, and undeleting files in the DOS and Windows environments.

DOS 6 Data Protection Overview

Microsoft's move to bundle Backup, Anti-Virus, and Undelete with DOS 6 frees you from the hassle and expense of purchasing third-party data protection programs. However, you may not need or want all three optional programs. Because DOS 6 Setup offers you the choice of installing only the programs you desire, here's an overview of each program's key features and how they facilitate data protection.

For more information on DOS 6 and Windows, check out
Chapter 16, "Setting Up DOS for Windows."

Benefits of Microsoft Backup

The benefits of Microsoft Backup are the following:

- Accessible in DOS or Windows

- Can assess backup media reliability

- Provides archival options

- Has configurable backup strategies

- Provides the ability to set up and save 50 backup types

- Easily identifiable backup catalog written to target and source media

Benefits of Anti-Virus

The benefits of Anti-Virus are the following:

- Accessible in DOS or Windows

- Provides protection against known viruses

- Acts as a sentry against virus-like behavior

- Provides for future virus updates

- Lists virus descriptions that you can search or browse

- Virus glossary available through help menu

Benefits of Undelete

The benefits of Undelete are the following:

- Versions for both DOS and Windows

- Provides flexible file identification and recovery

- Can recover deleted directories (in Windows Undelete)

- Has preconfigurable file protection, in three degrees

Installing Backup, Anti-Virus, and Undelete

The DOS 6 Setup utility automates the installation of the optional programs that come with DOS 6. For an overview of the DOS 6 Setup procedure, turn to Part II, "Setting Up DOS."

DOS 6 Setup lets you install the Windows, MS-DOS, or both versions of Backup, Undelete, and Anti-Virus. To conserve room on your hard disk, Setup defaults to the Windows version when it detects Windows, and only defaults to the MS-DOS version for MS-DOS systems. Before installing either optional program, Setup prompts you for confirmation.

Installing the Optional Programs at Setup

To install the optional programs when you first install DOS 6, follow these steps:

1. Start your computer in the usual way (however you are accustomed to starting it).

2. Insert the Setup disk into drive A: or drive B:.

3. At the command prompt, type A:SETUP or B:SETUP.

4. Press Enter.

5. Follow the on-screen Setup instructions.

6. Review the programs listed in the Optional Programs dialog box.

7. To install the listed programs, press Enter.

8. To see an alternate program listing, highlight the program and press Enter.

Remember, DOS 6's Setup utility detects whether Windows is installed on a computer. If you have Windows installed, Setup lists only the Windows versions of these optional programs, to save hard disk space. For example, a Windows user with hard disk C: would see the Optional Programs dialog box as shown in Figure 18.1.

```
Backup:            Windows only
Undelete:          Windows only
Anti-Virus:        Windows only

Install the listed programs.
```

Figure 18.1. Setup's dialog box for installing the optional programs.

Choosing an Alternate Program Version

Say you have plenty of hard disk space and you decide you want both the Windows and DOS versions of the programs. If you want to install a different program version than the one supplied in the Default menu, or if you decide not to install a program at this time, follow these steps:

1. From the Optional Programs dialog box, highlight a program with the up- or down-arrow key.

2. Review the list of installation alternatives.

3. Highlight your selection with the up- or down-arrow key.

4. Press Enter.

For example, if you choose to bypass the default Windows Backup installation and install both the Windows and MS-DOS versions of Backup, highlight and select the first item on the screen, as shown in Figure 18.2.

```
Windows and MS-DOS
Windows only
MS-DOS only
None
```

Figure 18.2. Selecting an alternate backup version during DOS 6 Setup.

If you install the DOS version at Setup and then switch to the Windows operating environment at a later date, you can install Windows versions of the optional program at that time, using SETUP /E, discussed in the "Installing or Removing an Optional Program" section later in this chapter. Conversely, Windows users who find themselves frequently using DOS can add the DOS versions by using SETUP /E as well.

Installing both the Windows and MS-DOS versions of all three optional programs can take up almost 8M of hard disk space. It's best to install only one version at setup time, adding alternate versions only when you're sure you'll need them. If you don't have enough disk space to install the optional programs at setup time, turn to the troubleshooting section at the end of this chapter.

Installing or Removing an Optional Program

You will probably choose to install Backup, Anti-Virus, and Undelete when you run MS-DOS 6 Setup. However, you can easily add, remove, or change versions of these programs at any time by running an abbreviated version of Setup.

To run Setup to add or change the optional programs:

1. Start your computer in the usual way.

2. Insert DOS 6 Setup Disk #1 in drive A: or drive B:.

3. At the DOS prompt, type A:SETUP /E or B:SETUP /E, depending on which disk drive you're using.

4. Press Enter.

5. Follow the instructions on the screen.

> You may see an error message saying there is not enough hard disk space to add more than one version of a program. If you encounter this message, turn to the troubleshooting section at the end of this chapter.

Accessing DOS External Commands

DOS contains two types of commands—*internal* and *external*. DOS external commands are stored on disk as programs. MS-Backup, MS-AntiVirus, and Undelete are examples of DOS external commands. Because they're actually subprograms under DOS, external commands are accessible only when DOS can find the appropriate file on the current directory (or in the defined PATH statement).

If you plan to use MS-Backup, MS-AntiVirus, or Undelete from the DOS prompt, and you want them (and any other external DOS commands) to be available at all times, you need to take two actions. First, be sure that all the DOS external command programs, including Backup, AntiVirus, and Undelete, are stored in one directory, usually C:\DOS. Second, include that directory in your PATH statement.

Chapter 10, "Working with Files and Directories," covers directories in more detail. Chapter 6, "Getting It All Started with CONFIG.SYS and AUTOEXEC.BAT," discusses setting up your DOS PATH statement.

Microsoft Backup

As harsh as it may sound, your data integrity is only as solid as your last backup. Keeping an up-to-date backup on hand secures your data—as well as your sanity—should your hard disk fail or elude the system at boot-up.

DOS 6 eases the backup process by making it more automatic. Because it's easily accessible in both DOS and Windows, MS Backup encourages you to make backing up part of your daily routine. The new Backup is highly configurable, letting you customize backup routines to your own needs. If an important file seems to be missing or you require an older version of a file, Backup creates easy-to-read *catalog files* to help you restore single files as well as entire directories.

Improvements to DOS's Backup Capabilities

DOS 6 Backup, provided by Symantec, a well-known utility publisher, is both easier to use and much more powerful than the backup utility found in prior DOS versions. Among the improvements you'll enjoy are the following:

- Windows and DOS command-line versions that contain extensive online help

- A Compatibility Test feature that enables you to ensure a backup's reliability

- The ability to create and save up to 50 backup configurations

- Automatic backups using Setup files

- Full, incremental, and differential backups

- Target and source backup media stamped with Backup Catalog, to locate and restore files easily

- DoubleSpace compression option that saves time and reduces media needed for backup

- Error correction and file comparison options that ensure data integrity

Configuring Backup

Before you can rely on backups made with MS-Backup, take a moment to configure its settings. The most important part of that involves performing a compatibility test to ensure your hardware will work reliably in a backup session. The compatibility test performs a small backup. Then a test Compare is made, displaying the Compare Progress dialog box.

If Backup's compatibility test fails on your computer, backups may be unreliable.

At any point in the Configuration menu system, press Escape as many times as needed to return to Backup's Main menu.

You need two floppy disks of the same size and capacity to perform the compatibility test—for either DOS or Windows Backup versions. The disks don't have to be formatted, but they must be the rated density for your disk drive (that is, don't use a 720K floppy in 1.44M disk drive).

You need to remove all disks from your floppy drive(s) before you start this test. During the compatibility test, your floppy drive's drive light may remain on even after it stops making working noises. Don't attempt to access the floppy disk in the drive until the light goes out.

When you first try to use Backup, you are prompted to perform the compatibility test at that time. I highly recommend that you proceed with the automated test.

Once you've been using Backup, but you need to retest your PC's configuration—say, if you purchase a new floppy drive—follow the step-by-step directions in the appropriate DOS or Windows Backup section to perform subsequent compatibility tests.

Take time out to do a compatibility test for any new backup drive or device before performing backups to the device.

DOS Backup Compatibility Test

To perform the recommended compatibility test, perform the following steps:

1. Type MSBACKUP at the DOS prompt.

2. Press Enter.

3. Select Configure by clicking that button with your mouse, or pressing Alt+N and then pressing Enter.

4. You'll see Backup's Configure menu, shown in Figure 18.3.

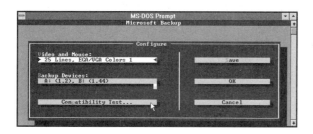

Figure 18.3. DOS 6 Backup Configure Menu.

5. Click the Compatibility Test button.

As mentioned in the preceding section, the first time you try to use DOS Backup, the program automatically prompts you to run the compatibility test. A screen similar to that in Figure 18.4 pops up.

Figure 18.4. The first time you run Backup, you are prompted to run its compatibility test.

Whether you perform the test as a first-time backup user or after buying a new drive or other hardware component, running the test activates a type of automated program called a macro, which checks various components and files on your system, prompting you at various points during the operation.

Compatibility Test in Windows Backup

Windows Backup, like DOS Backup, advises the first-time user to perform the compatibility test, and proceeds to automatically confirm your system's compatibility.

If you need to perform subsequent tests, click the Configure button and choose the Test option. In either case, follow the prompts on-screen to tell Backup which drives you'll be backing up to, as shown in Figure 18.5.

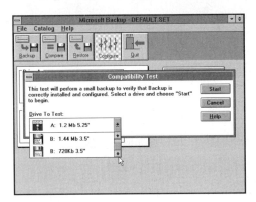

Figure 18.5. Selecting target drives for Windows Backup's compatibility test.

Other Backup Configuration Options

You can adjust the way Backup looks in either version, as well as select drive types and fine-tune mouse speeds and other settings.

Changing Settings in DOS Backup

To change settings in DOS Backup, perform the following steps:

1. Type MSBACKUP at the DOS prompt.

2. Press Enter.

3. Select Configure by clicking that button with your mouse, or by pressing Alt+N and then Enter.

4. Access pull-down menus in the Configuration dialog box by clicking the buttons with your mouse and then highlighting the desired item. Keyboard users can press Alt and the highlighted initial letter of the menu item, using arrow keys to move to the desired item and pressing Enter to select that item.

5. To save configurations permanently, select Save. To configure for current session only, click the OK button.

Video and Mouse Settings

Selecting Video and Mouse brings up the Video and Mouse Configuration dialog box, as shown in Figure 18.6. You can choose between a number of screen display options. Here, too, you can adjust your mouse's speed and responsiveness when working in Backup.

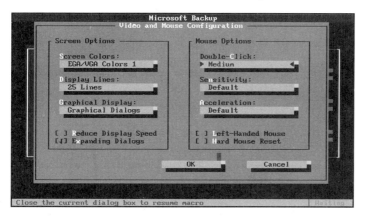

Figure 18.6. Changing video and mouse settings in DOS Backup.

The Default setting leaves the mouse sensitivity and speed as you find it within your other programs.

Screen Options contains Screen Colors, Display Lines, and Graphical Display options. Choosing Screen Colors reveals a number of display configurations, including Laptop, Black and White, and two sets of EGA/VGA palettes.

Laptop users will want to fine-tune their displays with the options available in Screen Colors.

If you're using an EGA or VGA video adapter, Display Lines enables you to increase the number of lines Backup displays on your screen.

Although the default 25 or 28 lines are easier to use with Backup, choosing more reveals a bigger directory tree and file list—handy when you're working in the Select Files dialog box, discussed in the "Setup Files in Backup" section later in this chapter.

Graphical Display gives you a way to fine-tune the way Backup looks; changing the mouse pointer from a rectangle to an arrow, for instance, or switching from expanding to static dialog boxes.

When Display Lines is set to 43 or 50 lines, graphics characters are not available, and the Graphical Display option and Display Speed default to Standard.

Backup Devices Settings

Choose floppy drives or other media you'll be backing up with this menu option, accessible with Alt key combinations or the mouse.

You must configure the drive types in the Backup Devices dialog box before performing the compatibility test. First-time Backup users are prompted to adjust these settings automatically, as part of the test.

Changing Settings in Windows Backup

The Configure button in Windows Backup lets you access the compatibility test. You can also select backup devices with the Floppy Drive Types option here. Configure's third option, Catalog File Path, lets you change the directory where Backup stores its catalog files.

Catalog File Path

Backup needs to record information about each backup session it performs, so it creates a Catalog file. The catalog, essential for restoring data, includes details on the files backed up and the hard disk's directory structure.

The Catalog files are normally stored in the same directory as the Windows Backup program. To store them elsewhere, create a new directory for them from File Manager and then type that pathname in Catalog File Path's text box.

For details on loading, retrieving, or rebuilding a Catalog, see the "Working with Catalogs in Windows Backup" section.

Video and Mouse Settings

If you want to change your mouse speed and video display settings while using Windows Backup, do so via Window's Control Panel.

Activating Backup, Restore, and Compare from DOS

Once you've ensured Backup's compatibility with your system, you can depend on the reliability of backups you create.

Backing Up from DOS

To backup from DOS:

1. Choose the Backup options from the Backup menu.

2. Select the drive to back up.

3. Choose Select Files and highlight the files to back up with the spacebar.

4. Choose OK.

5. Save a backup session's settings for future use by choosing File/Save Setup As, and naming the Setup file.

6. Choose Start Backup.

Backup estimates how many floppy disks you'll need if backing up to a floppy drive, as well as how much time the backup will take. Backup can automatically format unformatted floppy disks.

Label your floppy disks with the word Backup, and include the Catalog number Backup assigns to each backup session, for easy identification.

Restoring a File or Directory

To restore a backed up file or directory:

1. Select Backup Restore.

2. Locate the Backup Set Catalog containing the file(s) or directory you want to restore.

3. To restore select files, choose Restore Files.

4. Choose OK.

5. Select the path, drive, or backup destination directory.

6. Select Options and scan the Disk Restore Options menu to verify that Restore is set up optimally.

7. Choose Start Restore.

To be prompted before Restore overwrites existing files, click that item in the Disk Restore Options menu. Here's where you can tell Restore to verify restored data; prompt you before it creates directories and files, or overwrites existing files; or restore empty directories.

> You can enable audible prompts (beeps), which I recommend, or tell Restore to quit after it completes the procedure.

Compare

Backup's Compare feature lets you ensure that a backup set and a source of data match exactly. This feature is used primarily after a Backup is performed.

To Compare backups with their source files:

1. Select Backup Compare.

2. Locate the Backup Set Catalog containing the file(s) or directory you want to compare.

3. To compare select files, choose Compare Files.

4. Choose OK.

5. Select the path, drive, or backup destination directory from which and to which you want to compare.

6. Select Options to select Audible Prompt or Quit After Compare.

7. Choose Start Compare.

Activating Backup, Restore, and Compare in Windows

To access Backup within Windows, click the Backup icon in the Microsoft Tools Program Group, in the Program Manager. You might also notice that installing Backup has created a new Tools pull-down menu in File Manager, as shown in Figure 18.7, where Backup is one of the options you can highlight.

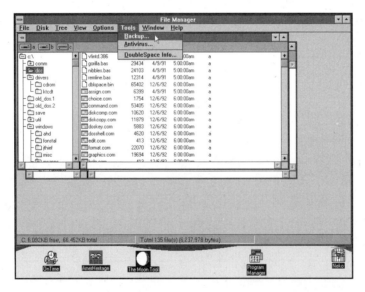

Figure 18.7. Tools pull-down menu in Windows' File Manager.

Accessing Backup in one of these ways brings up the Microsoft Backup main program window. Along the top, you see large buttons marked Backup, Compare, Restore, Configure (already discussed above), and Quit, as shown in Figure 18.8.

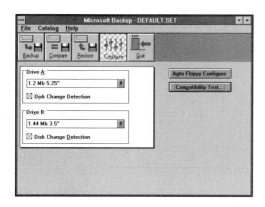

Figure 18.8.
Windows
Backup main
program
window.

You follow the prompts on screen to select target and source data for backup, compare, and restore. Options, available on the right of the window, are identical to those discussed above, in the DOS Backup section.

Backup enables you to backup individual files, as well as entire directories. To ease file selection, choose Windows Backup's Select Backup Files, using the Tree pull-down menus, as shown in Figure 18.9.

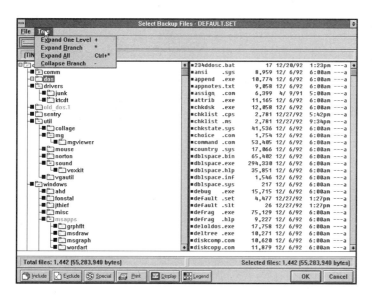

Figure 18.9.
Select Backup
Files screen.

Once you select source and target drives, Windows Backup displays the Backup Drive Selection Information screen, as shown in Figure 18.10. Here you see how long it will take to perform the backup, how many files (and how many total megabytes) are being backed up, and how many floppy disks are needed.

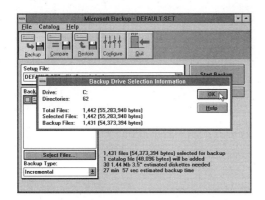

Figure 18.10. Backup Drive Selection Information screen.

Gauging a Backup's Progress

When a backup is in progress, a graphic display similar to the one in Figure 18.11 shows you how things are proceeding. When large backups can run into hours, it's handy to be able to see the backup's progress.

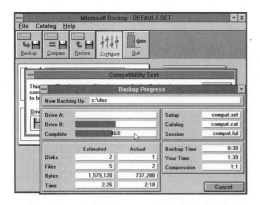

Figure 18.11. Backup Progress screen.

Backup Features Unleashed

MS-Backup for DOS and Windows contains several new features designed to give you flexibility in designing your backup strategy.

Backup Catalogs

Each time you perform a backup, Backup creates a catalog on both source and target media, in which it stores details about that particular backup. A backup catalog name, unique for each backup session, includes the date and type of backup, as well as the information listed in Table 18.1. When you need to restore one or more files, you can load the backup catalog and easily identify and restore backed up files.

A typical catalog name, such as CD30114ADIF, read from left to right, can be broken down as shown in Table 18.1.

Table 18.1. Anatomy of a Backup catalog file name.

Character	Meaning
C	First drive backed up in this set.
D	Last drive backed up in this set.
3	Last digit of the year.
01	Month backup set was created.
14	Day backup set was created.
A	Position in backup sequences for date (letters A-Z assigned to multiple backups made on a particular date).
DIF	Type of backup: FUL, full; INC, incremental; DIF, differential backup.

As the example illustrates, the catalog file name makes it easy to locate a particular backup, even if your directory contains several catalog files.

An overstuffed hard disk is a crash waiting to happen. Microsoft Backup's Catalog feature enables data archiving so you can copy rarely used data and programs on to floppy disks or tape and then delete them from your hard disk. In this way, Backup frees up valuable megabytes for other programs and data—simultaneously safeguarding your files and optimizing your hard disk's performance.

Working with Catalogs in Windows Backup

The following sections describe working with catalogs in the Windows Backup program.

Loading a Catalog

To load a catalog from your hard disk's Catalog Path for restoring or comparing a file, choose Load from the Catalog menu along the top of Backup's main program window. Then select the catalog you want from the Files list box on the left, as shown in Figure 18.12. Choose OK.

If the catalog you seek is unavailable, see Retrieving or Rebuilding a Catalog.

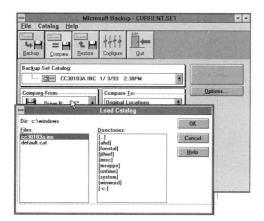

*Figure 18.12.
The Load
Catalog dialog
box.*

Retrieving Catalogs

If you can't locate a catalog on your hard disk, select the Retrieve option from the Catalog menu and insert the last disk of the backup set into the drive. Choose OK. The catalog is now loaded.

Rebuilding Catalogs

In the unlikely case that you lose the catalog and cannot retrieve it from the backup media, you can rebuild the catalog from the backup set. It's automatically loaded as it's rebuilt, ready for you to select files to restore.

To rebuild a catalog from backup media:

1. Access the Rebuild Catalog dialog box from the Catalog menu.

2. Select the disk drive to rebuild from.

3. Rebuild prompts you to insert the first disk of the set you're rebuilding. It's important to insert the disks in the same order as they were backed up.

Working with Catalogs in DOS

You can access catalogs in DOS Backup by choosing the Compare button from the Main Program dialog box, which opens the Select Catalog dialog box. From there, Load, Retrieve, and Rebuild are identical to those found in Windows Backup.

Setup Files in Backup

To reduce the risk of human error and automate the backup process, after configuring a backup session you can save the settings in a Setup File. Subsequent sessions don't need to be completely reconfigured from scratch. Instead, enable the Setup File with the configurations you desire.

Setting Up and Saving Setup Files

Backup lets you set up and save the particulars of your backup procedures. Figure 18.13 shows the selection of features in the Windows Backup Options screen, in fine-tuning a Setup File.

You can select the type of backup, the source and target drives, individual prompts, and other variables in up to 50 setup files. By preconfiguring backups in this manner, you can automate the backup procedure for non-technical users.

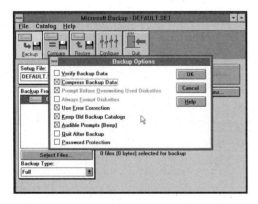

Figure 18.13.
Backup
Options menu
screen.

This powerful feature also enables you to implement a systems-wide backup policy that is standardized yet tailored to individual work stations.

From Windows or DOS, you can select Save Setup As and name the configuration as a Setup File. Invoking the Backup program, you see the last Setup File you used listed as the current Setup File in the Main Program screen. You can highlight and select others from this line.

If you do not save a configuration as a Setup File, Backup works from the "pot-luck" settings in the Default Setup file.

It's wise to make use of the Data Verification and Error Correction options found in Backup Options, to ensure the full reliability of your data.

Backup Types

You can choose between full, incremental, or differential backup types, streamlining the backup process yet ensuring you hold a current backup set at all times. Figure 18.14 shows the creation of a Setup File, and the selection of a backup type.

Depending on your needs, you probably want to combine more than one type of backup into a backup cycle. Here's what the backup types mean:

- *Full*—Creates a copy of all files selected on a drive, directory, or files of a particular type.

- *Incremental*—Copies only those files that have changed since the last full or incremental backup.

- *Differential*—Backs up files that have changed since the last full backup (includes incremental).

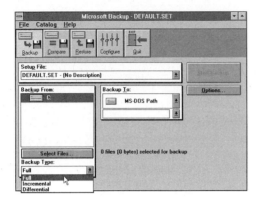

Figure 18.14. Choosing a backup type in Windows Backup.

Most experienced users recommend making a full backup at first, then augmenting that with a daily incremental backup. If you work with the same set of files each day, you may prefer to bolster your full backup with a differential backup each day.

Backup Help contains an in-depth discussion of backup strategies and information on automating the backup process further.

Microsoft Anti-Virus

Computers don't catch diseases, but they have been known to catch *viruses*—programs intentionally designed by malicious high-tech ne'er-do-wells to wreak havoc on your computer. Fortunately, viruses are extremely rare. No reputable software manufacturers would even consider selling infected programs, because doing so would immediately put them out of business. However, a few virus-infected programs have found their way into software and computers.

Some viruses have become so widespread and have infected so many computers that they've earned their own titles. Some well-known virus programs include the *Pakistani-Brain Teaser*, the *Trojan Horse*, the *Friday the 13th*, and the *Nuke*.

While a few viruses are relatively harmless and simply display a comical message on a given date and time, others may interfere with the PC's basic operations, causing a severe performance slow-down or a scrambling of data on the screen. Still others can damage all the files on a disk beyond any hope of recovery.

Whether pernicious or just plain silly, a virus is an unnecessary block to efficiency and productivity. Microsoft has incorporated Central Point Software's anti-virus utility into DOS 6 to protect against these unwanted data invaders.

Customizing Anti-Virus

You can configure a number of options in MSAV to customize the utility to your needs. If you install Windows MSAV, you will see an Options menu window similar to the one in Figure 18.15. Here's a brief summary of the options available and what they do.

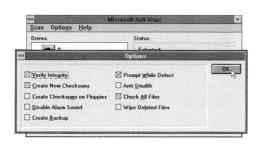

Figure 18.15.
Accessing the
Options menu
in Windows
Anti-Virus.

Verifying Integrity

Choosing this option gives you the best protection against new viruses that are unknown to MSAV. Verify Integrity alerts you to any changes that have taken place in executable files, by way of the CHKLIST.MS file created by the Create New Checksums option.

Combined with the Anti-Stealth option, MSAV provides you with extra protection against the Stealth family of viruses.

Creating New Checksums

Choosing this option causes MSAV to create a checklist file called CHKLIST.MS for each scanned directory. Information on each executable file in the directory is contained in the checklist file. Files not yet recorded in an existing CHKLIST.MS file are detailed in subsequent scans.

Creating Checksums on Floppy

Just like it sounds, MSAV creates the information files called CHKLIST.MS for each directory on a floppy disk as it's scanned.

Disabling Alarm Sound

You can choose to have MSAV's beeping sound in the Verify Error screen squelched with this option. The sound, not altogether unpleasant, works in combination with the screen to prompt you for an action during a scan, as shown in Figure 18.16. It's useful when you're working on other tasks while scanning your disks (a process that takes at least 10 minutes).

Figure 18.16. The alarm alerts you to the Verify Error screen.

Creating Backup

Selecting this option backs up files scanned as virus-infected before the files are cleaned. Backup files made with this option are renamed with the extension .VIR.

This option leaves virus-infected files on your disk, so it's not recommended, except under closely supervised conditions.

Creating Report

MSAV can create a report file after taking any action against viruses. You can find the filename, MSAV.RPT, in the root directory of the selected work drive, if this option is selected.

Prompt While Detect

This option displays a dialog box whenever MSAV encounters any questionable files during a scan. It's recommended that you leave the default for this option set to On.

Anti-Stealth Option

Enabling this option spurs MSAV to use a low-level verification technique to detect files approached by a Stealth-type virus, which evade normal detection methods by infecting files without changing them outwardly.

Because this method slightly impacts MSAV's performance during scans, the default for this option is Off.

Configuring Anti-Virus in DOS

The Options menu is visible from the Main Program window. You can choose between Set Options or Save Settings on Exit.

Configuring Anti-Virus in Windows

Access the Options Screen by clicking Options in the Anti-Virus Main Program window.

Activating Anti-Virus in DOS

To scan a disk for virus infections, type MSAV at the DOS prompt. You can select Detect or Detect and Clean from there.

Activating Anti-Virus in Windows

Clicking the Anti-Virus icon in the Microsoft Tools Program Group brings up the utility, and you can select Detect or Detect and Clean, as shown in Figure 18.17. Detect differs from Detect and Clean in that it merely announces the presence of a suspicious file change, instead of trying to remedy it.

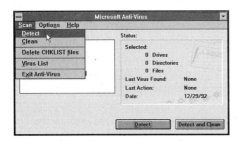

Figure 18.17. You can select Detect or Detect and Clean.

The display shows a Statistics Screen similar to that in Figure 18.18, providing information on the number of drives, directories and files scanned, how many were infected and/or cleaned, the scan's duration in minutes, plus today's date.

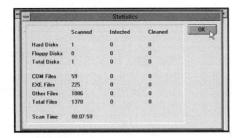

Figure 18.18. The Statistics Screen in Windows MSAV.

When scanning, MSAV shows its progress during the scan, as shown in Figure 18.19. The first time you scan your disk takes twice as long as subsequent scans.

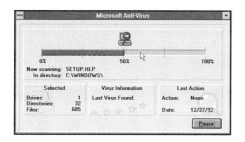

Figure 18.19. The Windows MSAV screen shows how the scan is progressing.

Besides extensive online help, the Anti-Virus program contains an extensive virus glossary, explaining difficult terms in an understandable way.

Those seeking to learn even more about viruses and similar destructive programs will enjoy the program's ability to search or browse through descriptions on 1,234 different viruses, as shown in Figure 18.20.

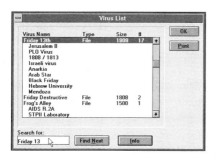

Figure 18.20. The Windows MSAV virus descriptions screen.

Searching for a particular virus name brings up a dialog box you can print for later reference.

Using VSafe

Anti-Virus can be effective when you use it periodically to scan disks, but it's most efficient when you set it to automatic mode.

To set up Anti-Virus as a constant sentry against suspicious activity, you must enable VSafe, a memory resident program that monitors your computer at all times.

Enabling VSafe Within DOS

To enable VSafe from the command prompt, type

VSAFE

VSafe is now loaded into memory. If you want the program to load into memory each time you start your computer, add the VSAFE command to your AUTOEXEC.BAT file.

A number of command-line switches help configure the VSafe program to your specifications. To list the switches and their functions, type the following command at the DOS prompt:

HELP VSAFE

Enabling VSafe Within Windows

To display VSafe messages from Windows, the VSafe Manager program must be loaded. To set up VSafe so it and WNTSRMAN load into memory each time you start Windows, use a text editor, like Notepad, to perform the following changes to these files:

1. Open your AUTOEXEC.BAT file and add the command VSAFE.

2. Open your WIN.INI file and add the command
   `LOAD=MWAVTSR.EXE`.

3. Restart your computer by pressing Ctrl+Alt+Del.

Automating Virus Scanning Within Windows

Scheduler, a program within the Windows Anti-Virus utility, lets you schedule unattended virus scans. To set up Scheduler within Windows to run an automatic virus scan, perform the following steps:

1. Choose the Scheduler button.

2. Choose the Anti-Virus button.

3. Type in the time and drives to scan.

4. Select the Detect or Clean options.

5. Minimize the Scheduler, but don't exit the program, because it must be running to start a scheduled event.

Microsoft Undelete

From time to time you may delete or erase unneeded files on your hard disk or floppies. As you saw in the Backup section, when it comes to the efficiency of your hard disk, less is definitely more. Because file deletion is a normal part of disk maintenance, it's not unusual for users to delete important files. As a safeguard against the DELETE command's unquestioning obedience, however, DOS Version 5.0 incorporated an UNDELETE command.

Users running earlier DOS versions took extra precautions when deleting files, because versions prior to DOS 5 contained no provision for undoing a DELETE. When DOS erased a file, it was gone. To protect their data, many users opted to buy and install a separate

Undelete utility. In fact, the acute need to recover accidentally or carelessly deleted files spurred the overwhelming success of programs like the Norton Utilities and follow-ons.

Undelete utilities retrieve deleted files because DOS doesn't actually erase the data in a file when it deletes a file—it simply removes references to that file on the disk. If you delete a crucial file, the UNDELETE command lets you restore these references.

Even with Undelete installed, you still need to take precautions when deleting files. Take an extra moment to be sure the file you're deleting won't be needed later. If you have any doubts, copy the file on to a spare floppy and then delete it from your hard drive.

If you do delete a file you need, try to perform the UNDELETE command right away. Performing other DOS commands before UNDELETE, like Copying new data to the affected disk, can destroy the file's potential for recovery by overwriting file clusters occupied by the deleted file.

Remember, the only sure way to recover accidentally deleted files is to maintain a current backup of all important files and programs.

Undelete in DOS 6 offers several improvements over DOS 5's Undelete capabilities:

- A Delete Sentry option saves deleted files in a hidden directory, thus guaranteeing file recovery.

- The ability to select between three levels of deletion protection lets you configure Undelete to your needs and system resources.

■ A Windows version removes the need for you to shell to DOS in order to Undelete a file.

■ Windows Undelete now provides for recovery of deleted directories, as well as files.

■ An Undelete option is available in the DOS 6 Shell.

Configuring DOS Undelete and Windows Undelete

Once you install Undelete in DOS or Windows, you're only half-way there. Before you can rely on Undelete, you must configure the level of deletion protection you want. Merely typing UNDELETE at the DOS prompt or clicking the Windows icon and expecting full recovery brings marginal results at best.

The DOS and Windows versions of Undelete offer three levels of file protection from which to choose:

■ *Delete Sentry*—top protection

■ *Delete Tracker*—medium protection

■ *Standard*—lowest level of protection

Using Delete Sentry

The Delete Sentry option offers the highest level of deletion protection by creating a hidden directory, /SENTRY, where Undelete stores deleted files. When you Undelete a file, DOS puts it back in its former location. Even though the file seems to have moved back and forth, DOS has left intact the file's directory information (*File Allocation Table*, or *FAT*) throughout the saving and recovery process—thereby making it impossible for another file to have accessed its clusters.

The tradeoff is that Delete Sentry requires the most system resources to do its job—some memory (13.5K) for its memory-resident portion, as well as some disk space for the \SENTRY directory (about 7 percent of your hard disk capacity). As it performs consecutive deletions, Delete Sentry purges older files in \SENTRY to make room for the most recently deleted one.

Activating DOS Undelete Delete Sentry

To enable Delete Sentry in the DOS version of Undelete:

1. Make sure MS-DOS Undelete is installed. If you need to install Undelete at this time, see the section "Installing or Removing an Optional Program."

2. At the DOS prompt, type UNDELETE /S. (If DOS responds with a Bad command or file name error message, type the full path name, C:\DOS\UNDELETE, and then type /S.)

To configure Delete Sentry from the DOS Shell:

1. Select Undelete from the Disk Utilities menu.

2. The Undelete dialog box appears on your screen, as shown in Figure 18.21. Note the Parameters line, where you can type in a number of switches to customize the undeletion process (see Using DOS Undelete Switches). For example, the /ds switch shown in the figure recovers only those files listed in the \SENTRY directory and prompts you to confirm the undeletion of each file.

3. Type /S in the parameters line, and press Enter.

Trying to activate a deletion method in the DOS Shell running in Windows results in memory conflicts. Instead, complete the following steps:

1. Start the DOS Shell, click on Undelete, and type /S.

2.   Exit the DOS Shell.

3.   Start Windows.

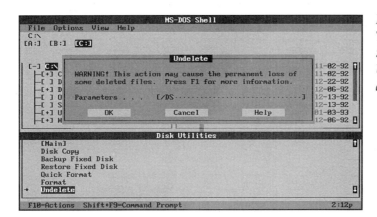

Figure 18.21. The DOS Shell's Undelete dialog box.

Accessing Windows Undelete

There are two ways to access Windows Undelete:

- From the File Manager, click the File pull-down menu. Under the Delete option you'll see a new Undelete option, as shown in Figure 18.22.

- From the Program Manager, you'll notice a new Microsoft Tools Program Group. Here, an icon for Windows Undelete displays, along with icons for the Windows Anti-Virus and Backup programs, as shown in Figure 18.23.

Activating Delete Sentry from Windows Undelete

To select Delete Sentry from Windows Undelete, start Undelete from the File Manager or Program Manager. Click the Options item in the menu bar, and highlight Configure Delete Protection in the pull-down menu. Click Delete Sentry in the dialog box, as shown in Figure 18.24.

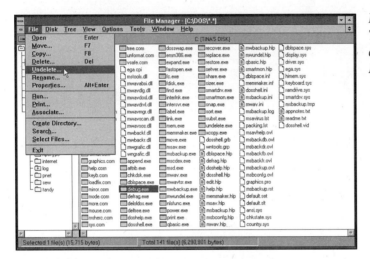

Figure 18.22.
The Undelete
option in File
Manager.

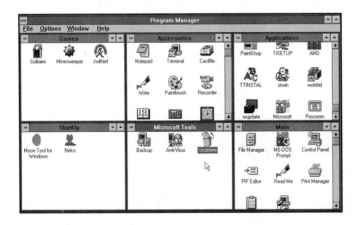

Figure 18.23.
The Undelete
icon in the
Microsoft
Tools Program
Group.

The program prompts you to add the Undelete/Load line to your AUTOEXEC.BAT file.

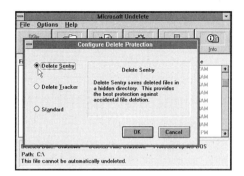

Figure 18.24.
The Configure
Deletion
Protection
dialog box.

Using Delete Tracker

Delete Tracker enables a medium level of protection through a hidden file, PCTRACKER.DEL, which records deleted files' locations. This allows for the partial recovery of a file even if another file has overwritten the deleted file's FAT.

Because it uses the same portion of Undelete's memory-resident program, Delete Tracker uses the same amount of memory as Delete Sentry: 13.5K. It requires only a small amount of disk space, however, used by the PCTRACKER.DEL file.

Enabling DOS Undelete Delete Tracker

To enable Delete Tracker from the DOS Prompt, substitute the command UNDELETE /T in the example for Delete Sentry.

To enable Delete Tracker from the DOS Shell, substitute the switch /T in the previous example for Delete Sentry.

A drive on which the JOIN or SUBST command is used cannot have deletion tracking installed on it. Also, reassign the default drive in a program with the ASSIGN command before installing deletion tracking.

Activating Windows Undelete Delete Tracker

To select Delete Tracker, start Undelete from the File Manager or Program Manager. Click the Options item in the menu bar, and highlight Configure Delete Protection in the pull-down menu. Click Delete Tracker in the dialog box.

The program prompts you to add the Undelete/Load line to your AUTOEXEC.BAT file.

Standard Deletion Protection

Because the Standard level of deletion protection is in effect from the time you turn on your computer, you don't need to do anything to enable it. If you installed the Windows version, you are asked to click the Standard item in the Configure Delete Protection menu. If switching from one of the other protection methods, you are prompted to alter your AUTOEXEC.BAT file as well.

Standard delete protection lacks memory-resident programs or disk files—minimizing its impact on your system resources, but also minimizing its effectiveness.

If you rely on Standard protection, you must be careful to attempt recovery the minute you become aware of an accidental deletion. (This is a good policy to follow in general.)

Changing Your Undelete Protection Method

Both the DOS and Windows versions of Undelete let you easily change the method of deletion protection used on your PC.

Changing a DOS Undelete Protection Method

Two methods of Undelete protection cannot be enabled at the same time. You must type the /U switch to unload the portion of Undelete that resides in memory, and then enable the new method by typing the appropriate switch.

For example, to change from Delete Sentry to Delete Tracker on your current drive, follow these steps:

1. At the DOS prompt, type UNDELETE /U and press Enter to unload Undelete's memory-resident portion.

2. Type UNDELETE /T and press Enter to enable Delete Tracker and reload the memory-resident portion of Undelete.

Changing a Windows Undelete Protection Method

To select a different data protection method, start Undelete from the File Manager or Program Manager. Click the Options item in the menu bar, and highlight configure Delete Protection in the pull-down menu. Choose between Delete Sentry, Delete Tracker, or Standard in the dialog box.

You are prompted to alter your AUTOEXEC.BAT file during this procedure.

> Whatever level of protection you settle on, if a file is deleted, use Undelete to recover it before you do anything else.

Using Undelete in DOS

Once you've configured Undelete, recovering a file in the current directory, whether from the DOS prompt or from DOS Shell, is fairly easy.

1. Move to the directory that contains the deleted files.

2. Type UNDELETE at the DOS prompt (or DOS Shell parameter line). (If typing UNDELETE at the DOS prompt results in a Bad command or file name error message, type the full path name C:\DOS\UNDELETE.)

3. When Undelete asks whether you want to recover the specified file, press Y (for Yes).

4. Follow the prompts on the screen to restore the initial letter of the file, if needed, as shown in Figure 18.25. (If you can't remember the original first letter, type any valid character that creates a unique file name in the current directory.)

5. Repeat the previous steps until you have undeleted all of the files you want to recover.

```
All rights reserved.

Directory: C:\UTIL\PKZ
File Specifications: *.*

    Delete Sentry control file contains     0 deleted files.

    Deletion-tracking file contains     0 deleted files.
    Of those,     0 files have all clusters available,
                  0 files have some clusters available,
                  0 files have no clusters available.

    MS-DOS directory contains     1 deleted files.
    Of those,     1 files may be recovered.

Using the MS-DOS directory method.

    ?MBUDSMN ASP      591 12-28-92  2:04a  ...A  Undelete (Y/N)?y
    Please type the first character for ?MBUDSMN.ASP: o

File successfully undeleted.


C:\UTIL\PKZ>
```

Figure 18.25. The DOS Undelete program prompts you to enter initial letters of deleted files.

Using DOS Undelete Switches

You can use a number of command-line switches to fine-tune Undelete. Table 18.2 lists UNDELETE's syntax and switches.

If you don't specify a switch, Undelete seeks the Delete Sentry directory. If the directory is not available, it looks for the Delete Tracker file. If Undelete doesn't find that, it reverts to the Standard or MS-DOS protection level.

The syntax for the UNDELETE command is

```
UNDELETE [[drive:][path]filename] [/DS¦/DT¦/DOS]
[/LIST¦/ALL¦/PURGE[drive]¦/STATUS¦/LOAD¦/UNLOAD¦/S[drive]¦
/T[drive][-entries]]
```

in which *drive* contains the file(s) you want to recover, *path* specifies the location of the file(s) you want to recover, and *filename* is the file name(s) you want to be recovered. Lacking these specifications, Undelete restores deleted files in the current directory.

Table 18.2. Undelete switches and their functions.

Switch	Function
/LIST	Lists recoverable files in the specified path, as determined by other switches.
/ALL	Undeletes all files in specified path without prompting you first. Undelete uses the Delete Sentry method if present, the Delete Tracker if Delete Sentry is not available, or recovers the files that DOS lists as deleted if the other two methods are not available.
/DOS	Undeletes files that DOS lists as deleted. This switch causes Undelete to ignore any existing delete-tracking file.

continues

565

Table 18.2. continued

Switch	Function
/DT	Undeletes only those files listed in the delete tracking file, prompting for confirmation on each file.
/DS	Undeletes only those files listed in the \SENTRY hidden directory, and prompts you to type the first letter of each file you want to recover.
/LOAD	Uses information from the Undelete.INI file to load the Undelete memory-resident program. Reverts to default values if the Undelete.INI file is not found.
/UNLOAD	Unloads memory-resident part of the Undelete utility, diminishing Undelete's effectiveness.
/PURGE[*drive*]	This purges the contents of the hidden \SENTRY directory. If the drive is unspecified, Undelete looks for SENTRY in the current directory.
/STATUS	Lists the level of data protection enabled for each drive.
/S[*drive*]	Activates Delete Sentry; uses information from the Undelete.INI file to load Undelete's memory-resident program, which tracks information used to Undelete files on the drive indicated. If no drive is indicated, Delete Sentry is enabled on the current drive.
/T[*drive*][-*entries*]	Activates Delete Tracker and uses information from the Undelete.INI file to load Undelete's memory-resident program, which tracks information

Switch	Function
	used to Undelete files on the indicated drive. You must specify the drive you want tracked. The *entries* parameter, a value between 1 and 999, is optional. If you don't specify a value, the maximum number of entries in the PCTRACKR.DEL file that tracks deletions will default to a value indicated in Table 18.3.
/help or /?	Brings up an Undelete switch help screen, similar to the one in Figure 18.26.

```
Copyright (C) 1987-1993 Central Point Software, Inc.
All rights reserved.
Restores files which have been deleted.

UNDELETE [[drive:][path]][filename] [/DS | /DT | /DOS]
UNDELETE [ /LIST | /ALL | /PURGE[DRIVE] | /STATUS | /LOAD |
         /UNLOAD | /S[DRIVE] | /T[DRIVE]-entrys ]

 /list          Lists the deleted files available to be recovered.
 /all           Undeletes all specified files without prompting.
 /dos           Uses only the MS-DOS directory.
 /dt            Uses only the deletion-tracking files.
 /ds            Uses only the deletion-sentry files.
 /load          Loads undelete using the UNDELETE.INI options.
 /unload        Unloads undelete from memory.
 /purge[drive]  Purge contents of the delete-sentry directory.
 /status        Display the status of Undelete.
 /s[drive]      Enables delete-sentry method of undelete protection.
 /t[drive][-entrys] Enables delete-tracking method of undelete protection.
 /?             Displays help on the undelete command.

UNDELETE, and UNFORMAT Copyright (C) 1987-1993 Central Point Software.


C:\WINDOWS>
```

Figure 18.26.
Undelete
switch help
screen.

Table 18.3. Default values for entries in PCTRACKR.DEL.

Disk Capacity	Entries	File Size
360K	25	5K
720K	50	9K
1.2M	75	14K
1.44M	75	14K
20M	101	18K
32M	202	36K
32M	303	55K

Advanced Undelete Commands

Advanced users may want to modify the Undelete.INI file with a text editor. By altering this file, you can change the number of drives protected, days between /SENTRY directory purges, or a number of other options. Details on this procedure are given in the MS-DOS Online Help file.

Windows Undelete users can find many of the same options in dialog boxes throughout Undelete. Consult Windows Undelete Help for more details.

Starting Undelete in Windows

From the File Manager, click the File pull-down menu. A new Undelete option appears under the Delete option. Click Undelete to activate the program.

Another way to access Undelete is from the Microsoft Tools Program Group in Program Manager. Here, click the icon for

Windows Undelete. A screen like the one in Figure 18.27 appears.
Notice that a list of deleted files appears for the current drive and
directory.

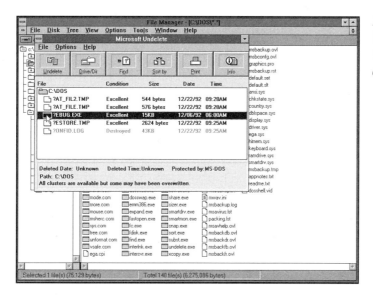

*Figure 18.27.
Windows
Undelete
opening screen.*

Accessing DOS Undelete from Windows

Like most DOS programs, DOS Undelete can be accessed from
Windows. Windows users with the DOS version of Undelete installed can access the utility in the following ways:

■ From Windows, activate the MS-DOS Shell. Undelete is
listed as one of the Disk Utilities on the Main Screen.

If you often run the DOS Shell from Windows, make the
Shell an icon in one of your Program Groups, as shown in
Figure 18.28, rather than shelling to DOS and typing
DOSSHELL. To learn more about the MS-DOS Shell under
Windows, turn to Chapter 16, "Setting Up DOS for
Windows."

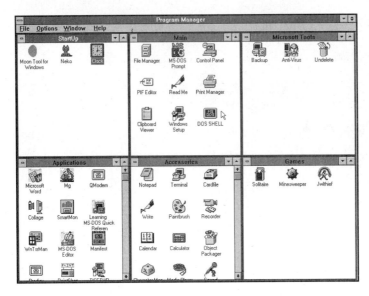

Figure 18.28.
DOS SHELL
icon in the
Main window.

> ■ From Windows, you also can shell to the DOS prompt,
> make the deleted file's directory current, and run Undelete.

Undeleting Files in Windows

Windows Undelete works best when you select either the Delete
Sentry or Delete Tracker method of data protection. Note that a listing of deleted files shows that Undelete puts a question mark at the
beginning of deleted file names that have not been protected by
Delete Protection, as shown in Figure 18.29. Only those files protected by the Delete Sentry method are in Perfect condition.

> Before you can feel completely safe deleting files, take a
> moment to preconfigure Undelete for one of these methods.
> You can find instructions for configuring each of these
> methods under About Delete Sentry and About Delete
> Tracker.

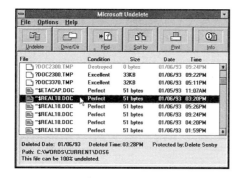

*Figure 18.29.
Undelete
indicates a
file's condition
by the initial
character in the
file name.*

To quickly Undelete a file:

1. Select the deleted file.

2. Click the Undelete button.

3. Type in the initial letter of the file name, if prompted (any letter will do, as long as there's no file by the same name in that directory).

To Undelete a file on a network:

1. Be sure to configure Delete Sentry as the deletion protection method.

2. Follow steps 1–3 from the instructions on how to quickly Undelete a file.

To Undelete a Directory

To Undelete a file from a deleted directory, first Undelete the directory as follows:

1. Use the Drive/Dir button to choose the drive and directory you want to recover.

2. Highlight the directory, and press Undelete.

If you attempt to Undelete a very large directory, you may see the Directory Undelete dialog box, as shown in Figure 18.30. Undelete needs your help in determining which files were part of the deleted directory. Choose Add to add the files listed on the screen if they were part of the directory you want to restore, or choose Skip to skip the file names that weren't in that directory.

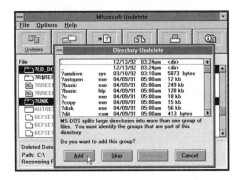

Figure 18.30.
The Directory
Undelete
dialog box.

The directory is labeled Recovered in the Undelete window.

Windows Undelete Commands

As a precautionary measure, you can use the File Menu's UNDELETE command to undelete files or directories to a location you specify.

Finding Files

If Undelete's opening screen doesn't list the file you want to recover, click the Drive/Dir button, or choose Change Drive/Directory from the File menu.

If you're not sure about the file's location, you can search for a file name with the File menu's Find Deleted File command, also accessed by clicking the Find button. Various options, detailed in this section, also help you find deleted files.

File Specification

When you know the deleted file's name, use the File Specification option in the Find Deleted File dialog box to type in the file name. File Specification supports wildcards.

Groups

When you don't know the file name but you know what program you used to create the file, look under the Groups option for the Search Groups dialog box, used to search for deleted files by specific applications. For example, to set up a search in a group of files saved or generated in MS Windows Notepad, click the Edit option and specify Notepad's typical .TXT and .INI extentions, as shown in Figure 18.31.

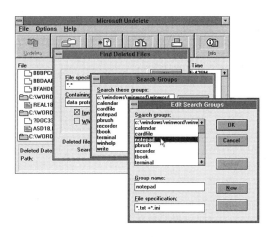

Figure 18.31. Editing Groups to enable a search of files associated with specific programs.

Containing

When you can't recall the exact file name, but remember some of the words in the deleted file, the Containing option lets you search by text content for deleted files. The Ignore Case and Whole Word items can further narrow the search. All files containing your text criteria are displayed in the file list, as shown in Figure 18.32.

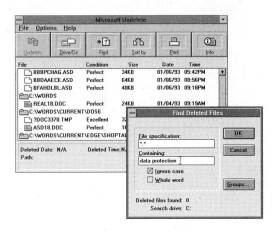

Figure 18.32. Find Deleted Files dialog box.

File Info

The File Info button (also accessed through the File menu) details information on the deleted file, such as the following:

- Deleted Date—Deletion protection allows the date a file was deleted to be listed. Under Standard protection, this information is unknown.

- First Cluster—The file's position on the disk is indicated by its first cluster, useful when attempting an undeletion in MS-DOS Undelete.

- Condition—A file's recovery potential ranges from Perfect, only enabled by the Delete Sentry protection method, Excellent, Good, Poor, or Destroyed. Recovered files from the current session are also listed.

Poor and Destroyed files are greyed out and unavailable for restoration under Windows Undelete, as shown in Figure 18.33. It may be possible to recover files in questionable condition under MS-DOS Undelete, however, because the DOS version differs slightly in the way it tracks file clusters.

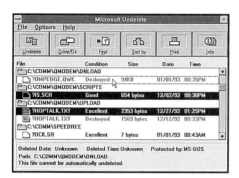

Figure 18.33.
Files that are
unavailable for
recovery in
Windows may
be recoverable
under DOS
Undelete.

Do not expect to recover these files if MS-DOS Undelete is not already installed on your computer, since installing the DOS version prior to recovery may overwrite some of the deleted file's clusters.

For more information, see the section "Using DOS Undelete Switches."

The Undelete Options Menu

Under the Options menu you find a Sort command that groups deleted files by name, extension, size, date, and condition. Sort comes in handy when you need to recover many files.

The Select by Name options are similar to functions found under Find File. Configure Delete Protection is located under the Options menu.

575

Additional Windows Undelete commands include the ability to Print Lists of deleted files, to perform a Printer Setup, and to Purge the Delete Sentry files in the hidden directory.

 Troubleshooting

If you make an error while trying the techniques in this chapter, you see one of the following messages on your PC's screen. Locate the appropriate error message and try the recommended solution.

- `Not enough room to install program`

  If you receive an error message that says you don't have enough free disk space to install the optional programs you want, and you have set up MS-DOS 6, you can free disk space by installing DoubleSpace. For more information on DoubleSpace, see Chapter 14, "Hard Disk Management Made Simple."

  If you choose not to run DoubleSpace but still need to make room for the optional programs, and you have one version of Backup installed, you can use Backup to archive some of your less frequently used data and programs. After deleting the archived programs off your hard disk, type SETUP /E (detailed at the beginning of this chapter) and follow the on-screen instructions.

- `DMA Buffer size too small`

  You will not be able to perform a backup, compare or restore until the DMA buffer size is increased. Increase the Buffers to 20 in your CONFIG.SYS file, then reboot your computer.

- `Insufficient memory`

  Backup requires at least 512K of memory. If you have that amount but still see a message that says you don't have enough memory, quit MS Backup, unload all memory-resident programs from memory, and activate MS Backup again. Disable the Compress Backup Data option from the Disk Backup Options dialog box in the Options section.

■ Bad command or file name

You either misspelled a command or the program is not available on the current diskette, directory, or in the currently defined path of directories.

■ General failure reading drive A

The disk in drive A: is probably not formatted. Press A to abandon the operation and then format the disk.

■ Invalid drive in search path

Your command includes a drive name that does not exist on your computer.

■ Last backup diskette not inserted

DOS requested that you put the last backup disk in the destination drive, but you put in a different disk. Try your highest-numbered backup disk.

Summary

This chapter focuses on data protection enabled by Backup, Anti-Virus, and Undelete, optional utilities that come with DOS 6. Here's a recap of the essentials:

■ Installing the optional programs requires quite a bit of room on your hard disk; be sure to add additional versions only when you're sure you'll use them.

■ The optional utilities are external DOS commands, so be sure to put them in a directory that's within the defined path. Otherwise, you'll have to change to the directory they're in to run them, or risk seeing the Bad command or file name error message.

■ Be sure to configure Backup and Undelete, as detailed in this chapter, before relying on their data-protection prowess.

■ Fire or other physical-site disasters can ruin backup disks or tape, as well as PCs. Be safe—keep a set of backup media off-site.

■ DOS 6 has been bolstered by the most extensive online help system known to software-dom to answer your questions about DOS commands in the DOS command line and Windows environments. Take advantage of the help system at any point in the utilities by pressing F1.

CHAPTER 19

DOS Compatibility Secrets and Surprises

Certain compatibility issues have surfaced between DOS 6 and its various components. Some of these problems relate to third-party programs and utilities and their incompatibility with DOS. Other problems exist between DOS's own programs under certain conditions. Still other conflicts arise between DOS 6 and the Windows operating environment.

If programs you run seem to be giving you trouble under DOS 6, scan the sections below to identify the cause. If a solution is not apparent from this chapter or the DOS online help system, call Microsoft's Technical Support for details on remedying the problem.

> It's a good idea to call anyway, because new solutions crop up once a product has been out awhile and in general use by a wider range of customers.

Hard Disk and Storage Issues

The following sections discuss possible compatibility problems with your hard disk.

Stacker and Other Disk-Compression Programs

Installing DOS 6 on a drive that's been compressed by Stacker or another disk-compression utility cancels your ability to uninstall DOS 6 during or after setup. To safeguard your data, make a thorough backup.

> It's wise to create a startup disk containing the system files of your previous DOS version, as well as the FDISK, SYS, and FORMAT commands.

Some disk-compression utilities cause DOS 6 to display this error message: Your computer uses a disk-compression program that must be removed.

You'll need to backup your data, remove the program, and reformat your hard disk. Follow the steps in Chapter 14, "Hard Disk Management Made Simple," to begin this procedure.

Converting from Stacker and Other Programs to DoubleSpace

You may experience problems when using DOS 6's disk compression conversion program that converts your computer from Stacker and other disk compression programs to DoubleSpace.

Running DoubleSpace from Other Programs

You cannot run DoubleSpace from Windows, DOS Shell, or any other shell program. Run DoubleSpace only from the DOS command line.

FDISK and Third-Party Partitioning Programs

You cannot use FDISK to repartition a hard disk that was partitioned by a third-party program such as those made by Disk Manager, SpeedStore, Priam, or Everex. In this case, repartition the disk using the same disk-partitioning program first used to partition the disk.

The reason you can't use FDISK in this case is that these programs replace the BIOS in interactions between DOS and your hard-disk controller. Also, FDISK cannot delete certain types of non-MS-DOS partitions. You have to use your original disk partitioning software to delete the partitions and then run FDISK.

You can determine whether you have a partition created by one of these programs by looking in a device line in your CONFIG.SYS file for any of the files shown in Table 19.1.

Table 19.1. Files created by disk-partitioning programs.

File	Program
DMDRVR.BIN	Disk Manager program
SSTOR.SYS	SpeedStor
HARDRIVE.SYS	Priam
EVDISK.SYS	Everex

You should contact the manufacturer of the original disk-partitioning program if you need help repartitioning your hard disk, or are unsure whether the BIOS is being replaced.

CHKDSK /F

Before using CHKDSK /F to scan for and delete lost file allocation units, make sure you aren't running any programs. You may need to disable memory-resident programs in your CONFIG.SYS and AUTOEXEC.BAT files and restart your system before running CHKDSK /F.

See the following caution on running CHKDSK /F under Windows.

Windows Compatibility Issues

A few commands should never be used once Windows has started. Become familiar with the commands in the following list; scan the text to see why they are incompatible under the Windows operating environment.

```
APPEND
DEFRAG
EMM386
FASTOPEN
NET STOP
NLSFUNC
SMARTDRV
SUBST
```

Activating a DOS Undelete Protection Method Under Windows

Trying to activate a DOS Undelete deletion protection method in a DOS Shell running in Windows, or when shelled to the DOS prompt, can create memory conflicts. Be sure to exit Windows before enabling a new protection method.

SMARTDrive, HIMEM.SYS, and Windows

DOS 6 includes the most recent version of the SMARTDrive Disk Caching utility, but Windows 3.1 doesn't know that. If you install Windows 3.1 subsequent to installing DOS 6, Windows will try to change references to SMARTDrive within your AUTOEXEC.BAT and CONFIG.SYS files to reflect an older (Windows) version.

Check your AUTOEXEC.BAT and CONFIG.SYS files after installing Windows to make sure they refer to the SMARTDrive file in your DOS 6 directory, not your Windows directory. One clue is to look for the file with the most recent creation date.

The same holds true for HIMEM.SYS.

APPEND, ASSIGN, JOIN, SUBST, and Windows

These commands trick DOS into recognizing drives and directories in different ways than intended. Don't use these commands with DOS applications running under Windows. If you want to create or delete virtual drives with SUBST, exit Windows first. After using the command you can safely load Windows again.

CHKDSK /F and Windows

CHKDSK helps in hard disk maintenance by uncovering lost file allocation units. Using the /F switch with CHKDSK lets you view the files and choose to delete them. If you use this command under Windows, however, you may lose data. Exit Windows (don't just shell to DOS) before using this command.

DBLSPACE and Windows

DOS 6 won't let you run the DBLSPACE program under Windows. Make sure you exit Windows (don't just shell to DOS) before running this disk-compression utility.

> When running DBLSPACE, leave from 1M to 8M of free space, uncompressed, where Windows can store its swap files. It's best to use DBLSPACE only after you install Windows. This gives Windows the chance to create its permanent swap file on an uncompressed portion of your hard drive. DBLSPACE, once activated, leaves Windows' portion untouched.

DEFRAG and Windows

Don't run the DEFRAG disk-optimizing utility from within Windows or a DOS Shell. Exit Windows first.

MemMaker and Windows

Don't run DOS 6's MemMaker memory-optimization utility under Windows. Make sure you exit Windows before you use MemMaker to sort out your PC's best memory configuration—not heeding this advice is bound to cause memory conflicts, because MemMaker will attempt to place programs into the same extended memory spaces already being used by Windows.

VSafe and Windows

VSafe, Anti-Virus' memory-resident virus scanning utility, should not be loaded from DOS when Windows is running. Exit Windows first and then add the VSafe line to your AUTOEXEC.BAT file.

> If you're planning to install Windows for the first time and you have VSafe in your AUTOEXEC.BAT file, be sure to disable VSafe first. Otherwise, VSafe will treat Windows installation commands as virus activity! To disable VSafe, you must edit your AUTOEXEC.BAT file, adding the letters REM to the beginning of the VSafe line. For example, type REM VSAFE.EXE.

Save your AUTOEXEC.BAT file, and then reboot your PC. After installing Windows, exit Windows, load AUTOEXEC.BAT into your text editor, remove the REM statement, and reboot your PC to restore VSafe.

DOS Shell and Windows

Attempting to start Windows from the DOS Shell graphical interface will result in memory conflicts. Be sure to start Windows first, and then you can start the Shell from Windows. You can even make the DOS Shell icon a member of one of Windows' Program Groups.

Error Messages After Uninstalling DOS 6

If you uninstall DOS 6 and revert to a former DOS version, and your PC has been installed with the Windows versions of the optional utilities Backup, Undelete, or Anti-Virus, you may receive error messages the next time you start Windows after uninstalling the DOS 6 program.

Press any key in response to the error message; Windows should start. If you're running Windows 3.1 and you see an error message that says Cannot open program-group C:\DOS\WNTOOLS.GRP, choose No. Windows should then start correctly.

Networking Issues

If your computer has a network card installed, you must make sure you specify the correct base memory address and interrupt (IRQ) for your particular network card. Make sure this interrupt does not conflict with your mouse.

Also, make sure the DEVICE command for EMM386 in your CONFIG.SYS file excludes the memory address used by your network card. If your CONFIG.SYS file contains a DEVICE command for EMM386, add to that command line

x=*mmmm*-*nnnn*

where *mmmm* equals the base memory address of your network card, and *nnnn* specifies a value that is 32K greater than *mmmm*.

DOS 6 Utilities Issues

The following sections discuss compatibility issues with DOS 6 utilities.

DOS Undelete from Windows

Trying to activate a DOS Undelete deletion protection method in a DOS Shell running in Windows, or when shelled to the DOS prompt, can create memory conflicts. Be sure to exit Windows before enabling one of DOS Undelete's other protection methods.

Changing a Windows Undelete deletion protection method from within Windows is fine.

Uninstalling VSafe

If you try and remove VSafe from memory and one or more memory-resident programs have been loaded after VSafe, you see the following error message:

```
Resident programs were loaded after VSafe
```

You must leave VSafe in memory and then attempt to remove other memory-resident programs from memory in reverse order of their installation. Then you can remove VSafe from memory.

DOS 6 on Floppy Disks and the Optional Programs

If you use a computer with no hard drive, setting up DOS 6 on floppy disks doesn't give you the optional utilities Backup, Anti-Virus, or Undelete. There is not enough room on the floppies for the optional programs.

ASSIGN, JOIN, SUBST, and Undelete

A drive on which the JOIN or SUBST command has been used cannot have deletion tracking installed. Also, if you reassign default drives within software by using the ASSIGN command, you must do so before installing Undelete's Delete Tracker.

Memory Management Issues

The following sections discuss compatibility issues with memory management.

RAMDrive and EMM386

DOS 6's memory-resident RAMDrive program lets you use part of your computer's RAM (Random Access Memory) as if it were a hard disk. If you use the EMM386 expanded-memory emulator, however, don't put RAMDrive in expanded memory. RAMDrive can use it, but it isn't as efficient under this emulated expanded memory as it is if using real physical memory.

MemMaker and Windows

If you use only Windows applications, don't bother running MemMaker. Windows applications need as much free extended memory as they can get, but, even though MemMaker frees conventional memory, it may lessen the amount of extended memory available to Windows.

You cannot run MemMaker from Windows, the DOS Shell, or another program. You must first exit to the DOS command prompt.

 # Troubleshooting

If you haven't noticed already, this chapter is one big troubleshooting chapter. Therefore, I can't stress enough that you re-read and thoroughly understand the following key points when using DOS 6:

- Compressing your disk with DoubleSpace

- Repartitioning your disk with FDISK

- Commands you should never use once Windows has started

- Running DEFRAG, MemMaker, Anti-Virus, and DOSSHELL from within Windows

Summary

The immense variety of personal computers, BIOS chips, and even software versions prevents the inclusion of each and every bug and incompatibility you may encounter during your computing sessions. Hopefully this chapter presents you with an idea of the kinds of conflicts that can occur, and gives you ideas for ways to solve them.

Managing Your Standard Devices

Alan Simpson's
DOS
SECRETS
UNLEASHED

C H A P T E R   2 0

Your Computer and DOS

You can drive a car without knowing anything about the internal workings of the transmission or the voltage regulator. Similarly, you can use a computer effectively without knowing a great deal about its technical internal workings. However, if you want to use advanced options, such as extended and expanded memory, or write complex programs of your own, you must have a basic understanding about DOS and the way things work in a computer.

How Computers Store Information

Although you interact with your computer with the same alphabet (A to Z) and numbers (0 to 9) that you use in your daily communications, the computer actually works on a different principle known as the *binary* numbering system. The binary system uses only two digits—0 and 1. Why only two digits? Because all the internal workings of the computer use electronic (or in the case of disks, magnetic) switches that can be in either of two states—off (0) or on (1).

Each of these on/off switches is called a *bit* (short for Binary digIT). Although on and off offer only two possible states, combining two binary digits offers four unique combinations:

    00
    01
    10
    11

A group of three bits offers eight possible unique combinations:

    000
    001
    010
    011
    100
    101
    110
    111

Notice the progression. One bit offers two combinations. Two bits offer four (2^2) unique combinations. Three bits offer eight (2^3) unique combinations.

Modern microcomputers use a group of eight bits to store an individual character. Using eight bits permits a total of 256 (2^8) unique combinations of bits. A group of eight bits is called a *byte*. As you might recall from Chapter 3, "Exploring the Basics of DOS," I pointed out that one byte equals one character. So the word *cat* uses three bytes of storage space.

The complete ASCII character set consists of 256 unique characters, numbered 0 to 255. Each of these characters is represented by a unique set of eight bits. For example, the letter *A* is represented by the byte 01000001, the letter *B* is represented by the byte 01000010, the letter *C* is represented by the byte 01000011, and so on.

Hexadecimal Numbering System

The hexadecimal numbering system is often used as a shorthand method of expressing binary numbers.

The decimal numbering system is based on 10 unique digits, 0 through 9. After you count to 9, you start using the two-digit numbers 10, 11, 12, 13, and so on to 99. Although the decimal numbering system is convenient for humans, who have 10 fingers to count on, it does not accurately reflect the computer's way of storing information, which is based on eight-bit bytes.

The hexadecimal numbering system uses 16 unique digits, 0 through 9 and A through F. In hex, you don't start using two-digit numbers until you get to F:

0
1
2
3

4
5
6
7
8
9
A
B
C
D
E
F
10

Because F is the largest single digit in hex, FF is the largest two-digit pair, just as 9 is the largest single-digit in decimal, and 99 is the largest two-digit number.

Simply stated, any character in the ASCII alphabet can be represented by a two-digit hexadecimal number. In fact, the first 16 hexadecimal numbers (0, 1, 2, 3, through F) are often expressed as 00, 01, 02, 03, through 0F, to maintain the two-digit consistency.

Converting Hex to Decimal

If you do not get involved in the technical aspects of DOS and your computer, you will probably never need to use hexadecimal numbers. In case you do, several tools are available to provide help.

If you frequently make conversions between hexadecimal and decimal numbers, you should purchase a calculator designed for programmers. You could also buy a program that offers a pop-up calculator, such as Borland's SideKick.

If you rarely make hexadecimal and decimal conversions and you don't want to spend money on such a specialized tool, you can use Table 20.1 to convert hexadecimal numbers as high as FFFF to their decimal equivalents.

Table 20.1. Converting hexadecimal numbers to decimal.

| Thousands Digit | | Hundreds Digit | | Tens Digit | | Ones Digit | |
Hex	Decimal	Hex	Decimal	Hex	Decimal	Hex	Decimal
0	0	0	0	0	0	0	0
1	4,096	1	256	1	16	1	1
2	8,192	2	512	2	32	2	2
3	12,288	3	768	3	48	3	3
4	16,384	4	1,024	4	64	4	4
5	20,480	5	1,280	5	80	5	5
6	24,576	6	1,536	6	96	6	6
7	28,672	7	1,792	7	112	7	7
8	32,768	8	2,048	8	128	8	8
9	36,864	9	2,304	9	144	9	9
A	40,960	A	2,560	A	160	A	10
B	45,056	B	2,816	B	176	B	11
C	49,152	C	3,072	C	192	C	12
D	53,248	D	3,328	D	208	D	13
E	57,344	E	3,584	E	224	E	14
F	61,440	F	3,840	F	240	F	15

To use Table 20.1, total the decimal values for each digit in the hex number. For example, the one-digit hex number F converts to 15 in decimal. The two-digit hex number 9F is 144 + 15, or 159 decimal. The hex number 100 is 256 + 0 + 0, or 256 decimal. The hex number CD1 is 3,072 + 208 + 1, or 3,281 decimal. The number 1010 hex is 4,096 + 0 + 16 + 0, or 4,112 decimal. The hex number FFFF is 61,440 + 3,840 + 240 + 15, or 65,535 decimal.

Converting Decimal to Hex

Converting decimal numbers to hex involves repeatedly dividing the number (and then subsequent quotients) by 16 while converting the remainder of each division to its hexadecimal equivalent until the quotient is zero. The result of the first division produces the ones digit in the hex number. The result of the second division produces the tens digit in the hex number, and so on. Figure 16.1 in Chapter 16 depicts how to convert the number 751 to hexadecimal.

How Memory Is Organized

Your computer's main memory (RAM) consists of *RAM chips*. If you were to remove the cover from your computer and look inside, you would see these RAM chips as small, black, rectangular wafers plugged into a larger board. Actually, the black wafer is the *chip carrier*, and it is much larger than the actual chip to make handling easier. If you could see through the chip carrier, you would see the RAM chip, which is actually small enough to fit on your thumbnail.

A RAM chip consists of thousands of tiny *transistors*, or switches, each of which can be turned either on (1) or off (0). A typical RAM chip contains 262,144 of these tiny switches (which gives you an idea of how small each switch is). Each switch represents one bit. As you know, it takes eight bits (a byte) to store one character, so a RAM chip that has 262,144 switches can store 32,768 bytes (or 32 kilobytes) of information. (From a purely technical standpoint, the bits on a single chip are not actually organized into bytes. Instead, a byte is spread across multiple chips.)

The switches in RAM operate very quickly, which enables the computer to run at amazing speeds. However, these switches work only when they receive electrical power. When you turn off the computer, all the switches go off. This is why RAM is volatile (as Chapter 3, "Exploring the Basics of DOS," discussed) and why you need to use disks to store information permanently.

Read-Only Memory (ROM)

There is more to memory than RAM. Your computer also contains read-only memory (ROM) in addition to RAM. A ROM chip is similar to a RAM chip, except that it is preprogrammed to perform certain tasks; it cannot be used for storing data or programs. ROM occupies certain areas of your computer's total memory, as you will see in a moment.

Memory Maps

The total memory (RAM and ROM combined) in a computer is often displayed in a *memory map*. A memory map shows how memory is divided into areas that perform specific jobs.

Memory above 640K is used for jobs that the computer needs to perform regularly. The first 128K above the 640K *address* (position in memory)—that is, from the 640K address to the 768K address—is usually used for managing the video display.

The remaining 256K at the high end of memory is partially unused and partially used by the ROM BIOS (the Basic Input/Output System), which controls the "traffic" of data being received from, and sent to, various devices such as the keyboard, screen, and printer.

DOS 6 offers the commands DOS, DEVICEHIGH, EMM386, and LOADHIGH to enable you to access reserved memory (see Chapter 15, "Getting the Most from Your Memory").

599

Prior to DOS 5, the 384K area above the 640K address (called *reserved memory*) was nearly off-limits to the ordinary user, because the computer reserves this area for its own "managerial" tasks. However, as discussed in Chapter 15, DOS 6 offers the LOADHIGH and DEVICEHIGH commands, which enable you to load device drivers and TSR programs into that area of memory. In this chapter, you'll also see how that area of memory is used to manage expanded memory.

How DOS and Programs Use RAM

As you know, DOS is a program. When you first start your computer, a part of DOS is stored in RAM automatically. (Incidentally, this explains why some DOS commands are *internal* commands, whereas others are *external* commands; the internal commands are already in RAM, and therefore DOS does not need to read instructions from a file stored on disk to perform an operation.)

The exact amount of RAM that DOS uses depends on the specific version of DOS that you are using, but all versions of DOS use some RAM. When you enter the CHKDSK or MEM command at the DOS command prompt, DOS displays both the total memory available (for example, 655360 bytes, which is 640K) and the total number of bytes free (for example, 565552). If you subtract the free (available) bytes from the total number of bytes, the difference is the number of bytes occupied by DOS (and perhaps other programs, as discussed later).

When you run a program, a copy of that program is loaded into RAM, which ensures maximum processing speed. The largest program that you can run is determined by how much memory is available after DOS has been loaded into RAM.

> This remaining area is sometimes called the Transient
> Program Area (or TPA), because it is used for programs that
> come and go.

For example, when you use your spreadsheet program, a copy
of that program is stored in RAM. When you exit your spreadsheet
program and load your word processing program, the copy of the
spreadsheet program in RAM is erased, and a copy of your word
processing program is stored in RAM. This is why you usually use
only one program at a time. However, as discussed in the next section, not all programs are transient.

Memory-Resident Programs

Some programs remain in memory after you start them so that you
can have quicker access to the features they offer. These are often
called TSR programs (for terminate-and-stay-resident). Some of the
DOS external commands, such as PRINT.COM, GRAPHICS.COM,
and MODE.COM, stay resident in RAM if you initialize them. When
you activate additional devices, such as a mouse, the mouse-driver
software also occupies some RAM.

In addition to the DOS TSR programs, many application programs stay resident in memory after loading. These programs remain in memory so that you can access them at any time just by
pressing a key (sometimes called a *hot key*). You don't even need to
be at the command prompt to run a loaded TSR program.

For example, SideKick Plus, a TSR program from Borland International, provides handy tools such as a phone list, an appointment
calendar, and a calculator. After you load SideKick into RAM, you
can access it by pressing a special key, even while you are running
another program such as your spreadsheet or word processor.

Typically, TSR programs are loaded into RAM from the top down. When you load multiple TSR programs, DOS automatically keeps track of where the current TSR program ends in memory and stores the next TSR immediately beneath the existing TSRs.

Some of DOS is actually stored near the top of the 640K mark. Nonetheless, it occupies a specific amount of memory.

All of these TSRs use additional memory, thus reducing the size of the remaining TPA. Of the original 640K, only 457K of memory remains after loading several TSR programs. Any program that requires more than 457K of RAM will not be able to run (DOS displays the message Insufficient Memory).

DOS 6 Memory Allocation

Chapter 15, "Getting the Most from Your Memory," discusses DOS 6 memory management in more detail.

One of the advantages DOS 6 has over its predecessors is that you can load TSRs (and device drivers) into the unused reserved memory above 640K, thereby saving conventional memory.

Granted, DOS 6 conserves precious conventional memory, but what if you really need a lot of memory, for example, to store a huge spreadsheet requiring several megabytes? As you might recall, spreadsheet programs store all the current spreadsheet's data in RAM. Even if you don't load the additional TSRs, you might not have enough RAM to create the spreadsheet model you want.

You might think you can solve this problem by buying more RAM chips. However, this is not the case. As the next section shows, for original IBM PCs, XTs, and compatibles, the 640K RAM limitation is not so easily expanded.

Why the 1M Memory Limit?

The reason for the 1M (RAM plus ROM) memory limit can be traced to the microprocessor that manipulates the data and instructions stored in RAM. As you might remember, RAM stores data for the microprocessor, but the microprocessor actually does all the work. For the microprocessor (the central processing unit, or CPU) to locate and manipulate the data stored in RAM, it needs to assign each byte an *address*.

The address of a particular byte in RAM is similar to the addresses of the houses in your community. Each house has a unique address so that the Post Office can deliver the mail. Each byte in memory also has a unique address so that the CPU can transfer information to and from RAM as needed.

The CPUs of computers that use the 8086 and 8088 microprocessors, such as the IBM PC, XT, and compatibles, use 20 bits for storing memory addresses. This provides for 2^{20}, or 1,048,576, directly addressable locations in memory. The number 1,048,576 is referred to as 1 megabyte. Because there is no way to express a number larger than 1,048,576 using 20 bits, 1M is the highest numbered memory location that the 8086 and 8088 microprocessors can address.

Overcoming the 640K RAM Limit

Throughout the years, many innovations have been developed to break the 640K RAM limit so that more space would be available for larger programs and bigger spreadsheets. The sections that follow discuss the three main approaches to overcoming this limitation.

Program Overlays

The oldest approach to running large programs in a smaller area of RAM has been to divide the program into a main file, which usually has the .EXE extension, and into separate *overlay* files, which often have extensions such as .OVL, .OVR, or .OV1, .OV2, .OV3, and so on.

In programs that use overlays, only the .EXE file is copied into RAM when you run the program. This file typically contains the most-often-used capabilities of the program so that these features are readily available when you want them. The .COM or .EXE file also reserves space in RAM, called the *overlay area*, that is meant to hold additional specialized instructions.

When you request a feature not currently available in RAM, the program quickly copies the overlay file which contains that feature into the overlay area, where it replaces the current overlay. That is, only one overlay file can be stored in RAM at a time.

Because only one overlay can be in use at a time in RAM, a program might need to swap overlays quite often, which involves copying the overlay from the disk into the overlay section of RAM. This can be a somewhat slow process (in the computer world, a two- or three-second delay is interminable), so it wasn't long before computer designers started seeking more efficient ways to extend the capabilities of RAM.

Extended Memory

The 80286 microprocessor, developed by Intel Corporation, offered a different solution to the 640K memory limit—*extended memory*. This microprocessor uses a 24-bit addressing scheme that can access as much as 16M of RAM. The IBM AT and compatible computers use the 80286 microprocessor.

The 80386 and 80486 microprocessors, which use a 32-bit addressing scheme, followed the 80286. The IBM PS/2 Model 80, the COMPAQ 386, and similar computers use the 80386 microprocessor. These computers also offer extended memory above the 640K limit.

Until version 5, DOS was never designed to take advantage of the additional memory made available by the 80286 and 80386 microprocessors. DOS was designed for the earlier 8086 and 8088 microprocessors, which use the 20-bit addressing scheme. Because most application programs were designed for use with DOS, these microprocessors also were incapable of using extended memory effectively.

DOS 5 and DOS 6, however, include an extended-memory manager program—HIMEM.SYS. This program enables you to access the enormous potential extended memory of the 80286 (16 megabytes) and 80386/80486 (4 gigabytes—4,000M) microprocessors. If your computer has one of these processors and more than 640K of RAM memory, and you are using DOS 5 or 6, refer to Chapter 15, "Getting the Most from Your Memory," to learn how to use HIMEM.SYS and extended memory most effectively.

One tool that allows DOS to take some advantage of the extended memory of the 80286 and 80386 microprocessors first appeared in version 3 of DOS. It offers a means of treating extended memory as though it were a disk drive. This disk drive in extended memory is often called a :RAM disk, or a *virtual disk,* because DOS interacts with it exactly as it does with all other disk drives in the computer.

DOS 3, 4, 5, and 6 can also use a part of conventional RAM memory as a virtual disk.

Fooling DOS into thinking that extended memory is a disk drive circumvents the problem of being able to address only 1M of memory. All versions of DOS can access as much as 32M from a disk drive, so by telling DOS that extended memory is another disk drive, you can easily access the 80286's maximum 16M of extended memory.

This virtual drive is actually composed of RAM chips and therefore does not use a spinning disk or moving drive heads. This feature makes it operate at speeds that are 10 to 20 times faster than a disk.

To take advantage of the extended memory as a virtual disk, you typically copy all the overlay files for a program or the data that you want to work with (or both, if they will fit) from a real disk to the virtual disk. Then you run the program as usual. DOS still runs the program in conventional memory (RAM) and still swaps overlays into and out of RAM from the virtual disk. However, the swapping is much quicker because there is no slow mechanical disk drive involved. Similarly, if the program needs to read and write data to a disk, these operations are also much quicker if the information is stored on the virtual disk.

Treating extended memory as though it were a disk does not really give you more RAM for running programs. It makes the movement of data into and out of RAM quicker, because no real disk drive is involved. As you'll see in the next section, a different technique, called *expanded memory,* was also devised to allow extra RAM to be treated as conventional RAM.

Expanded Memory

Most software developers were more interested in expanding RAM than in speeding the flow of information between RAM and a disk. This is particularly true of spreadsheet developers, because spreadsheet programs must store in RAM all the data for the current worksheet. The size of a spreadsheet was therefore limited to the amount of RAM available after DOS, any TSR programs, and the spreadsheet program itself were loaded into RAM.

Many spreadsheet users complained that 640K was not enough room for their spreadsheet applications. The only solution to this problem, with DOS as the operating system, was to find a means for allowing data beyond the 640K limit to spill over into additional RAM chips. Of course, data that was stored in these chips had to be as accessible as it was in conventional RAM. This presented a tricky problem, because DOS had no way of directly addressing the data beyond the 640K in RAM.

Three companies—Lotus Development Corporation, the maker of the 1-2-3 spreadsheet program; Intel, the maker of microprocessors; and Microsoft, the maker of DOS—joined forces to develop what is now known as the Lotus-Intel-Microsoft (LIM) standard for expanded memory. The word *expanded* is important here, because the LIM standard did, indeed, expand RAM beyond the 640K limit.

From a technical standpoint, this swapping of memory (also called *paging*) is trickier than you might think. As mentioned earlier, the area of addressable memory between 640K and 1M is typically reserved for video memory, hard disk management, and other BIOS operations.

In most systems, however, a good-sized chunk of memory in this area is unused. LIM controls 64K of this unused memory and uses it as a switching area for swapping data into, and out of, expanded memory as needed.

Even though the LIM technique involves some swapping of data into and out of the 1M of memory that DOS can address, it is very different from the technique of using extended memory as a virtual disk. In the virtual-disk approach, DOS sees whatever is in extended memory as being stored on a disk. If you try to copy a file from a virtual disk into RAM and there is not enough room in RAM to accommodate the data, DOS denies the request with the Insufficient Memory error message.

Specifically, the LIM approach sends data into memory in 16K chunks called *pages*. Thus, the 64K area in ROM can handle four pages at a time.

However, with the expanded-memory approach, the swapping is limited to the switching area memory, so DOS never issues the Insufficient Memory message. That's because the EMS approach, in a sense, tricks DOS into thinking that it's working with data stored within the 1M limit. In other words, the LIM approach lets DOS work with more RAM than it can actually handle by feeding it small chunks of data as needed.

Spreadsheet programs that take advantage of expanded memory could now enable users to create much larger worksheets. As a worksheet grows in size beyond the 640K limit, the LIM approach swaps the overflow quickly and automatically into and out of expanded memory so that conventional RAM is no longer a constraint.

The Current Standards

The basic LIM standard for expanded memory has evolved and improved since version 3.2. The two main standards used today are the EEMS (Enhanced Expanded Memory Specification) and the LIM 4.0 standard. Whereas the original LIM 3.2 specification allowed a maximum of 8M of expanded memory, the current specification allows as much as 32M of expanded memory.

Many alternatives are available for installing expanded memory on a computer. Before DOS 5 and DOS 6, the most common technique was to purchase a separate EMS board (hardware) and install it inside the computer. The board includes a *device driver* (a program) that manages the switching of data between expanded memory and addressable memory.

There are also EMS *emulators,* which mimic expanded memory using extended memory or even the hard disk. These are software-only products that do not require additional hardware, and DOS 5 includes one (EMM386.EXE) for use on 80386 and 80486 systems. If you own a computer that uses one of these microprocessors, see Chapter 15, "Getting the Most from Your Memory," for a detailed discussion of techniques for using HIMEM.SYS and EMM386.EXE to install and emulate expanded memory.

The Future of DOS?

One solution to breaking the 640K limit was the development of an entirely new operating system by IBM, called *OS/2* (for Operating System 2). A second solution has been the development of DOS "extenders" and new shells, such as Windows 3.1, developed by Microsoft, the same people who brought you DOS. Both OS/2 and Windows are specifically designed to work with new 80286-, 80386-, and 80486-based computers that offer two operating modes: *protected mode*, which takes full advantage of memory above 640K, and *real mode*, which runs most standard DOS programs in conventional RAM.

Protected mode allows multiple programs to run simultaneously in protected memory above the 1M limit of conventional memory. For example, with OS/2 or Windows, your computer can simultaneously print invoices, age your accounts receivable, and recalculate a large spreadsheet, all while you work with your word processing program.

Both OS/2 and Windows 3.1 offer more graphical user interfaces (GUIs), which are icon based rather than text based. The GUI interface is also more mouse oriented than DOS (much like the Macintosh, in case you are familiar with that machine).

How Disks Are Organized

A diskette or a hard disk stores information on a surface that is coated with hundreds of thousands—or millions—of tiny magnetic particles. As you might know, magnets have a positive pole and a negative pole. If you've ever played with two magnets, you know that when you push two positive (or two negative) poles toward each other, the magnets repel one another. When you push a negative pole toward a positive pole, the magnets attract each other.

609

Each magnetic particle on a computer disk can have one of two states—positive (represented as + or 1) or negative (represented as – or 0). Not surprisingly, each of these magnetic particles can represent one bit of data, and as you know, eight bits form a byte (a character).

Using binary numbers, you would express the + signs as 1s, and the minus signs as 0s, as shown here:

01000011 01000001 01010100

If you check an ASCII chart that shows the eight-bit byte for each character in the ASCII character set, you'll see that these are indeed the bytes used to represent the letters *C*, *A*, and *T*. Of course, the computer must convert these bytes to ASCII characters when it displays them on-screen or sends them to the printer, because the word *CAT* more meaningfully expresses to humans this feline animal than does 01000011 01000001 01010100.

How a Disk Drive Reads and Writes Data

Floppy diskette drives and hard disk drives use the same basic principle for reading information from and writing information to the magnetic medium of a disk. As the disk spins, the *read/write head* moves across the surface (although never actually touching the disk) in much the same way that a needle on a stereo turntable moves across a spinning album. As the recording head moves above the disk, it either reads the magnetic bits or changes their arrangement to store information.

Some older disk drives can read only one side of a diskette, because they have only one recording head. These drives use single-sided diskettes that can store only 160K or 180K of information.

Most modern disk drives have two recording heads, one for the top of the diskette and one for the bottom. These drives use double-sided diskettes, with the most popular storage capacities being 360K, 720K, 1.2M, and 1.44M.

A hard disk usually contains several spinning disks, referred to as *platters*. Each platter typically has two heads so that data can be read from or written to both sides.

> DOS can logically access the multiple platters as though they were one huge disk named C:. How DOS logically accesses a hard disk is determined by how you *partition* the hard disk using the FDISK program.

Versions of DOS prior to 4.0 could access a maximum of only 32 megabytes of information on any logical hard disk. Therefore, if the combined hard disk platters offered 40 megabytes of disk storage, DOS had to do something like accessing the first 32 megabytes as drive C: and then accessing the remaining 8 megabytes as drive D:. The physical number of platters in the hard disk is not important—only the storage capacity matters.

Low-Level Formatting

When DOS first formats a disk, it performs a *low-level format*, which divides the surface of the diskette into sectors (slices). Each sector represents one *allocation unit* of data and stores a specific number of bytes, usually either 512K or 1,024K.

Double-sided diskettes and hard disks are further divided into *cylinders*. A cylinder is the combination of all the corresponding tracks on each side of each platter. For example, a hard disk that has four double-sided platters contains eight tracks numbered "1." The combination of these eight tracks would be referred to as cylinder number 1.

When DOS writes a large file to a disk, it attempts to store data in a single cylinder of multiple sides (or platters) rather than in multiple tracks of a single platter. For example, when storing a file on the 10th track of a disk, DOS first fills track 10 of side 0, then track 10 of side 1, then track 10 of side 2, then track 10 of side 3, and so on. This makes reading and writing data quicker, because the heads are simultaneously positioned to the appropriate track (the heads always move in tandem, never independently).

High-Level Formatting

After the basic tracks, sectors, and cylinders are laid out on the surface of the disk, DOS performs a high-level format. During this phase, groups of sectors are set aside for storing information that DOS will later use to keep track of files. Each of these DOS information areas is discussed in the sections that follow.

The Boot Record

The first sector on a disk stores the *boot record.* This is where the computer looks for start-up information when you first turn it on. The boot record contains information about the format of the disk, such as the number of bytes per sector, the number of sectors per track and cylinder, and so on. The boot record also lists the names of the *system files* that contain the instructions that start the computer.

The system files needed to start DOS 6 on an IBM-clone computer are called IO.SYS, MSDOS.SYS, and DBLSPACE.BIN. The first two files are hidden; that is, their names do not appear when you list file names.

Another file, named COMMAND.COM, is also copied to a disk that has been formatted with the /S switch. COMMAND.COM interprets DOS commands and batch programs, issues prompts, and loads and executes other programs.

When you format a disk with the FORMAT /S command, DOS copies the two system files and COMMAND.COM to the disk so that you can use the disk to boot the computer. If you do not use the /S switch, the system files are not copied, and the disk cannot boot the computer. Furthermore, the space that would have been occupied by the start-up files is eventually allocated to other files, so you cannot copy the system files later. (Actually, you can use the /B switch to reserve space for the system files.)

The Directory Sectors

Another group of sectors on the disk is dedicated to storing the directory. In the directory sectors, the following information about each file is stored in a 32-byte area:

- The name and extension of the file

- The status of file attributes, such as Read-Only and Archive

- The time that the file was created or last changed

- The date that the file was created or last changed

- The size of the file

- The starting cluster number

All this information is stored in hexadecimal notation. However, when you use the DIR command to view the directory sectors of a disk, DOS converts the hex numbers to ASCII or characters before displaying them on-screen.

DOS never displays the starting cluster number on your screen. Instead, DOS uses this information to find the file. It would be a waste of time to have DOS search the entire disk each time you requested a file. Instead, it looks up the file name in the directory sectors and finds the corresponding *starting cluster number*, which pinpoints the track on the disk that contains the beginning of the file.

The File Allocation Table

Every disk also reserves a group of sectors that store the file allocation table (FAT). This table is a map that tells DOS where to find fragments of files that have been stored in *noncontiguous sectors*. Files are often fragmented into noncontiguous sectors when they are altered or expanded after new files have been stored next to them.

For example, suppose that you create a file that contains 50 names and addresses and name it CUSTLIST.DAT. Now, suppose that when you save this file, DOS stores it in sectors 5 through 10. Later, you create another file, which DOS stores in sectors 11 through 15. If you then add some names to CUSTLIST.DAT, the entire file will not fit into sectors 5 through 10 anymore, and because sectors 11 through 15 are already taken, DOS must store the rest of CUSTLIST.DAT elsewhere (perhaps starting at sector 16).

The FAT keeps track of the various sectors in which a fragmented file is stored. Actually, the FAT keeps track of the *clusters* (or groups of sectors) in which files are stored. When you tell DOS to retrieve a file, it finds the starting cluster number stored with the file's name in the directory sectors. Then it starts reading the file at that location.

After reading all the data in the starting cluster, DOS looks up the file's starting cluster number in the FAT. The FAT, in turn, tells DOS the next cluster number (if any) in which more of the file is stored. DOS then accesses this cluster and reads more of the file. This process is repeated until DOS encounters a special code in the file indicating that the entire file has been read.

The FAT is a crucial element of a disk. If the FAT is erased or destroyed, DOS can no longer access the files, because it doesn't know where they are stored. For this reason, DOS actually keeps two copies of the FAT on the disk. If the first table is ruined, DOS uses the other copy.

The Data Sectors

The data sectors are the sections of the disk in which the actual files and subdirectories beneath the root directory are stored. These remaining sectors are by far the largest area on the disk.

Table 20.2 shows the total number of sectors allocated to various data areas on different types of diskettes.

Table 20.2. Sector allotment for various diskette sizes and densities.

	5 1/4-inch		3 1/2-inch	
	Low	High	Low	High
Storage capacity	360K	1.2M	720K	1.44M
Boot record (sectors)	1	1	1	1
FAT sectors	4	14	10	18
Directory sectors	7	14	7	14
Data sectors	354	2,371	713	2,847
Bytes per sector	1,024	512	1,024	512
Sectors per cluster	2	1	2	1

The allocation schemes for the various sections of hard disks vary greatly from one disk to another. These are determined during formatting by taking into account the amount of available storage space, the partitioning, the number of cylinders and heads, and other factors.

Serial and Parallel Communications

Computers use two basic techniques for sending data through wires to peripheral devices: serial communication, in which bits are sent in a single-file stream, and parallel communication, in which eight bits are sent in parallel through eight wires.

Serial communication is sometimes called *asynchronous communication,* because the devices involved must take turns sending and receiving; they cannot do so in a simultaneous (that is, synchronized) manner.

The serial communication technique is used when multiple wires are not available. For example, when you send data through phone lines via a modem, serial communication is used because the phone lines do not have the eight wires necessary for parallel communications. Serial communications are generally slower because the receiving device receives only one bit at a time.

Parallel communication is faster than serial communication because the receiving device receives one byte (that is, eight bits) at a time. Most modern high-speed printers use parallel communications.

If you were to look at the back of your computer with all the plugs removed, you would see that some of the ports are male; that is, the pins protrude from the port. These are usually serial ports. The parallel ports on the back of the computer are usually female; the pins protrude from the plug at the end of the cable.

In most situations, you do not need to do anything special with DOS to use the serial and parallel ports. Other software automatically manages the ports. However, you can configure both the parallel and serial ports, if necessary, using the DOS MODE command.

Troubleshooting

Here are a few tips to follow if you experience problems with the technical information provided in this chapter.

■ If you find that you are not getting the performance you expected from your RAM disk, check your CONFIG.SYS file. To use extended memory rather than conventional RAM for a RAM disk, you must use the /E switch with the VDISK.SYS or RAMDRIVE.SYS device driver. To use expanded memory for a RAM disk, use the /X switch for VDISK.SYS and the /A switch for RAMDRIVE.SYS.

■ The 5¼-inch disk was standard among microcomputers until the 720K and 1.44M 3½-inch disk drives were installed in newer computers. These new drives cause compatibility problems for anyone who must use both types of machines. Unless you have a computer that has both 5¼-inch and 3½-inch drives installed, you have only two alternatives to solving the 5¼-inch versus 3½-inch compatibility problem:

If you have two computers, one with a 5¼-inch drive and one with a 3½-inch drive, you can solve the problem inexpensively with software. Ask your computer or software dealer for details.

If you have only one computer and one drive size, you'll need to resort to the most expensive hardware solution of adding another drive.

■ Understanding and effectively managing your memory depends on the type of computer you have:

If you have a 386 or higher computer, you can use HIMEM.SYS and EMM386.EXE to load DOS into high memory and put TSR programs and device drivers into high memory using the LOADHIGH and DEVICEHIGH commands. You can also create a RAM disk with RAMDRIVE.SYS and a disk cache with SMARTDRV.EXE.

If you have a 286 or higher machine, such as an IBM AT or clone, you can use HIMEM.SYS to put DOS in high memory. You can create a RAM disk with RAMDRIVE.SYS and a disk cache with SMARTDRV.EXE. You cannot use EMM386.EXE, nor can you load device drivers and TSRs into upper memory.

If you have an 8088-type machine, such as an IBM XT or clone, you can create a RAM disk (if you have expanded memory) and a disk cache, but you can't load DOS or TSR programs into high memory.

Summary

When you start using the more advanced features of your computer and DOS, you need a deeper understanding of the way things work. This chapter presented a brief overview of the technical inner workings of your computer. In summary:

- The basic unit of storage in a computer is a binary digit (*bit*), which can be either on (1) or off (0).

- A single character is stored as a group of eight bits, called a *byte*.

- Internally, computers use a binary (base 2) rather than a decimal (base 10) counting system. Programmers use the more convenient hexadecimal (base 16) numbering system.

- A computer's conventional memory consists of up to 640K of RAM and 384K of ROM, for a total of 1M of memory.

- Extended memory can be used as an effective extension of RAM by DOS 6's HIMEM.SYS memory manager. It can also be used as a virtual disk, which appears to DOS as any other disk but is much faster because there are no moving parts.

- Expanded memory (which can be created on a 386 or 486 computer with the DOS 5 EMM386.EXE program) can be used by DOS as though it were additional conventional RAM.

- During formatting, a disk is divided into tracks, sectors, and clusters, which organize data for rapid storage and retrieval.

- In serial (or asynchronous) communications, data is sent one bit at a time.

- In parallel communications, data is sent one byte at a time.

Alan Simpson's
DOS
SECRETS
UNLEASHED

C H A P T E R   2 1

Maximizing Your Disk Drives

Disk drives are very often the real culprit behind slow computer performance. In the next sections, I'll discuss techniques for improving and maximizing disk drive speed and performance.

Using a RAM Disk

As discussed in Chapter 14, "Hard Disk Management Made Simple," a RAM disk (or virtual disk) is a portion of memory set up to simulate a disk drive. The advantage of a RAM disk is that it is 10 to 20 times faster than a *physical* (that is, real) disk drive. A RAM disk does have disadvantages, however:

■ Everything is erased from the RAM disk when you turn off the computer.

■ Some programs might not have enough memory space after you assign part of memory to the RAM disk (depending on how you set up the RAM disk).

You can bypass the disadvantages of RAM disks if you 1) use the RAM disk only to store temporary files and 2) use extended or expanded memory, rather than conventional RAM, for the RAM disk, as I'll discuss in the sections that follow.

Creating a RAM Disk in Conventional Memory

You can use conventional memory for your RAM disk. However, you first need to realistically determine how much memory is available. Before you make this appraisal, be sure to load all of your usual memory-resident programs, such as SideKick, as well as any DOS memory-resident programs that you use regularly (such as PRINT.COM, MODE.COM, GRAPHICS.COM, and so on).

Next, at the command prompt, you can enter the CHKDSK or the DOS 6 MEM command. When you use CHKDSK, the last two lines displayed show the current available amount of conventional memory, as in the following example:

```
655360 total bytes memory
542832 bytes free
```

The DOS 6 MEM command displays three lines of information about conventional memory, as in the following example:

```
655360 bytes total conventional memory
655360 bytes available to MS-DOS
542832 largest executable program size
```

> To determine how much RAM an application program requires, check that program's documentation.

In the preceding examples, the computer has 655,360 total bytes of memory, of which 542,832 bytes are free. (Dividing 542,832 by 1,024 translates to about 530K.) To determine a realistic size for your RAM disk, subtract the amount of RAM that your largest program requires from the amount of available memory.

> Remember too that spreadsheet programs, such as Lotus 1-2-3, store data in RAM, and therefore you must also leave enough room to include your largest spreadsheet.

For example, assuming that Lotus 1-2-3 requires about 179K of RAM and that your largest spreadsheet requires 50K of RAM, the maximum amount of RAM available for a RAM disk would be about 301K (530K of available memory minus 179K for 1-2-3 and 50K for the largest spreadsheet). Because you wouldn't want to run out of memory during a crucial operation and because spreadsheets have a tendency to grow, play it safe and round that number down considerably, perhaps to 256K.

To create a RAM disk, you need to modify your CONFIG.SYS file to include the command DEVICE=*device driver*. If you are using MS-DOS, the *device driver* for creating a RAM disk is named RAMDRIVE.SYS. Therefore, the general technique for installing a RAM disk using MS-DOS is to add a command to your CONFIG.SYS file that uses the following syntax:

```
DEVICE=d:\path\RAMDRIVE.SYS size sectors entries
```

PC DOS users with IBM machines must use the VDISK.SYS device driver rather than RAMDRIVE.SYS. Check your start-up diskette or the root (C:) or C:\DOS directory of your hard disk to see whether it contains RAMDRIVE.SYS or VDISK.SYS. Use whichever device driver is available for your computer. (You might also need to check the documentation that came with your computer for additional details.)

VDISK.SYS uses the same syntax as RAMDRIVE.SYS, as follows:

```
DEVICE=d:\path\VDISK.SYS size sectors entries
```

Whether you use VDISK.SYS or RAMDRIVE.SYS, you need to replace the italicized parameters with the following information:

d:\path—Name of the drive and directory where the RAMDRIVE.SYS or VDISK.SYS file is located.

size—Size (in kilobytes) of the RAM disk (if omitted, DOS creates a 64K RAM disk).

sectors—Size of each sector on the RAM disk—128, 256, or 512 bytes.

entries—Maximum number of file names in the root directory of the RAM disk, within the range of 2 to 512 (if this parameter is omitted, DOS permits 64).

You can omit parameters only if you've specified parameters to the left. For example, if you want to allow 128 directory entries, you cannot use the command DEVICE=RAMDRIVE.SYS 128 or DEVICE=VDISK.SYS 128, because DOS will think that the 128 refers to the size of the disk in kilobytes. Instead, you must specify both the size of the disk and the size of each sector (even if they are equal to the defaults), as in the following example:

```
DEVICE=RAMDRIVE.SYS 64 256 128
```

When DOS creates a RAM disk, it automatically assigns the next available drive name to it. For example, if your computer has one hard disk named C:, the RAM disk is automatically named D:. If your computer has hard drives C:, D:, E:, F:, and G:, the RAM disk is automatically named H:.

Now, suppose that you want to create a 256K RAM disk in conventional RAM. If you are using MS-DOS and RAMDRIVE.SYS is stored on the \DOS directory of drive C:, you must add the following command to your CONFIG.SYS file:

```
DEVICE=C:\DOS\RAMDRIVE.SYS 256
```

If you are using MS-DOS and VDISK.SYS is stored on the root directory, you must add this command to the CONFIG.SYS file:

```
DEVICE=C:\VDISK.SYS 256
```

The exact information that appears on your screen depends on your version of DOS and other factors.

After you modify the CONFIG.SYS file, DOS automatically creates the RAM disk each time you start your computer in the future or after you reboot. Information about the RAM disk appears on your screen during the boot-up procedure, as follows:

```
Microsoft RAMDrive version 3.05 virtual disk D:
    Disk size Sector size adjusted
    Directory entries adjusted
    Buffer size: 256k
    Sector size: 512 bytes
    Allocation unit: 1 sectors
    Directory entries: 64
```

In this case, DOS named the RAM disk D: and gave it a 256K storage capacity. DOS used its internal default values for the sector size and directory entries, because you omitted values for these parameters in the DEVICE command in the CONFIG.SYS file. Each sector is 512 bytes, and you can store a maximum of 64 files on the RAM disk.

From now on, you can use the RAM disk exactly as you would any other disk drive. (Don't forget, however, that everything is erased from the RAM disk when you turn off the computer.)

> If you are using the DOS Shell, you'll notice that the drive name is included in the Drives area of the File System, with a special RAM icon in the Drives area.

Assume that your computer has one physical hard disk named C: and one RAM disk named D:. You can switch to the RAM disk from either the DOS Shell File System or from the command prompt by entering D: (as in this example). If you were to enter the command CHKDSK D: to check the RAM disk, your screen would show something like the following output:

```
Volume MS-RAMDRIVE created 6-06-93 12:00a

  258560 bytes total disk space
     512 bytes in 1 directories
  258048 bytes available on disk

     512 bytes in each allocation unit
     505 total allocation units on disk
     504 available allocation units on disk

  655360 total bytes memory
  279424 bytes free
```

As you can see, the RAM disk has about 256K of storage space available. Actually, it has a little less—256K is actually 262,144 (256 x 1024) bytes. However, some of the RAM disk sectors are formatted as the boot record, FAT, and directory area, and these occupy some of the disk space. DOS automatically adds the disk volume label, MS-RAMDRIVE in this example, when the RAM disk is created.

Notice that the CHKDSK display shows only 279,424 bytes of memory (RAM) available. That's because DOS and your TSR programs occupy memory and also because a large part of RAM is now dedicated to the RAM disk.

Installing a RAM Disk in Extended Memory

If your computer has extended memory, you should use that rather than conventional RAM for your RAM disk. Doing so saves precious conventional memory for running programs and generally enables you to create much larger RAM disks (because you're likely to have more than 640K of extended memory). As mentioned earlier, you can easily determine how much extended memory is available by entering the MEM command.

> To convert megabytes to kilobytes, multiply by 1024. For example, the maximum size of a RAM disk when 4M of extended memory is available is 4,096K (4 x 1024).

Before you can use extended memory for a RAM disk, the extended memory must be placed under the control of an extended memory driver. In DOS 6 (and machines that run Windows 3.x), this is easily accomplished using the HIMEM.SYS driver. The command that loads HIMEM.SYS (for example, DEVICE=C:\DOS\HIMEM.SYS in your CONFIG.SYS file) must come before the command that loads the RAM disk device driver.

To use extended memory for your RAM disk, activate the previously described VDISK.SYS or RAMDRIVE.SYS device driver in your CONFIG.SYS file, but follow the command with the /E (for extended memory) switch. For example, to use MS-DOS to create a 1M RAM disk with 512-byte sectors in extended memory, add the following command to your CONFIG.SYS file:

```
DEVICE=C:\DOS\RAMDRIVE.SYS 1024 512 /E
```

Note that the command assumes that the device driver is stored on the C:\DOS drive and directory. If your device driver is stored elsewhere, change C:\DOS\ to reflect the actual location of RAMDRIVE.SYS (or VDISK.SYS).

After you add the appropriate command to your CONFIG.SYS file, the RAM disk is automatically installed in extended memory every time you start your computer. For example, suppose that your computer has one hard disk named C:. After you add the appropriate DEVICE= command to your CONFIG.SYS file and boot up, your RAM disk is set up as drive D:. When you enter the command

```
CHKDSK D:
```

at the command prompt, your screen displays information using the following general format:

```
volume MS-RAMDRIVE created 6-06-93 12:00a

1042944 bytes total disk space
    512 bytes in 1 directories
1042432 bytes available on disk

    512 bytes in each allocation unit
   2037 total allocation units on disk
   2036 available allocation units on disk

 655360 total bytes memory
 603728 bytes free
```

In this example, the RAM disk has 1,042,944 bytes of storage space available. The boot record, FAT, and directory sectors of the RAM disk occupy 512 bytes in one directory, leaving 1,042,432 bytes for storage. Each sector (allocation unit) holds 512 bytes. Conventional RAM memory still has 603,728 bytes free, because the RAM disk is in extended memory.

If you are using DOS 4, 5, or 6, you could enter the MEM command to check available memory after installing this RAM disk in extended memory. You would notice that the "bytes available XMS memory" measurement is now smaller, because the RAM disk now uses some of that previously available extended memory.

Installing a RAM Disk in Expanded Memory

> DOS 6 includes the EMM386.EXE program, which lets 386 and 486 computers emulate expanded memory within the extended memory created by HIMEM.SYS.

If your computer has expanded rather than extended memory, you can use all or a portion of the expanded memory for a RAM disk. Keep in mind, however, that programs which use (or require) expanded memory cannot access the portion of expanded memory that you've designated for a RAM disk.

To convert expanded memory to a RAM disk, your CONFIG.SYS file must first install and activate the expanded memory, as discussed earlier in this chapter. If the commands in the CONFIG.SYS file for installing expanded memory are not executed before the DEVICE=RAMDRIVE.SYS command is used to install a RAM disk, an error occurs, and the RAM disk is not installed.

The exact command syntax required for installing a RAM disk in expanded memory depends on your version of DOS and whether you are using the DOS device driver, or a particular computer manufacturer's device driver, to install the RAM disk.

If you are using DOS 4, 5, or 6 and its VDISK.SYS device driver, you use the /X switch in the DEVICE=VDISK.SYS command to install the RAM disk in expanded memory. If you are using MS-DOS 3.2 or later, and the RAMDRIVE.SYS device driver, you use the /A switch in the DEVICE=RAMDRIVE.SYS command.

Because different expanded memory boards use different drivers, it's impossible to give a universally applicable example of using expanded memory for a RAM disk. Suppose, however, that you have a 2M expanded memory adapter in your computer, and the command DEVICE=C:\DOS\MYEMS.EXE in your CONFIG.SYS file activates that expanded memory. To use 1M of that expanded memory as a RAM drive, you would need to add this command to your CONFIG.SYS file (below the command that activates expanded memory):

```
DEVICE = C:\DOS\RAMDRIVE.SYS 1024 /A
```

In this line, 1024 is the size of the RAM drive (1M) and /A specifies expanded rather than conventional memory.

Using Upper Memory with RAMDrive

Even if you use extended or expanded memory for your RAM disk, the RAM disk device driver (which occupies about 1.2K of memory) remains in conventional memory (RAM). If you're using DOS 5, a 386 or 486 computer, and upper memory blocks, you can move this driver into upper memory, using the DEVICEHIGH command.

Just use the DEVICEHIGH command rather than the DEVICE command to load the RAM drive. Be sure all the commands for activating extended and upper memory precede the command for installing the RAM disk, as in the following example. This example installs a 1M (1024K) RAM disk in extended memory (due to /E) and puts the 1.2K driver for the RAM disk in upper rather than conventional memory:

```
****************************** CONFIG.SYS
DEVICE=C:\DOS\HIMEM.SYS
DOS=HIGH,UMB
DEVICE=C:\DOS\EMM386.EXE NOEMS
DEVICEHIGH = C:\DOS\RAMDRIVE.SYS 1024 /E
```

If you were to enter a MEM /C command and reboot after making this change to your CONFIG.SYS file, you would see that neither the RAM disk nor the device driver for the RAM disk occupies any conventional memory.

Installing Multiple RAM Disks

If you want to create multiple RAM disks—for example, drives D:, E:, and F:—include multiple DEVICE=RAMDRIVE.SYS (or VDISK.SYS) commands in your CONFIG.SYS file. DOS automatically assigns the next available drive name to each RAM disk.

However, you should also include a LASTDRIVE command in your CONFIG.SYS file to prepare DOS for the multiple virtual drives. Insert the LASTDRIVE command in your CONFIG.SYS file using the syntax

```
LASTDRIVE=drive letter
```

in which *drive letter* is the name (without the colon) of the last virtual drive. For example, if your computer has a hard disk named C: and you want to add three 512K RAM disks in 1.5M of extended memory, include the following commands in your CONFIG.SYS file:

```
LASTDRIVE=F
DEVICE=C:\DOS\RAMDRIVE.SYS 512 /E
DEVICE=C:\DOS\RAMDRIVE.SYS 512 /E
DEVICE=C:\DOS\RAMDRIVE.SYS 512 /E
```

DOS automatically assigns these drives the names D:, E:, and F:.

The first command prepares DOS to support drives named A:, B:, C:, D:, E:, and F:. The first DEVICE command sets up a 512K hard disk, named D: (because the name C: is already assigned to the physical hard disk). The second DEVICE command automatically assigns the name E: to the 512K RAM disk. The third DEVICE command assigns the name F: to the last 512K RAM disk.

Using a RAM Disk Safely

As mentioned earlier, a major disadvantage of using a RAM disk is that when you turn off the computer, all data stored on the RAM disk is immediately erased. A virtual disk acts so much like a physical disk drive that you can easily forget this important fact and lose all your data.

One of the best applications for a RAM disk is to use it only for temporary files that many programs create and erase automatically. You don't care about losing these files when you turn off the computer because they are useful only in the current session. In fact, you might not even be aware of their existence, because programs that use temporary files typically create and erase them behind the scenes.

> Many modern programs check the DOS environment for a variable named TEMP, which tells them what drive and directory to use to store temporary files. After your CONFIG.SYS file contains the command or commands required to activate a RAM disk, you can alter your AUTOEXEC.BAT file to both create a directory on the RAM disk and set the TEMP variable to that drive and directory.

For example, suppose that you've used whatever technique works for you to create a RAM disk, and that the RAM disk is drive D:. To use D: for temporary files, you would add these commands to your AUTOEXEC.BAT (not CONFIG.SYS) file:

```
MD D:\TEMPFILS
SET TEMP=D:\TEMPFILS
```

The first command creates a directory named TEMPFILS on drive D: (the RAM disk in this example). The advantage to creating a directory on the RAM drive is that the root directory of a RAM disk can hold only a limited number of files (usually 64), whereas a subdirectory below the root can hold any number of files.

The command SET TEMP=D:\TEMPFILS tells any program that searches the environment for the TEMP variable name to use the RAM disk for temporary files. Hence, that program can create and manage temporary files 10 to 20 times faster than it could when using the physical drive.

Using a Disk Cache to Speed Performance

Although a RAM disk is great for temporary files and some disk-intensive operations, most of your work will still involve interacting directly with your actual disk drives. Hence, you want to be sure your disks are always running at top speed to ensure maximum overall performance.

One way to maximize the speed of a disk drive is through a disk *cache* (pronounced "cash") to speed up processes that involve disk input/output (I/O). These processes include all operations that read data from the disk into RAM (input) and write data from RAM to the disk (output). The cache operates as an intermediary between the disk and RAM.

When a program requests data from the disk, DOS stores the data in the cache and then sends copies to the program (in RAM). When the program changes the data and returns it to the disk, DOS stores only the modified data in the cache. Although the program might change several items of data and send them to the disk for safekeeping, DOS actually stores these changes in the cache.

When the program finishes making changes to the data or the cache becomes filled, DOS copies all the modified data in the cache to the disk for safe storage. This single transfer is much more efficient than writing small chunks of modified data to the disk on a piecemeal basis.

Sophisticated caching programs also keep track of how often data in the cache is being used. When more space is needed in the cache to store new data, the least-used data is saved to disk and discarded from the cache to make room. This method makes the cache more efficient, because the cache tends to maintain data that is being modified frequently rather than only occasionally.

Some caching programs can also look ahead when a program requests data from the disk, reading a little more data than the program requests in anticipation that the program will soon request the additional data. Later, if the program requests the additional data, it's already in the cache and DOS doesn't need to access the disk. The only disadvantage to a disk cache is that it is usually stored in RAM, thereby consuming some of your valuable memory.

> You might be able to use extended or expanded memory for your disk cache, but this depends on your version of DOS and your specific disk cache program.

Some computers provide their own disk cache programs, which are separate from DOS. For example, the IBM PS/2 models 50 through 80 provide a disk cache program named IBMCACHE. Many COMPAQ computers provide a program named CACHE to manage disk caching. Refer to the owner's manual, or to the DOS manual, that came with your computer for information about using its unique disk-caching system.

DOS 6 (as well as Windows 3.x) provides the versatile SMARTDrive disk cache in extended, expanded, or reserved memory without wasting conventional memory.

Using the SMARTDrive Disk Cache

> If you are using both Windows and DOS 6, be sure you install the DOS 6 version of SMARTDRV.SYS—not the Windows version.

The SMARTDrive disk cache was originally developed for use with Microsoft Windows. Now, Microsoft has included it in the DOS 6 package. To use SMARTDrive, your computer must have extended or expanded memory and, of course, a hard disk. Consider using SMARTDrive if your system has 512K or more of free extended memory or 256K or more of free expanded memory. Whether you should install this cache on your system also depends on the type of computing you do.

DOS 6 includes an enhanced version of the SMARTDrive utility. SMARTDrive sets aside a portion of extended memory to act as a fast but temporary storage region for frequently accessed data. Originally designed to speed up only disk reads, the SMARTDrive in DOS 6 includes caching of disk writes, which speeds up writing to files as well as reading from them.

Remember, a disk-caching program speeds the reading and/or writing of data from and to your hard disk. If you use programs that perform many disk operations (databases, for example, which are notorious for their frequent disk reads), SMARTDrive will significantly increase the performance of your system. If, however, you use your computer primarily as a word processor or for running entertainment programs, a disk cache will be of little or no value.

SMARTDrive works equally well in either extended or expanded memory. If your system includes both types of memory, use whichever has the most available memory. However, do not use SMARTDrive if you are already using another disk cache; this wastes memory and also produces a cache-within-a-cache situation, which can actually slow down disk operations! Disable your original cache before you install SMARTDrive.

> For a complete discussion of the switches and usage of SMARTDrive, see Chapter 14, "Hard Disk Management Made Simple."

Activating SMARTDrive

To install the basic SMARTDrive disk cache in extended memory, add the following command in your CONFIG.SYS file:

```
DEVICE=C:\DOS\SMARTDRV.SYS
```

By default, SMARTDrive is installed in extended memory. To install the cache in expanded memory, add the /A switch to the preceding command, as follows:

```
DEVICE=C:\DOS\SMARTDRV.SYS /A
```

In either case, be sure that the command that activates extended or expanded memory precedes the command that loads SMARTDRV.SYS in the CONFIG.SYS file.

If you do not specify a size for the cache in your DEVICE= command, SMARTDrive uses a default cache size of 256K. Of course, if your system doesn't have that much extended or expanded memory, SMARTDrive simply uses whatever memory you have.

The size of the cache (which holds your data in RAM) directly affects the efficiency of the program. The more information that SMARTDrive can access from RAM (rather than from the slow mechanical disk drive), the more efficient it is. Although you can actually specify a cache size of 128K, the minimum effective cache size is probably about 512K. Microsoft recommends an optimum SMARTDrive cache of 2M. Note that unless you are working with huge data files, very large caches (from 2M to 8M) can actually degrade your system's performance!

If you have 2M of expanded memory, you can establish a large SMARTDrive disk cache with the following command in your CONFIG.SYS file:

```
DEVICE=C:\DOS\SMARTDRV.SYS 2048 /A
```

Note that the size follows the file name and must be expressed in kilobytes. To install this 2M cache in extended memory, simply omit the /A switch; SMARTDrive installs itself in extended memory by default.

Putting SMARTDRV.SYS in Upper Memory

Even though the SMARTDrive cache is placed in extended (or expanded) memory, the driver for the cache is still placed in conventional memory, occupying about 21K.

If you are using a 386 or 486 computer, DOS 6, and upper memory blocks, you can put that driver into upper memory by using DEVICEHIGH rather than the DEVICE command to install SMARTDrive, as in the sample CONFIG.SYS commands shown here:

```
REM**************************** Sample
CONFIG.SYS

DEVICE = C:\HIMEM.SYS
DOS = HIGH,UMB
DEVICE = C:\DOS\EMM386.EXE NOEMS
DEVICEHIGH=C:\DOS\SMARTDRV.SYS 1024
```

In the last line, a 1M (1024K) disk cache is placed in extended memory (automatically, because HIMEM.SYS has already activated extended memory), and the 21K driver is placed in upper memory.

Warnings About SMARTDrive

If you have partitioned your hard disk with some third-party disk-management programs (most notably ONTRACK's Disk Manager and the SPEEDSTOR disk manager), the SMARTDrive program will refuse to load. Instead, as your system boots, the following message will appear on your screen:

```
Microsoft SMARTDrive Disk Cache version 3.11
SMARTDrive: Incompatible disk partition detected.
```

If you later type MEM /P or MEM /C, you will see that the SMARTDrive cache was not installed in memory.

The mentioned third-party disk-management programs include routines that let hard disks work with computers which have outdated BIOS and that enable users to create larger partitions than earlier versions of DOS permitted. SMARTDrive is incompatible with these routines and can corrupt data if used in conjunction with them. As a safety feature, Microsoft by default won't permit SMARTDrive to work with these disk managers.

However, if you are using a newer computer with a recent BIOS and you have not created any partitions larger than 32M, SMARTDrive probably will work correctly on your system. You might need to add the /P (which stands for "partition") switch to the end of the DEVICE= command for installing SMARTDrive. This switch forces SMARTDrive to run with all disk-management programs.

> Because you risk losing data by forcing SMARTDrive to operate with potentially incompatible programs, be sure you contact the technical support personnel at Microsoft or at the makers of your disk-management software before you actually use this switch.

Other Ways to Improve Hard Disk Performance

There are a few additional techniques you can use to get maximum speed and performance from your hard disk. These techniques are described in the sections that follow.

Checking Your *PATH*

One of the most common causes of slow disk response times, particularly when you're trying to run a program, is a PATH statement that forces DOS to look through hundreds or thousands of file names before finding the program you want. For example, suppose that whenever you try to run WordPerfect 5.1 (stored on the C:\WP51 directory), there is an extremely long delay before the program starts.

Suppose that you then check the PATH statement in your AUTOEXEC.BAT file and find something like

```
PATH = C:\DOS;D:\UTILS;E:\WINDOWS;E:\TOOLBOOK;C:\WP51
```

Part of the delay in running in WordPerfect, in this case, might be the time required to search the current directory and every directory that precedes C:\WP51 in the PATH statement. If you changed that PATH statement to

```
PATH = C:\DOS;C:\WP51;D:\UTILS;E:\WINDOWS;E:\TOOLBOOK
```

DOS would be able to find WordPerfect much more quickly.

The sheer number of files on a directory can also affect performance. For example, referring to the preceding PATH statement, if both the C:\DOS and C:\WP51 directories contain 1,000 files each, that's up to 2,000 file names that must be searched when DOS looks for the WordPerfect program.

You can also greatly improve performance by deleting any unnecessary files, or by moving some files to other subdirectories to minimize the number of files in the directories that are listed in the PATH command.

For example, if you moved all the documents, graphics, macros, and other files from your C:\WP51 directory onto subdirectories (for example, C:\WP51\DOCS, C:\WP51\GRAPHICS, C:\WP51\MACROS, and so forth), DOS would no longer need to search through the names of all those files when looking for the WordPerfect program.

Incidentally, WordPerfect and many other programs make it especially easy to store files in this manner, via a "Location of Files" feature that you can use to specify subdirectories for storing various types of files. Check the documentation that came with your particular program to see what it has to offer along these lines.

Setting Up Buffers

> The BUFFERS command in DOS 4, 5, and 6 provides the look-ahead capabilities but not the frequency-checking of a disk cache.

The BUFFERS command, which acts as a sort of primitive disk cache system, is available in most versions of DOS. To use the BUFFERS command, add

BUFFERS=*buffers*

(in which *buffers* is a number in the range of 20 to 50) to your CONFIG.SYS file. The best values for buffers vary with the size of your hard disk:

Hard Disk Capacity	Value for Buffers
Less than 40M	20
40–79M	30
80–119M	40
120M or more	50

Using FASTOPEN

The FASTOPEN program, which comes with DOS 6, acts like a cache but is specifically designed for use with programs that regularly open and close large numbers of files, such as database management systems and language compilers.

> FASTOPEN cannot use extended memory, only conventional or expanded memory.

FASTOPEN uses the syntax

```
FASTOPEN drive:[=n] [...] [/X]
```

in which *drive:* is the name of the drive to track files on, *n* is the number of files to track, ... represents additional drives and numbers, and /X tells FASTOPEN to use expanded (not extended) memory.

You can use FASTOPEN right at the command prompt. For example, the following command tells FASTOPEN to track the names of 40 files on drive C: as they're being opened and closed:

```
FASTOPEN C:=40
```

Of course, you can also start FASTOPEN automatically at the beginning of each session by placing the FASTOPEN command in your AUTOEXEC.BAT file. For example, the following AUTOEXEC.BAT command tracks 10 files (each) on drives C:, D:, and E:, using expanded rather than conventional memory:

```
C:\DOS\FASTOPEN.EXE C:=10 D:=10 E:=10 /X
```

Note that for this command to work correctly, the CONFIG.SYS file must have already activated expanded (EMS, not XMS) memory.

If you have DOS 4, 5, or 6, you can use the INSTALL= command to load FASTOPEN from your CONFIG.SYS file, as in this example:

```
INSTALL=C:\DOS\FASTOPEN.EXE C:\20
```

Finally, if you're using DOS 6 with upper memory blocks, you can use LOADHIGH either from the command prompt or in your AUTOEXEC.BAT file to install FASTOPEN in upper memory, as in this example:

```
LOADHIGH=C:\DOS\FASTOPEN.EXE C:=10 D:=10 E:=10 F:=10
```

Defragmenting Your Hard Disk

As you erase old files and create new ones, DOS frees and reuses space as it becomes available. As a disk becomes older and fuller, many files can become fragmented, meaning that bits and pieces of a single file are spread throughout the disk rather than in consecutive factors. When this occurs, the drive head must move excessively (as you might actually be able to hear) when you read and write files. The result is slow disk speed.

To regain speed, you need to defragment the files. DOS 6 introduces the DEFRAG command for this purpose. Prior versions of DOS did not have much to offer in terms of defragmenting, other than the CHKDSK command with the /F switch. DEFRAG is discussed in detail in Chapter 14, "Hard Disk Management Made Simple."

Adjusting Your Hard Disk Interleave

Another means of increasing hard disk performance is by adjusting the drive's interleave, which is in essence the ratio of disk revolutions to read/write attempts. You need a third-party program to adjust your disk interleave; I can recommend this one:

SpinRite
Gibson Research Corporation
22991 La Cadena
Laguna Hills, CA 92653
(714)830-2200

 Troubleshooting

This section describes problems you might encounter while using the techniques described in this chapter.

- If you receive the message SMARTDrive: Incompatible disk partition detected, you have probably partitioned your hard drive with a third-party disk-management program that enabled you to create larger partitions than earlier versions of DOS permitted. SMARTDrive refuses to load.

  You can force SMARTDrive to run with all disk-management programs by adding the /P switch to the end of the DEVICE= command for installing SMARTDrive. You should contact Microsoft technical support personnel before using the /P switch to avoid losing your data.

■ If you receive the error message Invalid drive specification when loading files into RAMDrive, make sure the RAMDRIVE command in your CONFIG.SYS file is correct. You can also use the MEM /C command to see whether you have enough high memory available for the RAM drive.

■ If you specify RAM drives beyond the name E: in your CONFIG.SYS and your system does not create the RAM drive you specified, make sure you included the LASTDRIVE directive in your CONFIG.SYS file. The LASTDRIVE directive specifies a drive name beyond the last RAM disk. For example, if your computer has a drive beyond C: and you plan to create three RAM drives named D:, E:, and F:, your CONFIG.SYS file must contain the command LASTDRIVE=G.

Summary

You can use RAM disks, caching, and other features to speed up your system by minimizing disk access time. Many of these options are specific to a particular computer, and their features are made available to DOS through the use of device drivers. You might need to refer to the manuals that came with your computer or option board for information about using these features. In summary:

■ A RAM disk simulates a disk drive in conventional RAM, extended memory, or expanded memory and permits quicker disk operations.

■ On most computers, the device driver for installing a RAM disk is named RAMDRIVE.SYS or VDISK.SYS.

■ To use extended memory rather than conventional RAM for a RAM disk, use the /E switch with the VDISK.SYS or RAMDRIVE.SYS device driver. To use expanded memory for a RAM disk, use the /X switch for VDISK.SYS and the /A switch for RAMDRIVE.SYS.

■ Because files stored on a RAM disk are erased when you turn off the computer, use the safety procedure of creating batch programs that automatically copy data from a RAM disk to a physical disk when you exit a program.

■ Disk caching is a technique that speeds disk I/O by acting as an intermediary between RAM and the disk.

■ DOS 6 provides an enhanced, full-featured disk-caching program named SMARTDRV.SYS.

■ DOS 6 provides a new disk defragmenter program named DEFRAG.

Alan Simpson's
DOS
SECRETS
UNLEASHED

CHAPTER 22

Managing Your Screen

You have already seen how to change the colors of the DOS Shell and how to use the scroll bar and PgUp and PgDn keys to scroll through long lists of directory and file names (Chapter 10). This chapter focuses on techniques for managing the screen at the command prompt. These techniques work for all versions of DOS.

Clearing the Screen

> You cannot clear the screen while using EDIT.

Many times when you use the DOS command prompt, the screen becomes cluttered with old command lines and the output of those commands. You can eliminate that clutter by clearing the screen. Type the command CLS (short for *CLear Screen*) and press Enter. Everything but the command prompt (which now appears at the top left corner of the screen) is cleared from your screen.

Controlling Scrolling

Some DOS commands show far more lines of information than the screen can display at one time, and text scrolls off the screen too quickly for you to read. You've already seen how to use the /P switch with the DIR command so that DOS pauses after each full screen of information is presented. The next few sections discuss several more techniques to control scrolling.

Starting and Stopping Scrolling

Whenever large amounts of text are scrolling off the screen, you can always freeze the display by pressing Ctrl+S (hold down the Ctrl key and press the letter S). This key combination immediately stops the scrolling. To resume scrolling, press any character key, the Spacebar, or Ctrl+S.

If your keyboard has a Pause key, you can press that key instead of Ctrl+S to stop scrolling. To resume scrolling after pressing Pause, press any other key.

Using the *MORE* Command

In some cases, you need to be pretty quick on the keyboard to use the Ctrl+S or Pause key effectively, especially with today's high-speed computers. As an alternative, you can use the MORE command to have DOS automatically pause as each full screen of information is presented.

MORE is an *external* command. That is, it's actually a program stored in a file named MORE.COM. To use MORE, the MORE.COM file must be accessible from the current drive and directory. (If you get the Bad command or file name error when you first try to use the command, keep reading and try the alternative techniques discussed later in this section.)

There are two different syntaxes for using MORE. When you need to display the contents of lengthy text files, type MORE, followed by the < redirection symbol, followed by the name of the file whose contents you wish to view. The general syntax for this usage is

```
MORE < filename.ext
```

(*filename.ext* is the name of the file you wish to view).

When you want to use MORE in conjunction with another DOS command, use the second general syntax as shown in the following sentence. In this case, type the complete command, followed by the pipe character ¦ and the MORE command. This general syntax is as follows:

```
DOS command ¦ MORE
```

For example, assume that after you buy a new application program, you notice that a file named READ.ME is included on the program disk. You want the computer to pause each time the screen is filled with text so that you have time to read all the information. To do this, type either

```
MORE   < A:READ.ME
```

or

```
TYPE A:READ.ME ¦ MORE
```

> Notice how the MORE < READ.ME command uses the input redirection symbol to send the contents of the READ.ME file into the program invoked by the MORE command.

Although both commands use the MORE command in different ways, the result is the same. DOS displays one full screen of text and the prompt -- More --. When you see this prompt, press any key to see the next screen. Optionally, you can press Ctrl+C or Break to stop viewing the file. (To press Break, press Ctrl+Pause or Ctrl+Scroll Lock, depending on which key is marked *Break* on your keyboard.)

If the MORE command is not available on the current drive, directory, or path, change to the disk or directory that contains the MORE.COM file (usually the DOS directory in Versions 4, 5, and 6, or the root directory in earlier versions) and specify both the location and name of the file you want to view. For example, if you want to view the contents of a file named README.DOC in a directory named QUATTRO, first change to the drive and directory that contains the MORE.COM file. Then type the command

```
MORE < C:\QUATTRO\README.DOC
```

or

```
TYPE C:\QUATTRO\README.DOC ¦ MORE
```

If your computer doesn't have a hard disk, put the DOS disk that contains the MORE.COM program into drive A:, and insert the disk that contains the file with the contents you want to view in drive B:. Assuming that the file you want to view is named README.TXT and that the current drive is drive A:, type the command

```
MORE < B:README.TXT
```

or

```
TYPE B:README.TXT ¦ MORE
```

Remember, if you have a hard disk, you can make external commands, such as MORE, more accessible by setting up an appropriate PATH command, as discussed in Chapter 5, "Peak Performance in the DOS Environment."

You can use MORE with any command that displays data. For example, the TREE /F command can display the names of all files in all directories of your hard disk. To see its output one screen at a time, type the command

```
TREE C:\ /F ¦ MORE
```

Customizing the Command Prompt

You can type the command PROMPT PG to change the DOS command prompt so that it displays the current drive and directory. You can actually do quite a bit more to alter the command prompt. Table 22.1 lists all the codes that you can use with the PROMPT command to customize your command prompt.

Table 22.1. Symbols used with the PROMPT command.

Code	Effect
$$	Displays the $ character
$_	Breaks prompt onto a second line
$B	Displays the ¦ character
$D	Displays the current date
$E	Generates an escape character
$G	Displays the > character
$H	Backspaces one character
$L	Displays the < character
$N	Displays the current drive
$P	Displays the current drive and directory
$Q	Displays the = character
$T	Displays the current time
$V	Displays the current version of DOS
other characters	Other characters are displayed literally.

You can use these codes to change the prompt at any time. For example, the last entry in the table means that any characters other than the listed codes are displayed *literally*, or exactly as you type them in the prompt command. If at the command prompt you type

```
PROMPT At your service -- Please enter a command:
```

and press Enter, every command prompt that DOS displays thereafter will read At your service -- Please enter a command:.

Next, type this command:

```
PROMPT $D $B $T$G
```

When you press Enter, the command prompt displays the current date ($D) followed by a blank space, the ¦ symbol ($B), another blank space, the current time ($T), and the > symbol ($G). (Note that the blank spaces in the prompt correspond to the blank spaces you typed in the PROMPT command.)

```
Thu  01-14-1993 ¦ 10:31:42.70>
```

> The $_ code uses the underscore character, not the hyphen. That is, it's $_ rather than $-.

To break a lengthy prompt into two lines, use the $_ code where you want to split the prompt. For example, if you type the command

```
PROMPT $D$_$T$G
```

DOS displays a command prompt with the current date on one line and the current time and a > symbol on the second line, as follows:

```
Thu  01-14-1993
10:32:42:68>
```

The $V (version number) code does not break the command prompt into two lines, so you need to use the $_ code. For example, if you type

```
PROMPT $V$_$D$G
```

the command prompt displays the current version of DOS on one line, and the current date and the > symbol on the next, as follows:

```
IBM DOS Version 6.00
Thu 01-14-1993
```

You can use the Backspace code ($H) to erase parts of a prompt. For example, suppose that you want your command prompt to display the current date minus the year, followed by the ¦ character, the current drive and directory, and the > symbol. To do so, you must type this command:

```
PROMPT $D$H$H$H$H$H $B $P$G
```

When you press Enter, DOS displays a new prompt that resembles the following (of course, it will display today's date and your current directory):

```
Thu 01-14 ¦ C:\DOS>
```

Note that the command uses five Backspace ($H) symbols to erase the last five characters of the current date (/1993).

You can also combine text and codes in the PROMPT command. For example, type this command:

```
PROMPT Today is $D$_Current drive and directory is $P$G
```

When you press Enter, the prompt appears as follows (with today's date displayed in place of Fri 01-01-93 and your current drive and directory in place of C:\DOS):

```
Today is Fri 01-01-93
Current drive and directory is C:\DOS>
```

If you want to return to your more familiar command prompt, type PROMPT PG.

Using ANSI Codes to Control the Screen and Keyboard

Many years ago when computers were all room-size giants, the American National Standards Institute (ANSI) developed a standardized coding system for managing the interface between keyboards, computers, and monitors. They did so to make software more *portable*—that is, so that programs could be used without modification on many different types of computers and monitors.

DOS comes with a *device driver*, stored in a file named ANSI.SYS, that uses the ANSI coding system to send characters and images to your computer screen. The file is called a *device driver* because it literally drives a device; that is, it tells a device (in this case, the monitor) what to do.

To see whether your computer is currently set up to accept ANSI codes, you have to use the TYPE command to view the contents of your CONFIG.SYS file. Because CONFIG.SYS is always stored on the startup drive or directory, the file is easy to find—if it exists.

On a hard disk, type the following command at the DOS command prompt:

```
TYPE C:\CONFIG.SYS
```

On a computer that boots from a floppy disk, insert your Startup disk in drive A:, make sure that drive A: is your current drive, and type the following command:

```
TYPE CONFIG.SYS
```

If your computer can accept ANSI codes, the CONFIG.SYS file contains the command DEVICE = followed by the location and name of the ANSI.SYS file. For example, on a computer that boots from the hard disk, you should see either the command

```
DEVICE = C:\ANSI.SYS
```

or perhaps the command

```
DEVICE = C:\DOS\ANSI.SYS
```

On a computer that starts from a floppy disk, you should see the command

```
DEVICE = A:\ANSI.SYS
```

Some programs require that your CONFIG.SYS file load the ANSI.SYS file. The documentation of these programs will inform you of this requirement.

If your CONFIG.SYS file does not set up the ANSI.SYS device driver, you can modify the file using the general techniques described in Chapter 6, "Getting It All Started with AUTOEXEC.BAT and CONFIG.SYS." However, it is not absolutely necessary to do so, unless you want to customize screen colors at the command prompt or redefine keys on your keyboard (as discussed in Chapter 23, "Customizing Your Keyboard").

To modify your CONFIG.SYS file to include the ANSI.SYS device driver, you must first be sure that DOS can find the ANSI.SYS file as soon as you turn on the computer. That is, if you boot your computer from a floppy disk, the ANSI.SYS file must be stored on that disk. The CONFIG.SYS file must also contain the command

```
DEVICE = ANSI.SYS
```

If your computer boots from a hard disk, locate the directory that contains ANSI.SYS FILE (probably the root directory or the DOS directory). When you modify the CONFIG.SYS file, be sure to specify the complete path and file name in the DEVICE command, as in the following examples:

```
DEVICE = C:\ANSI.SYS
```

or

```
DEVICE = C:\DOS\ANSI.SYS
```

After you change the CONFIG.SYS file, remember that modifications do not take effect until you reboot the computer. However, from then on, DOS automatically issues these commands every time you start your computer.

Modifying Screen Colors and Attributes

DOS 6 users already know how to change the color scheme of the DOS Shell. If you are using another version of DOS (or you prefer the DOS 6 command prompt), you can use ANSI codes to customize the screen colors displayed at the command prompt, provided that your computer is set up to accept ANSI codes (as discussed in the preceding section).

To color the screen, you use the PROMPT command in conjunction with special codes called *escape sequences*. An escape sequence is a series of characters that begin with the Escape (or Esc) key character. Recall from Table 22.1 that you can use the $e symbol in the PROMPT command to specify the Escape key character.

The general syntax for using an escape sequence in the PROMPT command is

```
PROMPT $e[xxm
```

in which *xx* is a one-digit *attribute* number or a two-digit color number. Table 22.2 lists the complete escape sequences for controlling screen colors on monitors that are capable of displaying color.

Table 22.2. Escape sequences for changing screen colors.

Color	Foreground	Background
Black	$e[30m	$e[40m
Red	$e[31m	$e[41m
Green	$e[32m	$e[42m
Yellow	$e[33m	$e[43m
Blue	$e[34m	$e[44m
Magenta	$e[35m	$e[45m
Cyan	$e[36m	$e[46m
White	$e[37m	$e[47m

Table 22.3 lists the escape sequences for controlling special attributes on both color and monochrome screens. You can use these special attributes in conjunction with colors (on color monitors). Note that these one-digit escape sequences are similar to the two-digit codes used for coloring the screen.

Table 22.3. Escape sequences for changing screen attributes.

Attribute	Escape Sequence
None	$e[0m
High intensity	$e[1m
Underline (monochrome only)	$e[4m
Blinking	$e[5m
Reverse video	$e[7m
Invisible	$e[8m

Be sure to use the lowercase letters e and m in the escape sequences. If you make a mistake, the DOS prompt displays all characters literally from the point of the error to the right. Retype the command to correct it.

The following gives you practice using some of these escape sequences at the DOS command prompt. However, keep in mind that you might not see any changes until you either clear the screen or start typing again.

To switch the screen display to reverse video, type the following command:

```
PROMPT $e[7m
```

Reverse video reverses the foreground and background colors or shades used on the screen. For example, if your screen normally displays dark letters on a light background, reverse video displays light letters against a dark background.

Not much seems to happen at first (except that the command prompt disappears). However, watch what happens when you enter any command that displays text, such as DIR. The displayed text appears in reverse video, as shown in Figure 22.1.

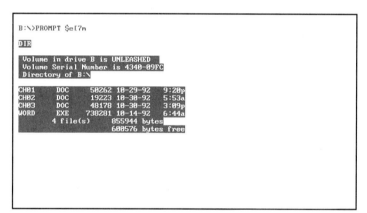

Figure 22.1.
Sample display
in reverse
video.

After changing screen colors or attributes, you can enter a new PROMPT command to redefine the command prompt, without losing the current attributes or colors. For example, to redisplay the familiar command prompt, type the command PROMPT PG.

Now try the blinking attribute; type the command

PROMPT $e[5m

To see the results, enter a command (such as DIR) that displays text on the screen. Notice that the reverse video attribute remains in effect, and now blinking has been added to that attribute.

To return to the normal screen display, remove all attributes by typing the command

```
PROMPT $e[0m
```

Then enter the CLS command to clear the screen and the PROMPT PG command to redisplay your command prompt.

> If you set the screen foreground and background to the same color, you won't be able to see what you are typing on the screen. If you cannot see what you are typing, carefully enter the command PROMPT $e[0m$P$G or press Ctrl+Alt+Del to reboot.

If you have a color monitor, try some different color schemes. Use any combination of the foreground and background color escape sequences shown in Table 22.2. For example, to display yellow text on a blue background, type the command

```
PROMPT $e[33m $e[44m
```

Then enter a command that displays text (such as DIR). If yellow looks more like brown, switch to high intensity by typing the command

```
PROMPT $e[1m
```

Again, enter a command to display text (such as DIR) and see the effects of these PROMPT commands.

You can use any combination of screen attributes, colors, and the command prompt style codes in a single PROMPT command if you wish. For example, to simultaneously set the screen colors to high-intensity red letters on a black background and also define the command prompt, type the command

```
PROMPT $e[40m$e[1m$e[31m$P$G
```

Keep in mind that DOS reads the code strings defined in the PROMPT command every time it displays the command prompt. Therefore, you can turn on an attribute at the beginning of the prompt and then turn it off at the end of the prompt, so that only the command prompt itself uses the defined attribute.

For example, suppose that you want to display your screen in normal colors, but you want to display the command prompt in reverse video. To do so, first return to the normal screen colors and attributes by typing the commands

```
PROMPT $e[0m$P$G
```

and

```
CLS
```

Next, type a PROMPT command that turns on reverse video, displays the command prompt, and then turns off reverse video, as follows:

```
PROMPT $e[7m$P$G$e[0m
```

As Figure 22.2 shows, only the command prompt displays in reverse video.

```
C:\DOS>PROMPT $e[7m$P$G$e[0m

C:\DOS>DATE
Current date is Thu 11-19-1992
Enter new date (mm-dd-yy):

C:\DOS>TIME
Current time is  3:06:24.20p
Enter new time:

C:\DOS>
```

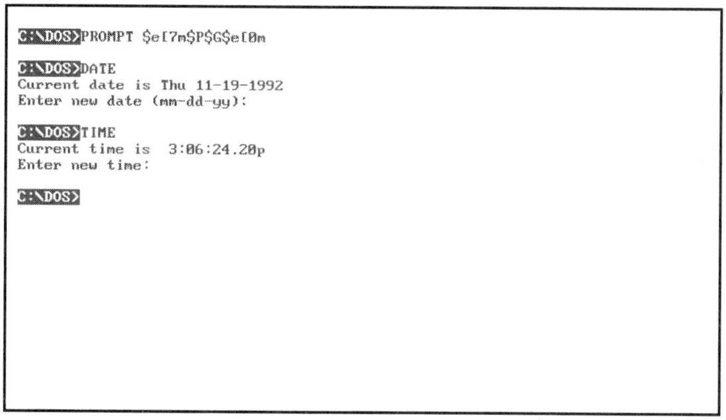

*Figure 22.2.
The command
prompt
displays in
reverse video.*

Saving *PROMPT* Settings

The one problem with designing a custom command prompt that uses fancy display attributes and colors is that DOS forgets it as soon as you turn off the computer. However, you can have DOS immediately activate your custom prompt at startup by including the PROMPT command in your AUTOEXEC.BAT file.

> Remember, you can only use screen attributes and colors if your CONFIG.SYS file loads the ANSI device driver.

You can place the PROMPT command on any line in the AUTOEXEC.BAT file. (However, DOS 4, 5, and 6 users must remember to leave the DOSSHELL command as the last command in AUTOEXEC.BAT.) Remember, you must edit the AUTOEXEC.BAT as a DOS text file, and you must store it in the root directory on the proper drive for your computer. The following is a sample AUTOEXEC.BAT file with a customized PROMPT command:

```
@ECHO OFF
SET COMSPEC=C:\DOS\COMMAND.COM
PATH C:\WP;C:\DOS;C:\UTILS;C:\DBASE;C:\WINDOWS
VERIFY OFF
PROMPT $e[7m$P$G$e[0m
C:\DOS ¦ MOUSE.COM
APPEND /E
APPEND C:\DOS
PRINT /D:LPT1
DOSSHELL
```

Controlling the Screen's Character Size

Normally, DOS displays 80 columns of text across the screen. However, you can double the size of the letters on the screen by telling DOS to display only 40 columns of text across the screen. To do so you must use the DOS MODE command. Table 22.4 lists the codes that you can use with the MODE command to control the display on your monitor.

You can also use the MODE command to configure other devices.

Table 22.4. Options for controlling the screen display with MODE.

Code	Effect
40	Sets the display width to 40 characters on a color graphics screen (does not affect colors)
80	Sets the display width to 80 characters on a color graphics screen (does not affect colors)
BW40	Sets the display width to 40 characters and the colors to black and white on a color graphics screen
BW80	Sets the display width to 80 characters and the colors to black and white on a color graphics screen
CO40	Sets the display width to 40 characters and allows color on a color graphics screen
CO80	Sets the display width to 80 characters and allows color on a color graphics screen
MONO	Sets the display width to 80 characters and allows only a monochrome display (the only setting available with monochrome display adapters)

Changing the character size affects command prompt
screens only, not the DOS Shell or EDIT.

MODE is an external DOS program. To use MODE, the MODE.COM
file must be accessible from the current disk or directory (otherwise,
DOS displays the Bad command or file name error message). If you
are using the DOS 5 Shell, you should exit the Shell using the F3
key (not the Shift+F9 key) so that the copy of the Shell remaining in
RAM does not conflict with the MODE program that will be loaded
into memory.

If you have a color monitor, and you are currently looking at the
command prompt, try the MODE command by typing the following:

MODE 40

Next, type any command that displays text (such as DIR). As
Figure 22.3 shows, the display uses much larger characters.

```
B:\>DIR

 Volume  in drive  B  is  UNLEASHED
 Volume  Serial  Number  is  4340-09FC
 Directory of  B:\

CH01        DOC        50262  10-29-92      9:20p
CH02        DOC        19223  10-30-92      5:53a
CH03        DOC        48178  10-30-92      3:09p
WORD        EXE       738281  10-14-92      6:44a
        4 file(s)         855944  bytes
                          600576  bytes  free


B:\>
```

Figure 22.3.
A screen
displaying 40
characters per
line.

To switch back to the 80-column display, type the command

MODE 80

Troubleshooting

The most common error message that DOS might display while you are trying some of the examples in this chapter is:

```
Invalid parameter
```

This means that a switch or option used in a command is misspelled, or that the forward slash (/), backslash (\), or pipe (¦) characters are used incorrectly.

Summary

This chapter presents commands and techniques for managing your screen.

- The CLS command clears the screen.

- The Ctrl+S key combination and the Pause key, as well as the MORE command, enable you to control the scrolling of text on the screen.

- You can use the PROMPT command to customize the command prompt.

- If your CONFIG.SYS file loads the ANSI.SYS file during startup, you can use the PROMPT command to control screen attributes and colors.

Alan Simpson's
DOS SECRETS UNLEASHED

C H A P T E R   2 3

Customizing Your Keyboard

If your CONFIG.SYS file includes the DEVICE=ANSI.SYS command, you can customize your keyboard to perform special tasks. It's extremely unlikely that you would want to redefine one of the standard keys, such as making the A key generate the letter Z (although you could do so if you had the desire). A more practical application uses the procedure to assign functions to special key combinations that are not already defined by DOS, such as Ctrl+F3 or Alt+F7.

Redefining Function Keys

The general procedure for redefining function keys is very similar to the one used for defining screen attributes and colors. You use the PROMPT command followed by an escape sequence. However, you must also include a code that indicates the key you want to redefine, the character or characters you want the key to display (enclosed in quotation marks), the number 13 (which is the code for the Enter key), and finally a lowercase p (rather than an m), which signals the end of the sequence. This general syntax is as follows:

```
PROMPT $e[0;key number;"characters to type";13p
```

Table 23.1 lists the numbers used to specify keys that you might want to redefine. Those marked with an asterisk already serve useful functions in DOS (and particularly the DOS Shell), so you should avoid redefining those keys.

Table 23.1. Numbers assigned to function keys.

Key	Number	Key	Number	Key	Number	Key	Number
F1*	59	Shift+F1	84	Ctrl+F1	94	Alt+F1*	104
F2*	60	Shift+F2	85	Ctrl+F2	95	Alt+F2	105
F3*	61	Shift+F3	86	Ctrl+F3	96	Alt+F3	106
F4*	62	Shift+F4	87	Ctrl+F4	97	Alt+F4	107

Key	Number	Key	Number	Key	Number	Key	Number
F5*	63	Shift+F5	88	Ctrl+F5	98	Alt+F5	108
F6*	64	Shift+F6	89	Ctrl+F6	99	Alt+F6	109
F7	65	Shift+F7	90	Ctrl+F7	100	Alt+F7	110
F8	66	Shift+F8	91	Ctrl+F8	101	Alt+F8	111
F9*	67	Shift+F9*	92	Ctrl+F9	102	Alt+F9	112
F10*	68	Shift+F10	93	Ctrl+F10	103	Alt+F10	113

Already assigned a function by DOS.

Suppose that you want to redefine the Shift+F10 key combination (number 93) so that it displays the names of files when you press it. First, type the following command at the command prompt:

```
PROMPT $e[0;93;"DIR";13p
```

After you press Enter, the command prompt is no longer visible, so enter the command PROMPT PG to redisplay it.

To test your new function key assignment, press Shift+F10 (hold down the Shift key and press the F10 key). Your screen displays the names of files on the current drive or directory.

Awkward commands that are difficult to remember are especially good candidates for redefinition as function keys. For example, in order to use the GRAPHICS command to prepare a wide-carriage IBM Personal Graphics Printer to print graphics screens, you might need to type the command GRAPHICS GRAPHICSWIDE /R /PRINTBOX:LCD. The following command assigns the appropriate command to the Shift+F8 key:

```
PROMPT $e[0;92;"GRAPHICS GRAPHICSWIDE /R /
PRINTBOX:LCD";13p
```

After you initially enter the command, your prompt will disappear. You can enter another PROMPT command, such as PROMPT pg to bring back your original command prompt.

To set up your printer to print graphics displays, you need only press Shift+F8. Note, however, that the function key works only during the current session (before you turn off the computer) and only if the GRAPHICS.COM program is available from the current drive and directory.

Assigning Multiple Commands to a Function Key

You can assign two or more commands to a function key, as long as you use the 13 (Enter) code to separate them. For example, the following command sets up the Shift+F7 key so that it first clears the screen (CLS) and then displays a wide directory listing (DIR /W):

```
PROMPT $e[0;90;"CLS";13;"DIR /W";13p
```

Using Function Keys to Type Text

Redefining function keys can be handy for more than entering commands. For example, assume that you regularly need to type your return address on envelopes. The following command sets up the Shift+F6 key to do this job for you, assuming of course, that you substitute your own name and address for John Q. Melon's. Note that you must type the command as one long line, even if it wraps to the next screen line. (Also, the entire escape sequence cannot exceed 128 characters.) Be sure that you include blank spaces only where indicated.

```
PROMPT $e[0;89;"COPY CON PRN";13;"John Q. Melon";13;"123 Oak Tree
Lane";13;"Glendora, CA 91749";13;26;13;"ECHO ";12;">PRN";13p
```

After you define the key, pressing Shift+F6 displays the output shown in Figure 23.1 on your screen. Of course, the name and address are also sent to the printer.

```
C:\>PROMPT $e[0;89;"COPY CON PRN";13;"John Q. Melon";13;"123 Oak Tree Lane";13;"
Glendora, CA 91749";13;26;13;"ECHO";12;">PRN";13p

PROMPT $P$G

C:\>COPY CON PRN
John Q. Melon
123 Oak Tree Lane
Glendora, CA 91749
^Z
        1 file(s) copied

C:\>ECHO^L>PRN

C:\>
```

Figure 23.1. Result of pressing Shift+F6 after redefining the key.

I'll review this key definition so that you can see how it works. First, COPY CON PRN;13 types the COPY CON PRN command and presses Enter so that the following text is sent to the printer. Then, the name, address, and city, state, zip lines are typed, each followed by the Enter key code so that they are placed on separate lines.

The 26 code that you see in the command causes DOS to press Ctrl+Z, the code necessary to end the COPY CON PRN command (it appears as ^Z in Figure 23.1). Then the sequence "ECHO ";12; " >PRN";13p types the ECHO ^L PRN command and presses Enter to eject the page from the printer.

How did I know that the 26 code types Ctrl+Z and that the 12 code types Ctrl+L? Easy—the Ctrl key combinations are numbered from 1 to 26, starting at A. That is, Ctrl+A is number 1, Ctrl+B is 2, and so on. Because L is the 12th letter of the alphabet, its numeric code is 12, and because Z is the 26th letter of the alphabet, its numeric code is 26.

The main problem with redefining function key definitions is that they are lost the moment you turn off your computer. Nor are key definition commands particularly good candidates for the

AUTOEXEC.BAT file, because other commands may reset them during the startup procedure. However, as you learned in Chapter 12, "Simple Batch Programs," you can store many key definitions in *batch programs*; then you need to type only one command to re-instate all your custom key definitions.

However, keep in mind that many application programs, including word processors and spreadsheets, assign their own commands to the function keys. Therefore, your custom key definition might work only when the DOS command prompt is displayed.

Resetting the Function Keys

To reset a function key to its original definition, follow the 0;*key number* portion of the command with a semicolon and a repeat of the 0;*key number*. For example, to reset the Shift+F10 key (number 93) to its original definition, enter the following command:

```
PROMPT $e[0;93;0;93p
```

DOSKEY and Commercial Keyboard Customizing Packages

In Chapter 13, "Customizing DOS," you learned how to use the DOS 6 DOSKEY command to create *macros*, which also let you quickly execute long, complicated commands. Because you can give these macros descriptive names, they are sometimes easier to remember and use than redefining the function keys.

You can also use commercial *keyboard macro* programs to customize your keyboard. Most of these programs enable you to redefine a key by recording a series of keystrokes; therefore, you don't have to deal with long strings of strange symbols. Many can also be used in conjunction with other programs on your computer, so your custom key definitions are not lost when you switch from one program to the next. Following are the names and manufacturers of some keyboard macro programs:

Keyworks
Alpha Software Corp.
1 North Ave.
Burlington, MA 01803
(617) 229-2924

ProKey
Rosesoft, Inc.
P.O. Box 45880
Seattle, WA 98145-0880
(206) 282-0454

SuperKey
Borland International, Inc.
4585 Scotts Valley Dr.
Scotts Valley, CA 95066
(408) 438-8400

 Troubleshooting

The most common error message that DOS might display while you are trying the examples in this chapter is

```
Invalid Parameter
```

This means that a switch or option used in a command is misspelled, or that the forward slash (/), backslash (\), or pipe (¦) characters are used incorrectly.

Summary

This chapter presents commands and techniques for customizing your keyboard.

- If your CONFIG.SYS file loads the ANSI.SYS file during startup, you can use the PROMPT command to assign text and commands to function keys.

- You can use the DOSKEY command to create macros, which enable you to quickly execute long, complicated commands.

- You can purchase commercial keyboard macro programs to customize your keyboard.

Alan Simpson's
DOS SECRETS UNLEASHED

C H A P T E R   2 4

Controlling Your Printers

If you have followed the command-prompt examples in this book, you've already seen redirection symbols and device names. For example, the command DIR > PRN sends output from the DIR command to the printer. The command TREE > PRN sends output from the TREE command to the printer.

Some device names define a *port*. You can think of a port as a plug on the back of your computer to which a device, such as a printer, is attached. For example, if you have two printers attached to your computer on ports LPT1 and LPT2, typing a command such as DIR > LPT2 sends output to your second printer rather than the first.

If you use the > PRN symbol and device name but it does not send output to the printer, perhaps you have a serial printer attached to the COM1 port. In that case, try typing the command DIR > COM1. In fact, if you are not sure which port your printer is hooked to, you can experiment with different device names and the DIR > command until you find the device name that is accessing the printer.

As you will see, DOS offers you great flexibility in using device names and redirection symbols.

Sending Information to Your Printer

Any text that you display on your screen can be easily sent to your printer. You've already used the > redirection symbol with the PRN device name to channel the output of some commands to the printer. For example, DIR > PRN prints all the file names in a directory. The command TYPE *filename.ext* > PRN prints the contents of a file. There are other ways to send information to the printer as well, as the following sections describe.

Copying Screen Text

When the command prompt is displayed, you can send a copy of whatever is on your screen (called a *screen dump*) to the printer by pressing the Shift+Print Screen key (on some keyboards, Print Screen is abbreviated Print Scrn or Prt Sc).

To try this procedure, be sure that the DOS command prompt is displayed on your screen, and then enter the command DIR /W. Then press Shift+Print Screen (hold down the Shift key and press the Print Screen key).

There are two points to keep in mind about using the Print Screen key to "dump" text from the screen to the printer. First of all, those of you who have laser printers might not see the printed results immediately. Instead, you might need to eject the current page from the printer to see the printed screen dump (as discussed in the next section).

Second, many printers cannot display graphics images (such as the DOS Shell) that are displayed on your screen. Read the section titled "Printing Graphics" later in this chapter before using the Print Screen key to print screen graphics.

Ejecting a Page

Most printers enable you to eject a page from the printer by pressing buttons on the front of the printer. However, it is often easier to let DOS do this task; use the DOS ECHO command with the form-feed character (Ctrl+L) and the printer redirection symbol (> PRN). To use this technique, follow these steps:

1. Type ECHO and press the Spacebar.

2. Press Ctrl+L; the screen displays ^L.

3. Press the Spacebar and type > PRN.

At this point, your command should look as follows:

```
ECHO ^L PRN
```

If it does, press Enter, and your printer will eject the current page.

Keeping Track of the Top of the Page

One of the most common complaints one hears about computers and printers is that the computer does not properly print text on pages. For example, your computer might start printing a new page in the middle of one piece of paper, keep printing that same page onto the second piece of paper, and then start printing the next page on the third piece of paper. This can be very irritating!

If your printer uses tractor-feed (continuous-form) paper, you can follow two simple rules to avoid this problem:

- Be sure that the page perforation is directly above the printer's printing head before you turn on the printer and the computer.

- After you turn on the printer and the computer, never manually crank the paper through the printer to get to the next page.

The reasoning behind these two rules is simple. First, whenever you start your computer, DOS assumes that the top of a page is aligned just above the printer head. Second, DOS keeps track of the top of each page by counting the number of lines it sends to the printer.

If the paper is not properly aligned when you start the computer, DOS is off the mark at the outset. Even if the paper is aligned properly when you turn on the computer, DOS cannot detect your manually cranking paper through the printer. When you do that, its count of how many lines of the page have been moved through the printer becomes incorrect, and it no longer can properly align text on the page.

Ctrl+J (^J) is called the *line feed* character because it feeds one blank line to the printer.

Now, you might be wondering how you can eject a partially printed page or insert extra blank lines without manually cranking the printer platen. Well, use the ECHO ^L > PRN command discussed previously to eject the entire page. If you want only to move the paper a few lines on the current page, use the command ECHO ^J > PRN (press Ctrl+J to type the ^J symbol). After you type the command and press Enter, you can print additional blank lines by pressing F3 and Enter. (Recall that F3 repeats the preceding DOS command.)

Note that some printers also provide buttons, such as "Set TOF" (Top Of Form), to help you keep track of alignment. See your printer manual for additional information about page alignment and the use of printer control buttons.

Slaving the Printer

Another way to send text to the printer is to *slave* the printer so that it prints all text as it appears on-screen. Use the Ctrl+Print Screen keys as a toggle to slave and *unslave* the printer.

For example, at the command prompt, hold down the Ctrl key and press the Print Screen (or Print Scrn or Prt Sc) key; then release both keys. Now enter any command that displays text, such as DIR. When you press Enter, the printer prints everything that appears on your screen (including the DIR command itself).

To unslave the printer, press Ctrl+Print Screen again. Now the printer is no longer a slave to the screen. (If you've been trying the examples, type the ECHO ^L > PRN command to eject the printed page from the printer.)

Another way to slave the printer is to make it copy exactly what you type at the keyboard. Although doing so turns your computer into an overpriced typewriter, the technique is handy for quick and easy jobs such as addressing envelopes. The basic procedure is to use the COPY command with CON (the DOS device name for the console) as the source and PRN as the destination.

For example, to address an envelope, put the envelope into the printer. Then type the command COPY CON PRN at the command prompt, as shown at the top of Figure 24.1. After you enter this command, the command prompt disappears, and you can type any text you want. (Use the Backspace key to make corrections.) In the figure, I inserted several blank lines by pressing Enter a few times; then I typed the name and address, which I indented using the Spacebar.

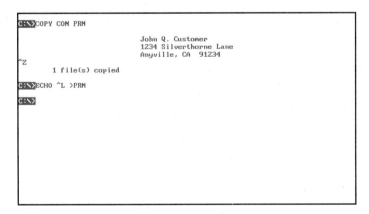

Figure 24.1. Using the computer to address an envelope.

After you type the name and address, press Ctrl+Z (which appears as ^Z), and press Enter. At this point, DOS prints the text on the printer and displays the message 1 file(s) copied on-screen.

To eject the envelope from the printer, type the ECHO ^L PRN command.

Copying Files to the Printer

You've already seen how to use the TYPE command and the > PRN redirection symbol to print the contents of a file. You can also use the COPY command to copy the contents of text files to the printer. In addition, because COPY (unlike TYPE) permits ambiguous file names, you can print several files with one command.

To copy a file to the printer, use the standard COPY command syntax, specifying the name of the file you want to print as the source, and the device name PRN (for printer) as the destination. For example, to print all the files that have the extension .BAT from the root directory of drive C:, type the command

```
COPY C:\*.BAT PRN
```

> Keep in mind that you can print only text files, not programs or files that use special formatting codes. When in doubt, first view the contents of the file using the TYPE command. If the file's contents look OK on-screen, they will look fine on the printer as well.

Printing Graphics

> All programs that are capable of displaying graphs are also capable of printing them on any dot matrix or laser printer, so you might never need to use the GRAPHICS program and Shift+Print Screen keys to print a graph.

If you have an IBM, an Epson, or a compatible printer that is capable of displaying graphics, you can use Shift+Print Screen to copy a graphics image from the screen to the printer only after you've loaded the DOS GRAPHICS program into memory. To load the GRAPHICS program, change to the directory that contains the file named GRAPHICS.COM, and then enter the command GRAPHICS at the command prompt.

After you run the GRAPHICS program, it stays in memory (RAM) until you turn off the computer. (It uses about 5K of memory while resident in RAM.) For the remainder of your session with the computer (that is, until you turn off your computer or reboot), you can use the Shift+Print Screen key combination to dump both text and graphics to your printer.

If your screen displays low-resolution graphics, graphics images are printed in the vertical format. If you use a high-resolution graphics screen, your graphics images are printed sideways (horizontally) across the page.

> If in doubt about low- and high-resolution graphics, try the procedure and see what happens; you can't do any harm.

If you always want to have the option to print graphs using Shift+Print Screen, include the GRAPHICS command in your AUTOEXEC.BAT file. In fact, if you are using DOS 6, the installation process might already have performed this step for you. Use the View option or the TYPE command to view the contents of your AUTOEXEC.BAT.

If you see the command A:\GRAPHICS or C:\DOS\GRAPHICS, the graphics program is automatically loaded when you start your computer. You can print graphics at any time by pressing Ctrl+Print Screen (provided that your printer is capable of printing graphics).

Entering the GRAPHICS command by itself is generally sufficient for printing graphs with Ctrl+Print Screen. However, you can use several options with the GRAPHICS command to control color printers and to reverse the colors on the printed copy.

Controlling Dot-Matrix Print Size

If you have an IBM or Epson dot-matrix printer (or any compatible printer), it is probably printing at the default setting of 80 characters per line and six lines to the inch. You can use the MODE command to change the number of characters per line to 132 or the number of lines printed per inch to eight.

If you have the right printer, and the MODE.COM file is available in the current drive or directory, you can try some combinations by entering the following commands (be sure to press Enter after typing each command):

```
MODE LPT1:COLS=132 LINES=6
DIR >PRN
MODE LPT1:COLS=132 LINES=8
DIR >PRN
MODE LPT1:COLS=80 LINES=8
DIR >PRN
MODE LPT1:COLS=80 LINES=6
DIR >PRN
```

Controlling Laser-Printer Print Size

If you have a Hewlett-Packard LaserJet printer, you can use a few tricks to take advantage of its special features, such as compressed print and landscape mode. However, the required codes are awkward to type at the command prompt. Therefore, in Chapter 29, "Batch Programs Unleashed," you will create your own program to facilitate using your laser printer's special features.

Background Printing

The main problem with using commands such as TYPE CONFIG.SYS
> PRN and COPY C:*.BAT PRN to print text files is that you have to
wait until the printing is done before you can use your computer
again. As an alternative, you can tell DOS to print *in the background*,
therefore enabling you to continue using the computer while the
printer is printing.

DOS accomplishes this background printing by using small slices
of time when the computer is doing nothing else to send some text
to the printer. For example, while you are reading something on-
screen or thinking about what you want to do next, DOS can send
quite a bit of text to the printer. Most printers, in turn, can store some
text in a *buffer* (memory inside the printer) and therefore can accept
data from the computer faster than the printer can print it. For example, in two seconds DOS might be able to send enough text to
keep your printer busy for a minute or two.

Although background printing with the PRINT command is easy,
each version of DOS uses a slightly different technique, so I'll discuss each version separately.

Using Print from the DOS Shell

To start background printing from the DOS Shell, you use the Print
option in the File pull-down menu in the File List section of the Shell.
This is usually a simple procedure. Use the following general steps
to print one or more files:

1. First, be sure the Shell is displaying the File List. If both the
   File List and the Program List are displayed, be sure that the
   highlight is currently in one of the File List areas.

2. Use the Drives area and the Directory Tree area of the Shell
   to select the drive and directory that contains the file you
   want to print.

The Print option (like the TYPE command) can reliably print only ASCII text files. If in doubt about the contents of a file, use the View File Contents option to preview the file. If the file's contents look OK on-screen, the printed copy will probably be fine as well. If your program has a print-to-file option, these files can be printed from the DOS Shell.

3. Move the highlight to the Files List, and select as many as 10 files to print by highlighting the appropriate file names.

4. After selecting files to print, press F10 (or Alt) and Enter to pull down the File menu (shown in Figure 24.2).

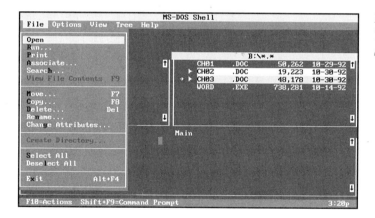

Figure 24.2.
The File pull-down menu.

If the Print option is shaded and unavailable on the File pull-down menu, press Esc to leave the menu, and continue reading the following instructions.

5. Select the Print option.

DOS immediately begins printing each file. If you selected multiple files, each file begins on a new page. Notice that you can continue to use your computer as DOS prints the files; you can even select additional files to print.

If you were unable to complete the preceding steps because the Print option on the menu was shaded and unavailable, but you are sure that you selected at least one file name to print, the PRINT command is not initialized. To initialize PRINT, press the F3 key to display the command prompt, type PRINT /D:LPT1, and press Enter. Then type the command DOSSHELL to return to the Shell. Select the files to print from the Files List again; then select Print from the File pull-down menu.

> You can add the PRINT /D:LPT1 command to your AUTOEXEC.BAT file provided that the PRINT.COM file is available from the start-up directory or diskette when you first turn on the computer. For example, if you boot from a hard disk and PRINT.COM is stored on the DOS directory, add the command C:\DOS\PRINT /D:LPT1 to your AUTOEXEC.BAT file.

If you start your computer from a diskette and PRINT.COM is on the Start-up diskette, add the command PRINT /D:LPT1 to your AUTOEXEC.BAT file. Be sure to place this command before the DOSSHELL command in AUTOEXEC.BAT.

Using *PRINT* from the Command Prompt

To use the PRINT command from the command prompt, first be sure that the PRINT.COM file is available on the current diskette or directory (or is in a directory defined in your path command). Then enter the command PRINT followed by the location and name of the file you want to print. For example, to print a copy of the AUTOEXEC.BAT file on a hard disk, type the command

```
PRINT C:\AUTOEXEC.BAT
```

If this is the first time you've used PRINT in the current session, DOS displays the message

```
Name of list device [PRN]:
```

PRN is the device name of your main printer. To use this suggested device name, press Enter. DOS then displays the message

```
C:\AUTOEXEC.BAT is currently being printed
```

and begins printing. In addition, the command prompt immediately appears on your screen, ready to accept new commands while DOS is printing your file.

You can even enter additional PRINT commands while DOS is printing a file. DOS puts other files that need to be printed in the queue, and it prints them when the printer becomes available. You can put a maximum of 10 files into the queue for printing (unless you use the /Q switch to expand the size of the queue).

Checking the Queue

If you want to see the names of the files that are currently lined up in the queue for printing, enter the command PRINT with no additional file names or switches.

Canceling a Print Job

PRINT provides two switches for canceling a print job: /T terminates all printing, and /C cancels the printing of a specific file or group of files. For example, suppose that you type the command

```
PRINT C:\DOSBOOK\CHAP?.TXT
```

to print a group of files (for example, CHAP1.TXT, CHAP2.TXT, and so on). After DOS displays a message such as

```
C:\DOSBOOK\CHAP1.DOC is currently being printed
C:\DOSBOOK\CHAP2.DOC is in queue
C:\DOSBOOK\CHAP3.DOC is in queue
```

the DOS prompt reappears, and you can type new commands. The printer then prints each file in the queue.

> DOS Shell users must exit the Shell and type the PRINT /C or PRINT /T command at the command prompt to terminate a printing job.

To remove a file from the queue so that it is not printed, use the PRINT command followed by the file name and the /C switch. For example, to remove CHAP2.DOC from the queue, type

```
PRINT C:\DOSBOOK\CHAP2.DOC /C
```

To cancel the printing of the current file and all remaining files in the queue, use the /T switch with the PRINT command, as follows:

```
PRINT /T
```

DOS then displays a message such as All files canceled by operator. Print queue is empty to inform you that all printing has stopped. (If your printer contains a buffer, it might continue to print for a short time.)

Using *PRINT* with Application Programs

> PRINT might not be able to use the formatting codes, such as boldface and underlining, that your word processor offers.

Most application programs, such as spreadsheets and word processors, store special codes in the files you create. If you try to print such a file directly, using the PRINT command, the output will probably be a mess. However, virtually all application programs provide the capability to print to a file or to store a copy of the file in

ASCII text format. (Refer to the application program's manual for specific instructions.) You can use the DOS PRINT command to print any file that has been stored in ASCII text format.

For example, suppose that you use the Lotus 1-2-3 program as your spreadsheet. Each month, you prepare a budgeted income statement. Furthermore, assume that at the end of the year, you want to print all 12 budget sheets, but you want to use the DOS PRINT command to print in the background so that you can continue to use your computer.

Now, suppose that the spreadsheet files are stored in files named BIS_JAN.WK1, BIS_FEB.WK1, and so on to BIS_DEC.WK1. To see what format these files are in, change to the directory that contains the files, and type the command

```
TYPE BIS_JAN.WK1
```

If your screen shows a lot of happy faces and other strange characters, you cannot use the PRINT command to print the file. You need to copy the file so that the copy contains only ASCII text characters.

As with most application programs, you can use Lotus 1-2-3 to store a copy of a file in ASCII text format. 1-2-3 provides this capability by enabling you to print the spreadsheet to a file rather than directly to the printer. (If you actually own Lotus 1-2-3, the command is /PF, which selects Print and File from the menus.) In this example, you need to print all 12 Budgeted Income Statement spreadsheets to files; for example, BIS_123.WKI for the spreadsheet and BIS_123.PRN for the ASCII file.

When you finish that job, you could exit 1-2-3 and return to DOS. To be sure the new .PRN files contain only ASCII characters, you could type the command TYPE BIS_123.PRN at the command prompt. Next, you would type the command

```
PRINT BIS_???.PRN
```

to print all 12 files. (This assumes that you used the /Q switch to initialize the PRINT command to handle more than 10 files.) Now DOS can print all 12 files in the background, and you are free to use your computer for other jobs.

Treating Files as Devices

You've already seen how to use a file as input to the MORE command (when you used the command MORE < READ.ME). You can also use file names as output devices. For example, instead of entering a command such as DIR > PRN to channel the output from the DIR command to the printer, you could enter a command such as DIR > MYFILES.TXT. This command stores the output from the DIR command in a file named MYFILES.TXT.

Storing the output from commands in files can be very handy. For example, when you use the > PRN directive to send output to the printer, you need to wait for printing to finish before you can use your computer. However, if you channel output to a file (which is much quicker than sending output to the printer), you can use the PRINT command to print the output file in the background.

Also, if you have a word processing program, you can use it to edit the output file in any way you want. That is, you can add special printer features (such as boldface or underline), reorganize the pagination, add margins, and so on. You can even merge the output file into an existing document. In fact, virtually all application programs, including spreadsheets and database managers, enable you to import these DOS output files for further use.

The following example demonstrates the power of using a file as a device that accepts output from a command. Assume that you want to print a listing of all the files in three directories on your hard disk—the root directory, the DOS directory, and the WP directory (the last two of which your computer might not actually have).

Instead of printing the file names immediately, you decide to store them in a file so that you can print them later using the PRINT command. Suppose that you want to store the output from the three DIR commands in a file named MYFILES.TXT in the WP directory.

Starting at the DOS command prompt, enter the following commands to change to the WP directory and send a list of all the file names in the root directory to the file named MYFILES.TXT:

```
CD \WP
DIR C:\ > MYFILES.TXT
```

The DIR command displays nothing on-screen, because its output was sent to the MYFILES.TXT file. Now, to add the file names from the DOS directory to the MYFILES.TXT file, you need to type the command

```
DIR C:\DOS >> MYFILES.TXT
```

Notice that this command uses the >> redirection symbol. This symbol adds (or *appends*) the new output to the MYFILES.TXT file, instead of replacing its contents. Again, the DIR command displays nothing on-screen, but when the DOS prompt reappears, you know that the output is stored in the file.

Finally, to add the list of file names from the WP directory to the MYFILES.TXT file, enter this command:

```
DIR >> MYFILES.TXT
```

Before printing the MYFILES.TXT file, be sure it actually contains the file names from all three directories. To do so, type the command

```
TYPE C:\WP\MYFILES.TXT
```

or the command

```
MORE < C:\WP\MYFILES.TXT
```

Now that you are convinced that MYFILES.TXT actually contains the text you want, you can type the final command:

```
PRINT C:\WP\MYFILES.TXT
```

You are now free to use your computer while the PRINT command prints the contents of the MYFILES.TXT file in the background.

You could also preview, edit, and print the MYFILES.TXT file with your word processing program. To do so, run your word processing program in the usual manner and specify C:\WP\MYFILES.TXT as the file to edit.

Troubleshooting

This section lists common error messages that DOS might display while you are trying some of the examples in this chapter. If you receive one of these messages, try the recommended solution.

- `Errors on list device indicate that it may be off-line. Please check it`: The printer is disconnected, turned off, or off-line. Check your printer to be sure it is on-line (see your printer manual if necessary).

- `Invalid parameter`: A switch or an option used in a command is misspelled, or the forward slash (/), backslash (\), or pipe (¦) characters are used incorrectly.

Summary

This chapter presented commands and techniques for managing and controlling your printer. To summarize the most important points covered in this chapter:

- The Shift+Print Screen key combination copies to your printer whatever is on-screen.

- The Ctrl+Print Screen key combination slaves the printer so that all future screen displays are sent to the printer. (You must press Ctrl+Print Screen again to unslave the printer.)

- To print ASCII text files in the background so that you can continue to use your computer during printing, use the `PRINT` command (or select the Print option on the DOS 6 File List's File pull-down menu).

Alan Simpson's
DOS
SECRETS
UNLEASHED

CHAPTER 25

Communicating with Modems and FAXes

If you need to communicate with remote computers via the telephone lines, you have two alternatives:

- Install a modem (short for MOdulator/DEModulator), which allows two computers to send and receive data and programs.

- Buy a FAX board, which allows a computer to send and receive text and graphics (but not programs) to and from any FAX machine or any other computer with a FAX board.

The sections that follow discuss the strengths and weaknesses of each type of communication capability. Of course, you are not limited to selecting only one. However, a FAX board does require that your computer have a slot available to hold the board, as does an internal modem. The only way to know for sure how many slots are available in your computer is to remove the cover on your system unit. These hardware matters are beyond the scope of this book, so if you are in doubt, consult a computer service technician.

Communicating with Modems

A modem is the most flexible means of sending data and programs from one computer to another. You also need a modem to communicate with large external database services such as The Source, CompuServe, Knowledge Index, Dow Jones, Prodigy, and the Official Airline Guides.

The Baud Rate Feature

Perhaps the single most important feature to consider when purchasing a modem is the *baud rate*. The baud rate is the speed at which data is sent and received (measured in bits per second). The most common baud rates used in serial communications (that is, transmissions through phone lines) are 300, 1200, 2400, and 9600 baud.

A modem's listed baud rate is its maximum rate of data transfer. Hence, buying a modem that can transmit and receive at 9600 baud provides the most flexibility for communicating with all other modems, both fast and slow.

Selecting Communications Software

A modem also requires communications software that manages the streams of data being sent and received by the connected computers. Two major types of communications software are available for modems. With the standard communications packages, you can perform basic communications operations, such as sending and receiving files.

Most modems are packaged with their own communications software. However, that software might offer only limited operations, especially compared to some of the more widely used communications packages available from independent software dealers. You might want to examine the following full-featured packages:

Crosstalk Mark IV
Crosstalk XVI
Crosstalk Communications
1000 Holcomb Woods Parkway
Roswell, GA 30076-2575
(404) 998-3998

ProComm Plus
Data Storm Technologies, Inc.
1621 Twone Drive, Suite G
Columbia, MI 65205
(314) 474-8461

If your job entails writing programs for others to use or training people to use computers, you might need to use remote access software with your modem rather than the standard communications packages. You can use these programs not only to send and receive files but also to control a remote computer from your own computer or watch the activity of a user on a remote computer. Here are a couple of vendors of remote access software:

Carbon Copy
Carbon Copy Plus
Meridian Technology, Inc.
7 Corporate Park, Suite 100
Irvine, CA 92714
(714) 261-1199

PC Anywhere
Dynamic Microprocessor Associates, Inc.
60 East 42nd St., Suite 1100
New York, NY 10165
(212) 687-7115

Modem Settings for Best Performance

The real trick to using a modem effectively is ensuring that the two communicating computers use the same settings for sending and receiving files. You can use your communications software to adjust numerous settings for communicating with other computers:

Baud Rate	Usually 300, 1200, 1400, 4800, or 9600
Parity	None, Odd, Even, Mark, or Space
Data Bits	5, 6, 7, or 8
Stop Bits	1 or 2

The *parity* setting represents the characters used to detect errors during communications. The *data bits* setting establishes the number of bits used to represent each character of transmitted data. The *stop bits* setting represents the number of bits used to separate groups of data bits.

Perhaps the most common setting used for sending and receiving files is 1200 N-8-1, which is an abbreviated way of expressing 1200 baud, None (parity), 8 data bits, and 1 stop bit. A common setting for communicating with remote database services is 1200 E-7-1 (1200 baud, Even parity, 7 data bits, and 1 stop bit).

> If you're not sure of the proper settings when you first access a remote computer, either one of these settings is a good first try.

Again, adjusting the settings for communications via modem is a matter of using your communications software correctly. For more information, consult your computer dealer or a book that specializes in communications.

Communicating with FAXs

A second way of communicating via telephone lines is through facsimile transmission (FAX). The beauty of FAX is that it enables you to communicate with a worldwide network of FAX machines and other computers with FAX boards without having to worry about settings such as baud rate, parity, and stop bits.

Selecting a FAX Board

The FAX standard for facsimile transmission has changed a few times throughout the years. Currently, the most widely used standard is named Group 3, although a new standard (Group 4) is emerging. When you select a FAX board for your computer, try to select one that supports at least Group 2 and Group 3 standards.

Using a FAX board in your computer is not exactly like owning a complete FAX machine. The main reason is that a FAX board can send and receive only files, not text or graphics that are already printed on paper. If you want to be able to send printed text, as well as files, you need to invest in an additional *scanner*. You can also buy a FAX machine that supports both paper and computer file transmissions.

Computer FAX is still in its infancy in many ways. Your computer dealer can offer up-to-date alternatives for installing a FAX board on your computer. If you want to survey the market on your own, contact the following FAX board manufacturers for additional information:

Connection CoProcessor
Intel PCEO
Mainstop CO3-07
5200 NE Elam Young Parkway
Hillsboro, OR 97124-6497
(800) 538-3373

JT-FAX 9600
Quadram Limited Partnership
1 Quad Way
Norcross, GA 30093
(800) 548-3420

FaxMail 96
Brook Trout Technology, Inc.
110 Cedar St.
Wellesley Hills, MA 02181
(617) 235-3026

FAX Users Beware

Be aware that, unlike with modems, when you receive a file via FAX, it is not a simple text file that can be edited with your word processor. Instead, it's a graphic file that can only be viewed and printed with certain programs. Therefore, if you need to transmit editable text from one location to another, a modem is preferable to a FAX board.

The same is true of scanners. They are a great way to "capture" printed graphics, diagrams, logos, signatures, and such, and to use them in your printed documents. However, the text they capture will probably be inaccessible to your word processor or other text editor. There are programs that can translate scanned text to editable ASCII files, but they tend to be expensive, slow, and only partially accurate.

Incidentally (speaking of scanners), I once saw a demonstration that used a scanner connected to a computer as an input device and also had a voice synthesizer as an output device. As the operator fed printed text into the scanner, the voice synthesizer read each word out loud, in perfect English. As the demonstrators pointed out, the implications of this demonstration are enormous for visually handicapped persons.

Troubleshooting

The most common problem modem users experience is failure to connect. You must ensure that the two communications computers use the same settings for sending and receiving files. Check the baud rate, parity, number of bits, and stop bits to be sure they are set the same on both computers.

If you need to transmit editable text from one location to another, do not use a FAX—use a modem.

Summary

This chapter presented a brief overview of communicating with modems and FAXs. In summary:

- A modem allows two computers to send and receive data and programs via telephone lines.

- Baud rate is the single most important feature to consider when purchasing a modem.

- Communications software manages streams of data being sent and received through modems.

- A FAX board allows a computer to send and receive text and graphics (but not programs) to and from any FAX machine.

- Unlike files you receive via modems, files you receive via FAX are not easily edited with your word processor.

The Network
Connection

PART VI

Alan Simpson's
DOS
SECRETS
UNLEASHED

C H A P T E R   2 6

Making the Workgroup Connection

The Workgroup Connection is a set of programs that let you connect to other computers in your organization and share applications, data, printers, and electronic mail.

What Is the Workgroup Connection?

The Workgroup Connection is available as a separate product apart from DOS 6. After it is installed (as you will see how to do in the next section), you can do the following:

- Share applications—Instead of having to walk to another computer to use a certain application, you can connect to that computer via the Workgroup Connection and run the application on your computer.

- Share data—You can connect to other computers and use data on their computers instead of using "sneakernet," or copying files to a floppy disk and walking them back to your computer.

- Share printers—With the Workgroup Connection, you can connect to printers on other workstations. Again, you can avoid "sneakernet," but more importantly, expensive printers can be shared.

- Exchange electronic mail—As you will see in Chapter 27, "Keeping in Touch with Electronic Mail," Workgroup Connection comes with Microsoft Mail for communicating electronically with other people in your company.

The Workgroup Connection only provides the *client software*—software that lets you connect to shared resources on other computers. It does not provide you with *server capabilities*—the capability to share your local resources with other computers.

Setting Up the Workgroup Connection

The Workgroup Connection Setup program identifies your hardware and software, configures Workgroup Connection to run on your computer, and copies the necessary files to your hard disk. The following sections detail what you need to do to start using the Workgroup Connection.

What You Need to Make the Connection

Before you can connect to other computers, you need to have a *network interface card* installed. This is simply an adapter, like a video or communications adapter, that fits inside your computer and connects you to a network. You will also need the proper type of cable to connect your network interface card to the network.

Your network administrator should be able to provide you with a card and cable. While you have the attention of your network administrator, talk to him or her to get the following required information:

- The *user name* you want to use. This choice is basically up to you, but it must be unique within your workgroup. Many people use a combination of first and last names, like MSMITH or MARYS for Mary Smith.

- The name of your computer. For example, IBMPC can be used to identify which computer in the workgroup is yours. Again, this is basically up to you, but your network administrator must make sure that no other computer on your network uses the same name.

- The name of your workgroup. This is simply a name that identifies the combination of all of the computers that make up your network. The network administrator should provide you with this name.

■ Whether your workgroup uses Microsoft Mail. The setup routine will ask you if you want to install Microsoft Mail. If you want to add mail at a later date, refer to Chapter 27.

Running WCSETUP

To start the SETUP process for the Workgroup Connection:

1. Insert the Workgroup Connection disk in drive A: or B:.

2. Type A:WCSETUP (if the disk is in drive A:) and press Enter.

The first screen after the introduction screen asks for the location of the Workgroup Connection files. It suggests the C:\NET directory by default, but any directory you choose is OK.

Your next step is to select the type of network interface card that is installed in your computer. As shown in Figure 26.1, you have a wide range of options. Select the one that you or your network administrator installed in your computer.

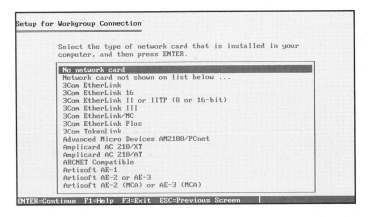

Figure 26.1. Selecting a network interface card.

On the next screen, enter the unique computer name that you chose for your computer. This name can be up to 15 characters long.

The next screen asks you for the workgroup name. Enter the workgroup name that your network administrator gave you. This can also be up to 15 characters long.

Finally, you will see a summary screen like the one in Figure 26.2.

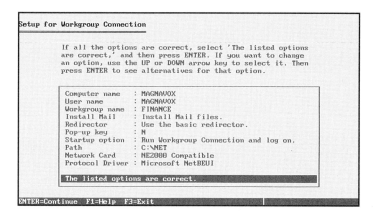

Figure 26.2. Summary of Workgroup Connection setup.

You can change most of the information you entered, as well as other configuration options, from this screen.

> User name—By default, the program makes your user name equal to your computer name. If you want to change this, use the arrows on your keyboard to move up and change it.

> If you made a mistake entering the computer name or workgroup name, you can change them now.

> Install mail—By default, Microsoft Mail is installed during the setup of the Workgroup Connection. If you don't want to install these files at this time, use the arrow keys to move up to this field and change the option.

Redirector—The default *redirector*, or memory-resident program that provides connectivity to other computers, is the Basic redirector. If you need advanced connection to equipment such as database servers or communications gateways, you may want to choose the Full redirector. See your network administrator if the Basic redirector does not handle all of your needs.

Pop-up key—The default key combination for popping-up the memory-resident NET utility, which you see in the next section, is Ctrl+Alt+N. If you want this to change this, you can choose another key combination here.

Startup option—WCSETUP offers you flexibility in determining how automated the startup process is. You have four options for starting the Workgroup Connection:

- Run Workgroup Connection only.
- Run Workgroup Connection and log on.
- Run Workgroup Connection, log on, load pop-up.
- Do not run Workgroup Connection.

The default startup option is `Run Workgroup Connection and log on`. Unless you have a special reason not to run the Workgroup Connection each time you start up, you should choose one of the other three options.

Network Card—If your network card is configured for any settings other than its default settings, you must tell the Workgroup Connection what the other settings are. Ask your network administrator for the correct settings for your card.

To view or change network card settings:

1. Move up to the Network Card field and press Enter.

2. Choose the option to edit settings. An example of the settings for a Novell NE2000 compatible network interface card is shown in Figure 26.3.

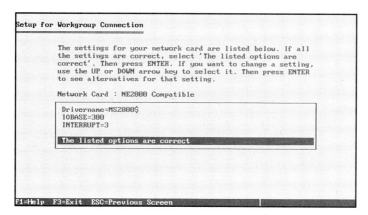

*Figure 26.3.
Configuring a
network
interface card.*

3. After changing your settings, choose `The listed options are correct` and press Enter.

4. Choose `Driver configuration is correct` and press Enter.

   Protocol Driver—The protocol determines the way that computers talk to each other. As with the choice of redirector, unless you have some special connectivity needs, you should leave this at the default of Microsoft NetBEUI.

   When you have all of the options configured, move to `The listed options are correct` line and press Enter.

   The Setup program finishes by copying the files to your hard drive and configuring your CONFIG.SYS and AUTOEXEC.BAT files appropriately. When the program is completed, you may either exit the program or reboot your computer.

Changing Your Workgroup Connection Settings

At any time after the initial installation, you can change Workgroup Connection settings:

1. Change to the directory where you installed the Workgroup Connection files.

2. Type WCSETUP and press Enter.

3. Make any necessary changes following the same procedures as outlined in the previous section, "Running WCSETUP."

Workgroup Basics

In this section, you will learn how to start the Workgroup Connection, use the NET utility and pop-up, connect to shared directories, and connect to and use shared printers.

Starting the Workgroup Connection

If you specified any of the first three options under "Startup option," the Workgroup Connection will start each time you turn on your computer. However, only the Run Workgroup Connection and log on option and the Run Workgroup Connection, log on, load pop-up option actually prompt you to log on. The Do not run Workgroup Connection option automatically starts the pop-up utility.

To manually log on:

1. Type NET LOGON and press Enter.

   If the Workgroup Connection was not automatically started, you will see:

   ```
   The WORKSTATION service is not started.
   Is it OK to start it? (Y/N) [Y]:
   ```

   Press Enter to start the connection.

2. You should see the following prompt:

   ```
   Type your user name, or press Enter if it is MARYS:
   ```

   where MARYS is the name you specified during setup.

3. Press Enter or type another user name and press Enter.

4. Type your password and press Enter. If this is the first time you are logging on, choose a password up to 14 characters in length. You will be prompted to type it again to confirm it before moving on.

You are connected to the computer and your *persistent connections* (discussed later) are reestablished.

Using the Pop-up Menu

Most of the major functions of Workgroup Connection are done from the pop-up interface. Before looking at these functions, you need to understand the ways this pop-up is accessed.

To use the pop-up and have it unload from memory when you are done, just as any other application would, type

```
NET
```

To load the pop-up as a TSR (terminate-and-stay-resident program), type

```
NET START POPUP
```

The following message displays:

```
Pop-up for Workgroup Connection loaded into memory.
Use Ctrl+Alt+N to activate.
```

> If you specified during setup to automatically load the pop-up, you do not need to load it again.

To access the menu in this way, press Ctrl+Alt+N from any DOS prompt or from within any DOS application.

To unload the pop-up from memory, type

```
NET STOP POPUP
```

Connecting to a Shared Directory

A *shared directory* is a directory on another computer that has been made available to the network. A computer running Windows for Workgroups may "publish" its C:\WINWORD2 directory as WINWORD, whereas the D:\WINFILES directory on a LAN Manager server may be published as WORDDATA.

As a Workgroup Connection user, you can connect to these directories and use the applications and data files in each directory. To make the connection, you need to know the name of the computer and the name of the directory.

To connect to a shared directory using the pop-up utility:

1. Display the pop-up interface, and then type NET or press Ctrl+Alt+N. A screen similar to the one in Figure 26.4 displays.

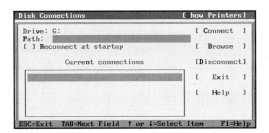

Figure 26.4.
The net pop-up
utility.

Use the Tab key to move between fields or press Alt+X where X is the highlighted letter for the field. For example, Alt+P moves the cursor to the Path field.

2. In the Drive field, type the letter of the drive you want to use for the connection. By default, it is the next available drive, but it can be any available drive.

You can only use drive letters up to the one specified in the LASTDRIVE parameter in the CONFIG.SYS file. If you do not have a LASTDRIVE line in your CONFIG.SYS file, the last available drive is E:.

3. In the Path field, enter the computer name and directory name using the following format:

   `\\computername\directoryname`

   For example,

   `\\IBMPC\WINWORD`

Use Alt+B to Browse through the computers and the shared directories available on each computer as shown in Figure 26.5.

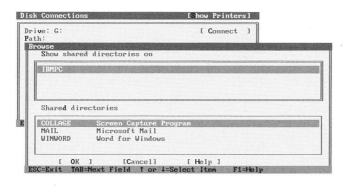

Figure 26.5. Browsing shared directories.

4. If there is a password required for accessing the shared directory, you may need to enter it now.

5. Use Alt+R to turn on Reconnect at startup if you want this to be a persistent connection, or one that is automatically reconnected each time you log on to the network.

6. Press Alt+C to make the connection. The connection should now show up in the Current connections list. Your screen should look similar to the one in Figure 26.6.

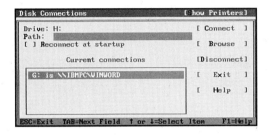

Figure 26.6. Connecting to a shared directory.

6. Press Escape to close the pop-up.

To disconnect from a shared directory using the pop-up utility:

1. Display the pop-up interface by typing NET or by pressing Ctrl+Alt+N.

2. Press Alt+N to display the Current connections list.

3. Select the shared directory to be disconnected.

4. Press Alt+D to disconnect.

5. Press Escape to close the pop-up.

Connecting to a Shared Printer

A *shared printer* is a printer on another computer that is made available to the network. A computer with an HP LaserJet may list it as LASERJET, whereas a LAN Manager server may publish an Epson dot matrix printer as EPSON.

As a Workgroup Connection user, you can connect to these printers and use them as if they were attached to your own computer. You just need to know the name of the computer and the name of the shared printer.

To connect to a shared printer using the pop-up utility:

1. Display the pop-up interface by typing NET or pressing Ctrl+Alt+N.

2. Press Alt+S to switch the display from shared directories to shared printers.

3. In the Port field, enter the name of the parallel port you want to use.

> If you have a printer attached to your own LPT1 port, use LPT2 or LPT3. You can use up to LPT9 with Workgroup Connection, but many applications only recognize LPT1 through LPT3.

4. In the Path field, enter the computer printer names using the following format:

    `\\computername\printername`

    For example,

    `\\IBMPC\LASERJET`

> Use Alt+B to Browse through the available computers and the shared printers available on each computer, as shown in Figure 26.7.

5. If there is a password required for accessing the shared printer, you may need to enter it now.

6. If you want this connection to be persistent, press Alt+R to turn on Reconnect at startup.

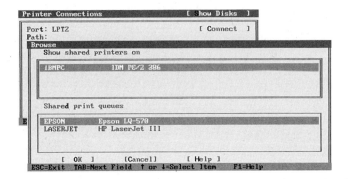

*Figure 26.7.
Browsing
for shared
printers.*

7. Press Alt+C to make the connection. The connection should now show up in the Current connections list. Your screen looks similar to the one in Figure 26.8.

8. Press Escape to close the pop-up.

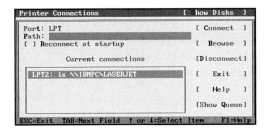

*Figure 26.8.
Connecting to
a shared
printer.*

To disconnect from a shared printer using the pop-up utility:

1. Display the pop-up interface by typing NET or pressing Ctrl+Alt+N.

2. Press Alt+S to switch the display from shared directories to shared printers.

3. Press Alt+N to display the Current connections list.

4. Select the shared printer to be disconnected.

5. Press Alt+D to disconnect.

6. Press Escape to close the pop-up.

Viewing and Controlling Print Queues

When multiple users can print to the same printer over a network, there has to be some mechanism for controlling which jobs are printed and when. Workgroup Connection uses print *queues* to manage this.

When you print to your own printer, the job goes straight to your printer. When you print to a shared printer, however, your job goes into a print queue.

To view a print queue using the pop-up utility:

1. Display the pop-up interface by typing NET or pressing Ctrl+Alt+N.

2. Press Alt+S to switch the display from shared directories to shared printers.

3. Press Alt+Q to show the print queues. A screen similar to Figure 26.9 displays.

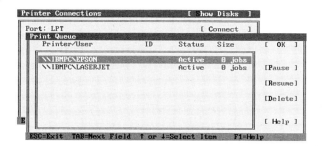

Figure 26.9. Viewing printer queues.

Notice that there are options to Pause, Resume, and Delete print jobs. Pausing a print job holds it until Resume is chosen. Delete simply deletes a print job from the queue.

To pause, resume, or delete a print job:

1. Select the print job.

2. Choose Pause by pressing Alt+P, choose Resume by pressing Alt+R, or choose Delete by pressing Alt+D.

715

Workgroup Commands

All of the functions that you can perform using the pop-up utility can be performed from the command line. In fact, there are additional commands that give you functions not included in the pop-up.

These commands give you additional information about your configuration, allow you to start and stop additional services, and even get help on network functions. Perhaps most importantly, as with DOS commands, these commands can be used in batch programs to automate network tasks.

The syntax for each command follows basically the same pattern:

- When you see a parameter enclosed in brackets ([]), it is optional.

- When you see parameters enclosed in braces ({}) and separated by a pipe (¦), you can only use one of the parameters in the group.

For example,

```
NET LOGON [user [{password ¦ ?}]] [/YES]
```

means that you can issue the NET LOGON command by itself, or you can add the *user* name. If you add the *user* name, you also have the option of specifying the *password* or the ? parameter. (You will see these parameters in the "NET LOGON" section—right now this is just for a syntax example.)

NET CONFIG

This command displays your current workgroup settings, producing output as follows:

```
Computer name                  \\IBMPC
User name                      MARYS
```

```
Software version              3.1
Redirector version            2.50
Workstation root directory    C:\NET

Workgroup                     FINANCE
The command completed successfully.
```

NET LOGON

If you chose the Run Workgroup Connection And Log On option or the Run Workgroup Connection, Log On, Load Pop-Up option during Startup, the NET LOGON command is automatically issued. However, if you log off and need to log on again, issue this command. You will be prompted for your user name and password. Once you are logged on, any persistent connections will be reestablished.

If you want to use this command in a batch program and don't want it to stop and ask you for a name and password, you can type

```
NET LOGON [user [{password ¦ ?}]] [/YES]
```

where

> *user* is your user name in the workgroup.
>
> *password* is the password for your user name.
>
> ? makes sure that you are prompted for your password, even if the /YES parameter is specified.
>
> /YES automatically answers Yes to any Yes/No prompts.

> Putting your password in a batch program is not very secure, as anyone can use your computer to view the file. It's better to have the batch program enter your user name and then stop for password entry.

NET LOGOFF

This command breaks all connections between you and the shared resources to which you are connected. All drive letters mapped to shared directories and all printer ports captured to shared printers are released. You can also use the /YES parameter to bypass any Yes/No prompts.

> In any command that asks you a Yes or No question, you can add the /YES or /Y parameter to automatically answer *Yes*.

NET PASSWORD

This command enables you to change your network password. In a Windows for Workgroups network, you can use the following parameters:

```
NET PASSWORD [oldpassword [newpassword]]
```

> Using this syntax may allow someone to look over your shoulder and see your old and new passwords as you type them. If you just type NET PASSWORD, your old and new passwords do not appear on the screen as you type.

If you are using a LAN Manager server, you can use these parameters:

```
NET PASSWORD [{\\computer | /DOMAIN:name}]
[user[oldpassword [newpassword]]]
```

In this case, you can specify either the particular LAN Manager server or a LAN Manager domain.

NET PRINT

This command provides functions similar to what you saw in the pop-up for viewing and controlling print queues and jobs. The syntax is as follows:

```
NET PRINT {\\computer[\queue] ¦ port} [/YES]
```

or

```
NET PRINT {\\computer ¦ port} [job# [{/PAUSE ¦ /RESUME ¦
/DELETE}]] [/YES]
```

where

computer is the name of the computer with the print queue.

queue is the name of the printer with the queue.

port is the name of the LPT port on your computer that is captured to the network printer.

job# is the number assigned to the print job.

For example, the command

```
NET PRINT \\IBMPC\LASERJET
```

displays the following output:

```
Printer queues at \\IBMPC

Name                        Job #     Size          Status
- - - - - - - - - - - - - - - - - - - - - - - - - - - - - - - - - - - - - - -
LASERJET Queue              0 jobs                  *Queue Active*
```

NET START

This command starts all or parts of Workgroup Connection. Issuing the command by itself starts all of the functions that you specified in the Startup options during Setup. However, the following are individual parameters you can use to start specific functions:

POPUP loads the pop-up utility into memory.

BASIC starts the basic redirector.

FULL starts the full redirector.

WORKSTATION starts the default redirector (usually Basic).

NETBIND binds network protocols to the network interface card.

NETBEUI starts the NetBIOS interface.

Issuing NET START /LIST gives you a list of services that have been started. For example:

```
These services are started:
BASIC  POPUP  NETBEUI
```

NET STOP

This command is very similar to NET START, except that it stops services and removes them from memory. Issuing the command alone stops all services currently running. However, the following are individual parameters you can use to stop specific functions:

POPUP unloads the pop-up utility from memory.

BASIC stops the basic redirector.

FULL stops the full redirector.

WORKSTATION stops the default redirector (usually Basic).

NETBEUI stops the NetBIOS interface.

NET TIME

This command synchronizes your computer's clock with that of a LAN Manager time server. The syntax is

```
NET TIME [\\computer ¦ /WORKGROUP:wgname] [/SET] [/YES]
```

where the parameters are as follows:

> *computer* is the name of the LAN Manager server with which you want to check or synchronize your time.
>
> /WORKGROUP enables you to pick another workgroup clock.
>
> *wgname* is the name of the other workgroup.
>
> /SET synchronizes your clock with the chosen timeserver.

NET USE

This command is the most important command of all, encompassing most of the functionality of the pop-up utility. It is used to connect and disconnect your computer from shared directories and printers and to view current connections. Type NET USE to view all current directory and printer connections. For example:

```
Status          Local name      Remote name
- - - - - - - - - - - - - - - - - - - - - - - - - - - - - - - - -
OK              F:              \\IBMPC\COLLAGE
OK              H:              \\IBMPC\WINWORD
OK              M:              \\IBMPC\MAIL
OK              LPT2            \\IBMPC\EPSON
OK              LPT3            \\IBMPC\LASERJET
```

To connect to a shared directory:

```
NET USE [{drive: ¦ *}] [\\computer\directory [{password ¦ ?}]]
[/PERSISTENT:{YES ¦ NO}] [/SAVEPW:NO] [/YES]
```

The new parameters are as follows:

> *drive* enables you to either specify a drive letter or use the asterisk to let Workgroup Connection pick the next available drive letter.
>
> /PERSISTENT makes the connection persistent so that next time you type NET LOGON, it will automatically reconnect (see discussion of persistent connections).

/SAVEPW automatically saves the password you enter in your password file. By using /SAVEPW:NO, you will be prompted for the password each time you reconnect.

To connect to a shared printer:

```
NET USE [port:] [\\computer\queue [{password ¦ ?}]]
[/PERSISTENT:{YES ¦ NO}] [/SAVEPW:NO] [/YES]
```

Except for specifying a queue instead of a directory, the options are the same as for connecting to a shared directory.

To disconnect from a shared directory or shared printer:

```
NET USE {drive: ¦ \\computer\directory} /DELETE [/YES]
```

or

```
NET USE {port: ¦ \\computer\queue} /DELETE [/YES]
```

You can specify the drive letter or shared directory to be disconnected and you can specify either the port (LPTx:) or the shared printer. For example,

```
NET USE D: /D
```

has the same effect as

```
NET USE \\IBMPC\MAIL /D
```

To delete all current connections:

```
NET USE * /DELETE [/YES]
```

To view and control your list of persistent connections:

```
NET USE /PERSISTENT:{YES ¦ NO ¦ LIST ¦ SAVE ¦ CLEAR}[/YES]
```

The individual parameters are as follows:

YES specifies that any connections from this point forward are to be made persistent.

NO specifies that any subsequent connections are not to be made persistent.

LIST lists all persistent connections.

SAVE saves all current connections as persistent.

CLEAR clears all persistent connections.

You can also use /P: instead of /PERSISTENT:.

> By default, issuing a NET USE command adds the connection to the list of persistent connections. However, when using the NET or pop-up utility, you must specify "Reconnect at startup" to make the connection persistent.

NET VER

This command simply displays the type and version of the workgroup redirector you are using. For example, NET VER may display the following:

```
Microsoft Workgroup Client Basic Redirector Version 3.1
Copyright (c) Microsoft Corp 1992.  All rights reserved.
```

NET VIEW

This command lists all computers in a workgroup or the shared resources available on a particular computer. Typing NET VIEW returns a list of computers in your workgroup. However, additional parameters are available:

```
NET VIEW [\\computer] [/YES]
```

or

```
NET VIEW [/WORKGROUP:wgname] [/YES]
```

will list all shared resources on a particular computer or within a particular workgroup.

Troubleshooting

As with all software, unfortunately, there will come a time when you forget functions or syntax or need help diagnosing a problem with the Workgroup Connection. Fortunately, there is quite a bit of help built into the Workgroup Connection itself.

Getting Help

There are three ways to get to the same help information for each network command. For example, to view help on the NET VIEW command, you can type any of the following commands:

HELP NET VIEW—This puts you into the DOS Help facility. From there, you can use the keyboard or mouse to move to subtopics or to related topics. This is the most useful way to get help.

NET HELP VIEW—This simply outputs help information to the screen.

NET VIEW /?—This produces the same information in the same way as NET HELP VIEW.

There is also a database of error messages, along with their possible causes and solutions, built into the Workgroup Connection. For example, after issuing the NET VIEW command, you get the following message:

Error 6118: The list of servers for this workgroup is not currently available.

You can use the NET HELP command to obtain further help on this error condition by typing

NET HELP 6118

which produces the following information:

EXPLANATION

```
The computer(s) that share resources in this workgroup
cannot be located. The computer(s) might have been
restarted.

ACTION

Wait a few minutes, and then check the workgroup for shared
resources again. If the problem persists, make sure your
network card settings are correct.
```

First and foremost, be sure and look at the README.TXT file in your DOS directory. In many cases, it addresses a specific hardware configuration or covers a particular condition or error.

Problems Running WCSETUP

If your computer hangs up during the Workgroup Connection setup, it could be a hardware or software problem. Try one or both of the following:

1. If WCSETUP was unable to correctly identify your hardware, it could be causing problems. Try typing WCSETUP/I to tell it to skip the hardware connection procedure.

2. Memory-resident programs could be causing problems. Try putting REM statements in front of TSR (terminate-and-stay-resident) programs in the AUTOEXEC.BAT file and DEVICE statements in the CONFIG.SYS file. Do this for as many programs as it takes to get WCSETUP running successfully.

Problems Starting Workgroup Connection

If the Workgroup Connection won't start after a successful installation, you should try the following:

1. Make sure that all cables and connectors are securely fastened to the network.

2. Try running the network card's diagnostic program (if one was included).

3. Make sure that you have specified the correct base memory and interrupt settings for your network card.

4. Make sure that your network card settings do not conflict with any other devices in your computer.

5. Try loading the Workgroup Connection drivers into conventional memory instead of upper memory.

6. Make sure that the device command for EMM386.EXE excludes any memory that your network card may use.

Problems Running Workgroup Connection with Windows

To use Windows correctly with the Workgroup Connection, you must tell Windows that you are running on a Microsoft network.

1. Start Windows.

2. Double-click the Windows Setup icon in the Main group.

3. Choose `Change System Settings` from the Options menu.

4. Choose `Microsoft Network` (or `100% compatible`) from the Network field.

5. Choose `OK`.

Summary

The Workgroup Connection is a powerful set of utilities for sharing resources on other computers. With it, you can use directories and printers on many kinds of Microsoft networks as if they were on your own local computer. Moreover, you can make connections through a user-friendly pop-up interface or automate them through the use of batch programs.

The next chapter looks at one of the most important uses of the Workgroup Connection—electronic mail.

Alan Simpson's
DOS
SECRETS
UNLEASHED

Keeping in Touch with Electronic Mail

In this chapter, you will learn about electronic mail (E-mail) and how it can help you in your day-to-day communications. Microsoft's implementation of electronic mail is called *Microsoft Mail* and is included in the Workgroup Connection.

Introduction to Electronic Mail

What exactly is electronic mail? It's quite simple. Think of everything you can do with an interoffice memo or with a letter sent via the U.S. Postal Service. Now multiply the speed at which you can do that by a large number, add a dozen or so more functions, and you've got E-mail.

Like a memo or a letter, you use E-mail to address the message to a sender, you can include things other than the message itself in the "envelope," and when you receive E-mail you can file it away like you can regular mail.

That's about where the similarity to regular mail ends. Although the postal service provides some additional functionality, it usually comes at an extra cost. With electronic mail, many additional functions are built in—and they're free. For example, you can carbon copy another person on your message, register mail so you are notified when the recipient reads it, forward mail to other users, search your files for old messages, reply to messages, print messages, and secure your mail with a password.

Setting Up Microsoft Mail

Now that you have a basic understanding of the power of E-mail, you're ready to configure Microsoft Mail and learn to use it to its fullest.

If you did not copy the mail files during the setup of Workgroup Connection:

1. Change to the directory where you installed Workgroup Connection.

2. Type WCSETUP and press Enter.

3. Using the arrows, move up to the Install Mail option and press Enter.

4. Select Install Mail Files and press Enter.

5. Choose The listed options are correct and press Enter.

6. Insert the Workgroup Connection disk in the specified drive and press Enter.

7. Press F3 to exit to DOS.

Once Mail is installed, you need to configure it for your local *post office*, the place where your mailbox is located. Your network administrator should provide you with this name.

Make sure that you are logged on to your workgroup. When you have done so:

1. Type MAIL and press Enter.

2. You will be prompted to enter your post office name. It should be in the format *computer**directory*. For example, if the computer with the post office is called IBMPC and the shared directory is called MAIL, you would type \\IBMPC\MAIL as shown in Figure 27.1.

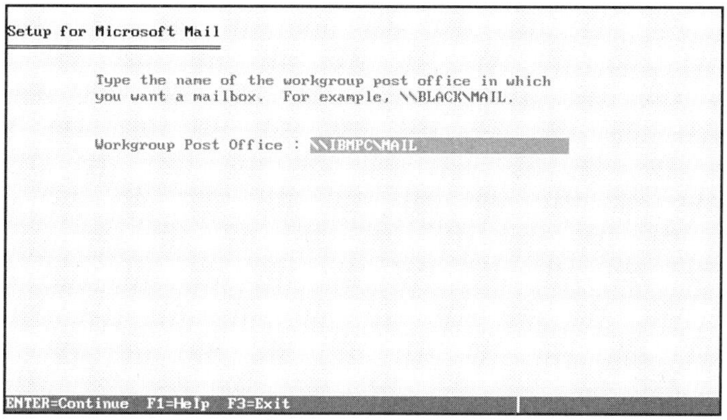

Figure 27.1. Configuring Mail for your post office.

3. The shared directory containing the post office may require a password the first time you connect. When prompted, enter the password given to you by the post office administrator.

4. A mailbox is created using your Workgroup Connection user name (MARYS, for example). You are then asked to enter information about yourself and your Mail account, such as the following:

   Full name (required)
   Password (recommended)
   Work phone (optional)
   Second phone (optional)
   Office (optional)
   Notes (optional)

A summary of this information is shown in Figure 27.2.

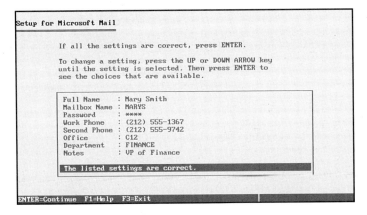

Figure 27.2.
Entering
Mail setup
information.

At this point, you may either enter Mail or exit to DOS. To practice entering Mail now that you are set up as a user, choose to exit to DOS.

Starting Mail

From now on, all that you need to do to start Mail is type MAIL and press Enter. A log-on screen similar to the one in Figure 27.3 appears.

```
          Microsoft (R) Mail for PC Networks V3.0b
              MS-DOS Workstation Version




              Mailbox:  ▒▒▒▒▒▒▒▒▒



  Copyright 1991-1992 Microsoft Corporation.  All rights reserved.
```

Figure 27.3. Starting Microsoft Mail.

When you start Mail for the first time, a persistent connection, M:, is made to the shared Mail directory. If you need to use M: for another purpose, start Mail by typing

MAIL G:

where G: is the drive you mapped to the Mail directory.

To enter Mail:

1. Enter your mailbox name (your user name) and press Enter.

2. Enter your password and press Enter.

You are now in Microsoft Mail!

You can check your mail at someone else's computer by choosing Login from the Options menu and logging in as yourself. You can also change your password by choosing Password from the Options menu.

The Mail Interface

Before you can use Mail effectively, you need to understand how the user interface works. There are three main actions that will get you through just about everything you need to do in Mail.

- You can select menu options in two ways—by using the arrow keys to move to an option and pressing Enter, or by pressing the highlighted letter of the option. For example, to choose Compose from the Main menu, you can move the arrows to Compose and press Enter, or you can press the C key.

- The Escape key takes you to the menu. If you are composing a message, for example, pressing the Escape key puts the cursor up on the Compose menu. Additionally, pressing the Escape key takes you back up a level in the menus, eventually leading to the prompt to quit.

- The arrow keys and the Spacebar are used to select multiple items from a list. To select a name from an address list, a message from your mailbag or a folder, or a file from a directory, you can use the arrows to highlight the item and press the Spacebar to select or deselect it.

Sending Mail

As with regular mail, there are two parts to an E-mail message—the address and the body of the message.

Addressing Mail

The following are the basic steps to addressing a new mail message. The more advanced options dealing with priority and attachments are looked at in detail in the following sections.

1. From the Main menu, choose Compose.

2. Choose To.

3. The list of users in your workgroup appears as shown in Figure 27.4. You can either use the up and down arrows to select a name or type the first few letters of the name to move quickly up and down the list.

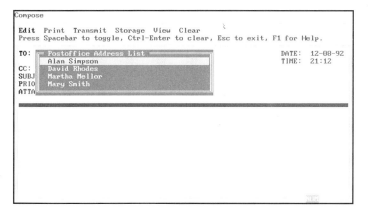

Figure 27.4. Microsoft Mail user list.

Pressing the right arrow reveals detailed information about the user.

4. Press Enter when the user name or names are selected.

When practicing Microsoft Mail, you may want to address messages to yourself so that you will have messages to read and respond to in the next sections.

5. If you wish to carbon copy other users on this message, choose CC. Select the user name or names and press Enter.

6. In the Subject field, type the subject of your message and press Enter.

7. If you want this message to be a certain priority, choose Priority. The priorities are 1 through 5 (low to high), and Registered (R).

8. Finally, if you want to attach any external files, choose Attachments. Enter the path and name of the file you want to send, and press Enter.

Pressing Enter in a field that asks for a path or file name enables you to browse through directories and select files.

Priority

This setting enables the sender to specify a priority, indicating how urgent a message is. To indicate a priority from low to high, you can select a number from 1 to 5. To request that you be notified when the message is received, select Registered (R). To remove priority from a message, press the Del key.

A receipt from a registered message will appear to be from a user called POSTOFFICE.

Attachments

An attachment is an additional file that you wish to mail. Think of it as an enclosure in a regular mail message. You can send one or more files with an E-mail message.

To send one or more files, you can type the file names manually or follow these steps:

1. In the Attachments field, press Enter and a directory list appears.

2. Select the files you want to send by pressing the Spacebar to mark them.

3. Press Enter when the file or files are selected.

If you change your mind, you can unattach the files. To remove all of the files you selected:

1. Move the cursor to the Attachments field.

2. Press Ctrl+Enter.

If the attached file is not in ASCII format, IBM Revisable Form Text (.RFT), or Microsoft Mail Fax (.DCX), the recipient will not be able to view it from within Mail. However, the recipient can still copy the attachment to a file for later use.

Creating the Message

Now that the message is addressed, you are ready to create the body of the message itself. The more complex steps of editing and importing files are examined in detail in the following sections.

1. Press the down arrow to move into the open message field.

2. Type your message as you would using a regular word processor.

3. If you wish to include an external ASCII (text) file in your message, press F5 to import the file.

4. After you type and edit the message, press Escape. Your screen should look similar to the one in Figure 27.5.

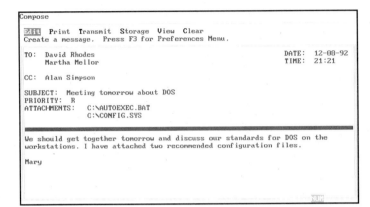

*Figure 27.5.
Composing
and sending
a message.*

At any point in addressing or composing a message, you
can use the up- and down-arrow keys to move between the
address fields and the message itself.

5. Choose Transmit from the Compose menu to send the
   message.

Editing Messages

As with any word processor, you will find that there are times when
you want to move, copy, or delete entire sections of a message.
Microsoft Mail has some of these basic editing functions built in. The
function keys that relate to these are shown in Table 27.1.

Table 27.1. Microsoft Mail editing keys.

Key	Description
F2	Realign text
F5	Include an ASCII text file
F6	Select text

Key	Description
F7	Copy selected text
F8	Paste selected text
F9	Move selected text
F10	Delete selected text

If you want to erase a whole message and start over, choose Clear from the Compose menu.

To move a block of text:

1. Press F6 at the start of the text.

2. Using the arrow keys, move the cursor to the end of the text.

3. Press F9 to move the text to the Clipboard.

If text already exists on the Clipboard, you see the following message:

`There is text in the paste buffer: Append Replace`

If you want to add to the text, choose Append. If you want to overwrite the text on the Clipboard, choose Replace.

4. Move the cursor to where you want to insert the text and press F8.

To copy a block of text:

1. Press F6 at the start of the text.

2. Using the arrow keys, move the cursor to the end of the text.

3. Press F7 to copy the text to the Clipboard.

4. Move the cursor to where you want the text and press F8.

To delete a block of text:

1. Press F6 at the start of the text.

2. Using the arrow keys, move the cursor to the end of the text.

3. Press F10 to delete the text.

Importing Text Files

Text files are files of unformatted text, as opposed to files created in word processor format that include codes for things like boldface, underline, tabs, and margins. You may want to import files into mail messages to avoid retyping them manually. You may also find it easier to create long mail messages in a word processor that you are comfortable with and then export to a text file for importing into your mail message.

To import an entire text file:

1. Move the cursor to the location in your message where you want to import the file.

2. Press F5.

3. Enter the path and name of the file you wish to import, or press Enter and select it from the directory list.

To import only part of a text file:

1. Press Escape to highlight the Compose menu.

2. Choose View.

3. Enter the path and name of the file you wish to import, or press Enter and select it from the directory list.

4. Move the cursor to the beginning of the text you want to import and press F6.

5. Press F7 to copy the text to the Clipboard.

6. Press Escape to return to the mail message.

7. Move the cursor to where you want to insert the text and press F8.

In the same way that you can use external text files, you can also copy text from a message that you have received and stored in a folder. Folders are discussed in the "Using Mail Folders" section later in this chapter.

Reading and Responding to Messages

Now that you have learned how to address, compose, and send E-mail messages, you are ready to learn how to read and respond to them. This section discusses the more advanced options of working with attachments, and replying to and forwarding mail.

Upon entering Microsoft Mail, you see all of the mail in your inbox, or *mailbag*. Unread messages are highlighted as shown in Figure 27.6.

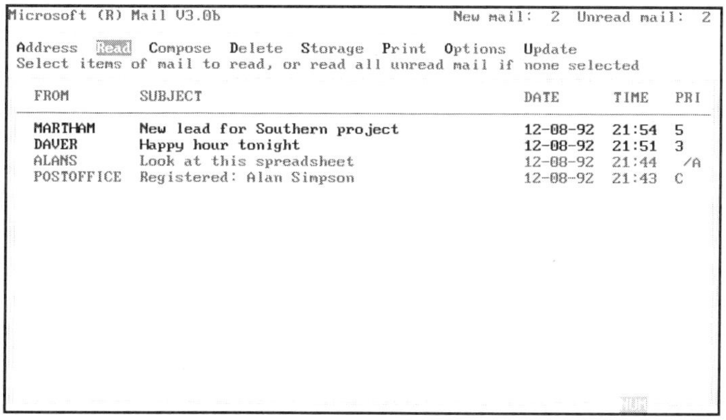

```
Microsoft (R) Mail V3.0b                     New mail:  2  Unread mail:  2

Address  Read  Compose  Delete  Storage  Print  Options  Update
Select items of mail to read, or read all unread mail if none selected

   FROM        SUBJECT                          DATE      TIME   PRI

   MARTHAM     New lead for Southern project    12-08-92  21:54  5
   DAVER       Happy hour tonight               12-08-92  21:51  3
   ALANS       Look at this spreadsheet         12-08-92  21:44  /A
   POSTOFFICE  Registered: Alan Simpson         12-08-92  21:43  C
```

*Figure 27.6.
The main Mail
screen.*

The options Read, Delete, Storage, and Print on the main menu have one important thing in common—multiple messages can be selected and these actions can be performed on them at once. For example, if you choose Delete from the main menu, you can choose one or more messages to delete.

On the other hand, as you will see in this section, Delete, Storage, and Print are also options on the Read menu so that they can be performed on single messages as well.

To read a message:

1. From the main menu, choose Read.

2. Use the arrows to select the message or messages and press Enter.

> If there are unread messages in your mailbag, pressing Enter without selecting any specific messages with the Spacebar scrolls you through your unread messages one at a time.

3. If the message has an attachment, you can view it (if it is in ASCII, .RFT, or .DCX format as discussed earlier) or save it to a file.

To view an attachment:

1. From the Read menu, choose Attachments.

2. Choose View. If there is only one attachment, it displays for you to view. If there are many attachments, you can select which one to view.

To save an attachment:

1. From the Read menu, choose Attachments.

2. Choose Save. If there is only one attachment, enter the path and file name where you want to store it. If there are many attachments, you can mark and save each one individually.

At this point, you can hold the message, print it, delete it, save it to a text file, reply to it, forward it to someone else, or save it to a folder.

To hold a message, choose Hold from the Read menu. If you selected multiple messages to read, this takes you to the next message. If you selected only one message, this has the same effect as pressing Escape, taking you back to the main Read menu.

To print a message:

1. From the Read menu, choose Print.

2. Choose Printer from the Print menu.

To delete a message:

1. From the Read menu, choose Delete.

2. To make sure that you don't accidentally delete a message, you are given the following prompt:

   Delete? Yes No

To save a message to a text file:

1. From the Read menu, choose Print.

2. Choose File from the Print menu.

3. Enter the path and file name for the text file you want to save and press Enter.

To reply to a message:

1. From the Read menu, choose Reply.

2. You are given the following option:

   Copy read message into reply text? Yes No

   If you want to have the original text in the response, choose Yes. If you think that the recipient will know what you are replying to and doesn't need to see the original text again, choose No.

3. Type your comments. If you chose to include the original text, you can also move down into the message and include comments there.

4. Press Escape and choose Transmit.

Forwarding is similar to replying, except that you cannot edit the original text and you are sending it to someone other than the original sender.

To forward a message:

1. From the Read menu, choose Forward. If the message has attached files, you will see the following prompt:

```
Forward attached files? Yes No
```

If you choose Yes and the message has multiple files, you are also given a chance to select or deselect individual files to be forwarded.

2. Choose the To option to see the address list.

3. Select the user or users you want to forward the message to and press Enter.

4. Press Escape and choose Transmit to forward the message.

The final option is to save the message to a folder, which the next section discusses.

Using Mail Folders

Microsoft Mail provides you with the ability to file your messages away for later usage. Unlike most people's manual filing systems, this one is quite structured. It provides an easy way to manipulate the folders and a quick way to find the messages you need.

Creating Folders

There are two types of folders—*shared* and *private*. A shared folder is a lot like a bulletin board. By saving mail messages to shared folders, you make them accessible to anyone who wishes to read them. In contrast, a private folder is just that—private. Only you can access the messages you store in private folders.

Folders can also contain subfolders. For example, a folder called PROJECTS might contain subfolders called MARKETING, FINANCE, and SITEPLAN.

To create a private folder or subfolder:

1. From the main menu, choose Options.

2. Choose Folders from the Options menu.

3. If you are creating a main folder, choose Create. If you are adding a subfolder to a main folder, choose Modify, select the main folder, and press the right-arrow key. A Create screen appears as shown in Figure 27.7.

A private folder can only contain private subfolders. Likewise, a shared folder can only contain shared subfolders.

```
Folders

Create  Modify  Delete  Folders  Items  Private-Storage
Add a new folder to the mail system


  Create
 Folder Name:
 Comment:
 Mode:          Private
 Sort Key:      Date


 Enter Folder Name
```

*Figure 27.7.
Creating a
folder.*

4. In the Folder Name field, enter a name for the folder and press Enter. This name can be up to 23 characters in length.

5. You can type an optional description of up to 24 characters in the Comments field. Press Enter when finished.

6. In the Mode field, select Private and press Enter.

7. Finally, you must choose a method for displaying the messages. The folder can be sorted by the person it's from, its subject, its date, or its priority. Press Enter when you have chosen a Sort option.

To create a shared folder, follow steps 1 through 5 for creating a private folder, and then follow these steps:

6. In the Mode field, select Shared and press Enter.

7. Choose a Sort option for the folder and press Enter. A box similar to the one in Figure 27.8 appears.

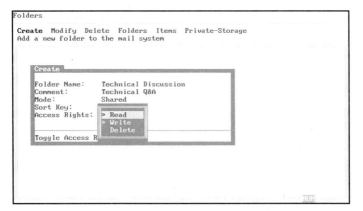

*Figure 27.8.
Determining
access rights to
a shared folder.*

8. You must now choose what access users will have to the folder. Select any combination of Read, Write, and Delete. Press Enter when finished.

Storing Mail in Folders

Now that you have created folders and subfolders, you can save or copy messages to them.

To copy a message you are composing to a folder, you carbon copy the folder:

1. When addressing your message, choose CC for Carbon-Copy and press the left-arrow key.

2. From the Address Lists box, select FOLDERS and press Enter.

3. Select one (or more) folders to copy the message to and press Enter.

4. Upon completion of your message, press Escape and choose Transmit to send as you normally would.

To save a message that you have received to a folder:

1. From either the main menu or the Read menu, choose Storage.

2. Choose Save from the Storage menu.

> Pressing the Insert key at this point also enables you to create a new folder.

3. Select the folder and press Enter.

4. If there are any attachments to the message, you can save any or all of them as well.

Finding and Using Mail in Folders

Microsoft Mail provides you with tools to read and even reuse mail in your folders and gives you an easy way to quickly search folders for just the right message.

To view a message saved in a folder:

1. Choose Storage from the Main, Compose, or Read menus.

2. Choose View from the Storage menu.

3. Select the folder and press Enter.

4. Select the message or messages you want to read, and press Enter.

5. When done reading the messages, choose Quit.

> You have most of the same options with stored messages as you do with new ones (print, delete, and work with attachments, for example).

To reuse a message:

1. Choose Compose from the Main menu.

2. Press Escape and choose Storage from the Compose menu.

3. Choose Load from the Storage menu.

4. Select the folder and press Enter.

5. Select the message you want to reuse and press Enter.

6. Choose Edit from the Compose menu.

You can now modify the message and send it as you would a regular mail message.

To search folders for a message:

1. Choose Options from the Main menu.

2. Choose Folders from the Options menu.

3. Choose Items from the Folders menu.

4. Choose Find from the Items menu.

5. Choose Pattern from the Find menu.

6. In the Pattern field, type up to 25 characters of the word or words for which you want to search and press Enter.

7. At this point, you can tell Mail whether to search all folders, just private folders, just shared folders, or only folders that you specify. If you want to search fewer than all folders, choose Folders from the Find menu. Next, choose the types of folders to search.

Choose Toggle to select individual folders. Using the arrow keys and Spacebar, select the folders to search, and press Enter.

Choose Private to search only private folders.

Choose Shared to search only shared folders.

8. Choose Go from the Find menu to begin the search.

All messages matching the criteria are retrieved. Use the arrow keys or the PageUp and PageDown keys to scroll through a message, and press Enter to move to the next message.

Archiving Mail

As your folders grow larger and more complex, you may find it necessary to *archive* some of your old messages—store them somewhere else for later use. Microsoft Mail provides tools to archive and de-archive (bring back into use) messages.

To archive a folder:

1. Choose Options from the Main menu.

2. Choose Folders from the Options menu.

3. Choose Folders from the Folders menu.

4. From the Folders menu, choose Archive.

5. Select the folder or folders you wish to archive and press Enter.

6. Type a path and file name for the archive file and press Enter.

Use an extension such as .ARC to make it easier to identify and keep track of archive files.

Now that the folder is archived, you can delete the folder from your mail account if you wish.

To delete a folder:

1. Choose Options from the Main menu.

2. Choose Folders from the Options menu.

3. Choose Delete from the Folders menu.

4. Select the folder you want to delete and press Enter.

At a later date, you may need to bring the messages back into your mail account, or de-archive them. To de-archive a folder:

1. Choose Options from the Main menu.

2. Choose Folders from the Options menu.

3. Choose Folders from the Folders menu.

4. From the Folders menu, choose Dearchive.

5. Type the path and file name of the archive file and press Enter.

6. Select the folder into which you want to de-archive the messages and press Enter.

Address Lists and Groups

As you use Mail more and more, you will come to realize that there are certain people that you send mail to more often than others. To make it easier to communicate with these users, Mail provides you with two tools—address lists and groups.

Address Lists

A personal *address list* works exactly the same as the master list but only includes the names you want to see.

To add users to your personal address list:

1. Choose Address from the Main menu.

2. Choose Browse from the Address menu.

3. Select the user or users that you want to add to your list and press Enter.

To delete users from your personal address list:

1. Choose Address from the Main menu.

2. Choose Delete from the Address menu.

3. Select the user or users that you want to delete from your list and press Enter.

You can also change the way that the user appears in your personal list. For example, if you know John Thompson as *Jack*, you can give him an *alias* of *Jack* in your list.

To create or change an alias:

1. Choose Address from the Main menu.

2. Choose Modify from the Address menu.

3. Select the user that you want to give an alias and press Enter.

4. Type the alias for the user and press Enter.

Personal Groups

Mail provides yet another way to combine users—personal groups. A *personal group* contains names from your personal address list that you would like to address as one group. For example, the group SOFTBALL might contain the names of everyone on the company softball team. To send a message about an upcoming game, you just select SOFTBALL from the list instead of each individual name.

To create a personal group:

1. Choose Address from the Main menu.

2. Choose Group from the Address menu.

3. Choose Create from the Group menu.

4. Select the users you wish to group together and press Enter.

5. Enter a name for the group in the Group Name field (up to 30 characters) and press Enter.

You can also add or delete users from the group and change the group name. To modify the group:

1. Choose Address from the Main menu.

2. Choose Group from the Address menu.

3. Choose Modify from the Group menu.

4. Select the group name and press Enter.

5. Select the users you wish to add or delete and press Enter.

6. Modify the group name if necessary and press Enter.

Configuring Mail

Microsoft Mail offers you a great deal of flexibility in configuring your electronic mail environment, from the way that Mail displays your messages to if and how it keeps records of all incoming and outgoing mail.

To configure Mail:

1. Choose Options from the Main menu.

2. Choose Configure from the Options menu. A screen similar to the one in Figure 27.9 appears.

```
Configure

Display  Headers  Preferences  Log  Sortkey  Useful-Life
Configure address list to show in Compose TO and CC fields

   Mailbox:      MARYS           Name:  Mary Smith
   Postoffice:   IBMPC           Network:  FINANCE
   Privileges:   Mail:           Delete, Read, Send, Urgent
                 Folders:        Private/Shared, View shared
                 Remote:         None

   Display:      Postoffice Address List
   Headers.      Number      50   Sorting          Date
   Useful life:  Regular mail  24   Urgent mail      2

   File log:     Compose
                    Auto log    No
                 Read
                    Auto log    No
   Folder log:   Compose
                    Auto log    No
                 Read
                    Auto log    No
```

*Figure 27.9.
Configuring
Microsoft
Mail.*

3. Select the option you wish to configure and press Enter. The user-configurable options are

   Display—This determines which address list is the default. Your choices are Personal Address List, Postoffice Address List (default), and FOLDERS.

   Headers—This is the number of messages that are retrieved and displayed in your mailbag. The default is 50, but it can be anywhere from 0 to 999.

   Preferences—There are a number of options here dealing with a variety of program prompts. Many are Yes/No choices, such as `Reply to sender only?`, whereas many are Ask/Always/Never options such as `Forward attached files?`

   Log—By default, no log is kept of your incoming or outgoing messages. However, you can configure Mail to keep track of incoming and/or outgoing messages in text format and/or Mail folders.

   Sorting—This option determines how your mailbag is sorted, by Date, who From, Subject, or Priority.

   Useful life—This option is only valid when sending mail to post offices other than your own. Given in days, it determines how long a message can reside at your local post office before delivery to the recipient is said to have failed.

Using the Mail Notifier

While using other DOS applications, you may want to be notified that you have received mail. Microsoft Mail provides a small memory-resident program to do just that. To load the notification pop-up, from the DOS prompt type `MICRO` `MAILBOXNAME` and press Enter. `MAILBOXNAME` is your mailbox name (for example, `MARYS`).

> You still have to quit your DOS application and run the full Mail program to read and respond to your mail.

To remove the notification pop-up, from the DOS prompt, type `MICRO` `/U` and press Enter.

 Troubleshooting

As with most DOS 6 applications, getting help with Microsoft Mail is as close as the F1 key. Extensive context-sensitive help is available on all menu and submenu options. However, if you can't get into Mail to begin with, this type of help doesn't really help much.

When you try to start Microsoft Mail, you might get the message `Could not find mail system database`. If this message displays, you probably do not have your M: drive mapped to the mail directory on the server. Try either of the following:

- Map drive M: to your post office directory. For example, type `NET USE M: \\IBMPC\MAIL`.

- Start Mail with the `-D` option and specify the drive letter for the post office. For example, if drive P: is mapped to the directory containing the post office, type `MAIL -DP`.

Once you are in Microsoft Mail, you may also run into problems that F1 can't help you solve. For example, if you have a color monitor, but Mail displays in monochrome, follow these steps:

1. Exit Microsoft Mail.

2. Restart Mail by typing `MAIL -C`.

Finally, if you are using the Task Swapper with the MS-DOS Shell, you can't switch away from Microsoft Mail once you have passed the Mailbox screen (first screen displayed when starting Mail).

Summary

As you use the Workgroup Connection and Microsoft Mail more, you will begin to wonder how you ever got along without them. Communicating with people via electronic mail is much faster than regular mail and memos. The extra functionality that Mail adds, including the electronic filing system and personalized address lists, makes this one application you'll never want to give up.

Alan Simpson's

DOS
SECRETS
UNLEASHED

C H A P T E R   2 8

The POWER of INTERLNK

DOS 6 has two new features designed specifically for use with laptop and notebook computers. POWER is a utility designed to conserve the battery life of your laptop, and INTERLNK is used to connect your laptop to another computer, generally your desktop computer.

Installing and Using the POWER Utility

The POWER utility conforms to the Advanced Power Management (APM) specification and is basically designed to reduce the consumption of power by the devices connected to your computer when your applications are idle. If your laptop or notebook computer conforms to this specification, you can save up to 25% of your battery life. If it does not conform, you can still save up to 5% of your battery life by using this utility.

To setup your computer to use the power conservation feature, add a device driver to your CONFIG.SYS file as follows:

1. Using EDIT or another text editor, open your CONFIG.SYS file.

2. Add the following line anywhere in your CONFIG.SYS file:

    ```
    DEVICE=C:\DOS\POWER.EXE
    ```

3. Save the changes and reboot your computer.

POWER attempts to load itself into upper memory by default. If you want it to run in conventional memory, add the /LOW parameter to the DEVICE command.

Once the computer restarts, you can type

```
POWER
```

at the DOS prompt for current power settings. You can also change power settings by including any of the POWER parameters, as follows:

```
POWER [[ADV [:] MAX ¦ REG ¦ MIN] ¦ STD ¦ OFF]
```

To change the Advanced Power Management settings, use the ADV parameter in conjunction with one of the following:

:MAX sets maximum power conservation, potentially at the expense of application performance.

:REG is the default setting, balancing power conservation with application performance.

:MIN sets minimum power conservation, used only if MAX and REG make applications run too slow.

For example, to set power consumption to the maximum level, type

```
POWER ADV:MAX
```

If you are using an APM-compliant computer, issuing the following command enables your hardware to use only the built-in power consumption features:

```
POWER STD
```

If your machine is not APM-compliant, the following command turns off all power management:

```
POWER OFF
```

You can also use each of these commands as parameters in the DEVICE command of the CONFIG.SYS file. For example, if you want maximum conservation when you turn on your laptop, add the following command to your CONFIG.SYS file:

```
DEVICE=POWER.EXE ADV:MAX
```

Setting Up INTERLNK

The INTERLNK program comes in two parts—one for the *client* (your laptop computer) and one for the *server* (your desktop computer). When connected, the client sees the server's drives and printers as if they are part of the laptop computer itself.

This is a very useful utility. For example, suppose you're using your laptop at home or on the road to update a calendar or contact management database. When you return to your office, you can connect your laptop computer with your desktop computer and use INTERLNK to transfer your updated laptop files to your desktop computer. Additionally, you can run any application on your desktop computer from your laptop without copying the whole application to your laptop computer.

Requirements

To run INTERLNK, you need the following:

- A serial or parallel port on both computers. A serial port on one computer won't work with a parallel port on the other computer because each computer must have the same type of port available.

- A three-wire serial cable, seven-wire null-modem serial cable, or a bidirectional parallel cable. These cables are easily built or purchased from a computer store.

- 16K of available memory on the client and 130K of available memory on the server. INTERLNK runs as terminate-and-stay-resident (TSR) on the client, while the server portion, INTERSVR, runs full-screen.

- MS-DOS Version 3.0 or later on both computers. Although INTERLNK comes with DOS 6.0, it works with previous versions. I recommend that you install DOS 6 on your server.

If you are running MS-DOS 3.x on the client and your server has large hard disk partitions, you may not be able to use your partitions because MS-DOS 3.x only supports partitions up to 32M in size.

Setting Up the Client

Setting up your laptop computer to run INTERLNK is as easy as it is for POWER. You just need to add a device driver (INTERLNK.EXE) to your CONFIG.SYS file.

The INTERLNK.EXE file must be installed on your client computer, even if you are running a prior version of DOS on your client computer.

1. Using EDIT or another text editor, open your CONFIG.SYS file.

2. Add the following line to your CONFIG.SYS file:

   ```
   DEVICE=C:\DOS\INTERLNK.EXE
   ```

3. Save the changes and exit the editor.

INTERLNK starts with the first free drive. If other device drivers set up drives like a RAM drive, you may want to put the INTERLNK driver after these device drivers. For example, if you have a C: and D: drive, INTERLNK starts with E:. If you want your RAM drive to be E:, put its device driver first.

As with any changes made to the CONFIG.SYS file, you must reboot for the changes to take effect. However, because you have not set up the server yet, wait to reboot.

Setting Up the Server

Setting up the server is even easier. To start the server portion of INTERLNK, type

```
INTERSVR
```

at the server computer. A screen similar to the one in Figure 28.1 appears.

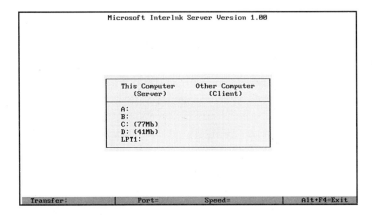

Figure 28.1. The INTERSVR screen.

Using INTERLNK

Now that both computers are configured and connected, you can reboot the client computer to begin the connection. As the device driver loads, you should see messages similar to the following:

```
Microsoft Interlnk version 1.00

    Port=COM1
    Drive letters redirected:  3 (F: through H:)
    Printer ports redirected:  2 (LPT2: through LPT3:)
```

```
This Computer        Other Computer
  (Client)              (Server)
- - - - - - - - - - -  - - - - - - - - - - - - - - - - - - - - - - -
  F:    equals    A:
  G:    equals    B:
  H:    equals    C: (77Mb)  DESKTOP
LPT2: equals      LPT1:
```

When the device driver loads, it redirects three drive letters, beginning with the first free letter, to the first three drives of the server. It also redirects any free printer ports on the client to any free printers on the server.

Once the device driver is loaded, type

```
INTERLNK
```

at a DOS prompt. The following will display:

```
  Scanning                              Port=COM1

This Computer        Other Computer
  (Client)              (Server)
- - - - - - - - - - -  - - - - - - - - - - - - - - - - - - - - - - -
  F:    equals    A:
  G:    equals    B:
  H:    equals    C: (77Mb)  DESKTOP
LPT2: equals      LPT1:
```

This shows you which port you are using for the connection (COM1), as well as the redirection of your client drives and printers to your server drives and printers.

To redirect additional drives, you use INTERLNK from the command line as follows:

```
INTERLNK [client[:]=[server][:]]
```

For example, to redirect the F: drive on your laptop computer to the D: drive on your desktop, type

```
INTERLNK F=D
```

or

```
INTERLNK F:=D:
```

> The redirected drive must be one that was redirected when you started INTERLNK. For example, you can't redirect drive I: if only F: through H: were redirected when you started INTERLNK.

To delete a redirected drive, type the client drive letter. For example, to delete the connection between the client's drive F: and the server's drive D:, type

```
INTERLNK F:=
```

Using a redirected drive or printer is, for all practical purposes, the same as using a local one. There are, of course, a few exceptions. You can't use any of the following commands on a redirected drive:

```
CHKDSK
DEFRAG
DISKCOMP
DISKCOPY
FDISK
FORMAT
MIRROR
SYS
UNDELETE
UNFORMAT
```

The INTERSVR screen provides you with a great deal of information about what's going on with the client computer. Figure 28.2 shows the current transfer operation, the port the server is using and the speed of the connection (*Turbo* for a parallel port). INTERSVR also places an asterisk by the server drive or printer being accessed.

> If you are running INTERSVR in a task-switching environment like the DOS Shell, the switching capability is disabled until you stop the server.

To stop the server, press Alt+F4.

> Pressing Alt+F4 will delete all client connections. Make sure that the client is finished using the server before stopping the server.

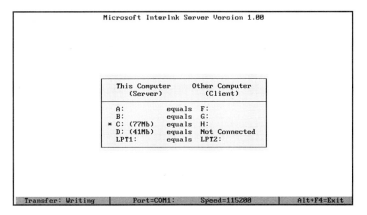

```
           Microsoft Interlnk Server Version 1.00


          This Computer        Other Computer
            (Server)             (Client)

          A:            equals  F:
          B:            equals  G:
        * C: (77Mb)     equals  H:
          D: (41Mb)     equals  Not Connected
          LPT1:         equals  LPT2:



  Transfer: Writing  |    Port=COM1:    Speed=115200  |  Alt+F4=Exit
```

*Figure 28.2.
The
INTERSVR
screen during a
disk access.*

Advanced INTERLNK Configurations

Using INTERLNK from the command line is very straightforward. However, INTERLNK can be configured in a number of ways through the device driver itself.

The syntax for using the device driver is as follows:

```
DEVICE=[drive:][path] INTERLNK.EXE [/DRIVES:n] [/NOPRINTER]
[/COM[:][n¦address]] [/LPT[:][n¦address]] [/AUTO]
[/NOSCAN][/LOW] [/BAUD:rate] [/V]
```

The *drive* and *path* point to the location of the INTERLNK.EXE file. The other configuration parameters do the following:

/DRIVES:*n* specifies the number of drives redirected during startup. By default, this is 3. If you specify 0, only printers are redirected.

/NOPRINTER specifies that printers are not redirected.

/COM[:][*n*¦*address*] specifies a serial port for the connection. You specify either the serial port number (COM1:) or the hexadecimal address (COM:3F8). If you enter COM, INTERLNK searches for the connection on serial ports only.

/LPT[:][*n*¦*address*] specifies a parallel port for the connection. Again, you can specify port number or hexadecimal address. Entering LPT searches for the connection on parallel ports only.

By specifying /NOPRINTER, /LPT and/or /COM, you can save memory. By default, INTERLNK loads all functions into memory. Specifying these parameters tells INTERLNK not to worry about redirecting printing or managing parallel and serial ports; therefore, less code is loaded into memory.

/AUTO means that INTERLNK only installs in memory if the connection is found.

Use the /AUTO parameter in the CONFIG.SYS file on your laptop computer. When it is not connected to the server (for example, if you are on the road), you save about 9K of memory because the INTERLNK driver does not load. When it is connected to your desktop, INTERLNK will initialize as usual.

/NOSCAN installs the INTERLNK driver in memory without making any connections. To establish a connection, you only need to attempt to access one of the redirected drives or ports.

/LOW performs the same function as when you use it with the POWER command. It loads into conventional memory instead of upper memory.

/BAUD:*rate* sets a maximum baud rate for serial communications. The default is 115,200. You don't need to change the baud rate unless you have problems making a connection.

/V prevents a conflict with the computer's timer. You use this parameter if your serial connection breaks when accessing a server. For example, the following command loads when a connection is available, only searches serial ports, and does not redirect printers.

```
DEVICE=INTERLNK.EXE /AUTO /COM /NOPRINTER
```

Advanced INTERSVR Configurations

The server is configured from the command line in the same way that INTERLNK is configured from the device driver in your CONFIG.SYS file.

The syntax for using INTERSVR is

```
INTERSVR [drive:] [/X=drive:] [/COM[:][n¦address]]
[/LPT[:][n¦address]] [/BAUD:rate] [/B] [/V]
```

where

drive: specifies a drive to redirect. By default, all drives are redirected. Use this parameter to change the order in which drives are made available—for example, INTERSVR C: D: A:.

/X=*drive*: specifies a drive that is not redirected.

If you have a small number of drives and want to exclude one, list the drives you want to redirect. However, if you have a large number of drives and want to exclude one, it is easier to use the /X:=drive: parameter than to list all of the other drives.

/B displays the server screen in black and white instead of color. For example, INTERSVR C: D: /LPT2 /B makes the server's C: and D: drives available to the second parallel port (LPT2), and displays the server screen in black and white.

Setting Up a Server from a Client

If the server you wish to connect to doesn't have the INTERSVR program on it, and you can't or don't want to copy it from a disk, you can remotely install INTERSVR from the client.

Use a seven-wire, null-modem serial cable to remotely install INTERSVR.

To install INTERSVR on the server from the client, type the following at the command prompt on the client:

```
INTERSVR /RCOPY
```

The result is the screen in Figure 28.3.

Select the serial port on the server that the cable is connected to and press Enter.

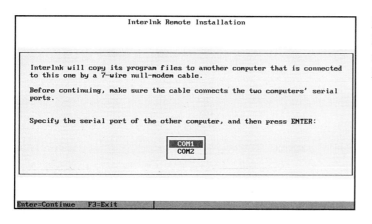

Figure 28.3.
Remotely
installing
INTERSVR.

At the server, perform the following (if the cable is connected to COM1):

1. Type MODE COM1:2400,N,8,1,P.

2. Press Enter.

3. Change to the directory where you want to copy the files.

4. Type CTTY COM1.

5. Press Enter.

The two files, INTERLNK.EXE and INTERSVR.EXE, are copied to the current directory on the server.

 Troubleshooting

If you experience a problem using the remote copy procedure, the following may be causing the problem:

■ You did not connect the computers through their serial ports with a seven-wire, null-modem serial cable. Remote copy will not work if you use a three-wire serial cable or a bidirectional parallel cable.

767

■ The MODE command is not available on the computer on which you are installing the INTERLNK program.

Summary

With these two new features of DOS 6, your laptop computer becomes an even more powerful tool. The POWER utility lets you work longer on each battery, and INTERLNK helps you effectively manage two computers—your desktop computer at the office and your laptop computer on the road.

Programming for
Non-Programmers

PART VII

Alan Simpson's
DOS SECRETS
UNLEASHED

C H A P T E R   2 9

Batch Programs Unleashed

Batch programs are also known as batch files, although *batch program* is Microsoft's preferred term.

This chapter presents some advanced techniques that you can use to create bigger and better batch programs. The sample batch programs that you will develop are practical enough to use in your own work.

This chapter assumes that you already know how to use the EDIT text editor described in previous chapters. Therefore, I will no longer present the step-by-step instructions required to create each batch program. Remember, Chapter 11, "Creating and Editing Files," provides general information about creating and editing any DOS text file.

Decision Making in Batch Programs

You can try out many of the IF and IF NOT commands shown in this chapter by typing them at the DOS prompt.

A batch program can use two commands—IF and IF NOT—to make a decision about whether to perform some operation. The basic syntax for the IF command is as follows:

```
IF condition command
```

in which *condition* is some situation that DOS can evaluate as being either true or false. If the condition proves true, it executes the *command* next to it. If the condition proves false, it ignores the *command* next to it.

You can reverse the effects of the condition by using the `IF NOT` command, as follows:

```
IF NOT condition command
```

In this command, if the *condition* is not true, it executes the *command*. If the *condition* is true, it ignores the *command*.

The three basic techniques for using the `IF` command are discussed in the sections that follow.

Using *IF* to Check for Files and Directories

The `IF EXIST` *filename* version of `IF` checks to see whether the file specified in *filename* exists. For example, the following command looks for a file named MYDIARY.TXT in the current directory. If the file exists, the command `TYPE MYDIARY.TXT` is executed; otherwise, the `TYPE MYDIARY.TXT` command is ignored.

```
IF EXIST MYDIARY.TXT TYPE MYDIARY.TXT
```

The next command checks to see whether a file named CHAP1.TXT already exists in a directory named \BAKFILES. If the file does not exist, the `COPY` command copies CHAP1.TXT from the current directory to the \BAKFILES directory; if the CHAP1.TXT files does exist on the \BAKFILES directory, the `COPY` command is not executed.

```
IF NOT EXIST \BAKFILES\CHAP1.TXT COPY
CHAP1.TXT \BAKFILES
```

As an alternative to using `IF NOT EXIST` to make sure a file does not exist before using `COPY`, you can use the `REPLACE` command, which enables you to confirm the replacement of existing files and to update older files without replacing newer files. The `XCOPY` command enables you to copy files in subdirectories and can also request permission to copy a file.

This general syntax is useful in batch programs when you want to be sure that a COPY operation does not overwrite an existing file. (You'll soon see an example of this usage.)

You also can use wildcard characters in the *filename* portion of the command. For example, the following command displays the message No batch programs here if the current directory does not contain any files with the .BAT extension:

```
IF NOT EXIST *.BAT ECHO No batch programs here
```

If you want to test for the presence of a *directory*, you can add the special device name \NUL after the name of the directory you're checking for. In the following command, the message Yep, it's here! appears if the directory C:\WOMBAT exists:

```
IF EXIST C:\WOMBAT\NUL ECHO Yep, it's here!
```

Using *IF* to Compare Strings

Recall that a *string* is any character or group of characters. You can use the IF command to compare two strings by using the general syntax

```
IF string1 == string2 command
```

which (in English) says, "If the first string matches the second string, do *command*." Alternatively, you can use the syntax

```
IF NOT string1 == string2 command
```

which says, "If the first string does not match the second string, do *command*."

The IF command recognizes two strings as identical if they are exactly the same, including uppercase and lowercase letters. For example, SMITH matches SMITH, but SMITH does not match Smith.

You can test the value of a passed parameter or environmental variable from batch programs only (not from the DOS prompt).

Typically, you use IF to see whether a passed parameter or an environmental variable equals a set value. For example, the command

```
IF %1 == Martha ECHO Hello Martha!
```

displays the message Hello Martha if the %1 variable contains the name Martha.

If either string is left blank, DOS returns the error message Syntax error. If one of the strings might be left blank, follow both strings in the IF command with an extra character, such as a period. For example, suppose you create a batch program that requires you to type a parameter at the command prompt. The following command checks to see whether the parameter is blank and, if so, displays the message A parameter is required.

```
IF %1. == . ECHO A parameter is required
```

Remember that %1 is merely a placeholder for the first option entered at the command prompt. Therefore, if %1 contains Joe, the previous command becomes IF Joe. == . ECHO A parameter is required before it is executed. Because Joe. is not the same as ., the ECHO command is ignored.

However, if you don't include a parameter at the command prompt, the command becomes IF . == . ECHO A parameter is required before execution. In this case, the two strings (. and .) are identical, so the ECHO command is executed. You'll see a practical example of this technique in SAFEMOVE.BAT and other batch programs presented in this chapter.

Testing for Values Returned by Commands

The commands BACKUP, DISKCOMP, DISKCOPY, FORMAT, GRAFTABL, KEYB, MOVE, REPLACE, RESTORE, and SETVER all return values for ERRORLEVEL. The "Notes" jump topic in the online help for each of these commands lists valid ERRORLEVEL values (also called *exit codes*). For example, to list the exit codes for BACKUP, type HELP BACKUP and press Enter. Press Enter again to select the "Notes" jump topic, and then press PgDn to scroll down to the list of exit codes. To return to the DOS prompt, press Alt+F and then X.

A third variation of the IF command is used in conjunction with commands such as BACKUP, FORMAT, and RESTORE. These commands all return an ERRORLEVEL value after they are executed. If the operation is completed successfully, ERRORLEVEL is zero. If the operation could not be completed, ERRORLEVEL is some number greater than zero.

Another command, CHOICE, also returns an ERRORLEVEL value when it is executed; however, the value returned depends on which key is pressed in response to a prompt. You'll learn how to use the CHOICE command later in this chapter.

The general syntax for using ERRORLEVEL in an IF command is as follows:

```
IF ERRORLEVEL number command
```

The *command* is executed only if the ERRORLEVEL value is greater than or equal to the *number*.

Alternatively, you can use the following syntax to reverse the test:

```
IF NOT ERRORLEVEL number command
```

In this case, the *command* is executed only if the ERRORLEVEL value is *not* greater than or equal to the *number*. In other words, the command is executed only if the ERRORLEVEL value is less than the number.

The BACKUP command, for example, returns an ERRORLEVEL value in the range from 1 to 4 when the backup operation cannot be completed, and a value of 0 if the backup is successful. In the following sample batch program, the IF commands signal DOS to display the message Backup not fully completed! if an error occurs during the BACKUP command. No message appears if the backup completes successfully.

```
REM ********************** QUICKBAK.BAT
REM Backs up new and modified files only.
BACKUP C:\*.* A: /S /M
IF ERRORLEVEL 4 ECHO Backup not fully completed!
IF ERRORLEVEL 3 ECHO Backup not fully completed!
IF ERRORLEVEL 2 ECHO Backup not fully completed!
IF ERRORLEVEL 1 ECHO Backup not fully completed!
```

In English, the IF ERRORLEVEL 4... command says "If the ERRORLEVEL is greater than or equal to 4, display the error message Backup not fully completed!". Thus, the error message will appear if the BACKUP command returns an ERRORLEVEL value of 4 or higher. The IF ERRORLEVEL 3... command says "If the ERRORLEVEL is greater than or equal to 3, display Backup not fully completed!". In this case, the message will appear if the BACKUP command returns a value of 3 or higher. Similarly, the IF ERRORLEVEL 2... command displays Backup not fully completed! if the BACKUP command returns a value of 2 or higher. Finally, the IF ERRORLEVEL 1... command displays the error message Backup not fully completed! if BACKUP returns a value of 1 or higher.

Depending on the value returned by the BACKUP command, the QUICKBAK.BAT batch program may display the message Backup not fully completed! up to four times. Of course, you could make each message more specific, so that the user (the person who happens to be running the batch program at the moment) knows which ERRORLEVEL value was returned. And after you learn about the GOTO command, you'll be able to refine batch programs like QUICKBAK.BAT so that they skip unnecessary error messages.

Notice how the QUICKBAK.BAT batch program checked for ERRORLEVEL values in reverse order, from highest to lowest. What do you think would happen if you tried to cut corners by creating the QUICKBAK.BAT batch program shown below?

```
REM *********************** QUICKBAK.BAT
REM Backs up new and modified files only.
BACKUP C:\*.* A: /S /M
IF NOT ERRORLEVEL 0 ECHO Backup not fully completed!
```

To understand the answer to this question, consider that the English meaning of this IF NOT ERRORLEVEL 0... command is "If the ERRORLEVEL is not greater than or equal to zero (that is, if the value is less than 0), display the message Backup not fully completed!" In fact, the ECHO command on the IF NOT ERRORLEVEL 0... line will *never* be executed because DOS commands always return an ERRORLEVEL value that is greater than or equal to zero. The bottom line is this: If you want to test for successful completion of a DOS command such as FORMAT, BACKUP, or RESTORE, you must first test for a ERRORLEVEL value that's greater than zero.

The following version of QUICKBAK.BAT does exactly what we want:

```
REM *********************** QUICKBAK.BAT
REM Backs up new and modified files only.
BACKUP C:\*.* A: /S /M
IF ERRORLEVEL 1 ECHO Backup not fully completed!
```

This version says "If the ERRORLEVEL is greater than or equal to 1, display the Backup not fully completed! message." Any returned value of 1 or higher causes the batch program to display just one error message letting us know that the backup was incomplete. If the backup completes successfully, no message appears.

Many of the batch programs presented later in this chapter contain practical examples of the IF command. First however, you need to learn about the GOTO command, which adds even more decision-making power to your batch programs.

Skipping a Group of Commands in a Batch Program

> You can use GOTO only in batch programs; it is not valid at the command prompt or in a DOSKEY macro.

As you know from Chapter 12, DOS usually executes commands in a batch program from the top down. However, you can force DOS to skip commands or repeat commands by using the GOTO command to perform a technique called *branching*.

The GOTO command tells DOS to skip a group of commands until it finds a *label*. When it finds the label, it resumes execution at the first command after the label. The label itself must be preceded by a colon in the batch program (but you do not include the colon in the GOTO command).

For example, the following sample batch program contains the command GOTO NearBottom and the label :NearBottom.

```
@ECHO OFF
ECHO I'm line 1
ECHO I'm line 2
GOTO NearBottom
ECHO I'm line 3
ECHO I'm line 4
:NearBottom
ECHO I'm line 5
ECHO I'm line 6
```

If you run this batch program, your screen displays this:

```
I'm line 1
I'm line 2
I'm line 5
I'm line 6
```

Notice that the two ECHO commands between the GOTO NearBottom command and the :NearBottom label were completely ignored. That's because the GOTO command branched execution to the first command after the NearBottom label, and therefore DOS never "saw" the ECHO commands for lines 3 and 4.

Copying Files Without Overwriting

To demonstrate a practical application of the IF and GOTO commands, Listing 29.1 shows a batch program named SAFECOPY.BAT that copies files from one drive or directory to another, but only if no files at the destination will be overwritten. (This is different from the DOS COPY command, which will overwrite files at the destination.)

Copy the SAFECOPY.BAT program from the add-in disks if you want to use it as a safe version of Copy—or, of course, you can type it in yourself.

Listing 29.1. The SAFECOPY.BAT batch program.

```
@ECHO OFF
REM *********************** SAFECOPY.BAT
REM Checks for overwriting before copying files
IF EXIST %2\%1 GOTO ErrMsg
COPY %1 %2\%1
GOTO Done
:ErrMsg
ECHO Files on %2 will be overwritten!
ECHO Copy aborted
:Done
```

Take a look at how SAFECOPY.BAT works. Assuming that you create this batch program on your own computer, you would type the command SAFECOPY *.BAT \DOS to use SAFECOPY.BAT to copy all the .BAT files from your current directory to a directory named \DOS.

First, in the command IF EXIST %2\%1 GOTO ErrMsg, the %1 and %2 variables are replaced with the source and destination for the copy. Hence, the command becomes IF EXIST \DOS*.BAT GOTO ErrMsg before execution. This checks to see whether any files on the \DOS directory have the extension .BAT. If that extension is found, control branches to the label :ErrMsg, thereby skipping the COPY command.

If the GOTO command did not branch control to the :ErrMsg label, the command COPY %1 %2\%1 becomes COPY *.BAT \DOS*.BAT after substitution. When this command executes, it copies all .BAT files to the \DOS directory.

> As an alternative to using SAFECOPY.BAT, you can use the XCOPY command with the /P switch or the REPLACE command with the /P and /A switches to prompt for confirmation before adding each destination file to the destination directory.

After a successful copy, the GOTO Done command passes control to the label named :Done, which bypasses the ECHO commands that display the error message. (These commands must be skipped to prevent the batch program from displaying the error messages after a successful copy operation.)

The :ErrMsg label (short for *error message*) marks the location to which the GOTO ErrMsg command passes control when the IF EXIST %2\%1 command proves true. Because this label is beneath the COPY command, the COPY command is not executed when control is passed to this label.

The commands ECHO Files on %2 will be overwritten! and ECHO Copy aborted display the error message on the screen. Note that if the COPY command is executed, the GOTO Done command skips over these commands, so the error message is not displayed. The :Done label marks the end of the batch program, where execution ends and control returns to the command prompt.

As you will see, asking questions with IF and branching with GOTO can help you to build more intelligent batch programs. But first, look at a few more optional techniques that can make your batch programs even smarter.

Pausing for a Keystroke

The CHOICE command, described in the "Requesting Input from the User" section, offers a more refined way to get input from the person using a batch program.

PAUSE is another command that you'll find useful when writing batch programs. This command temporarily stops execution of the batch program and displays the standard message Press any key to continue.... This pause is usually used to give a person a chance to insert a disk in a drive. However, you can also PAUSE to give you a chance to press Ctrl+C to terminate the batch program in the event of an unexpected situation.

NUL is sometimes called the "garbage can" device, because anything sent to it just disappears.

You can redirect the message displayed by PAUSE to a device called NUL (for null) if you want to hide the standard message and create your own. For example, look at the following commands:

```
@ECHO OFF
ECHO File(s) will be overwritten!
ECHO Press Ctrl+C, then Y, to abandon the operation
ECHO or any other key to proceed and overwrite...
PAUSE > NUL
COPY %1 %2
```

When executed, these commands display the following on the screen:

```
File(s) will be overwritten!
Press Ctrl+C, then Y, to abandon the operation
or any other key to proceed and overwrite...
```

Pressing any key other than Ctrl+C (or Ctrl+Break) resumes processing normally so that the COPY command below the PAUSE command is executed normally. However, pressing Ctrl+C (or Ctrl+Break) during this pause cancels execution of the batch program and displays this confirmation message:

```
Terminate batch job (Y/N)?
```

Pressing Y at this point finally terminates the batch program and returns to the command prompt. The COPY command is not executed. In essence, the PAUSE command enables the user to make a decision based on information provided by the messages on the screen.

Listing 29.2 shows a modified version of SAFECOPY.BAT that uses this alternate technique. Rather than absolutely refusing to overwrite files during a copy procedure, the batch program explains that files will be overwritten and asks for permission to proceed with the operation.

Listing 29.2. The modified SAFECOPY.BAT batch program.

```
@ECHO OFF
REM *********************** SAFECOPY.BAT
REM Modified version that gives the user the
REM choice about whether to proceed.
```

continues

Listing 29.2. continued

```
REM -- If no files will be overwritten, proceed to GoAhead.
IF NOT EXIST %2\%1 GOTO GoAhead

REM -- Present message and opportunity to cancel...
ECHO File(s) will be overwritten!
ECHO Press Ctrl+C, then Y, to abort operation
ECHO or any other key to proceed and overwrite...
PAUSE > NUL

REM -- If Ctrl+C was not pressed during pause,
REM -- execution proceeds with rest of commands.
:GoAhead
COPY %1 %2\%1
```

This version of SAFECOPY.BAT begins with the command IF NOT EXIST %2\%1 GOTO GoAhead, which sends control directly to the label :GoAhead and bypasses the messages that directly follow.

The ECHO commands present the messages warning that a file (or files) will be overwritten. Then a PAUSE waits for a key press. Pressing Ctrl+C during the pause and then pressing Y terminates execution of the batch program so that the COPY command is never reached.

Use the EDIT editor to create both versions of SAFECOPY.BAT (or retrieve these files from the Add-on disks included with this book). Test each one by trying to copy the same file to the same directory twice. On the second attempt, one batch program will not enable you to recopy the file, and the other will warn you about the operation.

Requesting Input from the User

You can experiment with the CHOICE command by typing it at the DOS prompt. However, if you want CHOICE to return ERRORLEVEL values, you must execute it from a batch program.

The CHOICE command is new in DOS 6. This handy batch program command displays a prompt, waits for the user to type a single-character response, and then returns an ERRORLEVEL value that reflects the user's choice.

For example, the simple command CHOICE displays the following prompt:

```
[Y,N]?
```

If the user responds by typing Y, the command returns ERRORLEVEL 1 to the batch program. If the user types N, the command returns ERRORLEVEL 2. If the user presses any key other than Y or N (the only allowable keys), the computer will beep and wait until the user types the correct response or presses Ctrl+C to terminate the batch program.

You can display a message preceding the prompt by typing the message text (optionally followed by a space) after the CHOICE command, like this:

```
CHOICE Are we having fun yet
```

Assuming you typed a space following the word yet, the CHOICE command would display the following message and prompt:

```
Are we having fun yet [Y,N]?
```

Notice how the message precedes the standard [Y,N]? prompt.

If you want to offer the user choices other than Y or N, or if you want to provide more than two options from which to choose, you can follow the CHOICE command with the switch /C: and the allowable keys for the user's response. The allowable responses can be letters or numbers. Consider this example:

```
CHOICE /C:YNQ Delete all files (Yes, No, Quit)
```

The colon (:) following the /C switch is optional, although it makes your batch program easier to read. Omitting the /C: switch is the same as specifying /C:YN.

(Again, there is a space at the end of the command line.) The preceding command displays the following prompt:

```
Delete all files (Yes, No, Quit) [Y,N,Q]?
```

Notice that the letters following the /C: switch are separated by commas and displayed in uppercase when the CHOICE command is executed. A user response of Y returns ERRORLEVEL 1 to the batch program; a response of N returns ERRORLEVEL 2; and a response of Q returns ERRORLEVEL 3. As you can see, the ERRORLEVEL returned depends on the position of the options that follow the /C: switch. If you omit the /C switch, a Y response always returns ERRORLEVEL 1 and an N response always returns ERRORLEVEL 2.

> If CHOICE detects an error, the ERRORLEVEL is set to 255. If you press Ctrl+Break or Ctrl+C, the ERRORLEVEL is set to 0.

When using an IF command to test for the ERRORLEVEL returned by the CHOICE command, remember that you must test in descending order. Hence, if the user can choose one of three options, you would type the CHOICE and IF ERRORLEVEL commands as shown in this partial example:

```
CHOICE /C:ynq Delete all files (Yes, No, Quit)
IF ERRORLEVEL 3 GOTO QUIT
IF ERRORLEVEL 2 GOTO SKIPDELETE
IF ERRORLEVEL 1 GOTO DELETE
```

Now, if the user types Q (the third option), execution branches to the batch program label :QUIT, which presumably is the last line of the batch program. If the user types N (the second option), execution branches to the label :SKIPDELETE, which bypasses the commands to delete all files. Finally, if the user types Y, the program executes the DEL commands following the label :DELETE.

Listing 29.3 illustrates another version of the SAFECOPY.BAT program. Suppose you ran the revised batch program by typing SAFECOPY *.BAT \DOS at the command prompt. As usual, the program tests for the existence of the .BAT files in the \DOS directory.

If the files do not exist, they are copied without further ado. However, if the files do exist, the CHOICE command displays the prompt Do you want to overwrite \DOS*.BAT [Y,N]? and waits for a response. If you type Y, CHOICE returns ERRORLEVEL 1 and control transfers to the label :GoAhead, which performs the copy. If you type N, CHOICE returns ERRORLEVEL 2, which transfers control to the label :Done at the end of the program.

Listing 29.3. The SAFECOPY.BAT batch program modified to use the CHOICE command.

```
@ECHO OFF
REM ************************ SAFECOPY.BAT
REM Modified version using CHOICE command.
REM Lets the user decide whether to overwrite existing files.

REM -- If no files will be overwritten, proceed to GoAhead.
IF NOT EXIST %2\%1 GOTO GoAhead

REM -- Present message and opportunity to cancel...
REM -- User must respond with Y (to overwrite) or N (to cancel).
CHOICE /C:YN Do you want to overwrite %2\%1
IF ERRORLEVEL 2 GOTO :Done
IF ERRORLEVEL 1 GOTO :GoAhead

REM -- If user chose Y when asked about overwriting files, the COPY
REM -- is executed; if user chose N, execution skips to :Done...
:GoAhead
COPY %1 %2\%1

:Done
```

You can use any combination of switches and text with the CHOICE command. As with most commands, the switches and message can appear in any order on the command line. All switches, as well as the text message, are optional.

CHOICE offers several other switches for extra flexibility. The switch /N prevents CHOICE from displaying the prompt that would otherwise appear in brackets ([ ]). Hence, the command CHOICE / C:12 Type 1 to edit or 2 to Quit: displays the prompt Type 1 to edit or 2 to Quit: [1,2]?. However, the command CHOICE /C:12 Type 1 to edit or 2 to Quit: /N (with the /N switch at the end) displays Type 1 to edit or 2 to Quit: instead.

By default, the user can respond with an uppercase or lowercase letter, and the prompt following the /C: switch is always displayed in uppercase. In contrast, if you include the /S switch with the CHOICE command, the user's response must match the case specified in the /C: switch exactly. Moreover, the prompt following the /C: switch will appear exactly as you entered it in the batch program. For example, the CHOICE command CHOICE /C:ynq /S will appear on the screen as [y,n,q]? and will accept only lowercase y, n, or q as a response.

As for the /S: switch, the colon (:) following the /T switch is optional, but makes your program easier to read and understand.

You can choose a default response to the CHOICE command by using the /T: switch. The format of this switch is

/T:c,nn

where c is the default response that is assumed if the user doesn't make a choice after nn seconds. Acceptable values for nn are from 0 (do not pause at all) to 99 (pause for 99 seconds). This option is handy for choosing the "safest" option if the user isn't paying attention or takes a coffee break while a batch program is running. For instance, suppose you want to have the option of defragmenting drive D: when you start your computer. You could add the following lines to your AUTOEXEC.BAT file:

```
CHOICE Defragment drive D: /T:N,5
IF ERRORLEVEL 2 GOTO NoDefrag
DEFRAG D:
:NoDefrag
```

This example prompts with `Defragment drive D: [Y,N]?` and waits for the user to respond. If the user doesn't respond after 5 seconds, the program assumes a response of `N` and transfers to the label `:NoDefrag`, which bypasses the `DEFRAG` command.

Now that you know how to make decisions in batch programs, take a look at a few tricks that will make your batch programs display more readable messages.

Improving Batch Program Messages

If you develop batch programs that display many messages and warnings on the screen, you should use some of the techniques discussed in the sections that follow.

Making Your Batch Program Beep

> You can also enter the beep in the message text of the `CHOICE` command.

You can easily make your batch program sound a beep when it presents an important message. If you are using the EDIT editor to create your batch programs, type the `ECHO` command, followed by a blank space and the message. However, before you press Enter to move to the next line, you have to insert a Ctrl+G control character. You insert this character while in EDIT by following these steps:

1. Press Ctrl+P (which enables you to use the Alt key to enter an ASCII control character).

2. Hold down the Alt key.

3. Type 007 (the ASCII code for Ctrl+G) on the numeric keypad.

4. Release the Alt key.

Your screen now displays a bullet character (●), as in the following example:

```
ECHO Files will be overwritten!●
```

Later, when you run the batch program, DOS sounds the beep whenever the message is displayed on the screen. (This technique is often used by programs to get your attention and warn you of a potential problem.)

Displaying Blank Lines from a Batch Program

If you want a batch program to display a blank line on the screen, follow the ECHO command with a period (no blank spaces). You can try this directly at the command prompt. That is, if you type the command

```
ECHO
```

DOS displays the message ECHO is on (or ECHO is off). However, if you type the command

```
ECHO.
```

DOS displays only a blank line.

A Batch Program to Move Files to a New Directory

> The MOVE command is new in DOS 6. If you're using Version 5 or an earlier version of DOS, you need to use the COPY and ERASE commands instead of MOVE, as discussed in the section "Making SAFEMOVE.BAT Even Safer." You can also use the Move option in the File pull-down menu of the File List in the DOS Shell to move files from one directory to another.

Combining most of the techniques discussed in the preceding sections help you to develop a powerful batch program named SAFEMOVE.BAT that can move files from one directory to another. On the surface, you might think that you could use the MOVE command for this purpose, and, indeed, the MOVE command is fine in many cases.

Suppose that you want to move the files named CHAP1.TXT, CHAP2.TXT, and so on up to CHAP19.TXT, to a directory named \DONE. You could enter the command MOVE CHAP*.TXT C:\DONE, which would copy all the files from the current directory to the directory named \DONE and erase them from the current directory immediately.

However, what if you entered the MOVE command without realizing that you had not yet created a directory named \DONE? Because DOS would not find the directory, it would assume you meant to move all those files to a file named DONE on the root directory! In this case, the MOVE command would display the message Cannot move multiple files to a single file and return to the DOS prompt without moving your files. To avoid this problem, the SAFEMOVE batch program verifies that the directory you're moving files to already exists.

> If you move just one file—by typing MOVE CHAP1.TXT
> C:\DONE—and the \DONE directory does not exist yet, the
> MOVE command would behave just like a RENAME command,
> changing the name of CHAP1.TXT to DONE (which is
> probably not what you want).

Now, think about what would happen if CHAP1.TXT, CHAP2.TXT, and so forth were present in the \DONE directory before you typed the MOVE command. That's right! The existing files in \DONE would be overwritten with the files being copied from the current directory faster than you could say "Oops!" For that reason, the batch program asks whether you want to replace any existing files in the destination directory with the source files.

Listing 29.4 shows the completed SAFEMOVE.BAT batch program, which has many safety features to prevent problems. It even warns you if the SAFEMOVE operation is going to overwrite files on the destination directory so that you can bail out before any overwriting takes place. (Blank lines are included in the batch program to help you isolate individual groups of commands, or *routines*. Also, notice that the line beginning with the word CHOICE, and the line that follows it, *must* be entered as one line; the arrow icon is used to indicate that the line is too long to print on one line in this book.)

Listing 29.4. The SAFEMOVE.BAT batch program.

```
@ECHO OFF
REM *************************** SAFEMOVE.BAT
REM Move file(s) to a new destination.
REM %1 is source, %2 is destination.

REM Make sure two parameters were passed.
IF %2. == . GOTO ErrMsg1

REM Make sure source exists.
IF NOT EXIST %1 GOTO ErrMsg2

REM Check to see whether %2 is a valid directory.
IF NOT EXIST %2\nul GOTO ErrMsg3
```

```
REM Check to see whether overwriting will occur.
IF NOT EXIST %2\%1 GOTO MoveIt

REM Provide warning before overwriting; ● is Ctrl+G ...
REM If user chooses N (ERRORLEVEL 2), don't overwrite.
CHOICE /C:YN WARNING! %1 file(s) exist on %2!
➡Do you want to overwrite ●
IF ERRORLEVEL 2 GOTO Done

:MoveIt
MOVE %1 %2 > NUL
GOTO Done

:ErrMsg1
ECHO You must provide a source and destination. For example,
ECHO SAFEMOVE *.BAK \BAKFILES
ECHO moves all .BAK files to the \BAKFILES directory.
GOTO Done

:ErrMsg2
ECHO %1 does not exist!
GOTO Done

:ErrMsg3
ECHO %2 is not a valid directory!

:Done
```

As an example, suppose that you run SAFEMOVE.BAT with this command:

```
SAFEMOVE CHAP*.TXT C:\DOSBOOK
```

The first line turns off ECHO, and the next four lines are the usual comments. The first command, IF %2. == . GOTO ErrMsg1, checks for an initial error. This command verifies that two parameters were entered next to the SAFEMOVE command. If %2 (the second parameter) is blank, this command passes control to the :ErrMsg1 label. In the example above, the command would be IF C:\DOSBOOK. == . GOTO ErrMsg1 after substitution. Because C:\DOSBOOK. is not the same as ., execution resumes with the next command.

The next command, IF NOT EXIST %1 GOTO ErrMsg2, checks to see whether the files being copied exist in the current directory. In this example, after substitution takes place, the command becomes

`IF NOT EXIST CHAP*.TXT GOTO ErrMsg2`. If no files in the current directory match the ambiguous file name CHAP*.TXT, this command passes control to the `:ErrMsg2` label. Again, this is just a safety precaution to ensure that the command line was entered correctly at the DOS command prompt.

Next, the command `IF NOT EXIST %2\nul GOTO ErrMsg3` checks to see whether %2 is a valid directory. If it is not, execution branches to the label `:ErrMsg3`. After substitution, the command becomes `IF NOT EXIST C:\DOSBOOK\nul GOTO ErrMsg3`.

> Recall that you must add `\nul` to a directory name if you want to determine whether the directory exists.

Assuming that the directory C:\DOSBOOK does exist, the batch program can proceed to the next command, `IF NOT EXIST %2\%1 GOTO MoveIt`. This command checks to see whether any files in the destination directory have the same names as the files in the source directory. In this example, the command becomes `IF NOT EXIST C:\DOSBOOK\CHAP*.TXT GOTO MoveIt`. If none of the files on the C:\DOSBOOK directory matches CHAP*.TXT, the `GOTO` command transfers control directly to the `:MoveIt` label. However, if file names on the destination directory match files to be moved, the next commands are executed instead. (Notice that the first two lines of the following example *must* be typed in as one line.)

```
CHOICE /C:YN WARNING! %1 file(s) exist on %2!
➡Do you want to overwrite ●
IF ERRORLEVEL 2 GOTO Done
```

These commands display the message warning that files will be overwritten, cause the computer to beep, and wait for the user to type Y or N. (Remember, the ● symbol represents the control character Ctrl+G and causes the computer to beep.)

After substitution, the actual message displayed is as follows:

```
WARNING! CHAP*.TXT file(s) exist on C:\DOSBOOK! Do you want
to overwrite [Y,N]?
```

The CHOICE command waits for a Y or N keystroke. At this point, pressing N returns an ERRORLEVEL value of 2; pressing Y returns a value of 1. If the user pressed N, the command IF ERRORLEVEL 2 GOTO Done transfers control to the label :Done, which cancels the batch program and prevents any files from being moved. Pressing the Y key passes control to the next commands.

MoveIt is the label for the block of commands that perform the actual moving. First the command MOVE %1 %2 > NUL is converted to MOVE CHAP*.TXT C:\DOSBOOK > NUL. This moves all the files with the ambiguous name CHAP*.TXT from the current directory to the directory C:\DOSBOOK. (Ignore the > NUL for now; it just hides the messages that COPY normally displays. You can omit it from the batch program if you prefer.)

The next command, GOTO Done, branches control to the :Done label to bypass the error messages. Following this command are the labels and error messages to which the preceding IF commands would pass control in the event of an error. These are simple ECHO commands that provide information about the specific error that occurred. As you can see in the following code lines, each routine branches to the :Done label after displaying its error message, so that the ECHO commands below the routine are not executed.

```
:ErrMsg1
ECHO You must provide a source and destination. For example,
ECHO SAFEMOVE *.BAK \BAKFILES
ECHO moves all .BAK files to the \BAKFILES directory.
GOTO Done

:ErrMsg2
ECHO %1 does not exist!
GOTO Done

:ErrMsg3
ECHO %2 is not a valid directory!

:Done
```

In some ways, SAFEMOVE.BAT might seem almost paranoid in its concern with safety. However, considering that this batch program removes the source files from their original directory and could overwrite existing files, safety is certainly important! For even more paranoia, see the later section titled "Making SAFEMOVE.BAT Even Safer."

Tips for Using SAFEMOVE.BAT

Be aware that the SAFEMOVE.BAT batch program is designed to protect existing files *only* when you move files from the current directory to a different directory. If you specify a drive letter or another directory in the source, the command IF NOT EXIST %2%1 GOTO MoveIt always transfers control to the label :MoveIt. That's because the combination %2%1 results in a file name that cannot possibly exist.

For example, if you enter a command such as SAFEMOVE C:\WP\WPFILES\SALEMEMO.DOC \SALES to move the SALEMEMO.DOC file from the \WP\WPFILES directory to the \SALES directory, the IF command would be interpreted as IF NOT EXIST \SALES\C:\WP\WPFILES\SALEMEMO.DOC GOTO MoveIt. Clearly, such a weird file name cannot exist, so control transfers to the :MoveIt label. To avoid this pitfall, you should change to the \WP\WPFILES directory first by entering the command CD \WP\WPFILES at the command prompt. If you fail to do this, SAFEMOVE.BAT still moves the source files to the correct destination directory; however, it overwrites any existing files in the destination directory.

Making SAFEMOVE.BAT Even Safer

To avoid overwriting existing files in the destination directory and make SAFEMOVE even safer, you could revise the MoveIt routine so that it uses the COPY command followed by the ERASE command, instead of the MOVE command.

As an alternative to revising the SAFEMOVE.BAT program, you could copy SAFEMOVE.BAT to a new file named SAFER.BAT, and then make your changes to SAFER.BAT. To do so, at the command prompt type the command COPY SAFEMOVE.BAT SAFER.BAT. Then type the command EDIT SAFER.BAT and make your changes.

The steps for revising SAFEMOVE.BAT are simple. First replace the three lines of the MoveIt routine shown in Listing 29.4 with the longer (but safer) MoveIt routine shown here:

```
:MoveIt
COPY %1 %2\%1 > NUL
REM Double-check before erasing.
IF NOT EXIST %2\%1 GOTO ErrMsg3
ERASE %1
GOTO Done
```

Then replace the two lines in the ErrMsg3 routine with commands that display a more accurate error message, as follows:

```
:ErrMsg3
ECHO Source is invalid, destination directory doesn't exist,
ECHO or destination directory is the same as the current
directory.
ECHO -- Operation canceled --
```

Suppose that after saving the revised program, you type the command SAFEMOVE CHAP*.TXT C:\DOSBOOK (or SAFER CHAP*.TXT C:\DOSBOOK). How does the new MoveIt routine do its job. First the command COPY %1 %2\%1 > NUL is converted to COPY CHAP*.TXT C:\DOSBOOK\CHAP*.TXT > NUL (again, > NUL simply hides messages displayed by COPY).

Notice that the COPY command repeats the file name in the destination. This technique prevents COPY from overwriting existing files in the destination directory when a drive or directory name is given for the source files to be moved. For example, if you type SAFEMOVE C:\WP51\BOOKS\CHAP*.TXT C:\DOSBOOK, the COPY command becomes COPY \C:\WP51\BOOKS\CHAP*.TXT C:\DOSBOOK\C:\WP51\BOOKS\ CHAP*.TXT. In this case, DOS displays the error message Too many parameters and refuses to copy the files. That's because it interprets the parameter C:\DOSBOOK\C:\WP51\BOOKS\CHAP*.TXT as two separate destination parameters—C:\DOSBOOK\ and C:\WP51\BOOKS\ CHAP*.TXT. Recall that COPY is allowed only two parameters: the *source* and *destination*. But in this case, you end up with three parameters—one source (\C:\WP51\BOOKS\CHAP*.TXT) and two destinations. DOS, naturally, complains about this state of affairs.

Before erasing any files in the current directory, the command IF NOT EXIST %2\%1 GOTO ErrMsg3 becomes IF NOT EXIST C:\DOSBOOK\CHAP*.TXT GOTO ErrMsg3. This command checks the destination directory to verify that it contains the files that were (presumably) copied by the preceding COPY command. If anything went wrong during the COPY operation, the destination directory will not contain the copied files, and the GOTO command will transfer to the :ErrMsg3 label. Hence, the ERASE command will be bypassed and will not erase any files if the copy failed for any reason.

If (and only if) all went well up to this point, the ERASE %1 command expands to ERASE CHAP*.TXT. This erases all copied files from the source directory. Because every possible error has been checked, it is now safe to proceed with the ERASE command.

The next command, GOTO Done, branches control to the :Done label to bypass the error messages as usual.

Repeating Commands in a Batch Program

Another high-powered technique that you can use in a batch program is *looping*. Looping enables you to repeat a command several times. The command you use for looping is FOR, which uses the following general syntax:

```
FOR %%letter IN (items) DO command
```

where *letter* is a single letter (a through z or A through Z), *items* is either a list of items separated by blank spaces or an ambiguous file name (which represents several files), and *command* is the command that is executed during each pass through the loop.

Each time the loop is executed, the %%letter variable assumes either the next value in the list of items or the next file name in the list produced by the ambiguous file name.

Even though you normally use the FOR command in a batch program, you can actually try an example at the command prompt. However, when using FOR at the command prompt, you use %*letter* rather than %%*letter*.

Now test the command. Assuming that the command prompt is displayed on your screen, type the following line and press Enter.

```
FOR %c IN (Item1 Item2 Item3) DO ECHO %c
```

After you press Enter, your screen shows the following:

```
C:\UTILS>ECHO Item1
Item1

C:\UTILS>ECHO Item2
Item2

C:\UTILS>ECHO Item3
Item3

C:\UTILS>
```

where C:\UTILS> is simply the DOS command prompt.

Notice what happens. In the first pass through the loop, %c is replaced by the first item in the list, so the first command executed is ECHO Item1. During the second pass through the loop, %c is replaced by the second item in the list, so the command executed is ECHO Item2. In the third pass through the loop, Item3 is substituted for %c, so the command executed is ECHO Item3. The next section examines a more practical application of looping.

LOOKIN.BAT—A Batch Program to Search for a Word

LOOKIN.BAT is a batch program that can search through the contents of text files for a specific word. The more files and information you store on your computer, the more useful this batch program becomes. For example, suppose that you use EDIT to create a file, named PHONE.TXT, that contains people's phone numbers, as shown in Listing 29.5. (Your file would probably contain many more names and numbers.) If you created LOOKIN.BAT, you could quickly retrieve Bonnie Baker's number by entering this command:

```
LOOKIN PHONES.TXT Baker
```

Listing 29.5. A file containing names and phone numbers.

Arthur Adams	(213)555-0146
Bonnie Baker	(619)555-9302
Charlie Charisma	(415)555-0954
Donna Daring	(213)555-8765
Edie Estoval	(415)555-7676
Frankly Fastidious	(619)555-9443
Gina Garrog	(714)555-3232
Harry Hampton	(212)555-6543

Your screen would display the following:

```
------------- PHONES.TXT
Bonnie Baker                (619)555-9302

Do you want to print the results [Y,N]?
```

Another situation in which LOOKIN.BAT is useful is when you forget the name of a file you've created. If you know the directory in which the file is stored and can think of a distinctive word that is stored in the file, you can use LOOKIN.BAT to quickly search a large group of files for that word.

For example, if you wrote a letter to Albert Smith but cannot remember the name of that particular file (other than the fact that it probably had the extension .LET), you would enter the following command to search all .LET files on the current directory for the word `Albert`:

```
LOOKIN *.LET Albert
```

Listing 29.6 shows sample results of running LOOKIN.BAT for the theoretical example above. Note that the name `Albert` appears only in the QUIKNOTE.LET file.

Listing 29.6. Sample results of a search with LOOKIN.BAT.

```
C:\WP\WPFILES>LOOKIN *.LET Albert
Searching for Albert in *.LET...
Results of scanning *.LET files for Albert


---------- ACCTNG.LET

---------- COVER.LET

---------- GRANDMA.LET

---------- QUIKNOTE.LET
Albert J. Smith
Dear Albert:

---------- ZOO.LET

Do you want to print the results [Y,N]?
```

Listing 29.7 shows the entire LOOKIN.BAT batch program. Use the usual EDIT techniques to create LOOKIN.BAT on your own computer (or copy it from the Add-on disks).

Listing 29.7. The LOOKIN.BAT batch program.

```
@ECHO OFF
REM ***************************************** LOOKIN.BAT
REM Searches multiple text files for a word.
REM ---- %1 is the file(s) to be searched,
REM ---- %2 is the word to search for.

REM ---- Erase TEMPFILE.TXT if it exists.
IF EXIST TEMPFILE.TXT ERASE TEMPFILE.TXT

REM ---- Search files with FIND,
REM ---- redirect output to TEMPFILE.TXT
ECHO Searching for %2 in %1...
FOR %%c IN (%1) DO FIND /I "%2" %%c >> TEMPFILE.TXT

REM ---- Display the results.
ECHO Results of scanning %1 files for %2
MORE < TEMPFILE.TXT

REM ---- Present option to print the results.
ECHO.
CHOICE Do you want to print the results
IF ERRORLEVEL 2 GOTO Done
ECHO Results of scanning %1 files for %2 > PRN
TYPE TEMPFILE.TXT > PRN
ECHO ♀ > PRN

:Done
```

Versions of DOS prior to DOS 5 do not include the /I switch, which tells FIND to ignore case. If you are using those versions of DOS, you must use the command FOR %%c IN (%1) DO FIND "%2" %%c >> TEMPFILE.TXT in the previous batch program.

LOOKIN.BAT offers some unique features that you have not seen in previous batch programs. Therefore, I'll discuss the purpose of each command in LOOKIN.BAT (excluding the REM comment lines and the @ECHO OFF line). For the purposes of example, assume that you executed LOOKIN.BAT with the command LOOKIN *.LET Albert.

First, the command IF EXIST TEMPFILE.TXT ERASE TEMPFILE.TXT erases the file named TEMPFILE.TXT from the current directory (if it exists). As you will see, LOOKIN.BAT sends its output to this file so that you later have the option of printing the results of LOOKIN.BAT after viewing them on the screen.

Next, the command ECHO Searching for %2 in %1 displays a message that tells you what operation is taking place. In this example, the message on the screen would be Searching for Albert in *.LET.

The next command, FOR %%c IN (%1) DO FIND /I "%2" %%c >> TEMPFILE.TXT, executes the command FIND /I "%2" every time a new file name matches the *.LET ambiguous file name. For example, if the first file to be searched is ACCTNG.LET, this command becomes FIND "Albert" ACCTNG.LET. The >> TEMPFILE.TXT portion of the command sends the output to the end of file TEMPFILE.TXT, without erasing existing text in TEMPFILE.TXT. This loop is repeated until all *.LET files have been searched.

The next command, ECHO Results of scanning %1 files for %2, displays a message on the screen. In this example, the message is Results of scanning *.LET files for Albert. Then the command MORE < TEMPFILE.TXT displays the results of the search, which are stored in the file TEMPFILE.TXT. The MORE < part of the command pauses the display after each screenful of information displayed and waits for a key press.

The ECHO. command prints a blank line on the screen. The following CHOICE command displays the following message and pauses to wait for a response.

Do you want to print the results [Y,N]?

Pressing N sends an ERRORLEVEL of 2 to the batch program and causes the program to branch to the label :Done.

To enter Ctrl+L (^L) at the command line, press Ctrl+L. To enter Ctrl+L while editing your batch program with the EDIT editor, position the cursor as usual, press Ctrl+P, hold down the Alt key, type 012 on the numeric key pad, and then release the Alt key.

If you press Y to continue the operation, the next three commands send the message Results of scanning *.LET files for Albert and the contents of the TEMPFILE.TXT to the printer. The last command, ECHO ♀ > PRN, sends Ctrl+L to the printer to eject the page. You can omit this last command if you are not using a laser printer.

Tips for Using LOOKIN.BAT

The FIND command in versions of DOS prior to DOS 5 cannot ignore the case of text. When using FIND with these earlier versions of DOS, you must omit the /I switch and type your search text in the exact uppercase and lowercase letters you want to match. For example, the command LOOKIN PHONES.TXT BAKER would not find Baker, but LOOKIN PHONES.TXT Baker would. (Another version of LOOKIN.BAT, named LOOKIN2.BAT, is presented in the "Passing More Than Nine Parameters" section later in this chapter to illustrate a way around this limitation for users of earlier versions of DOS.)

LOOKIN.BAT can search any file or group of files in any directory for any single word. The /I switch on the FIND command makes the search *non-case-sensitive*, which means that you can enter the word you're searching for in any combination of uppercase and lowercase letters. That is, the command LOOKIN PHONES.TXT BAKER would find Baker, BAKER, BaKer, and so forth.

Be aware that the results might not be accurate if you use LOOKIN.BAT to search files that you created with a word processor. Word processors may use formatting codes that change the word FIND is looking for. If in doubt, use the TYPE command to view the contents of your word processing file to see how it is stored.

If your word processor changes the last character of every word, you should use LOOKIN.BAT to search for all the characters in a word except for the last. Suppose that you want to search through a group of files with the extension .DOC for the word *banana*. However, you created these .DOC files with WordStar, which alters the last character of many words in a document. Entering the command LOOKIN *.DOC banan would yield more accurate results than the command LOOKIN *.DOC banana.

LOOKIN.BAT displays only the Searching... message while the search is taking place. Depending on the speed of your computer and the amount of text being searched, the delay might be anywhere from a few seconds to several minutes. In most cases, however, the search will be surprisingly fast.

COUNTIN.BAT—A Variation of LOOKIN.BAT

LOOKIN.BAT displays the name of every file searched and the lines of text in each file that contain the word you are looking for. As an alternative, you can create COUNTIN.BAT, which displays the names of files that contain the word you are looking for and the number of times the word appears in that file.

This can be a useful command in many situations. Imagine that you've stored each chapter for a book in files named CHAP1.TXT,

CHAP2.TXT, CHAP3.TXT, and so on. If you wanted to see which chapter first introduced the term *reboot*, you could enter the command COUNTIN CHAP*.TXT reboot. The results of this search, shown in Listing 29.8, reveal that the word *reboot* is first mentioned in Chapter 3 (CHAP3.TXT) and is also included in several other chapters.

Listing 29.8. Results of the command
`COUNTIN *.TXT reboot`.

```
C:\WP\WPFILES>COUNTIN *.TXT reboot
Counting for "reboot" in *.TXT files
"reboot" appears in the following *.TXT files

---------- CHAP3.TXT: 2
---------- CHAP5.TXT: 10
---------- CHAP10.TXT: 1

Do you want to print the results [Y,N]?
```

If you've created LOOKIN.BAT already, you can use it as a starting point for developing COUNTIN.BAT, because the two batch programs are very similar. To do so, at the command prompt type the command COPY LOOKIN.BAT COUNTIN.BAT. Then type the command EDIT COUNTIN.BAT. Now, you need to change only a few lines, rather than create an entirely new file. Listing 29.9 shows the complete COUNTIN.BAT file.

Listing 29.9. The COUNTIN.BAT batch program.

```
@ECHO OFF
REM ***************************************** LOOKIN.BAT
REM Searches multiple text files for a word.
REM ---- %1 is the file(s) to be searched,
REM ---- %2 is the word to search for.

REM ---- Erase TEMPFILE.TXT if it exists.
IF EXIST TEMPFILE.TXT ERASE TEMPFILE.TXT
```

```
REM ---- Search files with FIND /C
REM ---- redirect output to TEMPFILE.TXT
ECHO Counting for %2 in %1 files.
FOR %%c IN (%1) DO FIND /I /C "%2" %%c >> TEMPFILE.TXT

REM ---- Display the results.
ECHO "%2" appears in the following %1 files.
TYPE TEMPFILE.TXT ¦ FIND "-" ¦ FIND /V " 0" ¦ MORE

REM ---- Present option to print the results.
ECHO.
CHOICE Do you want to print the results
IF ERRORLEVEL 2 GOTO Done
ECHO "%2" appears in the following %1 files. > PRN
TYPE TEMPFILE.TXT ¦ FIND "-" ¦ FIND /V " 0" > PRN
ECHO ♀ > PRN

:Done
```

> Note that the FIND command in the line that begins FOR %%C... now includes the /C switch. This switch tells the FIND command to count rather than display the words for which it is searching.

The two lines that displayed results with a MORE command and printed results with a TYPE command have been changed to TYPE TEMPFILE.TXT ¦ FIND "-" ¦ FIND /V " 0" ¦ MORE. The TYPE command sends the results of the search (stored in TEMPFILE.TXT) to the filters that follow the command. The first filter, FIND "-", limits the output to lines that begin with a hyphen, because only those lines will contain file names (as you can see in Listing 29.8).

That output is passed through the second filter, FIND /V " 0", which filters out all lines that contain a zero preceded by a blank space. The leading blank space ensures that only lines with an exact count of zero are excluded; however, lines that contain a zero, such as those with a count of 10 or 20, or lines that contain a file name like SPRING90.TXT, will be included. In the line that displays output on the screen, the final output is passed through the MORE filter, which pauses the screen display every 24 lines. In the line that prints the results, the output is redirected to the printer (> PRN).

A few messages and comments also have been altered slightly. After making your changes, save your work and exit EDIT in the usual manner. The basic technique for using COUNTIN.BAT is identical to that for using LOOKIN.BAT. The only difference is the format of the displayed results.

Passing Multiple Parameters to DOS Commands

Looping is also valuable for passing multiple parameters to DOS commands that usually accept only a single parameter. For example, if you want to erase the files APPLE.TXT, BANANA.DOC, and CHERRY.LET using the DOS ERASE command, you must type three separate commands:

```
ERASE APPLE.TXT
ERASE BANANA.DOC
ERASE CHERRY.LET
```

However, with the next batch program, MERASE.BAT (Multiple ERASE), you can specify as many as nine files to erase, and any of those file names can contain wildcard characters. To erase the three files listed previously using MERASE, you need only type the following command:

```
MERASE APPLE.TXT BANANA.DOC CHERRY.LET
```

Listing 29.10 shows the complete MERASE.BAT file. To understand how the batch program works, assume that you created it and then typed the command MERASE APPLE.TXT BANANA.DOC CHERRY.LET to erase three files. This command stores the following values in the % variables:

```
%1= APPLE.TXT
%2= BANANA.DOC
%3= CHERRY.LET
```

%4 through %9 are empty (blank).

> In Listings 29.10 through 29.13, the last line, starting with
> FOR %%c, is broken only to fit within the margins of this
> book. If you type one of these batch programs, don't break
> that last line.

Listing 29.10. The MERASE.BAT batch program.

```
@ECHO OFF
REM ************************ MERASE.BAT
REM Accepts as many as nine file names to erase.
FOR %%c IN (%1 %2 %3 %4 %5 %6 %7 %8 %9) DO IF NOT %%c. == .
     ERASE %%c
```

In the first pass through the loop, %%c assumes the value of %1, or APPLE.TXT in this example. Therefore, the command IF NOT %%c. == . ERASE %%c expands to IF NOT APPLE.TXT == . THEN ERASE APPLE.TXT. Because APPLE.TXT and . are not the same, the command ERASE APPLE.TXT is executed, and the file is erased.

During the next pass through the loop, %%c takes the value of %2, or BANANA.DOC. Once again, the IF test proves true, so the ERASE BANANA.DOC command is executed, and the BANANA.DOC file is erased. In the third pass through the loop, %%c assumes the value of %3, or CHERRY.LET. Again, the IF test proves true, and CHERRY.LET is erased.

During the fourth pass through the loop, %%c takes the value of %4, which is empty. In this case, the command IF NOT %%c. == . proves false (because %%c. does equal .), so the ERASE command is ignored. In fact, in all remaining passes through the loop, the IF NOT command proves false; therefore, no more files are erased and the batch program ends, returning control to the command prompt.

There are no built-in safety features in this batch program. It is as immediate in its erasing as the regular DOS ERASE command. However, users of DOS 4 and later can add the /P switch to the right of the ERASE %%c command. This forces the ERASE command to pause and ask for permission before deleting each file. Listing 29.11 shows this safer version of MERASE.BAT.

Listing 29.11. Safer version of MERASE.BAT (works only with DOS 4 and later).

```
@ECHO OFF
REM ************************* MERASE.BAT
REM Accepts as many as nine file names to erase.
FOR %%c IN (%1 %2 %3 %4 %5 %6 %7 %8 %9) DO IF NOT %%c. == .
    ERASE %%c /P
```

You can use this general looping technique to pass as many as nine parameters to any DOS command. However, it's a little trickier to pass multiple parameters to a command that requires two or more parameters, such as COPY. For example, if you try to create a batch program named MCOPY that can accept multiple file names, as in the command

```
MCOPY LETTER.TXT MYFILE.DOC A:
```

and also the command

```
MCOPY APPLE.TXT BANANA.DOC Qtr1_90.WKS ABC.LET A:
```

you might have a difficult time, because in the first command, the destination (A:) is the third parameter (%3), but in the second command, the destination is the fifth parameter (%5). However, there is a simple solution to this problem. If you place the destination first, your batch program can always "assume" that the destination is %1.

For example, you could create a batch program named COPYTO.BAT that accepts as many as eight file names to copy, using the general syntax

```
COPYTO destination file1 file2...file8
```

where any of the eight file names can contain wildcards. That is, you could type the command

```
COPYTO A: APPLE.TXT BANANA.DOC CHERRY.LET
```

where A: is the destination and the rest are file names to be copied to drive A:. Alternatively, you could type the command

```
COPYTO A: *.LET *.LET *.DOC *.BAK LETTER?.TXT
```

to copy all the specified files to drive A:.

Listing 29.12 shows the COPYTO.BAT batch program. It works on the same basic principle that MERASE.BAT does; however, the %1 variable is not included in the list of items for the loop command. The FOR loop processes only the file names (%2 through %9), whereas the destination (%1) is used repeatedly as the destination in the COPY command.

Listing 29.12 shows the COPYTO.BAT batch program.

```
@ECHO OFF
REM ************************* COPYTO.BAT
REM Accepts as many as eight file names to copy.
FOR %%c IN (%2 %3 %4 %5 %6 %7 %8 %9) DO IF NOT %%c. == .
     COPY %%c %1
```

You can use this looping technique to pass multiple parameters to a batch program as well. However, this technique is a little different, and it also varies with different versions of DOS, as the next section explains.

Passing Control from One Batch Program to Another

Because batch programs are essentially customized DOS commands, they can be used like any other DOS command, either at the command prompt or in a batch program. In all versions of DOS, one batch program can pass control to another batch program, but in doing so, the first batch program relinquishes all control to the second batch program, and any additional commands in the first batch program are not executed. Take a look at a simple example.

The following BAT1.BAT file contains two ECHO commands. However, note that a command between them executes a batch program named BAT2.BAT:

```
@ECHO OFF
REM ****** Bat1.BAT
ECHO I am the first line in BAT1.BAT.
BAT2
ECHO I am the last line in BAT1.BAT.
```

BAT2.BAT, shown here, contains one ECHO command:

```
@ECHO OFF
REM ****** Bat2.BAT
ECHO      I am the only line in BAT2.BAT.
```

If you were to create both of these batch programs and then type the command BAT1, your screen would display the following:

```
I am the first line in BAT1.BAT.
    I am the only line in BAT2.BAT.
```

As you can see, the second ECHO command in BAT1.BAT was never executed. That's because after the BAT2 command was executed, all control passed to BAT2.BAT. When BAT2.BAT finished its job, all execution stopped.

If you are using a version of DOS prior to Version 3.3, replace the command CALL BAT2 with COMMAND /C BAT2 in the sample batch programs that follow. Be sure to follow the /C with a blank space. Note that COMMAND /C still works in DOS 3.3 and later, although CALL is the preferred command.

With DOS Version 3.3 and later versions, you can have one batch program call another, so that when the second batch program finishes, it returns control to the first. That way, execution resumes normally and the first batch program can finish executing its remaining commands. To use this technique, use the CALL command.

For example, look at the following BAT1.BAT file. Notice that the only difference between this version and the previous version is that BAT1.BAT uses the command CALL BAT2, rather than just BAT2, to pass control to the BAT2.BAT batch program:

```
@ECHO OFF
REM ******* Bat1.BAT
ECHO I am the first line in BAT1.BAT.
CALL BAT2
ECHO I am the last line in BAT1.BAT.
```

With this version of BAT1.BAT, typing the command BAT1 produces these messages on the screen:

```
I am the first line in BAT1.BAT.
     I am the only line in BAT2.BAT.
I am the last line in BAT1.BAT.
```

Notice in this example that when BAT2.BAT finished its job, it returned control to BAT1.BAT, and execution resumed normally at the first command beneath the CALL BAT2 command.

With this latter technique you easily can create batch programs that use other batch programs. When used in conjunction with the FOR command, CALL can pass multiple parameters to batch programs that normally accept only a fixed number of parameters.

For example, the previously described SAFEMOVE.BAT batch program accepts only two parameters—the source of the move and the destination of the move. Now, SAFEMOVE.BAT can be used together with a similar batch program named MOVETO.BAT. To run MOVETO.BAT, you use a slightly different syntax:

```
MOVETO destination file1 file2...file8
```

where *destination* is the drive or directory to which files are being moved, and *file1 file2...file8* represents as many as eight file names to be moved. Therefore, the single command

```
MOVETO C:\WP\WPFILES *.TXT *.DOC *.LET
```

moves all .TXT, .DOC, and .LET files from the current directory to the WP\WPFILES directory.

The command

```
MOVETO A: *.BAK LETTER.TXT NOTE.TXT JUNE90.WKS
```

moves all .BAK files, plus the files LETTER.TXT, NOTE.TXT, and JUNE90.WKS, to drive A:. Again, you can list as many as eight file names, and any or all of those can contain wildcard characters.

The real beauty of this technique is that you don't even need to modify the existing SAFEMOVE.BAT batch program to use it. Instead, you can call it from the MOVETO.BAT batch program and still get all the benefits of the safety features it offers. Listing 29.13 shows the MOVETO.BAT batch program.

If you prefer to use the SAFER.BAT batch program discussed earlier, replace the CALL SAFEMOVE command with CALL SAFER in the last line of the MOVETO.BAT batch program shown in Listing 29.13.

Listing 29.13. The MOVETO.BAT batch program.

```
@ECHO OFF
REM ************************** MOVETO.BAT
REM Moves multiple files.
REM %1 is destination, %2 through %9 are file names.

FOR %%c IN (%2 %3 %4 %5 %6 %7 %8 %9) DO IF NOT %%c. == .
    CALL SAFEMOVE %%c %1
```

MOVETO.BAT uses the same basic technique to pass multiple parameters that COPYTO.BAT uses. The only real difference is that it uses the CALL command in the FOR loop.

Now, take a closer look at how MOVETO.BAT does its job. The following discussion assumes that you type the command MOVETO \WP\WPFILES APPLE.TXT BANANA.TXT CHERRY.TXT.

First, the % variables immediately receive these values:

```
%1= \WP\WPFILES
%2= APPLE.TXT
%3= BANANA.TXT
%4= CHERRY.TXT
```

%5 through %9 are blank

On the first pass through the loop, %%c is replaced with %2, which is APPLE.TXT. The command IF NOT %%c. == . proves true, so the command CALL SAFEMOVE %%c %1 becomes CALL SAFEMOVE APPLE.TXT \WP\WPFILES. This executes the SAFEMOVE command with these parameters, and SAFEMOVE.BAT moves the file.

When control returns to MOVETO.BAT, the next pass through the loop is executed, and %%c takes the value of %3, which is BANANA.TXT. The IF NOT %%c. == . test proves true, so the command expands to CALL SAFEMOVE BANANA.TXT \WP\WPFILES. Once again, SAFEMOVE.BAT moves the file and returns control to MOVETO.BAT.

On the next pass through the loop, `%%c` takes on the value of `%4`, which is CHERRY.TXT. Once again, the `IF` test proves true, the command `CALL SAFEMOVE CHERRY.TXT \WP\WPFILES` is executed, and SAFEMOVE.BAT moves the file. Again, it returns control to MOVETO.BAT.

During the next pass through the loop, `%%c` assumes the value of `%5`, which is empty. The test `IF NOT %%c. == .` proves false in this case, so the `CALL SAFEMOVE` command is not executed. In fact, because all remaining `%` variables are empty, the `CALL SAFEMOVE` command is never executed again. After the last pass through the loop, execution ends and control returns to the command prompt.

Passing More Than Nine Parameters

A tenth variable, named `%0`, initially contains the name of the batch program as it was typed at the DOS command prompt. Suppose you create a batch program, TEST.BAT, that contains the command `ECHO -- %0 %1 %2 %3 --`. Typing `TEST Isn't this fun?` at the DOS prompt would display the message -- `TEST Isn't this fun?` -- on your screen. (The value of `%0` is overwritten when you use SHIFT.)

As mentioned earlier, you can use up to nine `%` variables (`%1` through `%9`) in a batch program. However, you can pass more than nine parameters to a batch program and gain access to those above `%9` by *shifting* all other parameters to the left (that is, to a smaller `%` variable number). The command to shift parameters is (not surprisingly) `SHIFT`.

The `SHIFT` command is much different than the `FOR...IN...DO` looping method you used in previous examples to pass multiple parameters to a command, so let me take a few moments to discuss SHIFT in its own light.

Suppose that you create a batch program named SAMPLE.BAT and type the following command to execute the batch program:

```
SAMPLE A B C D E F G H I J K
```

The first nine % variables would receive the following values:

```
%1 = A
%2 = B
%3 = C
%4 = D
%5 = E
%6 = F
%7 = G
%8 = H
%9 = I
```

The SHIFT command shifts all the parameters from their current positions to the next lower-numbered % variable. For example, if SAMPLE.BAT contains a SHIFT command, after that command is executed, the % variables would contain the following:

```
%1 = B
$2 = C
%3 = D
%4 = E
%5 = F
%6 = G
%7 = H
%8 = I
%9 = J
```

Executing the SHIFT command again would have this effect:

```
%1 = C
%2 = D
%3 = E
%4 = F
%5 = G
%6 = H
%7 = I
%8 = J
%9 = K
```

The next SHIFT command would result in the following:

```
%1 = D
%2 = E
%3 = F
%4 = G
%5 = H
%6 = I
%7 = J
%8 = K
%9 =
```

Notice that because there were no additional parameters on the command line, %9 is now blank. Each time a SHIFT command is executed in the future, the variables continue to be shifted, and the blanks follow accordingly. If you execute SHIFT enough times, all the % variables would eventually be empty.

> The maximum number of parameters that you can pass to a batch program is limited by the maximum allowable length of any DOS command, which is 127 characters.

To use the SHIFT command effectively, you usually couple it with the decision-making power of the IF command and the branching ability of the GOTO command. Look at an example of this by creating a modified version of the LOOKIN.BAT batch program, named LOOKIN2.BAT, that can accept any number of parameters.

In its current state, LOOKIN.BAT can search for only one word. If you are using a version of DOS other than DOS 5 or later, LOOKIN.BAT is case-sensitive; therefore, a truly thorough search for all occurrences of a word such as *tomato* would require at least three commands, as follows:

```
LOOKIN *.TXT tomato
LOOKIN *.TXT Tomato
LOOKIN *.TXT TOMATO
```

With LOOKIN2.BAT, you can accomplish this same goal by typing this single command:

```
LOOKIN2 *.TXT tomato Tomato TOMATO
```

In fact, you can search for any number of words using this same basic syntax.

Listing 29.14 shows the LOOKIN2.BAT batch program. Many of the commands in LOOKIN2.BAT are identical to the commands in LOOKIN.BAT. This section focuses on commands that are unique to LOOKIN2.BAT.

As mentioned previously, you'll need to omit the /I switch on the FIND command if you're using a version of DOS prior to DOS 5.

Listing 29.14. The LOOKIN2.BAT batch program.

```
@ECHO OFF
REM *************************************** LOOKIN2.BAT
REM Searches multiple text files for a multiple words.
REM ---- %1 is the file(s) to be searched,
REM ---- %2 is the word to search for.

REM ---- Erase TEMPFILE.TXT if it exists.
IF EXIST TEMPFILE.TXT ERASE TEMPFILE.TXT

REM Put %1 in the environment for future use.
SET FileName=%1

REM ---- Search files with FIND,
REM ---- redirect output to TEMPFILE.TXT
:NextWord
ECHO Searching for %2 in %FileName%...
ECHO *** Search for "%2" in %FileName% *** >> TEMPFILE.TXT
FOR %%c IN (%FileName%) DO FIND /I "%2" %%c >> TEMPFILE.TXT

REM Store a form-feed in TEMPFILE.TXT.
ECHO ♀ >> TEMPFILE.TXT
```

continues

Listing 29.14. continued

```
REM Shift and repeat search if more words to search for.
SHIFT
IF NOT %2. == . GOTO NextWord

REM ---- Clean up the environment. It's the right thing to do.
REM ---- Display the results.
SET FileName =
MORE < TEMPFILE.TXT

REM ---- Present option to print the results.
ECHO.
CHOICE Do you want to print the results
IF ERRORLEVEL 2 GOTO Done
ECHO Results of scanning %1 files for %2 > PRN
TYPE TEMPFILE.TXT > PRN
ECHO ♀ > PRN

:Done
```

To understand the basic technique that LOOKIN2.BAT uses to search for multiple words, assume that you execute the batch program with the command LOOKIN2 *.TXT Apple Banana Cherry. This sets up the % variables as follows:

```
%1= *.TXT
%2= Apple
%3= Banana
%4= Cherry
```

%5 through %9 are blank.

The command SET FileName=%1 stores the first parameter (for example, *.TXT) in the environment, using the variable name FileName. This ensures that the batch program can still gain access to *.TXT if a later SHIFT command erases the *.TXT value stored in %1 from the list of parameters.

:NextWord is a label that marks the beginning of the commands used for printing messages and performing the search. The next two ECHO commands display messages. The first displays its message on the screen; the second sends its message to the TEMPFILE.TXT file, where it is displayed later as a heading for TEMPFILE.TXT. Note that both commands use %FileName% to display *.TXT, rather than %1. On the first search, therefore, the message displayed on the screen is this:

```
Searching for Apple in *.TXT...
```

The command FOR %%c IN (%FileName%) DO FIND /I "%2" %%c >> TEMPFILE.TXT searches all files that match the file name *.TXT for the word currently stored in %2. This is similar to the same command in LOOKIN.BAT, but %FileName% is used in place of %1 so that *.TXT is taken from the environment. This loop searches all .TXT files for the word Apple and then stores the results in TEMPFILE.TXT.

When the batch program displays the contents of TEMPFILE.TXT on your screen, the form-feed appears as a small ♀ character.

The next command, ECHO ♀ >> TEMPFILE.TXT, sends a form-feed to TEMPFILE.TXT. (Remember, ♀ represents Ctrl+L and is generated in EDIT by pressing Ctrl+P and then Alt+0+1+2 on the numeric keypad when you create the batch program.) This form-feed ejects the paper from the printer after the batch program prints the contents of TEMPFILE.TXT. Ejecting the page after printing ensures that the results of each word-search start printing on a new page.

Next, the SHIFT command shifts all parameters to the left (or to the next lower number). Therefore, the % variables now contain the following values:

```
%1= Apple
%2= Banana
%3= Cherry
%4=
```

The next command, IF NOT %2. == . GOTO NextWord, checks to see whether %2 is blank. In this example, %2 currently contains the word Banana, so the command GOTO NextWord is executed, and control branches to the :NextWord label.

The commands below :NextWord are executed, but because %2 now contains Banana (not Apple), the message, heading, and FIND search are adjusted accordingly. For example, the command ECHO Searching for %2 in %FileName% now displays this message:

```
Searching for Banana in *.TXT...
```

After the FOR loop searches the *.TXT files for the word Banana and stores the results in the TEMPFILE.TXT file, the SHIFT command is executed again. Now the % variables contain the following:

```
%1= Banana
%2= Cherry
%3=
%4=
```

The command IF NOT %2 == . GOTO NextWord once again passes control up to the :NextWord label, and once again the message, heading, and search are updated. However, %2 now equals Cherry, and that is the word searched for. The command ECHO Searching for %2 in %FileName% now displays the following message on the screen:

```
Searching for Cherry in *.TXT...
```

Once again, after completing the search for the word Cherry, the SWITCH command is executed. Now the % variables contain the following:

```
%1= Cherry
%2=
%3=
%4=
```

This time, the command IF NOT %2. == . GOTO NextWord does not pass control to the :NextWord label, because %2 is empty. Therefore, processing resumes with the next command in the batch program.

The command SET FileName= sets the FileName variable to "nothing" and thus removes it from the environment. Then the command MORE < TEMPFILE.TXT displays the results of the searches, all of which have been stored in the TEMPFILE.TXT. The remaining commands print the TEMPFILE.TXT file, exactly as they did in the original LOOKIN.BAT batch program.

Including Escape Sequences in Batch Programs

Many printers require that you send Escape-key sequences to activate special features. For example, the Hewlett-Packard LaserJet printers use the Escape-key sequences shown in Table 29.1 to activate various printing modes. The table signifies the Escape-key character as {ESC}, as your printer manual might.

Table 29.1. Escape-key codes that control the HP LaserJet printer.

Print Mode	Escape Sequence
Portrait (normal)	{ESC}E{ESC}&l0O
Landscape	{ESC}E{ESC}&l1O
Compressed Portrait	{ESC}E{ESC}&l0O{ESC}&k2s
Compressed Landscape	{ESC}E{ESC}&l1O{ESC}&k2s
Reset to default mode	{ESC}E

Different printers require different codes to activate their features; check your printer manual for a complete list of these codes.

Note that the characters used for portrait modes (l0O) are a lowercase l, the number zero (0), and an uppercase letter O. The characters used for the landscape modes (l1O) are a lowercase letter l, the number 1, and an uppercase letter O.

If you want your batch program to send Escape-character sequences to the printer, you might have trouble typing them into your batch program. For example, if you use the EDIT editor, when you press the Esc key, EDIT assumes that you want to cancel a command.

> If you use an editor other than EDIT, refer to that program's documentation for instructions on how to enter the Escape character into a file.

If you are using EDIT, you must use the following procedure to enter an Escape character:

1. Press Ctrl+P (to disable any special meaning for the next command).

2. Press Escape. This displays a small left-arrow character (←).

Note that even though Escape looks like a left-arrow character when you are in EDIT and whenever you use the TYPE or MORE command to list the file, DOS interprets it as an Escape-key character.

Creating JETSET.BAT

This section shows you how to create a batch program named JETSET.BAT that you can use to set the print mode for a LaserJet printer. Listing 29.15 shows the entire JETSET.BAT file as it appears when displayed in EDIT. This is a tricky batch program to type; remember, when you see the ← character in the following figure, you must press Ctrl+P and then press Escape to generate it.

Listing 29.15. The JETSET.BAT batch program.

```
@ECHO OFF
REM *************************** JETSET.BAT
REM ----------------- Sends printer control codes to LaserJet.

REM ---- Make sure parameter passed is valid.
FOR %%c IN (P p L l CP cp CL cl) DO IF %1. == %%c. GOTO Ok
```

```
REM -- If parameter matches none of the items checked in the loop
REM -- above, there must be an error. Display help below.

ECHO JETSET requires one of the following codes:
ECHO.
ECHO      P Portrait (normal)
ECHO       L Landscape
ECHO      CP Compressed Portrait
ECHO      CL Compressed Landscape
ECHO.
ECHO Example: To switch to Compressed Landscape mode, enter JETSET CL.
ECHO.
GOTO End

REM Valid parameter was entered; send appropriate code to the printer.

:Ok
IF %1. == P. ECHO ←E←&l00 > PRN
IF %1. == p. ECHO ←E←&l00 > PRN
IF %1. == CP. ECHO ←E←&l00←&k2s > PRN
IF %1. == cp. ECHO ←E←&l00←&k2s > PRN
IF %1. == L. ECHO ←E←&l10 > PRN
IF %1. == l. ECHO ←E←&l10 > PRN
IF %1. == CL. ECHO ←E←&l10←&k2s > PRN
IF %1. == CL. ECHO ←E←&l10←&k2s > PRN

REM ---- Ask about performing a test to verify success.
ECHO.
CHOICE Printer set. Do you want to try it
IF ERRORLEVEL 2 GOTO End

REM -- Proceed with test (print test message if user pressed
Y)
ECHO -- This is a test of JETSET %1. How does it look? -- >
PRN
ECHO ♀ > PRN
ECHO.
ECHO Remember that other programs might set the
ECHO printer back to Portrait (normal) mode!
:End
```

Remember, you can use EDIT's Copy and Paste commands to copy similar lines. Then you can make only a few changes to those lines instead of typing the lines from scratch.

> Be sure to pay close attention to the differences between the lowercase letter *l* and the number *1*, and between the uppercase letter *O* and the number *0*.

To enter line 41, type ECHO followed by a blank space. Then press Ctrl+P, hold down the Alt key, type 012 on the numeric keypad, and release the Alt key. Finally, type another blank space, and then > PRN. After you have typed the entire batch program, press Alt+F. Then type X and press Y to save your work and return to the command prompt.

Using JETSET.BAT

After you create JETSET.BAT, you can select a print mode for an HP LaserJet by entering the command JETSET followed by a one- or two-letter code in upper- or lowercase letters, as follows:

JETSET P switches to Portrait (normal) mode

JETSET L switches to Landscape (horizontal) mode

JETSET CP switches to Compressed Portrait mode

JETSET CL switches to Compressed Landscape mode

If you enter the command JETSET without a code (or with an invalid code), the screen displays the following help message:

```
JETSET requires one of the following codes:

   P   Portrait (normal)
   L   Landscape
   CP  Compressed Portrait
   CL  Compressed Landscape

Example: To switch to Compressed Landscape mode, enter
JETSET CL
```

When you enter a valid code, JETSET displays the following message:

```
Printer set. Do you want to try it [Y,N]?
```

If you press Y, JETSET sends the line -- This is a test of JETSET %1. How does it look? -- to the printer and then ejects the page so that you can verify that the proper mode has been set. (The variable %1 is expanded to whatever code you typed on the command line.) If you type N, the newly selected print mode stays in effect, but the test sentence is not printed.

If you proceed with the test, the screen also displays the reminder message:

```
Remember that other programs might set the
printer back to Portrait (normal) mode!
```

You should test each of the possible codes that JETSET offers. If a particular command, such as JETSET CL, does not set the correct mode for your printer, you might have typed the wrong escape sequence in JETSET.BAT. Use EDIT to make corrections, referring to Listing 29.15 as a guide.

How JETSET.BAT Works

When you first run JETSET.BAT, the %1 variable takes the value of the parameter entered next to the JETSET command. The command FOR %%c IN (P p L l CP cp CL cl) DO IF %1. == %%c. GOTO Ok compares %1 to each acceptable option (both uppercase and lowercase). If the %1 parameter matches one of the acceptable options, the GOTO command passes control to the label :Ok.

If the %1 variable does not match one of the acceptable options, the help messages beneath the FOR loop (lines 11 through 19 in Listing 29.15) are displayed instead. After the help messages are displayed, the GOTO End command skips the IF commands that send escape sequences to the printer, and therefore the print mode is not altered.

Lines 25 through 32 compare %1 to each acceptable option. When an IF command finds a match between %1 and an acceptable option, the ECHO command sends the appropriate escape sequence to the printer (that is, > PRN). Line 35 displays a blank line. Line 36 presents the message that explains the optional test, and then execution waits for a key press. When you press Y or N, line 37 tests the value returned. If the value is Y, line 40 sends a simple sentence to the printer, and line 41 ejects the page from the printer. Lines 42 through 44 display the reminder message on the screen.

Accessing Batch Programs from the Shell

You learned in Chapter 8 how to create new groups in the DOS Shell and how to access programs from a group. You can use those same basic techniques to create a group screen for your batch programs.

Figure 29.1 shows the Main Group screen with the addition of a new group called *Custom Utilities*. Figure 29.2 shows an example of how you could design the Custom Utilities group screen. Note that the options on this screen refer to the batch programs created in this chapter and Chapter 12.

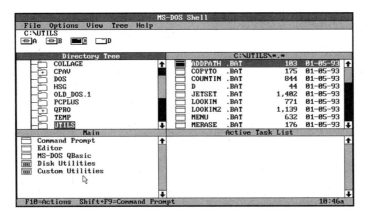

Figure 29.1. DOS Shell Main Group with a new group added.

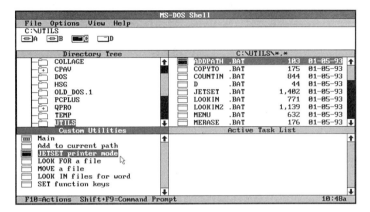

*Figure 29.2.
A new group
screen for
accessing batch
programs.*

Figure 29.3 shows the Program Item Properties dialog box for the JETSET printer mode option. Enter JETSET as the Program Title, enter JETSET %1 as the startup command, and toggle off the Pause After Exit check box. When you select OK, you must fill in the Program Item Properties dialog box for the %1 parameter, as shown in Figure 29.4.

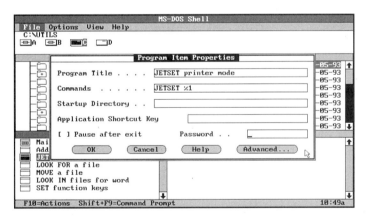

*Figure 29.3.
The Program
Item Properties
screen for
JETSET.BAT.*

This set of fields creates the dialog box that appears when you select the JETSET program. Type JetSet as the Window Title, type Enter mode (P, L, CP, or CL) as the Program Information, and type Mode... as the Prompt Message. If you want the batch program to display a default value (perhaps L), enter that value in the Default Parameters field.

*Figure 29.4.
The Program
Item Properties
screen for
JETSET's %1
parameter.*

> The startup sequence assumes that the directory that
> contains JETSET.BAT is listed in the current path setting.
> Therefore, the startup sequence does not change directories
> before running JETSET.

Once you've created the dialog boxes for running JETSET.BAT, you can run it from the Custom Utilities Program Group by highlighting its name and pressing Enter or by double-clicking its name. You'll see the dialog box shown in Figure 29.5. See Chapter 8 if you need additional help with creating program groups and items in the DOS 6 Shell.

Creating Your Own Shell

If you are the principal user of a computer that other users share, you might want to create your own DOS Shell. This shell won't be as fancy as the DOS 6 Shell, but it can give less knowledgeable users much easier access to programs. In addition, you can also restrict beginners to certain directories (at least, until they learn how to use DOS on their own).

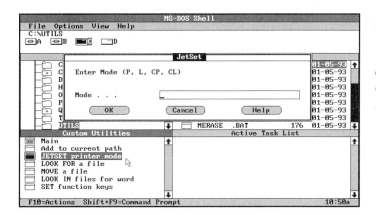

Figure 29.5.
The dialog box
that appears
after selection
of the JETSET
Printer mode.

The basic idea is straightforward. Create a batch program (perhaps named MENU.BAT) that displays a menu of all the programs that you want to make available to other users. Label the options by assigning a number or a letter to each option, as in the example shown in Listing 29.16.

Next, create a batch program that uses the option number or letter as its name, that contains the necessary commands to run the requested program, and (optionally) re-executes the MENU.BAT batch program when the user exits the requested program.

Listing 29.16. The MENU.BAT batch program.

```
@ECHO OFF
REM ********************************* MENU.BAT
REM Provide a "shell" for running programs.
CLS
ECHO =====================================================
ECHO.
ECHO          What do you want to do?
ECHO.
```

continues

Listing 29.16. continued

```
ECHO            1. Use WordPerfect
ECHO            2. Use Microsoft Excel
ECHO            3. Use dBASE IV
ECHO            4. Show what the function keys do
ECHO            5. Go to DOS Command Prompt
ECHO.
ECHO ========================================================
ECHO.
ECHO Enter a number (1-5); then press Enter...
ECHO.
ECHO ========================================================
PROMPT $e
```

For example, the user must select option 1 from the menu to run the WordPerfect program. Therefore, you need to create a batch program named 1.BAT that will go through the steps required to run the WordPerfect program (because when the user types 1 and presses Enter, DOS naturally will look for a program named 1.EXE, 1.COM, or 1.BAT). Listing 29.17 shows a sample 1.BAT batch program.

Listing 29.17. The 1.BAT batch program.

```
@ECHO OFF
REM ********************************** 1.BAT
REM Run WordPerfect from the \WP\WPFILES directory.
CD \WP\WPFILES
WP
CD \UTILS
MENU
```

When the user types 1 and presses Enter, DOS assumes that 1 is a normal command, and it looks for a file named 1.BAT (or 1.COM or 1.EXE). This executes 1.BAT, which first changes to the \WP\WPFILES directory and then runs the

> WordPerfect program. When the user exits WordPerfect, the
> CD \UTILS directory changes back to the \UTILS directory
> and then the MENU command executes the MENU.BAT batch
> program again.

You could create similar batch programs, named 2.BAT and
3.BAT, to run Microsoft Excel, dBASE IV, or any other program that
is available on your system.

Option 5 uses the batch program 5.BAT, shown in Listing 29.18,
to remove the menu from the screen and redisplay the command
prompt.

Listing 29.18. The 5.BAT batch program redisplays the command prompt.

```
@ECHO OFF
REM ********************************* 5.BAT
REM Return to command prompt from MENU.BAT.
PROMPT $P$G
CLS
```

> You'll need to delete any DOSSHELL or WINDOWS
> command lines from your AUTOEXEC.BAT file if you want
> your custom shell to be used instead of the DOS Shell or
> Windows.

As an alternative to making users enter the command MENU,
you could add the following two lines to the very end of your
AUTOEXEC.BAT file:

```
CD \UTILS
MENU
```

These commands display the help screen automatically when you start the computer.

When you consider that you can customize the function keys (if ANSI.SYS is installed) to have them enter DOS commands automatically and you can also create batch programs such as MENU.BAT to create a simple type of DOS Shell, you can see that DOS is indeed a very flexible and powerful tool. These techniques let you customize your system in just about any way you can imagine, and they make your personal computer very personal indeed.

 # Troubleshooting

Just about anything that can go wrong when typing commands from the command prompt can also go wrong when you use those commands in batch programs. So, for the most part, troubleshooting techniques for batch programs are similar to the techniques presented in previous chapters. For instance, if you see the message Bad command or file name when you execute the batch program, the batch program may be trying to run a program that is not in the current directory or disk and is not in the PATH statement; or perhaps you misspelled a command or batch program name when typing it into the batch program.

Anything else that goes wrong with your batch program probably is the result of a *logic error*—that is, you get an incorrect result. Logic errors can have a number of causes, such as using the wrong command, not taking safety issues into consideration, or executing commands in the wrong order.

The following tips will help you track down and eradicate logic errors:

- Print a copy of your batch program so that you can follow its logic on paper. For example, to print a program named SAFECOPY.BAT, type the command TYPE SAFECOPY.BAT > PRN.

■ Get a printed record of everything that your batch program displays on the screen while it's running. To do this, press Ctrl+P before you run the batch program, run the batch program as usual, and then press Ctrl+P again. If you're using a laser printer, you may need to eject the last page of the listing. Now you can compare the listing of your batch program with the messages it prints and the actions it takes to gain a better understanding of where things might have gone haywire.

■ Temporarily suspend a batch program by pressing Ctrl+S or pressing the Pause key. This will give you time to read messages that it displays before they scroll off the screen. (To cancel the batch program completely, press Ctrl+C or Ctrl+Break and type Y.)

■ If you're having trouble deciding what is wrong with the batch program and you have turned echo off, try turning the echo on again, either by deleting the @ECHO OFF command or by changing it to a comment (REM @ECHO OFF). This will show you each command as it is executed and will reveal how DOS has expanded each command that uses variables.

■ If your batch program used to work properly, but suddenly has stopped doing so, make sure that you've specified the correct parameters on the command line and have typed them in the proper order. For example, if the general syntax for your batch file is

```
COPYTO source destination
```

be sure that you type the source parameter first, a space, and then the destination parameter. If you type the parameters in the reverse order, the batch program will not work properly. Likewise, if your batch program is calling another batch program, make sure that you've specified the parameters for the called program correctly.

■ If your batch program is not executing commands in the correct sequence, make sure that your labels are not misplaced and that GOTO commands are branching to the correct labels.

■ When using the IF ERRORLEVEL and IF NOT ERRORLEVEL commands, remember to test the values in order from highest to lowest.

■ When using the CHOICE /C: command, remember that the values returned when the user chooses an option will correspond to the position of the characters in the list of choices. For instance, the command CHOICE /C:ynq will return a value of 1 if the user responds with y or Y, a value of 2 if the response is n or N, and a value of 3 if the response is q or Q. The following IF ERRORLEVEL commands should check these values accordingly (again in order from highest value to lowest).

■ When using the FOR and SHIFT commands, be careful to use the correct variable numbers. Referencing %2 when you really mean %1 definitely will cause problems. Likewise, be sure to use SET to preserve the value of variables that otherwise might be overwritten by SHIFT.

Summary

This chapter presents advanced commands and techniques for creating batch programs and develops several useful batch programs to demonstrate their use. As you gain experience with DOS, you certainly will be able to create some interesting customized commands of your own.

■ The IF command allows a batch program to test for a condition and then react accordingly.

■ The GOTO command reroutes the normal sequence of execution in a batch program.

■ The PAUSE command temporarily stops batch program execution and waits until you press a key.

- Redirecting output of a command to the NUL device hides any messages that the command normally displays.

- The CHOICE command temporarily stops batch program execution and waits until you press a specific key.

- The ERRORLEVEL command lets you test the value returned by the CHOICE command and other DOS commands such as FORMAT, BACKUP, and RESTORE.

- To make a batch program display a blank line, type ECHO followed by a period (ECHO.).

- To make a message in a batch program sound a beep, use the Ctrl+G character. To enter Ctrl+G in EDIT, press Ctrl+P, hold down the Alt key, type 007 on the numeric keypad, and release the Alt key.

- To send a form-feed character to the printer, type ECHO, a space, the form-feed character (Ctrl+L), a space, and > PRN. To enter the form-feed character in EDIT, press Ctrl+P, hold down the Alt key, type 012 on the numeric keypad, and release the Alt key.

- The FOR command sets up a loop to repeatedly execute a command in a batch program.

- The CALL command passes execution to another batch program, but it permits execution to resume at the next command in the calling batch program.

- To use EDIT to enter Escape-key sequences in a batch program, press Ctrl+P and then press Escape.

Alan Simpson's
DOS SECRETS
UNLEASHED

C H A P T E R   3 0

A QBasic Primer

Like its ancestors, the latest version of DOS includes a version of the BASIC programming language. QBasic (short for QuickBasic) gives the DOS user a powerful structured programming tool to develop applications. Often used to develop programs quickly to meet simple needs, QBasic is also used to develop larger applications that rival those developed in such languages as Pascal, C, and COBOL.

The QBasic Environment

Because QBasic is included and installed with DOS 6, to start QBasic you need only type `qbasic` at the DOS prompt. The screen in Figure 30.1 appears.

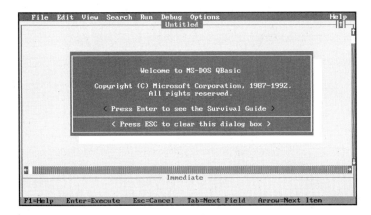

Figure 30.1. The QBasic start-up screen.

At the start-up screen, you can immediately access QBasic Help by pressing Enter. The QBasic Help system is the only way to get help, because no paper documentation is provided with DOS 6. The Help environment is covered later in this section.

Editing a Program

Notice that the QBasic screen is divided into two parts: the program window and the Immediate window. Pressing F6 toggles you between these windows. You use the program window to edit your application code, and you use the Immediate window to instantly test a command.

In the program window (named "Untitled" until you save your program), type the following line and press Enter:

```
if a=1 then print "OK"
```

QBasic automatically formats the line, putting all *reserved* words, or words that QBasic uses, in capital letters and putting spaces between words, symbols, and numbers as shown here:

```
IF a = 1 THEN PRINT "OK"
```

Immediate Commands

Sometimes you might want to test a command quickly to see its results without running the entire program. Typing a command in the Immediate window does just that.

To use the Immediate window, follow these steps:

1. Press F6 to toggle between the program window and the Immediate window.

2. Type print "Hello, world!" and press Enter.

3. The screen changes to one that looks like your DOS screen and prints "Hello, world!".

You can use a ? rather than the PRINT command to save keystrokes. QBasic automatically converts the symbol to the full PRINT command.

Structure of Programs

If you are familiar with the BASIC programming language, you know that with previous versions of BASIC, all lines had to be numbered. When you needed your program to move from one area of code to another, you used a GOTO (or GOSUB) command and a specific line number.

By adding *subprocedures* and *functions,* QBasic no longer requires line numbers. When it is necessary to jump to a specific line, a *label,* or descriptive tag, is used. Throughout this chapter, subprocedures, functions, and labels are used wherever possible.

Getting Help

The online help for QBasic is as good as, if not better than, that of DOS itself. All functions, statements, operators, and keywords are covered, along with their syntax, examples, and related topics.

To get help on a particular topic, move the cursor to the keyword and press F1. For example, pressing F1 while the cursor is on print brings up the help screen for the PRINT command.

To get general help at any time, press Shift+F1. From there, you can choose to access the Table of Contents, shown in Figure 30.2, or the Index, shown in Figure 30.3.

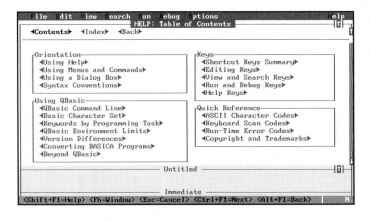

*Figure 30.2.
The Help Table
of Contents.*

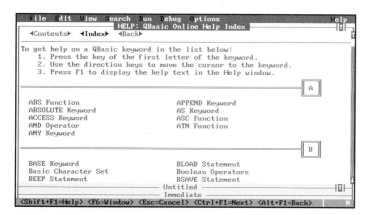

Figure 30.3.
The Online
Help Index.

As noted earlier, QBasic can be used for the simplest programs and the most complex applications. Both levels of programming, however, build on fundamental commands and structures. In the rest of this chapter, we will look at many of these fundamentals in building an application to calculate and schedule payments for a loan.

Using Comments

Always try to use good programming *style*. Style deals with the way your code looks and reads not only to you but to anyone else who might need to work on it. Perhaps the most important element of programming style is the *comment*, which you use to describe what you are doing and why.

QBasic uses the REM statement or simply the ' character to denote a comment. In the interest of style, start your program something like this:

```
' Title: Loan Calculator and Payment Scheduler
' Author: Your name
' Date: Today's date
' Version: 1.0
'
' Input: Loan amount, number of years, annual interest rate
' Output: Monthly payment, payment schedule (screen and/or file)
```

You can change this as much or as little as you want. Remember, nothing after a REM or a ' is even looked at by QBasic itself—it simply enables you to describe what your program is doing.

Getting Input

Now consider the things that you'll need as input to your program. When applying for a loan, a customer has a certain amount in mind. A car might be $25,000, or a mortgage might be $80,000. The bank probably has several payment options available, ranging from 3 years for a car to 30 years for a house. Finally, the bank also has an interest rate it charges for loaning the money. This rate, generally somewhere between 5 percent and 15 percent, is usually compounded monthly because payments are made monthly.

In QBasic, you can get input into a program in several ways. You can input information from the keyboard. You can use the INPUT command to input relatively short lines of data, or the LINE INPUT command to input up to 255 characters at a time. You can also input information from a file on a disk using the INPUT and LINE INPUT commands.

For this example, a simple INPUT command will do. Add these lines to your program (remember, capitalization of keywords and spacing don't matter, but do press Enter at the end of each line):

```
' clear the screen and begin getting the input
CLS
INPUT "Loan amount"; Loan
INPUT "Number of years"; Years%
INPUT "Annual interest rate (percent)"; AnnualRate
```

The CLS command clears the screen, just as it does in DOS.

Variables

Loan, Years, and AnnualRate are *variables.* Variables are simply place-holders in memory for numbers, characters, and other things that you use in your programs. A variable name can be up to 40 characters, can include the letters A–Z and the numbers 0–9, and must be one of the five data types.

> A variable name must begin with a letter.

These are the five QBasic data types:

- Integer—Whole numbers only (no decimals), ranging from –32768 to 32767.

- Long—Also an integer, but 32 bits in length. Ranges from –2,147,483,648 to 2,147,483,647.

- Single—Single-precision number, used for numbers that require fractions and decimal places.

- Double—Double-precision number, used for intensive scientific calculations that require extreme precision.

- String—Used for letters, words, and numbers that don't need calculations performed on them. Can have up to 32,767 characters.

Notice that the variable Years ends with a percent (%) symbol. This is a data type *suffix* that tells QBasic that this variable is an integer. The list of data types and suffixes is shown in Table 30.1.

Table 30.1. Data types and suffixes.

Data Type	Suffix
Integer	%
Long integer	&
Single-precision	!
Double-precision	#
String	$

By default, any variable that does not have a suffix becomes a single-precision number. The functions DEFINT, DEFLNG, DEFSNG, DEFDBL, and DEFSTR enable you to change these defaults, but a data type suffix always overrides any default.

Notice that in the INPUT statements, Loan and AnnualRate are allowed to have decimal places (they are single-precision by default), but the Years variable is an integer. In this example, whenever reference variables other than single-precision are used, data type suffixes are used.

Entering a decimal number for an integer variable does not produce an error or round the number—it simply *truncates* it, or cuts off the digits after the decimal.

Checking Conditions and Taking Action

Before going any further, you must make sure that you don't allow anyone to input a value that won't work. For example, a negative interest rate or zero loan value just doesn't make sense. To check these conditions and take action if they are wrong, use the IF...THEN statement.

Using the *IF...THEN* Statement

The IF...THEN statement can take three basic forms.

```
if condition1 then action1
```

works if just one condition needs to be checked and only one action needs to be taken. If an alternative action should be taken,

```
if condition1 then action1 else action2
```

does the job. If *condition1* is true, then *action1* takes place. If *condition1* in not true, *action2* occurs. Finally, if more than one action needs to take place for any condition you can use

```
if condition1 then
    action1
    action2
end if
```

You must use an END IF statement if you have only one action to be taken but the action is coded on a separate line from the IF...THEN statement.

These can all be combined for more complex checking:

```
if condition1 then
    action1
    action2
elseif condition2 then
    action3
    action4
else
    action5
    action6
end if
```

Operators

The conditions in the IF...THEN statements can take many forms, but all end up evaluating to either true or false. QBasic provides *operators,* or functions that compare or operate on variables, to return true or false results. Table 30.2 lists the mathematical operators, and Table 30.3 lists the Boolean operators.

Table 30.2. Mathematical operators.

Symbol	Function
*	Multiplication
/	Division
\	Integer division
+	Addition
-	Subtraction
^	Exponentiation
=	Equals (also used to assign)
<	Less than
>	Greater than

Table 30.3. Boolean operators.

Operator	Function
AND	Conjunction
OR	Disjunction
NOT	Bit-wise complement
XOR	Exclusive OR
EQV	Equivalence
IMP	Implication

Boolean operators are very useful in IF...THEN statements. For example, the statement

```
IF a = 1 AND b = 2 THEN PRINT "Both conditions met."
```

prints the message only if both conditions are met. The statement

```
IF a = 1 OR b = 2 THEN PRINT "One or both conditions met."
```

prints the message if either condition or both conditions are true. The results of Boolean operations are shown in Table 30.4.

Table 30.4. Boolean operations and results.

Expr	Expr2	NOT	AND	OR	XOR	EQV	IMP
T	T	F	T	T	F	T	T
T	F	F	F	T	T	F	F
F	T	T	F	T	T	F	T
F	F	T	F	F	F	T	T

Now that you have seen how to compare variables and take action accordingly, you can add some error checking to your program. Modify your program to add error checking to the input as shown here (comments are optional):

```
' clear the screen and begin getting the input
CLS
EnterLoan:
INPUT "Loan amount"; Loan
' check that the loan amount is greater than zero
IF Loan <= 0 THEN
        BEEP
        GOTO EnterLoan
END IF

EnterYears:
INPUT "Number of years"; Years%
' check that the number of years is greater than zero
IF Years% <= 0 THEN
        BEEP
        GOTO EnterYears
END IF
' convert the number of years into months
Months% = Years% * 12

EnterRate:
INPUT "Annual interest rate (percent)"; AnnualRate
' check that the rate is greater than zero but less than 100
IF AnnualRate <= 0 OR AnnualRate >= 100 THEN
        BEEP
        GOTO EnterRate
END IF
' convert the annual rate into a monthly percentage
Rate = AnnualRate / 1200
```

> You can use a colon (:) to separate commands on a single line. For example, the line could read
>
> ```
> IF Years% <= 0 THEN BEEP: GOTO EnterYears.
> ```

Take a look at all you did in these changes. You made it impossible for a user to enter a zero or a negative number for Loan, Years, or AnnualRate. You also used an OR statement to make sure that the annual interest rate is not greater than or equal to 100.

By adding labels to each section, you made it possible for the program to return to a specific spot and try again. The BEEP command simply sounds the computer's buzzer to let the user know he made a mistake. After Years is entered correctly, a new variable, Months, holds the number of periods for the loan. After AnnualRate is entered correctly, a new variable, Rate, converts the annual rate to a monthly decimal value.

> Save your work frequently by choosing Save from the File menu.

Functions

Now that you have the numbers in the format that you need, you're ready to perform some mathematical operations on them. Because your sample application is fairly small, you can probably get away with coding these steps right into the body of the main program. However, in a bigger program, you might want to use the same set of calculations for another set of numbers, and that would mean coding the same steps again in another place.

QBasic has the perfect mechanism for removing such complex calculations from the main body of the program—the *function*. From the main program, using the function requires only one line of code.

Creating the Function

In your program, you need a function to give you the monthly payment for your loan. To do this, your function will need to know the number of months, the interest rate per month, and the amount of the loan. These are the *parameters* you must pass to the function from your main program.

To create the function, follow these instructions:

1. From the Edit menu, choose New FUNCTION.

2. Call the new function `CalcMonthlyPayment`, and press Enter.

3. The cursor sits as the end of the function name, waiting for the parameters. Type `(Months%, Rate, Loan)` and press Enter.

You are now ready to code the function itself. The formula for the monthly payment is shown in Figure 30.4.

Monthly Payment = Loan / Present Value Factor

$$\text{Present Value Factor} = \frac{1 - \frac{1}{(1+r)}^n}{r}$$

r is the interest rate per period
n is the number of periods

Figure 30.4. Formula for the monthly payment.

The code for this formula is as follows:

```
' determines the present value of a $1 annuity
PresentValueFactor = (1 - (1 / (1 + Rate) ^ Months%)) / Rate

' divides the loan amount by the present value and
' returns the value of the monthly payment
CalcMonthlyPayment = Loan / PresentValueFactor
```

The function should now look similar to the one in Figure 30.5.

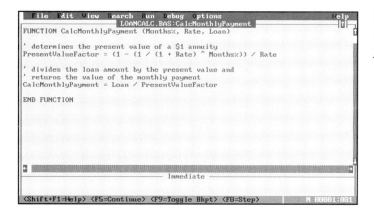

Figure 30.5.
Creating a
function.

Saving your program after creating a function automatically places a DECLARE statement at the beginning of your main program. This statement lets your main program know that the function exists and what parameters it needs.

Using the Function

Now that the function is created, you're ready to use it. To switch back to the main program, take these steps:

1. Choose SUBS from the View menu, or press F2.

2. Select the main program (shown by its file name), and press Enter.

   At the end of your main program, type the following lines:

```
' call the function to calculate the monthly payment
MonthlyPayment = CalcMonthlyPayment(Months%, Rate, Loan)
```

When QBasic reaches these lines, it passes the *parameters* to the function, executes the function, and places the return value in the new single-precision variable, MonthlyPayment.

Getting Output

So far, you've seen how to get data into the program, check it, and do calculations on it, but you haven't seen how to get the results. QBasic's PRINT command is very versatile and, as you will see in this and later sections, can print to the screen, a printer, or a file on a disk.

Using the *PRINT* Command

To print the monthly payment, you want to do more than just throw a number out on the screen. You should print a message telling what it is, get the result in the right format, and print the result to the screen.

Printing the message is easy. Add the following lines to the end of your program:

```
PRINT
PRINT "Your monthly payment will be ";
```

The first PRINT command simply adds a blank line between the preceding screen output and the new output. The second PRINT command prints a nice message. When you use the semicolon, QBasic knows that the next thing to print should go directly beside this message and not on a new line.

> You can use a comma (,) rather than a semicolon to place the next output one tab stop away from the end of the message.

The *PRINT USING* Command

To properly format your printed output, QBasic offers an addition to the PRINT command. With PRINT USING, you can format numeric or string output in various ways. The monthly payment should be displayed with a dollar sign, commas (for those who can afford a monthly payment of over three digits!), and two decimal places.

The following lines go next:

```
' format the monthly payment figure
PRINT USING "$#####,.##"; MonthlyPayment
```

This gives you a dollar sign, five digits to the left of the decimal point, a comma if necessary, and two decimal points. In the next section, you'll also see a way to use the PRINT and PRINT USING commands with tab stops and with files on disks.

> PRINT and PRINT USING have sister commands that work the same way with the printer as they do with the screen: LPRINT and LPRINT USING.

Subprocedures

Subprocedures and functions are very similar. They are both coded separately from the main program, and both use parameters passed from the main program. However, a subprocedure is designed to actually do a piece of work, whereas a function just does some calculations and returns a value.

You are now ready to print a monthly payment schedule. Because this task involves a fair amount of coding and might also be called from a number of places in a larger program, you'll make printing a monthly payment schedule a subprocedure.

To create the subprocedure, follow these steps:

1. From the Edit menu, choose New SUB.

2. Call the new function Schedule, and press Enter.

3. The cursor sits at the end of the subprocedure name, waiting for you to type the parameters. Type `(Months%, Rate, Loan, MonthlyPayment)` and press Enter.

> Saving your program after creating a subprocedure automatically places a `DECLARE` statement at the beginning of your main program.

Before you begin to code the procedure for calculating and displaying the payment schedule for the loan, you need to understand the logic behind the process.

Consider the following example:

Loan amount—$50,000
Number of years—15
Annual interest rate—8.0%
Monthly payment—$477.83

In month one of the loan, you pay $477.83. Of that amount, only part actually applies to paying off the original $50,000—the rest applies to paying off the interest. The amount that applies to interest is one-twelfth of the annual rate times the balance of $50,000. That amounts to $333.33. The remaining amount of the payment, $477.83–$333.33 = $144.50, applies to paying off the balance.

In month two of the loan, you still pay $477.83. Of that amount, the interest rate applies to only $50,000–$144.50 = $49,855.50 of the loan, so your interest payment is only $332.37. The rest of the payment, $477.83–$332.37 = $145.46, applies to paying off the principal.

Your schedule for the first two months looks as shown in Table 30.5.

Table 30.5. Two months of a sample payment schedule.

Period	Payment	Principal	Interest	Balance
1	477.83	144.50	333.33	49,855.50
2	477.83	145.46	332.37	49,710.04

As the months go on, the amount of interest paid decreases and the amount applied to the principal increases. At the end of 180 periods, or 12 months times 15 years, the balance is zero and the loan is paid in full. It is obvious that you need a procedure to repeat these tedious calculations many times.

Control Loops

QBasic has several different kinds of *loops* that help to iterate through this process as many times as needed. These include DO WHILE...LOOP, DO UNTIL...LOOP, WHILE...WEND, and FOR...NEXT.

The first three looping techniques are basically the same—statements are executed while a certain condition exists or until a specified condition occurs:

```
i%=0
DO WHILE i% < NumberOfMonths%
    i% = i% + 1
    actions
LOOP
```

or

```
i%=0
DO UNTIL i% = NumberOfMonths%
    i% = i% + 1
    actions
LOOP
```

or

```
i%=0
WHILE i% < NumberOfMonths%
    i% = i% + 1
    actions
WEND
```

You could use one of these methods to loop until the end of the loan, but the fourth looping method, FOR...NEXT, provides a better way.

A FOR...NEXT loop would look something like this:

```
FOR period = 1 TO NumberOfMonths%
    action1
    action2
NEXT
```

The FOR...NEXT loop provides its own counter, and you don't have to track a certain condition to see whether you should still be looping. In your example schedule, you loop exactly 180 times.

The user of the program might not want to see all 180 periods, so you let the user enter the number of months she wants to see. Add the following lines to the body of the Schedule subprocedure, paying attention to (but not necessarily typing) the comments:

```
PRINT "Number of periods to view ("; Months%; " max)";
INPUT NumberOfMonths%
' if the requested number of months is greater than the length
' of the loan or is not entered, set the requested number to
' the length of the loan
IF NumberOfMonths% > Months% OR NumberOfMonths% = 0 THEN
        NumberOfMonths% = Months%
END IF

' clear the screen and print the headings for the table
CLS
PRINT "Period"; TAB(15); "Payment"; TAB(30);
PRINT "Principal"; TAB(45); "Interest"; TAB(60); "Balance"
PRINT

' set the initial balance to the amount of the loan itself
Balance = Loan
```

```
' begin the loop
FOR Period% = 1 TO NumberOfMonths%

' calculate the amount of interest paid
InterestPaid = Rate * Balance
' calculate the amount of the payment that goes to principal
Principal = MonthlyPayment - InterestPaid
' calculate the remaining balance on the loan
Balance = Balance - Principal

' print the numbers for the period
PRINT Period%; TAB(15);
PRINT USING "######,.##"; MonthlyPayment; TAB(30);
PRINT USING "######,.##"; Principal; TAB(45);
PRINT USING "######,.##"; InterestPaid; TAB(60);
PRINT USING "######,.##"; Balance

' repeat the loop
NEXT
```

Notice the use of the TAB function. After printing the Period, the cursor moves to the 15th column. After printing Principal there, the cursor moves to the 30th column.

The output for the first six months of the example program is shown in Listing 30.1.

Listing 30.1. Sample payment schedule.

Period	Payment	Principal	Interest	Balance
1	477.83	144.49	333.33	49,855.51
2	477.83	145.46	332.37	49,710.05
3	477.83	146.43	331.40	49,563.63
4	477.83	147.40	330.42	49,416.22
5	477.83	148.38	329.44	49,267.84
6	477.83	149.37	328.45	49,118.46

That's basically it for a simple loan calculator and payment scheduler. To show you more of QBasic's advanced functions, though, I'll have you jazz up the program a little.

Arrays

Instead of simply displaying the number of the period, it would be more informative to display the month and year of the payment. There are two parts to displaying the month—getting a number from 1 to 12 out of the period, and matching that number with the name of the month. The display of the year is easier, because it changes only every 12 months.

A variable that holds all the month names and corresponding numbers would be nice. QBasic provides *arrays* to do just that. An array is basically a list of variables that can be accessed by a number. The third value in the list would be March, the fifth, May, and so on.

To set up an array of month names, add the following statements immediately after the DECLARE statements in the main program:

```
' set up an array of month names to be shared among all
' functions/procedures
DIM SHARED MonthName$(12)
```

The array is created (or dimensioned) to hold 12 strings. It is also *shared*, meaning that functions and subprocedures can reference it. If you didn't declare it as shared, it would be available only to the main program itself.

To put the values for the months into this array, you manually assign each month as shown here:

```
MonthName$(1) = "Jan"
MonthName$(2) = "Feb"
MonthName$(3) = "Mar"
```

And so on. This is a bit tedious for 12 values, let alone for a larger array such as StateName$ that would hold 50 values. Can you use some sort of loop to automate the process? Of course.

Using *READ* and *DATA* Commands

QBasic uses two statements, READ and DATA, to facilitate using large quantities of similar data. The READ command simply pulls the next value from the DATA statement.

After setting up the array with the DIM statement, add the following lines:

```
' read the month names into the array
DATA Dec,Jan,Feb,Mar,Apr,May,Jun,Jul,Aug,Sep,Oct,Nov
FOR MonthNum% = 0 TO 11: READ MonthName$(MonthNum%): NEXT
```

Yes, you would normally start with Jan and end with Dec and loop from 1 to 12, but as you will see in the next section, there is a reason for doing it this way. January is still month 1, August is still month 8, but December needs to be month zero.

If you are to give the user the months and years of the payments, you need to know what month and year the loan starts. In the Schedule subprocedure, add the following lines at the beginning of the body:

```
EnterStartMonth:
INPUT "Starting month of loan (1-12)"; StartMonth%
' check that the month is valid
IF StartMonth% < 1 OR StartMonth% > 12 THEN
        BEEP
        GOTO EnterStartMonth
END IF

EnterStartYear:
INPUT "Starting year of loan"; StartYear%
' check that the year is valid
IF StartYear% < 1900 THEN
        BEEP
        GOTO EnterStartYear
END IF
```

Special Division Functions

Now that you know the starting month and year, you can get the month and year for each subsequent period. The `Period` counter in the `FOR...NEXT` loop and the starting month can be divided by 12 to get the proper month. Then, if that month is December, the year changes for the next month.

Sounds straightforward enough, but there's a problem with the division—these are all integer values. You can't simply divide a number like 3 or 17 evenly into 12.

To solve this problem, QBasic provides two special integer division functions, \ and `MOD`. The statement

```
PRINT 17 \ 5
```

returns the number 3, because 5 goes into 17 three times. On the other hand, the statement

```
PRINT 17 MOD 5
```

returns the number 2, because after 5 goes into 17 three times, a remainder of 2 is left.

For your calculations, you want to `MOD` a number by 12, because its remainder will be between 0 and 11. This is why you rearranged the months from 0 to 11 beginning with December—12 `MOD` 12 is 0, not 12.

Add the following lines just inside the FOR...NEXT loop of the `Schedule` subprocedure:

```
' determine the number of the current month
PeriodMonth% = (StartMonth% + Period% - 1) MOD 12
```

If your starting month is May (the fifth month) and you are in the second period of the loan, (5+2-1) `MOD` 12 = 6, or June. If you are in the eighth month of the loan, (5+8-1) `MOD` 12 = 0, or December.

String Manipulation

Now that you have a way to get the month name from the array, you need a way to print it and the year. QBasic provides string functions that you can use to join or manipulate string values.

Directly after the lines previously added, type the following lines:

```
' create the label for the current month
PeriodLabel$ = MonthName$(PeriodMonth%) + STR$(StartYear%)
```

This statement creates a string called `PeriodLabel` that holds the name of the month and the year. Notice that you couldn't just add `StartYear` to the string, because it's an integer data type. You used the `STR$` function to convert it to a string first.

QBasic also gives you functions to trim characters from a string (`LTRIM$`, `RTRIM$`), manipulate or extract parts of a string (`LEFT$`, `MID$`, `RIGHT$`), and change the case of a string (`UCASE$`, `LCASE$`). You'll see the `UCASE$` function a bit later.

Next, you need a little logic to see whether the year needs to be incremented. If it is December, the `PeriodMonth` variable will be 0, because a multiple of 12 MOD 12 is 0.

```
' if it is the last month, change the year
IF PeriodMonth% = 0 THEN StartYear% = StartYear% + 1
```

Finally, you need to edit the PRINT command that originally printed just the `Period` variable. Change the line in the `Schedule` subprocedure from

```
PRINT Period%; TAB(15);
```

to

```
PRINT PeriodLabel$; TAB(15);
```

If you haven't saved your program in a while, now would be a good time to do so.

Working with Data Files

Finally, now that you've put all of this work into calculating and scheduling payments, it would be nice to be able to store a final schedule on a disk.

QBasic can read from and write to three types of files:

- Sequential—Stores and retrieves data one line at a time and only in the order in which they are stored. Simplest of the three file types.

- Random—Data can be accessed from anywhere in the file at any time. Commonly used in database-oriented applications.

- Binary—Data can be accessed from any individual byte in the file. Used when elaborate storage measures are needed.

For your simple payment schedule, a sequential file will do.

To ask the user whether he wants to save the table to a file, add the following lines to the Schedule subprocedure after the NumberOfMonths is input:

```
INPUT "Print schedule to a file (Y/N)"; YN$
' convert response to uppercase
FileYN$ = UCASE$(YN$)
IF FileYN$ = "Y" THEN
        ' get a file name and open it for writing
        INPUT "Filename"; FileName$
        OPEN FileName$ FOR OUTPUT AS 1
END IF
```

If you have trouble following the program segments, the final program is listed at the end of this chapter.

Notice that the answer is converted to uppercase. This way, QBasic only has to check to see whether it's equal to Y and not y as well. The OPEN statement is simple. The FOR OUTPUT keyword sets up the program to write to a sequential file, and the AS 1 keyword assigns this file a number that will be used later.

Writing to a file is as easy as printing to the screen. In fact, the same PRINT and PRINT USING commands are used. Whereas a PRINT command reads

```
PRINT "This goes to the screen."
```

a file command reads

```
PRINT #1, "This goes to a file."
```

in which 1 is the file number assigned in the OPEN statement. To get the Schedule subprocedure to write to a file, you need to duplicate the PRINT and PRINT USING commands, modify them for file writing, and check to see whether the user requested that the schedule be saved.

After printing the headings to the screen in the Schedule subprocedure, add the following lines:

```
' if printing to a file, write the headings for the table
IF FileYN$ = "Y" THEN
        PRINT #1, "Period"; TAB(15); "Payment"; TAB(30);
        PRINT #1, "Principal"; TAB(45); "Interest";
TAB(60);
        PRINT #1, "Balance"
        PRINT #1,
END IF
```

In the loop, after printing the monthly data to the screen, add the following lines:

```
' if printing to a file, write the numbers for the period
IF FileYN$ = "Y" THEN
        PRINT #1, PeriodLabel$; TAB(15);
        PRINT #1, USING "######,.##";
MonthlyPayment;TAB(30);
        PRINT #1, USING "######,.##"; Principal; TAB(45);
        PRINT #1, USING "######,.##"; InterestPaid;
TAB(60);
        PRINT #1, USING "######,.##"; Balance
END IF
```

Finally, at the end of the body of the Schedule subprocedure (just before END SUB), add the following lines:

```
' if printing to a file, close the file
IF FileYN$ = "Y" THEN CLOSE #1
```

Running Your Program

That's it! Your program is ready to go! To run your program, press F5.

Troubleshooting

QBasic makes it easy to debug (troubleshoot) your programs. If any error messages pop up, you can take one of the following actions:

- Press Enter to clear the message.

- Press F1 or select Help and press Enter to receive help on the particular error message.

If you are having problems with your program or don't understand why it's not working, you can have QBasic walk you through the program step-by-step.

To step through your program, follow these instructions:

1. Press F8 to start the process.

2. Press F8 to step through one line at a time, or press F5 to continue the program.

QBasic also enables you to specify where you want a program to stop. For example, you can set a *breakpoint* after a function has been called, toggle to the Immediate window, and print the value the function returned. This can help a great deal in troubleshooting specific sections of code.

To set a breakpoint, take the following steps:

1. Move the cursor to the line of code you want to stop on.

2. Press F9.

You can set as many breakpoints as you need to troubleshoot your program. When you are ready to run the program, press F5. QBasic will stop when it detects a breakpoint. Pressing F5 again continues the program.

Summary

Listing 30.2 shows the complete code for the main program, function, and subprocedure used as the sample application.

Listing 30.2. Main program, LOANCALC.BAS.

```
' Title: Loan Calculator and Payment Scheduler
' Author: David Rhodes
' Date: December 25, 1992
' Version: 1.0
'
' Input: Loan amount, number of years, annual interest rate
' Output: Monthly payment, payment schedule (screen and/or file)
' declarations are automatically done by QBasic when functions
' or subprocedures are created
DECLARE SUB Schedule (Months%, Rate!, Loan!, MonthlyPayment!)
DECLARE FUNCTION CalcMonthlyPayment! (Months%, Rate!, Loan!)

' set up an array of month names to be shared among all
' functions/procedures
DIM SHARED MonthName$(12)
' read the month names into the array
DATA Dec,Jan,Feb,Mar,Apr,May,Jun,Jul,Aug,Sep,Oct,Nov
FOR MonthNum% = 0 TO 11: READ MonthName$(MonthNum%): NEXT

' clear the screen and begin getting the input
CLS
EnterLoan:
```

continues

Listing 30.2. continued

```
INPUT "Loan amount"; Loan
' check that the loan amount is greater than zero
IF Loan <= 0 THEN
        BEEP
        GOTO EnterLoan
END IF

EnterYears:
INPUT "Number of years"; Years%
' check that the number of years is greater than zero
IF Years% <= 0 THEN
        BEEP
        GOTO EnterYears
END IF
' convert the number of years into months
Months% = Years% * 12

EnterRate:
INPUT "Annual interest rate (percent)"; AnnualRate
' check that the rate is greater than zero but less than 100
IF AnnualRate <= 0 OR AnnualRate >= 100 THEN
        BEEP
        GOTO EnterRate
END IF
' convert the annual rate into a monthly percentage
Rate = AnnualRate / 1200

' call the function to calculate the monthly payment
MonthlyPayment = CalcMonthlyPayment(Months%, Rate, Loan)

PRINT
PRINT "Your monthly payment will be ";
' format the monthly payment figure
PRINT USING "$#####,.##"; MonthlyPayment

' call the procedure to print the payment schedule
CALL Schedule(Months%, Rate, Loan, MonthlyPayment)

FUNCTION CalcMonthlyPayment (Months%, Rate, Loan)

' determines the present value of a $1 annuity
PresentValueFactor = (1 - (1 / (1 + Rate) ^ Months%)) / Rate
```

```
' divides the loan amount by the present value and
' returns the value of the monthly payment
CalcMonthlyPayment = Loan / PresentValueFactor

END FUNCTION

SUB Schedule (Months%, Rate, Loan, MonthlyPayment)

EnterStartMonth:
INPUT "Starting month of loan (1-12)"; StartMonth%
' check that the month is valid
IF StartMonth% < 1 OR StartMonth% > 12 THEN
        BEEP
        GOTO EnterStartMonth
END IF

EnterStartYear:
INPUT "Starting year of loan"; StartYear%
' check that the year is valid
IF StartYear% < 1900 THEN
        BEEP
        GOTO EnterStartYear
END IF

PRINT "Number of periods to view ("; Months%; " max)";
INPUT NumberOfMonths%
' if the requested number of months is greater than the length
' of the loan or is not entered, set the requested number to
' the length of the loan
IF NumberOfMonths% > Months% OR NumberOfMonths% = 0 THEN
        NumberOfMonths% = Months%
END IF

INPUT "Print schedule to a file (Y/N)"; YN$
' convert response to uppercase
FileYN$ = UCASE$(YN$)
IF FileYN$ = "Y" THEN
        ' get a file name and open it for writing
        INPUT "Filename"; FileName$
        OPEN FileName$ FOR OUTPUT AS 1
END IF

' clear the screen and print the headings for the table
CLS
PRINT "Period"; TAB(15); "Payment"; TAB(30);
PRINT "Principal"; TAB(45); "Interest"; TAB(60); "Balance"
PRINT
```

continues

Listing 30.2. continued

```
' if printing to a file, write the headings for the table
IF FileYN$ = "Y" THEN
        PRINT #1, "Period"; TAB(15); "Payment"; TAB(30);
        PRINT #1, "Principal"; TAB(45); "Interest"; TAB(60);
        PRINT #1, "Balance"
        PRINT #1,
END IF

' set the initial balance to the amount of the loan itself
Balance = Loan

' begin the loop
FOR Period% = 1 TO NumberOfMonths%

' determine the number of the current month
PeriodMonth% = (StartMonth% + Period% - 1) MOD 12
' create the label for the current month
PeriodLabel$ = MonthName$(PeriodMonth%) + STR$(StartYear%)

' if it is the last month, change the year
IF PeriodMonth% = 0 THEN StartYear% = StartYear% + 1

' calculate the amount of interest paid
InterestPaid = Rate * Balance
' calculate the amount of the payment that goes to principal
Principal = MonthlyPayment - InterestPaid
' calculate the remaining balance on the loan
Balance = Balance - Principal

' print the numbers for the period
PRINT PeriodLabel$; TAB(15);
PRINT USING "#####,.##"; MonthlyPayment; TAB(30);
PRINT USING "#####,.##"; Principal; TAB(45);
PRINT USING "#####,.##"; InterestPaid; TAB(60);
PRINT USING "#####,.##"; Balance

' if printing to a file, write the numbers for the period
IF FileYN$ = "Y" THEN
        PRINT #1, PeriodLabel$; TAB(15);
        PRINT #1, USING "#####,.##";
MonthlyPayment;TAB(30);
        PRINT #1, USING "#####,.##"; Principal; TAB(45);
        PRINT #1, USING "#####,.##"; InterestPaid; TAB(60);
        PRINT #1, USING "#####,.##"; Balance
END IF
```

```
' repeat the loop
NEXT

' if printing to a file, close the file
IF FileYN$ = "Y" THEN CLOSE #1

END SUB
```

Alan Simpson's
DOS SECRETS UNLEASHED

Simple Programming Tools

This chapter takes a look at two programming tools that, while not part of DOS 6, can greatly enhance the appearance and utility of your batch programs and Basic applications.

The first tool, named *Batch Enhancer,* is part of *The Norton Utilities Version 6* by Symantec. Batch Enhancer, or simply *BE,* provides commands to make your batch programs more attractive and interactive. Although this chapter discusses only BE, The Norton Utilities includes many other features for performing data recovery and disk repair, speeding performance, adding security to your system, and navigating the DOS file system.

The package even includes *NDOS,* a complete replacement for the DOS command processor (COMMAND.COM).

The second tool is *Visual Basic for MS-DOS* (Version 1.0) by Microsoft. Visual Basic provides a complete programming system that lets you design jazzy-looking windows, dialog boxes, menus, command buttons, option buttons, and other Windows-style elements for an application, and then attach just enough program code to perform the actions specific to your application.

The Norton Utilities and Visual Basic are *not* part of DOS 6. You must purchase them separately.

Both The Norton Utilities and Visual Basic come with complete documentation that shows how to use these tools from A to Z. The goal here is just to whet your appetite for the possibilities offered by these tools, in case you wish to explore (and purchase) them on your own. I'm assuming that you already know how to use the EDIT text editor described in previous chapters and that you're comfortable with the material in Chapters 29 and 30.

Using Norton Batch Enhancer

The Batch Enhancer (BE) consists of about 20 commands that you can add to your batch programs or store in special BE *script files*. Before using the Batch Enhancer, you must purchase and install *The Norton Utilities Version 6* according to the manufacturer's instructions. Also, be sure that the directory containing the BE commands—usually C:\NU—is in your search path.

> Files, directories, and the PATH command are covered in Chapter 10.

What Batch Enhancer Can Do for You

Most people use BE commands to display fancier screens and prompts from batch programs, to provide more flexible decision-making within the program, and to interact with the user. The Batch Enhancer includes commands to do the following:

- Prompt for responses to questions (much like the DOS 6 CHOICE command)

- Draw boxes and windows on the screen, position text exactly where you want it, and control screen colors and other attributes

- Pause for a specified amount of time, or resume execution at a specified time

- Branch to one of several labels, depending on the exit code (ERRORLEVEL) returned by a previous Batch Enhancer command

■ Make decisions based on the day of the month or week

■ Perform a warm boot of the system

Summary of Batch Enhancer Commands

Table 31.1 lists all of the BE commands, along with an example and explanation of what each one does. Notice how each command begins with the word BE and a space, followed by the rest of the command.

> If you place the BE commands in a script file (discussed later), you can include or omit the BE prefix as you wish; however, you must include the prefix when typing the commands at the command line or in a batch program.

Table 31.1. Batch Enhancer commands and examples.

BE Command	Sample Command and Explanation *
ASK	BE ASK "Continue (Y/N)? " YN DEFAULT=N TIMEOUT=10
	Prompts with Continue (Y/N)? and waits until the user responds with Y (or y) or N (or n). If the user presses Enter or doesn't respond after 10 seconds, the default choice of N is assumed. ERRORLEVEL 1 is returned if the user chooses 1 and ERRORLEVEL 2 is returned if the user chooses N.

BE Command	Sample Command and Explanation *
BEEP	BE BEEP /F440 /R3 /D36 /W9
	Sounds the note "A" (/F440) three times (/R3) for a duration of 2 seconds (/D36) and waits 0.5 seconds between beeps (/W9). Duration and wait are specified in 18ths of a second; thus 36 represents 36/18ths or 2 seconds.
BOX	BE BOX 5 10 15 70 BLUE
	Draws a transparent (unfilled) rectangle with a blue, double-line border. The top left corner is at row 5 column 10, and the bottom right border is at row 15 column 70.
CLS	BE CLS WHITE ON RED
	Clears the screen and specifies the color as white text on a red background. You can specify the same color attributes as for SA, but you don't have to load ANSI.SYS first.
DELAY	BE DELAY 36
	Pauses execution for 2 seconds (36/18ths) and then resumes.
EXIT	BE EXIT
	Terminates execution of a BE script file before reaching the end of the file. Works only in script files.

continues

Table 31.1. continued

BE Command	Sample Command and Explanation *
GOTO	`BE MYSCRIPT.BE GOTO THURSDAY` Starts executing the BE script file named `MYSCRIPT.BE` at the label named `THURSDAY`, instead of starting at the beginning of myscript.be as usual. Works only to start BE script files.
JUMP	`BE JUMP YES, NO /DEFAULT:OTHER` Transfers control to the label `:YES` if the previous command returned an exit code (`ERRORLEVEL`) of 1, to the label `:NO` if exit code 2 was returned, or to the label `:OTHER` if any other exit code was returned. Works only in BE script files.
MONTHDAY	`BE MONTHDAY /DEBUG` Returns the day of the month (1-31) as an exit code. The `/DEBUG` switch displays the exit code.
PRINTCHAR	`BE PRINTCHAR *, 80, BLUE` Repeats a blue asterisk (*) 80 times at the current cursor location.
REBOOT	`BE REBOOT /VERIFY` Displays the message `Reboot the computer now?` and reboots the computer if the user types `Y` or `y`.
ROWCOL	`BE ROWCOL 15 25 "Hello World!" BLINKING WHITE ON RED` Displays the message `Hello World!` in blinking white text on a red background on row 15 column 25 of the screen. You

BE Command	Sample Command and Explanation *
	can specify the same color attributes as for SA, but you don't have to load ANSI.SYS first.
SA	BE SA BRIGHT WHITE ON RED /CLS
	Sets the screen colors to bright white text foreground on a red background and clears the screen. The ANSI.SYS driver must be loaded in CONFIG.SYS before using this command.
	Valid colors are WHITE, BLACK, BLUE, CYAN, GREEN, MAGENTA, RED, and YELLOW. You can add the word BRIGHT or BLINKING before the foreground color. Use BE SA NORMAL to reset the screen to normal attributes.
SHIFTSTATE	BE SHIFTSTATE /DEBUG
	Returns an exit code that can be used to determine whether the Shift, Ctrl, or Alt key was active when the SHIFTSTATE command was run. The /DEBUG switch displays the exit code.
TRIGGER	BE TRIGGER 05:00 pm
	Suspends execution of the next command until 5 p.m.
WEEKDAY	BE WEEKDAY /DEBUG
	Returns the day of the week as an exit code between 1 (Sunday) and 7 (Saturday). The /DEBUG switch displays the exit code.

continues

Table 31.1. continued

BE Command	Sample Command and Explanation *
WINDOW	BE WINDOW 5 10 15 70 BLUE ZOOM SHADOW Draws a solid (filled) rectangle with a blue, double-line border. The top left corner is at row 5 column 10, and the bottom right border is at row 15 column 70. The window will zoom as it displays and a black drop shadow will appear if the background color isn't black.

*You can omit the BE prefix when you use Batch Enhancer commands in a Batch Enhancer script file. Unless otherwise specified, all BE commands can be used at the command prompt, in a BE script file, or in a batch program.

If you've installed BE on your system, you can try out most of the Batch Enhancer commands shown in this chapter by typing them at the DOS prompt.

Getting Help with Batch Enhancer

After installing The Norton Utilities, you can list the available BE commands by typing BE ? and pressing Enter at the command prompt. For help on a specific command, type BE *command* ? where *command* is the name of the command in which you're interested. For example, typing BE ASK ? displays the following information on your screen:

```
Batch Enhancer, Norton Utilities 6.01, Copyright 1992 by
Symantec Corporation

BE ASK "prompt" [key-list] [DEFAULT=key] [TIMEOUT=n]
[ADJUST=n] [color]
```

The BE help uses the same syntax conventions as normal DOS 6 help. That is, square brackets ([ ]) enclose optional parameters (do not type the brackets when entering commands). Uppercase letters represent text that you must type exactly as shown. Lowercase letters represent text that you must replace with values. You can type BE commands in uppercase letters, lowercase, or a mixture of the two.

The following sample ASK command follows these syntax rules:

```
BE ASK "Continue? (Y/N) " yn default=n
```

This command prompts with Continue? (Y/N) and waits until you type y or Y, n or N, or press Enter. Because the parameter default=n was added to the command, pressing Enter is the same as choosing n or N.

For more detailed information on using each BE command, please refer to The Norton Utilities *User's Guide* or *Command Line Usage Guide* that comes with your package.

Entering BE Commands at the DOS Prompt

You can type BE commands at the DOS prompt, just as you would any other command. Simply type BE and a space followed by the rest of the command, and then press Enter. Typing BE commands at the DOS prompt is a handy way to try out new commands before adding them to a batch program or BE script file.

The Norton Utilities commands must be in your PATH statement, or you must switch to the directory that contains Norton Utilities (typically by typing CD C:\NU and pressing Enter). Otherwise, DOS isn't able to run the BE commands.

Entering BE Commands in a Batch Program

You enter the BE commands in a batch program just as you would enter any DOS or batch command—type the complete BE command on a line of its own. Later you'll see some examples of batch programs that contain BE commands.

Creating Batch Enhancer Script Files

You can use Batch Enhancer script files to execute BE commands directly, instead of going through DOS. When used in script files, Batch Enhancer commands run much faster—especially when you're drawing fancy screens—and are easier to type.

Anatomy of a Script File

Batch Enhancer script files contain a series of BE commands that normally would appear in batch programs; the BE prefix is optional in scripts. You can create script files with any DOS text editor (such as EDIT) or word processor that creates ASCII text files. Like normal batch programs, script files can include labels, which are preceded by a colon (:).

The BE JUMP and BE ... GOTO commands are used in BE
script files to transfer control to labels.

Script files also can contain comments, which are preceded by a
semicolon (;). The sample Batch Enhancer script file in Listing 31.1
contains a comment on the first line, and the label Skip1 on the fifth
line.

Listing 31.1. A simple Batch Enhancer script file named SkipTest.

```
; Usage: BE Skiptest or BE Skiptest GOTO Skip1
cls
rowcol 20 40 "Start"
exit
:Skip1
cls
rowcol 20 40 "Skip1"
```

If DOS commands are present in a Batch Enhancer script
file, they are ignored completely.

Running a Script File

You can run a script file from the command prompt or from a batch
program. The complete syntax for running a script file is

```
BE pathname [[GOTO] label]
```

where pathname is the drive, directory, and file name of the BE script
file. Normally the script file begins execution at the first line and

continues until it reaches the end of file or it encounters an EXIT command. However, if you specify the name of a valid *label* when you start the script file, execution begins after that label instead.

> You can omit the word GOTO and specify just the label name.

Suppose you created the script file shown in Listing 31.1 and then ran it by typing BE SkipTest (without GOTO or the label name) and pressing Enter. The script would clear the screen (cls), display the message Start at row 20 column 40 of the screen, and then exit.

In contrast, you could start the SkipTest script file at the Skip1 label by typing BE SkipTest Skip1 and pressing Enter. This would clear the screen, display the message Skip1 at row 20 column 40 of the screen, and exit normally.

Now look at some ways to spice up two batch programs with fancier screen displays and speedier execution. First we'll revise LOOKIN2.BAT, which searches for text in one or more files. Then we'll look at two ways to "batch enhance" the menu shell named MENU.BAT.

> Both LOOKIN2.BAT and MENU.BAT are explained in Chapter 29, and you may wish to review the explanations there for a quick refresher.

Supercharging LOOKIN2.BAT

Recall from Chapter 29 that the LOOKIN2.BAT batch program can search for one or more words in a file or group of files (see Listing 29.13). The search results are stored in a temporary file named

TEMPFILE.TXT, which is displayed on the screen and optionally printed. Listing 31.2 shows a revised version of LOOKIN2.BAT that includes several Batch Enhancer commands.

> The Batch Enhancer commands in Listing 31.2 are shown in lowercase letters, beginning with the word be.

Listing 31.2. LOOKIN2.BAT with Batch Enhancer commands to control the screen display.

```
@ECHO OFF
REM ***************************************** LOOKIN2.BAT
REM Searches multiple text files for multiple words.
REM ----- %1 is the file(s) to be searched,
REM ----- %2 is the word to search for.

REM ----- Erase TEMPFILE.TXT if it exists.
IF EXIST TEMPFILE.TXT ERASE TEMPFILE.TXT

REM Put %1 in the environment for future use.
SET FileName=%1

REM ----- Search files with FIND,
REM ----- redirect output to TEMPFILE.TXT
:NextWord
REM ----- Display "Searching..." message in a BE window
be cls black on white
be window 5 10 15 70 zoom shadow
be rowcol 10 15 "Searching for '%2' in %FileName%..."
REM ----- Pause for 2 seconds while user views BE window
be delay 36
ECHO *** Search for "%2" in %FileName% *** >> TEMPFILE.TXT
FOR %%c IN (%FileName%) DO FIND /I "%2" %%c >> TEMPFILE.TXT

REM Store a form-feed in TEMPFILE.TXT.
ECHO 
 >> TEMPFILE.TXT
```

continues

Listing 31.2. continued

```
REM Shift and repeat search if more words to search for.
SHIFT
IF NOT %2. == . GOTO NextWord

REM ----- Clean up the environment. It's the right thing to do.
REM ----- Display the results.
SET FileName =
REM ----- Clear screen with white text on black (normal)
be cls white on black
MORE < TEMPFILE.TXT

REM ----- Present option to print the results.
ECHO.
REM ----- Prompt for input and accept only Y, N, or Enter
be ask "Do you want to print the results? " yn Default=n
timeout=10
IF ERRORLEVEL 2 GOTO Done
REM ----- Clear screen with black text on white (reverse).
be cls black on white
REM ----- Display "Results..." message in a BE window
be window 5 10 15 70 zoom shadow
be rowcol 10 15 "Results of scanning %FileName% files > PRN"
TYPE TEMPFILE.TXT > PRN
ECHO
 > PRN
REM ----- Give user time to view message in a BE window
be delay 54

:Done
REM ----- Return screen to normal colors
be cls white on black
```

Now, suppose you want to use this new LOOKIN2.BAT batch program to search for *tomato* in files with a .DAT extension. Type LOOKIN2 *.DAT TOMATO and press Enter at the command prompt.

After performing some preliminary housekeeping chores, the batch program displays the screen shown in Figure 31.1. This figure illustrates the power of Batch Enhancer to produce fancy windows and control screen colors (for now, just take it on faith that screen colors can be changed).

I won't explain *every* command in LOOKIN2.BAT here, because Chapter 29 covers its operation in detail.

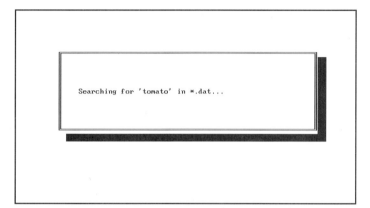

*Figure 31.1.
The first screen
displayed by
LOOKIN2.BAT
has a drop-
shadowed,
zooming
window style.*

Now, take a look at Listing 31.1 again and find the :NextWord label, followed by the BE commands that displayed the screen in Figure 31.1. First, the BE CLS command clears the screen and sets it to show black text on a white background. The BE WINDOW command displays a window with the top left corner at row 5 column 10 and the bottom right corner at row 15 column 70. The window will zoom (or explode) open and will have a drop shadow at the right. Next, the BE ROWCOL command displays the Searching... message at row 10 column 15 (roughly the middle of the window). Then the BE DELAY 36 command pauses execution for 2 seconds (36/18ths) so that the user has a chance to read information on the window.

Windows have a solid color and overwrite any text they cover. That's why the Searching... text was displayed after opening the window. If you want existing text to show through, you need to use the BE BOX command instead.

Following the BE commands, the FOR command searches each file for the word you specified on the command line, saves the results in TEMPFILE.TXT, and shifts the command line parameters and returns to the NextWord label until the program has searched for all the words you specified.

After completing the searches, the program is ready to display the result. First, the command BE CLS WHITE ON BLACK resets the screen to white text on a black background, then the MORE command displays the contents of TEMPFILE.TXT (Figure 31.2). Next, the BE ASK command asks if you want to print the results and awaits your answer. If you type y or Y within ten seconds, the results are printed. If you type n or N, or press Enter, or wait too long, the program transfers control to the :Done label and once more clears the screen and sets it to show white text on a black background.

Notice how similar the ASK command is to the new CHOICE command in DOS 6. The main differences are that ASK does not display the valid keys in the prompt, it always accepts uppercase or lowercase responses, and it can display the prompt in color.

```
*** Search for "tomato" in *.dat ***

---------- FRUIT.DAT
Tomatoes
TOMATOS
TOMATo

---------- SALAD.DAT
Tomato
Tomatoes
♀

Do you want to print the results?
```

Figure 31.2. The search results appear next, along with a prompt asking if you want to print the file.

If you chose to print the contents of TEMPFILE.TXT, you'll see the window and `Results...` message shown in Figure 31.3. To produce this display, the batch program again clears the screen and sets it to black text on a white background, draws the drop-shadowed zoomed window, displays the `Results...` message in the middle of the window, prints the output, and delays for 3 seconds before proceeding to the `:Done` label and clearing the screen.

A window's drop shadow is always black, and therefore appears only if the screen background color is *not* black.

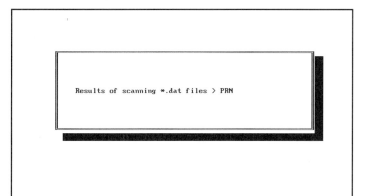

Figure 31.3. The final window tells you that LOOKIN2.BAT is printing your search results.

```
Results of scanning *.dat files > PRN
```

Supercharging MENU.BAT

Listing 29.16 in Chapter 29 illustrates a simple shell for running programs. The shell displays a series of numbered options for each program a user might want to run. When the user types a number, DOS executes a batch program that uses the option number as its name, contains the necessary commands to run the requested program, and (optionally) re-executes the MENU.BAT batch program when the user exits the requested program.

Figure 31.4 shows a supercharged version of the menu presented in Chapter 29, and Listing 31.3 shows the batch program that displays the fancier menu.

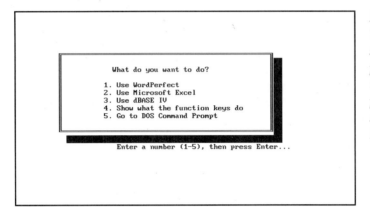

Figure 31.4. This menu screen is produced by the batch program shown in Listing 31.3.

Listing 31.3. A fancier version of the MENU.BAT program.

```
@ECHO OFF
REM ********************************** MENU.BAT
REM ----- Display "shell" for running programs in a BE
window.
be cls black on white
be window  5 10 15 60 zoom shadow
be rowcol  7 23 "What do you want to do?"
be rowcol  9 21 "1. Use WordPerfect"
be rowcol 10 21 "2. Use Microsoft Excel"
be rowcol 11 21 "3. Use dBASE IV"
be rowcol 12 21 "4. Show what the function keys do"
be rowcol 13 21 "5. Go to DOS Command Prompt"
be rowcol 17 24 "Enter a number (1-5), then press Enter... "
prompt $e
```

The revised MENU.BAT batch program really is quite simple. When you type MENU and press Enter at the command prompt, the batch program displays a zoomed window, with the top left corner at row 5 column 10 and the bottom left corner at row 15 column 60.

If your CONFIG.SYS file includes the command
DEVICE=ANSI.SYS, you can get even better results by replacing the BE CLS command with the command BE SA BLACK ON WHITE /CLS, which will clear the screen and set the attributes to white text on a black background. (Of course, you can choose other colors, depending on the monitor you're using.)

After displaying the window, the batch program uses a series of ROWCOL commands to print each line of the menu at a specific row and column position on the screen. Finally, the PROMPT command turns off the prompt character.

You can type PROMPT PG to have the prompt show the current drive and path.

Super Supercharging MENU.BAT

If you've tried the MENU.BAT example shown in Listing 31.3, you might have discovered that the menu doesn't appear instantaneously on the screen. To supercharge a sluggish screen and speed up the execution of Batch Enhancer commands, move the BE commands into a separate script file, and then run the script file from your batch program or the command prompt.

This technique is especially useful with enhanced batch programs that display many windows, boxes, or prompts on the screen.

For instance, you can make just a few changes to MENU.BAT that will display the menu much faster. Begin by copying MENU.BAT to MENU.BE. Then edit MENU.BAT, remove the BE commands, type be menu.be on a new line preceding the PROMPT command, and save the file again. Here's what remains in MENU.BAT after making these changes:

```
@ECHO OFF
REM ********************************** MENU.BAT
REM Provide a faster "shell" for running programs.
be menu.be
prompt $e
```

Now edit the MENU.BE file. Change the REM commands to Batch Enhancer comments (;), remove the @ECHO and PROMPT commands, remove the BE prefix from each Batch Enhancer command if you wish, and save the file. Your MENU.BE file should now look something like this:

```
; ********************************** MENU.BE
; BE script file provides a faster "shell" for running
programs.
cls black on white
window  5 10 15 60 zoom shadow
rowcol  7 23 "What do you want to do?"
rowcol  9 21 "1. Use WordPerfect"
rowcol 10 21 "2. Use Microsoft Excel"
rowcol 11 21 "3. Use dBASE IV"
rowcol 12 21 "4. Show what the function keys do"
rowcol 13 21 "5. Go to DOS Command Prompt"
rowcol 17 24 "Enter a number (1-5), then press Enter... "
```

When you type MENU and press Enter to execute the revised MENU.BAT program, you should notice that the menu appears on the screen much faster than it did when the BE commands were embedded within the batch program.

Microsoft Visual Basic for MS-DOS

Microsoft Visual Basic for MS-DOS (VBDOS) is a powerful programming environment that lets you create graphical applications that respond to events such as clicking your mouse on a command button, selecting options from menus, changing values in a text box, and so forth. You use the Visual Basic Form Designer to draw your application's user interface, and then switch to the programming environment to write just enough Basic code to bring your application to life.

Visual Basic for MS-DOS comes in two versions. The *Standard Edition* offers an easy-to-use system for beginning programmers who want to develop sophisticated applications with a minimum of fuss. The *Professional Edition* adds tools to enhance speed, capacity, and access to databases that professional developers require.

The Standard Edition is compatible with QBasic and QuickBasic programs. The professional Edition runs all Basic Professional Development System programs designed for MS-DOS. The event-driven aspects of Visual Basic for MS-DOS are highly compatible with Visual Basic for Windows.

What Visual Basic Can Do for Your Applications

Designing an attractive, easy-to-use application in a traditional programming language like QBasic can be a slow, tedious process that requires a huge amount of code. But Visual Basic makes that job easy, because you can design attractive forms simply by drawing them on the screen. All the coding for the user interface is built-in, so you never need to worry about writing commands to specify how or where to place text and other design elements on the screen.

Suppose you want to design a program that converts a temperature from Fahrenheit to Centigrade, or Centigrade to Fahrenheit. A very simple user interface might look like this:

```
Enter the temperature you want to convert: 100
Type C to convert to Centigrade,
or F to convert to Fahrenheit,
or Q to Quit (C/F/Q): F
The answer is: 212.00
```

BORING!!! But in Visual Basic, you can design an application that looks like Figure 31.5 and requires you to write very little Basic code. In essence, Visual Basic frees you from the tedium of coding attractive user interfaces and allows you to work more quickly and creatively.

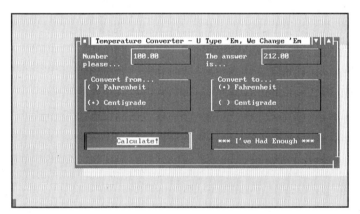

Figure 31.5. This Visual Basic application is much more interesting and intuitive for the user, and requires very little Basic code.

To use the temperature converter in Figure 31.5, you would click Fahrenheit or Centigrade in the Convert from... area of the window, and then click the appropriate conversion option in the Convert to... area. Now type your number into the Number please... box and click the Calculate! button. When you're finished, click the

*** I've Had Enough *** button. The application will play some music through your computer's speaker, display a friendly closing message, and wait for you to press Enter or click OK before it returns to the command prompt.

Getting Started with Visual Basic for DOS

After purchasing the package, the quickest way to get started with Visual Basic for MS-DOS is to follow the steps below:

1. Install the program according to the manufacturer's instructions.

2. Switch to the directory where you want to work. For example, type CD \MYAPPS if you've created a directory named MYAPPS on drive C to store your VBDOS applications.

3. To start Visual Basic, type VBDOS and press Enter at the command prompt. You'll see the opening screen shown in Figure 31.6.

4. Take the interactive tutorial, which offers eight lessons. To start the tutorial, open the Help menu and select Tutorial.

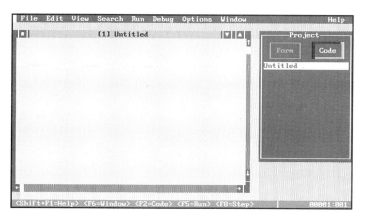

Figure 31.6. The Visual Basic opening screen.

A Quick Tour Through Visual Basic for DOS

Before diving into our sample temperature converter application, take a quick tour through Visual Basic.

Understanding Projects

All the files that make up an application are grouped into a *project*. Each project can contain form files and basic code files such as modules, include files, and libraries. (Many projects just contain a single form file.)

Project files have a .MAK extension.

The Programming Environment

Initially, an empty programming environment window appears (Figure 31.6). When the programming environment window contains code, it looks like Figure 31.7.

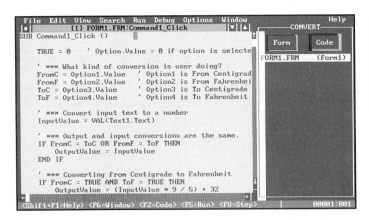

Figure 31.7. The programming environment window with code added.

The programming environment features a "smart" code editor and many debugging features. If you make a syntax error, Visual Basic alerts you as soon as you press the Enter key or move to another line. For example, the error message shown Figure 31.8 popped up when TRUE @= 0 was accidentally typed instead of TRUE = 0.

You can click the Help button if you're not sure about how to correct the error.

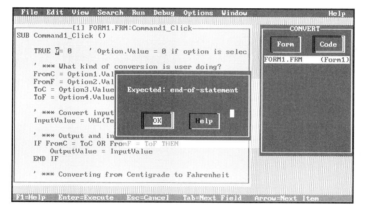

*Figure 31.8.
The programming environment features a smart code editor that informs you immediately when you make syntax errors.*

Getting Help in the Programming Environment

If you need help while working in the programming environment, you can highlight a Basic keyword (such as VAL) and press F1. You also can select options from the Help menu, or press Shift+F1 to view information on using help. Figure 31.9 shows a help screen for the STR$ and VAL functions.

Most help screens provide examples, which you can access by clicking the Example topic at the top of the screen. You can paste the code examples into your own code, and then make changes as necessary.

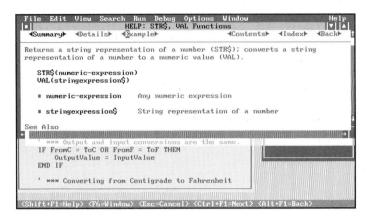

Figure 31.9. A help screen for the STR$ *and* VAL *functions.*

> The Help system in Visual Basic is almost identical to the Help system in QBASIC.

The Form Designer

The Form Designer provides an intuitive tool for designing forms-based DOS applications. Forms are windows that serve as backgrounds for your application. Each form consists of the form itself and various objects called *controls*.

> A form file has a .FRM extension.

Adding Controls to a Form

To add a control to your form, select the control you want from the Toolbox or Tools menu, and then draw it on your form. After creating a control, you can move and resize it as needed, or delete it.

Figure 31.10 shows a completed form for your temperature converter. This form includes two Text Box controls, two Frames, two Labels, four Option Buttons, and two Command Buttons.

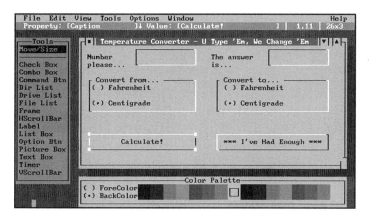

Figure 31.10.
The completed
form for your
temperature
converter
application.

You can switch quickly from the programming environment to the Form Designer by highlighting the form you want to work with in the list of project files and then clicking the Form button.

Changing Properties

All forms and controls have properties, such as name, size, and position that determine the object's position on the screen and its behavior. You can set properties by selecting the form or control you want to change, selecting a Property in the Properties Bar, and then changing the Value in the Value box.

Responding to Events

Applications created in Visual Basic are *event-driven*. That is, they can respond to events such as clicking a button, pressing a key, or waiting for a certain amount of time. To make an application respond to an event, you switch to the programming environment and write Basic code for your forms and controls. This code is called an *event procedure*.

> You only have to write Basic code for events to which you want the application to respond.

Creating an Executable Application

When you've finished creating your form and controls, added the necessary Basic code, and tested the application, you can create a standalone .EXE file that can run on any MS-DOS computer, whether or not it has Visual Basic. Your original files aren't changed in any way.

Creating a New Application

Here's a summary of the general steps for creating an application:

1. Use the CD or CHDIR command to switch to the directory where you want to create the application.

2. Start Visual Basic by typing VBDOS and pressing Enter at the command prompt.

3. When the opening screen appears (Figure 31.6), open the File menu. If you're creating a new application, select New Project. If you're changing an existing application, select Open Project and select the project you want.

4. To create a new form, open the File menu and select New Form. Type a name for your new form (such as MYFORM) and press Enter.

> If you want to change an existing form, click the form name in the Project window, and then click the Form button.

5. Draw the controls for your form.

6. Set properties for the form and each control.

7. Create event procedures in the programming environment. To switch to the programming environment, open the Edit menu and select Event Procedures, or press F12.

8. Save the project by opening the File menu and selecting Save Project. If this is a new project, type in the project name and press Enter.

9. To test the application, open the Run menu and select Start, or press Shift+F5. Now test the application. When you're finished, press Ctrl+F4, then press any key to close the test application and return to the programming environment. Make any corrections and changes you wish, and run and retest as needed.

> If you're testing the sample temperature converter application, click the `*** I've Had Enough ***` button instead of pressing Ctrl+F4.

10. When you've finished designing and testing the application, create an executable file by opening the Run menu and selecting Make EXE File.

Creating the Temperature Converter Application

Now that you have a general idea of what Visual Basic can do, you might want to try creating the sample temperature converter application shown in Figure 31.5. You already should have tried out the tutorial that comes with Visual Basic for MS-DOS, so that you'll be familiar with the general techniques involved.

To begin, switch to the directory where you want to create your application. Next, type VBDOS and press Enter. Open the File menu and select New Project. Now open the File menu again and select New Form. Type a name for your form (the name HEATCOLD might be nice) and press Enter. The empty form shown in Figure 31.11 will appear.

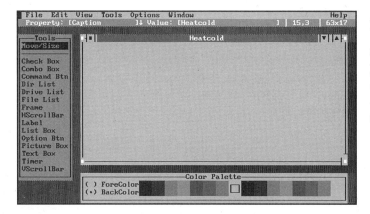

Figure 31.11. The new form appears after you select New Form from the File menu and name the form.

I assume here that you're familiar with the general programming topics discussed in Chapter 30. I also assume that you're comfortable using your computer's mouse. Although Visual Basic does provide keyboard equivalents for mouse actions, the mouse generally provides the quickest and easiest way to work in the Form Designer and programming environment.

If you just want to *use* the sample application, you'll find it on the floppy disk that came with this book. Simply copy the file named CONVERT.EXE to your computer, and then type CONVERT and press Enter at the command prompt.

Drawing Controls for the Sample Application

The next step is to draw the controls on the form. To draw a control, select the control you want from the Toolbox or the Tools menu, and then click and drag your mouse until the control is the size you want. Alternatively, you can just double-click the control you want in the Toolbox and drag the control to its new position.

Table 31.2 lists all the controls you can create.

Table 31.2. Controls that you can create in the Form Designer.

Control Name	What It Does
Check Box	Toggles selection of an option on and off
Combo Box	Allows a user to enter text or select items from a list
Command Button	Performs an action
Custom Control	A control that you design
Directory List Box	Enables user to select a directory path
Drive List Box	Enables user to select a disk drive
File List Box	Enables user to select a file or files
Frame	Groups controls

continues

903

Table 31.2. continued

Control Name	What It Does
Horizontal Scroll Bar	Enables selection from a range of values
Label	Displays text that the user cannot change
List Box	Enables user to select options from a list
Menu	Displays items the user can choose from
Option Button	Enables user to select one item in a group
Picture Box	Displays ASCII characters on a form
Text Box	Displays text that the user can change
Timer	Specifies a time interval for timer events
Vertical Scroll Bar	Enables selection from a range of values

Now go ahead and draw the controls as indicated in Figure 31.12. Be sure to create the Label1 control before creating Label2, create Text1 before Text2, and so on.

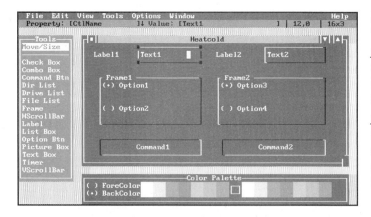

Figure 31.12. The HEATCOLD form after drawing two labels, two text boxes, two frames, four option buttons, and two command buttons.

When you get to the frames and option buttons, follow these steps to ensure that the option buttons are *grouped* within their respective frames:

1. Select Frame in the Toolbox, then click your form and drag the frame outline so that it's large enough to hold the option buttons.

2. Select Option Btn in the Toolbox, and then click inside the frame and drag so that the option button outline stays within the frame border.

3. Repeat Step 2 for the second option button in the frame.

Repeat these three steps to create the second frame.

You should draw the frame first, and then add the controls so that you can move the frame and controls together. If you try to move existing controls onto a frame, the controls will not move with the frame, and they will be obscured by the frame when you run the program. If the frame and option buttons don't move together, you can delete them and try creating them again.

You don't need to worry too much about getting the initial size or position of each control exactly right. You can make adjustments later.

Changing the Controls

Now that you've created the controls, you should save your work by opening the File menu and selecting Save Project. Type a name for your project, such as CONVERT, and press Enter.

When you're ready to adjust the appearance of a control, use the techniques listed below.

- To select the control, click it. Resizing handles will appear in each corner when you select a control (see Figure 31.13).

- To delete a control, select it and press Del.

- To resize the control, select it and drag the resizing handles.

- To move a control, select it and then drag the object to its new location (do not drag the object by a resizing handle).

- To change the properties of a control, select it and use the Properties Bar as described in the next section.

Now, make any desired adjustments to the size and position of the form's controls and save your work again (from the File menu select Save Project).

Setting the Properties for the Sample Application

Properties define an object's *characteristics*—such as size, color, and screen location—or *behavior*—such as whether the object is enabled or not. You can set properties with the Properties Bar at design time, or with Basic code at run time. For example, if you assign blank text to the text boxes when designing the form, at run time, after the user clicks Calculate!, the program will update the text boxes to contain formatted numbers for the input and output temperatures.

The general procedures for changing a property are

1. Select the object you want to change by clicking it. For example, select the form by clicking in an empty area of the form or by clicking the form's title bar.

2. Click the ↓ symbol next to the Property box in the Properties Bar. A drop-down menu will appear, as shown in Figure 31.13. Now select the Property you want to change. You can type the first letter of the property, or highlight it

with the arrow keys; then press Enter. Alternatively, you can use the scroll bar to locate the property you want, and then click the property name with your mouse.

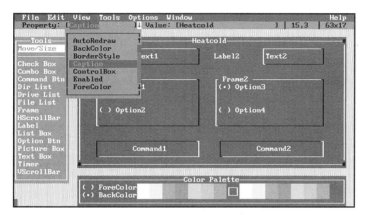

Figure 31.13. Click the ↓ next to the Property list box to open the Property menu in the Properties Bar.

Each time you press the first letter of the property name, the next option beginning with that letter will be highlighted.

3. Change the Value for the selected property in the Value box of the Property Bar. You can make changes by clicking the Value: title and typing a value or, if a ↓ appears to the right of the Value list box, you can select values as you did in Step 2.

The CtlName property is used in Basic code to identify the control. After creating a control, you can change its CtlName property if you wish; however, you should not change the CtlName property after you create Basic code that refers to the control.

Changing the Form Caption

Our first task is to change the caption that appears on the form's menu bar. To do this, click the form. Notice that the Caption property is selected in the Property Bar automatically. If it isn't selected, click the ↓ to the right of the Property box, and select Caption. Now, click `Value:` to select the existing caption (`HeatCold`), or drag your mouse across the existing text in the Value box. Now type the following text, then press Enter.

```
Temperature Converter - U Type 'Em, We Change 'Em
```

Notice how the title bar changes as you type the new value.

Changing the Remaining Captions

Next, change the captions in the Label controls. To do this, select a label control by clicking it, select the Caption property in the Property box, and then type the appropriate value for the label. The values for the labels are as follows:

- Change `Label1` to `Number please...`
- Change `Label2` to `The answer is...`

> You may need to resize and move the objects after changing their captions. Please refer to Figure 31.10 if you need a reminder about how the form should look.

Now, change the captions for the frames, option buttons, and command buttons. Here are the values to use:

- Change `Frame1` to `Convert from...`
- Change `Frame2` to `Convert to...`
- Change `Option1` to `Fahrenheit`
- Change `Option2` to `Centigrade`

- Change `Option3` to `Fahrenheit`

- Change `Option4` to `Centigrade`

- Change `Command1` to `Calculate!`

- Change `Command2` to `*** I've Had Enough ***`

If necessary, adjust the size and locations of these controls, and then save your work again by opening the File menu and selecting Save Project.

Changing the Text Box Values

Initially, the text boxes have the values `Text1` and `Text2`, respectively. The application will look (and work) much better if you make the initial values blank. To do so, select the Text Box you want to change, click the ↓ next to the Property list box in the Properties Bar, and type the letter `T` until you select the `Text` property. Press Enter. Now click `Value:` in the Property Bar, press the Del key to erase the existing value, and press Enter. Repeat this procedure for the other text box.

At this point, your form will resemble Figure 31.10. Before moving on to the event procedures, you should save the project once more.

Creating Event Procedures for the Sample Application

All objects in Visual Basic can recognize a predefined set of events automatically. For example, command buttons can recognize when you've clicked them with your mouse. However, it's your job to determine how or whether the objects respond. You do this by writing Basic code, called an *event procedure*, for the control and the event to which it responds.

The temperature converter needs to respond when the user clicks the `Calculate!` and `*** I've Had Enough ***` command buttons. The `Calculate!` button performs the temperature conversion, using as input the number typed into the `Number please...` text box, the option selected in the `Convert from...` frame, and the option selected in the `Convert to...` frame. The results will appear in the text box labeled `The number is...`. The *** I've Had Enough *** button enables the user to exit the application.

Switching to the Programming Environment

To begin writing event procedures, switch to the programming environment by opening the Edit menu and selecting Event Procedure, or pressing F12. You'll be asked if you're sure you want to exit to the programming environment. Press Enter or click OK to continue.

The Event Procedures dialog box shown in Figure 31.14 will appear next. To begin writing code for an event (or to change existing code for an event), follow these steps:

1. If necessary, select the file you want to work with in the Files list box.

2. Select the object you want to work with in the Objects list box. All the objects for the selected file are listed by their `CtlName` in the order in which they were created. The valid events for the object will appear in the Events box as soon as you select the object.

3. Choose the Edit in Active button.

Writing the Calculation Event Procedure

To create the event procedure that converts temperatures, complete the previous three steps, selecting the object named `Command1` in Step 2. Your screen will resemble Figure 31.15.

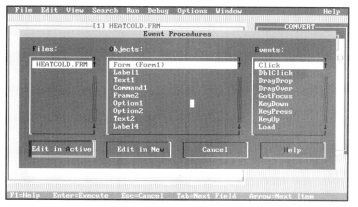

Figure 31.14. The Event Procedures dialog box enables you to select the file, object, and event for event procedures that you write.

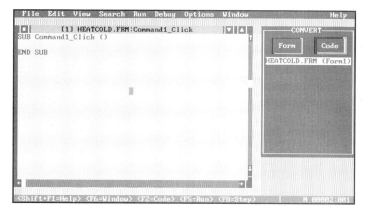

Figure 31.15. Your screen after you create the event procedure that converts temperatures.

The SUB and END SUB statements are created automatically to mark the beginning and end of a procedure named Command1_Click. The Command1 portion of the procedure name refers to the object for which you're writing code. The Click portion refers to the event to which the procedure will respond.

You can quickly switch back to the Form Designer by clicking the Form button. If prompted, press Enter or click OK to save your changes. To return to the programming environment window, press F12, then Enter, and then press Esc.

Now, type the Basic code shown in Listing 31.4. You can maximize the editing window by double-clicking its title bar. To restore the window to its original size, double-click the title bar once more.

The SUB and END SUB statements are shown in the listing just for completeness; you shouldn't type them again, because Visual Basic supplies those statements automatically.

Editing in Visual Basic is a lot like editing in QBasic (see Chapter 30). If you need help with editing procedures, open the Help menu, select Index, then double-click the letter E in the index that appears. Now double-click the topic Guidelines for Entering and Editing Code.

The code in Listing 31.4 is commented in detail, so you probably won't have much trouble figuring out what's going on (comments are introduced by an apostrophe). If you need more information about a keyword, highlight it on the screen and press F1.

You can press Esc to exit help.

Listing 31.4. The Basic code for converting Centigrade to Fahrenheit and vice versa.

```
SUB Command1_Click ()

    TRUE = 0    ' Option.Value = 0 if option is selected.

    ' *** What kind of conversion is user doing?
    FromC = Option1.Value    ' Option1 is From Centigrade
    FromF = Option2.Value    ' Option2 is From Fahrenheit
    ToC = Option3.Value      ' Option3 is To Centigrade
    ToF = Option4.Value      ' Option4 is To Fahrenheit

    ' *** Convert input text to a number
    InputValue = VAL(Text1.Text)

    ' *** Output and input conversions are the same.
    IF FromC = ToC OR FromF = ToF THEN
        OutputValue = InputValue
    END IF

    ' *** Converting from Centigrade to Fahrenheit
    IF FromC = TRUE AND ToF = TRUE THEN
        OutputValue = (InputValue * 9 / 5) + 32
    END IF

    ' *** Converting from Fahrenheit to Centigrade
    IF FromF = TRUE AND ToC = TRUE THEN
        OutputValue = (InputValue - 32) * 5 / 9
    END IF

    ' *** Convert InputValue & OutputValue to text & display
    Text1.Text = FORMAT$(InputValue, "#,###,###.00")
    Text2.Text = FORMAT$(OutputValue, "#,###,###.00")
END SUB
```

After typing the code, save the project by opening the File menu and selecting Save Project.

Writing the Exit Procedure

When you're ready to create the event procedure for the second command button (labeled *** I've Had Enough ***), press F12 to open the Event Procedures dialog box, select the object named

Command2 from the Objects list box, and choose the Edit in Active button. Now add the code shown in Listing 31.5.

This button's main job is to exit the application, and you could simply have typed the keyword END between the SUB and END SUB statements. However, this spices up the exit routine with commands that play a series of musical notes through the computer's speaker, and display a message box with an OK button on the screen. When you run the application and click the *** I've Had Enough *** button, you'll see a dialog box like the one shown in Figure 31.16.

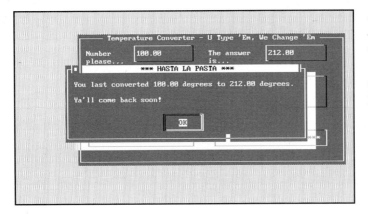

*Figure 31.16. A closing dialog box like this one will appear when you click the*** I've Had Enough *** *button when testing or running the sample application.*

Listing 31.5. The Basic code for exiting the application.

```
SUB Command2_Click ()
  scale$ = "CEG"           ' *** Arpeggio with notes C
                           ' *** E G
  PLAY "L16"               ' *** Play 16th notes
  FOR i% = 0 TO 3          ' *** Play 3 octaves of
                           ' *** arpeggios up
    PLAY "O" + STR$(i%)     ' *** Set the octave
    PLAY "X" + VARPTR$(scale$) ' *** Play the notes
  NEXT i%

  FOR i% = 3 TO 0 STEP -1   ' *** Play 3 octaves of
                           ' *** arpeggios down
```

```
    PLAY "O" + STR$(i%)          ' *** Set the octave
    PLAY "X" + VARPTR$(scale$)   ' *** Play the notes
  NEXT i%

  '*** Set up a closing message in Msg$
  BlankLine$ = CHR$(13) + CHR$(10) + CHR$(13) + CHR$(10)
  '*** Two CR/LFs
  Msg$ = "You last converted " + Text1.Text + " degrees to "
  Msg$ = Msg$ + Text2.Text + " degrees. "
  Msg$ = Msg$ + BlankLine$ + "Ya'll come back soon!"
  '*** Display message box with message, OK button, & title
  MSGBOX Msg$, 0, "*** HASTA LA PASTA ***"
  END
END SUB
```

After you type the Basic code, save the project once again. Now you're ready to begin testing.

Testing the Temperature Converter Application

To test your application, open the Run menu and select Start, or press Shift+F5. Now, test your application. You can try entering some of the input values and options listed in Table 31.3. Whenever you're ready to perform the calculation, click the `Calculate!` button to display the answer. When you're ready to return to the programming environment, click the `*** I've Had Enough ***` button, listen to the music and look at the closing message box, press Enter to clear the message, and then press any key.

> You can also return to the programming environment by pressing Ctrl+F4, then pressing any key.

Table 31.3. Sample values for testing the temperature conversion.

Input Number	Convert from...	Convert to...	Expected Answer
100	Centigrade	Fahrenheit	212.00
212	Fahrenheit	Centigrade	100.00
47	Centigrade	Centigrade	47.00
47	Fahrenheit	Fahrenheit	47.00
98.6	Fahrenheit	Centigrade	37.00
0	Centigrade	Fahrenheit	32.00

If you need to make any corrections to your code, return to the programming environment. If the window doesn't contain the code that you need to change, click the Code button in the Project window, and then double-click the event procedure that you want to change. Be sure to save your work when finished and test your application again.

Creating an Executable Temperature Converter

After testing your application thoroughly, you can create an executable file (.EXE) so that the application can be run from the command prompt or a batch program. Here are the steps:

1. From the Run menu in the programming environment, choose Make EXE File. The Make EXE File dialog box shown in Figure 31.17 will appear.

2. If you wish, change the suggested name in the EXE File Name text box.

3. Select Stand-Alone EXE File in the EXE Type area of the dialog box.

4. Click the Make EXE and Exit button.

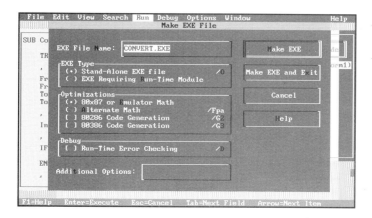

Figure 31.17.
The Make EXE
File dialog box.

Visual Basic will compile and link the executable file in the current directory, and then exit to the command prompt. To run the executable file, type CONVERT (or whatever name you chose in Step 2) and press Enter.

Troubleshooting Norton Batch Enhancer

Troubleshooting an enhanced batch program or Batch Enhancer script file is basically the same as troubleshooting any normal batch program, so all the tips given in Chapter 29 apply here as well. As with normal batch programs, logic errors such as using the wrong command, not taking safety issues into consideration, or executing commands in the wrong order are the most common sources of trouble.

Consider the following additional tips when trying to figure out what's wrong with an enhanced batch program:

- If the commands are whizzing by too quickly for you to read them, try adding some BE DELAY or BE ASK commands to strategic areas of the program, and then run the program again. BE DELAY pauses execution long enough for you to see what's happening, whereas BE ASK pauses the program and enables you to interact with it.

- When using the BE TRIGGER time command to pause batch program execution until a certain time, be sure to specify AM or PM or express the time using a 24-hour clock. For example, suppose that it's currently 5:01 p.m. and you start a batch program that contains the command BE TRIGGER 5:04. If you were hoping to start the program three minutes from now, you'd be sorely disappointed—your batch program won't actually start executing the next command until 5:04 *tomorrow morning!* (Just press Ctrl+Break to cancel the TRIGGER command and resume the program.) To start the next command at 5:04 in the evening, you'd need to specify BE TRIGGER 5:04pm or BE TRIGGER 17:04 instead.

- If a BE WINDOW command obscures text that you've displayed on the screen, try using a BE BOX command instead. Remember that windows are always opaque, whereas boxes are always transparent. Alternatively, you can move the BE WINDOW command *above* any BE ROWCOL, BE PRINTCHAR, or ECHO commands that display text that should be visible through the window.

Troubleshooting Visual Basic

Visual Basic is a rich language that offers many features, as well as many opportunities for making programming errors. Because most of the general troubleshooting concepts discussed in Chapter 30 apply to Visual Basic as well, I won't repeat them here. Don't forget that the old standbys—printing out your code, using PRINT statements and message boxes (MSGBOX) to display values at strategic places in your program, and careful deskchecking of your program's logic—can help you find many errors quickly.

You can use Visual Basic's online help to learn the correct syntax for any command. Type the command that you need help with or move the cursor to an existing command and press the F1 key, or press Shift+F1 and search for the command you're interested in. The online help also offers correctly typed sample code that you can paste into your programs and modify as needed.

Like QBasic, Visual Basic has its own debugging system, which is fully documented in the online help and the *Microsoft Visual Basic Programmer's Guide*. Debug menu options and function keys enable you to step through your program statement by statement, trace execution history, monitor the value of specific variables, and set breakpoints at specific places in your program. If you'd like a hands-on introduction to debugging techniques and tools, try the debugging tutorial. To start the tutorial, open Visual Basic's Help menu and select Tutorial. Make sure your Num Lock key is turned OFF, and then type 6 to select Debugging Your Application.

Summary

This chapter presents two software packages—The Norton Utilities Version 6.0 by Symantec, and Visual Basic for MS-DOS by Microsoft—that will enhance your batch programs and Basic applications. This only scratches the surface of features offered by these programming tools, but you should know enough now to decide whether they're worth adding to your computer's bag of tricks.

- The Batch Enhancer (BE) is part of the Norton Utilities Version 6.0. You can use BE commands to display fancy screens and menus in your batch programs, restart the computer, get user input, and control the order in which program statements are executed.

- You can usually enter BE commands at the command prompt, within a batch program file, or within a special Batch Enhancer script file. BE commands execute fastest from within script files.

■ The general form of a BE command is BE, followed by a space, and then the rest of the command. When used in script files, you can omit the BE prefix.

■ Visual Basic for MS-DOS, by Microsoft, offers a programming environment for creating graphical applications that respond to events. To start Visual Basic, switch to the directory where you want to create or change your application, and then type VBDOS and press Enter at the command prompt.

■ To create a Visual Basic application, follow these general steps:

1. Create a new project or open an existing project.

2. Create (or edit) a form. Add command buttons, text boxes, option buttons, or other *controls* (objects) to the form.

3. Set properties for the objects.

4. Switch to the programming environment and write event procedures for the application.

5. Save and test the application.

6. Create an executable file that enables you to run the application from the command prompt.

Low-Cost and
Free Software

Alan Simpson's
DOS
SECRETS
UNLEASHED

C H A P T E R   3 2

Using Shareware to Enhance DOS

Shareware is a unique method for marketing and distributing software that has a rich history. This chapter describes shareware and the programs that are on the add-in disks that accompany this book. This chapter also describes how to begin using the shareware programs.

What Is Shareware?

Shareware is a good deal for both software users and developers. Users can try shareware products for a period of time to make sure they like it before they pay for it. Authors benefit because shareware is a low-cost method of marketing software. That enables individual developers and small companies to succeed in the software business without investing a lot of money. The low-cost marketing method also keeps prices for shareware products much lower than prices for similar software sold through the normal commercial methods.

Low price, however, does not mean low quality. Many shareware products are as full-featured as their commercial competitors, but often are sold at a fraction of the price. In addition, the best-selling products in some product categories are shareware. This is particularly true for certain types of utilities, such as those that compress programs so they take up less space on your disk.

The concept of shareware started to flourish in the 1970s, even before DOS was invented. Shareware grew rapidly in the early 1980s as use of DOS-based PCs began to mushroom. In fact, it could be argued that the availability of low-cost, high-quality shareware helped fuel the PC boom.

Certainly, the PC boom spurred a lot of creative minds to create excellent software and to market it as shareware. From the beginning, shareware products have contributed more than their share of innovations to the software industry.

Although shareware accounts for far fewer sales than commercial software, it still is widely accepted and used. Virtually all large organizations use shareware products. Some shareware vendors have graduated to distributing their products through more mainstream means, making their products available through computer stores and mail order operations.

The software in the add-in disks that accompany this book are shareware products. I've included a variety of shareware products ranging from basic applications, to utilities, and even to games and entertainment software. Some of the products accompanying this book, such as PC-File, are updated versions of pioneering shareware products. Others were developed more recently by authors keeping the shareware tradition alive.

There are literally thousands of shareware programs that are easily available to you. Chapter 33 provides more information about obtaining additional shareware products. This chapter provides brief descriptions of the shareware products included with this book. Also read Chapter 33 for more details about how to register shareware products.

Registering Shareware

Shareware remains a grass roots tradition. Because shareware vendors often distribute their software through user groups and electronic bulletin boards, and because they usually are individuals or small companies, they tend to be much closer to their users than are commercial software companies. Don't be surprised if, after you register and pay for your shareware product, you call for technical support and the owner of the company answers the telephone.

Because the programs accompanying this book are shareware, you may use them for a trial period. However, if you continue to use the products past that time, you need to register with the developer and pay for the software. Remember, even though you can use shareware products for a period of time without paying, they are not free. Using shareware products for more than a trial period without paying for them is a form of theft, and can serve to damage this fine tradition.

In addition to it being the honest thing to do, there are other reasons to register your shareware if you are going to use it regularly:

- In most cases, registration entitles you to more complete documentation than comes with the shareware disks.

- In many cases, you will receive a more powerful version of the program, with special features that the evaluation version did not have.

- Many shareware authors will provide technical support to registered users.

- You will be notified about updates and other important news about your shareware program.

Preparing to Use the Shareware Programs

The programs on the enclosed floppy disks are stored in a compressed form—you must run the installation program before you can use them. Installing the programs means that they will be decompressed and copied to your hard drive. To install the programs on the disks, follow these steps:

1. Insert one of the disks into your floppy disk drive.

2. Change your default directory to this floppy drive. For example, if the disk is in drive A:, type A: and press Enter.

3. Type INSTALL and press Enter.

4. The installation program gives you the choice of installing all the programs on this disk, or just one program of your choosing.

5. Once you make your choice, the installation program asks you to what drive you want to copy the program. You need to type the drive letter of your hard drive (for example, C:), and press Enter.

The program you choose (or the entire disk) is then installed to your hard drive. It is copied to a directory named \UNLEASH.

The installation program will tell you how much space each particular program (or the entire disk) will take up on your hard drive. Be sure you have enough free space on your hard drive before attempting to install the disks.

Location of Programs

Each individual program is stored in its own subdirectory, as you can see from the following list.

Program	Directory on your hard drive	Disk #
As-Easy-As	\UNLEASH\ASEASYAS	1
Blank-It	\UNLEASH\BLANKIT	3
Chinese Checkers	\UNLEASH\CHECKERS	1
Design Shell	\UNLEASH\DESIGN	2

continues

Program	Directory on your hard drive	Disk #
Jill of the Jungle	\UNLEASH\JILL	1
List	\UNLEASH\LIST	3
NeoPaint	\UNLEASH\NEOPAINT	3
Odyssey	\UNLEASH\ODYSSEY	3
PCFile	\UNLEASH\PCFILE	2
PKZip	\UNLEASH\PKZIP	3
SkyGlobe	\UNLEASH\SKYGLOBE	1
Target	\UNLEASH\TARGET	1
Sample batch programs	\UNLEASH\CHAP29	2
QBasic programs	\UNLEASH\CHAP30	2
Visual Basic and Batch Builder programs	\UNLEASH\CHAP31	2

You must go through the installation procedure for each of the three disks to install all the software. If you only want to install one application, check Table 32.1 to see what disk it's on and run the INSTALL program for that disk.

You can then start using these excellent programs. In the next section, you learn about each program in detail.

Once you determine that you like using a particular utility program, such as Target or PKZIP, move these files to a directory that's in your DOS path. This enables you to use these utilities from any drive and directory.

Programs Included with this Book

I worked hard to include some of the best shareware programs available. Enjoy trying them out and remember, if you like them and want to continue using them, you need to register and pay for them.

For each program, I've listed the name of the executable file and the main manual. To read the manual, you can open it within the EDIT program that comes with DOS. Type EDIT filename, where filename is the name of the manual.

As-Easy-As

Program: ASEASY.EXE

Manual: ASEASY.MAN

Author:
TRIUS, Inc.
P.O. BOX 249
N. Andover, MA 01845
(508) 794-9377
(800) GO-TRIUS (orders only)

This award-winning spreadsheet is a good example of how shareware products can actually surpass many commercial products. As-Easy-As uses spreadsheets that are compatible with Versions 2.01 and 1A of Lotus 1-2-3. It includes nearly every Lotus function, such as range names and macros.

Before you can begin using As-Easy-As, you need to run its installation program.

To run the installation program, follow these steps:

1. Type CD \UNLEASH\ASEASYAS and press Enter.

2. Type INSTALL and press Enter.

3. When the installation program starts, you are given a choice of where to install As-Easy-As. You can accept the default (C:\ASEASY), or you can type in another directory. Once you agree with the location, press F10 to begin the installation.

4. When the installation program pauses, you are asked to press Esc to continue. You are then asked to enter your name (or your company name).

5. Next, you're asked to enter a number from inside the manual cover. Because this is a shareware copy, follow the on-screen instructions and enter 99-999.

6. A message will ask you to insert disk #2—simply press any key and the installation will continue.

7. The installation program will then ask you if you want to continue with extracting the sample worksheet files and the manual. Type Y to continue.

8. After all the files have been installed, you'll find yourself in the As-Easy-As directory, ready to start!

In addition to working like Lotus 1-2-3, As-Easy-As offers a wealth of advanced features, including the following:

- A complete macro language
- Math, statistical, logical, financial, string, date, time and user functions
- Matrix operations and frequency distribution tables (bins)
- File linking
- Up to six resizeable and moveable spreadsheet views
- Database operations, data input forms, and read/write database files

- Goalseeking lets the computer solve for the input value

- Spreadsheet auditing capabilities

- Multiple planes (3-D simulation)

To get a quick start with As-Easy-As, read the READ.ME file. It contains information on starting the program, command-line options, and more. Once you start As-Easy-As, you select menu commands by pressing the / key. This displays the menu; you select the choices with the keyboard or with a mouse.

Try loading some of the sample files that are included—they will show off some of the program's windowing and graphics capabilities (Figure 32.1). To load a file, press /, select File Retrieve, highlight a file, and press Enter.

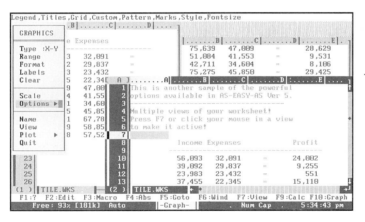

Figure 32.1.
As-Easy-As
allows multiple
files to be open
at one time.

If you need to enter a lot of text into a spreadsheet cell, try using the built-in word processor. Press / and select Sheet Text Word to start this feature.

Blank-It

Program: BLANK-IT.ZIP

Manual: BLANK-IT.DOC

Author:
Rhode Island Soft Systems, Inc.
PO Box 748
Woonsocket, RI 02895
(401) 658-4632

BLANK-IT is a flexible screen-blanking utility. You can set it to automatically blank your screen after a pre-set period of time. This avoids screen burn-in and increases the life of your monitor. For a quick overview of BLANK-IT, you can read the text file called DESCRIBE.DOC.

To load Blank-It, type BLANK-IT at the command prompt. You will see a screen that tells you that BLANK-IT is loaded in memory. If you don't add any parameters to BLANK-IT, it will automatically blank your screen after your keyboard has been inactive for 10 minutes.

It's easy, however, to specify a different period of time that should elapse before BLANK-IT blanks your screen. To do so, type a space after the command to load BLANK-IT, and then add a number to represent the number of minutes that should pass before BLANK-IT goes to work. For example, if you type BLANK-IT 4, BLANK-IT blanks your screen after four minutes.

Include BLANK-IT and all appropriate parameters in your AUTOEXEC.BAT. This will ensure that BLANK-IT will automatically load and provide protection for your monitor.

Chinese Checkers

Program: CHINESE.EXE

Manual: CHINESE.TXT

Author:
ImagiSOFT, Inc.
Computer Games Division
P.O. Box 13208
Albuquerque, NM 87192
(505) 275-1920
1-800-767-1978 (Orders only)

This version of the classic Chinese Checkers game has some of the nicest graphics you'll see in a VGA board game (see Figure 32.2). Each player is represented by an animal, and the player can be a human or the computer; you can set up the game for 2 to 6 players. A mouse is required.

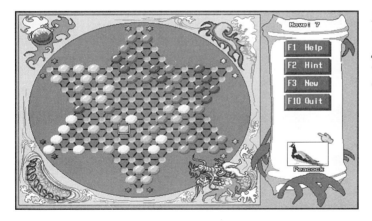

Figure 32.2. The middle of a game of Chinese Checkers.

Playing the game is simple. Once you set up the players, each player tries to move their marbles from their side of the board to the opposite side. When it's your turn, you choose which marble to use by clicking it with the mouse. You choose your path of movement by clicking each square in turn. When you click the final square a second time, your marble hops and moves to your chosen location.

If you're stuck during a game and you don't know how to move, click the Hint button (or you can press the F2 key). You'll receive a hint on how you might move.

Design Shell

Program: DESIGN.EXE

Manual: README.1ST

Author:
jwh: SoftWare
6947 Haggerty Road
Hillsboro, Ohio   45133
(513) 393-2402

Design Shell is a complete graphical menu system. It provides the user with colorful picture icons for selecting sub menus or executing applications or DOS commands.

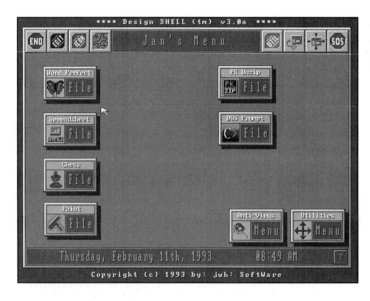

*Figure 32.3.
A sample
Design Shell
menu.*

You can create up to 30 menus or applications on the opening page; sub menus may be nested three levels deep. Design Shell gives you the option of up to eight different color combinations and up to six different 3D or flat-faced fonts.

A number of icons are included with the program, but you can edit and create your own with the built-in Icon editor (there are also hundreds of additional icons available—see the manual for for details).

You can fully password protect all options in Design Shell— even exiting the program. This makes Design Shell a good program to use if other people who are inexperienced with DOS use your computer. You can even use it as a menu for your children to use.

Jill of the Jungle

Program: JILL.BAT

Manual: JILL.DOC

Author:
Epic MegaGames
10406 Holbrook Drive
Potomac, MD 20854
1-800-972-7434 (orders only)

Jill of the Jungle is one of the hottest shareware games of the past year. This 256-color VGA arcade adventure game (see Figure 32.4) is on a level with the top Sega Genesis and Super Nintendo hits. Jill features digital sound effects and a musical soundtrack for the Sound Blaster and compatible cards.

*Figure 32.4.
Guide Jill
through 16
game levels.*

You guide Jill through 16 smooth-scrolling levels, each filled with vivid scenery and animated creatures. Jill can run, jump, and use objects; she can also magically transform into other creatures such as birds, fish, and frogs.

> If you're having a hard time guiding Jill to victory, you can press T to enter Turtle mode. This slows the game to half speed.

Be sure to read the online instructions when you start the program. You'll find out how to play the game, and you'll get some hints on how to play smarter.

List

Program: LIST.EXE

Manual: LIST.DOC

Author:
Buerg Software
139 White Oak Circle
Petaluma CA 94952
(707) 778-1811

The List utility has become somewhat of a classic in shareware. It started its life as a simple program to view text files, and it has evolved into a powerful text file viewer and file management utility.

If you type LIST and press Enter, you'll see a listing of files in your current directory (Figure 32.5). If you move the highlight to one of the files and press Enter, you can view the contents of the file. However, this just scratches the surface of what List can do.

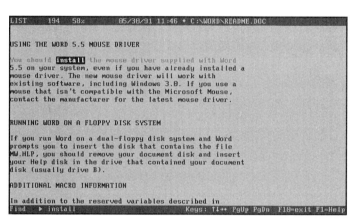

Figure 32.5.
A document
file with a
word searched
for and found.

For example, typing LIST \UTILS*.DOC enables you to browse through all *.DOC files in your \UTILS directory. You'll see the first file on your screen, and you can switch to view the next file by pressing Ctrl+PgDn.

LIST enables you to customize the program in an incredible variety of ways—colors, display style, and much more. Once you configure the program to your taste, press Alt+C to save your changes.

NeoPaint

Program: NEOPAINT.EXE

Manual: README.DOC

Author:
OSCS Software Development, Inc.
354 NE Greenwood Avenue, Suite 108
Bend, OR 97701-4631
(503) 389-5489

NeoPaint is a paint and image editing program that offers features usually found only in very expensive commercial programs. It supports graphics modes from EGA up to 1024x768 SVGA, and enables you to edit and view multiple images at one time (see Figure 32.6)

You can begin creating a masterpiece yourself, or you can edit existing PCX, GIF or TIFF graphics files. In addition to standard paint features, NeoPaint has a number of special effects that you can apply to your image: smudge, blur, pixelize, fade, streak, and more.

NEOGRAB.EXE is a screen capture program that comes with NeoPaint. You can use this program to grab images from existing programs, save them, and edit them within NeoPaint. See the manual for more details.

When you first start the program, it will be running in the lowest resolution graphics mode that your system can support. One of the first things you should do is select the highest resolution you can display. Select the Video Mode box in the top middle of the screen, and set it to the highest setting.

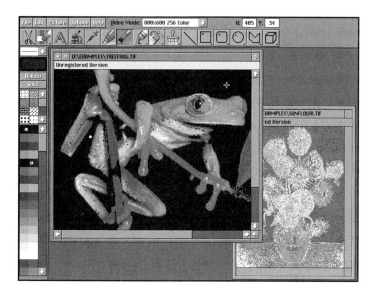

*Figure 32.6.
NeoPaint
enables you to
open multiple
graphics files.*

Odyssey

Program: ODY.EXE

Manual: ODY150SH.DOC

Author:
TRIUS, Inc.
P.O. BOX 249
N. Andover, MA 01845
(508) 794-9377
1-800-GO-TRIUS (orders only)

Odyssey is a powerful modem communications program that's also easy to use. If you're a newcomer to communications, you'll find Odyssey easy to set up and use. Figure 32.7 shows Odyssey being used to connect to the CompuServe Information Service.

If you're an advanced user, you'll appreciate some of Odyssey's more sophisticated features. For example, file transfers can be completed in the background while you work within other DOS programs.

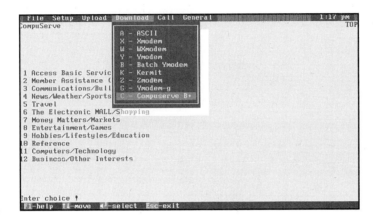

*Figure 32.7.
Odyssey
being used to
connect to
CompuServe.*

Odyssey also comes with the most popular transfer protocols, such as Zmodem and CompuServe B+. A protocol is a method a computer uses to transfer a file to another computer without errors. Both computers must use the same method.

When you are transferring files to or from your computer, use the Zmodem protocol if possible. This protocol is faster than most others, and if your connection with the other computer should fail during the file transfer, you won't have to send the whole file again. Zmodem looks at what's been transferred so far, and continues from where it stopped.

Before you can begin using Odyssey, you need to run its installation program.

To run the Odyssey installation program, follow these steps:

1. Type CD \UNLEASH\ODYSSEY and press Enter.

2. Type INSTALL and press Enter.

3. When the installation program starts, you are given a choice of where to install Odyssey. If you want to accept the default (C:\ODYSSEY), press Enter. If you want to install to another directory, type the full directory name and press Enter.

4. After the files are installed, the installation program continues, setting up Odyssey for your particular modem. It first asks you to make sure your modem is turned on. Once the modem is on, press any key. The program will attempt to detect to which COM port you have your modem attached.

> If your modem is not turned on at this point, the installation will proceed, but your modem will not be properly set up. You'll need to choose your modem settings manually the first time you run Odyssey.

5. The program will tell you that it has detected a modem on either COM port 1 or COM port 2. If this information is correct, press Enter. If it is not correct, type 1 or 2 to identify to which COM port your modem is connected.

6. You will then be asked to identify your brand of modem. Use the arrow keys to highlight the correct choice and press Enter. If you don't find your modem on this list, choose Hayes Generic.

7. Next, you'll need to choose Tone or Pulse dialing. Press T or P to identify your choice.

8. Finally, you need to choose whether or not Odyssey will use color. Press Y or N to indicate yes or no.

Now that the installation of Odyssey is complete, you can begin to explore the world of telecommunications.

PC-File

Program: PCF.EXE

Manual: PCF65.MAN

Author:
ButtonWare
PO Box 96058
Bellevue, WA 98009-4469
(206) 454-0479

PC-File is a pioneering shareware program that has gotten more and more powerful as the years progressed. In fact, the mark of this program's popularity is the fact that it also is available from retail distributors. This is a full-featured database manager that has all the features you need for virtually any home or business.

To get started with PC-File, read the file READ.ME with any text editor or file viewer. This gives you a quick overview of the product. If you want to read the documentation first, that information is in the PCF65.MAN file.

Once you start PC-File, you're ready to create your first database. You can create databases using either PC-File's Fast option, or you can select Draw, which takes more time but gives you more flexibility designing the layout of the database fields on your screen. Figure 32.8 shows a record in a sample database provided with PC-File.

If you want to get going quickly, select the Fast option. This option provides a fill-in-the-blanks approach to database creation. When you are done, save your new database and you will be ready to start filling in information. Figure 32.9 shows the Fast database creation screen.

Once you are up and running in PC-File, you will find that it is both full-featured and easy to use. One feature of particular interest is PC-File's ability to search for duplicate files. This feature is

exceptionally simple to use and solves the recurring problem of
duplicate records in databases.

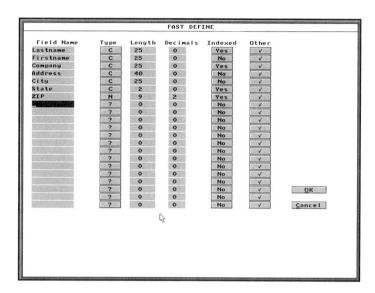

*Figure 32.8.
A record in a
newly created
database.*

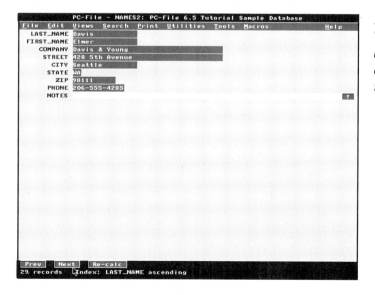

*Figure 32.9.
The Fast
database
creation screen
in PC-File.*

PKZIP/PKUNZIP

Programs: PKZIP.EXE, PKUNZIP.EXE

Manual: MANUAL.DOC

Author:
PKWARE, Inc.
9025 N. Deerwood Dr.
Brown Deer, WI 53223-2437
(414) 354-8699

PKZIP has practically become the standard for compressing and decompressing files. Using PKZIP/PKUNZIP, you save disk space and toll charges when you transfer files onto floppies or use a modem. To get started, read the file named README.DOC.

PKZIP.EXE is the program file that compresses files; PKUNZIP.EXE is the program file that decompresses files. Both work from the command line. The syntax for using both programs is similar. Figure 32.10 shows the command line syntax for decompressing a file, and the result.

```
C:\UTILS>pkunzip mywork.zip

PKUNZIP (R)    FAST!    Extract Utility    Version 2.04c  12-28-92
Copr. 1989-1992 PKWARE Inc. All Rights Reserved. Shareware version
PKUNZIP Reg. U.S. Pat. and Tm. Off.

 ■ 80486 CPU detected.
 ■ EMS version 4.00 detected.
 ■ XMS version 3.00 detected.

Searching ZIP: MYWORK.ZIP
   Inflating: FAX_BOOK.DOC
   Inflating: JANELET.DOC
   Inflating: PAGEKEEP.DOC
   Inflating: PAPRLES1.DOC
   Inflating: PAPRLESS.DOC
   Inflating: PCC_PROP.DOC
   Inflating: PKEPPROP.DOC
   Inflating: SLEEPTIM.DOC

C:\UTILS>
```

Figure 32.10
PKUNZIP tells you which files have been decompressed.

The syntax for compressing files is similar. If you want to compress all files in a directory with the .DOC file extension, and assuming you are in that same directory, you would type the following:

```
PKZIP filename *.DOC
```

The new version of PKZIP included with this book has many advanced features. One feature of particular interest is the program's ability to compress files across more than one disk. This is useful if the compressed file is larger than a single floppy disk can handle. Read the documentation to learn how to use this advanced feature.

SkyGlobe

Program: SKYGLOBE.EXE

Manual: SKYGLOBE.DOC

Author:
KlassM SoftWare
284 142nd AVE
Caledonia MI 49316
75020,1431
1-800-968-4994 (orders only)

SkyGlobe is an award-winning desktop planetarium that provides a realistic and beautiful display of the splendor of the heavens (Figure 32.11). You can instantly change your computer view of the cosmos to suit your own tastes, or you can use one of the many animation modes to simulate celestial motion.

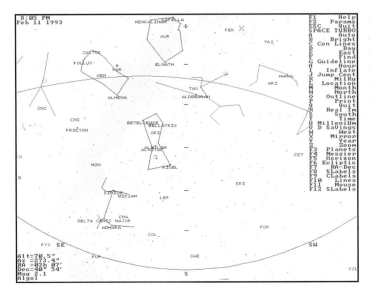

*Figure 32.11.
A view of the
night sky with
constellation
names, star
names, and
other details
displayed.*

SkyGlobe can display 25,000 stars, constellation lines, the planets, the Sun, the Moon, the Milky Way, the Messier objects, and much more. One of the program's strongest features is how you can customize the display of the heavens, making it as simple or complex as you wish. You can change these settings quickly with hot-key commands, or through the use of the mouse.

When you start SkyGlobe, it displays the stars that residents of Caledonia, Michigan (the home of the author) would see. To change the sky to your location, press L for Location. You are presented with a list of major cities to choose from—choose the city nearest your home.

If you're not familiar with stars and constellations, read through the manual to familiarize yourself with SkyGlobe. You'll also learn a little bit about astronomy in the process.

Target

Program: TARGET.EXE

Manual: TARGET.DOC

Author:

McAfee Associates
3350 Scott Boulevard, Building 14
Santa Clara, California
95054-3107
(408) 988-3832}

Target is a powerful utility for finding and manipulating files. It finds selected files across all drives, including logged network drives. It also can initiate actions on those files. It can conduct searches based on date ranges, file sizes, archive condition, file types or duplicate files, and other search expressions. It can even search within compressed archive files, such as those created with PKZip.

Target is an extremely powerful and flexible program that enables you to find files, and also to manage them in a variety of ways. It is run from the command prompt with the following basic syntax:

```
TARGET [filespec] [parameters] [switches]
```

The most common usage of Target is to find files on your hard drive. The search shown in Figure 32.12 is looking for all files with the .BAK file extension name.

```
C:\>target *.bak

Target v1.5  Copyright 1992 by McAfee Associates.  (408) 988-3832
All ARC files will be bypassed.

 autoexec.bak      585   2-08-93    7:51   c:\
 config  .bak      597   2-10-93   13:34   c:\
 image   .bak   140800   2-11-93    8:21   c:\
 schedule.bak      382   2-06-93   15:41   c:\ndw\
 system  .bak     2609   2-10-93   13:49   c:\windows\
 win     .bak    21486   2-10-93   16:17   c:\windows\

6 matches found, occupying 166459 bytes.


Target v1.5  Copyright 1992 by McAfee Associates.  (408) 988-3832

   This program may not be used in a business, corporation, organization,
   government or agency environment without a negotiated site license.

C:\>
```

Figure 32.12. The results of a search using Target.

Notice that Target shows the location of each file that was found and the total amount of disk space taken by all the files that were found.

> Target also can be used for finding files and then managing them. For example, you can use Target to find and then delete files wherever they are on your hard drive. This is useful, for example, for tasks in which the files you want to manage are spread out throughout your hard drive. Read Target's documentation for directions on how to use Target to manage files in multiple directories.

Basic and Batch Program Listings from the Book

Also included on the add-in disks are all the batch program examples from Chapter 29, "Batch Programs Unleashed," and the LOANCALC.BAS loan payment calculator program developed in Chapter 30, "A QBasic Primer." The Visual Basic for DOS source code for the Metric conversion application from Chapter 31, "Simple Programming Tools," is on the disk as well.

 Troubleshooting

When you install the programs from the three companion disks, you probably won't experience any problems. The installation program makes the process an easy one.

It is possible, however, that you might run up against some common difficulties. If you have run the INSTALL program on one of the disks and it doesn't seem to work, here are some possible solutions:

- Make sure you change drives to the drive containing the floppy disk. The install program won't work properly unless you do this.

- When the program asks you to enter the `Installation_Drive?`, be sure you type in the correct drive letter. For example, if you type `C`, the program won't work (`C:` would be correct).

- Be sure to check how much hard drive space each program requires. You'll see this when you run INSTALL for each disk. If you don't have enough space on your hard drive, the program will not install properly.

- After you install an application, be sure to read the section in this chapter about that application. It will tell you how to start the program and which file to read for more information.

- Some of the programs have their own installation routine that must be run before you can use the program. See the section about that program for more information and instructions.

Summary

In this chapter, you learned the following:

- Shareware is an innovative way of marketing and distributing software that has a rich history in the software industry. With shareware, you try programs before you buy them.

- The add-in disks accompanying this book include many different types of shareware programs, ranging from basic applications to games and educational software.

Alan Simpson's
DOS
SECRETS
UNLEASHED

C H A P T E R   3 3

How to Obtain Shareware

There are literally thousands of shareware software titles available to you. The add-in disks included with this book contain a few of those titles. This chapter tells you how to obtain even more shareware, and how to register shareware when you decide you want to keep it and use it on a regular basis.

Collecting Shareware

Obtaining shareware is easy. One way to obtain shareware is to order it over the phone directly from vendors. In addition, a number of companies specialize in selling shareware disks at a low price. If you have a modem, obtaining shareware is particularly easy. Online bulletin boards and information services usually have hundreds, if not thousands, of shareware titles available for you to download. This section describes the various methods of collecting shareware.

Obtaining Online Shareware

The most common method of distributing shareware is via online bulletin boards. Electronic bulletin boards are computers to which you can connect via your modem. To do this, all you need is a modem attached to your computer and communications software. Bulletin boards are designed so that you can download shareware or participate in online conversations about a variety of topics.

There are two broad classes of online bulletin boards from which you can download shareware—locally run bulletin boards and large national information services.

There is much more to do on electronic bulletin boards than just download shareware. Most bulletin boards have sections in which you can exchange messages about various topics with people who have similar interests, whether those interests are computers, sports, politics, or virtually any other subject.

Bulletin boards sometimes are confusing for new users. So whether you are logging on to a local bulletin board or the huge national and international information services, take some time to learn your way around, and how to get from one section to another.

Local Bulletin Boards

These days, bulletin boards abound even in smaller towns and cities. Some are run by local computer user groups, whereas others are run by computer bulletin board enthusiasts. Many bulletin boards have shareware programs and discussion areas about a wide variety of topics. However, some bulletin boards specialize in certain topics, such as games, computer programming, or even professional or social issues. If you have a special area of interest, somewhere in the world there is probably a bulletin board specializing in your interest area.

If you do not know the telephone number of your local bulletin boards, contact a local computer user group, ask in a local computer store, or (if you know one) ask a computer enthusiast. When you call a bulletin board for the first time, you usally must register to use the board by answering a short series of questions. In most cases, registration is free, although there are a number of subscription-only local bulletin boards.

The subscription-only boards often have more shareware titles to download than other local bulletin boards.

It might take a couple of days for the bulletin board system operator (or SYSOP, as they are called) to process your registration. Often, during that time you cannot download software, although you can log on and get acquainted with the various aspects of the bulletin board. Figure 33.1 shows a typical main menu from an online bulletin board service.

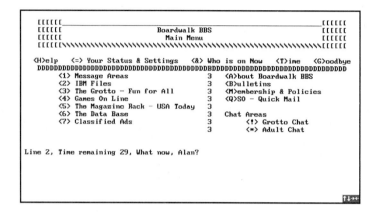

```
[[[[[[                                                            [[[[[[
[[[[[[                    Boardwalk BBS                          [[[[[[
[[[[[[                    Main Menu                              [[[[[[
[[[[[[\\\\\\\\\\\\\\\\\\\\\\\\\\\\\\\\\\\\\\\\\\\\\\\\\\\\\\\\\\\[[[[[[

<H>elp   <=> Your Status & Settings   <&> Who is on Now   <T>ime   <G>oodbye
DDDDDDDDDDDDDDDDDDDDDDDDDDDDDDDDDDDDDDDDBDDDDDDDDDDDDDDDDDDDDDDDDDDDDDDDDDDDDD
       <1> Message Areas                3    <A>bout Boardwalk BBS
       <2> IBM Files                    3    <B>ulletins
       <3> The Grotto - Fun for All     3    <M>embership & Policies
       <4> Games On Line                3    <Q>SO - Quick Mail
       <5> The Magazine Rack - USA Today 3
       <6> The Data Base                3    Chat Areas
       <7> Classified Ads               3        <!> Grotto Chat
                                        3        <*> Adult Chat


Line 2, Time remaining 29, What now, Alan?


                                                                    [↑↓←]
```

*Figure 33.1.
A typical main
menu from a
local bulletin
board.*

Unlike national information services, rarely are there printed instruction manuals for using local bulletin boards. Instructions would be useful, because the interface of most bulletin boards can be confusing to new users.

Online help is often available, and sometimes you can download text files with instructions.

National Information Services

National information services offer an astounding array of online opportunities. In fact, it may take quite a while after you first log on to a national bulletin board to discover all the opportunities that await you. Special forums are available in which you can discuss virtually any topic and access shareware of specific interest to that topic. Software and hardware companies have special forums that provide technical support for their products. You can chat live or play games in "real time" with other users. You can exchange electronic mail and files with other users. You can even order products from a wide variety of merchants, ranging from clothes to coffee to software. The first time you log on to a national information service, it may feel a bit like leaving a small town and standing in the hustle and bustle of midtown Manhattan for the first time.

In some ways, national information services are like huge versions of local bulletin boards. However, there are a couple of important differences. First, you must pay to use the national information services, whereas most local bulletin boards are free. The trend in recent years has been for the national information services to charge a flat monthly fee for access to basic services, usually about $5 to $10, and then charge an additional hourly fee for using more advanced features. In most cases, downloading shareware is considered a service for which you are charged extra.

Offsetting the extra charges is the fact that virtually every shareware product is available from the national information services. And usually you don't have to make a toll call to log on to the national information service. In most locations, local access or toll-free numbers are available for subscribers.

The second difference is that the national information services, because of the vast array of products and services they offer, are much more complex than local bulletin boards. Figure 33.2 shows the opening menu screen for CompuServe, one of the largest national information services. Although it looks simple, each option leads to many other options, each of which leads to more options still, and so on.

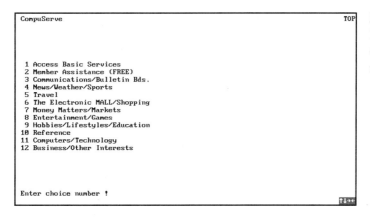

```
CompuServe                                          TOP

    1 Access Basic Services
    2 Member Assistance (FREE)
    3 Communications/Bulletin Bds.
    4 News/Weather/Sports
    5 Travel
    6 The Electronic MALL/Shopping
    7 Money Matters/Markets
    8 Entertainment/Games
    9 Hobbies/Lifestyles/Education
   10 Reference
   11 Computers/Technology
   12 Business/Other Interests



Enter choice number !
```

*Figure 33.2.
The opening
CompuServe
menu screen.*

> Because national information services are so complex, special communications programs designed for specific information services are available. These special programs combine an intimate knowledge of the intricacies of the national information service you are using with a much-simplified interface. When you join a national information service, ask about the special communications software that is available for that service.

Table 33.1 provides toll-free telephone numbers for some of the better-known national information services. You can use those numbers to ask for more information or to sign up.

Table 33.1. Toll-free telephone numbers of national information services.

Information Service	Toll-Free Number
America Online	(800) 227-6364
CompuServe	(800) 848-8990
GEnie	(800) 638-9636
Prodigy	(800) 776-3449

Shareware Vendors

As the popularity of shareware grew, special for-profit services sprang up to distribute disks of shareware products. Shareware vendors often sell disks of shareware at low prices, sometimes as low as a dollar or two per disk, depending on the programs.

Purchasing disks from shareware disk services does not free you from the obligation to register and pay for shareware. Rather, these services merely provide a convenient way to get shareware disks at a low price, and are particularly useful for those who do not have a modem for downloading shareware from online services.

There are dozens of shareware disk vendors. Most of them stock thousands of shareware titles and will send you a catalog of their listings for free or at low cost. As with shareware developers themselves, some are large companies and others are comprised of just a few individuals.

Table 33.2 provides the names and toll-free telephone numbers for a few shareware disk services. This is meant to be a sampler of vendors, not a comprehensive listing.

Table 33.2. Shareware disk vendors and their toll-free telephone numbers.

Shareware Disk Vendor	Toll-Free Number
Big Byte Software	(800) 879-2983
PC Shareware	(800) 447-2181
PC-SIG	(800) 245-6717
Pendragon Software Library	(800) 828-3475
Public Brand Software	(800) 426-3475
Public Software Library	(800) 242-4775

Obtaining Shareware from User Groups

Another good source of shareware is your local computer user group. Many communities have user groups that have regular meetings. At these meetings, computer users gather to discuss a variety of computer-related issues and exchange shareware. As with bulletin boards, there are many reasons to join a user group besides collecting shareware. At user groups, you can band together with other computer users who have similar interests in Special Interest Groups (SIGs). If you are a newcomer to computing, you will find many people who will help you understand the intricacies of DOS and your applications.

To find the user group in your area, ask computer enthusiasts or inquire at your local computer store.

How to Register Your Shareware

If you try a shareware product and decide you will use it regularly, you must register and pay for it. That is because shareware is not free. Shareware is a method of marketing software that enables you to try it before you buy it.

There are a number of different methods for registering your shareware product, and they vary among shareware vendors. Typically, though, when you receive a shareware product, it includes a separate text file with instructions and often a form for registering. The name of this file varies, but it usually has an obvious name such as REGISTER.DOC. The file will include the amount of the registration fee and an address and phone number of the vendor. To register, print the registration form and mail it to the vendor along with your payment. In some cases, you can call the vendor and register over the phone.

Although some shareware vendors are companies with full-time staff members, others are individuals who work out of their homes and often have other jobs. In the latter case, information accompanying your shareware may not include a telephone number, and you will have to correspond by mail or via an online service.

 Troubleshooting

If you have problems using shareware, perhaps the following resolutions can help:

■ If, after you start using shareware, your system or the shareware program starts acting erratically by displaying strange screen messages or destroying your files, a virus may have been lurking in your shareware. Although relatively rare, there are hundreds of viruses that currently plague PC users. If you suspect your problem might be a virus, use Anti-Virus to search for and remove viruses, as detailed in Chapter 18, "Protecting Your System."

■ If you download a program, but it doesn't do what you expect it to do, it may only be a demonstration version. Usually, shareware that you download from a bulletin board is completely functional. However, sometimes shareware vendors only make demonstration versions of their products available for downloading. Contact the shareware vendor to be sure you are loading a complete version of the product.

■ If, when you first try to start a shareware product, it doesn't load, or you get error messages saying certain files are missing, the file might have been damaged during downloading. Try downloading the file again. If the problem continues, ask the shareware vendor for another evaluation copy.

Summary

In this chapter, you learned the following:

- If you have a modem, you can obtain shareware from local bulletin boards or national online information services.

- You also can obtain shareware from shareware disk vendors and from your local user group.

- If you try shareware and continue to use it, you must register and pay for it. Shareware programs usually include information about how to do this.

Customer Support

Alan Simpson's
DOS
SECRETS
UNLEASHED

A   P   P   E   N   D   I   X   A

Installing DOS 6

Chances are you won't have to install DOS for the first time on your computer. If you use a computer at work or school, DOS is probably already installed. Even if your computer is fresh out of the box and you've never even turned it on before, your computer dealer might have already installed DOS for you. (Nearly all computer dealers install DOS so that they can test the computer before they ship it to you.) If, however, you need to install DOS 6, this appendix provides you with the necessary guidance.

Before You Upgrade to DOS 6

If DOS is already installed on your computer, upgrading your current version of DOS to DOS 6 is a relatively easy procedure. Microsoft's installation program, Setup, has automated the process to such an extent that you might need only to press Enter a few times and insert disks as prompted. In addition, if you ever need clarification of what Setup is telling (or asking) you, press F1 to display the program's built-in, context-sensitive help system.

Do not run Setup from Windows.

If DOS 6 is already installed on your computer, you can still run Setup again—perhaps to install features which you chose not to install during your previous installations.

If you have OS/2 on your computer, see the section "Upgrading from OS/2 to MS-DOS 6" later in this appendix.

Your current system must meet three requirements before you upgrade to DOS 6:

- Your computer must have at least 640K of RAM.

- Your current version of DOS must be Version 2.11 or later.

- Your hard disk should have at least 420K of free space.

You may be able to resolve this potential problem by simply moving non-system files to another logical drive on your hard disk if you have previously created an extended partition. You can also repartition your hard disk (see Chapter 14, "Hard Disk Management Made Simple").

If your boot drive does not have 420K of available space, you might be able to delete unnecessary files or move them to floppy disk storage. If this still does not provide you with the needed space, you must then perform a minimum installation. Minimum installation consists of first upgrading your system files, installing the rest of DOS 6 onto floppy disks, and then copying selected programs to your hard disk. (For details about this process, see the section "Handling Installation Problems.")

All disk-caching, deletion-protection, anti-virus programs, and screen automatic message services (such as network pop-up or printing notification) must be disabled. Some of these programs conflict with Setup. If any of these programs are loaded when you start your computer, edit your CONFIG.SYS and AUTOEXEC.BAT files, and disable (type REM followed by a space at the beginning of each command line that starts one of these programs) or remove the start-up commands for these programs. Be sure to save your changes and reboot before continuing.

Be sure to read the README.TXT files on the DOS 6 distribution disks. These files contain important hardware and software specific information to help ensure that your installation is successful. The file named PACKING.LST, located on the Setup disk, is a DOS text file that contains a directory showing what programs are on which DOS 6 distribution disk.

What Setup Does

Most files on the DOS 6 distribution disks are compressed. The Setup program automatically decompresses them into usable files by using the DECOMP utility (formerly the EXPAND program).

Once you get the Setup program started, it performs the following series of operations:

- Determines your system's hardware configuration

- Saves all of your current DOS's files in a directory called OLD_DOS.1

- Stores your original system information (File Allocation Tables, root directory entries, AUTOEXEC.BAT, CONFIG.SYS, and so on) on an UNINSTALL disk(s)

- Decompresses compressed files on your DOS distribution disks and copies all files to your DOS 6 directory (usually C:\DOS)

- Creates a new CONFIG.SYS file that includes commands and installs device drivers that let DOS 6 utilize available extended memory

- Modifies your AUTOEXEC.BAT file to include a correct DOS 6 PATH entry and possibly insert specific driver load commands

In addition, when you start Setup, it determines your system's hardware configuration and then displays the results of its findings on a screen similar to the one in Figure A.1

This screen enables you to verify the following information:

- The manufacturer of your current version of DOS (which you can learn before you start Setup by typing VER at the DOS prompt)

- The directory in which DOS files will be stored (Setup defaults to the C:\DOS directory)

- Your video monitor type

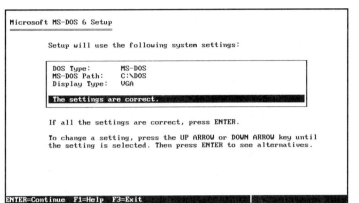

*Figure A.1.
The Setup
verification
screen.*

Setup supplies additional help information whenever you press the F1 function key or enables you to exit the Setup process with the F3 function key each time Setup pauses with a screen display.

Backup, Anti-Virus, and Undelete

Setup provides an option screen for the new DOS 6 data protection tools: Backup, Anti-Virus, and Undelete. The screen options enable you to install these utilities to function under MS-DOS Only, Windows Only, Windows and MS-DOS, or None. The screen also provides you with the amount of storage required for DOS 6 and each option, as depicted in Figure A.2.

Table A.1 shows the total hard disk space requirements for DOS 6 and the data protection tools.

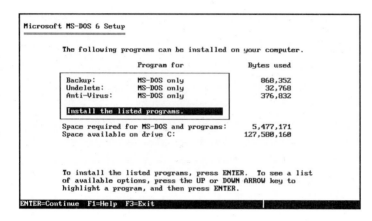

Figure A.2. Data protection tools selection screen.

Table A.1. Data protection space requirements.

Operating Environment	Space Required for DOS and Programs (in Bytes)
DOS 6 Only	5,477,171
Windows Only	6,935,347
Windows & DOS 6	8,114,995

Try to determine how you want to respond to these entries before you start.

As reliable as most hardware and software is, accidents do happen. Brownouts, power failures, and loose plugs can interrupt the installation process at critical times. Hard drives can crash, and devices and plug-in boards can fail. Protect your data. A system-backup is an insurance policy that you cannot afford to be without.

One last thing before you begin installing DOS 6 on your hard disk: you will need one blank 720K, 1.2M, or 1.44M disk (or two blank 360K disks). The disks may be formatted or unformatted. Label the disk(s) UNINSTALL (or UNINSTALL 1 and UNINSTALL 2).

Installing DOS 6 on Floppy Disks

In today's world, a computer without a hard disk drive is like a car with a one-pint gas tank—it's usable, but not very efficient. I assume, therefore, that you're probably upgrading DOS 6 on a hard disk. However, before you do so, I strongly suggest that you install DOS 6 on floppy disks.

The files on the DOS 6 Setup disks are compressed; therefore, you cannot boot directly from the Setup disks. Installing DOS 6 on floppy disks makes a decompressed version of DOS 6 and assures that you'll have a bootable copy of DOS 6 in case you run into problems in the future.

Installing DOS 6 on floppy disks takes some additional time, and, at first, you might think it unnecessary. However, this operation serves several important purposes:

- It gives you another backup of your DOS 6 files.

- It creates a Start-up disk (a bootable system disk that you can use to start your computer if your hard drive fails).

- It gives you a convenient source of decompressed DOS 6 programs that you can copy to your hard disk if you ever need them (that is, you won't have to use the DECOMP command and your original DOS disks to retrieve a DOS file).

Although installing DOS 6 on floppy disks is a simple procedure, it is a little time-consuming. Take the time. You only need to do it once. After all, as I stressed previously, you can never take too many precautions with your computer, your programs, and your data.

Today's de facto floppy disk density is *high* (1.2M or 1.44M). Do yourself a favor and upgrade or order your system with these high-density drives. The savings realized in your increased efficiency and storage considerations can easily justify the purchase.

Whether you are using 5¼-inch 1.2M disks or 3½-inch 1.44M floppy disks, Setup installs DOS 6 on three floppy disks. Label them with the following names:

- Startup/Support

- Help/Basic/Edit

- Supplemental

There are two different procedures you can use when installing DOS 6 on floppy disks, as the following sections describe.

When Your Drive Capacity Is at Least as Great as Your Setup Disks

Use this procedure to install DOS 6 when the disk capacity of the drive that contains your labeled disks is at least as great as that of the drive containing the DOS 6 Setup disks.

When you start Setup for installation on high-density floppy disks, Setup displays a screen similar to the one in Figure A.3 indicating that you should indeed be installing on high-density disks. To install DOS 6 on floppy disks:

1. Start your computer using your current version of DOS.

2. Insert Setup Disk 1 in your A: or B: drive.

3. Type the following at the command prompt (the /F switch tells Setup that this is a floppy installation):

    A:SETUP /F

    or

    B:SETUP /F

4. Follow the instructions on your screen.

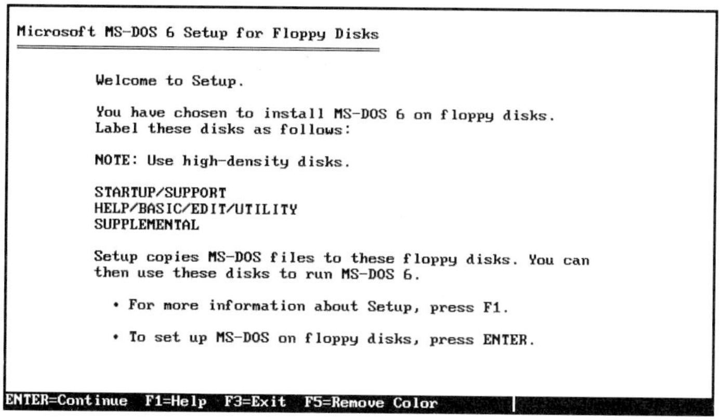

```
Microsoft MS-DOS 6 Setup for Floppy Disks
━━━━━━━━━━━━━━━━━━━━━━━━━━━━━━━━━━━━━

    Welcome to Setup.

    You have chosen to install MS-DOS 6 on floppy disks.
    Label these disks as follows:

    NOTE: Use high-density disks.

    STARTUP/SUPPORT
    HELP/BASIC/EDIT/UTILITY
    SUPPLEMENTAL

    Setup copies MS-DOS files to these floppy disks. You can
    then use these disks to run MS-DOS 6.

       • For more information about Setup, press F1.

       • To set up MS-DOS on floppy disks, press ENTER.


ENTER=Continue   F1=Help   F3=Exit   F5=Remove Color
```

Figure A.3. The Setup screen for floppy disk installation.

At the end of the Setup process you have a complete set of de-compressed DOS 6 floppy disks. You can run DOS 6 from the floppy disks by inserting the Startup/Support disk in your A: or B: drive, and then restarting your computer by pressing Ctrl+Alt+Del.

When the Setup Disks Are of a Higher Density Than Your Drive

This procedure is used when the DOS 6 Setup disks are of a higher density than the disk capacity of the drive containing the labeled disks. A system disk, as well as three high-density disks with MS-DOS 6 files, is created. To install DOS 6 on floppy disks:

1. Start your computer using your current version of DOS.

2. Insert Startup Disk 1 of your DOS 6 Setup disks into your high-density drive (for example, drive B:), and a formatted floppy disk in drive A:, labeled Startup/Support.

3. Type the following at the command prompt (the /M specifies minimum installation):

   `B:SETUP /F /M`

> Be sure you leave a space between the /F and /M switches, because without a space DOS 6 does not recognize this to be a floppy installation and defaults to a hard disk installation.

Setup will display a screen (see Figure A.4) indicating that you are about to perform a minimum floppy disk installation.

4. Follow the instructions on your screen.

5. Restart your computer by pressing Ctrl+Alt+Del.

6. After your computer restarts, insert Startup Disk 1 into your high-density drive (for example, drive B), and type the following at the command prompt:

   `B:SETUP /F`

7. Follow the instructions on your screen.

You can run DOS 6 from the floppy disks by inserting the disk you created in step 3 in your startup drive, and then restarting your computer by pressing Ctrl+Alt+Del. Use the disks you created in step 6 when you want to use a wider range of DOS 6 commands.

The installation process is nearly bullet-proof; that is, it's automated to the extent that all you need to do is press Enter and insert the various numbered Setup disks and your own labeled disks into the proper drive(s). The Setup program checks each DOS 6 Setup disk's volume label (Disk 1, Disk 2, and so on) as you insert them to ensure that the proper disk is being processed. If you don't insert them in the order requested, the Setup program informs you of this problem and waits for you to insert the proper disk.

```
Microsoft MS-DOS 6 Setup for Floppy Disks

    Welcome to Setup.

    You have chosen to perform a minimal installation of
    MS-DOS 6 on a floppy disk. You must provide a formatted
    or unformatted floppy disk that works in your computer's
    drive A. Label the disk as follows:

    STARTUP/SUPPORT

    Setup copies the MS-DOS system files and a few important
    utilities to this disk. You can use this disk to run
    MS-DOS 6.

        • For more information about Setup, press F1.

        • To exit Setup without installing MS-DOS, press F3.

        • To set up MS-DOS on a floppy disk, press ENTER.

ENTER=Continue  F1=Help  F3=Exit  F5=Remove Color
```

Figure A.4.
DOS 6 Setup
for floppy disks
screen.

After programs are copied to the disk labeled Supplemental, Setup will signal that the process is complete and suggest that you reboot with your new Startup disk. If you are now ready to install DOS 6 on your hard disk, press F3 to exit Setup and return to the command prompt.

Setup does not incorporate the new DOS 6 Backup, Anti-Virus, or Undelete programs in a floppy disk installation.

Installing DOS 6 on Your Hard Disk

If you are upgrading your current version of DOS to DOS 6, first label one blank disk with the name UNINSTALL. (Note that if you use a 360K disk, you need two disks—label them UNINSTALL 1 and

UNINSTALL 2.) Setup saves important files and system data on these disks so that you can restore your system to its original state if the installation process is interrupted or if you later have difficulty using your programs with the new operating system. A sample directory listing reflecting the types of files written by Setup to the UNINSTALL disk(s) is shown in Figure A.5.

```
Volume in drive A is UNINSTALL 1
Volume Serial Number is 196F-7CD3
Directory of A:\

COMMAND  COM    53022 10-26-92   6:00a
DOSSETUP INI    13295 10-26-92   6:00a
UNINSTAL EXE   126366 10-26-92   6:00a
BIOS     OLD    33430 04-09-91   5:00a
DOS      OLD    37394 04-09-91   5:00a
MBOOT0   DAT      512 11-15-92   3:39p
PBOOT    DAT      512 11-15-92   3:39p
BPB0     DAT       86 11-15-92   3:39p
GLOBAL   DAT      876 11-15-92   3:39p
AUTOEXEC BAT        8 11-15-92   3:39p
COMMAND  DAT    47845 04-09-91   5:00a
AUTOEXEC DAT       54 11-15-92   3:24p
CONFIG   DAT       71 11-15-92   3:24p
WINA20   386     9349 04-09-91   5:00a
ROOT     DAT    16384 11-15-92   3:39p
FAT      DAT   126976 11-15-92   3:39p
       16 file(s)      466180 bytes
                       666112 bytes free

C:\>
```

Figure A.5. Sample UNINSTALL directory listing.

If you are presently using a disk compression program on your startup drive, you will not be able to create an UNINSTALL disk(s) or restore your previous version of DOS during or after Setup. Give yourself a "fail-safe out" by backing up all of your files before you run Setup. Also create a system disk of your previous DOS version with its system files and include the FDISK, FORMAT, and SYS commands.

The first time you install DOS 6, Setup creates a directory named OLD_DOS.1 on your hard disk. Setup copies your previous DOS files to this directory. The OLD_DOS.*n* directory name extension is incremented and a new directory is created each time you install DOS 6. For example, if you install DOS 6 a second time, you will see two directories: one named OLD_DOS.1 (still containing your previous DOS files) and the other named OLD_DOS.2 containing your first installation of DOS 6 files.

Setup creates the UNINSTALL disk(s) as another insurance policy to protect your system, programs, and data. After the UNINSTALL disk is created, it can be a lifesaver. If the installation process is later interrupted (by a power failure, for example), you can reboot your computer with the UNINSTALL disk in drive A: and then continue the DOS 6 installation from exactly where you left off.

Most importantly, you can use UNINSTALL to restore your previous version of DOS and your original system files if you later determine that DOS 6 is incompatible with your current hardware or software. For details, see the later section "Restoring Your Previous Version of DOS."

To upgrade your previous version of DOS to Version 6, use the following steps:

1. Start your computer with your previous version of DOS (even if you've already created DOS 6 floppy disks).

2. Insert Setup Disk 1 (not the disks you previously labeled) into either the A: or B: drive.

3. Type A:SETUP or B:SETUP, which displays the screen shown previously in Figure A.1.

4. When Setup prompts you for the Uninstall disk(s), insert the disk(s) in drive A:. This is done because Setup copies the files needed to start your computer if you need to restore your previous version of DOS or if Setup cannot complete the installation of DOS 6.

If any of the new Windows optional programs (Anti-Virus, Backup, or Undelete) are installed during Setup, Setup automatically creates a Microsoft Tools group in the Program Manager and adds their icons to the group.

If Setup refuses to install DOS 6 on your hard disk because you don't have the required free space, press F3 to exit Setup; then read the "minimal installation" discussion in the later section "Handling Installation Problems."

5. Follow the instructions on each of the next screens. These guide you through the process of creating an UNINSTALL disk and upgrading your system to DOS 6. Actually, all you have to do is swap floppy disks and press Enter every once in a while. It's as simple and as painless a process as you'll find.

When the installation process is complete and successful, a screen prompt will inform you.

Restoring Your Previous Version of DOS

In addition to your important system files and other information, the UNINSTALL disk also contains a program called UNINSTAL.EXE. This program lets you restore your previous version of DOS if you encounter technical problems using DOS 6. (This is not likely, however, because DOS 6 is perhaps the most-tested program ever released.)

You can use the UNINSTALL disk to restore your system to its original state only if you have not performed certain operations with your computer. The following operations negate UNINSTAL's power to restore your system:

■ If you ran the new DOS 6 DoubleSpace disk compression program

■ If you reformatted or repartitioned your hard disk

■ If you deleted or moved one or both of the hidden DOS system files, IO.SYS or MSDOS.SYS

■ If you used the DELOLDOS command (which deletes your original DOS files (OLD_DOS.1) from your hard disk)

If you performed one of the previous procedures, do not try to uninstall DOS 6. The UNINSTAL program will not function correctly and might even damage your data and hard disk file structure.

To restore your previous version of DOS (or recover from an installation problem such as a power loss), insert the UNINSTALL disk in drive A: (if you needed to use two 360K diskettes, insert UNINSTALL 1). Then press Ctrl+Alt+Del to reboot your system. The UNINSTAL program immediately runs and displays easy-to-use instructions for restoring your original version of DOS. That's it—the process is nearly automatic, and you will need to do little else than confirm that you actually want to proceed with the operation.

> Because the UNINSTALL disk is bootable (contains DOS 6 system files), you can also use it to restart your computer if your hard disk fails. Start your computer with the UNINSTALL disk in drive A, press F3 twice, and then press Y to exit the UNINSTAL program. When the DOS prompt appears, you can again work with your system.

Although booting your system with the UNINSTALL disk works fine, you should be more cautious with your data and create a specialized disk for this purpose. That is, use either a Startup disk (created during a floppy installation) or a System or Emergency disk (created by using the SYS command). See Chapter 4, "Installation Secrets and Surprises," for full details.

Performing a Manual Installation

There are some situations where you may have to install DOS 6 manually because of some types of disk partitions or partition software. The following steps accomplish this task:

1. Setup DOS 6 on floppy disks if you haven't already done so.

2. Insert the disk labeled Startup/Support in drive A: or B: and press Ctrl+Alt+Del to reboot your system.

3. At the command prompt, type either `A:SYS A:\C:` or `B:SYS B:\C.`

4. Create a directory named C:\OLD_DOS.

5. Copy your current or original DOS files into the C:\OLD_DOS directory.

6. Delete all the DOS files in your original DOS directory.

7. Copy all the files from the Startup/Support and Help/Basic/Edit/Utility disk(s) to your original DOS directory.

8. Edit your CONFIG.SYS and AUTOEXEC.BAT files and ensure that the locations of the files for your device drivers are correct and that the PATH statement reflects the correct location of the DOS 6 files.

9. Remove all floppy disks from your drives and reboot your system by pressing Ctrl+Alt+Del.

Performing a Minimum Installation

A minimum installation updates your hard disk's system files (IO.SYS, MSDOS.SYS, and COMMAND.COM), creates an UNINSTALL floppy disk, and then creates new AUTOEXEC.BAT and CONFIG.SYS files. However, it does not expand and transfer to your hard disk any of the other DOS 6 programs. (To expand the DOS 6 files, you need to perform a floppy disk installation with the SETUP /F command and then transfer the programs on those disks to your hard disk.)

To perform a minimum installation, follow these steps:

1. Perform a floppy disk installation.

2. Insert Disk 1 of your DOS 6 distribution disks and type SETUP /MIN.

3. Make a backup of your system if you haven't already done so.

4. Follow the instructions to create an UNINSTALL disk.

5. After Setup copies the three DOS 6 system files to your hard disk, follow the instructions that tell you to reboot your computer.

6. Copy to your hard disk drive as many essential DOS 6 programs from your expanded DOS 6 floppy disks as you can fit in the available space (Normally, you will copy those files and programs into the C:\DOS directory.)

7. Rename your current AUTOEXEC.BAT and CONFIG.SYS files to AUTOEXEC.OLD and CONFIG.OLD.

8. Rename the AUTOEXEC.NEW and CONFIG.NEW files (which Setup created) to AUTOEXEC.BAT and CONFIG.SYS.

9. Reboot your computer by pressing Ctrl+Alt+Del.

Deleting Your Previous Operating System

When (and if) you are certain that DOS 6 will work fine on your system, you can delete your previous operating system, which is stored in a directory named OLD_DOS.1. At the command prompt type DELOLDOS (for DELete OLD Disk Operating System) and press Enter.

This command deletes all of the previous operating system files, the directories they were stored on, and itself (so this is a once-in-a-lifetime command!).

Windows Considerations

DOS 6 was designed to be tightly integrated with Windows. The new Backup, Anti-Virus, and Undelete data protection utilities come in both DOS and Windows versions. They are accessible from icons in a Microsoft Tools Program Group created during Setup.

Do not run Setup from Windows.

Installing Backup, Anti-Virus, and Undelete

Typically, you install these programs when you set up DOS 6. However, if you later want to install some of the programs you didn't install during Setup, you can run Setup again just to install the programs. For example, if after setting up DOS 6 you install Windows, you can run DOS 6 Setup again to install Backup, Anti-Virus, and Undelete for Windows.

If you do not have Windows installed on your computer, you cannot set up the optional programs for Windows.

To run Setup to install the optional programs:

1. Insert Setup Disk 1 in drive A: or B:, then type the following at the command prompt:

```
A:SETUP /E
```

or

```
B:SETUP /E
```

2. Follow the instructions on your screen.

Chapter 18, "Protecting Your System," provides detailed information on these data protection programs.

Potential UNINSTALL Problems With Windows

If you installed Backup, Undelete, or Anti-Virus for Windows, you might receive error messages when you start Windows after uninstalling DOS 6.

If you receive the `Cannot find a device file that may be needed to run Windows in 386 enhanced mode` message, press any key if instructed to do so; otherwise, wait for Windows to start. If the message appears again, press any key again. Windows should start.

If you use Windows 3.1 and receive the `Cannot open program-group C:\DOS\WNTOOLS.GRP` message, choose No. Windows should work correctly. If you use Windows 3.0, and receive this message, choose OK. Windows should work correctly.

Upgrading from OS/2 to DOS 6

Read this section if you want to set up DOS 6 on a computer that already has OS/2 installed on it. This section contains information about setting up DOS 6 if you:

- Have neither OS/2 Dual Boot nor OS/2 Boot Manager on your computer

- Have OS/2 Dual Boot with DOS or OS/2 Boot Manager with DOS on your computer

- Have only OS/2 Boot Manager with OS/2 on your computer

- Want to install DOS 6 on floppy disks

If You Have a 360K or 720K Floppy Disk Drive

If the floppy drive capacity of your computer is 360K or 720K, you need to order 360K or 720K Setup disks. To order the disks, either contact your dealer or use the coupon at the back of the Microsoft *MS-DOS 6 User's Guide and Reference* manual.

If You Have Neither OS/2 Dual Boot nor OS/2 Boot Manager

Perform the following procedures if you have neither the OS/2 Dual Boot nor the OS/2 Boot Manager:

1. Insert Setup Disk 1 in drive A: (the startup drive).

2. Restart your computer by pressing Ctrl+Alt+Del.

3. If you want to remove OS/2 from your computer without saving the data on your hard disk, choose to remove OS/2 or OS/2 files when Setup displays the screen about OS/2.

   If you want to remove OS/2 from your computer but want to save your hard disk data first, see the following section, "Removing OS/2 and Saving the Data On Your Computer."

4. Follow the instructions on your screen.

If you have any questions about any of the procedures or options you encounter during Setup, press F1 for Help. If you have problems running Setup, see "Troubleshooting During Setup" later in this appendix.

If You Have OS/2 Dual Boot or OS/2 Boot Manager with DOS

This section describes how to set up DOS 6 if you have OS/2 Dual Boot or OS/2 Boot Manager and one of your operating systems is DOS. It also describes how to remove OS/2 from your computer.

Before running DOS 6 (OS/2) Setup, ensure that the following checklist items are performed if they are applicable:

- Disable disk-caching, deletion-protection, and anti-virus programs.

- Disable automatic message services.

- Prepare the UNINSTALL disk(s).

> For explanations of each of the preceding items, see the previous section, "Before You Upgrade to DOS 6".

Running DOS 6 (OS/2) Setup

Setup detects the type of hardware and software you have on your computer and notifies you if your computer does not meet the minimum requirements. Setup also notifies you if it detects system features that are incompatible with DOS 6.

To set up DOS 6 if you have OS/2 Dual Boot or OS/2 Boot Manager and one of your operating systems is DOS:

1. Boot your computer with your current version of DOS.

2. Insert Setup Disk 1 into drive A: or B:.

3. Type the following at the command prompt:

   A:SETUP

   or

   B:SETUP

4. When Setup displays the "OS/2 Partition Detected" or "OS/2 Files Detected " screen and you want to keep OS/2 on your computer, choose the "Continue Setup" option then proceed to Step 5.

   If you want to remove OS/2 from your computer but want to save your hard disk data first, skip to the following section, "Removing OS/2 and Saving the Data on Your Computer."

> If you have a version of OS/2 Dual Boot that prompts you to select an operating system each time you start your computer, and you want to keep OS/2, you must re-install OS/2 after you install DOS 6.

5. Follow the instructions on your screen. If you have any questions about any of the procedures or options you encounter during Setup, press F1 for Help.

6. When Setup prompts you for the UNINSTALL disk(s), insert the disk(s) in drive A:. You must use drive A, because Setup copies files to the UNINSTALL disk that DOS 6 needs to start your computer if you need to use it to restore your previous version of DOS.

7. If you are using OS/2 Boot Manager, make the Boot Manager partition active after you complete Setup and restart your computer. To make the Boot Manager partition active, use the FDISK program. FDISK will identify the Boot Manager partition as a 1M non-MS-DOS partition.

If you install any of the Windows programs during the Setup, Setup automatically adds their icons to the Microsoft Tools group in Program Manager. If you have problems running Setup, see the section "Troubleshooting During Setup."

If You Have OS/2 Boot Manager Without DOS

This section describes how to set up DOS 6 on a computer that has OS/2 Boot Manager and does not have DOS. It also describes how to remove OS/2 from your computer.

To set up DOS 6, you use the original Setup disks. Setup detects the type of hardware and software you have on your computer and notifies you if your computer does not meet the minimum requirements. Setup also notifies you if it detects system features that are incompatible with DOS 6.

To set up DOS 6 if you have OS/2 Boot Manager without DOS:

1. Insert Setup Disk 1 in drive A: (the startup drive).

2. Restart your computer by pressing Ctrl+Alt+Del.

3. If you want to remove OS/2 from your computer without saving the data on your hard disk, choose "Remove OS/2 and reconfigure your hard disk" when Setup displays the screen about OS/2. Then proceed to step 4.

   If you want to remove OS/2 from your computer but want to save the data on your hard disk first, skip to the section "Removing OS/2 and Saving the Data on Your Computer."

   If you want to keep OS/2, see your OS/2 documentation for information about setting up OS/2 and MS-DOS on the same computer. In general, you will first need to install DOS 6 on drive C:.

4. Follow the instructions on your screen.

If you have any questions about any of the procedures or options you encounter during Setup, press F1 for Help. If you have any problems running Setup, see the section "Troubleshooting During Setup."

Removing OS/2 and Saving the Data on Your Computer

When Setup detects OS/2, it displays an "OS/2 Partition Detected" and/or "OS/2 Files Detected" screen. Make a note of which screen Setup displays—the procedure you use to remove OS/2 from your computer depends on which screen Setup displays. For instructions on removing OS/2 from your computer, contact your dealer or Microsoft Product Support Services.

Handling Installation Problems

Several configurations of your current system may prevent Setup from working correctly:

- The hard disk doesn't contain enough free space to perform a complete DOS 6 upgrade.

- The hard disk drive has been compressed by an incompatible disk-compression program.

- The primary DOS partition (boot hard disk drive) is too small to accommodate all of DOS 6's files and programs.

- The hard disk drive has been partitioned by a third-party disk-manager program that is not compatible with DOS 6.

- The current DOS partition is no longer valid under DOS 6's new partitioning scheme.

Disk Partitioning Problems

The last four problems in this list need to be corrected by re-partitioning your hard disk. For detailed instructions about this complex (and widely varying) procedure, see Chapter 14, "Hard Disk Management Made Simple."

> The README.TXT file on your DOS 6 Setup disks contains information about many third-party, hard-disk-manager programs. This information might help you install DOS 6 on a system that originally balks at the operation.

Insufficient Disk Space Problems

You can easily overcome insufficient hard disk space problems. The best way to eliminate the problem is to delete any old or unnecessary files on your boot drive. If you still don't have enough free space, you must perform a minimal installation as detailed in the section "Performing a Minimal Installation."

Summary

Installing or upgrading to DOS 6 is normally a straight-forward process. If you experience problems, I hope you will find the solution to your difficulties in this appendix. Enjoy your new operating system—Microsoft just keeps making it better!

Alan Simpson's
DOS SECRETS UNLEASHED

Solutions to Common Problems

This appendix discusses tips and techniques for using DOS to solve common computer problems. The seemingly unrelated topics in this appendix represent the most commonly asked questions about how DOS can handle "real world" problems. I hope the following sections will save you hours of frustration while you are fiddling with the pesky problems that can plague your computing sessions.

The purpose here is to flag problems, propose solutions, and refer you to the chapters where you'll find step-by-step directions to implement the solutions. The material in the referenced chapters provides all you need to know about the various DOS commands and options.

The following topics are likely to cover most of the questions you'll encounter. However, even if you don't have a specific question or an unresolved problem at the moment, reading about the solutions to these common problems will better prepare you to resolve them when they arise.

Upgrading from Older DOS Versions

MS-DOS Version 3.3 and earlier couldn't access a hard disk partition bigger than 32M. Older versions of DOS's file allocation table (FAT) couldn't handle a bigger space in which to store files. DOS 6 enables you to configure any size hard disk partition.

To combine several partitions into one large partition, use the DOS 6 FDISK command. If Setup can install MS-DOS 6 on your computer, go ahead and install it before using FDISK. You must delete all the logical drives, the extended partition, and the primary partition, then create a new primary partition and make it active. Turn to Chapter 14, "Hard Disk Management Made Simple," to learn more about using the FDISK command.

You cannot use FDISK to repartition a hard disk that was partitioned by a third-party program such as those made by Disk Manager, SpeedStore, Priam, or Everex. These programs replace the BIOS in interactions between DOS and your hard disk controller. In this case, repartition the disk using the same disk-partitioning program first used to partition the disk. See Chapter 19, "DOS Compatibility Secrets and Surprises," for more information.

Recovering from "Crashes" with a System Disk (Boot Disk)

A system disk enables you to restart your PC in case it *crashes,* or falters, during a procedure and cannot find the hard disk containing its system files. A system disk contains essential DOS commands and is *bootable,* meaning it contains hidden files that DOS uses to boot the computer. A good system disk should contain copies of your current AUTOEXEC.BAT and CONFIG.SYS files, a root directory listing, and a copy of your PC's CMOS settings.

A system disk will help you out of many a jam. The small amount of time it takes to make a system disk will be amply repaid when your PC takes a fall.

To create a system disk, turn to Chapter 4, "Installation Secrets and Surprises." Remember to copy the Anti-Virus program onto the disk to enable virus detection and deletion.

Transferring Information Between Computers with Incompatible Disk Formats

From the gradual extinction of the 8-inch floppy in the early 1980s until 1986's unveiling of the IBM PS/2 line of computers, the 5 ¼-inch diskette was the standard among microcomputers. Since then, many computers, particularly laptops, have been equipped to handle the smaller-sized, larger-capacity 720K and 1.44M 3 ½-inch diskettes. Often these drives cause compatibility problems for anyone who must use both types of computers.

If you have access to a PC with both types of drives, you can easily transfer data between diskettes of both formats. Otherwise, getting data from a 5 ¼-inch disk to a 3 ½-inch disk can be done in three ways:

■ If you have two computers that are each fitted with a different-sized drive and a cable, you can use INTERLNK, a file-transfer software program that comes with DOS 6.

■ If each computer is fitted with communications software, a modem, and a phone line, you can transfer the data from one computer to another through the phone lines or a null modem cable.

■ If you have only one computer and it has the wrong-sized drive to read your diskette, you must consider the more expensive hardware solution of adding a floppy drive with the right dimensions.

INTERLNK

Suppose you have a laptop that has one or two 3 ½-inch disk drives, and a desktop computer that uses 5 ¼-inch diskettes. How do you get data from one machine to another? Because you can transport the laptop, put it next to the desktop model, connect the two through cables linking their serial or parallel ports, and load the INTERLNK software that comes with DOS 6 onto both com-puters.

INTERLNK removes the need to copy files from one PC to the other via floppies. The PCs must be close to each other to allow a cable connection. The two computers can be loaded using INTERLNK, thereby establishing a client/server relationship—the client computer receives your typed commands, and the server responds.

You can learn how to set up and use INTERLNK in Chapter 28, "The POWER of INTERLNK." You can purchase the cable inexpensively from a computer store. Several third-party software companies market similar data-transfer software/cable packages.

High-Density/Low-Density Conversions

All disk drives can read diskettes that are the appropriate size and the same or lower density. For example, a 1.2M high-density disk drive can read 5 ¼-inch diskettes in both 1.2M (high-density) and 360K (low-density) capacities. A 360K 5 ¼-inch drive, in comparison, can read only 360K diskettes (and not the higher-density 1.2M diskettes).

Similarly, a 1.44M 3 ¼-inch disk drive can read 3 ¼-inch diskettes in both 720K (low-density) and 1.44M (high-density) formats. However, a 720K 3 ¼-inch diskette drive cannot read a higher-density 1.44M 3 ¼-inch diskette.

DOS enables you to format diskettes that can be used in the same types of drives or in those of lower density. For example, suppose that your desktop computer uses 1.44M 3 ¹/-inch drives, but your laptop uses 720K 3 ½-inch diskette drives. How would you format a diskette and copy files to it so that you could use it with your laptop?

One solution is to use the laptop to format a 720K diskette and then copy files from the desktop computer's hard disk onto that diskette.

An alternative solution, if your laptop is not available, is to tell DOS to format the blank 3 ½-inch diskette in the 1.44M drive for use in a 720K drive. (Check the FORMAT command in Chapter 14, "Hard Disk Management Made Simple," to learn how.) Then use the COPY command to copy files from your 720K diskette in drive A:. Your laptop will have no problem using this diskette and the copied files.

The same solution can be effected with most 5 ¼-inch diskettes. Again, consult the step-by-step directions for FORMAT in Chapter 14 to learn how.

The brand-name, IBM PC AT, poses an exception to this rule. With the AT you can still use the FORMAT command to format the disk in the 1.2M drive A: as a 360K diskette, but when you copy a file onto that diskette, it is no longer readable in a 360K drive!

This problem has caused much frenzied hair-pulling among IBM AT users who need to share data on PCs with 360K drives. Fortunately, a fairly inexpensive software solution exists. COPY AT2PC, a software program that converts files saved in the IBM AT's high-density format to low-density format, solves this problem. You can purchase the program from the following source:

COPY AT2PC
Microbridge Computers International
655 Sky Way, #125
San Carlos, CA 94070
(800)523-8777

Modem Communications

If two computers need to share data housed in incompatible disk formats and they are remote, or in separate sites, you can accomplish data transfer via modem communications.

This solution requires that each computer has communications software installed, because each computer is set up to receive data in a "host" mode. The sending computer calls the receiving PC and uploads the data to it. Each computer must also have a modem, and a phone line must be handy, temporarily, for each computer.

Turn to Chapter 25, "Communicating with Modems and FAXs," to learn more about communicating with modems.

Hardware Solution: A New Drive

If you have access to only one computer with only one size of drive, but you need the convenience of using data on both 5 ¼-inch and 3 ½-inch diskettes, you would do well to install a drive for each diskette size you require. Although this solution is considerably more expensive than the software solutions mentioned previously, it might be the only alternative for some users.

If your computer's system box has room for an additional floppy disk drive, either above, below, or beside existing drives, you can purchase and install another internal drive. If you have no room inside the system box, you can get an external drive.

TEAC's Combo Floppy drive combines both 5 ¼-inch and 3 ½-inch drives in one half-height internal drive. So even if your PC accommodates only a single drive, you can remove the old one and add the new dual-drive model in the same space. This two-size, four-capacity disk drive might sport a slightly higher price tag than single-size models, but you can use extra internal drive bays later for tape backup units and other hardware additions to your computing arsenal. Be sure to consult a qualified hardware consultant or dealer before making any purchases.

Regardless of how you configure the multiple floppy drives on your computer, remember these two tips:

- A computer equipped with a hard disk, one 1.44M 3 ½-inch disk drive, one 1.2M 5 ¼-inch drive, and a modem provides total accessibility to data of all kinds, in all formats.

- If you decide to install your own extra disk drive, follow the manufacturer's instructions carefully. You'll need to inquire about floppy controller cards and all sorts of worrisome stuff. If the manufacturer does not supply a specific device driver to activate an external drive, see Chapter 21, "Maximizing Your Disk Drives."

Computer dealers, manufacturers, and service technicians are good sources for help in determining what drive solution is best for you. For information on the dual diskette drive, contact

TEAC America, Inc.
Data Storage Products Division
7733 Telegraph Road
Montebello, CA 90640
(213)726-0303

Solving Data Incompatibility Problems

Different software products use various formats to store data, formats that are most efficient within that particular program. Unfortunately for users, all these various formats are incompatible with each other, which hinders your ability to get data from one application program, say WordPerfect, into another application, such as Lotus 1-2-3.

Many of the leading applications contain facilities for importing and exporting data to and from other leading packages. Microsoft Word for Windows contains a file menu that enables you to easily import a WordPerfect file for editing within Word for Windows, for example. Word even enables you to save, or export, that file back into WordPerfect when you're done.

In a few cases, you might not be able to import or export data directly. But almost all software can import and export DOS text files (or ASCII text files). Some products also enable you to choose between various ASCII formats, such as delimited or fixed-length for text files (delimited is usually easier to work with).

For example, say you use an older database program, GoodBase, and decide to switch to a newer product, GreatBase. You don't want to lose all the work you did in GoodBase, right? What you want to do is export data from your obsolete GoodBase program into GreatBase, but GoodBase, being older, has no direct exporting facility to put your data into GreatBase format. GoodBase can, however, export ASCII text files (nearly every product can). So run GoodBase, save your old data in ASCII format, and then run GreatBase and import the ASCII data into your new program. (Real-life programs might differ slightly in this procedure.)

Importing and exporting data among word processing programs is a little more complicated, because each uses a very different method for storing formatting codes such as boldface, underline, and so on.

As mentioned previously, some word processors (usually the major programs) offer programs that enable you to import and export documents in various leading formats. But for each program that contains this capability, 10 others do not. There's always the option of saving a document in ASCII text and porting it between the two word processors, but you'll lose the formatting codes.

Several independent software companies offer programs that transfer documents between many, many word processing programs. Before you purchase, be sure to determine whether the word processing formats you require are supported. Your computer store or software dealer might be able to provide some alternatives, and so can the following companies:

R-Doc/X
Advanced Computer Innovations
30 Burncoat Way
Pittsford, NY 14534-2216
(716)383-1939

Software Bridge
Systems Compatibility Corp.
401 North Wabash #600
Chicago, IL 60611
(800)333-1359

Word for Word
Design Software, Inc.
1275 West Roosevelt Road
West Chicago, IL 60185
(312)231-4540

Using Older Programs with Newer Computers

Some very old ("dinosaur," in computerese) DOS programs will not run under later versions of DOS. This is particularly true of programs designed to run under version 1 of DOS, which was created for the first IBM PC.

You might be able to run these older programs under current versions of DOS by experimenting with several DOS commands designed to handle this situation. In particular, review the entries in each chapter featuring the following commands:

ASSIGN—Reroutes program requests to a different disk drive. For example, use ASSIGN to run a program that insists on reading and writing data on drive B: (even if your PC has no such drive).

FCBS—Tells DOS to use the Version 1 File Control Block system of managing files rather than the file handles approach used by later version of DOS. Use this command when DOS displays the error message FCB unavailable.

JOIN—Tells DOS to treat a disk drive as though it were a directory for a program on another drive.

STACKS—Tells DOS to allocate more stacks than normal (the default is 9). Use this when DOS displays the error message Fatal: Internal Stack Failure, System Halted.

SUBST—Forces DOS to access a subdirectory as though it were a separate disk drive. Use this command when running DOS Version 1 programs on a hard disk subdirectory rather than on a floppy disk.

ASSIGN, JOIN, and SUBST should not be used in Windows.

Using the DOS commands in this list can be risky, because these commands trick DOS into actions it wouldn't normally perform. Therefore, treat these commands with the utmost caution. Use these commands only when you have no alternative, and heed the warnings in each chapter discussion of the commands.

Running Older Programs with DOS 6

Some programs designed to run with earlier versions of DOS might not be able to run properly under DOS 6. The SETVER command, included with DOS 6, can fool these programs into behaving as if an earlier version of DOS were running. For more information, check Chapter 15, "Getting the Most from Your Memory," for a discussion of the SETVER command.

Similarly, some older programs cannot run in the extra memory space that DOS 6 offers. Such programs often return the message Packed File Corrupt when you try to run them in DOS 6. Refer to the LOADFIX command, also covered in Chapter 15, if you run across this problem while using DOS 6.

When Programs Can't Find Their Overlays

Most, but not all, programs are designed to be accessed easily from a hard disk. These programs can be activated from any drive or directory as long as the application's home directory is included in the current PATH setting. However, there is no guarantee that this always works as expected, especially if you name a program's directory something other than the manufacturer's recommended directory name.

For example, suppose that you use an early version of WordStar (version 4) as your word processing program, and you install it on a directory named \EDITOR rather than the WordStar-recommended name, \WS4. If you include the \EDITOR directory in your PATH command, DOS can always find the main WordStar program, WS.EXE, in the path.

However, WordStar is designed to search only the current directory and the (nonexistent) \WS4 directory for its overlay files (such as WSMSGS.OVR). If your current directory is not \EDITOR (where the overlay files are housed), when you enter the WS command, WordStar appears to get started, but then the following error messages appear on-screen:

```
Cannot find overlay c:WSSPELL.OVR
Cannot find messages C:WSSPELL.OVR
```

Because WordStar can't find its overlay (.OVR) files in either the current or the nonexistent and renamed \WS4 directory, it gives up and returns control to DOS.

If the PATH command tells DOS to search the \EDITOR directory, why can't WordStar find these overlay files? The PATH command searches only for files with the .BAT, .COM, and .EXE extensions. Because the overlay files missed by WordStar have .OVR extensions, they can't be detected by the DOS PATH command.

The APPEND command offers a solution to this problem. APPEND, searches directories for all files except those with the .BAT, .COM, or .EXE extension. To solve problems like the one just mentioned, simply keep the \EDITOR directory in the current PATH settings so that DOS searches the \EDITOR directory for WordStar's main program, WS.EXE. Then list the \EDITOR directory in an APPEND command so that DOS searches that directory for the required overlay files.

See Chapter 11, "Creating and Editing Files," if you need help editing your AUTOEXEC.BAT file.

This entire WordStar problem example (assuming WordStar's files are all stored in a directory named \EDITOR on hard disk C:) can be resolved by adding the following commands to your AUTOEXEC.BAT file:

```
PATH C:\EDITOR
APPEND C:\EDITOR
```

After DOS detects these commands, you can access the WordStar program and all its overlay files from any directory. The PATH command tells DOS to search the \EDITOR directory for the main program (WS.EXE, in this example). The APPEND command tells DOS to search the \EDITOR directory for any other files (WSSPELL.OVR, for example) that WordStar needs.

Do not use the APPEND command in Windows.

Increasing Hard Disk Efficiency

As a hard disk drive becomes older and more packed with programs and data, you might notice a decrease in the speed at which it accesses files. A large part of this loss of efficiency is caused by file fragmentation, in which portions of files are scattered throughout the disk by the repeated saving, modifying, and erasing of files (as discussed in Chapter 14, "Hard Disk Management Made Simple").

When a file is severely fragmented, the drive head must move around the disk a great deal to read the many scattered sectors which constitute that complete file. When this happens, you will notice that the hard disk drive light remains on for a long time when reading the file. (You might also hear the drive head mechanism grinding away within the unit as it searches the disk for stray sectors.)

DOS 6 contains a disk defragmenter utility, DEFRAG, a program that reorganizes files on your hard disk to minimize the degradation described previously. DEFRAG rearranges the files so that each is stored in a contiguous series of sectors and the drive head doesn't need to search the entire disk to read a file. To learn how to employ DEFRAG to tidy up your hard disk, see Chapter 14.

Before you use DEFRAG, or third-party disk defragmenting utilities, to reorganize your hard disk, you should take these steps:

■ Back up your entire hard disk, using the new DOS 6 Backup for DOS or Backup for Windows programs, to safeguard your data lest something goes awry.

■ De-install any copy-protected programs before using Defragmenter or similar programs.

If you fail to heed the second warning, you probably will no longer be able to use the copy-protected program on your hard disk without inserting the key diskette beforehand.

Alternatives to Defragmenting

File fragmentation is not the only cause of inefficient hard disk accessing, and using DEFRAG is not the only solution. Scan the following tips to see whether you (and your hard disk) could be working more effectively.

If your PATH command forces DOS to search directories that contain many files, extensive file searches will slow access time. Put the most crowded directories near the end of your PATH statement, forcing DOS to search them only as a last resort. To learn more about the PATH command, see Chapter 14.

The SMARTDrive disk-caching program included with DOS 6 reduces the time your computer spends reading data from your hard disk. SMARTDrive sets aside an area in extended memory to store information it reads from your hard disk. A program can use the data it retrieves from memory much faster than data retrieved from the hard disk, simply because a hard disk, being mechanical in nature, works more slowly than electronic RAM.

SMARTDrive also uses its section of RAM to temporarily store data to be written to your hard disk, choosing a time when system resources are more available to write to the disk. If your computer has extended memory available and a hard disk, turn to Chapter 14 to see how SMARTDrive can speed data access.

Even if you don't have extended memory, DOS 6 provides a way to install a disk-caching system. FASTOPEN, discussed in Chapter 14, can speed data access for those with no extended memory.

The DOS Shell Task Swapper speeds disk access and enables you to switch back and forth between open programs quickly. If you don't use Windows 3.1 or another type of Shell program, Task Swapper will show immediate benefits in the area of program access. Turn to Chapter 8, "Using the Shell," to find out more about Task Swapper.

Freeing Disk Space

A hard disk doesn't necessarily have to be fragmented to work poorly. In some cases, your hard disk might simply be too full to work as well as it should. DOS 6 offers several ways to help you remove infrequently used programs and files from your hard disk. After you pare down your disk to the essentials, double your hard disk's capacity with DoubleSpace, a new disk-compression program featured in DOS 6. Scan the following tips to see how DOS 6 can enhance your hard disk's performance, and then turn to the chapters mentioned to start streamlining your data.

Microsoft Backup, a new backup program included with DOS 6, enables you to archive infrequently used files and directories onto floppies or other storage media. The program is highly configurable and offers Backup Catalog Files that enable you to identify and re-store selected files quickly. Turn to Chapter 18, "Protecting Your System," to see how Backup can help you archive data and clean up your hard disk.

Deleting Unnecessary Files

You can use the DELETE command (DEL) to remove unwanted files and free up disk space. Consider deleting programs and data you no longer want or need: temporary files deposited on your hard disk by a program that terminated unexpectedly; MS-DOS files that you don't need; and lost file allocation units, also deposited on a hard disk after a program's sudden termination.

To remove unwanted files and programs, consider getting a good third-party file viewer that enables you to navigate the entire hard disk subdirectory structure, file by file, and view the contents of each file. If you haven't used a file or program in ages, you can use Backup to archive it onto a floppy disk or other backup media, and then delete it off your hard disk. Backup can even compress such files. Normally, you would want to save only data files, because you already own the program and can reinstall it from its original disks at any time.

To identify and delete temporary files, search for any files con-taining a .TMP extension. Some programs store their temporary files in a specific directory, which you should clean out periodically.

Delete temporary files and clean out directories only when you are not running any programs. Windows users must exit Windows and delete files only from the DOS prompt (not when shelled to DOS).

You can delete unneeded DOS files and programs that install themselves automatically when you first install DOS 6. For example, if you're sure you never intend to use DOS Shell, DOS's graphical user interface, you could delete DOSSHELL.VID, DOSSHELL.COM, DOSSHELL.GRB, DOSSHELL.EXE, and DOSSHELL.HLP from your DOS subdirectory. By doing so, you would gain 416,204K (almost half a megabyte) in hard disk space. Chapter 13, "Customizing DOS," provides more information on which DOS files are safe to delete. Do not delete any DOS files unless you've made a Start-up Disk, as outlined previously. As always, use utmost caution when deleting any files from your hard disk, especially DOS files.

Never delete these files from your DOS subdirectory or root directory; doing so will disable your computer: COMMAND.COM, DBLSPACE.BIN, IO.SYS, and MSDOS.SYS. (The latter two are usually hidden files.)

Using *CHKDSK* to Free Disk Space

The CHKDSK command, used with the /F switch, can recover lost allocation units taking up space on your hard disk. Allocation units, the smallest portion of a hard disk that can be allocated to a file, get lost when the program terminates suddenly and unexpectedly. When this happens, temporary files are left on the disk without being saved or deleted properly. Over time, lost allocation units can accumulate and take up disk space.

You cannot use CHKDSK /F when programs are running on your computer. Doing so might result in losing data off your hard disk. Before using CHKDSK, read over the subject matter in Chapter 14, "Hard Disk Management Made Simple."

Using CHKDSK's /F switch enables CHKDSK to convert lost allocation units to visible files that you can examine and delete. To learn how to use CHKDSK, turn to Chapter 14.

Creating Disk Space with DoubleSpace

DOS 6 offers a way to double your storage capacity, by using its disk compression program, DoubleSpace. This program stores data on a disk more densely than normal. DoubleSpace can double or even triple your hard disk's storage space.

Before you attempt to use DoubleSpace or third-party disk compression programs, take a moment to back up your hard drive and make a system disk. It's not likely that anything will go wrong, but better to be safe than sorry!

Read more about how DoubleSpace works in Chapter 14.

Sharing Data, Printers, and Other Devices

As a company expands its investment in microcomputer technology, the capability to share resources among computers becomes increasingly important. For example, a four-computer office will get much more value from sharing one laser printer, if all four computers are able to access it, than from purchasing a separate printer for each computer.

The solutions to the resource-sharing problems that follow are but a few of the alternatives possible, which vary in cost and convenience. The following sections briefly describe some alternatives to look into when these situations occur.

Peripheral Sharing Devices

The most inexpensive (and most limited) device for connecting several computers and peripherals is called the *peripheral sharing device*.

This allows multiple computers to share printers and other devices and send files to one another. Peripheral sharing devices don't enable multiple users to access data simultaneously, however.

Suppose that you have several users who need access to a printer, plotter, and modem. You can use a peripheral sharing device to give an inexpensive means of providing all connected computers with access to a single printer, plotter, and modem.

The names of several peripheral sharing devices, and the companies that manufacture them, are listed next. Your computer dealer might be able to offer other alternatives.

The Logical Connection
Fifth Generation Systems Inc.
11200 Industriplex Blvd.
Baton Rough, LA 70809
(800)873-4384

EasyLAN
Server Technology, Inc.
140 Kifer Court
Sunnyvale, CA 94086
(800)835-1515

ManyLink
ManyLink for Work Groups
NetLine
2155 North 200 West, Suite 90
Provo, UT 84604
(801)373-6000

Another product, Microsoft's Workgroup Connection, facilitates data and resource sharing. This program makes it easier for you to access files, directories, and printers on PCs and laptops equipped with Microsoft Workgroup Connection, Microsoft Windows for Workgroups, or Microsoft LAN Manager. To learn more about Workgroup Connection, read Chapter 26, "Making the Workgroup Connection."

True multiuser capability, in which several users on separate computers not only share devices but also have simultaneous access to the same data, requires either a local area network (LAN) or a multiuser operating system. These vary considerably in price and performance.

Selecting which alternative best meets your needs involves researching a potentially complex system and matching your findings with your cost and system resources. A thorough investigation is beyond the scope of this book, but you can glean much through LAN-oriented periodicals and books, as well as through visits to LAN User Groups, where you can discuss your situation with real-world users who might share some of your concerns.

Summary

This appendix offers resolutions to common problems all computer users can experience from time to time. If you experience one of the problems listed in this appendix, be sure to review more detailed information in the referenced chapters. See Appendix C, "DOS Error Messages and What to Do," for resolutions to common DOS error messages.

Alan Simpson's
DOS
SECRETS
UNLEASHED

A P P E N D I X   C

DOS Error
Messages and
What to Do

This appendix defines some of the DOS 6 error messages you will have to contend with from time to time, and offers applicable solutions. Most of these problem resolutions are accomplished without any serious ramifications; however, a few could be costly both in time and money. Probably the best piece of advice I can give you is to always have not only a current backup of your applications but a System Recovery disk as well. See Chapter 4, "Installation Secrets and Surprises," for a detailed discussion on creating a System Recovery disk.

> DOS 6 Shell users can press the Help key (F1) for instant help whenever the error message window is displayed on-screen.

The error messages in this appendix are grouped into the following categories:

- *DOS Critical Error Messages*—Typically affect more than one program.

- *DOS Noncritical Error Messages*—Normally affect your currently executing program.

- *Backup Error Messages*—Generated during the DOS 6 MS Backup operations.

- *INTERLNK Error Messages*—Appear while you are using INTERLNK and INTERSRV to transfer files.

- *Anti-Virus Error Messages*—Warnings of possible virus infections on your disks.

DOS Critical Error Messages

The following messages typically affect more than one of your programs.

Bad or missing Command Interpreter. Enter correct name of Command Interpreter

DOS 6 is unable to locate your COMMAND.COM file. One reason for this error indicator is that you might have a SHELL= statement in your CONFIG.SYS file or a SET COMSPEC command in your AUTOEXEC.BAT file that has an incorrect path indication of where the COMMAND.COM file is located. Also check to be sure that at least one command-interpreter command is present.

You might need to boot from your System disk (containing your DOS IO.SYS, MSDOS.SYS, and COMMAND.COM files) to correct this problem.

Bad partition table

This error typically occurs when you are in the process of formatting a partition and the FORMAT program is unable to recognize the partition table information that FDISK has previously provided. You will need to run FDISK again before attempting to format.

Cannot start command, exiting

DOS is attempting to load another copy of COMMAND.COM, and either there isn't enough memory available or the FILES= statement in your CONFIG.SYS file does not have enough open files defined. Use MEM /C to see what TSRs you might be able to remove, or increase the number of files in your FILES command.

Disk boot failure

Your disk boot record has possibly become corrupted. Attempt to reboot. If that fails, you should boot from your System disk (containing your IO.SYS, MSDOS.SYS, and COMMAND.COM files), and then type SYS C:.

Disk error writing *FAT* n

Your DOS file allocation table has become corrupt. Try running a third-party disk-repair utility. If that doesn't work, you will have to reformat your disk.

Divide overflow

This error is caused by a bug in an application program. Debug your program, or if you purchased this particular program, contact the software manufacturer.

Error in loading operating system

This error occurs when you are booting up your system. It is an indication that the DOS bootstrap routine is unable to load the IO.SYS and MSDOS.SYS system files because they have been corrupted. Boot with your System disk in drive A, and type SYS C:. If your system files do not transfer, type FORMAT /S.

Fail on *INT 24*

You normally see this message when DOS has attempted a hardware access, typically three times, and has been unsuccessful. It is also displayed if you select the Fail option from an Abort, Retry, Ignore, Fail? prompt. If the failure occurs when DOS is accessing your hard disk, you most likely have a hardware problem with either your hard disk itself or its controller, in which case you should contact your dealer.

File allocation table bad, drive %1

Your file allocation table has become corrupted. Hopefully, you have a current backup of your critical files. You should initially try to use a third-party disk-repair utility in hopes of recovering this vital data with the second copy of the FAT. If that doesn't work, you will have to reformat your disk.

General failure reading drive

See Sector not found error message.

Insufficient disk space

Your disk is full. You can either back up and delete some infrequently used files, utilize the DOS 6 DECOMP disk-compression program, or buy a new disk with high capacity.

Insufficient memory

A program is attempting to execute and doesn't have the required amount of internal memory. Try running the MemMaker program, or remove any noncritical TSRs. If that doesn't work, you might have to purchase additional memory.

Internal stack overflow

Either DOS or an application program has experienced an overflow of its stack space. Edit your CONFIG.SYS file, and increase the DOS 6 STACK statement to an appropriate value.

Invalid *COMMAND.COM*

Most likely an application or power spike/drop has corrupted the transient portion of DOS's COMMAND.COM file. Insert your DOS 6 System disk, reboot, and copy the COMMAND.COM file to your hard disk.

Invalid drive specification

This message normally indicates that you typed the incorrect drive letter. Sometimes, however, it can indicate that DOS cannot find the "logical" disk defined by the partition table on the physical hard disk. You need to run the UNFORMAT command with the /PARTN switch (see Invalid partition table error message).

Invalid environment

You have specified an environment size in your CONFIG.SYS file that isn't between 160 and 32,768 bytes. Check your /E option on the COMMAND.COM command line.

Invalid partition table, Bad partition table, Error reading partition table, Non-standard, missing, or bad partition table, or Disk unsuitable

All of these errors indicate that you should run the UNFORMAT program with the /PARTN switch included. This will rebuild your partition table. To be assured that your partition table will be re-built accurately and with the most current state, you should have the MIRROR /PARTN command line included in your AUTOEXEC.BAT file.

Memory allocation error

A program has corrupted the DOS memory tracking tables. DOS is completely unstable. Reboot and the problem should go away. If you are testing new software, check it very carefully for this type of violation.

Missing operating system

Your operating system file IO.SYS or MSDOS.SYS, or both, has become corrupted. Boot with your System disk in drive A, and type SYS C:. If your system files do not transfer, type FORMAT /S.

No free file handles

All the DOS file identifier codes for all simultaneous open files have been utilized. Increase the size parameter in the FILES= statement in the CONFIG.SYS file, and reboot.

Non-System disk or disk error, Replace and press any key when ready

You have inserted the wrong diskette in a floppy drive, the diskette is not inserted properly, or your hard disk does not have DOS installed on it. Remove any diskette that is in a floppy drive. Place your Start-up/Support disk in the floppy drive, and press any key to continue.

Not enough memory

DOS doesn't have enough memory to load in a program. Run MEM.EXE with the /C switch, and review your memory map. Unload any unnecessary TSRs and try again. Maybe you really need to get some additional memory!

Out of environment space

You can increase the environment space by using the /E option on the COMMAND.COM command line in your CONFIG.SYS file.

Sector not found or General failure reading drive

This error will most likely occur when an aging (over a year old) hard disk's magnetic images such as Sector IDs fade over time. You should run a low-level format utility on your disk. If that doesn't work, contact your dealer for warranty status on your hard disk!

System files restored. Target disk may not be bootable

Versions of DOS prior to 3.3 copy the system files during backup and restore operations. You probably need to use the SYS command to recopy system files from DOS 6 to the root directory. (This makes your hard disk bootable again.)

Unrecoverable error in directory, Convert directory to file (Y/N)?

CHKDSK is informing you that your directory structure has become corrupted. If you have a current system backup, answer no, delete the directory, and restore. If you do not have a current system backup, answer yes and locate a third-party disk editor to repair the directory.

DOS Noncritical Error Messages

The following error messages normally affect your currently executing program.

A20 Hardware error

This seldom-seen error can occur at start-up when your system is attempting to execute the DOS=HIGH command in your CONFIG.SYS file. This command normally loads as much of DOS as possible into the high memory area (HMA). The most immediate solution is to remove the DOS=HIGH statement in your CONFIG.SYS file. The A20 refers to the A20 address line that enables programs to access nearly 64K of memory while in real mode. Another probably less desirable solution would be for you to buy a 386/486 computer, which would allow this accessibility without special hardware.

Abort, Retry, Ignore or Abort, Retry, Fail

This error occurs when you type a command that the computer cannot carry out, such as when you attempt to access an empty floppy disk drive or when DOS attempts to write to your printer and it's not in a ready state.

1. If you can determine the cause of the problem based on the brief message that appears above the Abort, Retry, Ignore or Abort, Retry, Fail options, correct the problem if possible, and then press R to retry the command.

2. If you cannot correct the situation, press I to select Ignore, or F to select Fail (whichever is displayed on your screen as an option). If this problem occurs with a floppy disk operation, you must switch to a valid drive. For example, if you have a hard disk named C:, type C: and press Enter. If your disk drive A: contains a diskette, type A: and press Enter. The command prompt redisplays the current drive name.

Access denied

You have attempted to modify a file (by copying over or by editing) that is protected by the read-only attribute. If you really want to modify this file, you must turn off the read-only attribute with the ATTRIB -R command.

All files in directory will be deleted!— Are you sure (Y/N)?

You entered a command that will erase all the files in a directory. Proceed with this command by pressing Y (for Yes), or cancel the command by pressing N (for No).

Bad command or file name

This error can occur in several situations. You might have misspelled a command or program name, or attempted to run a program that is not available on the current disk drive or directory, or utilized an invalid command line.

1. If you simply misspelled a command (such as typing DOR rather than DIR), type the command again and press Enter.

2. If you are certain that you typed the command properly and you still see the error message, you are attempting to run a program that is not available on the current disk drive or directory. Be sure the file name is in the current directory on the current drive.

Directory already exists

You tried to create a directory that already exists. DOS returns you to the prompt and doesn't enable you to proceed with the command.

Drive types or diskette types not compatible

You tried to use incompatible disk drives or incompatible diskette types during a Disk Copy procedure. Try using one diskette drive (for example, a: a:) rather than two (for example, a: b:). If that does not work, the diskettes are incompatible and cannot be copied using that procedure. You'll need to use the Copy option from the File pull-down menu or the XCOPY or COPY command at the command prompt instead.

Duplicate file name or file not found

During a renaming operation, DOS was unable to find the file that you want to rename or was unable to rename the file because the file name already existed in the current directory. Use the DIR command to check current file names to determine which error is creating the problem; then, retry the command using an acceptable file name.

Error in *EXE* file

COMMAND.COM is informing you that your .EXE file is non-executable due to either errors originating from your compilation process or a corrupted file. Try recompiling if the file is one that you have just created; otherwise, locate the original .EXE file, and copy over the corrupted version.

File cannot be copied onto itself

The source and destination in a copy operation are identical, thus asking DOS to store two files with the same name in the same directory. Try again, being sure to specify a valid source and destination for the copy operation.

File creation error

You exceeded the maximum number of directory entries for the disk.

File not found

DOS cannot locate the file that you named in a command, or you used an ambiguous file name that does not match any of the file names on the disk.

General failure reading drive

The diskette in the drive is not formatted and therefore cannot be accessed. You could also have a bad diskette, in which case you should try a new diskette.

Invalid directory

You tried to access a directory that does not exist or that does not exist beneath the current directory. Perhaps you merely misspelled the directory name in the command line. Try reentering the command with the directory name spelled properly.

Invalid drive specification

You specified a disk drive that does not exist on your computer. For example, you specified drive B: with a computer that has no drive named B:. Try again, using a valid disk drive name.

Invalid filename or file not found

You tried to create or rename a file using an illegal file name. DOS also displays this error when you try to use the wildcard characters ? or * in a TYPE command, which can accept only a single, unambiguous file name.

Invalid number of parameters

You used too many optional switches with a command, or perhaps you used a backslash (\) rather than a forward slash (/) to identify a switch.

Invalid path, not directory, or directory not empty

While attempting to remove a directory, you misspelled the directory name, attempted to delete the current directory, specified a directory that has subdirectories, or specified a directory that still contains files.

Invalid switch

A switch specified in your command is not available with the current command. This message is also caused when you use a forward slash (/) rather than a backslash (\) in directory names.

Last backup diskette not inserted

DOS requested that you put the last backup diskette in the destination drive, but you put in a different diskette. Try your highest-numbered diskette.

No subdirectories exist

You ran the TREE command from a directory that has no subdirectories. Type the command CD \ to access the root directory, and then retry the TREE command.

Packed file is corrupt

A program is attempting to load into the first 64K of memory. Run LOADFIX.COM to circumvent this problem.

Parameter format not correct...
Do not specify filename(s)

Most likely, you omitted a parameter or left out a blank space. For example, when you are using the Disk Copy and Disk Comp utilities, entering a:a: or b:b: produces this error because the drive names are not separated by a space. Try the command again, this time inserting the required blank space between the drive names (for example, a: a: or b: b:).

Path not found

The path you specified in the command does not exist on your current disk. For example, you entered a command such as COPY C:\SALES*.* A:, but your hard disk does not have a directory named SALES.

Required parameter missing

You tried to use a command without specifying a parameter. Try again, but include the required parameter.

Syntax error

You used the wrong format when you typed a command. This problem typically occurs within batch program commands. Review your batch program command lines carefully.

Terminate batch job (Y/N) Cannot execute %1

COMMAND.COM is informing you that you have a fatal error in your batch program (%1). Review your batch commands.

Unable to create directory

DOS displays this message when you try to create a directory beneath a nonexistent directory, or when you specify a directory name that contains invalid characters or has the same name as a reserved device. Check the existing directory tree structure, using the DOS 6 File List, the DIR command, or the TREE command, to determine which error occurred in your situation.

Write fault error writing device *PRN* Abort, Retry, Ignore, or Fail?

You attempted to send data to your printer, and it is either disconnected or not in a ready state. Check your cabling and the ready indicator on your printer.

Write protect error writing drive (n)

You tried to copy data onto (or to format) a write-protected diskette. If you are using 5^1/$_4$-inch diskettes, remove the write-protect tab (if possible), or use a different diskette. If you are using 3^1/$_2$-inch diskettes, close the write-protect slot or slots (if possible), or use another diskette.

Backup Error Messages

The following error messages can occur if you use MS-DOS Backup.

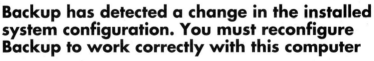

Backup has detected a change in the installed system configuration. You must reconfigure Backup to work correctly with this computer

Backup has determined that you have copied its files from a computer with a configuration different from this one. You will have to configure Backup to work with your present system. Choose Cancel and continue.

Backup/Restore Module: module_name, Missing. Backup cannot find one of the program files

All of your Backup program files must be within the same directory. Choose Cancel and continue.

Cannot access subdirectory during handle log. A subdirectory is not available during disk logging

This error indicates a cross-linked problem with DOS's file allocation table. You should run CHKDSK immediately. Choose Cancel and continue.

Cannot allocate memory for catalog version information

You will have to free at least 512K of memory before trying again. Choose Cancel and continue.

Cannot allocate memory for directory index buffers

Backup requires 512K of internal memory. You will have to free more memory and try again. Choose Cancel and continue.

Cannot create file in the installed directory

This error could be the result of a lack of disk space or a network accessibility problem. Choose Cancel and continue.

Cannot create *SLT* path or file

There isn't enough room to create the file that holds your keyboard and mouse selections. Check your hard disk to see whether it is full or whether there is a network conflict. Choose Cancel and continue.

Cannot create the setup file...*c:\DOSBACK\MYDOCS.SET*

This error could be the result of the following problems:

- You might have a full hard disk.

- You might have exceeded the root directory file limit (512).

- You might not have the network authority to access the file.

- Your path might be incorrect.

Cannot find an entry in setup file

Your setup file is missing an option setting. Choose Cancel and continue. You will have to delete this setup file before you restart the Backup program.

Cannot open catalog file

You should check to see whether you have a network conflict. Choose Cancel and continue.

Cannot open log file

Under normal circumstances, you should not see this internal diagnostic message. You should record the displayed data and contact Microsoft Product Support.

Cannot open setup file: *WP51.SET*

Ensure that your setup file is not read-only or that it is a network file for which you do not have write access. Choose Cancel and continue.

Cannot read volume from virtual memory

Under normal circumstances, you should not see this internal diagnostic message. You should record the displayed data and contact Microsoft Product Support.

Catalog file: catalog_name is missing!

Backup is unable to locate one of the Incremental or Differential catalogs listed in the master catalog that you are using for selection of files to be restored. You should note the missing catalog name and either retrieve or rebuild the catalog from the original backup set. Choose Cancel and continue.

Catalog file count is corrupt

Backup has determined that this file is corrupt. You should still be able to compare or restore files from this backup set, however. Catalog files can be retrieved or rebuilt from the backup set, and compares and restores can be performed without a catalog. Choose Cancel and continue.

Divide overflow error

This should not occur during normal operations. If it does, however, the contents of the CPU registers are displayed. Note the identification and content of the registers, and contact Microsoft Product Support Services. Choose Cancel and then Exit Program to continue.

DOCSFILE.SET entry file not found

The setup file you specified cannot be found. Choose Cancel and then Exit Program to continue.

Error writing setup file c:\DOSBACK\doc.set

You might have a full hard disk, or you might have a hardware problem. Choose Cancel and continue.

Incompatible configuration file version

The configuration file MSBACKUP.INI in which Backup stores your system configuration and personal preferences is not the correct version. If you want to reconfigure now, choose Reconfigure (press Enter), and if you want to exit Backup, press Esc.

Insufficient disk space available for the restore/capture process

You need to free approximately 100K of hard disk space. Choose Cancel and continue.

Insufficient disk space for log file

You need to free approximately 100K of hard disk space. Choose Cancel and continue.

Insufficient disk space to create catalog

Your hard disk needs about 100K of available space. Choose Cancel and continue.

Insufficient disk space to save backup selections

Your hard disk needs about 100K of available space for the SETUP.SLT file, which holds previously entered directory and file selections. Choose Cancel and continue.

Insufficient disk space to save setup file

You will have to provide about 100K of available space. Choose Cancel and continue.

Insufficient memory for catalog buffer

You will have to free at least 512K of memory before trying again. Choose Cancel and continue.

Insufficient memory for catalog merging buffers

There isn't enough memory available for merging multiple catalogs using a master catalog. You will either have to free more memory or restore or compare individual backup sets to individual catalogs. Choose Cancel and continue.

Insufficient memory for catalog processing

You will have to free more memory before trying again. Choose Cancel and continue.

Insufficient memory for directory log

There isn't enough memory to contain the largest directory's list of contents. You will need to either free more memory or divide the largest directory into two or more smaller directories. Choose Cancel and continue.

Insufficient memory for direct logging buffers

You will have to free at least 512K of memory before trying again. Choose Cancel and continue.

Insufficient memory for merged *DIR* information

You will have to free at least 512K of memory before trying again. You might have to compare or restore each backup set individually in lieu of utilizing the merged catalog. Choose Cancel and continue.

Insufficient memory or disk space to rebuild/retrieve

There is either insufficient memory available to load the catalog processing program or insufficient disk space to create a temporary file. If you have at least 500K disk space available, the problem is probably memory. Choose Cancel and continue.

Insufficient memory to continue backup. Backup requires 512KB Memory

You will have to free more memory and try again. Choose Cancel and continue.

Insufficient memory to load directory information

You will have to free at least 512K of memory before trying again. Choose Cancel and continue.

Insufficient memory to log selected drive

You will have to free at least 512K of memory before trying again. Choose Cancel and continue.

Insufficient memory to process setup file

There isn't enough memory to hold your keyboard and mouse settings. Choose Cancel and continue.

Insufficient memory to process the directory index

There isn't enough memory to process the directory index within the catalog. You will have to free more memory and try again. Choose Cancel and continue.

Insufficient memory to read setup file

You will have to free at least 512K of memory before trying again. Choose Cancel and then Exit Program to continue.

Insufficient memory to save *DIR* information

You will have to free at least 512K of memory before trying again. Choose Cancel and continue.

Insufficient memory to verify catalog checksums

You will have to free at least 512K of memory before trying again. The checksums are used to verify the integrity of the catalogs. Choose Cancel and continue.

Invalid drive specifier...

The Include/Exclude list within the setup file contains a statement referencing an invalid drive letter. If applicable, make sure you are logged on to your network and have access rights to that drive. Choose Cancel and continue.

Maximum subdirectories per drive reached

Backup has a limit of 1,023 subdirectories per drive. You will need to divide your drive into two logical drives, or combine some of your directories before backing up your drive.

Module_name: Engine Module Missing.
Backup cannot find one of the program files

All of your Backup program files must be in the same directory. Choose Cancel and continue.

No room for new catalog name

You are exceeding the maximum of 26 backups a day of the same drives using the same backup type. Choose Cancel and continue.

Only the first 49 setup files
in this directory can be listed

You are trying to exceed the maximum of 49 files that can be listed in the Setup Files list box. Either delete some of your files or move them to a different directory. Choose Cancel and continue.

Out of memory

Backup is unable to continue due to lack of available memory. You will have to free at least 512K of memory before trying again. Choose Cancel and continue.

Out of memory can also be displayed when there isn't enough memory to hold logging data. You should have at least 512K of memory. Choose Cancel and continue.

Setup file *MYWORK.SET* was not found

The setup file you specified in the Open Setup File dialog box was not found by Backup. This error could have resulted because you don't have network authorization to use the file, the file doesn't exist, or a hardware problem exists. Choose Cancel and continue.

The catalog file *C:\DOSBACK\TEST.CAT* is corrupt

You are attempting to load a corrupt catalog file. By choosing the Catalog button in the Compare or Restore dialog box, you can still compare or restore files in this backup set by rebuilding the catalog.

The current system date is not set properly

Backup has detected that your system date is incorrect. Choose Cancel and continue.

The include/exclude list is full. No more items can be added

The Include/Exclude list has a limit of 50 statements. Choose Cancel and continue.

The MS-DOS path you entered has an invalid destination drive. Please re-enter it

This error occurs when you choose Start Backup. Enter the path correctly, or choose Cancel and continue.

The password you entered doesn't verify

Backup doesn't recognize what you entered. Remember that the password check is case-sensitive. Choose Cancel and continue.

The password you entered is incorrect. The catalog will not be loaded

The backup set that you protected with a password is not loaded because Backup doesn't recognize what you entered. Remember that the password check is case-sensitive. Choose Cancel and continue.

Unable to open the catalog file C:\DOSBACK\FULL.CAT

Under normal circumstances, you should not see this internal diagnostic message. You should record the displayed data and contact Microsoft Product Support.

Unable to create the catalog file C:\DOSBACK\TEST.CAT

Your system does not have enough disk space (it needs a minimum of 100K), or it has a full root directory. Or there might be a network conflict or lack of network rights to create the file.

Version mismatch between *MSBACKUP.EXE* and *MSBACKUP.OVL*

Backup has detected different versions of itself in its directory. You must ensure that all Backup program files have the same date and time stamps. If you are unable to correct the problem by reviewing the directory listing, you should reinstall using the DOS 6 Setup Distribution diskettes. Choose Cancel and then choose Exit Program.

Version mismatch between program files

You have two or more versions of Backup installed. The date and time stamps must be consistent for Backup to work. If you are unable to correct the problem after a review of the directory, you should reinstall using the DOS 6 Setup Distribution diskettes. Choose Cancel and continue.

INTERLNK Error Messages

The following messages can appear while you are using INTERLNK and INTERSRV to transfer files.

Directory is full

The number of files and subdirectories in your Server's root directory has exceeded 512. Copy off or back up the appropriate files or directories from your Server, remove them, and try again.

Error sending file to remote system

This problem typically occurs when the validation algorithm computed value on the remote file doesn't match that of the sending file. Try retransmitting the file. Also make sure that your remote computer is turned on.

Insufficient disk space

Your Server's disk is full. Copy off or back up the appropriate files from your Server, remove them, and try again.

Anti-Virus Error Messages

The following messages display warnings about a possible virus infection.

Virus found

You have several options at this point. You can choose Clean to clean the virus from the file and restore it to its original condition. Choose Continue to ignore the virus and continue scanning. Choose Stop to stop the scan and return to the Anti-Virus program. Or choose Delete to erase the file from your system.

Verify error

This error message might be the result of an intentional change you made. If you know you changed the file, you can choose Update to register the change. Information displayed includes the attribute assigned to the file, time, date, and size of file, and checksum. You have the following options:

- If the attribute, time, or date has changed, choose Repair to return the file to its original condition.

- If you know that the change is legitimate, choose Update to avoid receiving this message again during subsequent scans.

- Choose Continue if you know about the change and you don't want to update the anti-virus program.

- Choose Stop to abort the scan.

File was destroyed by the virus!!! Recovery for this file is impossible. Delete this file in order to prevent further infection and damage?

If a file is destroyed by a virus, you can choose Delete to delete the infected file from the system, choose Continue to ignore the situation, or choose Stop to stop the scanning process.

Invalid signature - checksum does not match

A signature uniquely identifies a virus. If the virus signature you enter when updating the Virus List has an error in it, you will receive this message. To correct the signature, check the signature code for accuracy and completeness, correct the codes, and choose OK.

Program is trying to modify system memory

This message displays when a program tries to modify the system memory without using the standard MS-DOS calls for TSR programs. Modifying system memory this way generally indicates that a virus is attempting to infect the system. This is an added safety measure to ensure that no virus is present. If you know that a network program is being loaded after VSafe was loaded, choose Continue. If you don't know what is causing the message, choose Stop, then run the anti-virus program to check for viruses.

Resident programs were loaded after VSafe

VSafe displays this message if you try to remove VSafe from memory. Choose Stop to leave VSafe resident in memory.

Since a virus was detected, rebooting is recommended to minimize the possibility of further infection

Choose reboot to restart your system after a virus is detected.

The xxxxxx virus is known to infect DATA files as well as executable files

This message is displayed if you have not checked the Check All Files option and a virus is detected. You should check all the files on this disk.

Alan Simpson's
DOS
SECRETS
UNLEASHED

APPENDIX D

Technical Support Numbers and Product Directory

This appendix tells you how to get technical support for DOS 6 from virtually anywhere in the world. It also includes a listing of all software vendors who developed software products contained on the add-in disks.

Getting Technical Support for DOS 6

Microsoft provides technical support for all registered users of DOS 6 for 90 days after you purchase it. The company asks that you be at your computer when you call and that you be prepared to provide support personnel with the following information:

- Your version of DOS

- Your hardware configuration, including your network configuration if appropriate

- The precise wording of any error messages that have appeared

- A description of what happened when the problem occurred and what you tried to do to solve it

Technical Support Numbers

For technical support for DOS for users in the United States, call (206) 646-5104. Microsoft support offices are open between 6 a.m. and 6 p.m. Pacific time, Monday through Friday.

The following numbers are for technical support for the rest of the world. Microsoft does not have technical support personnel in every country, so in some cases you must call another country in your region that does have a technical support office.

Country	Phone
Argentina	(54)(1)814-0356
Australia	(61)(02)870-2131
Austria	0660-65-17
Baltic States	089-3176-1152
Belgium (Dutch)	02-5133274
Belgium (English)	02-5023432
Belgium (French)	02-5132268
Bolivia	(54)(1)814-0356
Brazil	(55) (11) 533-2922
Canada	1 (416) 568-3503
Caribbean Countries	0058.2.914739
Central America	0058.2.914739
Chile	(54)(1)814-0356
Columbia	0058.2.914739
Denmark	(45) (44) 89 01 00
Ecuador	0058.2.914739
England	(44) (734) 271000
Finland	(358) (0) 525 501
France	(33) (1) 69-86-10-20
French Polynesia	(33) (1) 69-86-10-20
Germany	089-3176-1152
Hong Kong	(852) 804-4222
Ireland	(44) (734) 271000
Israel	972-3-752-7915
Italy	(39) (2) 26901364
Japan	(81) (3) 3363-0160
Korea	(82) (2) 553-9230
Liechtenstein	01-342-2152
Luxembourg (Dutch)	(31) 2503-77877
Luxembourg (English)	(31) 2503-77853
Luxembourg (French)	(32) 2-5132268
Mexico	(52) (5) 325-0912

continues

Country	Phone
Netherlands (Dutch)	02503-77877
Netherlands (English)	02503-77853
New Zealand	64 (9) 357-5575
Northern Ireland	(44) (734) 271000
Norway	(47) (2) 18 35 00
Papua New Guinea	(61)(02)870-2131
Paraguay	(54)(1)814-0356
Peru	0058.2.914739
Portugal	(351) 1 4412205
Puerto Rico	0058.2.914739
Republic of China	(886) (2) 504-3122
Republic of Ireland	(44) (734) 271000
Scotland	(44) (734) 271000
Spain	(34) (1) 803-9960
Sweden	(46) (071) 21 05 15
Switzerland (German)	01-342-2152
Switzerland (French)	022-738-96 88
Uruguay	(54)(1)814-0356
Venezuela	0058.2.914739
Wales	(44) (734) 271000

Other Ways to Get Help

Microsoft offers additional ways to get help using DOS. The company's FastTips line provides recorded answers to commonly asked questions. Using the FastTips line, you also can order technical information that Microsoft can FAX or mail to you. In the United States, the FastTips number is (206) 646-5103. It is available at all times.

If you use a modem, you have two additional alternatives for support. The Microsoft Product Support Download Service enables you to access technical notes and other information about DOS and any other Microsoft product. That number is (206) 936-6735. Also,

Microsoft maintains a number of support forums on CompuServe Information Service, the large international bulletin board and information service. If you already are a CompuServe member, type GO MICROSOFT at any ! prompt. If you would like information about joining CompuServe, call (800) 848-8990.

If you are hearing impaired, call TDD/TT (Text Telephone) Support. Using a special TDD/TT modem, dial (206) 635-4948. This service is available between 6 a.m. and 6 p.m. Pacific time, Monday through Thursday.

Software Product Directory

Following are addresses for authors of the software products included with this book. The individual software is described in greater detail in Chapter 32, "Using Shareware to Enhance DOS." Telephone numbers are not included for some authors who only develop software part-time.

Crossdown
Bellotto, Sam Jr.
133 Akron Street
Rochester, NY 14609-7618

PC-File
ButtonWare
P.O. Box 96058
Bellevue, WA 98009
(800) 528-8866

Batutil/Stackey
CTRLALT Associates
260 South Lake Avenue
Suite 133
Pasadena, CA 91101
(800) 872-4768

FileBuddy
Dean, Lenard
Box 73094
Woodbine Postal Outlet
Calgary, AB T2W 6EO

DOS-CALC
DOS-CALC
3120 Homestead Drive
Erie, PA 16506

DMP
DMP Software
204 E. Second Avenue
Suite 610
San Mateo, CA 94401

Target
McAfee Associates
3350 Scott Blvd.
Building 14
Santa Clara, CA 95054-3107
(408) 988-3832

PKZIP/PKUNZIP
PKWARE, Inc.
7545 N. Port Washington Road
Glendale, WI 53217-3422
(414) 352-3670

Metric-X
Orion Development Corp.
P.O. Box 2323
Merrifield, VA 22116-2323
(800) 992-8170

PC-Write Lite
Quicksoft
300 Queen Anne Avenue N., #224
Seattle, WA 98109
(800) 888-8088

BLANK-IT
Rhode Island Soft Systems, Inc.
P.O. Box 748
Woonsocket, RI 02895
(401) 658-4632

I.Q. Challenge
R.K. West Consulting
P.O. Box 8059
Mission Hills, CA 91346

Type Trek and WordTrix
Tea Time Software
92 Acorn Circle
Oxford, OH 45056

OMNIDay
Unicorn Software Ltd.
P.O. Box 911
Wabash, IN 46992-0911
(800) 242-4775

Index

error messages (continued)
  The xxxxxx virus is known to infect DATA files as well as executable files, 1034
  Unable to create directory, 189, 258, 1021-1022
  Unable to create the catalog file C:\DOSBACK\TEST.CAT, 1031
  Unable to open the catalog file C:\DOSBACK\FULL.CAT, 1031
  Unrecognized Command in CONFIG.SYS, 74
  Unrecoverable error in directory, Convert directory to file (Y/N), 1016
  Verify error, 1033
  Version mismatch between MSBACKUP.EXE and MSBACKUP.OVL, 1031
  Version mismatch between program files, 1031
  Virus found, 1032
  Write fault error writing device PRN Abort, Retry, Ignore, or Fail?, 1022
  Write protect error writing drive (n), 1022
  Write protect error writing to drive A: Abort, Retry, Fail?, 188
  Write-protect error writing drive n -Abort, Retry, 258
Error reading partition table error message, 1014
Error sending file to remote system error message, 1032

Error writing setup file c:\DOSBACK\doc.set error message, 1025
ERRORLEVEL command, 776
errors, logic, 834
Escape key characters, 655
escape seqences, 655
  in batch programs, 823-824
  screen
    attributes, 656-659
    colors, 655
event procedures, 900, 909
event-driven applications, 899
.EXE file name extension, 113, 195
exit codes, 776
EXIT command, 877
exiting
  EDIT command, 279
  Shell program, 159-160
    with F3 key, 662
expanded memory, 66-67, 447, 606-608
  activating, 457-458
  installing, 608
    RAM disks in, 629-630
    SMARTDrive, 635-636
  utilizing, 617
expanding, branches, 248-250
EXPATH environmental variable, 305
Express mode (MemMaker), 6, 471-474
extended memory, 66-67, 446, 604-606
  activating, 455-457
  installing
    RAM disks in, 627-628
    SMARTDrive, 635-636
  utilizing, 617

IF YOUR COMPUTER USES 3½-inch DISKS...

Although many personal computers use 5¼-inch disks to store information, some newer computers are switching to 3½-inch disks for information storage. If your computer uses 3½-inch disks, you can return this form to SAMS to obtain 3½-inch disks to use with this book. Complete the remainder of this form and mail to the following address:

Alan Simpson's DOS Secrets Unleashed

Disk Exchange
Sams Publishing
11711 N. College Ave., Suite 140
Carmel, IN 46032

We will send you, free of charge, the 3½-inch version of the book software.

Name_____Phone_____

Company_____Title _____

Address _____

City_____State____ZIP _____

What's on the Disks

The three disks included with this book contain some of the best shareware products available, including:

AsEasyAs (spreadsheet)

PKZip (file compression)

Jill of the Jungle (arcade game)

Odyssey (communications)

Chinese Checkers (board game)

Design Shell (graphical menu)

PC-File (database)

NeoPaint (paint/image editing)

SkyGlobe (planetarium)

List (file viewing)

Target (disk searching)

Blank-It (screen blanker)

The disks also include sample QBasic, Visual Basic, and batch programs from Alan Simpson.

Installing the Floppy Disks

The software included with this book is stored in a compressed form. You cannot use the software without first installing it on your hard drive.

1. From a DOS prompt, change to the drive that contains the installation disk. For example, if the disk is in drive A:, type A: and press Enter.

2. Type INSTALL and press Enter. The installation menu program will appear.

3. You can choose to install the entire disk, or you can choose to install a single program. To select a menu option, press the letter next to the choice. You can also highlight the choice with the arrow keys and press Enter.

4. After you make your choice, you will be prompted to type the letter of your hard drive. Type the drive letter and press Enter. For example, if you want to install the programs on drive C:, type C: and press Enter.

5. When you finish installing programs from a disk, press X to exit the install program. You can then proceed to installing programs from the other disks.

The installation program installs the programs in a directory named \UNLEASH on your hard drive. This directory is automatically created during the installation.

For more information, read Chapter 32, "Using Shareware to Enhance DOS." The file README.TXT, found on each disk, also contains important information.

To install all the disks, you need at least 8M of free space on your hard drive.

DOS 6 Survival Guide

Feature/Action	Command(s)	Feature/Action	Command(s)
Backup hard disk	BACKUP	File (update or replace)	REPLACE
Resore files from DOS 5 backup	RESTORE	File (view contents)	TYPE
Batch file (create or edit)	EDIT	File (view names)	DIR
Batch file (run)	*batch filename*	Files open (maximum)	FILES
Batch file (run other)	CALL, COMMAND	Format a disk	FORMAT
Bootup Disk (create)	FORMAT /S, SYS	Function keys (change)	ANSI.SYS, PROMPT
CD-ROM driver access	MSCDEX	Help	HELP, *command*? or F1 in shell
Change alphabet	CHCP	High memory (use)	DOS=HIGH
Check disk	CHKDSK	Install DOS 6	SETUP
Choices in batch programs	CHOICE	Interupt process	Ctrl+Break
Clear screen	CLS	Macro (create/change)	DOSKEY
Command prompt (change)	PROMPT	Memory maker	MEMMAKER
Compare files	FC	Memory status	MEM, CHKDSK
Compare diskettes	DISKCOMP	Move file(s) (or rename)	MOVE
Configure devices	DEVICE, MODE	Packed file corrupt (fix)	LOADFIX
Connect two computers	INTERLNK	Path to search nonprograms	APPEND
Copy File(s)	COPY, XCOPY	Path to search programs	PATH
Copy diskette	DISKCOPY	Pause screen scroll	MORE
Date/time format (change)	COUNTRY	Pause batch file	PAUSE
Date (set or change)	DATE	Print text file(s)	PRINT, COPY
Double space	DBLSPACE	Printer (eject page)	ECHO
Debug executables	DEBUG	Printer (graphics)	GRAPHICS
Defragment files	DEFRAG	Printer settings	MODE
Delete files	DEL	Program (run)	*program filename*
Delete a directory	DELTREE	Power management (laptop)	POWER
Directory (change)	CHDIR or CD	RAM Disk (create)	RAMDRIVE.SYS
Directory (make/create)	MKDIR or MD	Record keystrokes	DOSKEY
Directory (remove/delete)	RMDIR or RD	Repeat command(s)	FOR
Directory (view structure)	TREE	Reserved memory (used)	LOADHIGH, DEVICEHIGH
Disk cache	SMARTDRIV, FASTOPEN	Screen colors	ANSI.SYS, PROMPT
DOS Shell (activate)	DOSSHELL	Screen mode	MODE
Drive names	LASTDRIVE, ASSIGN	Sort file or output	SORT
Drive (change)	*drive:*	Substitute drive/directory	SUBST
Edit text file	EDIT	System disk (create)	FORMAT /S, SYS
Environment (DOS)	SET	Time (set/change)	TIME
Expanded memory (activate)	EMM386	Undelete file	UNDELETE
Extended memory (activate)	HIMEM.SYS	Unformat disk	UNFORMAT
File (attributes)	ATTRIB	Upper memory (see reserved memory)	DOS
File (change name)	RENAME or REN	Verify files	VERIFY
File (compare)	FC	Version of DOS (set)	SETVER
File (copy)	COPY, XCOPY	Version of DOS (view)	VER
File (combine)	COPY	View files	(see File)
File (delete)	DEL, ERASE	Virus monitor	VSAFE
File (find text in)	FIND	Virus scan	MSAV
File (print)	PRINT, COPY	Volume label (set/change)	LABEL
File (protect/unprotect)	ATTRIB	Volume label (view)	VOL
File (search for)	DIR, TREE, CHKDSK	File (undelete)	UNDELETE

DOS 6 Shell Survival Guide

Action	Option(s)
Activate Shell	Type EXIT and press Enter or type DOSSHELL and press Enter
Move highlight bar	Press Tab to move from area to area; ↑, ↓, ←, → moves within area
Move mouse pointer	Roll your mouse
Pull down a menu	Hold down Alt key and press underlined letter or click desired option
Select a drive	Highlight and press Enter or click drive
Select a directory	Highlight and press Enter or click directory name
Expand/contract directory	Highlight directory name and press + or – or click directory icon
Select a file for operation	Press Add (Shift+F8), highlight, and press the Spacebar, or hold down Ctrl and click the file name
Run a program (file with .EXE, .COM, or .BAT)	Highlight and press Enter or double-click extension
Get Help	Select an option from Help pull-down menu and press F1
Run a Program or select a program group	Highlight and press Enter or double-click
Activate or deactivate task swapper	Select Enable Task Swapper from the Options pull-down menu
Change overall view	Select an option from the View pull-down menu
Exit the Shell	Select Exit from the File pull-down menu, or press F3

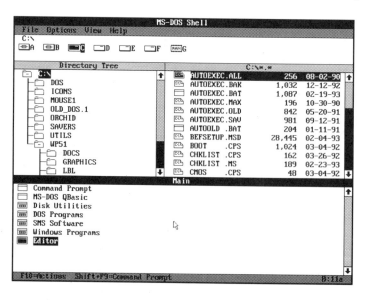